FINNEY AND MILLER'S

Principles of ACCOUNTING

INTRODUCTORY

BY **GLENN L. JOHNSON,** PH.D., CPA
THE UNIVERSITY OF KANSAS

AND **JAMES A. GENTRY, JR.,** PH.D., CPA
EMORY UNIVERSITY

FINNEY AND MILLER'S

Principles of
ACCOUNTING

INTRODUCTORY

SEVENTH EDITION

PRENTICE-HALL, INC.

Englewood Cliffs, New Jersey

Finney and Miller's
Principles of ACCOUNTING, Introductory
Seventh Edition
Glenn L. Johnson and James A. Gentry, Jr.

© 1932, 1936, 1938, 1940, 1948, 1953, 1957, 1963, 1970, by
PRENTICE–HALL, INC., *Englewood Cliffs, N.J.*

13-317388-7
Library of Congress Catalog Card No.: 79-113046

PRINTED IN THE UNITED STATES OF AMERICA

Current Printing (last digit):
10   9   8   7   6   5   4   3   2   1

PRENTICE-HALL INTERNATIONAL, INC., *London*
PRENTICE-HALL OF AUSTRALIA, PTY. LTD., *Sydney*
PRENTICE-HALL OF CANADA, LTD., *Toronto*
PRENTICE-HALL OF INDIA PRIVATE LTD., *New Delhi*
PRENTICE-HALL OF JAPAN, INC., *Tokyo*

PREFACE

This introduction to accounting was written for the prospective career accountant as well as for potential administrators, for investors, and for anyone who needs to understand the function that accounting performs in our society.

This edition, the seventh, presents a blending of *financial* accounting, which deals primarily with formal statements showing the financial position of a business firm and the results of its operations, with *managerial* accounting, which emphasizes the use of accounting data for managerial decisions. The organization of the text is flexible enough to permit the reader to concentrate, should he wish to do so, on either financial or managerial accounting.

The seventh edition is more conceptual and less procedural than previous editions. For greater clarity we have maintained a separation, in the early chapters, between the conceptual and the procedural, postponing briefly the introduction of procedural matters until the reader has been exposed to certain basic accounting concepts. Procedural matters are included primarily for their usefulness as tools to facilitate the understanding of accounting concepts.

We have included a wide assortment of questions, short exercises, and problems at the end of each chapter to assist in the learning process. Special forms designed to reduce the time required for solutions are available for half of the problems. A workbook of objective test exercises is available separately; also a practice case in two stages, separately bound. The practice case will provide experience in carrying out all phases of the accounting process equivalent to that obtained from two separate practice cases, one long and the other short. The two-stage arrangement will enable the user to control the time devoted to this activity.

Accounting research studies and bulletins copyrighted by the American Institute of Certified Public Accountants are quoted in the text by permission of the Institute.

GLENN L. JOHNSON
JAMES A. GENTRY, JR.

CONTENTS

FINNEY AND MILLER'S

Principles of ACCOUNTING

INTRODUCTORY

Accounting as an
Information System

Introduction. What might a college student with little knowledge of business matters want to know if he inherited 2,000 shares of capital stock in a company called Sight & Sound Corporation? His questions might include some of the following:

What is a share of stock?
What are the Sight & Sound shares worth?
In what business is Sight & Sound Corporation engaged?
Is the company in good financial condition?
Has it been profitable?
What is involved in managing a business?
Should the 2,000 shares of stock be sold or retained?

What is a share of stock? When a business is organized as a corporation, the resources which enable it to commence operations are acquired through shares of capital stock issued to investors. When Sight & Sound Corporation was organized one year ago it issued 2,500 shares of capital stock for $25,000 cash.

Ownership of shares of capital stock is evidenced by a stock certificate. An illustration of a stock certificate appears on page 2.

Certificate No. __2__   __2,000__ *Shares*

SIGHT & SOUND CORPORATION
CAPITAL STOCK

THIS CERTIFIES THAT _____(Name of college student)_____ *is the*
owner of _____two thousand_____ *shares at $10 par value of*
the Capital Stock of

SIGHT & SOUND CORPORATION

transferable on the books of the Corporation in person or by duly authorized
attorney upon surrender of this Certificate properly endorsed.

IN WITNESS WHEREOF *the said Corporation has caused this Certificate to be signed*
by its duly authorized officers, and to be sealed with the seal of the Corporation at
_____(Name of city)_____ *, this* __Second__ *day of* __January__ *, 19+2*

Secretary   *President*

STOCK CERTIFICATE

As indicated, only one certificate is needed to establish ownership of any number of shares.

Although the stockholders are the owners of a corporation, they have no authority to transact any corporate business. The authority to conduct corporate business rests with the board of directors, whose members are elected by the stockholders. As a general rule, the board delegates many of the responsibilities associated with managing the operations of the business to the corporate officers who are appointed by it. The appointed officers are often referred to collectively as the management. The board establishes broad policies and, at periodic meetings, reviews the results of management's efforts.

Employees of corporations may also be stockholders, and those employees holding important managerial positions often own a significant number of shares. An employee, if elected, may serve on the board of directors. However, the law generally specifies that board members must be stockholders.

Stockholders may receive income, known as dividends, from their shareholdings. Dividend distributions are made by corporations only when so ordered by the board of directors; hence dividend income should never be counted on as a certainty. In the year just ended the directors of Sight & Sound Corporation authorized the payment of four quarterly dividends of 20 cents per share. Thus, a stockholder owning 2,000 shares would have received a total of $1,600 (2,000 × $.20 × 4) in dividends for the year.

What are the Sight & Sound shares worth? As a general rule, shares of stock are transferable; that is, they may be bought and sold or given away. If a company's stock is listed on a stock exchange, the buying and selling of its shares thereon establishes a market value. The market value of a share of stock will change, often frequently and sometimes significantly, for a number of reasons. Basically, the market value of a share of stock is affected by the earnings prospects of the company, by the prospective dividend payments to stockholders, and by the relative attractiveness of alternative investment opportunities.

The shares of Sight & Sound Corporation are not actively traded; however, a securities dealer has offered to pay $16 a share for the 2,000 shares held by the college student, thus indicating an aggregate market value of $32,000. Incidentally, if the directors continue the existing dividend payments, the dividend yield based on the market value of the investment will amount to 5 per cent per annum ($1,600 annual dividends divided by $32,000 market value).

In what business is the corporation engaged? Sight & Sound Corporation operates a retail store dealing in television and audio equipment. However, in the recent annual report to stockholders, management indicated that consideration is being given to the opening of a service center, which could significantly expand the company's volume of business.

Is the company in good financial condition? Has it been profitable? A stockholders's primary source of information concerning the financial condition and profitability of his company is the firm's financial statements. The financial statements of Sight & Sound Corporation for the year just ended are presented on the following pages. Some background comments and definitions are offered at this point to indicate why financial statements are helpful whenever there are questions about financial condition and profitability.

Balance sheet. The balance sheet on page 4 shows the assets of the business, its liabilities, and the owners' equity. Thus it portrays financial position as of the date stated in the heading of the statement. Observe the equality of the total assets ($48,500) and the total equities ($48,500)—hence the name balance sheet. The assets of a business are always equalled by claims against assets, which accountants refer to as equities. If the balance sheet fails to "balance," at least one error has been made.

Assets. *Assets are future economic benefits, the rights to which are owned or controlled by an organization or individual.* The assets included in a firm's balance sheet are those for which the rights have been acquired by a current or past transaction. Cash, accounts receivable (amounts owed to the business by its customers), merchandise, office supplies, land, buildings, machinery and other equipment, and patents are typical business assets.

Assets may provide future economic benefits for several reasons; for instance:
(1) Because the asset may be used as purchasing power.
  Cash is an example. It is valuable because other assets can be acquired with it.
(2) Because the asset is a money claim.
  Accounts receivable and United States savings bonds are examples, the

holder or claimant being entitled to receive money for them, usually at some specified date.

(3) Because the asset can be sold and thus converted to cash or to a money claim.

Merchandise held for sale by a merchant is an example.

(4) Because the asset offers some potential services, or rights, to the owner. A building is an example. It provides shelter or a place in which business activities may be conducted. Land, machinery, equipment, patents, and supplies are other examples. Assets of the type described under (4) are acquired by a business with the expectation of earning something from their use.

Liabilities. *Liabilities are obligations of an organization or individual,* such as debts owed to creditors. They arise from a variety of business events such as the borrowing of money or the purchase of goods and services through the use of credit. Accounts payable, notes payable, mortgages payable, salaries and wages payable, and taxes payable are some of the liabilities that may be owed by a business. The "size" and due dates of liabilities must be carefully watched by management because, should a business fail to pay its liabilities when they fall due, it may be thrown into bankruptcy by the creditors.

Note content of
statement heading:
1. Name of business ——→ **SIGHT & SOUND CORPORATION**
2. Name of statement ————→ **Balance Sheet**
3. Date ————————————→ **December 31, 19+1**

Assets			Equities		
Current assets:			Current liabilities:		
Cash	$16,500		Accounts payable	$20,000	
Accounts receivable	10,000		Salaries payable	1,500	$21,500
Merchandise inventory—at cost	12,000	$38,500	Stockholders' equity:		
			Capital stock, 2,500		
Long-term investment:			shares issued and		
Investment in land—at cost		10,000	outstanding	$25,000	
			Retained earnings	2,000	27,000
		$48,500			$48,500

Notes about the financial statements:

19+1 denotes the first year of the corporation's existence, which year has just ended; 19+2 will be used later to denote the second year, and so forth.

Corporations are subject to income tax, but to keep the illustrative financial statements relatively simple, such taxes are ignored in the early chapters. For the same reason, the dollar amounts in the illustrative statements are small.

Owners' equity. *The excess of the assets over the liabilities of a business is the owners' equity.* For instance,

If a business has assets in the amount of	$48,500
And has liabilities of.	21,500
Then the owners' equity is	$27,000

Unlike the fixed dollar claims of creditors, the equity held by the owners is in the nature of a residual claim or interest. If a corporation goes out of business, the creditors' claims come first. Any assets that remain after the creditors' claims have been satisfied may be distributed to the owners.

The owners' equity in a corporation may come from the following sources:

From stockholders' investments—Shown in the illustrative balance sheet on page 4 as:

Capital stock	$25,000

From profitable operations—Shown in the illustrative balance sheet on page 4 as:

Retained earnings.	2,000
Total stockholders' (owners') equity	$27,000

Brief appraisal of company's financial position. The strong financial position of Sight & Sound Corporation becomes evident from an inspection of its balance sheet. Items:

The current assets (cash and those assets which will be converted to cash in the near future during the normal course of business operations) exceed the current liabilities (those payable in the near future) by a comfortable margin.

The cash balance seems adequate.

The receivables are a source of cash inflow in the near future. The year-end balance ($10,000) does not seem excessive in relation to the sales volume (which was $80,000 for 19+1, as shown by the income statement which follows), particularly in view of the fact that the company allows its customers sixty days to pay their accounts. A large accounts-receivable balance in relation to sales volume might indicate doubtful collectibility.

The inventory is another near-term source of cash, assuming normal sales activity. In relation to the sales volume, the investment in inventory does not appear excessive. A large inventory balance in relation to sales volume might indicate "slow moving" merchandise.

The long-term investment, though probably made for some good business reason such as to acquire a future building site or to participate in rising real estate values, is nevertheless a source of cash, should an urgent need for cash arise.

The company has no long-term debt.

Income statement. Most businesses are engaged in a continuing "stream" of operations which are conducted for the purpose of producing net income (also called profit), which is defined as the excess of revenues over expenses. The success of a business is judged largely by its profitability, as shown in the income statement below—not only by the *amount* of net income, but by its *trend* and by how it *compares* with the net income of comparable businesses.

Note the special feature of the heading for an income statement:
It indicates a period of time rather than a date ⟶

SIGHT & SOUND CORPORATION
Income Statement
For the Year Ended December 31, 19+1

Revenue:
Sales of merchandise $80,000
Deduct expenses:
Cost of goods sold $48,000
Salaries expense 18,000
Rent expense 4,800
Other expense 5,200   76,000
Net income . . . . $ 4,000

Some of the common uses of income statements are set forth below:

They may be included in a report to stockholders and used by the stockholders in forming an opinion regarding the progress of the business and the effectiveness of the management group.

They may be submitted to banks in support of a request for a loan for the banks' use in judging the earnings prospects of the borrower.

They may be used by investors in reaching decisions whether to acquire, to continue to hold, or to dispose of securities issued by the corporation—for example, the corporation's capital stock.

They may be used by management to judge the effectiveness of its past policies and decisions, to detect unfavorable trends and developments, and to provide data upon which to base decisions regarding a wide variety of matters, such as whether to expand production, whether to change advertising policy, whether to introduce a new product, whether to alter selling prices, and whether to merge with another corporation.

For many of the above uses, the balance sheet also will be examined. The balance sheet and the income statement should be thought of as companion statements, each supplementing the other.

Revenue. *Revenue is an inflow of assets in the form of cash, receivables, or other property from customers or clients, which results from sales of merchandise or the rendering of services, or from investments;* for instance, interest may be earned on bonds or on savings deposits. In contrast, revenue does not arise from an inflow of capital funds from stockholders investing in the capital stock of a corporation. Nor does an inflow of borrowed funds qualify as revenue.

Observe that Sight & Sound Corporation has only one kind of revenue: from sales of merchandise.

Expense. *Expense is the cost of goods or services used for the purpose of generating revenue.* A businessman advertises with the expectation of attracting customers; he engages employees so that customers may be served; and he rents space so that he will have a place to conduct the operations of the business. In all such activities he is utilizing goods or services for the purpose of generating revenue, and hence is incurring expenses.

Sight & Sound Corporation's expenses for the year just ended amounted to $76,000.

Brief appraisal of the company's profitability. It is apparent from an examination of the income statement that the management of Sight & Sound Corporation operated the company profitably in the year 19+1. From the merchandising activity $4,000 was earned, as shown by the following schedule, which also sets forth some profit percentages.

Sales of merchandise	$80,000	100%
Cost of goods sold	48,000	60
Gross margin	$32,000	40%
Deduct operating expenses:		
Salaries $18,000		
Rent 4,800		
Other 5,200	28,000	35
Net income from merchandising activity	$ 4,000	5%

The net income of $4,000 represents approximately a 15 per cent return on the December 31, 19+1 stockholders' equity ($4,000 ÷ $27,000).

Whether such profit percentages and the rate of return indicate a truly excellent managerial performance cannot be determined merely by an examination of one set of financial statements. As indicated earlier, the success of a business is judged largely by its earnings—but to "evaluate" the earnings, consideration should be given to their trend and how they compare with the earnings results of comparable businesses. The statements of past years will provide the data needed to determine the trend of earnings. (Earlier statements are not available in this instance because Sight & Sound Corporation is only one year old.) Several organizations publish financial data, classified by industry, which enable anyone interested to make comparisons and thus form an opinion about the relative performance of a particular company.

The analysis of earnings data should not be based solely on absolute amounts. For instance, the relationship between earnings and balance-sheet data is an important consideration. A company with $10,000 earnings and $100,000 of stockholders' equity ($10,000 ÷ $100,000 is a 10% return) has operated more successfully, other things being equal, than a company with larger earnings of $24,000 but stockholders' equity of $300,000 (only an 8% return).

Statement of retained earnings. The third statement illustrated is the statement of retained earnings. Retained earnings are that portion of the stockholders' equity attributable to profitable operations, and equal the aggregate net income minus any net losses and dividends to date.

Note: This statement   **SIGHT & SOUND CORPORATION**
also covers a period   **Statement of Retained Earnings**
of time ──────────→ **For the Year Ended December 31, 19+1**

Retained earnings—beginning of year	$ -0-
Net income for 19+1	4,000
Total	$4,000
Deduct dividends	2,000
Retained earnings—end of year	$2,000

This statement shows the changes that have occurred in the retained earnings during the period covered by the statement. One of the changes is dividends. Dividends are distributions of assets (usually cash) to stockholders as a result of profitable operations. Profitable operations increase assets and retained earnings; therefore, dividends decrease assets and retained earnings. Although dividends reduce retained earnings, they are *not* an expense: they are not paid for the purpose of generating revenue.

Observe that the net income shown in the statement of retained earnings agrees with the net income shown by the income statement and that the year-end retained earnings of $2,000 shown in the statement of retained earnings agree with the amount shown in the balance sheet. Thus the retained earnings statement serves as a connecting link between the income statement and the balance sheet.

The interconnection among the three financial statements can be depicted as follows:

Shown in the income statement (page 6):

Net income for the period . . . . $4,000 ⌐

Shown in the statement of retained earnings above:

Net income for the period . . . . $4,000 ◄
Less the dividends paid to stockholders   2,000
Retained earnings at the end of the period . . . . $2,000 ⌐

Shown in the year-end balance sheet (page 4):

Retained earnings at the end of the period . . . . $2,000 ◄

To return to the questions that might be raised by the college student who has just inherited stock in Sight & Sound Corporation, if it is management that "runs" the company, what is involved in managing a business? Stated simply, those who manage a business:

Set goals for the enterprise.
    This function usually requires extensive and careful planning.
Control and coordinate the activities of employees as they work to attain the
    goals established by management.
Evaluate performance.
Make decisions.

In pursuing the above activities, management is more or less continually evaluating alternative courses of action. Choosing among alternatives is facilitated by the use of relevant information. Much of the information that is relevant for managerial decision-making purposes is quantitative and is supplied by the company's accounting system. After management has made a decision, the subsequent financial effects of the decision can be determined through the analysis of relevant accounting data. Thus, accounting data help management make decisions and to control the business by feeding back information on the economic results of past and current decisions. This decision-making process is illustrated below.

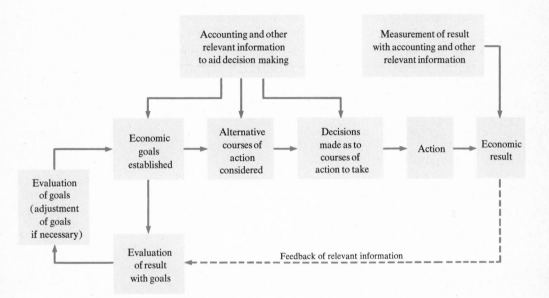

Those involved in management usually acknowledge the value of a good understanding of the accounting process by which data relative to a business are gathered, classified, and set forth in financial reports.

Should the 2,000 shares of stock be sold? By acquiring the shares of stock, the student has become an investor. He should periodically review his holding of "S & S" shares to determine whether a better investment alternative exists.

A number of considerations bear on the question whether the stock should be sold. Some of them are briefly set forth below. It would be up to the student to place his own evaluation on the relevance of such considerations.

He owns 80 per cent of the issued and outstanding shares of capital stock of Sight & Sound Corporation. If he keeps the stock he is in a position to control the company by voting his shares at stockholders' meetings and thus electing those he favors to the board of directors. He could even elect himself to the board of directors and, if he so desired, could become president of the corporation—if his interest, knowledge, and ability suggested such a course of action would be wise.

If he should sell the stock, the opportunity to start at the top would be eliminated; if he desired to be employed by the company he would probably have to start at the bottom and work up.

The shares of stock currently yield a 5 per cent return on market value, as noted earlier. Could he obtain a higher yield if he sold the shares and invested the proceeds elsewhere? A relevant consideration here is that, by controlling the board of directors of Sight & Sound Corporation, he can have some influence on the dividend policy. Of course, there must be profitable operations in the first place before there can be any distributions in the form of dividends. But the proportion of earnings to be retained in the business and used for expansion or investment is a matter for the board of directors to decide. As indicated by the illustrative balance sheet of Sight & Sound Corporation, $2,000 of earnings have been retained in the business.

Another relevant consideration concerns the future prospects of the company. In this connection the following factors seem pertinent:

The market for color television is far from saturated.

Trade publications indicate that, as a result of recent emphasis on research by manufacturing companies, many new products for the home entertainment field are in the final stages of development.

Population of the city in which Sight & Sound Corporation is located is growing at an above-average rate.

As a general rule it takes several years for a new business to attain a satisfactory profit level. Thus, the profit level achieved by the management of Sight & Sound Corporation during its first year of operations can be viewed as a most encouraging sign for the future.

The company has not as yet established a service department. Thus an additional source of profit is available for management's consideration.

The company has no long-term debt. Thus long-term debt can probably be counted on as a source should additional financing be required.

Whether or not he sells his stock, the student will continue to face investment decisions. Knowledge of accounting will enable the student to analyze the financial statements of business firms in order to derive useful information for making investment decisions.

Objectives of this text. Evidence shows that a large proportion of college graduates become involved with business matters either as investors or as members of a management team. Businessmen currently engaged in investing and managing make extensive use of accounting data, and their performance indicates that they have considerable knowledge of the accounting process. It is the objective of this text to provide the kind of knowledge about accounting that will be useful to investors and managers. Such knowledge can also serve as a base upon which prospective career accountants (including those who plan to become certified public accountants) can build a body of specialized knowledge.

Accounting defined. Broadly speaking, accounting is an information-gathering system. The information is economic in character—that is, it involves dollars and cents.

From the preceding discussion in response to the questions raised by our hypothetical college student, it should be apparent that information gathered by the accounting process may serve many purposes. To summarize, such information:

Provides a record of property owned, debts owed, and money invested;
Enables the accountant to prepare reports indicative of the financial position
  of a business and the profitability or unprofitability of its operations;
Facilitates the managing of business activity;
Provides a basis for the evaluation of managerial effectiveness;
Assists those who must make business decisions.

The accounting process. An understanding of the accounting process will be achieved more readily if the following basic relationship is kept in mind:

$$\textbf{Assets} = \textbf{Equities}$$

Such equality does not prevail only at the end of a period when the balance sheet is prepared; the equality prevails continuously.

A business engages in transactions. To cite several kinds of transactions: it makes sales, purchases merchandise, borrows money, pays salaries, and buys equipment. Transactions may be thought of broadly as financial events which result in changes to the assets and/or equities of a business firm. Because of transactions, there are *increases* and *decreases* in the assets and equities. But after each transaction the assets will continue to equal the equities, as can be demonstrated by noting the effects of the first year's transactions of Sight & Sound Corporation.

19+1 Transactions

(1) Issued capital stock for cash, $25,000.
  Result: The corporation acquired $25,000 cash, which was an asset, and in exchange issued capital stock, which resulted in $25,000 of stockholders' equity.

	Assets =	Equities
Before	$ -0-	$ -0-
Changes	+25,000	+25,000
After	$25,000	$25,000

(2) Purchased land as a long-term investment for $10,000 cash.
  Result: The asset cash was decreased $10,000, but the decrease was offset by the new asset, land.

	Assets =	Equities
Before	$25,000	$25,000
Changes	−10,000	
	+10,000	
After	$25,000	$25,000

(3) Purchased merchandise on account, $60,000.

Result: An asset, merchandise inventory, was acquired, and a liability, called accounts payable, was incurred in the amount of $60,000.

	Assets =	Equities
Before	$25,000	$25,000
Changes	+60,000	+60,000
After	$85,000	$85,000

(4a) Made sales of merchandise on account for $80,000.

Note: Sales are revenue transactions; revenues *increase* retained earnings, which are part of the stockholders' equity.

Result: An asset, accounts receivable, was acquired, and the revenue increased retained earnings by $80,000.

	Assets =	Equities
Before	$ 85,000	$ 85,000
Changes	+80,000	+80,000
After	$165,000	$165,000

(4b) The merchandise sold and delivered to the customers from the company's inventory cost the company $48,000.

Note: The cost of the merchandise sold is an expense; expenses *decrease* retained earnings, which are part of the stockholders' equity.

Result: The asset merchandise inventory was decreased $48,000, and the expense decreased the retained earnings by $48,000.

	Assets =	Equities
Before	$165,000	$165,000
Changes	−48,000	−48,000
After	$117,000	$117,000

(5) Collected $70,000 from customers who owed money to the company as a result of the sales made on account.

Result: The asset cash was increased $70,000, and the asset accounts receivable was decreased $70,000.

	Assets =	Equities
Before	$117,000	$117,000
Changes	+70,000	
	−70,000	
After	$117,000	$117,000

(6) Paid $40,000 on the amount owing as a result of the merchandise purchases made on account.

Result: The asset cash was decreased $40,000, and the liability accounts payable was decreased $40,000.

	Assets	=	Equities
Before	$117,000		$117,000
Changes	−40,000		−40,000
After	$ 77,000		$ 77,000

(7) Paid rent for the year 19+1, $4,800.

> Note: This is an expense transaction, so retained earnings are reduced.
> Result: The asset cash was decreased $4,800, and the expense decreased the retained earnings by $4,800.

	Assets	=	Equities
Before	$77,000		$77,000
Changes	−4,800		−4,800
After	$72,200		$72,200

(8) Paid other expenses, $5,200.

> Result: The asset cash was decreased $5,200, and the expense decreased the retained earnings by $5,200.

	Assets	=	Equities
Before	$72,200		$72,200
Changes	−5,200		−5,200
After	$67,000		$67,000

(9) Employees' salaries amount to $1,500 per month, or $18,000 per annum. They are paid monthly on the first business day of the following month. For example, salaries for last January were paid on February 1. Thus salaries for the eleven months January through November have been paid by the disbursement of $16,500 cash, and salaries of $1,500 for December are owed as of December 31.

> Note: Salaries are an expense.

(a) Result: The $16,500 disbursement for salaries reduced the asset cash and the retained earnings.

	Assets	=	Equities
Before	$67,000		$67,000
Changes	−16,500		−16,500
After	$50,500		$50,500

(b) Result: The $1,500 owed for December salaries increased the liabilities and decreased the retained earnings; thus one type of equity (liabilities) was increased and the other type of equity (stockholders' equity) was decreased.

	Assets	=	Equities
Before	$50,500		$50,500
Changes			+1,500
			−1,500
After	$50,500		$50,500

Combined result: The expense for salaries for the year amounts to $18,000:

(a) $16,500 (paid)
(b) __1,500__ (owed)
$18,000

(10) The board of directors authorized the payment of $2,000 cash dividends.
Note: Dividends reduce the retained earnings but, as indicated earlier, they are not an expense.
Result: The asset cash was decreased $2,000, and the retained earnings were decreased $2,000.

	Assets	=	Equities
Before	$50,500		$50,500
Changes	− 2,000		− 2,000
After	$48,500		$48,500

Transaction worksheet. The increases and decreases resulting from the 19+1 transactions which have been analyzed in the preceding paragraphs are noted in the transaction worksheet on the following page. The transaction worksheet is nothing more than the basic accounting equation

Assets = Equities

subdivided for the individual assets and equities, as follows:

Cash + Accounts Receivable + Merchandise Inventory + Land = Accounts Payable + Salaries Payable + Capital Stock + Retained Earnings.

Financial statements for 19+1. Referring to the transaction worksheet, it can be seen that the revenues earned and the expenses incurred during the year were listed in the Retained Earnings column. Revenue and expense items can be thought of as subdivisions of retained earnings. One can, therefore, prepare the income statement for the year ended December 31, 19+1, by summarizing the changes affecting retained earnings caused by revenue and expense transactions.

Compare the data shown in the income statement on page 6, the statement of retained earnings on page 8, and the balance sheet on page 4 with the data set forth in the transaction worksheet on page 15.

The agreement of the financial statements with the data accumulated in the transaction worksheet should be readily apparent. For example, the ending balance of the Cash column, $16,500, agrees with the cash balance shown in the balance sheet. Concerning the normal sequence associated with the accounting process, it is probably equally apparent that the data are recorded in accounting forms and records before the financial statements are prepared. In this chapter, however, the financial statements were presented first to help answer some of the questions raised by the hypothetical college student.

SIGHT & SOUND CORPORATION
Transaction Worksheet
Year 19+1

Explanation	ASSETS				=	EQUITIES				
	Cash	+ Accounts Receivable	+ Merchandise Inventory	+ Land	=	Accounts Payable	+ Salaries Payable	+ Capital Stock	+ Retained Earnings	
Beginning balances	-0-	-0-	-0-	-0-		-0-	-0-	-0-	-0-	
(1) Issued capital stock for cash	+25,000							+25,000		
(2) Purchased land for cash	−10,000			+10,000						
(3) Purchased merchandise on account			+60,000			+60,000				
(4a) Sales on account		+80,000							+80,000	Sales
(4b) Cost of goods sold			−48,000						−48,000	Cost of goods sold
(5) Cash receipts from customers	+70,000	−70,000								
(6) Cash payments on account	−40,000					−40,000				
(7) Paid rent	− 4,800								− 4,800	Rent expense
(8) Paid other expenses	− 5,200								− 5,200	Other expense
(9a) Paid salaries	−16,500								−16,500	Salaries expense
(9b) Liability for December salaries							+ 1,500		− 1,500	Salaries expense
(10) Paid dividends	− 2,000								− 2,000	Dividends
Ending balances	16,500	+ 10,000	+ 12,000	+ 10,000	=	20,000	+ 1,500	+ 25,000	+ 2,000	
		48,500					48,500			

Some customary practices. Dollar signs are generally used in financial statements, although rarely in any other form or record associated with accounting. In the financial statements it is customary to place a dollar sign:

> Beside the first amount in each money column.
> > Look at the balance sheet on page 4 and observe the dollar signs with $16,500, $38,500, $20,000, and $21,500.
> Beside each amount appearing below an underline.
> > Look at the same balance sheet and observe the dollar signs with $48,500 and $25,000.

It is also customary to list detail figures in an inside column with the total carried to the right on the same line. A final figure is usually double underlined. These customs have been followed in the preparation of the balance sheet on page 4.

ASSIGNMENT
MATERIAL

QUESTIONS

1. What is a *balance sheet?*
2. Define *assets.* Prepare a list of ten assets.
3. List four reasons why assets may provide future economic benefits.
4. Define *owners' equity.*
5. What constitutes an indication of "slow moving" merchandise?
6. List several of the common uses made of income statements.
7. Define *revenue.*
8. What is the special feature of the heading for an income statement in contrast to that for a balance sheet?
9. What is involved in managing a business?
10. List some purposes served by the information gathered by the accounting process.
11. Describe transactions that would cause the results set forth below.
    (a) Decrease in cash; increase in some other asset. *Long TERM INVESTMENT*
    (b) Increase in accounts payable; increase in an asset. *PURCHASE OF MERCHANDISE ON ACCOUNT*
    (c) Increase in capital stock. *ISSUE CAPITAL STOCK*
    (d) Decrease in retained earnings. *PAYMENT OF DIVIDENDS*
    (e) Increase in cash; decrease in some other asset. *COLLECTED FROM CUSTOMERS WHO MADE SALES ON ACCOUNT.*
12. State the basic accounting equation.

SHORT EXERCISES

E1-1. What is wrong with the following statement of retained earnings?

QUICK CORPORATION
Statement of Retained Earnings
December 31, 19+1

Retained earnings—beginning of year	$ -0-
Net income for 19+1	8,000
Total	$8,000
Deduct dividends	3,000
Retained earnings—end of year	$5,000

E1-2. If you were asked to prepare an income statement from the following information, which two items among those listed should you not use? (Remember, only revenues and expenses are proper elements for an income statement.)

Cost of goods sold	$30,000
Rent expense	6,000
Sales of merchandise	60,000
Dividends paid to stockholders	2,000
Salaries expense	18,000
Advertising expense	1,800
Patents owned	6,000

E1-3. The total expenses during 19+1 for CD Corporation amounted to $45,000. Use what you need of the following data to determine the total revenue for the year.

Cash receipts for 19+1	$46,000
Net income for 19+1	4,000
Total assets as of December 31, 19+1	80,000

(It might be helpful to denote the elements of an income statement in the form of a simple algebraic equation.)

E1-4. The following transactions occurred after North Slope Corporation was organized.

Issued capital stock for cash, $30,000.
Purchased merchandise on account, $3,000.
Purchased land for cash, $8,000.
Sales of merchandise on account, $5,000.
Cost of goods sold, $2,500.
Collected $1,200 from customers.
Paid salaries, $1,800.

If a balance sheet were prepared after the above transactions, what would be the total shown thereon for all of the assets? Would this amount be equal to any other total shown in the financial statements? (Remember the basic relationship set forth by a simple equation.)

PROBLEMS   NET INCOME 7,000   ENDING R.E. 4000   BALANCE 40,000

Problem A1-1. Prepare the income statement, the statement of retained earnings, and the balance sheet from the following data of First Corporation.

Related to the Year Ended December 31, 19+1

	Retained earnings—beginning of year	$ -0-
B, A	Cash	4,000
I, R	Sales of merchandise	160,000
I, E	Cost of goods sold	100,000
I, E	Salaries expense	35,000
I, E	Rent expense	12,000
I, E	Advertising expense	6,000

B, A	Accounts receivable	14,000
B, A	Merchandise inventory	22,000
SRE	Dividends	3,000
B, L	Accounts payable	5,000
B, L	Rent payable	1,000
B, SE	Capital stock	30,000

Problem A1-2. The following transactions relate to the affairs of Block Corporation, a newly organized firm. Prepare a schedule showing the cumulative dollar total for the assets and equities after each transaction.

Transactions

Issued capital stock for cash, $15,000.
Purchased merchandise on account, $800.
Purchased land for cash, $5,000.
Purchased merchandise for cash, $600.
Purchased additional land giving a mortgage payable, $3,000.
Sales of merchandise on account, $1,000.
Cost of goods sold, $700.
Paid for merchandise purchased earlier on account, $800.
Paid salaries, $500.
Paid dividends, $150.

Suggested solution form:

	Assets	Equities
Issuance of capital stock		
Balances after issuance of stock		
Changes from purchase of merchandise		
Balances after purchase		
Etc.		

Problem A1-3. The following data relate to the year ended December 31, 19+1. Prepare the financial statements (income statement, statement of retained earnings, and balance sheet). Note that you will have to determine the figure for capital stock.

Second Corporation

B, SE		Capital stock	$?
	A	Cash	4,000
	A	Accounts receivable	11,000
B,	*A*	Merchandise inventory—at cost	22,000
	A	Land (Long-term investment)	10,000
I,	*R*	Sales	100,000
I,	*E*	Cost of goods sold	62,000
I,	*E*	Salaries expense	22,000
I,	*E*	Rent expense	9,000
I,	*E*	Miscellaneous expense	2,000
B,	*L*	Accounts payable	3,000
B	*L*	Salaries payable	500
SRE,		Dividends	1,500
SRE		Retained earnings—beginning of year	-0-

Problem A1-4. Use what you need of the following data covering the first year of operations of Alpha Corporation to prepare the statement of retained earnings for 19+1.

Accounts payable	$ 40,000
Accounts receivable	20,000
Capital stock	50,000
Cash	33,000
Cost of goods sold	96,000
Dividends	4,000
Land	20,000
Merchandise inventory, December 31, 19+1	24,000
Rent expense	9,600
Retained earnings—beginning of year	-0-
Other expense	10,400
Salaries expense	36,000
Salaries payable	3,000
Sales	160,000

Problem A1-5. Renewal Corporation was organized at the beginning of 19+1. Show the increases and decreases resulting from the 19+1 transactions on a transaction worksheet. Also prepare the 19+1 financial statements.

19+1 Transactions

(1) Issued capital stock for cash, $40,000.
(2) Purchased merchandise on account, $50,000.
(3) Purchased merchandise for cash, $10,000.
(4a) Made sales of merchandise on account for $60,000.
(4b) Cost of goods sold on account, $40,000.
(5a) Made cash sales, $8,000.
(5b) Cost of goods sold for cash, $5,000.
(6) Collected $52,000 from customers.
(7) Paid $41,000 on the amount owed for merchandise.
(8) Paid rent for the year 19+1, $3,000.
(9) Paid salaries for the year 19+1, $15,000.
(10) Other expenses for 19+1 amounted to $2,500, of which $2,100 had been paid and $400 was owed as of December 31, 19+1.
(11) Paid cash dividends, $1,000.

Problem A1-6. Transactions covering the first year of operations of Starter Company are listed below.

19+1 Transactions

(1) Issued capital stock for cash, $50,000.
(2) Purchased merchandise on account, $70,000.
(3) Paid for advertising expenses, $500.
(4) Paid rent for 19+1, $3,000.
(5a) Made sales of merchandise:
      On account, $80,000.
      For cash, $7,000.
(5b) Cost of goods sold, $51,000.

(6) Salaries for 19+1 total $21,000:
    Paid in cash, $19,500.
    Owed at year end, $1,500.

(7) Other expenses for 19+1 total $2,200, of which $1,900 have been paid for.

(8) Cash collections from customers, $71,000.

(9) Cash payments for merchandise purchased on account, $64,000.

(10) At year-end the company made long-term investments in bonds in the amount of $12,000, and in land in the amount of $18,000, paying cash therefor.

(11) Paid cash dividends, $2,000.

Required:
    (a) Transaction worksheet covering 19+1.
    (b) Financial statements for 19+1.

Problem B1-1. Using the following data, prepare the income statement, statement of retained earnings, and balance sheet of Initial Company. The data relate to the year ended December 31, 19+1.

Cash	$ 4,000
Sales of merchandise	90,000
Cost of goods sold	54,000
Retained earnings—beginning of year	-0-
Salaries expense	22,000
Other expense	9,000
Dividends	1,000
Merchandise inventory	15,000
Accounts receivable	8,000
Accounts payable	3,000
Capital stock	20,000

Problem B1-2. Determine the dollar balance of the assets and equities at the end of the period during which the following transactions occurred.

ABC Corporation was organized, and capital stock was issued for $20,000 cash.
Purchased merchandise on account for $2,000.
Paid rent for the period, $500.
Sold merchandise on account for $1,900.
The merchandise sold cost ABC Corporation $1,100.
Paid $2,000 on account for the merchandise purchased above.
Purchased land for $4,000 cash.
Paid salaries, $250.
Sold merchandise for cash, $300.
The merchandise sold cost ABC Corporation $200.
Collected $400 on account from customers.
Paid dividends, $100.

Suggested form for solution:

	Assets	Equities
Changes resulting from transactions:		
Issuance of capital stock	$ xx	$ xx
Purchase of merchandise on account	xx	xx
Etc.		

Problem B1-3. (a) Use what you need of the following data covering the first year of operations of XYZ Corporation to prepare the income statement for 19+1.

Cash	$ 3,000
Salaries payable	500
Salaries expense	15,000
Merchandise purchased	40,000
Cost of merchandise sold	32,000
Sales	55,000
Rent expense	3,600
Advertising expense	800
Telephone expense	100
Electricity expense	200
Dividends	1,200
Amount owed for merchandise purchased	2,000
Merchandise inventory on hand at year end	8,000
Other expense	400
Retained earnings—end of year	1,700

(b) Prepare a computation showing the accuracy or inaccuracy of the $1,700 amount for retained earnings.

Problem B1-4. Novel Corporation was organized at the beginning of 19+1. The following transactions occurred during the year.

> Issued capital stock for cash, $75,000.
> Purchased merchandise on account, $180,000.
> Made sales of merchandise on account, $240,000.
> Cost of goods sold, $144,000.
> Purchased land as a long-term investment for $30,000, giving $10,000 cash and a $20,000 mortgage payable.
> Collected $210,000 from customers.
> Paid rent for eleven months, $13,200.
> Paid other expenses, $15,600.
> Paid $120,000 of the amount owed for merchandise.
> Paid salaries, $46,000.
> Paid $1,800 in local taxes for 19+1.
> Paid $3,000 in dividends.

At year end the corporation owed $1,200 for one month's rent (December, 19+1). It intends to pay this obligation during the first week of 19+2.

Determine the retained earnings as of December 31, 19+1.

Problem B1-5. The results of the 19+1 transactions of Fresh Company are summarized below.

> (1) The company was organized and capital stock was issued for cash, $30,000.
> (2) Purchased merchandise for cash, $5,000.
> (3a) Made cash sales, $6,000.
> (3b) Cost of goods sold for cash, $4,000.
> (4) Purchased merchandise on account, $35,000.
> (5) Paid for advertising expenses, $800.
> (6a) Made sales of merchandise on account, $36,000.

(6b) Cost of goods sold on account, $24,000.
 (7) Paid rent for the year, $2,400.
 (8) Cash payments for salaries, $8,000.
 (9) Cash receipts from customers, $31,000.
(10) Cash payments for merchandise purchased on account, $29,000.
(11) At year end securities were acquired as a long-term investment for a cash outlay of $10,000.
(12) At year end the company owed $700 for unpaid salaries.
(13) Paid cash dividends, $1,200.

Required:
(a) Completed transaction worksheet.
(b) Financial statements for 19+1 (income statement, statement of retained earnings, and balance sheet).

Problem B1-6. Glisten Company commenced regular operations as of January 2, 19+1. During the preceding month it had issued capital stock for $70,000, but no other transactions occurred prior to January 2, 19+1. Prepare a transaction worksheet which will provide the information needed for the 19+1 financial statements. Also determine the following amounts:

Net income for 19+1
Total assets as of December 31, 19+1
Stockholders' equity as of December 31, 19+1

19+1 Transactions

 (1) Purchased merchandise on account, $60,000.
 (2) Paid rent for 19+1, $3,600.
(3a) Sales for 19+1, $85,000, of which $7,000 were cash sales.
(3b) Cost of goods sold, $52,000.
 (4) Salaries for 19+1 totaled $21,000:
     Paid in cash, $20,200.
     Owed at year end, $800.
 (5) Paid local taxes, $2,300. (Such taxes are a business expense.)
 (6) Collections from customers for sales on account, $71,000.
 (7) Cash disbursements for merchandise purchased on account, $55,000.
 (8) Paid miscellaneous expenses, $1,800.
 (9) Purchased land as a long-term investment for $12,000; terms: $6,000 in cash and $6,000 noninterest-bearing note payable due January 31, 19+2.
(10) Paid travel and entertainment expenses, $1,100.
(11) Paid cash dividends, $3,000.

Introduction
to Accounting Theory

Accounting theory. Accounting, like other academic subjects, needs a theoretical structure to unify its underlying logic or system of reasoning. Such a structure provides a frame of reference that gives meaning to and justification for the concepts and procedures identified with a given subject matter area. Thus the manner in which accountants gather, record, classify, report, and interpret financial data is given meaning and is explained by accounting theory. For example, accounting theory explains the reasoning followed by accountants when they determine the dollar amounts shown in financial statements.

Accounting operates in an economic environment in which uncertainty is an element. Complete or perfect knowledge cannot exist when there is uncertainty; therefore, we must make assumptions when building a theoretical structure for accounting. Assumptions are made to fill the unknowns in knowledge, and the assumptions plus observable facts are woven together to form the theoretical structure. Consequently, to understand accounting and the theory associated therewith, the student must be aware of the following underlying assumptions.

The measuring-unit assumption. It was noted in the discussion of the accounting process in
Chapter 1 that accounting records the changes in assets and equities from business
transactions. Therefore, it is necessary to decide upon some means of measuring
such changes. Accountants assume that, for their purposes, money is the best measur-
ing unit. This means that accountants gather, record, classify, report, and interpret
only that financial information which is quantifiable in terms of money. As a result,
the accounting information about a particular firm does not include such pertinent
information as the state of its personnel relations, the health of its top executives,
the quality of its products relative to competing products, and the status of its
research and development programs. Accounting simply does not provide all of the
information about a firm; it provides only that economic information that can be
expressed in terms of money.

Ideally the dimensions or "size" of whatever is adopted as a unit of measurement
should remain constant over time. Thus the distance of an inch or the weight of
an ounce or the general purchasing power of the dollar, to cite three familiar
measuring units, should remain constant. In fact, the purchasing power of the dollar
varies over time because of changes in the general price level; however, accountants
assume that such fluctuations in the purchasing power of money will be immaterial
or inconsequential. In effect, accountants use the dollar as though it were a stable
unit of measurement.

During certain periods this assumption regarding the stability of money has
squared substantially with reality. It is also true that, during other periods, the
purchasing power of the dollar has changed significantly, as during the twenty years
from 1950 to 1970 when the purchasing power of the dollar declined considerably.
In other words, during that period the purchasing power, or size, of the dollar
changed. Accounting makes no allowance for such a change; it treats all dollars
as though they were of equal size. Such accounting could result in misleading infor-
mation being set forth in the financial statements. For example, assume that Com-
pany A paid $100,000 for land in 1940 and that Company B paid the same amount
for land in 1960. Their current balance sheets, assuming that the companies con-
tinued to own the land, would show the asset land as follows:

Company A Balance Sheet

Land $100,000

Company B Balance Sheet

Land $100,000

A reader of the balance sheets could be misled if he concluded that both companies
had made an *equal* investment in land in terms of general purchasing power invested,
or that the two companies owned land of comparable present value. The fact is that
1940 dollars are not the same as 1960 dollars, because during this particular 20-year
period the purchasing power of the dollar declined by approximately 50 per cent.
So the companies did not make equal investments in land; and historical cost, the
amount shown in the balance sheets of the two companies, is not usually a good
indicator of what something is worth now.

Some accountants, dissatisfied with the stable-dollar assumption, have advocated that the various-sized dollars shown in the financial statements should be converted to current-sized dollars. After conversion, each dollar shown in such modified financial statements would represent the same amount of purchasing power. Thus all of the dollars shown in financial statements would be the "same size" dollars. However, most accountants continue to support the stable-dollar assumption. More attention will be given to this important matter in a later chapter.

The going-concern assumption. The accountant assumes that the business for which he is accounting will continue in operation indefinitely, or at least will remain in business long enough to complete current plans and fulfill existing commitments. This assumption has been used traditionally to justify what is known as the cost basis of accounting, in contrast to a value basis of accounting, for those assets not being held for sale. For example, land being used as an employee parking lot would, following the cost basis of accounting, be shown in the balance sheet at its cost, even though there was reliable evidence that the land could be sold for more than its cost. For a going concern that intends to continue using its assets to carry on its regular business operations, the accountant traditionally assumes that realizable values are not particularly relevant because such assets will continue to be used and will not be sold.

On the other hand, if a business is failing and it seems likely that its assets will be subject to sale rather than continued use, the application of conventional accounting principles and procedures would probably result in inadequate or misleading financial statements. Under such circumstances the accountant is expected either to discontinue the cost basis of accounting or to make it known to the statement-user, by suitable disclosure accompanying the financial statements, that the going-concern assumption has not been abandoned and, therefore, that the financial statements may not provide an indication of realizable values.

The fiscal-period assumption. A primary objective of accounting is to provide economic information useful for financial decision making. If that objective is to be fulfilled, the accounting data must be timely. Obviously, the accounting data relevant for a particular decision must be available to the decision-makers before the deadline for making the decision.

Earnings data are relevant for many business decisions. Income determination would be quite easy if the accountant could delay it until business operations were discontinued and all assets were converted to cash. The net income for the entire life span of a business would be the excess cash received by the owners, including that received upon liquidation, over their investment in the business. No estimates or assumptions would be required because there would be no uncertainty. But it obviously would be unsatisfactory to postpone the determination of net income until after liquidation. Management and other users of financial data want such information currently; they want to plan and adapt their courses of action in the light of such information. In short, users want timely accounting data.

The accountant tries to meet this need by assuming that he can segment the business operations of a firm into time periods. Such time intervals are known as accounting periods or fiscal periods. Thus the accountant determines the firm's financial position at the end of each fiscal period (shown by the balance sheet) and measures the results of operations for each fiscal period (reported in the income statement). However, most businesses are engaged in continuous activity which does not stop at the end of each fiscal period. So, in a sense, the fiscal-period concept is based on an assumption that business activity "stops" at periodic intervals, which allows the accountant to prepare financial statements and thus provide a report on the firm's progress during the period just ended and its financial position at the end of the period. In fact, because of the continuous nature of most business activity, accounting data associated with fiscal periods should be viewed as short-run approximations of the firm's position and progress.

To make the short-run approximations shown in the financial statements as meaningful as possible, revenue and expense must be identified with the proper time periods. Revenues and expenses for 19+1 have to be kept separate from those of 19+2; otherwise the net income of each year would be distorted and those who use accounting data for decision making would be misled. To avoid such distortion the accountant relies on the *matching concept:* expenses are incurred to generate revenue, and the two are matched to determine net income for the period. Such matching is known as accrual accounting. In contrast, under cash accounting, revenue is reported in the period when the related cash collection is made, and expenses are reported in the period when the cash disbursements are made. Accrual accounting will continue to be the primary concern of this text. However, in some instances, usually among small businesses and professional practices, cash accounting is used.

ILLUSTRATION OF ACCRUAL ACCOUNTING: The following will illustrate the application of the matching concept. The illustration covers four fiscal periods, and during that time there were $1,500 of revenue and $1,150 of expense. A proper matching requires that the revenue and expense be shown in the income statement for the period when the revenue is earned and the expense is incurred. In the illustration below this occurred in the third period.

Event	Effect on Financial Statements
	First Fiscal Period
The business ordered merchandise costing $1,000.	No effect. Placing an order for merchandise results in a future transaction, not a present transaction, because the changes in assets and equities as a consequence of the order will occur in the future.

Second Fiscal Period

Event	Merchandise Inventory	Accounts Payable
The merchandise ordered was delivered.	+1,000	+1,000

Event	Cash	Accounts Payable
The bill for the merchandise was paid.	−1,000	−1,000

Third Fiscal Period

	Accounts Receivable	Merchandise Inventory	Retained Earnings	
The merchandise was sold on account for $1,500.	+1,500		+1,500	Sales
		−1,000	−1,000	Cost of goods sold

	Sales Commissions Payable	Retained Earnings	
Salesmen's commissions of 10% are payable in the fiscal period following sale.	+ 150	− 150	Sales commissions

These transactions are summarized in the partial financial statements below.

Partial Income Statement
For the Third Fiscal Period

Revenue:
  Sales $1,500
Expenses:
  Cost of goods sold $1,000
  Sales commissions   150

Partial Balance Sheet
At End of Third Fiscal Period

Assets:
  Accounts receivable $1,500

Liabilities:
  Sales commissions payable . . . .$ 150

Fourth Fiscal Period

	Cash	Accounts Receivable	Sales Commissions Payable
Paid commissions on third fiscal period sales.	− 150		−150
Collected $1,500 from customer.	+1,500	−1,500	

OBSERVATION: Cash receipts and disbursements are often the result of revenue and expense transactions. However, the time when the cash receipt or cash disbursement occurs is not necessarily the proper time, following accrual accounting, to give recognition to the revenue or expense. The relevance of this observation was demonstrated by the preceding illustration, in which the cash receipts and disbursements occurred during the second and fourth fiscal periods while the related revenue and expense were applicable to the third fiscal period.

Accrual accounting applied to business transactions. To illustrate further the nature of accrual accounting, the transactions of Sight & Sound Corporation relating to its second year of operations (19+2) will be analyzed. Remember that the equality of assets with equities is not disturbed by the increases and decreases caused by transactions. Such continuing equality of the accounting equation is depicted by the following diagram. Studying it may further clarify why the assets will always equal the equities.

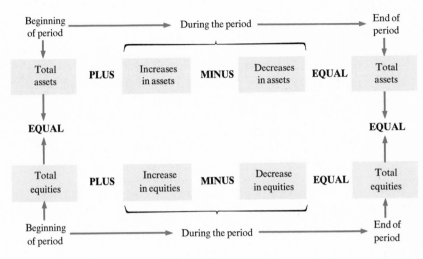

19+2 Transactions

(1) Paid the liability for December 19+1 salaries, $1,500.

   Reasoning: Although salaries are expenses, they apply to the period that received the benefit of the services performed by the salaried employees, which may or may not coincide with the period during which the salary payments are made. In this instance the salaries for December 19+1 were properly treated as a 19+1 expense and the liability therefor was shown in the December 31, 19+1 balance sheet. The payment made in 19+2 merely removed the outstanding liability.

   Result: The asset cash was decreased $1,500 and the liability salaries payable was satisfied.

ASSETS	EQUITIES
Cash	Salaries Payable
	1,500 Outstanding balance
−1,500	−1,500
	-0-

(2) Purchased a small delivery truck for cash, $4,000. Management believes the truck will last four years.

   Reasoning: By acquiring the delivery truck, the business has secured the right to some future economic benefits and, since the benefit period extends beyond the current fiscal period, the transaction should be handled as an asset acquisition.

Result: The asset cash was decreased $4,000 and a new asset was acquired costing $4,000.

	ASSETS
Cash	Delivery Truck
−4,000	+4,000

(3) Purchased merchandise on account, $60,000.
   Comment: Satisfying inventory needs with only one purchase a year would be most unusual. But, since each purchase of merchandise would be handled in the same way, presenting annual data eliminates repetitive transactions.
   Result: The asset merchandise inventory and the liability accounts payable were increased $60,000.

ASSETS	EQUITIES
Merchandise Inventory	Accounts Payable
+60,000	+60,000

(4a) Sales on account, $90,000.
   Comment: Here also, annual data are given to eliminate repetitive transactions.
   Result: Accounts receivable and retained earnings (revenue) were both increased $90,000.

ASSETS	EQUITIES
Accounts Receivable	Retained Earnings
+90,000	+90,000 Sales

(4b) Cost of goods sold, $54,000.
   Result: Merchandise inventory and retained earnings were both decreased $54,000.

ASSETS	EQUITIES
Merchandise Inventory	Retained Earnings
−54,000	−54,000 Cost of goods sold

(5) Collections from customers, $85,000.
   Result: Cash was increased and accounts receivable decreased $85,000.

	ASSETS
Cash	Accounts Receivable
+85,000	−85,000

(6) Payments to creditors on account, $55,000.

Result: Cash and accounts payable decreased $55,000.

ASSETS	EQUITIES
Cash	Accounts Payable
−55,000	−55,000

(7) Paid two years' rent in advance, $9,600. At the beginning of 19+2 the company signed a rental agreement covering a two-year period which specified that rent for the two-year period was to be paid in advance.

Reasoning: By making the payment in advance the company has acquired the right to some future economic benefits, namely, the benefits arising from the use of the rented property for business purposes. Thus the prepaid rent qualifies as an asset acquisition.

Result: One asset increased and another asset decreased $9,600.

ASSETS	
Cash	Prepaid Rent
−9,600	+9,600

(8) Paid other expenses, $5,500.

Result: Cash and retained earnings were both decreased $5,500.

ASSETS	EQUITIES
Cash	Retained Earnings
−5,500	−5,500 Other expense

(9) Paid salaries for the eleven months January through November 19+2, $18,700.

Result: Cash and retained earnings were both decreased $18,700.

ASSETS	EQUITIES
Cash	Retained Earnings
−18,700	−18,700 Salaries expense

(10) The board of directors authorized the payment of $2,000 cash dividends.

Result: Remember, dividends reduce retained earnings, but they are not an expense.

ASSETS	EQUITIES
Cash	Retained Earnings
−2,000	−2,000 Dividends

(11) Received $1,400 "cash in advance" from a customer when he ordered a custom TV-stereo unit. The unit was special-ordered by Sight & Sound Corporation but had not been received as of December 31, 19+2.

Reasoning: Because the article ordered has not been delivered to the customer, the $1,400 received cannot be considered as revenue for 19+2. Pending performance, the company has an obligation to its customer, which liability is generally labeled as Advances from Customers. Alternative labels sometimes found in published financial statements are "Revenue Received in Advance" and "Deferred Revenue."

Result: Cash and the liability advances from customers increased $1,400.

ASSETS	EQUITIES
Cash	Advances from Customers
+1,400	+1,400

Transaction worksheet for 19+2. The increases and decreases resulting from the 19+2 transactions that have been analyzed in the preceding paragraphs are presented in the transaction worksheet on page 33. Observe that the first line of the transaction worksheet is used for the beginning-of-year balances, which data are taken from the bottom line of the 19+1 transaction worksheet presented in Chapter 1, page 15.

The last line of the transaction worksheet shows the balances (accountants call them account balances) after all 19+2 *transactions* have been given recognition. However, a proper matching of revenue and expense would not be achieved if these balances were used to prepare the financial statements for 19+2, because of the following:

(A-1) No recognition has been given to the December salaries.

As previously noted the company records and pays the monthly salaries on the first business day of the following month. As a consequence, December salaries would not be included among the 19+2 transactions listed in the transaction worksheet.

(A-2) No recognition has been given to the fact that one-half of the rent paid in advance is rent expense for 19+2.

The $9,600 rent payment made by the company at the beginning of 19+2 and recorded as Prepaid Rent covered the two-year period 19+2 and 19+3. Thus the rent expense amounts to $4,800 per year.

(A-3) No recognition has been given to depreciation on the delivery truck.

Required adjustments to year-end balances. To achieve a proper matching of revenue and expense for 19+2, the following adjustments or modifications need to be made to the year-end balances shown on the transaction worksheet:

SIGHT & SOUND CORPORATION
Transaction Worksheet
Year 19+2

Explanation	ASSETS						=	EQUITIES					
	Cash	+ Accounts Receivable	+ Merchandise Inventory	+ Prepaid Rent	+ Land	+ Delivery Truck	=	Accounts Payable	+ Salaries Payable	+ Advances from Customers	+ Capital Stock	+ Retained Earnings	
Beginning balances	16,500	10,000	12,000	-0-	10,000	-0-		20,000	1,500	-0-	25,000	2,000	
(1) Paid liability for salaries	− 1,500								−1,500				
(2) Purchased delivery truck	− 4,000					+4,000							
(3) Purchased merchandise on account			+60,000					+60,000					
(4a) Sales on account		+90,000										+90,000	Sales
(4b) Cost of goods sold			−54,000									−54,000	Cost of goods sold
(5) Collections from customers	+85,000	−85,000											
(6) Payments on account	−55,000							−55,000					
(7) Prepayment of rent	− 9,600			+9,600									
(8) Paid other expenses	− 5,500											− 5,500	Other expense
(9) Paid salaries for 11 months	−18,700											−18,700	Salaries expense
(10) Paid dividends	− 2,000											− 2,000	Dividends
(11) Advances from customers	+ 1,400									+1,400			
Balances	6,600	15,000	18,000	9,600	10,000	4,000		25,000	-0-	1,400	25,000	11,800	

63,200 = 63,200

(A-1) Liability for December salaries, $1,700.

	EQUITIES		
	Salaries Payable	Retained Earnings	
Balances per trans- action worksheet . . .	-0-	− 18,700	Salaries expense for eleven months
Adjustment (A-1)	+ 1,700	− 1,700	December salaries
Adjusted balances	1,700	20,400	Salaries expense for the year

Reasoning: Without the above adjustment, the expenses for 19+2 and the year-end liabilities shown in the financial statements would be understated.

(A-2) Half of the rent payment made in advance applies to the year 19+2. Therefore, half of the prepaid rent balance must be transferred to expense.

	ASSETS	**EQUITIES**	
	Prepaid Rent	Retained Earnings	
Balances per transaction worksheet	+ 9,600	—	
Adjustment (A-2)	− 4,800	− 4,800	Rent expense
Adjusted balances	4,800	4,800	Rent expense for the year

Reasoning: When the $9,600 payment was made in advance to cover the rent for the years 19+2 and 19+3, the disbursement was properly analyzed as an asset acquisition because the company put itself in a position to benefit from the use of the rented property for a two-year period. However, by the end of 19+2, one-half of the rental benefits had been used. A December 31, 19+2 balance sheet that showed prepaid rent among the assets at $9,600 and an income statement that showed no rent expense for 19+2 would be incorrect. There would be an improper matching of revenue and expense.

(A-3) Depreciation for 19+2 on the delivery truck is computed as follows:

Cost of depreciable asset	$4,000
Deduct estimated scrap value	400
Amount subject to depreciation	$3,600
Useful life—4 years.	
Depreciation per annum	$ 900

	ASSETS		EQUITIES
	(Delivery _ Accumulated) Truck Depreciation		Retained Earnings
Balances per transaction worksheet	4,000	-0-	—
Adjustment (A-3)		−900	−900 Depreciation expense
Adjusted balances	(4,000 −	900)	Depreciation expense 900 for the year

Reasoning: As noted, the delivery truck is expected to have a four-year useful life. Because the truck will be used during that period to assist in the business activities carried on to earn revenue, a portion of the cost should be transferred to expense during each accounting period. That is, the cost of the truck's services during the fiscal period is a legitimate expense incurred in the generation of revenue. Such expense is called depreciation and, if it were ignored, net income would be overstated because of the improper matching of revenue and expense.

For purposes of providing more useful information, the accumulated depreciation deduction ($900) is accounted for separately from the original cost of the asset ($4,000) in order to avoid showing only the undepreciated cost ($3,100) in the balance sheet.

Depreciation is discussed in greater depth elsewhere in the text.

Financial statements for 19+2. The financial statements for 19+2, prepared after consideration of the three year-end adjustments just discussed, are set forth below. Observe how the accumulated depreciation is shown in the balance sheet, i.e., it is contra to (deducted from) the related asset. Also note that the rent prepayment (often called prepaid expense) is properly listed as the last item under the Current Assets caption.

SIGHT & SOUND CORPORATION
Income Statement
For the Year Ended December 31, 19+2

Revenue:		
Sales of merchandise		$90,000
Deduct expenses:		
Cost of goods sold	$54,000	
Salaries expense	20,400	
Rent expense	4,800	
Other expense	5,500	
Depreciation expense	900	85,600
Net income		$ 4,400

SIGHT & SOUND CORPORATION
Statement of Retained Earnings
For the Year Ended December 31, 19+2

Retained earnings, December 31, 19+1	$2,000
Net income for 19+2	4,400
Total	$6,400
Deduct dividends	2,000
Retained earnings, December 31, 19+2	$4,400

SIGHT & SOUND CORPORATION
Balance Sheet
December 31, 19+2

Assets			Equities		
Current assets:			Current liabilities:		
Cash	$ 6,600		Accounts payable	$25,000	
Accounts receivable . . .	15,000		Salaries payable	1,700	
Merchandise inventory—			Advances from		
at cost	18,000		customers	1,400	$28,100
Prepaid rent	4,800	$44,400			
			Stockholders' equity:		
Long-term investment:			Capital stock, 2,500		
Investment in land—at			shares issued and		
cost		10,000	outstanding	$25,000	
			Retained earnings	4,400	29,400
Property, plant, and					
equipment:					
Delivery truck	$ 4,000				
Less accumulated de-					
preciation	900	3,100			
		$57,500			$57,500

The historical-cost assumption. A fairly common question, and a highly relevant one, is: Does the balance sheet indicate what the assets are worth? A brief answer is: In most cases it does not.

To some extent, the answer depends on the kinds of assets held by a business. Obviously the cash balance indicates value. Also, the amounts shown for the money claims held by a business, such as accounts receivable, being indicative of prospective cash inflow, in most cases will approximate their value. But in most businesses the dollar amount of assets acquired by purchase, such as merchandise inventory, investments, and depreciable assets, far exceed the cash and money claim balances. And the purchased assets generally are shown at their cost, which usually will not closely approximate their values as of the balance sheet date.

The reliance on cost as the accounting basis for assets acquired by purchase rather than their present value can be attributed in part to the indefinite nature of value. Value is subjective. Frequently it is merely someone's opinion—often affected by optimism or pessimism. Value is something that people often argue about. It may be quite difficult to find several businessmen who would agree on the value of a building, or a patent, or a complicated machine. In contrast, the accountant views cost as being an objective measurement because it is the result of a bargained transaction and is verifiable. Furthermore, the cost basis of reporting has the merit of showing on subsequent balance sheets what management paid in acquiring various assets.

In most cases it would be wrong to conclude from the above that cost and value differ greatly at acquisition date. Under normal conditions, cost is a reliable indication of value at the date the transaction is completed because, as a general rule, a seller would not sell an asset for an amount less than its worth, nor would a purchaser pay more than an asset is worth. In a sense, the two amounts (cost and value) can be said to coincide, at least approximately, at acquisition.

What happens with the passage of time? No predictions can be offered regarding the trend of values. It may develop in some cases that acquisition cost and value will remain close together. It is just as likely that "old" costs will become a poor indication of "current" values. An important point to remember is: It should not be assumed that a balance sheet discloses current values. Whether historical cost will closely approximate current value depends on the nature of the asset and the economic changes that have occurred since the asset was acquired.

Does the above observation destroy the usefulness of balance sheets? Usually not. When a disparity exists between historical costs shown in the balance sheet and current values, the usefulness of the balance sheet is not completely destroyed, because in most cases the assets with current values significantly different from historical cost have been acquired to be used and not to be resold. The accountant traditionally assumes that current values often are of slight significance to a "going concern" because, in most cases, assets with current values differing materially from their actual cost would be such things as buildings, machinery, and equipment that were acquired to be used and not to be resold.

Classified balance sheet. The financial statements of many companies are widely circulated, often as a part of an annual report to stockholders. (An example of an annual report to stockholders is presented in Appendix 1.) Stockholders, banks, stockbrokers, investment analysts, governmental agencies, and investors are frequent users of financial statements. Many concerned with business matters review and analyze a considerable number of financial statements in the regular course of their work. Consider the confusion and inconvenience that statement-users might suffer if every business followed its own preference concerning the form and content of financial statements.

To minimize the misunderstanding and annoyance that would be likely to prevail if no uniformity existed, accountants and businessmen have developed some classification and disclosure practices that have become rather widely used. Their application to the balance sheet will be noted at this time.

The classifications used in a balance sheet depend upon the nature of the business, upon the kinds of assets held and liabilities owed, and upon the type of business organization adopted. In general, the principal balance sheet categories are

Assets:
Current assets
Long-term investments
Property, plant, and equipment
Intangible assets

Equities:
Liabilities:
Current
Long-term
Stockholders' equity (This classification caption is used for corporations. Business operations also may be conducted by an individual proprietorship or a partnership. Captions for such alternative forms of organization will be introduced later.)

CURRENT ASSETS: Cash and other assets, such as temporary investments in securities, accounts and notes receivable, inventory, supplies, and prepayments that presumably will be converted into cash, or will be used, or will expire during a normal *operating cycle*. Such items are viewed as being indicative of short-term debt-paying ability.

An operating cycle can be described as follows: Business operations consist of a round of conversions—cash to inventories, to receivables, and back to cash; the average time required to complete this round is an *operating cycle*. The time period of an operating cycle depends on the nature of the business.

The current assets are customarily listed in the following order: Cash, short-term holdings of marketable securities, receivables from customers, other receivables, inventories, supplies, and short-term prepayments. Short-term prepayments are regarded as current assets because a company with, say, $18,000 of cash and a $500 rent prepayment for one month is in essentially the same position as a company with $18,500 of cash but faced with the necessity of immediately spending $500 for rent.

LONG-TERM INVESTMENTS: Investments other than those properly classifiable as current assets. Examples include investments in the capital stock of other companies and in land held for resale.

PROPERTY, PLANT, AND EQUIPMENT: Land and depreciable property of a relatively long-term nature used in the operations of the business and not intended for sale. Examples are employee parking lots, buildings, machinery, furniture and fixtures, office equipment, and delivery equipment. Such assets are customarily listed according to their use-life, assets with the longest use-life being listed first and assets with the shortest use-life being listed last.

INTANGIBLE ASSETS: Noncurrent assets lacking physical substance that have future economic benefits because of the rights they afford the possessor. Examples are patents, franchises, copyrights, and goodwill.

CURRENT LIABILITIES: The debts or obligations that, according to reasonable expectations, are to be satisfied within the operating-cycle period (as described in connection with the discussion of current assets) or one year, whichever is longer. Advances from customers, which are to be earned by the future performance of services or future delivery of merchandise within the operating-cycle period, are properly classifiable as current liabilities, because the earning of such revenue normally requires the utilization of current assets.

The excess of the current assets over the current liabilities is called *working capital,* and the ratio of current assets to current liabilities is called the *current ratio.* Because current assets normally are used to pay the current liabilities, the relationship between current assets and current liabilities is indicative of the ability of the company to meet its short-term financial obligations. Thus a firm with $300,000 in current assets and $100,000 in current liabilities has a current ratio of 3 to 1, which indicates that its current assets could shrink two-thirds and still meet the current liabilities owed, other things being equal. For the purpose of financial analysis, the current ratio of a company should be compared with the current ratios of similar companies, and the trend of the current ratio over several years should be noted. Finally, a current ratio that looks very high may indicate that the company has too much of its money tied up in current assets.

LONG-TERM LIABILITIES: Bonds, mortgages, and other long-term financial obligations not classifiable as current liabilities.

STOCKHOLDERS' EQUITY: In accounting for the elements of stockholders' equity, the emphasis is placed on the *source:* how much of the stockholders' equity is traceable to

- Investments by stockholders, shown as capital stock.
- Gifts—such as the gift of a plant to a company to induce it to locate in the donor city, shown as additional paid-in capital.
- Earnings, shown as retained earnings.

Definitions and accounting procedures relating to the above balance sheet items will be developed in reasonable depth later in the text.

Alternative form for the balance sheet. A balance sheet customarily is prepared showing the assets at the left and the liabilities and stockholders' equity at the right. Such an arrangement is referred to as the account form.

If space limitations make it desirable, the liabilities and stockholders' equity may be presented below the assets. This arrangement is known as the report form, which is used in the following, more comprehensive illustration of a balance sheet.

HYPOTHETICAL COMPANY
Balance Sheet
December 31, 19—

Assets

Current assets:

Cash	$ 18,000	
Temporary investments in marketable securities, at cost	8,000	
Accounts receivable	24,000	
Notes receivable	5,000	
Interest receivable	100	
Inventory, at cost	30,000	
Prepaid rent	500	
Unexpired insurance	400	$ 86,000

Long-term investments:

Land (held for future use)	$ 15,000	
Government bonds	12,000	27,000

Property, plant, and equipment:

Land—Parking lot		$ 25,000	
Buildings	$150,000		
Less accumulated depreciation	30,000	120,000	
Furniture and fixtures	$ 40,000		
Less accumulated depreciation	8,000	32,000	
Delivery equipment	$ 9,000		
Less accumulated depreciation	5,000	4,000	181,000

Intangible assets:

Patents	6,000
	$300,000

Equities

Current liabilities:

Accounts payable	$ 15,000	
Notes payable	10,000	
Salaries payable	1,500	
Interest payable	300	
Estimated income tax payable	2,800	
Liability for payroll taxes	1,400	
Advances from customers	3,000	
Rent received in advance	1,000	$ 35,000

Long-term liability:

6% Bank loan, due in five years	50,000

Stockholders' equity:

Capital stock—authorized, 10,000 shares;		
issued and outstanding, 6,000 shares	$120,000	
Additional paid-in capital	25,000	$145,000
Retained earnings	70,000	215,000
		$300,000

Disclosure matters. Financial statements are rarely limited to a listing of money amounts. To give added meaning to the financial statements, various kinds of informative material are included, by means of parenthetical comment or footnotes.

Some matters that may require disclosure are the following:

- Valuation bases for certain assets such as inventories, investments, and property, plant, and equipment.
- Contingent liabilities.
- Interest rates and maturity dates on long-term liabilities.
- Descriptive features of the company's capital stock.
- Matters concerning any litigation involving the company.
- Changes in accounting methods.
- Any limitation on the availability of retained earnings for dividends (for example, as a condition for a long-term loan, a bank may require that dividends in any year not exceed one-half of that year's net income).

No specific rules can be offered regarding what should be disclosed. No useful purpose would be served by the disclosure of insignificant information; on the other hand, a fair presentation of the financial position and results of operations rarely can be achieved by "bare-boned" financial statements. One criterion that has merit, although it does not eliminate the need for the use of judgment on the part of those preparing financial statements for circulation to stockholders, is that any factual information which, if known, could influence an investor's decision to hold or to sell a company's stock should be disclosed.

As a general rule, homework problems included in this book will not include the kind of informative material that would be shown in footnotes or parenthetical comments.

ASSIGNMENT

MATERIAL

QUESTIONS

1. What does the accountant assume with regard to the unit of measurement used in accounting?

2. The December 31, 19+1 balance sheets of Companies X and Y both show among the assets an investment in land of $200,000. Identify two basic things about the investments which a reader of the balance sheets cannot safely conclude.

3. State the going-concern assumption.

4. The going-concern assumption is cited as justification for the use of cost as the basis for certain assets. Give the reasoning that is followed in connection with the justification.

5. Briefly contrast the accrual basis of accounting and the cash basis of accounting.

6. Assuming that accrual accounting was properly followed during the year 19+1, will a payment made in January of 19+2 for December, 19+1, salaries reduce the retained earnings?

7. Assume that during the first year of operations of a new corporation all transactions for that year were properly recorded on a transaction worksheet. Does it follow that a proper matching of revenue and expense will have been achieved? Explain.

8. Describe the approach followed to compute "depreciation per annum."

9. How and where is the accumulated depreciation shown in the financial statements?

10. Does the balance sheet indicate what the assets are worth?

11. List the principal categories used when preparing a classified balance sheet.

12. Which assets are current assets?

13. List some matters that may require disclosure in conjunction with the financial statements.

SHORT EXERCISES

E2-1 (a). The following is a partial listing of balances taken from a transaction worksheet. Determine the total of the current assets.

Cash	$10,000
Land (held for future use)	25,000

Inventory	14,000
Unexpired insurance	1,000
Salaries payable	2,000
Retained earnings	18,000
Advances from customers	500
Delivery equipment	4,000
Accumulated depreciation—Delivery equipment	1,200
Accounts receivable	7,000
Prepaid rent	600
Temporary investments	5,000

(b). Determine the new total for current assets after giving consideration to the following adjustments. (Remember: Not every adjustment affects current assets.)

Interest receivable of $100.
Liability for unpaid salaries of $500.
Expired insurance premiums of $300.

E2-2 (a). The following is a partial listing of balances taken from a transaction worksheet. Determine the total of the current liabilities.

Government bonds	$ 4,000
Accounts payable	7,000
Retained earnings	22,000
Estimated income tax payable	1,100
Patents	5,000
Advances from customers	800
Prepaid rent	1,200
Rent received in advance	300
Bank loan due in three years	10,000
Notes payable	2,000

(b). Determine the new total for current liabilities after giving consideration to the following adjustments.

Interest payable of $200 on the bank loan.
Interest payable of $30 on the notes payable.
Liability for unpaid salaries of $300.
Depreciation expense of $600.

E2-3. Several transactions or adjustments are listed below.

Transactions or Adjustments

(1) Purchased merchandise on account.
(2) Purchased delivery equipment and signed a five-year note payable in favor of the seller.
(3) Issued capital stock for cash.
(4) Purchased office equipment for cash.
(5) Depreciation expense.
(6) Purchased temporary investments for cash.
(7) Purchased office furniture on account.
(8) Borrowed from a bank by signing a four-year note payable.
(9) Sold unneeded delivery equipment for cash.
(10) Liability for interest.

(11) Purchased land as a long-term investment and signed a five-year note payable in favor of the seller.

(12) Paid salaries.

(13) Purchased securities maturing in five years with cash not needed for operations in the near future.

(14) Paid liability for income tax.

(15) Cash received for matured long-term investments.

(16) Paid long-term bank loan.

Identify by number which transactions or adjustments cause each of the following results:

	Current Assets	Long-term Investments	Property, Plant, and Equipment	Current Liabilities	Long-term Liabilities	Stockholders' Equity
(a)	+					+
(b)	+				+	
(c)	+			+		
(d)	+		−			
(e)	+	−				
(f)	−	+				
(g)	−		+			
(h)	−			−		
(i)	−				−	
(j)	−					−
(k)		+			+	
(l)			+	+		
(m)		−				−
(n)				+		−

Answer for (a) is (3).

(Note: Some of the transactions or adjustments may not cause results of the kind indicated above.)

E2-4. Data taken from a transaction worksheet before year-end adjustments have been grouped according to balance-sheet categories, as follows:

Current assets	$ 40,000
Long-term investments	30,000
Property, plant, and equipment	50,000
Intangible assets	10,000
	$130,000

Current liabilities	$ 30,000
Long-term liabilities	20,000
Stockholders' equity	80,000
	$130,000

Adjustments are required for the following:

(a) Depreciation on equipment, $1,000.

(b) Interest payable, $500 (on long-term liabilities).

(c) Rent receivable, $300.
(d) Use of $200 of office supplies (classified as a current asset).
(e) To reduce advances from customers from $800 to $400.

Show the revised totals for the balance-sheet categories after giving consideration to the above adjustments.

PROBLEMS

Problem A2-1. For each of the following separate cases, indicate the increases and decreases caused by any needed year-end adjustment. Adopt the solution format suggested for Problem B2-1.

(a) Balances before adjustment:

Rent expense (for 11 months) $3,300
Rent payable . . . . -0-

Data

The company owes $300 for the December rent.

(b) Balances before adjustment:

Prepaid truck rental . . . . $ 400
Truck rental expense . . . . -0-

Data

On December 1, the company leased a truck from Rent-A-Truck Corporation under the following terms: 20 cents per mile, payable monthly, with an initial prepayment of $400, which may be applied to pay for the first 2,000 miles used. December mileage: 900 miles.

(c) Balances before adjustment:

Travel advances . . . . $ 200
Travel expense 900

Data

Employees are granted travel advances to cover certain expenses while away on company business. When the employee completes a trip, he reports the amount of the advance used for company expenses. In this case, half of the travel advances has been used at year-end.

(d) Balances before adjustment:

Office equipment $8,000
Depreciation expense . . . . -0-

Data

Cost of equipment $8,000
Scrap value 800
Useful life: 6 years.
Purchased at the beginning of the current year.

(e) Balances before adjustment:

Taxes expense $1,300
Taxes payable . . . . -0-

Data

The company is liable for unrecorded taxes in the amount of $200.

Problem A2-2. From the following, prepare a classified balance sheet of Georgia Company as of September 30, 19+3.

✓ CA.	Cash	$ 2,345
✓	Interest expense	120
PPE.	Accumulated depreciation—Buildings	2,400
	Sales	40,000
✓ CA.	Prepaid rent	60
	Depreciation expense—Equipment	400
✓ CL	Accounts payable	3,210
✓ CA	Temporary investments	900
SE.	Capital stock	25,000
✓ LTL	Mortgage payable, due March 31, 19+12	3,000
PPE	Land	2,500
PPE.	Accumulated depreciation—Equipment	800
	Cost of goods sold	21,000
	Wages and salaries expense	9,600
✓ CL.	Wages and salaries payable	240
CA	Inventory	2,850
PPE	Buildings	20,000
CL.	Estimated income tax payable	500
SE.	Retained earnings, September 30, 19+3	6,885
CA.	Accounts receivable	1,980
LTI	Land (held for future use)	4,000
PPE	Equipment	2,400
	Depreciation expense—Buildings	800
I A.	Patents	5,000
	Rent expense	240

(handwritten left margin: Liabilities; ASSETS: 38,835)

Problem A2-3. Set up a column for each of the following balance-sheet categories:

> Current assets
> Long-term investments
> Property, plant, and equipment
> Current liabilities
> Long-term liabilities
> Stockholders' equity

Allow one line for each transaction or adjustment and indicate by the use of plus (+) and minus (−) signs the changes, if any, which result from the following.

(1) Issued capital stock for cash.

Suggested form for answer:

Trans-action	Current Assets	Long-term Investments	Property, Plant, and Equipment	Current Liabilities	Long-term Liabilities	Stockholders' Equity
(1)	+					+

(2) Purchased merchandise on account.
(3) Paid cash for land to be held for future use.

  (4) Paid cash for a two-year insurance policy.
(5a) Sold merchandise on account.
(5b) Cost of goods sold.
  (6) Purchased on account fifteen-months' supply of wrapping and packaging material.
  (7) Purchased office equipment for cash.
  (8) Borrowed money on a long-term bank loan.
  (9) Paid office expenses.
(10) Paid interest expense.
(11) Paid the amount owed for merchandise purchased on account.
(12) Recorded depreciation expense on the office equipment.
(13) Recorded liability for unpaid rent.
(14) Made an adjustment for the expired portion of prepaid insurance. (See 4 above.)
(15) Recorded liability for interest on long-term bank loan.
(16) Paid cash dividend.
(17) Recorded estimated liability for income tax.
(18) Sold for cash the land being held for future use, recovering the amount invested therein.
(19) Received cash from a customer as a down payment for a future sale (within six months).
(20) Made an adjustment to show that 80 per cent of the wrapping and packaging material had been used.

Problem A 2-4. The person who prepared the following balance sheet made several mistakes. Prepare a corrected balance sheet.

CACTUS COMPANY
Balance Sheet
December 31, 19+2
Assets

Current assets:

Cash	$ 36,000	
Additional paid-in capital	20,000	
Temporary investments in marketable securities	16,000	
Inventory	60,000	
Accounts receivable	48,000	
Notes receivable	10,000	
Interest receivable	200	$180,200

Property, plant, and equipment:

Land—parking lot	$ 15,000	
Building	300,000	
Furniture and fixtures	80,000	385,000

Intangible assets:

Patents	$ 12,000	
Land (held for future use)	30,000	
Prepaid rent	1,000	
Advances from customers	700	
Interest payable	100	43,800
		$609,000

Equities

Current liabilities:

Accounts payable . . . . $ 15,000
Notes payable.   20,000
Salaries payable   3,000
Unexpired insurance . . . .   800 $ 48,800

Long-term liabilities:

Bank loan—due in 5 years $175,000
Accumulated depreciation—Building.   60,000
Accumulated depreciation—Furniture and fixtures. . . .   16,000   261,000

Stockholders' equity:

Capital stock $250,000
Retained earnings   49,200   299,200
                                                                          $609,000

Problem A2-5. Prepare a transaction worksheet and financial statements for Service Company for 19+2.

December 31, 19+1 balances:

Cash. $14,000
Accounts receivable   18,000
Prepaid rent   4,800
Service trucks   15,000
Accumulated depreciation . . . .   -0-
Salaries payable   2,000
Advances from customers . . . .   -0-
Capital stock   40,000
Retained earnings   9,800

19+2 transactions:

(1) Sales of service on account, $48,000.
(2) Payment of December 31, 19+1 liability for salaries, $2,000.
(3) Collections from customers, $50,000.
(4) Payment of salaries, $23,000.
(5) Receipt of advances from customers, $1,100.
(6) Payment for supplies and parts used in the performance of services for customers, $9,000.
(7) Payment for other expenses, $6,000.
(8) Payment of dividend, $4,000.

Adjustments:

(a) Salaries payable as of December 31, 19+2, $2,200.
(b) Rent expense applicable to 19+2, $2,400.
(c) Depreciation:
  Service trucks were acquired as of December 31, 19+1.
  Estimated useful life, 5 years.
  Estimated value at end of useful life, $1,000.

Problem B2-1. For each of the following separate cases, indicate the increases and decreases caused by any needed year-end adjustment.

Use the following solution format for each case:

	Salaries Payable	Retained Earnings	
Balances before adjustment	-0-	−22,000	Salaries expense
Adjustment	+2,000	− 2,000	
Adjusted balances.	+2,000	−24,000	

(a) Balances before adjustment:

Prepaid rent $14,400

Rent expense. . . . .   -0-

Data

At the beginning of the current year, rent was prepaid for a three-year period.

(b) Balances before adjustment:

Unexpired insurance . . . . $ 600

Insurance expense . . . .   -0-

Data

At the beginning of the current year a two-year insurance policy was acquired by payment of a $600 premium.

(c) Balances before adjustment:

Light and power expense . . . . $ 800

Liability for light and power . . . .   -0-

Data

At year-end there was an unpaid bill for one month's light and power, $90.

(d) Balances before adjustment:

Delivery expense . . . . $ 480

Truck rent payable . . . .   -0-

Data

A delivery truck was rented during the year from Transport Rental Company at the rate of 15 cents a mile. The truck was driven 500 miles during December; hence $75 is owed to Transport Rental Company.

(e) Balances before adjustment:

Office equipment $12,000

Depreciation expense . . . .   -0-

Data

At the beginning of the year the company purchased office equipment that has an expected useful life of six years. No salvage or trade-in value is anticipated at the end of the equipment's useful life.

Problem B2-2. The following data are available regarding Kansas Corporation as of June 30, 19+2:

(1) Cash on hand, $1,400.

(2) Capital stock issued, 6,000 shares, par $10.

(3) Cost of merchandise on hand, $40,300.

(4) Wages and salaries payable, $750.

(5) Amounts owed to creditors on purchases of merchandise, $4,300.

(6) Store building: value, $25,000; cost, $30,000; accumulated depreciation, $9,000.

(7) Store equipment: value, $10,000; cost, $10,000; accumulated depreciation, $3,000.

(8) Face amount of 5%, 60-day note, dated June 15, 19+2, and payable to City Bank, $480. (Interest payable thereon as of June 30, 19+2, is $1.)

(9) Amount owed by customers on merchandise sold on account, $12,500.

(10) Unexpired insurance premiums, $110.

(11) Cost of U.S. Government bonds, $10,000; interest amounting to $200 for six months is collectible July 1, 19+2. (Bonds are held as a long-term investment.)

(12) Cost of land, $5,000; value, $4,000.

(13) Mortgage payable on land and store building, due January 1, 19+10, $10,000.

(14) Interest payable on mortgage, $200.

(15) Retained earnings, $21,779.

Prepare a classified balance sheet. (Use the report form.)

Problem B2-3. The following income statement is incorrect because it was prepared before year-end adjustments were taken into consideration.

IMPROBABLE SERVICE COMPANY
Income Statement
For the Year Ended December 31, 19+2

Revenues:
Sales of service $50,000
Interest revenue 400 $50,400

Deduct expenses:
Salaries expense $33,000
Cost of repair parts used   8,000
Miscellaneous expense   2,000   43,000
Net income . . . . $ 7,400

The assets and liabilities before and after adjustment are listed below.

	December 31, 19+2 Balances	
Assets	Before Adjustment	After Adjustment
Cash	$10,000	$10,000
Marketable securities	15,000	15,000
Interest receivable	-0-	300
Inventory of repair parts	1,000	1,000
Prepaid rent	2,400	1,200
Equipment	20,000	20,000
Accumulated depreciation	-0-	1,500
Liabilities		
Accounts payable	4,000	4,000
Salaries payable	-0-	3,000
Advances from customers	700	700

Prepare a corrected income statement, which should show the net income for 19+2 as $2,000.

Problem B2-4. The following data have been taken from the 19+2 transaction worksheet before year-end adjustments.

Terminal Company

Cash	$ 8,000
Accounts receivable	12,000
Merchandise inventory	20,000
Prepaid rent	9,000
Long-term investment in securities	5,000
Equipment	15,000
Accounts payable	24,000
Advances from customers	2,000
Capital stock	30,000
Retained earnings	13,000

Adjustments are required for the following:

(1) Liability for salaries, $400.
(2) Depreciation on equipment, $1,500.
(3) Interest receivable, $500.
(4) At the beginning of 19+2, the $3,000 annual rental was prepaid for three years.
(5) Liability for local taxes, $300.

Required:

The December 31, 19+2 classified balance sheet.

Problem B2-5. The financial statements below are incorrect for two reasons:

(a) Some of the assets are improperly positioned in the balance sheet.
(b) No provision was made for the following adjustments:
    (1) Liability for December salaries, $4,000.
    (2) Annual depreciation of building acquired at the beginning of 19+2, $7,500.
    (3) Liability for December rent, $1,000.
    (4) Interest receivable, $200.

Required:

Corrected financial statements.

GENERAL CORPORATION
Income Statement
For the Year Ended December 31, 19+2

Revenues:		
Sales	$240,000	
Interest revenue	800	$240,800
Deduct expenses:		
Cost of goods sold	$160,000	
Salaries expense	32,000	
Rent expense	11,000	203,000
Net income		$ 37,800

GENERAL CORPORATION
Statement of Retained Earnings
For the Year Ended December 31, 19+2

Retained earnings, December 31, 19+1	$36,000
Net income for 19+2	37,800
Total	$73,800
Deduct dividends	9,000
Retained earnings, December 31, 19+2	$64,800

GENERAL CORPORATION
Balance Sheet
December 31, 19+2

Assets

Current assets:

Cash	$ 16,800	
Inventory	60,000	
Accounts receivable	28,000	$104,800

Property, plant, and equipment:

Land (held for future use)	$ 30,000	
Land	15,000	
Building	300,000	345,000

Intangible assets:

Temporary investment in marketable securities		10,000
		$459,800

Equities

Current liabilities:

Accounts payable	$ 35,000

Stockholders' equity:

Capital stock	$300,000	
Additional paid-in capital	60,000	$360,000
Retained earnings	64,800	424,800
		$459,800

Problem B2-6. The December 31, 19+1 balances applicable to Fresh Company are as follows:

Cash	$10,600
Accounts receivable	5,000
Merchandise inventory	12,000
Unexpired insurance	-0-
Securities	10,000
Equipment	-0-
Accumulated depreciation	-0-
Accounts payable	6,000
Salaries payable	700
Capital stock	30,000
Retained earnings	900

The 19+2 transactions are as follows:

(1) Purchased merchandise on account, $36,000.

(2a) Made sales of merchandise on account, $41,000.

(2b) Cost of goods sold on account, $27,000.

(3) Cash receipts from customers, $42,000.

(4) Cash payments for merchandise purchased on account, $30,000.

(5) As of January 1, 19+2, purchased equipment for cash, $6,000. The equipment is expected to last for ten years and have a scrap value of $1,000.

(6) As of January 1, 19+2, paid $600 cash for a three-year fire insurance policy on the equipment.

(7) Paid for advertising expenses, $900.

(8) Paid rent for the year, $2,400.

(9) Cash payments for salaries:
    For December 31, 19+1 liability, $700.
    For eleven months ended November 30, 19+2, $8,800. (Salaries for 19+2 amount to $800 per month.)

(10) Received $400 dividend revenue from long-term investments.

(11) Paid cash dividends, $1,200.

Required:

(a) Transaction worksheet for 19+2.

(b) Statement of retained earnings for 19+2 and the December 31, 19+2 classified balance sheet.

3

Income Measurement

Emphasis on income measurement. For many decades accountants regarded the balance sheet as of primary importance and the income statement as of secondary importance—possibly a reflection of the attitude then held by bankers and other grantors of short-term credit. Grantors of credit were concerned with the margin of security for their loans. They were primarily interested in two questions: What assets does the applicant for credit own? What liabilities does he already owe? The answers to those questions were found in the balance sheet.

Over the years a shift in emphasis—from the balance sheet to the income statement—has taken place. In part, this shift can be traced to a change in the point of view of credit grantors, their current approach placing more emphasis on the earnings (net income) potential as an indication of debt-paying ability. Another factor has been the increase in the number of investors in corporate securities. Investors and speculators are disposed to measure the attractiveness of securities by the earnings of the issuing company. As net income goes up, security values tend to increase; as net income goes down, security values tend to decrease.

With the increasing emphasis on the income statement, the determination and reporting of net income have become the central objectives of the accounting process. As a result, a significant portion of accounting theory is devoted to the development of concepts, standards, and criteria regarding income measurement, which, as previously noted, is often described as a process of matching revenue and related expense.

How is revenue measured? Revenue has been previously defined as an inflow of assets. This leaves unanswered the question of how revenue is measured; that is, what number of dollars and cents should be used when revenue transactions are entered in the company's records and reported in the company's income statement.

In a sense, revenue is measured in the market place. The actions of buyers and sellers establish the dollar amounts of revenue transactions. In typical situations this means that the amounts are determined objectively, being a product of bargained transactions and supported by various kinds of evidence such as legal contracts, bills of sale, and checks made out in favor of the seller.

It should be pointed out that the process of revenue measurement also results in measuring, initially, certain assets, namely, those arising from revenue-producing transactions. In other words, the revenue figure is used not only as a measure of revenue but also as a measure of the assets received in connection with revenue transactions. This use of the revenue figure follows from the basic equation: Assets = Equities.

The assets most commonly acquired through revenue transactions are cash and accounts and notes receivable. Occasionally securities, or even property, plant, and equipment, are acquired from revenue transactions, in which case they are recorded initially in the company's records at the cash transaction price established for the goods or services sold in exchange by the business. Thus revenue measurement and asset valuation are not completely separate activities. However, it should be recognized that not all asset balances are traceable to revenue transactions. Many asset balances are the result of purchases by a business. For example, this is typically the case for machinery and equipment and for inventory.

The revenue-recognition assumption. When should revenue be given recognition in the accounting records and hence included in the income statement? There are several possibilities. Revenue could be recognized when orders are secured from customers, when the manufacturing process is completed, when the goods are delivered to the customer, or when cash or some other asset is received in payment for the goods sold.

The several events or activities noted in the preceding sentence all contribute to the revenue-earning process. Unless orders are secured there is no revenue. Unless goods are manufactured or otherwise acquired for resale, there can be no deliveries to customers. If a business fails to generate a cash inflow from customers, it will, in time, cease being a going concern. In short, the earning of revenue is based on several coordinated, and often complicated, activities such as selling, financing, purchasing, manufacturing, and distribution. It is difficult, both theoretically and practically, to determine which event or activity is the critical one which, when completed or fulfilled, justifies the recognition of revenue.

For retail, wholesale, and manufacturing businesses, the accountant generally uses the point of sale as the basis for revenue recognition. In essence, the accountant *assumes* that recognizing revenue at the point of sale will provide a meaningful measurement of the results of management's efforts directed toward the generation of revenue. The following facts support that assumption:

> Generally, by the time the point of sale has been reached, the firm has performed the major economic effort required by the sale transaction and any remaining expense associated with the sale will be negligible.
>
> At the point of sale, the exchange price provides an objective measurement for revenue.
>
> At the point of sale a conversion takes place—one asset is exchanged for another.

Legally, the point of sale occurs when title to the goods passes to the buyer. For expediency, the accountant assumes that passage of title coincides with delivery of the goods to the customer or the customer's agent.

Revenue is earned by service-type businesses as services are performed. In some cases—usually when the rendering of services extends over a fairly long time period and involves more than one accounting period—estimates may be used in order that revenue may be recorded and reported during the periods when the work is being performed. Practical considerations may lead to the adoption of a policy of postponing the recognition of any revenue from services until the services are completed; the amount to be charged for the entire service may not be determinable until completion and, as a consequence, the revenue applicable to services rendered during the periods prior to completion may not be determinable.

Revenue received in advance. It was stated previously that, at the point of sale, there is performance accompanied by the acquisition of an asset. It should be noted that in some circumstances the asset acquisition may precede the performance, in which case the revenue recognition is postponed until the required performance, whether it be the delivery of merchandise or the rendering of some specified service, has been undertaken. Such a situation occurred in 19+2 in the case of Sight & Sound Corporation. In transaction number 11 the company received $1,400 cash in advance from a customer when he ordered a custom TV-stereo unit. The mere receipt of the asset in a revenue-type transaction does not justify the recognition of revenue; performance is the essential test for revenue recognition. As noted in Chapter 2, pending performance, the company has an obligation to its customer. Thus the receipt of "revenue in advance" creates a liability. Actually it is the asset that has been received in advance, but businessmen and accountants generally refer to such an event by using the phrase "revenue received in advance."

Now assume that during 19+3 Sight & Sound Corporation delivered to the customer the unit ordered in 19+2. Delivery, which constitutes the required performance, satisfies the obligation. Hence, in the company's records, the liability should be eliminated and the revenue should be recognized.

Result of delivery of merchandise:

	EQUITIES	
	Advances from Customers	Retained Earnings
Outstanding balance	1,400	—
Merchandise delivered	−1,400	+1,400 Sales

Of course, there may be partial performance in connection with such revenue-received-in-advance transactions; and, when the accountant is able to make reasonable determinations of the extent of such partial performance, a portion or fraction of the revenue received in advance may be considered as earned. Perhaps the most common example is that of magazine subscriptions. Assume that the annual subscription price for a monthly magazine is $12, payable in advance. The publisher earns one-twelfth of the subscription price with the delivery of each monthly issue of the magazine. Accordingly, the liability resulting from the revenue received in advance, recorded initially at $12, would be reduced as recognition is given for partial performance under the subscription agreement.

To illustrate, assume that the publisher prepares financial statements at the end of each calendar year, that the $12 subscription was received in August of 19+2, and that monthly deliveries of the magazine started in the following month, September of 19+2. Four monthly issues would have been delivered by year end.

The December 31, 19+2 balance sheet would include the following under the Current Liabilities caption:

Subscriptions received in advance $8

The income statement for 19+2 would include the following in its revenue earned for the year:

Revenue from subscriptions $4

YEAR-END ADJUSTMENT. The August subscription transaction would produce the following results in the accounting records:

ASSETS	EQUITIES
Cash	Subscriptions Received in Advance
+12	+12

At year end, unless the following adjustment was made to give recognition to partial performance under the subscription agreement, financial statements prepared from the accounting records would be in error. Specifically, liabilities would be overstated and revenue understated.

	EQUITIES	
	Subscriptions Received in Advance	Retained Earnings
Outstanding balance	12	
Adjustment for partial performance	−4	+4 Revenue from subscriptions
Amounts included in year-end financial statements	8	4

Unrecorded revenue. Revenue may be earned before it is entered in the accounting records. At year end, or whenever financial statements are prepared, any such unrecorded, though earned, revenue should be entered in the records. Otherwise the financial statements would be in error, because the revenue shown thereon would be understated. Consider the following example.

During 19+3 the management of Sight & Sound Corporation sold the land owned by the company for $10,200. On October 1, 19+3, the proceeds were invested in 4% bonds. As long as the bonds are held the company will earn $408 interest per year ($10,200 × 4% = $408).

Assume that the bonds specify that interest will be paid semiannually on April 1 and October 1. Accordingly, the company will not receive any bond interest until April 1, 19+4. Although not received until 19+4, a portion (half in this case) of the six months' interest was earned in 19+3, because interest is earned with the passage of time. April 1 and October 1 are merely the collection dates for the revenue which has been earned during the preceding six months.

During the year, entries are made in the accounting records only when transactions occur. The first transaction relating to the bond interest would occur on April 1, 19+4, when the interest check for the period October 1, 19+3, to March 31, 19+4, in the amount of $204, is received. Therefore, the following adjustment would be required at the end of 19+3 in order that the 19+3 financial statements based on the accounting records would include the interest earned for the three months ended December 31, 19+3:

	ASSETS	EQUITIES	
	Interest Receivable	Retained Earnings	
Adjustment for 3 months' interest	+102	+102	Interest revenue

Computation: Amount at interest × Rate of interest × Period of time = Interest

$$\$10,200 \times .04 \times \frac{3(\text{months})}{12(\text{months})} = \$102$$

Accountants generally refer to unrecorded revenue as "accrued revenue."

To carry the illustration into 19+4, the recording of the 19+4 interest collection transactions are indicated below.

		ASSETS		EQUITIES	
		Cash	Interest Receivable	Retained Earnings	
19+3	Outstanding balance as a result of December 31, 19+3 adjustment		102		
19+4	April 1, 19+4 collection	+204	−102	+102	Interest revenue
	October 1, 19+4 collection	+204		+204	Interest revenue

Observe the treatment accorded the April 1 interest collection. The half earned during 19+4 (for January, February, and March) was recorded as 19+4 revenue, while the half earned in 19+3 and reported as earned during that year in the 19+3 financial statements was treated as the collection of a previously recorded receivable.

Assets and expenses. A satisfactory net income figure is a primary objective of a business enterprise. In carrying on the numerous and varied activities aimed at "generating" income, a business spends money for a wide variety of things and services. Such expenditures are made in the belief that they will contribute to the profitability of the enterprise (advertising, for example) or because they cannot be avoided without curtailing the activities of the business (taxes, for example). In either case economic benefits are expected from the expenditures, or they would not have been made.

If it is known at the time of making an expenditure that the related economic benefit will not extend beyond the current accounting period (as when a year's rent is paid in advance at the beginning of the year), it is customary and expedient to record the transaction as an expense. One could reach the same result by recording the transaction as an asset acquisition, and then later during the period, when the benefit had expired or been consumed, making a transfer of the amount involved from its asset status to an expense status. The recording plan described first is favored because it entails less work.

If there is a reasonable expectation at the time of making an expenditure that the related economic benefits will extend beyond the current accounting period (as when a delivery truck is purchased), it is customary to record the transaction as an asset acquisition. As the benefits expire or are consumed, an appropriate portion of the asset cost is transferred to expense. Such transfers are usually made at the end of the accounting period before the annual financial statements are prepared. If such transfers were omitted or overlooked, the financial statements would be incorrect.

Accounting for asset acquisitions. *Cost* is the measure used to account for assets acquired by purchase and, ultimately, for the transfers to expense to give recognition to the consumption or expiration of the economic benefits embodied in assets. Costs are a product of the actions of buyers and sellers and, therefore, costs are established objectively.

INCIDENTAL COSTS: The cost of an asset includes not only the basic or purchase price but also related incidental costs, such as the cost of a title search and legal fees incurred in the acquisition of real estate; transportation, installation, and breaking-in costs incident to the acquisition of machinery; storage, taxes, and other costs incurred in aging certain kinds of inventories, such as wine; and expenditures made in the rehabilitation of a plant purchased in a run-down condition.

ASSETS ACQUIRED FOR NONCASH ASSETS: Some difficulty may be encountered in determining cost if assets other than cash are used in payment. For instance, suppose that a new machine selling for a price listed at $1,500 is acquired by the payment of $1,000 in cash and the trade-in of the following old machine:

Original cost of old machine	$1,000
Less accumulated depreciation	600
Undepreciated cost (often called book value)	$ 400

Assume that the old machine being traded in could have been sold by the owner for $250. Did the new machine cost $1,500 (the list price), or $1,400 (the sum of the cash payment and the undepreciated cost of the old machine), or $1,250 (the sum of the cash payment and the cash value of the old machine)?

A figure of $1,250 appears most truly to represent cost, because it is the sum of the cash paid and the cash value of the old asset.

In the determination of cost, the general rule may be stated as follows: cost equals the cash value of the consideration parted with. This rule would apply when any noncash asset, such as securities, is used as part or full payment for the asset acquired.

Accounting for asset expirations. Through use or with the passage of time, most economic benefits expire. Their expiration converts the cost paid for the benefits from an asset status to an expense or loss status. The accounting problem is to determine *when* such asset expirations occur and to give recognition thereto in the accounting records and in the financial statements. Should the accountant do a poor job of determining when the asset, or cost, expirations occur, both the assets and the expenses shown in the financial statements will be misstated.

> One of the features of the accounting process that is commonly misunderstood or overlooked is the direct relationship between certain asset balances and expenses (and losses). For accounting purposes, asset valuation and expense determination are, in many instances, one and the same process. Incurred costs either are applicable to the future or are assignable as expenses or losses. If assets are misstated, it follows that cost expirations are misstated.

To illustrate, consider the asset-expense relationship resulting from the following expenditures:

Beginning-of-Period Expenditures	Resulting Asset Balances	Cost Expirations During Period		End-of-Period Asset Balances	
		Description	Amount	Description	Amount
1. Advances to salesmen	$ 8,000	Salesmen's commissions	$7,000	Advances to salesmen	$ 1,000
2. Rent prepayment . . .	12,000	Rent expense	6,000	Prepaid rent	6,000
3. Equipment purchased	20,000	Depreciation expense	5,000	Equipment	15,000
4. Office supplies purchased	3,000	Office supplies expense	2,400	Office supplies on hand	600

If an amount in the cost expiration column is incorrectly determined, the amount in the asset balance (last) column will also be wrong, and vice versa.

Measurement of cost expirations. The amounts of cost properly assignable to expense may be determined by any of the following approaches, the accountant using the one that he regards as the most suitable (reliable) in the given circumstances:

(1) Identification with revenue transactions.

Salesmen's commissions are an example. Such expenses would not exist if sales were not made; therefore, they are directly associated with the revenue from sales and should be recorded as expenses in the period in which the sales are reported as revenue.

Such a case was illustrated on line 1 of the table on page 60.

(2) Identification with a period of time.

Annual dues paid to a trade association are an example. Although there may be some connection between such expenses and revenue, the relationship is usually so indirect that it is impracticable to attempt to establish it. However, there is a clear identification with a period of time. Rent payments provide another example of a period expense, as was illustrated on line 2 of the table on page 60.

(3) Apportioning the cost outlay (expenditure) between cost expiration and cost residue in either of two ways:

(*a*) By computing the cost expiration (expense) and accepting the remainder as a proper balance for the unexpired cost (asset balance). This is the procedure normally applied to depreciable assets. The cost expiration (depreciation expense) is computed and the remaining balance, the undepreciated cost, is reported as an asset.

Such a case was illustrated on line 3 of the table on page 60.

(*b*) By computing the unexpired cost (asset balance) and accepting the remainder as the proper amount for the cost expiration. If the accountant can establish the portion of a cost outlay that is assignable to the future, he has, in effect, established the cost expiration. This procedure is illustrated by the following apportionment of an expenditure for office supplies, which is based on the data shown on line 4 of the table on page 60.

Office supplies purchased	$3,000
Office supplies on hand at end of period—determined by counting the items on hand and valuing them at their cost	600
Office supplies expense	$2,400

(4) Estimating cost recoverability.

Costs should not be carried in the accounting records as assets at amounts exceeding those that can be recovered through sales or utilization. For example, if merchandise costing $1,000 becomes out of style and only $700 can be expected from its sale, the accountant will regard as an acceptable balance for the asset only an amount consistent with its recoverability prospects.

Lost costs. Accountants recognize, in theory, two classes of cost expirations: expenses and lost costs. Lost costs, in contrast to expenses, are those cost expirations which have *no traceable association* with the generation of revenue. However, except in rare and special circumstances discussed in a later chapter, both are shown in the income statement and are deducted from revenue in the computation of net income.

Two examples of lost costs are given below:

A flood causes merchandise costing $50,000 to be unsalable. The business carries no insurance covering flood damage. There is a $50,000 lost cost.

A business obligates itself under a five-year lease for a warehouse at an annual rental of $4,000. At the end of the third year, the business changes its location and, as a result, makes no further use of the warehouse. The rental payments for the remaining two years of the lease do not help generate revenue and therefore are lost costs.

Unrecorded expense. Just as there may be unrecorded revenue (discussed on page 57) there may be unrecorded expense. A business may have incurred an expense, that is, used some economic benefits, before a record thereof was made in the accounting records. At year-end, or whenever financial statements are prepared, any such unrecorded, though incurred, expense should be entered in the records. Otherwise the financial statements would be in error because the expenses shown thereon would be under-stated. Consider the following familiar example:

Employees' salaries are paid monthly on the first business day of the following month. At year-end, the balances shown in the accounting records would not include the expense for December salaries. Such expense would have been incurred, that is, the business would have received the benefit of the employees' services for December, but in the normal course of recording business transactions it is unlikely that the expense for December salaries would have been recorded. Therefore, the following adjustment would be required:

	EQUITIES	
	Salaries Payable	Retained Earnings
Adjustment for unrecorded salaries . .	+1,500	−1,500 Salaries expense

Adjustments and income measurement. As previously noted, income measurement in accounting is a matter of matching, or associating, revenues with related expenses (and, occasionally, lost costs). Revenue is a gross concept, whereas income is a net or resultant amount. If revenues exceed expenses, the business earns income, the dollar amount thereof being shown in the income statement usually as "net income." If expenses exceed revenues, a loss results.

To achieve a proper matching it often is necessary, in addition to recording the transactions of the business, to make certain adjustments of the records at the end of the accounting period before the financial statements are prepared. Such adjustments have been previously discussed and illustrated; they are required for:

Unrecorded revenues: Revenues that have been earned but not recorded.
Unrecorded expenses: Expenses that have been incurred but not recorded.

Earned revenues: Revenues that have been earned but are shown in the records as revenue received in advance.

Cost expirations: Expenses that have been incurred but are shown in the records as assets (prepayments).

Often the process of matching requires the use of judgment and estimates, as is indicated by the following illustrations involving proper matching.

Assume that commissions are paid to salesmen when orders are received for future delivery; to obtain a proper matching, the commissions should not be reported as an expense until the period in which the sales are reported as revenue. If the commissions were deducted from revenue in the period when paid, instead of being deferred until the period in which the sales are reported as revenue, there would not be a proper matching of related revenue and expense. The rule may be stated as follows:

> If revenue is deferred because it is regarded as not yet earned, all reasonably measurable expense related to such deferred revenue must be deferred also, in order to achieve a proper matching and a proper determination of income for the period.

Or, assume that products are sold with agreements to provide service thereon for a period of time without additional cost to the purchaser. If expenses incurred in connection with the service agreements were deducted from revenue in a subsequent period when paid, net income for the period when such sales were made would be overstated, because a portion of the expense associated with the revenue would not as yet have been deducted. The rule may be stated as follows:

> In cases where a "future" expense is associated with current revenue, provisions for such future outlays should be made by charges to expense in the period when the related revenue is earned.

Incidental transactions. As a general rule, accountants believe that informative reporting of the regular operations of the business requires that both revenues and related cost expirations in appropriate detail, not merely net amounts, be shown in the income statement. Thus, it usually would be considered unacceptable to omit sales and cost of goods sold from the income statement and show merely the gross margin on sales, that is, the difference between the sales and the cost of goods sold. The sales of $120,000 and the cost of goods sold, $72,000, are properly set forth in the Sight & Sound Corporation income statement on page 64. It would be incorrect to omit the sales and cost of goods sold and substitute therefor gross margin on sales of $48,000.

However, in the case of extraneous or incidental transactions, it is considered acceptable, even preferable, to report only the resulting gain or loss. For example, during 19+3 the management of Sight & Sound Corporation sold the land owned by the company for $10,200. A $200 gain resulted because the company had paid $10,000 for the land. Only the $200 gain would be shown in the 19+3 income statement.

Illustrative income statement. The 19+3 income statement of Sight & Sound Corporation is presented below. Note the statement location of the following items which were not shown in previously illustrated income statements:

Interest revenue
Gain on sale of land
Interest expense
Income tax

SIGHT & SOUND CORPORATION
Income Statement
For the Year Ended December 31, 19+3

Sales	$120,000	
Interest revenue	102	
Gain on sale of land	200	$120,302
Expenses and losses:		
Cost of goods sold	$ 72,000	
Salaries and commissions	24,000	
Rent expense	4,800	
Other operating expense	6,352	
Depreciation expense	900	
Interest expense	50	
Income tax	2,700	110,802
Net income		$ 9,500

Alternative form of income statement. The income statement form just illustrated is known as the *"single-step"* form; that is, no intermediate income totals are shown. An alternative "multiple-step" form is illustrated below, using the same 19+3 data of Sight & Sound Corporation. As is evident, the multiple-step form sets forth three intermediate income figures, namely the gross margin on sales, the net operating income (only the expenses associated with the selling and administrative activities of the business are classified as operating expenses), and the net income before income taxes. Separate captions are used for incidental revenues, expenses, and relatively small gains and losses. Some items that are properly classified under such separate captions are: revenues from rent and dividends, interest income and expense, and relatively small gains and losses from the sale or disposal of assets other than the merchandise inventory acquired for resale in the normal course of business. The proper way to show extraordinary, and relatively large, gains and losses in the financial statements will be discussed in Chapter 15.

The multiple-step form often appears in annual reports to stockholders, although statistics on current accounting practice indicate that the multiple-step form is steadily giving way to the single-step form. In both forms the income stop tax is the last item before net income. Frequently the single-step format is modified slightly in annual reports to stockholders to show the subtotal "net income before income taxes," from which the income tax is deducted to arrive at net income.

SIGHT & SOUND CORPORATION
Income Statement
For the Year Ended December 31, 19+3

Sales			$120,000
Cost of goods sold			72,000
Gross margin			$ 48,000
Operating expenses:			
Salaries and commissions		$24,000	
Rent expense		4,800	
Other operating expense		6,352	
Depreciation expense		900	36,052
Net operating income			$ 11,948
Other revenue and gains:			
Interest revenue	$102		
Gain on sale of land	200	$ 302	
Other expense and losses:			
Interest expense		50	252
Net income before income taxes			$ 12,200
Income tax			2,700
Net income			$ 9,500

ASSIGNMENT

MATERIAL

QUESTIONS

1. State two developments which possibly explain the shift in emphasis from the balance sheet to the income statement.
2. Explain the following statement: The process of revenue measurement also results in the measurement, initially, of certain assets.
3. When should revenue be given recognition in the accounting records and hence included in the income statement?
4. The text states that "the mere receipt of the asset in a revenue-type transaction does not justify the recognition of revenue." What is the missing element which, if supplied, will justify recognition of revenue?
5. Under what circumstances does the receipt of an asset in a revenue-type transaction create a liability?
6. Is the following statement true or false? Revenue may be earned before it is shown in the accounting records.
7. Some expenditure transactions are recorded as asset acquisitions while in other cases similar expenditure transactions are recorded as expenses. What considerations contribute to the difference in treatment?
8. Name some examples of incidental costs. What accounting treatment should be accorded them?
9. State the general rule to apply in the measurement of cost when assets are acquired for noncash assets.
10. List the approaches used by the accountant to determine the amounts of cost properly assignable to expense.
11. Make a list of the different kinds of adjustments and give an example of each.

SHORT EXERCISES

E3-1. The following disbursements were made at the beginning of 19+3.

    (a) Shipping supplies were purchased for $6,000.
    (b) Office furniture was purchased for $30,000. (You may assume that the useful life is ten years with no scrap value.)
    (c) A three-year insurance policy was purchased for $900.
    (d) Travel advances of $500 were made to employees.

Status at year end:

(a) Half of the shipping supplies had been used.
(d) Eighty per cent of the travel advances had been used; the remainder is being held for travel scheduled during the next month.

Indicate the proper amount and balance-sheet category for each of the above four items as of December 31, 19+3.

E3-2. As of January 1, 19+3, a company signed rental agreements covering three properties—A, B, and C. The terms of the agreements and payments thereunder made during 19+3 are noted below.

A—Rented for five years. The rent is $400 per month.
  Rental payments made during 19+3 totaled $4,400.
B—Rented for two years. The rent is $2,000 per year.
  Rental payments made during 19+3 totaled $4,000.
C—Rented for five years. The rent is $500 per month.
  Rental payments made during 19+3 totaled $6,500.

Indicate how all items relating to the above rental payments will be presented in the 19+3 financial statements.

E3-3. The following data were taken from the Retained Earnings column of the 19+3 transaction worksheet of Introspection Company.

Balance, December 31, 19+2	$ 8,000
Sales	160,000
Cost of goods sold	90,000
Salesmen's commissions	30,000
Insurance expense	1,200
Office salaries	20,000
Dividends	4,000
Balance	$ 22,800

After giving consideration to the following, prepare the 19+3 income statement using the multiple-step form.

The employment agreements with the salesmen specify that the commissions payable will amount to 20% of sales.

The $1,200 insurance expense resulted from the payment of the premium on a three-year policy dated January 1, 19+3.

The sales include $1,000 of advances received from customers

E3-4. All of the assets and liabilities affected by year-end adjustments are shown below.

	December 31, 19+3	
	Before Adjustment	After Adjustment
Interest receivable	$ 100	$ 300
Prepaid rent	800	400
Unexpired insurance	-0-	300
Accumulated depreciation	1,200	1,800
Miscellaneous expenses payable	-0-	700
Subscriptions received in advance	3,000	2,000

Before the year-end adjustments for 19+3 were considered, the net income was computed as $15,000. Determine the net income after giving consideration to the year-end adjustments.

PROBLEMS

Problem A3-1. From the data given, prepare the 19+3 income statement of Symphony Company in multiple-step form.

Retained earnings, December 31, 19+2	$ 25,000
— Sales	200,000
— Cost of goods sold	125,000
— Interest revenue	300
— Loss on sale of real estate	250
— Salaries expense	42,000
— Traveling expense	14,000
— Advertising expense	2,100
— Dividends received	400
— Telephone and telegraph expense	580
— Depreciation expense	3,450
Accumulated depreciation	8,000
— Insurance expense	300
Unexpired insurance as of December 31, 19+3	600
— Other expense	1,720
Cash receipts for 19+3	203,000
Cash disbursements for 19+3	195,000
— Income tax	3,300

Problem A3-2. Prepare a list of the elements that make up the cost of each of the assets identified below.

A used machine was purchased for a cash payment of $5,400. It cost the company $60 to transport the machine to a warehouse, where it was stored for six months. The storage cost amounted to $90, and it cost another $60 to transport the machine to the company's premises. The machine was overhauled at a cost of $480, and accessories costing $120 were added for use with the machine. An electrician was paid $210 to check the wiring in the machine and for his services in connection with the installation. Shortly after the machine was installed, it received a new coat of paint, as did all of the machines owned by the company. The company paints all of its machines annually. The cost of painting applicable to the used machine was $50. Insurance covering the first year after purchase, including the storage period, cost $40.

A used delivery truck advertised for $3,500 was acquired under the following terms: $2,000 cash along with a trade-in of a used truck owned by the purchaser, on which a $1,500 trade-in allowance was granted. The truck traded in had a market value of $1,400. The purchased truck was immediately driven to a garage in order that certain specified work could be performed on it. The garage submitted the following bill:

Overhauling motor	$120
New body panels	615
New battery	30
Gas and oil	9
Total	$774

The annual premium for insurance on the truck amounted to $250. Cost of new license plates was $90. After the truck had been used for three months, an automatic loader was installed thereon at a cost of $800.

Problem A3-3. Webster Company, publishers of a monthly magazine, began operations on July 1, 19+1, and established the calendar year as the time period to be used in accounting for its operations.

The publication, issued at the end of each month, was available by the copy for 40 cents, through a one-year subscription for $4, or through a two-year subscription for $7. Magazines were sent to subscribers in the month in which subscriptions were received.

All receipts from single-copy sales and from subscriptions were credited to income. The income statement for the six months ended December 31, 19+1, showed Magazine Revenue Earned to be $66,345. Details for single-copy sales and subscriptions are given below.

Month	Single-copy Sales	One-year Subscriptions	Two-year Subscriptions
July	$ 1,750	$ 4,000	$ 1,400
August	2,625	6,000	1,680
September	3,500	4,800	2,100
October	3,150	6,400	1,960
November	3,850	6,900	2,100
December	3,570	7,200	3,360
	$18,445	$35,300	$12,600

Compute the correct amount of magazine revenue earned for the six months ended December 31, 19+1.

Problem A3-4. At the beginning of 19+1, Eastinghouse Corporation purchased a truck for $3,400, paying cash. The corporation immediately added a refrigeration system to the truck at a cost of $800. This system was expected to last for the expected life of the truck.

Data concerning the truck and the corporation's accounting therefor:

Expected useful life—5 years.
Expected value at end of 5 years, $400.
Depreciation rate used—20%.

Data from the corporation's financial statements:

	Year-end Balance Sheet		Income Statement		
Year	Truck	Accumulated Depreciation	Maintenance Expense	Depreciation Expense	Net Income
19+1	$3,400	$ 680	$800	$680	$3,000
19+2	3,400	1,360		680	3,600
19+3	3,400	2,040		680	4,000
19+4	3,400	2,720		680	3,500
19+5	3,400	3,400		680	4,200

At the beginning of 19+6, the corporation traded in the old truck on a new one, paying $3,600 in cash and receiving a trade-in allowance on the old truck of $400.

(a) Modify the above data from the corporation's financial statements applying proper accounting methods. (Ignore income taxes.)
(b) Compute the cost of the new truck acquired in 19+6.

Problem A3-5. The following data have been taken from the 19+3 transaction worksheet before year-end adjustments.

Southwest Company

Cash	$ 10,000
Merchandise inventory	20,000
Shipping supplies	1,000
Long-term investment in real estate	100,000
Store building	60,000
Accumulated depreciation	2,400
Capital stock	150,000
Retained earnings.	38,600

The retained earnings balance was the result of the following:

Balance, December 31, 19+2	$ 16,400
Sales	170,000
Rent revenue.	15,200
Cost of goods sold	110,000
Salaries expense	38,500
Property taxes expense	4,000
Miscellaneous expense	3,000
Dividends	7,500
Balance, per above	$ 38,600

Set up a transaction worksheet. Enter on the first line the balances in the assets and equities before year-end adjustments. Record on the transaction worksheet any required adjustments based on the following data, and show the adjusted December 31, 19+3 balances. Also prepare the statement of retained earnings for the year ended December 31, 19+3.

Additional Data

(a) Depreciation expense for 19+3, $1,200.

(b) A physical count of the shipping supplies on hand as of December 31, 19+3, reveals that the unused supplies cost $400.

(c) Salaries payable as of December 31, 19+3, $3,500.

(d) During 19+3 the company was able to rent to three tenants parcels of the real estate it owns as a long-term investment. Rent collections from the tenants during 19+3 are detailed below.

From A.	$ 2,000

A's rent is $200 per month. He has paid rent for ten months and owes two month's back rent as of December 31, 19+3, which the company believes is collectible.

From B	3,600

B's rent is $300 per month and is paid through December 31, 19+3.

From C.	9,600

When C signed his rental agreement as of January 1, 19+3, covering a two-year period, he paid the $4,800 annual rental for the two-year period in advance.

Recorded as rent revenue	$15,200

(e) The applicable income-tax rate may be assumed to be 30%.

Problem B3-1. Use what is relevant of the following data to prepare the 19+3 income statement of Computation Corporation in multiple-step form.

Cash	$ 10,000
Dividends	4,000
Retained earnings, December 31, 19+2	40,000
Sales	180,000
Interest revenue	800
Rent revenue..	1,200
Gain on sale of securities	300
Cost of goods sold	110,000
Merchandise inventory, December 31, 19+3	30,000
Wages and salaries	35,000
Rent expense...	4,800
Rent payable as of December 31, 19+3	400
Depreciation expense	8,000
Accumulated depreciation	16,000
Miscellaneous expense.................................	7,000
Interest expense	200
Income tax	5,100

Problem B3-2. Determine the cost of the asset from the data given.

Case A—Vending Machine:

New vending machine, invoice cost	$10,000
Payment to a general contractor to reinforce floor in vending area	800
Cost of fire insurance policy on vending machine—3-year term ..	45
Cost of transportation of vending machine...............	125
Cost of installation	
Employees' labor	90
Supplies used	4
Cost of repairs to make the vending machine perform properly, 50% of which will be reimbursed by manufacturer of the vending machine	120

Case B—Used Building:

Seller's price.......................................		$30,000
Paid for by transferring securities owned:		
Cost	$28,000	
Market value	29,500	
Cost of title search		300
Cost of improvements to interior before occupancy		5,500
Cost of new roof....................................		3,000
Property taxes covering first 12 months after purchase; however, 3 months were devoted to making the improvements noted above.......................................		1,800
Payment for custodial service to clean the building before occupancy....................................		500

Problem B3-3. At the beginning of 19+1, Acme Company acquired two assets, as described below.

(1) A machine was purchased for $2,600 cash. In addition to the payment to the manufacturer of the machine, $150 was paid for freight on the shipment of the machine from

the manufacturer's plant and $350 was paid to install the machine. In an effort to be conservative, Acme Company recorded the freight and installation costs as 19+1 maintenance expense. The machine had an estimated service life of ten years and an estimated scrap value of $200. For 19+1 and 19+2, the company recorded depreciation expense at $260 per year.

(2) A building was acquired in exchange for 1,000 shares of Acme Company $10 par value common stock. Acme Company recorded the building in its records at the aggregate par value of the stock issued for it. On the date the building was acquired, the common stock was being traded on the market for $18 per share. The estimated service life of the building was 20 years.

(a) Compute the amount at which the two assets described above should have been recorded initially in the records of Acme Company.
(b) Compute the net error in net income for 19+1 and 19+2 caused by the accounting procedures employed by Acme Company.

Problem B3-4. The following data have been taken from the 19+3 transaction worksheet before year-end adjustments.

Northeast Company

Cash	$ 9,000
Merchandise inventory	21,000
Advances to salesmen	1,000
Prepaid rent	3,000
Office supplies	2,000
Equipment	20,000
Accumulated depreciation	2,000
Advances from customers	500
Capital stock	40,000
Retained earnings	13,500

The retained earnings balance was the result of the following:

Balance, December 31, 19+2	$ 3,500
Sales	200,000
Cost of goods sold	120,000
Salesmen's commissions	30,000
Office salaries	25,000
Miscellaneous expense	10,000
Dividends	5,000
Balance, per above	$ 13,500

Adjustments are required for the following:

(a) The sales include $2,000 of advances received from customers. As of December 31, 19+3, a total of $2,500 has been received in advance.
(b) Half of the $1,000 advanced on future commissions has been earned by the company's salesmen.
(c) Office salaries owed at year-end amount to $400.

(d) One-third of the prepaid rent applies to 19+3.

(e) The unused office supplies amount to $500 at year-end.

(f) Unrecorded depreciation for 19+3, $1,000.

(g) Income taxes (use 30% as the appropriate rate).

Required:

The 19+3 financial statements.

Problem B3-5. The following tentative draft of the condensed income statement of Crisp Company covers the first year of the company's operations.

CRISP COMPANY
Income Statement
For the Year Ended December 31, 19+1

Sales		$300,000
Cost of goods sold		200,000
Gross margin		$100,000
Operating expenses:		
Salaries expense	$60,000	
Depreciation expense	15,000	
Interest expense	700	
Other operating expense	33,000	108,700
Net loss		$ 8,700

You are asked to review the accounting procedures to satisfy the management of the company that those followed are acceptable. You discover that the company has treated all incidental costs associated with the purchase of merchandise and equipment as other operating expense. You also note with approval that the equipment, all of which was acquired at the beginning of the year, is being depreciated over a ten-year period and that no scrap value is anticipated.

The following data have been taken from the company's records:

Merchandise purchased during 19+1—Invoice cost	$250,000
Merchandise on hand at year-end (20% of purchases)	50,000
Incidental costs relating to merchandise	1,000
Equipment acquired at beginning of 19+1	$150,000
Incidental costs (such as transportation and installation)	2,000
Advances from customers for merchandise ordered for delivery in 19+2 included in 19+1 sales	$ 1,500

Prepare a revised, and improved, draft of the 19+1 condensed income statement, following the multiple-step form.

Problem B3-6. The following income statement is incorrect because it was prepared before year-end adjustments were taken into consideration.

IMPROBABLE SALES AND SERVICE COMPANY
Income Statement
For the Year Ended December 31, 19+3

Revenues:

Sales of merchandise	$145,000	
Sales of service	55,000	
Interest revenue	400	$200,400

Deduct expenses:

Cost of goods sold	$ 95,000	
Cost of repair parts used	7,000	
Salaries expense	60,000	
Miscellaneous expense	3,400	165,400
Net income		$ 35,000

The assets and liabilities before and after adjustments are listed below.

	December 31, 19+3	
Assets	Before Adjustment	After Adjustment
Cash	$12,000	$12,000
Marketable securities	15,000	15,000
Accounts receivable	8,000	8,000
Interest receivable	-0-	500
Merchandise inventory	18,000	18,000
Inventory of repair parts	1,500	1,200
Prepaid rent	1,200	-0-
Unexpired insurance	900	600
Equipment	20,000	20,000
Accumulated depreciation	1,500	3,000
Liabilities		
Accounts payable	9,000	9,000
Salaries payable	-0-	4,000
Estimated income tax payable	-0-	8,300
Advances from customers (Note 1)	900	1,500

Note 1. During 19+3, $600 of advances from customers were improperly treated as sales of merchandise. This error was corrected by an adjustment.

Prepare a corrected income statement, which should show the net income for 19+3 as $19,300.

Traditional
Record-keeping Procedures

The value of understanding the accounting process. Part of the accounting process deals with procedural matters; that is, with record keeping. A career accountant, of course, should be well-versed in procedural matters, not because any significant portion of his time will be devoted to keeping records but because others view him as an expert and thus expect him to have the ability to plan and install record-keeping systems, to evaluate existing systems, and possibly to assume administrative responsibility over such activity. Whether a business is large or small, whether the procedures are simple or complex, and whether manual, machine, or electronic devices are utilized, the task of record keeping, that is, data gathering, is extremely important. Many important decisions are based on the data accumulated in the accounting records of a business.

Whether or not a student intends to become an expert accountant, a knowledge of accounting procedures can be valuable. With such knowledge he will more easily understand accounting theory. In turn, a good foundation in accounting theory will lead to a better understanding of accounting data, particularly that set forth in the form of financial statements.

The accounting system. As a general rule, the first accounting work performed for any business involves the development of an accounting system. The accountant studies the nature of the business, determines the types of transactions that probably will occur and the kinds of assets and equities that will result from the expected transactions. He takes cognizance of the needs of those who will make use of accounting data, and he plans or selects the necessary forms and records in which the transactions of the business may be recorded. An obvious objective of any accounting system is to provide for each kind of asset and equity a record of the increases and decreases caused by transactions.

In the case of Sight & Sound Corporation for its first year of operations, the record-keeping arrangement should be designed to keep track of the increases and decreases for the following assets and equities:

Assets	Equities
Cash	Accounts payable
Accounts receivable	Salaries payable
Merchandise inventory	Capital stock
Land	Retained earnings

The record maintained for each asset and equity is known as an *account*. If the increases and decreases are correctly processed in the accounting records, the dollar amounts (account balances) needed for the $19+1$ financial statements will be available.

The recording process. The recording process may be accomplished in a variety of ways, ranging from the use of pen and ink to electronic devices, and the resulting record can be maintained on paper, punched cards, or magnetic tapes, to mention the most commonly used record forms. The transaction worksheet used in the first two chapters is an acceptable record-keeping device, although it would be cumbersome and impractical for a business of even moderate size when one considers the large number of accounts and the volume of transactions present-day business activity entails.

The point is, the increase-decrease plan illustrated in the first two chapters is applicable whether accounting records consist of hand- or machine-written entries on paper forms, data punched into cards, or data stored on magnetic tapes. If one has acquired an understanding of the accounting process, such knowledge is effective and useful no matter how modern or how old-fashioned is the accounting system for a particular business enterprise.

Debit and credit. Exposure to the traditional hand-written record-keeping procedures associated with the double-entry method of accounting has the following in its favor:

The knowledge gained by such exposure is transferable to other, more modern record-keeping systems.

Hand-written systems continue to be used by many small businesses.

Most large companies still use some hand-written records in combination with computer records.

The traditional account form set forth below can be used for purposes of demonstrating the basic features of the double-entry method. One such form would be used for each account. Observe that the form has two sides—left and right—with identical columns. Thus increases can be recorded on one side of the form and decreases on the other.

Sheet No.			*Account Title*					Account No.
DATE	EXPLANATION	REF.	AMOUNT	DATE	EXPLANATION	REF.	AMOUNT	

The column headings (*Date, Explanation, Ref.,* and *Amount*) shown in the preceding illustration usually do not appear in accounts, but are included in the illustration to indicate the kind of data put in each column. Completed accounts will be illustrated later in the chapter.

To simplify illustrations and problem assignments, the account form is often depicted as follows:

Accountants call this abbreviated form a "T-account" because it is shaped like the capital letter T.

The recording plan. Increases in assets and decreases in equities are recorded on the left side of the account, called the debit side. Increases in equities and decreases in assets are recorded on the right side of the account, called the credit side. Many nonaccountants seem to think that debit means something unfavorable and credit means something favorable. This is not the case. The words debit and credit merely refer to the two sides of an account.

The difference between the total debits and the total credits in an account is called the *balance.* If the dollars debited exceed the dollars credited, the account has a debit balance; if the credits exceed the debits, the account has a credit balance.

When the above recording plan is followed, asset accounts will have debit (left-hand) balances and equity accounts will have credit (right-hand) balances. This account balance arrangement, namely, left-side balances for assets and right-side balances for equities, ties in with the customary form of the balance sheet, in which the assets are shown on the left side and the equities are shown on the right side.

The increase-decrease-balance plan for accounts outlined above can be restated as follows by the use of T-accounts.

ASSET ACCOUNTS

(They will have debit balances)

T-Account

Debit	Credit
Balance . . . . $ xxx	
Increases recorded as debits	Decreases recorded as credits

EQUITY ACCOUNTS

(They will have credit balances)

T-Account

Debit	Credit
	Balance . . . . $ xx
Decreases recorded as debits	Increases recorded as credits

The application of the recording plan is illustrated in the following asset and equity accounts.

Data for cash account:
    Beginning balance, $1,000
    Cash receipt, $500
    Cash disbursement, $400

Cash

Balance . 1,000	400
500	

Data for accounts payable account:
    Beginning balance, $600
    Purchase of merchandise on account, $300
    Payment to reduce accounts payable, $400

Accounts Payable

400	Balance . . 600
	300

To repeat, increases in assets, and
    decreases in equities
        are recorded as debits.
And, increases in equities, and
    decreases in assets
        are recorded as credits.

	Assets		Equities	
+	−	−	+
Debits	Credits	Debits	Credits

Recording transactions. To illustrate the debiting and crediting of accounts, let us return to the first year's transactions of Sight & Sound Corporation mentioned in Chapter 1, analyze the transactions, and observe the resulting debit and credit entries. Color is used to identify each additional debit and credit when entered in the T-accounts. Accounts with debit balances (the asset accounts) are shown at the left; accounts with credit balances (the equity accounts) are shown at the right.

(1) Issued capital stock for cash, $25,000.

Accounts Affected	Kind of Account	Change in Balance	Debit	Credit
Cash	Asset	Increase	25,000	
Capital stock	Equity	Increase		25,000

Cash		Capital Stock	
25,000			*25,000*

(2) Purchased land as a long-term investment for $10,000 cash.

Accounts Affected	Kind of Account	Change in Balance	Debit	Credit
Land	Asset	Increase	10,000	
Cash	Asset	Decrease		10,000

Land	
10,000	

Cash	
25,000	*10,000*

(3) Purchased merchandise on account, $60,000.

Accounts Affected	Kind of Account	Change in Balance	Debit	Credit
Merchandise inventory	Asset	Increase	60,000	
Accounts payable	Equity	Increase		60,000

Merchandise Inventory		Accounts Payable	
60,000			*60,000*

(4a) Made sales of merchandise on account for $80,000.

Accounts Affected	Kind of Account	Change in Balance	Debit	Credit
Accounts receivable	Asset	Increase	80,000	
Retained earnings	Equity	Increase		80,000

Accounts Receivable		Retained Earnings	
80,000			*80,000*

(4b) Cost of goods sold, $48,000.

Accounts Affected	Kind of Account	Change in Balance	Debit	Credit
Retained earnings	Equity	Decrease	48,000	
Merchandise inventory	Asset	Decrease		48,000

Merchandise Inventory		Retained Earnings	
60,000	*48,000*	*48,000*	80,000

(5) Collections from customers, $70,000.

Accounts Affected	Kind of Account	Change in Balance	Debit	Credit
Cash	Asset	Increase	70,000	
Accounts receivable	Asset	Decrease		70,000

Cash	
25,000	10,000
70,000	

Accounts Receivable	
80,000	*70,000*

Recording plan restated: increases in assets, and
decreases in equities
are recorded as debits;

increases in equities, and
decreases in assets
are recorded as credits.

(6) Paid on account, $40,000.

Accounts Affected	Kind of Account	Change in Balance	Debit	Credit
Accounts payable	Equity	Decrease	40,000	
Cash	Asset	Decrease		40,000

Cash		Accounts Payable	
25,000	10,000	*40,000*	60,000
70,000	*40,000*		

(7) Paid rent for the year, $4,800.

Accounts Affected	Kind of Account	Change in Balance	Debit	Credit
Retained earnings	Equity	Decrease	4,800	
Cash	Asset	Decrease		4,800

Cash			Retained Earnings	
25,000	10,000		48,000	80,000
70,000	40,000		*4,800*	
	4,800			

(8) Paid other expenses, $5,200.

Accounts Affected	Kind of Account	Change in Balance	Debit	Credit
Retained earnings	Equity	Decrease	5,200	
Cash	Asset	Decrease		5,200

Cash			Retained Earnings	
25,000	10,000		48,000	80,000
70,000	40,000		4,800	
	4,800		*5,200*	
	5,200			

(9) Paid employees' salaries for eleven months, $16,500.

Accounts Affected	Kind of Account	Change in Balance	Debit	Credit
Retained earnings	Equity	Decrease	16,500	
Cash	Asset	Decrease		16,500

Cash			Retained Earnings	
25,000	10,000		48,000	80,000
70,000	40,000		4,800	
	4,800		5,200	
	5,200		*16,500*	
	16,500			

(10) Payment of cash dividend, $2,000.

Accounts Affected	Kind of Account	Change in Balance	Debit	Credit
Retained earnings	Equity	Decrease	2,000	
Cash	Asset	Decrease		2,000

Cash			Retained Earnings	
25,000	10,000		48,000	80,000
70,000	40,000		4,800	
	4,800		5,200	
	5,200		16,500	
	16,500		*2,000*	
	2,000			

Adjustment for December salaries, $1,500.

Accounts Affected	Kind of Account	Change in Balance	Debit	Credit
Retained earnings	Equity	Decrease	1,500	
Salaries payable	Equity	Increase		1,500

Retained Earnings

48,000	80,000
4,800	
5,200	
16,500	
2,000	
1,500	

Salaries Payable

	1,500

The above determination of the debits and credits required to record the $19+1$ transactions reveals a basic rule of double-entry accounting: For each transaction the dollar amount of the debit (or debits, if more than one account is debited) will equal the dollar amount of the credit (or credits).

In short, debits must equal credits.

The working of this rule is demonstrated by the following summary of the transactions.

Transaction	Increases in Assets	Decreases in Equities	Debits	Increases in Equities	Decreases in Assets	Credits
1	X		$ 25,000	X		$ 25,000
2	X		10,000		X	10,000
3	X		60,000	X		60,000
4a	X		80,000	X		80,000
4b		X	48,000		X	48,000
5	X		70,000		X	70,000
6		X	40,000		X	40,000
7		X	4,800		X	4,800
8		X	5,200		X	5,200
9		X	16,500		X	16,500
10		X	2,000		X	2,000
Adjustment		X	1,500	X		1,500
			$363,000			$363,000

Revenue and expense accounts. As explained earlier, revenues are inflows of assets from the sale of goods or the rendering of services that increase the owners' equity, or, more specifically, that increase the retained earnings of a corporation. Expenses decrease the retained earnings of a corporation and are the cost of services or resources used for the purpose of generating revenue.

The increases and decreases to retained earnings that result from revenue and expense transactions can be recorded in the retained earnings account, as was the practice in the preceding illustration which introduced the debit-credit procedure.

However, revenue and expense transactions usually occur in such volume that this recording practice would unduly clutter up the retained earnings account. Furthermore, it would be exceedingly time consuming to extract from the retained earnings account the revenue and expense data therein needed to prepare the income statement. For such reasons, separate accounts are used for each type of revenue and expense.

It may be helpful to think of revenue and expense accounts as "offshoots" or subdivisions of the retained earnings account. By so relating revenue and expense accounts to the retained earnings account, the debit-credit procedure for revenue and expense accounts follows logically:

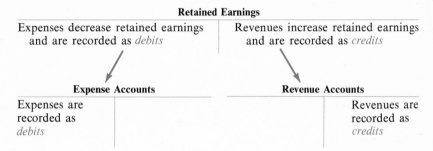

Retained Earnings

| Expenses decrease retained earnings and are recorded as *debits* | Revenues increase retained earnings and are recorded as *credits* |

Expense Accounts

Expenses are recorded as *debits*

Revenue Accounts

Revenues are recorded as *credits*

The recording practice previously illustrated resulted in revenue and expense transactions for 19+1 being recorded in the retained earnings as shown below:

Retained Earnings

(Cost of goods sold)	48,000	(Sales)	80,000
(Rent expense)	4,800		
(Other expense)	5,200		
(Salaries expense)	16,500		
(Salaries expense)	1,500		

Such use of the retained earnings account will henceforth be discarded in favor of individual revenue and expense accounts, which, in the case of Sight & Sound Corporation, would appear as follows:

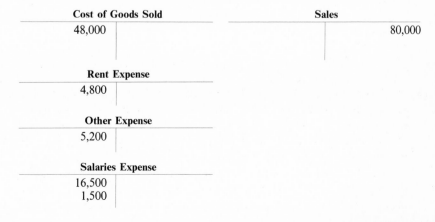

Cost of Goods Sold		**Sales**	
48,000			80,000

Rent Expense	
4,800	

Other Expense	
5,200	

Salaries Expense	
16,500	
1,500	

Although dividends are not an expense, they are usually recorded in a separate account.

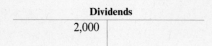

Dividends

2,000	

Consequently, the retained earnings account would have no debits or credits therein for dividends, expenses, or revenues. It would appear as follows after the 19+1 transactions of Sight & Sound Corporation had been recorded in the accounts:

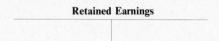

Retained Earnings

As will be shown later, other kinds of entries are made in the retained earnings account.

Summary of debit-credit plan. The debit-credit plan just illustrated will result in the following groupings:

Debit Balance Accounts	Credit Balance Accounts
Assets	Liabilities
Expenses	Owners' equity
Dividends	Revenues

Also, the use of the debit (left-hand) and credit (right-hand) sides of the accounts for recording increases and decreases works out as follows:

Debits	Credits
Increases in assets	Decreases in assets
Increases in expenses	Decreases in expenses
Decreases in liabilities	Increases in liabilities
Decreases in owners' equity	Increases in owners' equity
Decreases in revenues	Increases in revenues
Increases in dividends	

or:

ASSETS	=	LIABILITIES	+	OWNERS' EQUITY
+ | −		− | +		− | +
dr. | cr.		dr. | cr.		dr. | cr.

EXPENSES	REVENUES
+ | −	− | +
dr. | cr.	dr. | cr.

DIVIDENDS
+
dr.

Alternative account form. Observe the following cash account of Sight & Sound Corporation. The data therein agree with that set forth in the T-account on page 81.

CASH

Relevant dates would be entered in this column	This space used when it seems desirable to describe some unusual feature of a transaction	25,000 70,000	Relevant dates would be entered in this column	This space used when it seems desirable to describe some unusual feature of a transaction	10,000 40,000 4,800 5,200 16,500 2,000

The account has a balance because there is a difference between the total debits and the total credits:

Total debits $95,000
Total credits $78,500

Because the debits exceed the credits, the account has a debit balance; the balance is $16,500.

One disadvantage of the account form just shown is that there is no convenient way to keep track of and display the current balance of the account. The following account form, widely used in manual accounting systems, overcomes this weakness. The third money column is used as a balance column. To show the use of balance columns, a few of the cash transactions from the previous illustration have been entered in the account.

Account Title Cash   **Account No.** 111

			Debit	**Credit**	**Balance**
19+1 Jan.	2 3 5	←For explanation, if needed→	25,000	10,000 4,800	25,000 Dr. 15,000 Dr. 11,200 Dr.

The accounts, like the cash account just illustrated, usually are kept in a loose-leaf binder or in a file. The binder or the file, together with the accounts therein, is called a *ledger*. It is helpful if the accounts in the ledger are arranged in the order in which they will appear in the financial statements.

Journal and ledger. Although transactions *could be* recorded directly in the ledger accounts, it is customary to use at least two accounting records:

(1) A *Journal.*
>The first record of a transaction is made in a journal. It provides a *chronological* record of all transactions.
>A journal is a ruled form designed to provide suitable spaces in which to record such pertinent details as: the date of the transaction, the accounts affected, and the amounts debited and credited.

(2) A *Ledger.*

The debits and credits to the various accounts, as shown by the journal entries, are entered in the accounts by a process called *posting.*

Journal illustrated. The following illustration of a journal, although based on only three transactions of Sight & Sound Corporation, should be sufficient to indicate the clerical process of journalizing.

		JOURNAL		(Page 1)
19+1				
Jan.	2	Cash	25,000	
		Capital stock		25,000
		Issued capital stock for cash.		
	3	Land	10,000	
		Cash		10,000
		Purchased land as a long-term investment, for cash.		
	5	Rent expense.............................	4,800	
		Cash		4,800
		Paid rent for the year.		

In connection with the above journal, note the following conventional recording practices:

· The year, month, and day of the month are shown with the first journal entry on each page; entries on the same page for subsequent transactions in the same year and month need show only the day of the month.
·· Always record the debit part of the entry first.
··· Indent the account credited.
···· Support each journal entry with a concise explanation of the transaction.
····· Leave a space between entries.

Advantages of the journal. The journal serves three useful purposes. In the first place, it reduces the possibility of error. If transactions were recorded directly in the ledger, there would be considerable danger of omitting the debit or the credit entry, or of making two debit entries or two credit entries. This danger is reduced to a minimum by use of the journal. In the journal, the debits and credits for each transaction are recorded together, making any such errors more obvious.

In the second place, the journal shows offsetting debit and credit entries for each transaction, and thus provides a complete record of the transaction in one place. Also, the journal provides ample space for an explanation of the transaction.

In the third place, the journal contains a record of transactions in their *chronological* order.

Posting. *Posting* is the process of transferring data from the journal to the ledger accounts. It is a clerical operation, as can be seen by examining the following posted journal entry and the relevant ledger accounts. The data entered in the records by the posting operation are shown in color.

JOURNAL (Page 1)

19 + 1						
Jan.	2	Cash	111	25,000	
		Capital stock	311		25,000
		Issued capital stock for cash.			

Account Title   **Cash**   **Account No.**   **111**

19 + 1					
Jan.	2		1	25,000	25,000 Dr.

Account Title   **Capital Stock**   **Account No.**   **311**

19 + 1					
Jan.	2		1	25,000	25,000 Cr.

In the journal and ledger account forms, the small column at the left of the money columns is known as the reference column. A number placed in the journal reference column during the posting operation indicates the number of the account in the ledger *to* which the entry was posted. A number placed in the ledger account reference indicates the journal page *from* which the entry was posted.

Recording the journal page number in the ledger and the account number in the journal serves two purposes:

During the posting operation, it shows how much of the posting has been done. Thus, if the posting work is interrupted, the notations, called *posting references,* indicate where the work was discontinued and where it should be resumed.

After the posting has been completed, the notations serve as cross references between the journal and the ledger. Such cross references can be helpful in the event that errors make it necessary to trace the entries in ledger accounts.

The trial balance. The accounting process being described herein is known as the double-entry method because the recording of each transaction requires debit and credit entries of equal amount. Because the debit and credit entries for each transaction are equal, it follows that the total debit entries in all of the accounts should be equal to the total credit entries. It is equally true that *the total of the debit balances in the accounts should be equal to the total of the credit balances.*

It is customary to check periodically the equality of the debit and credit balances in a ledger by listing and totaling them. Such a list is called a *trial balance.* Many businesses prepare a trial balance at the end of each month. The December 31, 19 + 1 trial balance of Sight & Sound Corporation, prepared after the 19 + 1 journal entries had been posted, follows.

SIGHT & SOUND CORPORATION
Trial Balance
December 31, 19+1

	Debit	Credit
Cash	16,500	
Accounts receivable	10,000	
Merchandise inventory	12,000	
Land	10,000	
Accounts payable		20,000
Salaries payable		1,500
Capital stock		25,000
Dividends	2,000	
Sales		80,000
Cost of goods sold	48,000	
Salaries expense	18,000	
Rent expense	4,800	
Other expense	5,200	
	126,500	126,500

Uses of the trial balance. A trial balance is useful in checking the *mathematical* accuracy of the ledger. But it should be understood that a trial balance proves nothing more than the equality of the debit and credit balances. For example, the trial balance will still "balance" even though a transaction was not journalized, or a wrong account was debited or credited in the journal.

A trial balance is also useful to an accountant whenever periodic statements are to be prepared. Although it is possible for the accountant to prepare such statements by working directly from the ledger, it is much easier to use the account balances shown by a trial balance. For example, the above trial balance would provide the information needed for the preparation of the financial statements shown on pages 3, 6, and 8.

Compound journal entries. Sometimes the recording of a transaction requires more than a single debit and credit. For instance, assume that land which cost $10,000 was sold at cost, and that $6,000 in U.S. Government bonds and $4,000 in cash were received in settlement; the entry to record the transaction would be:

U.S. Government bonds	6,000	
Cash	4,000	
Land		10,000
Sale of land.		

Such entries, having more than one debit and/or more than one credit, are called *compound journal entries.*

ASSIGNMENT

MATERIAL

QUESTIONS

1. What function is served by an *account?*

2. State briefly the debit-credit recording plan as it relates to asset and equity accounts.

3. Under what circumstances does an account have a debit balance?

4. State briefly the debit-credit recording plan as it relates to revenue and expense accounts.

5. What is a *journal?*

6. Recite the three useful purposes served by a journal.

7. What is *posting?*

8. What is a *trial balance?*

9. Of what use is a trial balance?

SHORT EXERCISES

E4-1. Indicate your knowledge of the debit-credit plan by completing the following with one of the words: *debits* or *credits.*

    (a) Increases in assets are recorded by _____.

    (b) Decreases in expenses are recorded by _____.

    (c) Increases in liabilities are recorded by _____.

    (d) Increases in expenses are recorded by _____.

    (e) Increases in revenues are recorded by _____.

    (f) Increases in dividends are recorded by _____.

    (g) Decreases in owners' equity are recorded by _____.

    (h) Decreases in assets are recorded by _____.

    (i) Decreases in liabilities are recorded by _____.

    (j) Decreases in revenues are recorded by _____.

    (k) Increases in owners' equity are recorded by _____.

E4-2. The following accounts and amounts were taken from the trial balance of Zoomer Corporation. Put the debit balances in one column and the credit balances in another. Add the columns to see if the trial balance was in balance.

Accumulated depreciation	$ 900
Cash	6,600
Depreciation expense	900
Accounts receivable	15,000
Rent expense.	4,800
Merchandise inventory	18,000
Salaries payable	1,700
Prepaid rent	4,800
Other expense	5,500
Land	10,000
Salaries expense	20,400
Delivery truck	4,000
Accounts payable	25,000
Cost of goods sold	54,000
Advances from customers	1,400
Sales	90,000
Dividends	2,000
Retained earnings	2,000
Capital stock	25,000

E4-3. The transactions listed below are those of Fences, Incorporated, which was organized on May 1, 19+8.

19+8
May 1—Capital stock with a par value of $8,000 was issued for cash.
2—One hundred dollars was paid for the use of office facilities for May.
5—A job was finished today and $250 was collected.
6—Paid $60 for materials used on the fence-building job.
10—A bill was delivered to A. O. Smith in the amount of $500 for work completed today. Smith agreed to pay in 10 days.
11—Paid $90 for materials used on the Smith job.
15—Paid wages in the amount of $225.
17—Purchased land as a future building site, paying $3,000.
19—Received $500 from A. O. Smith for the work completed on May 10.
22—A job was finished today; the bill was $600. The customer, R. J. Brown, promised to pay half of the bill before the end of the month and the balance within 30 days.
23—Paid $95 for materials used on the Brown job.
27—Received $300 from R. J. Brown.
31—Paid wages in the amount of $350.
31—Stockholders were paid a dividend of $80.
31—Purchased a tractor for $1,000 cash.

Indicate the accounts to be debited and credited for each of the above transactions. Use the account numbers shown below for the suggested accounts.

111—Cash	319—Dividends
113—Accounts Receivable	411—Revenue from Jobs
131—Land	511—Office Facilities Expense
135—Equipment	512—Materials Expense
311—Capital Stock	513—Wages Expense

E4-4. Prophet Company was organized on October 1, 19+8, for the purpose of leasing and operating an FM radio station. Data in summary form relating to the first month's operations are given below.

Advertising revenue earned for services performed, on account	$ 2,500

Cash receipts for the month:

From stockholders for shares of stock	$20,000
From customers representing collections on account	1,800
Total	$21,800

Cash disbursements for the month:

For salaries	$ 1,050
For October rent	1,000
For miscellaneous expenses	195
For dividends to stockholders	100
Total	$ 2,345

Equipment costing $3,500 was purchased on account.

Prepare the October 31, 19+8 trial balance.

PROBLEMS

Problem A4-1. Using the following information, prepare the December 31, 19+3 trial balance of Mixture Corporation. Place the accounts in financial-statement sequence, that is, balance sheet accounts first, starting with current assets and ending with stockholders' equity, and income statement accounts last, with revenues preceding the expenses.

December 31, 19+3 Account Balances
(Alphabetical Order)

Accounts receivable	$ 68,000
Accounts payable	25,000
Accumulated depreciation—Building	48,000
Accumulated depreciation—Equipment	11,500
Advertising expense	2,500
Building	105,000
Capital stock	275,000
Cash	50,000
Cost of goods sold	260,000
Depreciation expense—Building	2,100
Depreciation expense—Equipment	4,000
Equipment	40,000
Insurance expense	1,000
Inventory	44,100
Land	28,000
Patents	20,000
Retained earnings	12,350
Salaries expense . . . . :	80,000

(Continued)

Salaries payable . . . . $ 750
Sales   340,000
Taxes   9,000
Taxes payable   1,500
Unexpired insurance   400

Problem A4-2. The account balances of Air Distributors Corporation at the beginning of 19+2 are listed below.

Cash . . . . $ 6,105
Inventory   9,000
Prepaid rent (for January)   600
Commissions payable   400
Taxes payable   135
Capital stock   14,000
Retained earnings.   2,170

The inventory consisted of two airplanes costing $4,500 each.
Journalize the following January, 19+2 transactions.

19+2
January   2—Sold an airplane and collected cash for the sales price, $6,500.

5—Purchased from Willow Aircraft Company on account two airplanes costing $5,000 each.

7—Paid the taxes payable.

10—One of the company's salesmen sold the remaining airplane that was on hand at the beginning of the year. He collected $6,500 from the customer. He deducted his 10 per cent commission on this sale and the $400 commission owed him from an earlier sale and turned in $5,450 to the company.

15—Delivered one of the airplanes acquired from Willow Aircraft Company to a customer and collected the sales price, $6,400.

18—Paid the amount owed to Willow Aircraft Company.

25—Purchased from Willow Aircraft Company on account three airplanes costing $5,000 each.

31—Paid rent in advance for February, March, and April, $1,800.

Record the adjusting entry for the January rent expense.

Problem A4-3. The transactions listed below are those of a newly organized corporation. Journalize the transactions.

19+1
July   1—Smith and Jones each invested $4,000 for capital stock in Campus Auto Laundry Company.

1—An agreement was made whereby car-washing equipment and facilities were rented on a monthly basis. Rent of $1,125 was paid for July. Campus Auto Laundry assumed responsibility for repairs.

2—Paid $75 for a newspaper advertisement announcing the nature of the company's business, namely, the washing of automobiles and trucks owned and operated by businesses.

5—Signed an agreement with Regional Car Rentals, Inc., to keep its fleet of rental cars washed.

15—Billed Regional Car Rentals, Inc., for car-washing services performed during the last ten days, $810.

17—Received a bill for $19 from Mechanical Fixit Shop for repairs to equipment.

19—Received $810 from Regional Car Rentals, Inc.

20—Signed an agreement with Airport Cab Company to keep its fleet of cabs washed.

22—Paid miscellaneous expenses of $35.

25—Paid bill owed to Mechanical Fixit Shop.

31—Billed Regional Car Rentals, Inc., $1,120 and Airport Cab Company $680 for car-washing services performed during last half of month.

31—Salaries and wages were paid, $925.

Problem A4-4. (Problem A4-4 is continued as Problem A5-4.) The accounts in the ledger of Touch and View Company with their December 31, 19+1 balances are listed below.

Account Number	Account Title	Balance
111	Cash	$33,000
113	Accounts receivable.	20,000
115	Merchandise inventory.	24,000
116	Prepaid rent.	—
131	Land (Held as an investment)	20,000
152	Delivery truck	—
153	Accumulated depreciation	—
211	Accounts payable	40,000
212	Salaries payable	3,000
215	Advances from customers	—
311	Capital stock	50,000
315	Retained earnings	4,000
319	Dividends	—
411	Sales	—
511	Cost of goods sold	—
512	Salaries expense	—
513	Other expense	—

In order to reduce the repetition in the recording process (journalizing and posting), yearly totals are given below for certain kinds of transactions.

Dates	19+2 Transactions
19+2	
January	3—Paid the liability for the December, 19+1 salaries, $3,000.
	3—Purchased a delivery truck for cash, $8,000.
	3—Paid $19,200 rent in advance for 19+2 and 19+3.
November	1—Received $2,800 cash in advance from a customer who gave a special order for merchandise to be delivered in 19+3.
December	31—Purchased merchandise on account, $120,000.
	31—Sales on account, $180,000.
	31—Cost of goods sold, $108,000.
	31—Collections on accounts receivable, $170,000.
	31—Payments to creditors, $110,000.
	31—Paid other expenses, $11,000.
	31—Paid salaries, $37,400.
	31—Paid dividends, $4,000.

Required:

(a) Enter the December 31, 19+1 (beginning) balances in the ledger accounts.

   Allow fifteen lines for the cash account and five lines for all other accounts.

(b) Journalize the 19+2 transactions.

(c) Post.

(d) Prepare the December 31, 19+2 trial balance.

Problem A4-5. Journalize the July, 19+1 transactions of Air Overhaul Company, post to the ledger accounts, and take a July 31, 19+1 trial balance.

The company was organized to perform maintenance and repair services on aircraft. There will be two sources of revenue, one from the sale of parts (parts will be sold at twice their cost) and the other from the performance of maintenance and repair service. The following accounts can be used when recording the July transactions.

Account Number	Account Title	(X)
111	Cash	(19)
112	Accounts receivable	(9)
113	Parts inventory	(12)
114	Shop supplies on hand	(4)
115	Unexpired insurance	(4)
151	Equipment	(4)
211	Accounts payable	(7)
212	Advances from customers	(4)
311	Capital stock	(4)
411	Sales of parts	(10)
412	Service revenue	(10)
511	Cost of parts sold	(10)
512	Wages expense	(5)
513	Rent expense	(4)

(X) Suggested number of lines to allow when setting up the ledger accounts.

July 1—Issued $8,000 par value stock for $5,000 cash and equipment valued at $3,000.

2—Paid July rent, $180.

5—Purchased airplane spare parts on account from Curtis Company, $1,817.

7—Purchased shop supplies for $410, cash.

9—Billed Charter Airline $288 for parts and $470 for labor used in making a periodic check on one of its aircraft.

11—Purchased additional airplane parts from Wright Corporation, paying $421 cash.

12—Collected $45 for repair of landing gear on a private plane. No parts were used.

14—Paid the Curtis Company bill.

15—Billed World Air Flights $418 for parts and $614 for labor used in rebuilding a tail assembly.

15—Paid wages of $800 for first half of July.

18—Collected $100 for periodic overhaul of a private plane; this amount included $20 for parts.

20—Received $758 from Charter Airline.

20—Signed an agreement with XYZ Company to perform all required labor for maintenance on its company plane for $600 per quarter, starting today. All parts used will be extra.

21—Collected $600 in advance from XYZ Company.

23—Purchased a one-year fire insurance policy for cash, $30.

25—Received $1,032 from World Air Flights.

26—Billed Charter Airline $310 for parts and $580 for labor used in making a periodic check of one of its aircraft.

27—Purchased aiplane parts on account from Curtis Company, $622.

29—Completed rebuilding landing gear on plane belonging to A. Y. Junior. The total bill amounted to $690, of which $200 was for parts. Junior gave his check for the entire bill when he called today for his plane.

30—Purchased shop supplies on account from Modern Supply Co., $84.

31—Paid wages for last half of July, $825.

31—Billed XYZ Company, pursuant to agreement of July 20, for parts used in maintenance of company plane, $72.

Problem B4-1. Journalize the following transactions of Rapid Service Company.

19+2

May 1—Received $300 in cash as commissions on sales made today.

3—Paid office rent for May, $130.

5—Received a bill from Local Supply Co. for miscellaneous expenses, $17.

6—Received $50 rent for the balance of the month of May on land owned by the company.

9—Paid traveling expenses incurred by employees, $38.

10—Paid the bill owed to Local Supply Co. in the amount of $17.

15—Paid salaries for first half of May, $750.

16—Received $800 in commissions.

19—Invested $1,000 in municipal bonds.

23—Paid miscellaneous expenses, $12.

25—Received a bill for advertising from *The City Herald,* $21.

26—Paid repair expense in the amount of $24.

27—Purchased additional land worth $2,500 by issuing capital stock with a par value of $2,000 and paying $500 in cash.

29—Paid the bill received on May 25 from *The City Herald.*

31—Paid salaries for the last half of May, $750.

31—Paid dividends of $150 to stockholders.

31—Billed Metropolitan Realtors for $1,800 of commissions earned during May but remaining uncollected as of May 31.

Problem B4-2. Vision and Smell Company was organized early in 19+1. The 19+1 transactions are accumulated below by type of transaction.

Issued capital stock for cash, $50,000.

Purchased land as a long-term investment for $20,000 cash.

Purchased merchandise on account, $120,000.

Made sales of merchandise on account for $160,000.

Cost of goods sold, $96,000.

Collections from customers, $140,000.
Paid on account, $80,000.
Paid rent for the year, $9,600.
Paid other expenses, $10,400.
Paid salaries, $36,000.
Paid cash dividend, $4,000.

Required:

(a) Journalize the transactions, omitting explanations. (Dates have been omitted to lessen work.)
(b) Post. (Try to arrange the ledger accounts in financial-statement sequence. Assign numbers to the ledger accounts.)
(c) Take a December 31, 19+1 trial balance.

Problem B4-3. Journalize the following transactions of Commercial Refrigerator Sales Company, a newly organized corporation. The company will close its books annually on June 30.

19+1
July   1—Issued $10,000 par value stock for cash.
         2—Paid rent for July, $110.
         3—Purchased from Wholesale Supply Company, on account, five refrigerators for $200 each.
         7—Sold one refrigerator for $300 cash. (Remember to make a journal entry for the cost of goods sold.)
         8—Paid $40 as commission to the salesman.
         9—As an advertising feature, the company has agreed to place a new refrigerator in the local Girl Scout Home each July. According to the plan, when the new refrigerator is delivered each year, the Girl Scouts may sell the old refrigerator and keep the proceeds. A refrigerator is delivered to the Girl Scout Home today.
      10—Sold a refrigerator for $300 to R. S. Brown on account.
      15—Paid $1,000 to Wholesale Supply Company.
      18—Purchased for cash four refrigerators for $200 each.
      20—Paid $30 for newspaper advertising.
      24—Collected $300 from R. S. Brown.
      24—Paid $40 commission to the salesman.
      28—Cash sale of three refrigerators to Local Hospital for $860.
      30—Paid $50 in dividends to stockholders.

Problem B4-4. The beginning-of-year and end-of-year account balances of Ruler Company are listed below.

	19+4	
	January 1	December 31
Cash	$ 8,000	$ 9,100
Accounts receivable	12,000	13,000
Interest receivable	—	100
Inventory	10,000	10,000
Prepaid rent ($100 per month)	600	—
Investment in bonds	—	5,000
Land	4,000	—

	19+4 January 1	19+4 December 31
Equipment	$ 5,000	$ 5,000
Accumulated depreciation	1,000	2,000
Accounts payable	3,000	4,000
Salaries payable	500	600
Estimated income tax payable	800	900
Advances from customers	300	—
Capital stock	30,000	30,000
Retained earnings.....................	4,000	4,000
Dividends		2,000
Sales		80,300
Cost of goods sold		50,000
Salaries expense......................		25,000
Rent expense ($100 per month)		1,200
Depreciation expense		1,000
Interest revenue		200
Gain on sale of land...................		300
Income tax		900

The cash disbursements during 19+4 totaled $82,300, and were for the following purposes:

To suppliers for merchandise purchased on account	$49,000
Investment in bonds	5,000
Payment of 19+3 income tax liability	800
Dividends	2,000
Salaries	24,900
Rent	600
Total cash disbursements	$82,300

During 19+4, $79,000 was collected from customers.

Required:

(a) Present the December 31, 19+4 account balances in trial balance form.

(b) The journal entries for the 19+4 transactions and adjustments (omitting dates) of Ruler Company, which will account for all of the changes in the account balances between the beginning of the year and the end of the year. Entries will be required for the following:

> Sales of merchandise and cost of goods sold.
> Purchases of merchandise (all purchases were made on account).
> Payments to suppliers of merchandise.
> Collections from customers.
> The investment in bonds.
> The sale of the land.
> Payments to settle the $500 liability for salaries and the $800 liability for income taxes.
> Payment of dividends.
> The 19+4 expenses.
> The interest revenue.

Problem B4-5. (Problem B4-5 is continued as Problem B5-5.) On July 31, 19+1, Mr. Sam Teed and
Mr. John Tokay received a charter from the State of Wisconsin authorizing Totee Corpora-
tion to issue five thousand shares of $50 par value stock and to engage in the purchase, sale,
and servicing of refrigerators and allied products.

   The accountant for the new company plans to use the following accounts in the company's
ledger.

Account Number	Account Title	(X)	Account Number	Account Title	(X)
1	Cash	30	70	Sales	7
2	Accounts receivable	12	74	Repair revenue	5
10	Inventory	12	80	Cost of goods sold	7
20	Supplies and parts	6	84	Cost of supplies and parts used	5
26	Tools and equipment	5			
27	Accumulated depreciation	5	90	Rent expense	5
50	Accounts payable	10	91	Advertising expense	7
55	Advertising payable	5	92	Wages expense	7
56	Wages payable	5	93	Delivery expense	5
57	Delivery expense payable	5	94	Salaries expense	5
60	Capital stock	5	95	Depreciation expense	5
61	Retained earnings	5			

(X) Suggested number of lines to allow when setting up the ledger account.

   It will be the company's practice to bill the customer and record sales of merchandise
on the day of sale but, in the case of repair work, the billing and recording will be made
at month-end for the month's work.

19+1

August 1—Totee Corporation issued 300 shares of stock to Mr. Teed upon the in-
           vestment of $15,000, and issued 200 shares of stock to Mr. Tokay upon
           the investment of $10,000.

        1—A showroom and warehouse-servicing building was rented from the May
           Real Estate Agency for $300 per month, payable in advance. The
           August rent was paid.

        3—Received, per order, 15 O.K. Specials at an invoice price of $175 each,
           from the O.K. Cooling Equipment Co.

        4—Purchased for cash from Johnstone Hardware Co. tools and light repair
           equipment for $600. It is expected that these items will last approxi-
           mately two years.

        5—Paid O.K. Cooling Equipment Co. $2,000 on account and ordered $850
           worth of service supplies and parts.

        6—Sales for the day totaled two O.K. Specials. One was sold for $255 cash
           installed and the other was sold for $273 on credit to J. B. Stonehue.

        8—Supplies and parts ordered on August 5 from O. K. Cooling Equipment
           Co. were received.

       11—Paid balance owed O. K. Cooling Equipment Co. and ordered 12 O. K.
           Specials.

       12—Paid $48 for newspaper advertising for the week ended August 6.

       13—Paid employees' wages for the week, $350.

19+1

August 13—Sales for the day: Cash—3 units at $255 each.

Credit—1 unit at $273 to Frank Rae.

15—Collected $15 on account.

16—Paid $83 for window posters advertising next week's sale.

17—Received the 12 O. K. Specials ordered on August 11, at an invoice price of $175 each.

20—Paid employees' wages for the week, $350.

20—Sales for the day: Cash—4 units at $255 each.

Credit—1 unit at $273 to Henry Peel.

1 unit at $273 to H. E. Roberts.

22—Collected $30 on account.

23—Paid newspaper advertising for the week ended August 13, $63.

25—Paid O. K. Cooling Equipment Co. $1,000 on account.

26—Paid Local Drayage Co. $180 for deliveries of refrigerators to customers during the first three weeks.

27—Paid employees' wages for the week, $350.

27—Sales for the day: Cash—4 units at $255 each.

29—Purchased repair parts and supplies for $2,500 cash.

30—Received 10 O. K. Specials from O. K. Cooling Equipment Co. at an invoice price of $175 each.

30—Paid advertising for the week ended August 20, $105.

31—Paid salaries of $800.

31—Collected $60 on account.

31—Billed customers $2,899 for repair work completed during August.

31—Supplies and parts used on repair work during August cost $438.

Required:

(a) Journalize the August transactions.

(b) Post.

(c) Take a trial balance.

The Accounting Cycle

Sequence of accounting procedures. The various accounting procedures thus far explained are performed in the sequence shown below.

Journalize—thus providing a chronological record of transactions.

Post—thus accumulating the results of transactions in the accounts affected.

Take a trial balance—thus checking on the equality of the debit and credit balances in the ledger and setting forth in a convenient form the account balances needed for the preparation of the accounting statements.

Prepare an income statement—thus reporting on the results of operations for the period.

Prepare a statement of retained earnings—thus accounting for the changes in retained earnings during the period and showing the current balance of the account.

Prepare a balance sheet—thus showing the financial position at the end of the period.

The additional steps to complete the accounting cycle performed during each accounting (fiscal) period are:

Make and post the journal entries necessary to close the books.

Take an after-closing trial balance.

Closing the books. Refer to the December 31, 19+1 balance sheet of Sight & Sound Corporation on page 3. According to the balance sheet, the retained earnings amount to $2,000. However, if you refer to the trial balance for the same date, shown on page 88, you will not find among the data listed thereon a $2,000 balance for retained earnings. This condition is evident from the following columnar comparison of the December 31, 19+1 balance sheet amounts and the trial-balance amounts.

SIGHT & SOUND CORPORATION
December 31, 19+1

	Trial Balance		Balance Sheet	
Cash	16,500		16,500	
Accounts receivable	10,000		10,000	
Merchandise inventory	12,000		12,000	
Land	10,000		10,000	
Accounts payable		20,000		20,000
Salaries payable		1,500		1,500
Capital stock		25,000		25,000
Retained earnings.				2,000
Dividends	2,000			
Sales		80,000		
Cost of goods sold	48,000			
Salaries expense	18,000			
Rent expense	4,800			
Other expense	5,200			
	126,500	126,500	48,500	48,500

Since the trial balance is a list of the account balances as found in the ledger, it follows that the retained earnings ledger account had a zero balance when the trial balance was prepared. The reason for the lack of agreement is that the elements which make up the $2,000 of retained earnings have not been transferred to the retained earnings account. Those elements are found in the following accounts:

The Revenue and Expense Accounts

Revenue:
   Sales—this account has a credit balance $80,000
Expense:
   Cost of goods sold $48,000
   Salaries expense 18,000
   Rent expense 4,800
   Other expense 5,200
      The expense accounts have debit balances   76,000
      The difference (a net credit) is the net income . . . . $ 4,000

The Dividends Account

Dividends—this account has a debit balance   2,000
   The difference (also a net credit) is the retained earnings
   resulting from operating the business during 19+1 . . . . $ 2,000

These elements are transferred to the retained earnings account by the following journal entries, which are called *closing entries.*

		JOURNAL			(Page 10)
19+1					
Dec.	31	Sales	411	80,000	
		Cost of goods sold	511		48,000
		Salaries expense	512		18,000
		Rent expense	513		4,800
		Other expense	514		5,200
		Retained earnings	315		4,000
		To close the revenue and expense accounts and to transfer the net income to the retained earnings account.			
	31	Retained earnings	315	2,000	
		Dividends	319		2,000
		To close the dividends account.			

The account numbers in the Reference column of the journal indicate that the postings have been made. After the above entries have been posted, the retained earnings account will have a credit balance of $2,000, which agrees with the amount shown in the December 31, 19+1 balance sheet. The revenue, expense, and dividends accounts will have zero balances. This condition can be verified by reference to the accounts affected by the closing entries. (The amounts posted from the closing entries are shown in color.)

Account Title	Retained Earnings				Account No.	315
19+1						
Dec.	31		10		4,000	4,000 Cr.
	31		10	2,000		2,000 Cr.

Account Title	Dividends				Account No.	319
19+1						
Dec.	31	Year-end balance before closing				2,000 Dr.
	31		10	2,000		—

Account Title	Sales				Account No.	411
19+1						
Dec.	31	Year-end balance before closing				80,000 Cr.
	31		10	80,000		—

Account Title	Cost of Goods Sold				Account No.	511
19+1						
Dec.	31	Year-end balance before closing				48,000 Dr.
	31		10		48,000	—

Account Title		Salaries Expense				Account No. 512
19+1 Dec.	31	Year-end balance before closing				18,000 Dr.
	31		10		18,000	—

Account Title		Rent Expense				Account No. 513
19+1 Dec.	31	Year-end balance before closing				4,800 Dr.
	31		10		4,800	—

Account Title		Other Expense				Account No. 514
19+1 Dec.	31	Year-end balance before closing				5,200 Dr.
	31		10		5,200	—

Observe the use of a double rule in the revenue, expense, and dividend accounts to signal the end of an accounting period and that the books have been closed.

Closing the books annually serves to separate, by years, the data accumulated in the accounts relating to revenues, expenses, and dividends. The availability of revenue and expense data by years enables management and investors to make comparisons with earlier years to determine the extent of improvement or deterioration in the current year's operating performance. Since the books are closed annually, the revenue, expense, and dividend accounts start off each new year with zero balances. Closing the books also updates the retained earnings account by transferring thereto the net income (or loss) for the year just ended and the dividends declared for that year.

Trial balance after closing. After the books are closed, it is advisable to take an *after-closing* trial balance (sometimes called a *post-closing* trial balance) to make sure that the equality of debits and credits in the ledger has not been destroyed through errors made in closing the books. The after-closing trial balance of Sight & Sound Corporation is shown below.

SIGHT & SOUND CORPORATION
After-Closing Trial Balance
December 31, 19+1

Cash	16,500	
Accounts receivable	10,000	
Merchandise inventory	12,000	
Land	10,000	
Accounts payable		20,000
Salaries payable		1,500
Capital stock		25,000
Retained earnings		2,000
	48,500	48,500

Observe that only asset and equity accounts appear in the after-closing trial balance because revenue, expense, and dividend accounts have been closed to retained earnings.

Possible additional steps in the accounting cycle. Before preparing the financial statements, the accountant, or whoever has the responsibility for their accuracy, examines the account balances set forth in the trial balance to determine if any adjusting entries are required. As indicated in Chapter 3, adjusting entries are required if there is:

Revenue that was earned but not recorded.
Expense that was incurred but not recorded.
Revenue that was earned but is shown in the accounts as revenue received in advance.
Unrecognized cost expirations.

As a general rule, accounting entries are made when business transactions occur. Usually a customer or supplier or employee is a party to the transaction and some sort of business document, such as a check, a sales slip, or an invoice, is issued or received. Such documents serve as evidence in support of business transactions. Their issuance or receipt provides the justification for whatever entry is required to record the changes in the account balances caused by a business transaction. At the end of an accounting period, when it is time to take the trial balance and prepare the financial statements, it is unlikely that any transactions would be unrecorded. The same cannot be said about adjusting entries. They may or may not have been made before the trial balance was prepared. It does not matter whether the adjusting entries are made before or after the trial balance as long as they are made before the account balances are used to prepare the financial statements.

If adjusting entries were made after the trial balance was prepared, another trial balance often is prepared after the adjusting entries have been journalized and posted. Accountants differentiate between the trial balances by calling the first the "unadjusted trial balance" and the second the "adjusted trial balance."

To illustrate such trial balances, let us return to the Sight & Sound Corporation example for 19+2. A trial balance prepared after all 19+2 transactions had been journalized and posted would appear as shown at the top of the following page.

As noted earlier, a proper matching of revenue and expense would not be achieved if the December 31, 19+2 unadjusted trial balance figures were used to prepare the 19+2 financial statements because of three unrecognized expenses. These are discussed below the following unadjusted trial balance.

SIGHT & SOUND CORPORATION
Unadjusted Trial Balance
December 31, 19+2

Cash	6,600	
Accounts receivable	15,000	
Merchandise inventory	18,000	
Prepaid rent	9,600	
Land	10,000	
Delivery truck	4,000	
Accounts payable		25,000
Advances from customers		1,400
Capital stock		25,000
Retained earnings		2,000
Dividends	2,000	
Sales		90,000
Cost of goods sold	54,000	
Salaries expense	18,700	
Other expense	5,500	
	143,400	143,400

(a) No recognition has been given to the December salaries.

Adjusting entry:

19+2
Dec. 31   Salaries expense 1,700
     Salaries payable 1,700

(b) No recognition has been given to the fact that one-half of the rent paid in advance applies to 19+2.

Adjusting entry:

19+2
Dec. 31   Rent expense 4,800
     Prepaid rent 4,800

(c) No recognition has been given to depreciation on the delivery truck.

Adjusting entry:

19+2
Dec. 31   Depreciation expense 900
     Accumulated depreciation 900

To summarize, required adjusting entries may be journalized and posted either before or after the trial balance is prepared. The important point is: Consideration must be given to any required adjustments *before* the financial statements are prepared, whether the adjusting entries are made before or after the trial balance.

The schedule on the next page shows the relationship between the unadjusted trial balance and the adjusted trial balance.

SIGHT & SOUND CORPORATION
Trial Balances
December 31, 19+2

	Unadjusted Trial Balance		Adjustments		Adjusted Trial Balance	
Cash	6,600				6,600	
Accounts receivable	15,000				15,000	
Merchandise inventory	18,000				18,000	
Prepaid rent	9,600			(b) 4,800	4,800	
Land	10,000				10,000	
Delivery truck	4,000				4,000	
Accounts payable		25,000				25,000
Advances from customers		1,400				1,400
Capital stock		25,000				25,000
Retained earnings		2,000				2,000
Dividends	2,000				2,000	
Sales		90,000				90,000
Cost of goods sold	54,000				54,000	
Salaries expense	18,700		(a) 1,700		20,400	
Other expense	5,500				5,500	
	143,400	143,400				
Salaries payable				(a) 1,700		1,700
Rent expense			(b) 4,800		4,800	
Depreciation expense			(c) 900		900	
Accumulated depreciation				(c) 900		900
			7,400	7,400	146,000	146,000

Working papers. Working papers are a columnar device employed by accountants as a convenient and orderly way of organizing the accounting data to be used in the preparation of adjusting entries, periodic financial statements, and closing entries.

If the ledger contains only a few accounts and there are few adjusting entries, working papers are not necessary; if the ledger contains numerous accounts or if there are numerous adjustments, working papers are very useful. Even though a person may never have to prepare working papers, he should be generally familiar with them because they are often used as a way to present data promptly to management for its information or for decision-making purposes.

Illustrative working papers. The account balances of Sight & Sound Corporation at the end of 19+2 and the related adjustments referred to previously will be used to illustrate the preparation of working papers. There are so few accounts and adjustments that an experienced accountant probably would not consider it worth while to prepare working papers, but in a textbook it is desirable to begin with a relatively simple illustration.

The steps in the preparation of working papers are stated and illustrated on the pages following.

The data in the first six columns of the working papers coincide with the preceding schedule showing the unadjusted and adjusted trial balances of Sight & Sound Corporation.

First step. The account balances before adjustments were entered in the Trial Balance columns; the columns were totaled to determine their equality.

Second step. The required adjustments were entered in the Adjustments columns; the columns were totaled as a check against errors. Observe that the nature of each adjustment is set forth at the bottom of the working papers, with a key letter matching the debit and credit entries in the Adjustments columns with the explanatory material.

Third step. The Adjusted Trial Balance columns were completed by extending and, when necessary, combining the amounts in the Trial Balance and Adjustments columns; the Adjusted Trial Balance columns were totaled to determine their equality.

SIGHT & SOUND CORPORATION
Working Papers
For the Year Ended December 31, 19+2

	Trial Balance		Adjustments		Adjusted Trial Balance		Income Statement	Retained Earnings Statement	Balance Sheet
Cash	6,600				6,600				
Accounts receivable	15,000				15,000				
Merchandise inventory	18,000				18,000				
Prepaid rent	9,600			(b) 4,800	4,800				
Land	10,000				10,000				
Delivery truck	4,000				4,000				
Accounts payable		25,000				25,000			
Advances from customers		1,400				1,400			
Capital stock		25,000				25,000			
Retained earnings		2,000				2,000			
Dividends	2,000				2,000				
Sales		90,000				90,000			
Cost of goods sold	54,000				54,000				
Salaries expense	18,700		(a) 1,700		20,400				
Other expense	5,500				5,500				
	143,400	143,400							
Salaries payable				(a) 1,700		1,700			
Rent expense			(b) 4,800		4,800				
Depreciation expense			(c) 900		900				
Accumulated depreciation				(c) 900		900			
			7,400	7,400	146,000	146,000			

Adjustments

a—December salaries.
b—Rent expense applicable to 19+2.
c—Depreciation for the year.

107

Fourth step. Each account balance appearing in the Adjusted Trial Balance columns was entered in a column at the right corresponding to the statement in which it should appear. Debit balances were entered in the debit columns; credit balances were entered in credit columns.

SIGHT & SOUND CORPORATION
Working Papers
For the Year Ended December 31, 19+2

	Trial Balance		Adjustments		Adjusted Trial Balance		Income Statement		Retained Earnings Statement		Balance Sheet	
Cash	6,600				6,600						6,600	
Accounts receivable	15,000				15,000						15,000	
Merchandise inventory	18,000				18,000						18,000	
Prepaid rent	9,600			(b) 4,800	4,800						4,800	
Land	10,000				10,000						10,000	
Delivery truck	4,000				4,000						4,000	
Accounts payable		25,000				25,000						25,000
Advances from customers		1,400				1,400						1,400
Capital stock		25,000				25,000						25,000
Retained earnings		2,000				2,000				2,000		
Dividends	2,000				2,000				2,000			
Sales		90,000				90,000		90,000				
Cost of goods sold	54,000				54,000		54,000					
Salaries expense	18,700		(a) 1,700		20,400		20,400					
Other expense	5,500				5,500		5,500					
	143,400	143,400										
Salaries payable				(a) 1,700		1,700						1,700
Rent expense			(b) 4,800		4,800		4,800					
Depreciation expense			(c) 900		900		900					
Accumulated depreciation				(c) 900		900						900
			7,400	7,400	146,000	146,000						

Adjustments
a—December salaries.
b—Rent expense applicable to 19+2.
c—Depreciation for the year.

Fifth step. The net income for the year, amounting to $4,400, was determined as the balance of the Income Statement columns was computed. To facilitate this computation, the items in the two columns were totaled. The $4,400 was entered in the Income Statement debit column as a balancing figure; and, since the net income increases the retained earnings, it was also entered in the Retained Earnings Statement credit column. The Income Statement columns were again totaled and ruled.

SIGHT & SOUND CORPORATION
Working Papers
For the Year Ended December 31, 19+2

	Trial Balance Dr	Trial Balance Cr	Adjustments Dr	Adjustments Cr	Adjusted Trial Balance Dr	Adjusted Trial Balance Cr	Income Statement Dr	Income Statement Cr	Retained Earnings Statement Dr	Retained Earnings Statement Cr	Balance Sheet Dr	Balance Sheet Cr
Cash	6,600				6,600						6,600	
Accounts receivable	15,000				15,000						15,000	
Merchandise inventory	18,000				18,000						18,000	
Prepaid rent	9,600			(b) 4,800	4,800						4,800	
Land	10,000				10,000						10,000	
Delivery truck	4,000				4,000						4,000	
Accounts payable		25,000				25,000						25,000
Advances from customers		1,400				1,400						1,400
Capital stock		25,000				25,000						25,000
Retained earnings		2,000				2,000				2,000		
Dividends	2,000				2,000							
Sales		90,000				90,000		90,000				
Cost of goods sold	54,000				54,000		54,000					
Salaries expense	18,700		(a) 1,700		20,400		20,400					
Other expense	5,500				5,500		5,500					
	143,400	143,400										
Salaries payable				(a) 1,700		1,700						1,700
Rent expense			(b) 4,800		4,800		4,800					
Depreciation expense			(c) 900		900		900					
Accumulated depreciation				(c) 900		900						900
			7,400	7,400	146,000	146,000	85,600	90,000				
Net income							4,400			4,400		
							90,000	90,000				

Adjustments
a—December salaries.
b—Rent expense applicable to 19+2.
c—Depreciation for the year.

109

Sixth and final step. The retained earnings figure for the end of the year was computed, entered as a balancing figure in the Retained Earnings Statement debit column, and also entered in the Balance Sheet credit column. The two Balance Sheet columns were totaled and found to be in agreement. Lack of agreement would indicate an error somewhere in the working papers.

SIGHT & SOUND CORPORATION
Working Papers
For the Year Ended December 31, 19+2

	Trial Balance		Adjustments		Adjusted Trial Balance		Income Statement		Retained Earnings Statement		Balance Sheet	
	Dr	Cr	Dr	Cr	Dr	Cr	Dr	Cr	Dr	Cr	Dr	Cr
Cash	6,600				6,600						6,600	
Accounts receivable	15,000				15,000						15,000	
Merchandise inventory	18,000				18,000						18,000	
Prepaid rent	9,600			(b) 4,800	4,800						4,800	
Land	10,000				10,000						10,000	
Delivery truck	4,000				4,000						4,000	
Accounts payable		25,000				25,000						25,000
Advances from customers		1,400				1,400						1,400
Capital stock		25,000				25,000						25,000
Retained earnings		2,000				2,000				2,000		
Dividends	2,000				2,000				2,000			
Sales		90,000				90,000		90,000				
Cost of goods sold	54,000				54,000		54,000					
Salaries expense	18,700		(a) 1,700		20,400		20,400					
Other expense	5,500				5,500		5,500					
	143,400	143,400										
Salaries payable				(a) 1,700		1,700						1,700
Rent expense			(b) 4,800		4,800		4,800					
Depreciation expense			(c) 900		900		900					
Accumulated depreciation				(c) 900		900						900
			7,400	7,400	146,000	146,000	85,600	90,000				
Net income							4,400			4,400		
							90,000	90,000				
Retained earnings, December 31, 19+2.									4,400			4,400
									2,000	6,400	58,400	58,400
									6,400	6,400		

Adjustments
a—December salaries.
b—Rent expense applicable to 19+2.
c—Depreciation for the year.

Statements prepared from working papers. The working papers provide in a convenient form the information required for the financial statements. The financial statements prepared from the illustrative working papers would be in agreement with those shown on pages 35–36.

Closing entries. The closing entries can be prepared from the data in the Income Statement columns and the Retained Earnings Statement columns of the working papers. Refer to the completed working papers on page 110 for the data used to prepare the following closing entries.

> 19+2
>
> Dec. 31   Sales 90,000
>   Cost of goods sold 54,000
>   Salaries expense..................... 20,400
>   Other expense 5,500
>   Rent expense........................ 4,800
>   Depreciation expense 900
>   Retained earnings.................... 4,400
>   To transfer the net income to the retained earnings account.
>
>   31   Retained earnings....................... 2,000
>   Dividends 2,000
>   To transfer the dividends to the retained earnings account.

The accounting cycle. The fully developed accounting cycle is set forth below. It indicates the sequence in which accounting procedures are customarily performed.

- Make and post entries for all transactions.
- Take a trial balance (usually entered directly on the working papers, if they are prepared).
- (Optional) Complete the working papers.
- As needed, make and post adjusting entries.
- Prepare financial statements.
- Make and post closing entries.
- Take an after-closing trial balance.

These procedures, in total, constitute an *accounting cycle.* In practice the complete cycle usually is performed only once a year, because the books ordinarily are not closed more frequently. In some of the illustrations and problems in this text it is assumed, for convenience and simplicity, that the cycle is completed monthly.

When working papers are used, the financial statements may be prepared therefrom before the adjusting and closing entries are journalized and posted.

Determining when adjustments are required and the amounts thereof. In accounting courses, the data required for adjusting entries are usually given in the text. In business, the required information comes from many sources. As a first step, the accountant usually reviews the trial balance. The mere appearance of some accounts in the trial balance may suggest the necessity for certain adjustments. For instance, depreciable assets suggest adjustments for depreciation; investments in bonds suggest the possibility of earned, but unrecorded, interest revenue (income); a notes payable account suggests the need for an adjustment for interest payable.

If any prepayments (advance payments for services or revenues received in advance) appear in the trial balance, they should immediately draw the accountant's attention to the fact that adjustments for cost expirations and revenue earned may be required. Often a reference to the prior year's adjusting entries will disclose adjustments that are again appropriate.

Although an inspection of the trial balance and a review of earlier adjusting entries may suggest the *nature* of the required adjustments, to determine the *amounts* of the adjustments the accountant may need to refer to a variety of business documents, or he may make physical counts or other suitable quantitative measurements.

ASSIGNMENT

MATERIAL

QUESTIONS

1. Give the sequence of procedures for the accounting cycle.
2. When the books have been closed, which kinds of accounts will have zero balances?
3. Is the following statement true or false? "Closing the books updates the retained earnings account."
4. What does one achieve by taking an after-closing trial balance?
5. Does it matter whether adjusting entries are recorded before or after the trial balance has been prepared?
6. What are working papers?
7. Is it always desirable to prepare working papers before preparing the financial statements?
8. Is it possible to prepare the financial statements by reference only to completed working papers?

SHORT EXERCISES

E5-1 (a). A company's trial balance is shown below. Prepare journal entries to close the books as of May 31, 19+8.

FENCES, INCORPORATED
Trial Balance
May 31, 19+8

Cash	4,050	
Accounts receivable	300	
Inventory	1,000	
Land	3,000	
Capital stock		8,000
Dividends	80	
Sales		11,350
Cost of goods sold	6,000	
Store rent expense	900	
Advertising expense	245	
Salaries expense	3,775	
	19,350	19,350

(Remember that after closing entries have been posted the revenue, expense, and dividend accounts should have zero balances.)

(b). The company's trial balance one year later is shown below. This year the company suffered a net loss, that is, the expenses exceeded the revenues. As a result, the retained earnings would be reduced by the amount of the net loss. Prepare closing entries as of May 31, 19+9.

FENCES, INCORPORATED

Trial Balance
May 31, 19+9

Cash	6,900	
Accounts receivable	600	
Inventory	1,200	
Accounts payable		500
Capital stock		8,000
Retained earnings		350
Sales		12,000
Cost of goods sold	7,000	
Store rent expense	900	
Advertising expense	250	
Salaries expense	4,000	
	20,850	20,850

E5-2. Prepare the December 31, 19+3 after-closing trial balance.

DAYTIME COMPANY

Adjusted Trial Balance
December 31, 19+3

Cash	3,000	
Accounts receivable	4,000	
Inventory	5,000	
Supplies on hand	1,000	
Equipment	10,000	
Accumulated depreciation		1,500
Accounts payable		6,000
Taxes payable		300
Capital stock		10,000
Retained earnings		2,700
Dividends	400	
Sales		82,000
Cost of goods sold	50,000	
Salaries expense	25,000	
Rent expense	1,800	
Depreciation expense	500	
Supplies expense	1,200	
Taxes expense	600	
	102,500	102,500

E5-3. The following accounts and amounts are taken from those shown in the Adjusted Trial Balance columns of the working papers of Nightly Corporation. To demonstrate your knowledge of working papers, indicate, by the use of the numbers 1 through 6 shown in the columns, the column or columns in which you would place the amounts listed under "Adjusted Trial Balance." (You are not asked to enter the amounts in the columns. Just write the correct column number beside each account title.)

	Adjusted Trial Balance	Income Statement		Retained Earnings Statement		Balance Sheet	
		1	2	3	4	5	6
Cash	800						
Inventory	1,000						
Unexpired insurance	100						
Land	4,000						
Building	20,000						
Accumulated depreciation	2,000						
Accounts payable	1,200						
Salaries payable	700						
Capital stock	10,000						
Retained earnings............	1,800						
Dividends	400						
Sales	75,000						
Cost of goods sold	40,000						
Salaries expense.............	20,000						
Interest revenue	300						
Interest expense	200						

E5-4. Modern Electrical Company, engaged in inspection and repair work only, has been in business since 19+1. It closes its books on December 31. The company's trial balance at the end of 19+8 was as follows:

MODERN ELECTRICAL COMPANY
Trial Balance
December 31, 19+8

Cash	2,100	
Notes receivable.............................	1,000	
Electrical supplies...........................	800	
Unexpired insurance	240	
Land	6,200	
Building	18,800	
Accumulated depreciation—Building		5,264
Equipment	5,000	
Accumulated depreciation—Equipment		1,500
Accounts payable		350
Inspection fees received in advance		1,200
Capital stock		25,000
Retained earnings.............................	1,124	
Repair service revenue		13,250
Inspection fees earned........................		3,100
Salaries and wages expense	12,500	
Miscellaneous expense	1,900	
	49,664	49,664

The building had an expected useful life of 25 years when new, and the equipment an expected life of 5 years when new. The interest owed on the notes receivable amounted to $20 as of December 31, 19+8. The insurance coverage was acquired on January 1, 19+7, and the policy covered a 3-year term. The premium for the 3-year term was $360. One-third of the inspection fees received in advance has been earned as of December 31, 19+8. The year-end inventory of electrical supplies amounted to $150.

Prepare adjusting entries.

PROBLEMS

Problem A5-1. Using the trial balance and the data for adjustments given below, prepare the working papers for Consulting Corporation for the month of July.

CONSULTING CORPORATION
Trial Balance
July 31, 19+4

Cash	4,713	
Notes receivable	2,600	
Capital stock		6,000
Retained earnings		548
Dividends	60	
Fees		3,950
Salaries expense	3,000	
Advertising expense	125	
	10,498	10,498

Data for adjustments:

(a) Interest receivable, $13.
(b) Office rent payable for July, $215.
(c) Liability for advertising expense, $25.

Problem A5-2. Using the following information, prepare working papers for the year ended June 30, 19+4.

ARBORVIEW CORPORATION
Trial Balance
June 30, 19+4

Cash	3,200	
U.S. Government bonds	5,000	
Inventory	9,500	
Land	2,750	
Building	9,000	
Accumulated depreciation—Building		3,000
Equipment	2,800	
Accumulated depreciation—Equipment		1,200
Taxes payable		500
Capital stock		25,000
Retained earnings (deficit)	3,750	
Sales		35,000
Cost of goods sold	25,000	
Advertising expense	350	
Salaries expense	2,400	
Miscellaneous expense	950	
	64,700	64,700

Depreciation:

   (a) Depreciation of building, $225.
   (b) Depreciation of equipment, $140.

Accrued amounts as of June 30, 19+4:

   (c) Interest receivable, $25.
   (d) Salaries payable, $300.
   (e) Total taxes payable, $750.

Problem A5-3. Modern Electrical Company, engaged in inspection and repair work only, has been in business since 19—. It closes its books on December 31. The company's trial balance at the end of 19+8 was:

MODERN ELECTRICAL COMPANY
Trial Balance
December 31, 19+8

Cash	1,100	
Notes receivable.	1,000	
Electrical supplies.	800	
Unexpired insurance	240	
Land	6,200	
Building	18,800	
Accumulated depreciation—Building		5,264
Equipment	5,000	
Accumulated depreciation—Equipment		1,500
Accounts payable		350
Inspection fees received in advance		1,200
Capital stock		20,000
Retained earnings.		3,876
Dividends	1,000	
Repair service revenue		13,250
Inspection fees earned.		3,100
Salaries and wages expense	12,500	
Miscellaneous expense.	1,900	
	48,540	48,540

The building had an expected useful life of 25 years when new, and the equipment an expected life of five years when new. The interest receivable on the notes amounted to $20 as of December 31, 19+8. The insurance coverage was acquired on January 1, 19+7, and the policy covered a three-year term. One-third of the inspection fees received in advance has been earned as of December 31, 19+8. The year-end inventory of electrical supplies amounted to $150.

Prepare adjusting entries and closing entries.

Problem A5-4. This problem is a continuation of Problem A4-4 involving Touch and View Company.

Required:

Prepare working papers for the year ended December 31, 19+2.
Journalize and post the adjusting and closing entries. (Set up additional ledger accounts as needed and assign account numbers.)
Prepare the after-closing trial balance.
Prepare the financial statements.

Data for adjustments:

(a) Salaries payable as of December 31, 19+2, amount to $3,400.
(b) The delivery truck has an expected useful life of four years and a trade-in value of $800.
(c) The rent was prepaid for 19+2 and 19+3.
(d) Estimated liability for income taxes, $2,600.

Problem A5-5. Using the following data, prepare the December 31, 19+3 balance sheet.

TACOMA COMPANY
Unadjusted Trial Balance
December 31, 19+3

Cash	3,500	
Accounts receivable	8,500	
Inventory	12,000	
Supplies	900	
Investment in bonds (Long-term)	15,000	
Furniture and fixtures	20,000	
Accumulated depreciation		4,000
Accounts payable		13,940
Service fees received in advance		1,400
Capital stock		30,000
Retained earnings (deficit)	2,000	
Sales of merchandise		100,000
Revenue from service fees		18,000
Cost of goods sold	65,000	
Salaries and wages	28,000	
Rent expense	12,000	
Advertising expense	1,100	
Interest revenue		660
	168,000	168,000

Handwritten annotations: INTEREST RECEIVABLE (C); INTEREST RECEIVABLE +90; Supplies (D) 600; INCOME TAX PAYABLE (F); Accum. depr. (E) 5,000; Accounts payable (D) 13,540; Service fees (A) 1000; Retained earnings (G) 6500 (CREDIT); Revenue from service fees (A) 18,400; Salaries (B) 28,400; Interest revenue (C) 750

Closing Entry—December 31, 19+3

Sales of merchandise	100,000	
Revenue from service fees	18,400	(A)
Interest revenue	750	(C)
Cost of goods sold	65,000	
Salaries and wages	28,400	(B)
Rent expense	12,000	
Advertising expense	1,100	
Supplies used	300	(D)
Depreciation expense	1,000	(E)
Income tax	2,850	(F)
Retained earnings	8,500	(G)

To close the revenue and expense accounts and to transfer the net income to the retained earnings account.

Problem A5-6. Earth Moving Company was formed June 1 to engage in the specialty of digging trenches for municipalities and public utilities. The company planned to use the following chart of accounts.

Assets
 1—Cash
 3—Accounts receivable
 6—Prepaid rent
 10—Equipment
 11—Accumulated depreciation—
   Equipment

Liabilities
 21—Accounts payable
 22—Traveling expense payable
 24—Salaries and wages payable

Stockholders' Equity
 30—Capital stock
 31—Retained earnings
 38—Dividends

Revenue
 40—Service revenue

Expenses
 45—Salaries and wages expense
 46—Repairs expense
 47—Supplies expense
 48—Traveling expense
 49—Depreciation expense—Equipment
 50—Rent expense

The transactions for June are set forth below.

19+8

June 1—$60,000 par-value capital stock was issued to the incorporators for cash.
      1—Rent was paid for the use of land and building for the next 12 months, $1,500.
     15—Equipment with an expected useful life of five years and costing $45,000 was purchased. The company paid $40,000 in cash and agreed to pay the balance within 30 days.
     19—Received a bill from Mechanical Skills Corporation for machinery repairs, $89.
     25—Paid $97 for supplies which had been used on a large contract.
     27—Received a bill from an officer of the company for traveling expense, $115.
     28—Paid salaries and wages, $4,371. (The salaries and wages for June 29 and 30 will amount to $122; however, they will be paid during July.)
     29—Paid a dividend, $300.
     30—Completed a contract for X City. The city was billed in full for $7,141, pursuant to the terms of the agreement.

Required:

  (a) Journalize transactions and post to ledger accounts. (Plan for five lines in the ledger for each account except cash; allow ten lines for the cash account.)
  (b) Prepare working papers. (Take depreciation for one-half month.)
  (c) Prepare statements.
  (d) Make and post journal entries for any necessary adjustments.
  (e) Make and post journal entries to close the books.
  (f) Take an after-closing trial balance.

Problem B5-1. Following is the trial balance of Johnson Tractor Sales Company at the end of operations for the month of October, 19+3.

JOHNSON TRACTOR SALES COMPANY
Trial Balance
October 31, 19+3

Cash	6,000	
Inventory	22,000	
Prepaid insurance	300	
Land	19,000	
Building	60,000	
Accumulated depreciation—Building		18,000
Accounts payable		10,000
Capital stock		60,000
Retained earnings		14,600
Dividends	3,000	
Sales		91,000
Cost of tractors sold	53,000	
Advertising expense	2,100	
Miscellaneous expense	2,200	
Salaries and wages expense	26,000	
	193,600	193,600

Salaries and wages payable amount to $400. The building when new had an expected useful life of forty years. Insurance premium unexpired at the end of October is $75. Income tax on 19+3 earnings amounts to $1,600.

Prepare working papers covering the year ended October 31, 19+3, and closing entries.

Problem B5-2. The trial balance below was taken from the books of The Newton Company at the close of business for the year 19+6.

THE NEWTON COMPANY
Trial Balance
December 31, 19+6

Cash	5,438	
Accounts receivable	12,720	
Inventory	6,500	
Materials and supplies	2,250	
Prepaid insurance	270	
Land	5,000	
Buildings	50,000	
Accumulated depreciation—Buildings		10,000
Equipment	60,000	
Accumulated depreciation—Equipment		32,000
Accounts payable		4,450
Notes payable—5%, due 12/31/+9		16,000
Taxes payable		2,520
Capital stock		60,000
Retained earnings		12,500
Totals—forward	142,178	137,470

Totals—brought forward	142,178	137,470
Dividends.................................	3,600	
Sales		138,430
Cost of goods sold	82,400	
Selling commissions	6,900	
Delivery expense	2,380	
Wages and salaries	33,500	
Property taxes	4,542	
Interest expense	400	
	275,900	275,900

The following information was also obtained from the records maintained by The Newton Company.

(1) The building was put into operation on January 1, 19+1, and is expected to have a useful life of 25 years from that date.
(2) The equipment is to be depreciated at 20% per year.
(3) A count of the materials and supplies shows $460 as the cost of those on hand.
(4) The insurance policy was purchased on June 30, 19+5, and expires on June 30, 19+8.
(5) The notes payable bear interest of 5 per cent per year. Interest was last paid on July 1, 19+6.
(6) Wages payable amount to $110.
(7) Sales commissions payable are $332.

Required: Working papers and closing entries.

Problem B5-3. The trial balance given below was taken from the ledger of Steam Specialty Corporation before adjusting entries were posted at the end of operations for 19+3.

STEAM SPECIALTY CORPORATION
Unadjusted Trial Balance
December 31, 19+3

Cash	6,400	
Resale parts	9,000	
Supplies	900	
Service equipment	16,000	
Accumulated depreciation		3,200
Service fees received in advance		2,800
Capital stock		12,000
Retained earnings, December 31, 19+2		2,650
Dividends.................................	750	
Sales of parts..............................		30,000
Service revenue		80,000
Cost of parts sold...........................	18,000	
Salaries expense............................	74,000	
Rent expense..............................	3,900	
Miscellaneous expense........................	1,700	
	130,650	130,650

The following after-closing trial balance was taken from the same ledger after adjusting and closing entries had been posted.

STEAM SPECIALITY CORPORATION
After-Closing Trial Balance
December 31, 19+3

Cash	6,400	
Resale parts	9,000	
Supplies	400	
Prepaid rent	300	
Service equipment	16,000	
Accumulated depreciation		4,800
Service fees received in advance		1,000
Estimated income tax payable		3,500
Salaries payable		500
Capital stock		12,000
Retained earnings		10,300
	32,100	32,100

Make the closing entries which were entered in the journal of Steam Specialty Corporation at the end of 19+3.

Problem B5-4. The after-closing trial balance of Blend Corporation appears below.

BLEND CORPORATION
After-Closing Trial Balance
December 31, 19+8

Cash	6,100	
Rent receivable—Land	100	
Repair supplies on hand	200	
Land	3,000	
Equipment	8,000	
Accumulated depreciation—Equipment		4,000
Salaries payable		500
Taxes payable		85
Capital stock		12,000
Retained earnings		815
	17,400	17,400

The corporation closes its books monthly. Journalize the following transactions and all adjustments required for January, 19+9 financial statements.

19+9

January   3—The corporation rents out some of its land as a parking lot for $50 per month. Today the corporation received $200 from the renter covering the four months ending February 28, 19+9.

           10—Paid salaries for the month ending January 10, 19+9, $750.

           17—Received $800 cash for repair services completed today.

           19—Paid $75 for special supplies used on repair work completed January 17.

21—The corporation rented some of its equipment for the next 30 days ending February 20, receiving the $360 rental charge in advance.

31—Additional data required for adjustments:

Depreciation, 6% per annum of cost of equipment.

Taxes payable as of January 31, 19+9, $100.

Salaries payable as of January 31, 19+9, $510.

Repair supplies on hand, $175.

Repair services performed, not billed, $340.

Problem B5-5. This problem is a continuation of the Totee Corporation problem, B4-5. The following data are needed for the August 31 adjusting entries.

(a) The corporation owes $130 for advertising.

(b) The corporation owes one-half week's wages to employees.

(c) The tools and equipment are to be depreciated for one full month. See the transaction of August 4 in Problem B4-5.

(d) Delivery expense incurred but not yet paid amounts to $60.

Required:

(d) Prepare working papers.

(e) Prepare the income statement and balance sheet.

(f) Journalize and post the adjusting and closing entries.

Problem B5-6. Several mistakes were made in completing the following working papers. The trial balance and the supporting descriptions of the adjusting entries (a through g at the bottom of the working papers) are correct. Prepare corrected working papers for Award Company.

Account	Trial Balance Dr	Trial Balance Cr	Adjustments Dr	Adjustments Cr	Adjusted Trial Balance Dr	Adjusted Trial Balance Cr	Income Statement Dr	Income Statement Cr	Retained Earnings Statement Dr	Retained Earnings Statement Cr	Balance Sheet Dr	Balance Sheet Cr
Cash	8,000				8,000						8,000	
Corporate bonds	20,000				20,000						20,000	
Inventory	12,000				12,000						12,000	
Expense advances to employees	800			(c) 300	500		500					
Office supplies	600			(d) 350	250						250	
Equipment	15,000			(a) 1,500	13,500						13,500	
Accounts payable		14,000				14,000						14,000
Advances from customers		700				700		700				
Bank loans (One year loan due 9/1/19+3)		9,000				9,000						9,000
Capital stock		20,000				20,000						20,000
Retained earnings, December 31, 19+1		5,700				5,700				5,700		
Dividends	1,000				1,000							
Sales		85,000				85,000		85,000				
Cost of goods sold	50,000				50,000		50,000					
Salaries expense	22,000		(b) 2,000		20,000		20,000					
Traveling expense	3,000		(c) 300		3,300		3,300					
Office expense	2,000		(d) 350		2,350		2,350					
	134,400	134,400										
Depreciation expense—Equipment			(a) 1,500		1,500		1,500					
Salaries payable				(b) 2,000		2,000						2,000
Rent expense			(e) 6,000		6,000		6,000					
Rent payable				(e) 6,000		6,000						6,000
Interest expense			(f) 200		200		200					
Interest payable				(f) 200		200						200
Interest receivable			(g) 600		600						600	
Interest revenue				(g) 600		600		600				
			10,950	10,950	141,200	141,200	85,250	85,900				
Net income							650		-0-	650		
							85,900	85,900	6,350	6,350		6,350
Retained earnings, December 31, 19+2									6,350	6,350	55,950	55,950

Adjustments

a—Depreciation for the year—10% rate.
b—Salaries payable at year-end, $2,000.
c—Expense advances used as of December 31, 19+2, $300.
d—Unused office supplies as of December 31, 19+2, $250.
e—Rent owed as of December 31, 19+2, $6,000.
f—Interest on bank loans applicable to 19+2, $200.
g—Interest earned on the corporate bonds, $600.

Processing
Repetitive Transactions

MANUAL PROCEDURES

Special journals. In previous chapters business transactions were recorded in a journal form which required the listing of each account affected and the amounts debited and credited. A firm could record every transaction in this manner. However, the recording and posting time required would be considerable, even for a firm of only moderate size.

Any procedure that reduces recording and posting time is helpful. Journals specially designed to accommodate different classes of transactions may be used to save time. The special journals to be used in any particular business will depend upon the nature of its operations, and upon whether transactions of a particular kind occur often enough to warrant having a special journal in which to record them. In most firms the following special journals are useful because of the frequency with which certain transactions occur:

(1) Sales journal—for recording sales of merchandise on account.
(2) Purchases journal—for recording purchases on account.

(3) Cash receipts journal—for recording all receipts of cash.

(4) Cash disbursements journal—for recording all payments of cash.

Some transactions cannot be recorded in any *one* of the special journals, making it necessary to maintain the two-column journal illustrated in earlier chapters. This journal would also be used to record correcting, adjusting, and closing entries.

Advantages of special journals. There are two important advantages of special journals:

SAVING OF LABOR: Less time is required in *recording* transactions because it is unnecessary to write the account title for a debit or credit when the heading of a special column indicates the account affected by the transaction. Posting also requires less time because columnar *totals,* which represent several transactions, are posted to the accounts rather than individual amounts.

DIVISION OF LABOR: Special journals allow the division of labor in both the recording and posting of transactions. While one employee is recording sales transactions in the sales journal, another can be recording receipts of cash in the cash receipts journal. The same division is possible for posting.

Subsidiary ledgers. The procedure of recording all credit sales in a single accounts receivable account makes it very difficult to determine the amount receivable from each customer. To provide this information an account is needed for each customer who is indebted to the firm. These accounts are kept in a separate accounts receivable ledger, called a *subsidiary ledger.* The accounts receivable account previously used to show the total accounts receivable from all customers is still used in the *general ledger.*

The accounts receivable account in the general ledger is called a *controlling account* because its balance and the sum of the balances in the subsidiary accounts receivable ledger should be equal. This is so because the transactions affecting the controlling account also affect the accounts in the subsidiary ledger. The controlling account thus serves as a check on the accuracy of the subsidiary ledger. For this relationship to be maintained, the sum of all debits and credits to the *controlling account* must equal the sum of all debits and credits to the *subsidiary ledger.*

The same procedure can be used to maintain a separate record of the amounts owed to individual creditors. A subsidiary accounts payable ledger is established with an account for each creditor. The accounts payable account in the general ledger then becomes a controlling account.

It should be noted that the subsidiary-ledger-controlling-account arrangement can be used in areas other than accounts receivable and accounts payable. For example, individual accounts can be set up in a subsidiary ledger for each type of equipment owned, with a controlling account in the general ledger entitled Equipment. In any case in which an account requires record keeping in considerable detail, a subsidiary ledger may prove helpful.

References to special journals. When several journals are used, the ledger accounts must indicate the specific journal from which the entries were posted. Thus,

S 1   means sales journal, page 1.
P 1   means purchases journal, page 1.
CR 1   means cash receipts journal, page 1.
CD 1   means cash disbursements journal, page 1.
J 1   means journal, page 1.

Sales journal. A single-column sales journal is shown below. Only one amount column is needed because each credit sale results in a debit to Accounts Receivable and a credit to Sales for the same amount.

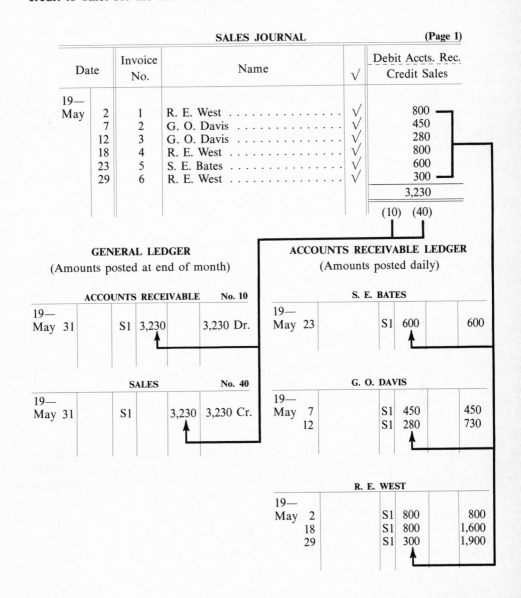

SALES JOURNAL   (Page 1)

Date	Invoice No.	Name	√	Debit Accts. Rec. Credit Sales
19—				
May 2	1	R. E. West	√	800
7	2	G. O. Davis	√	450
12	3	G. O. Davis	√	280
18	4	R. E. West	√	800
23	5	S. E. Bates	√	600
29	6	R. E. West	√	300
				3,230
				(10) (40)

GENERAL LEDGER
(Amounts posted at end of month)

ACCOUNTS RECEIVABLE   No. 10

19—			
May 31	S1	3,230	3,230 Dr.

SALES   No. 40

19—			
May 31	S1		3,230	3,230 Cr.

ACCOUNTS RECEIVABLE LEDGER
(Amounts posted daily)

S. E. BATES

19—			
May 23	S1	600	600

G. O. DAVIS

19—			
May 7	S1	450	450
12	S1	280	730

R. E. WEST

19—			
May 2	S1	800	800
18	S1	800	1,600
29	S1	300	1,900

POSTING THE SALES JOURNAL: Postings have been made as follows:

Debits:

Posted to the individual accounts (West, Davis, and Bates) in the subsidiary ledger. Since the accounts in the subsidiary ledger usually are arranged in alphabetical order and are not numbered, check marks are used (instead of account numbers) to indicate that postings have been made. In practice, debits to the customers' accounts in the subsidiary ledger might be made from copies of the invoices, which could be routed to the accounts receivable bookkeeper instead of being posted from the sales journal. The frequency of postings to the individual accounts varies. Many firms post the amounts daily.

The *total* of the debits to Accounts Receivable for the sales on account ($3,230) has been posted to the accounts receivable controlling account in the general ledger, as indicated by the account number (No. 10) at the foot of the money column.

The posting of column totals to the controlling account (instead of individual entries) is the reason why the use of subsidiary ledgers and controlling accounts does not double the work of posting.

Credits:

The *total* of the sales on account ($3,230) has been posted to the sales account (No. 40) in the general ledger, as indicated by the sales account number at the foot of the money column.

Purchases journal. The purchases journal illustrated on page 129 contains only one column for credits: the Accounts Payable credit column. Thus only purchases on account can be recorded in this journal. Provision was made, by the use of the Sundry Accounts section, for debits that cannot be entered in any of the special debit columns.

POSTING THE PURCHASES JOURNAL: Postings from the purchases journal are made as follows:

Credits:

These are posted to the individual accounts for each creditor (Price and Holmes, Henderson's, Inc., and Osborne Company) in the accounts payable subsidiary ledger. The check marks indicate such postings.

The *total* credits to Accounts Payable are posted to the accounts payable controlling account in the general ledger, as indicated by the account number (No. 20) at the foot of the Accounts Payable column.

Debits:

The *column total* is posted to each general ledger account for which there is a special money column. The account numbers below those column totals (No. 12 and No. 71) indicate the postings.

Debits are posted to the designated general ledger accounts for each entry in the Sundry Accounts section of the journal.

The sundry column total was not posted, and never would be, because the individual amounts therein would always be posted separately.

PURCHASES JOURNAL

Date	Subsidiary Ledger Account Credited	Invoice Date	✓	Credits Accounts Payable	Merchandise Inventory	Office Expense	General Ledger Accounts Debits — Sundry Accounts Name	L.F.	Amount
19— May 1	Price and Holmes..	May 1	✓	2,000	2,000				
9	Henderson's, Inc...	May 8	✓	200		200			
13	Osborne Company .	May 10	✓	2,600	2,600				
15	Price and Holmes..	May 14	✓	650	650				
20	Henderson's, Inc...	May 19	✓	1,300			Office equipment	15	1,300
				6,750	5,250	200			1,300
				(20)	(12)	(71)			

GENERAL LEDGER
(Amounts posted at end of month)

MERCHANDISE INVENTORY No. 12

19— May 31	P1	5,250	5,250 Dr.

OFFICE EQUIPMENT No. 15

19— May 24	P1	1,300	1,300 Dr.

ACCOUNTS PAYABLE No. 20

19— May 31	P1	6,750	6,750 Cr.

OFFICE EXPENSE No. 71

19— May 31	P1	200	200 Dr.

ACCOUNTS PAYABLE LEDGER
(Amounts posted daily)

HENDERSON'S, INC.

19— May 9	P1	200	200
20	P1	1,300	1,500

OSBORNE COMPANY

19— May 13	P1	2,600	2,600

PRICE AND HOLMES

19— May 1	P1	2,000	2,000
15	P1	650	2,650

Cash receipts journal. The cash receipts journal on page 131 is designed to accommodate the two primary sources of cash receipts for most firms—cash sales and cash received on account from customers.

POSTING THE CASH RECEIPTS JOURNAL: The posting procedure follows the pattern previously described.

Column totals:
Column totals, except the Sundry Accounts column total, are posted to the general ledger accounts designated by the column headings. In the case of the illustrative cash receipts journal, three column totals were posted. Specifically, $26,400 was posted as a *debit* to the cash account, $1,250 was posted as a *credit* to the accounts receivable account, and $150 was posted as a *credit* to the sales account.
Individual items:
Each amount in the Accounts Receivable column is posted to an individual account (Davis and West) in the subsidiary accounts receivable ledger.
Each amount in the Sundry Accounts section of the journal is posted to the designated general ledger account.
To repeat, the total of the sundry column was not posted, and never would be, because the individual amounts therein would always be posted separately.
Posting references in journals:
Account numbers indicate postings to accounts in the *general* ledger.
Check marks indicate postings to accounts in a *subsidiary* ledger.

Cash disbursements journal. The cash disbursements journal on page 132 is used to record all cash disbursements of the firm. Special debit columns are provided for recording the acquisition of merchandise inventory and payments to creditors on account. It will be noted that the posting procedure is quite similar to the posting of the cash receipts journal.

The journal. When special journals are used, only those transactions which cannot be recorded in a special journal are recorded in the general journal. Two such transactions are shown below.

		JOURNAL			Page 1
19—					
May	31	Cost of goods sold	50	2,100	
		Merchandise inventory	12		2,100
		Reduction in inventory for the cost of goods sold during the month of May.			
	31	Notes receivable.	11	600	
		Accounts receivable (S. E. Bates).	10/√		600
		Received 30-day, noninterest-bearing note for balance of invoice of May 23.			

Since the journal does not have special columns for controlling accounts, whenever a controlling account is debited or credited, it is necessary to post such debits or credits twice, once to the controlling account in the general ledger and again to an account in the subsidiary ledger. If such double posting is not performed, agreement

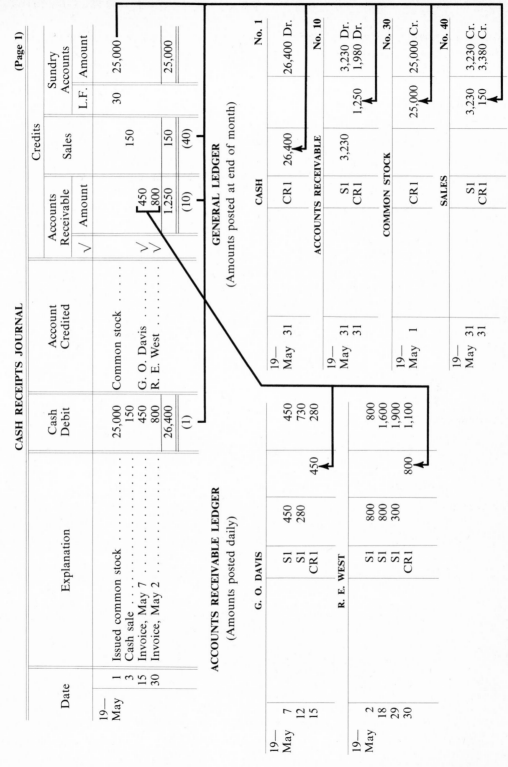

CASH RECEIPTS JOURNAL (Page 1)

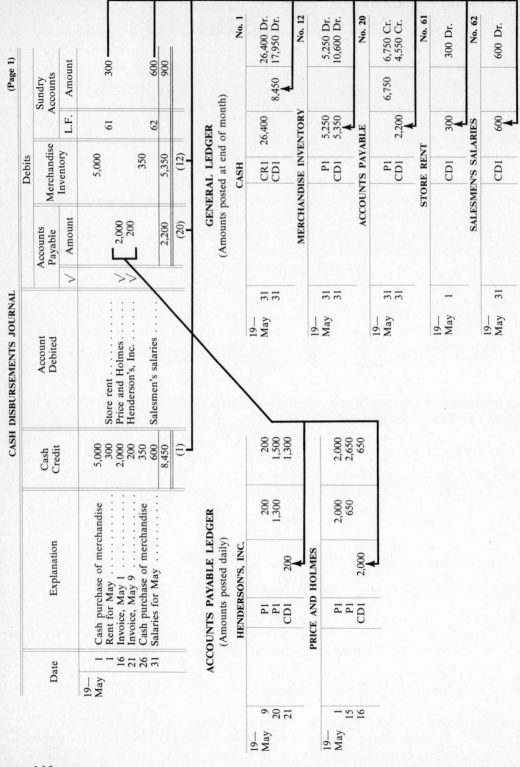

CASH DISBURSEMENTS JOURNAL

(Page 1)

Date	Explanation	Cash Credit	Account Debited	Accounts Payable		Merchandise Inventory	Sundry Accounts		
				✓	Amount		L.F.	Amount	
19— May 1	Cash purchase of merchandise	5,000				5,000			
1	Rent for May	300	Store rent				61	300	
16	Invoice, May 1	2,000	Price and Holmes	✓	2,000				
21	Invoice, May 9	200	Henderson's, Inc.	✓	200				
26	Cash purchase of merchandise	350				350			
31	Salaries for May	600	Salesmen's salaries				62	600	
		8,450			2,200	5,350		900	
		(1)			(20)	(12)			

ACCOUNTS PAYABLE LEDGER
(Amounts posted daily)

HENDERSON'S, INC.

19— May 9	P1		200		200
20	P1		1,300		1,500
21	CD1	200			1,300

PRICE AND HOLMES

19— May 1	P1		2,000		2,000
15	P1		650		2,650
16	CD1	2,000			650

GENERAL LEDGER
(Amounts posted at end of month)

CASH No. 1

19— May 31	CR1	26,400		26,400 Dr.
31	CD1		8,450	17,950 Dr.

MERCHANDISE INVENTORY No. 12

19— May 31	P1	5,250		5,250 Dr.
31	CD1	5,350		10,600 Dr.

ACCOUNTS PAYABLE No. 20

19— May 31	P1		6,750	6,750 Cr.
31	CD1	2,200		4,550 Cr.

STORE RENT No. 61

19— May 1	CD1	300		300 Dr.

SALESMEN'S SALARIES No. 62

19— May 31	CD1	600		600 Dr.

between the controlling account and the subsidiary ledger will not be maintained. Thus, in the foregoing illustration, it was necessary to post the credit member of the journal entry twice:

> To the accounts receivable controlling account in the general ledger, as indicated by the "10" in the L.F. column; and
> To S. E. Bates' account in the subsidiary accounts receivable ledger, as indicated by the check mark in the L.F. column.

Notice that the identity of the customer (S.E. Bates) must be included in the journal entry in order that the posting may be made to the subsidiary ledger.

Proving the subsidiary ledgers. The accounts receivable and accounts payable ledgers after posting from the illustrative journals are shown on page 134. To prove the subsidiary ledgers, schedules of their balances are prepared and the totals compared with the balances of the respective controlling accounts. This proof is presented below.

ACCOUNTS RECEIVABLE   No. 10

19—						
May	31		S1	3,230		3,230 Dr.
	31		CR1		1,250	1,980 Dr.
	31		J1		600	1,380 Dr.

Schedule of Accounts Receivable
May 31, 19—

G. O. Davis	280
R. E. West	1,100
Total (per balance of controlling account)	1,380

ACCOUNTS PAYABLE   No. 20

19—						
May	31		P1		6,750	6,750 Cr.
	31		CD1	2,200		4,550 Cr.

Schedule of Accounts Payable
May 31, 19—

Henderson's, Inc.	1,300
Osborne Company	2,600
Price and Holmes	650
Total (per balance of controlling account)	4,550

Advantages of controlling accounts. It might seem that when individual accounts are kept with debtors and creditors it is a useless duplication of work to maintain controlling accounts also. However, controlling accounts serve two very useful purposes:

> First, controlling accounts make it possible to determine the total accounts receivable and total accounts payable without listing the balances of the individual accounts.
> Second, controlling accounts help in locating errors. Without controlling accounts it would be necessary to take a combined trial balance of the general ledger and the subsidiary ledgers. If the combined trial balance did not

ACCOUNTS RECEIVABLE LEDGER

S. E. BATES

19—					
May	23	S1	600		600
	31	J1		600	—

G. O. DAVIS

19—					
May	7	S1	450		450
	12	S1	280		730
	15	CR1		450	280

R. E. WEST

19—					
May	2	S1	800		800
	18	S1	800		1,600
	29	S1	300		1,900
	30	CR1		800	1,100

ACCOUNTS PAYABLE LEDGER

HENDERSON'S, INC.

19—					
May	9	P1		200	200
	20	P1		1,300	1,500
	21	CD1	200		1,300

OSBORNE COMPANY

19—				
May	13	P1	2,600	2,600

PRICE AND HOLMES

19—					
May	1	P1		2,000	2,000
	15	P1		650	2,650
	16	CD1	2,000		650

balance, it might be necessary to check all of the postings in search of errors. With controlling accounts, errors often can be more readily located. For instance, if the general ledger is in balance, but the total of the balances in the accounts receivable ledger does not agree with the balance in the accounts receivable controlling account, an error presumably has been made in the subsidiary ledger.

Since, with a few possible exceptions (for instance, the posting of the credit to Accounts Receivable in the two-column journal on page 130), the controlling accounts are produced by the posting of column totals, very little additional work is required to obtain the above-mentioned benefits.

MACHINE PROCEDURES

Accounting machines. The manual procedures discussed up to this point offer the advantages of division of labor and saving of time in the recording and posting operations. However, where the number of transactions to be processed is large, manual procedures are impractical.

Accounting machines can further expedite the processing of a large number of transactions. As an illustration, consider the following sales and billing procedure. It is assumed that orders are secured by salesmen. When an order is obtained, the salesman completes an order form and sends one copy to the office. This copy ultimately reaches the accounting department, where it is used as a source document to prepare the following:

A customer's invoice—this is the bill that will be sent to the customer indicating the amount owed as a result of his order having been filled.

An office copy of the customer's invoice.

A shipping advice—this is routed to the shipping department, authorizing it to ship or deliver the described merchandise to the customer.

A record of the transaction in the customer's accounts receivable account.

A record of the transaction in the sales journal.

A billing machine can be used to accomplish the above. A new roll of paper, printed in the form of the company's sales journal, is inserted in the machine at the beginning of each month. It is also assumed that the pre-numbered invoice and shipping advice forms are purchased in three-page, carboned packets, assembled as follows:

1st sheet—customer's copy of invoice
2nd sheet—office copy of invoice
3rd sheet—shipping advice

The billing machine is designed so that a packet of forms and the customer's accounts receivable account sheet can be easily and simultaneously inserted in the machine. In one operation, the operator can record the facts relating to the sales transaction on the invoice forms, on the shipping advice, in the customer's account, and in the sales journal. As a result, the following steps will have been completed in one operation:

Invoice prepared.
Shipping advice prepared.
Recording in the sales journal.
Posting to the customer's accounts receivable account.

The billing machine just described can accumulate, by the use of built-in adding-machine registers, such aggregates as total debits to Accounts Receivable and total credits to Sales. In more elaborate systems, the machine may automatically compute and accumulate such amounts as sales taxes, salesmen's commissions, and shipping charges. Such totals might be printed out at the end of each day, week, or some other period and thus provide data for posting to the general ledger accounts.

As an alternative to posting directly from the machine record, summary general journal entries may be made on the basis of the machine-accumulated amounts. Returning to the sales journal shown on page 127, and assuming that the sales journal had been prepared as a by-product of the accounts receivable billing operation, the data could be used to prepare the following summary journal entry:

Accounts receivable 3,230
Sales   3,230

Posting to the general ledger would thus be made from the journal.

Other techniques or devices can be designed to accumulate data from which similar summary entries can be prepared. Mechanical accounting devices can be used to accumulate totals affecting other, or all, general ledger accounts, to develop subsidiary records, and to prepare statistical reports—and to do all this speedily and with the expenditure of a minimum amount of human effort.

Electronic data processing. The use of an electronic computer to processs accounting data has two important advantages over the use of accounting machines: (1) there is less human involvement once the processing begins and, therefore, less likelihood of error, and (2) data are processed much more rapidly.

The computer is the center of an electronic data-processing system. It processes data and may store information for future use. However, additional machines and equipment, referred to as *hardware,* are also needed. Some of this equipment performs the *input* function by preparing data for the computer and transferring the data to the computer for processing. Other equipment performs the *output* function by taking the processed data from the computer and preparing the information for users.

Input procedures. There are basically two means by which data can be prepared for processing by the computer: (1) punched cards, and (2) paper or magnetic tape.

PUNCHED CARDS: The computers widely used today are not capable of reading written information. Data to be processed must be presented to the computer in a language it can understand. Punched cards can be used for this purpose. Using a machine known as a keypunch and a predetermined coding system, data are transferred to the cards by a series of holes punched in appropriate places. The information on the punched cards may be checked for accuracy prior to processing by means of a machine known as a verifier.

Pertinent data concerning sales transactions, for example, may be "captured" by means of punched cards for processing by the computer. The data, recorded on a separate card for each sale, might include the customer's name, the order number, the invoice number, the salesman's name, the quantity bought, description of the goods, and price information. The illustration on page 137 shows the data which are transferred from a sales invoice to a punched card.

PAPER AND MAGNETIC TAPE: Rolls of tape, rather than punched cards, may be used to provide information to the computer for processing. As with punched cards, a predetermined code is used to place the data on the tapes, which are used as a direct input device for the computer.

SHERIDAN PAPER COMPANY **ROXBORO, NORTH CAROLINA 28806**

TERMS:
2% CASH DISCOUNT FOR PAYMENT BY
THE 15TH OF MONTH NEXT FOLLOWING
DATE OF SHIPMENT. NET 16TH.
1% PER MONTH SERVICE CHARGE ON
ALL ACCOUNTS OVER 60 DAYS.

SOLD TO
*

Apex Printing Company
River Road
Youngstown, Ohio 44514

SHIPPED TO
*

Same

Customer #127

INVOICE #	DATE	CUST. ORDER #	CUST. REQ. #	SLSM. BRCH.	CODE	SHIPPED
6903	1-8-71	980		14		Our truck

QUANTITY	DESCRIPTION	TOTAL WEIGHT	PRICE	AMOUNT
1	A-31 500 ft. roll		15.45	15.45
5	D-76 1,000 ft. roll		34.50	172.50
3	D-53 1,000 ft. roll		27.60	82.80

	GROSS	TAX%	TAX AMOUNT	FRT., P.P. & INS.	PAY THIS AMOUNT
					270.75

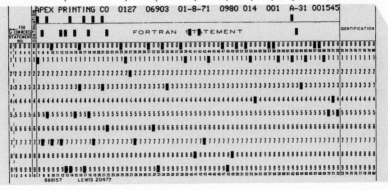

APEX PRINTING CO 0127 06903 01-8-71 0980 014 001 A-31 001545

FORTRAN STATEMENT

IDENTIFICATION

868157   LEWIS 20477

137

Both paper and magnetic tapes offer two important advantages over punched cards: (1) information on the tapes can be processed much faster by the computer than the same data on punched cards; and (2) much less space is needed to store a given amount of data on a tape than is required for punched cards.

Processing. The processing of data by a computer involves more than just the arithmetical calculations. The computer processes data according to a series of instructions, known as a *program.* The *control unit* of the computer is the key to the implementation of the program. If the program is properly written, the control unit will guide the computer through the required processing steps automatically. The computer also has a "memory," in that it can store data in a memory unit and recall the data when instructed to do so.

These characteristics of the computer enhance its usefulness tremendously. Once data are stored in the computer, additional processing may take place; one needs simply to instruct the computer as to what operations are required. Programmers are highly trained individuals who prepare the programs or instructions given to the computer.

Output procedures. Those procedures by which processed data are taken from the computer and prepared for the persons desiring the information are known as output procedures.

PUNCHED CARDS: Placing the processed information on punched cards offers a distinct advantage when the data require considerable handling after processing by the computer. The cards facilitate changing the sequence of the information for additional processing.

PAPER OR MAGNETIC TAPE: If a large quantity of processed data is to be stored, paper or magnetic tape is preferable to punched cards for the reason previously mentioned—much less space is needed to store a given quantity of data. Additional processing can also be done more rapidly because of the ability of the computer to read data from tapes more rapidly than from punched cards.

DIRECT PRINTOUT: Processed data may be prepared in prescribed typewritten form by use of an electric typewriter or line printer connected directly to the computer.

Accounting uses of the computer. Computers are most commonly used in those accounting operations that require the routine processing of a great amount of data. Examples are payrolls, inventories, receivables, and payables. The obvious advantages of the computer in these areas are its accuracy and speed. The potential accounting uses of the computer in the future are limited only by the ability of people to discover additional applications and instruct the computer in what is to be done.

A specific transfer of accounting data to the computer was shown on page 137. There is another major advantage of the computer in this case: once the sales data are in the computer, they can be retained by the memory or storage unit for further processing. For example, the computer could be instructed to prepare sales information classified by territories, by salesmen, by products, or in some other manner.

The illustration on page 139 shows the operation of a computer in a specific accounting application, the processing of a credit sales transaction.

OPERATION OF A COMPUTER IN PROCESSING A CREDIT SALES TRANSACTION

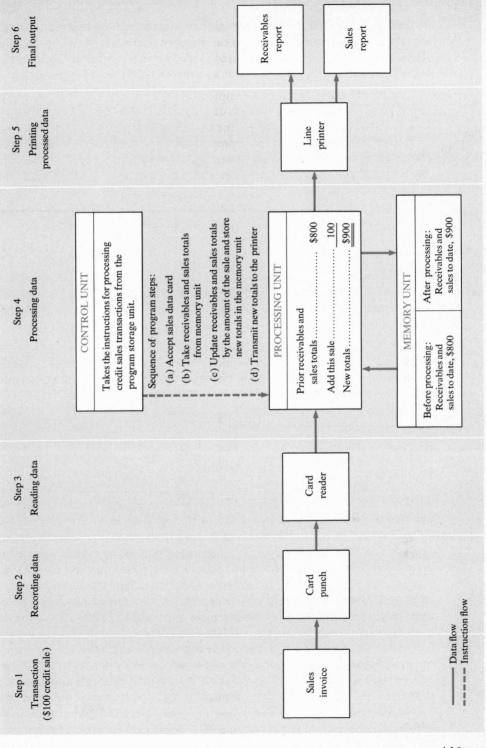

Matrix approach to accounting. The advent of electronic data-processing equipment allows the relationships expressed in the basic accounting equation (Assets = Equities) and the double-entry system of accounting to be stated in a completely different manner. Up to this point, we have seen that the accountant uses a device known as an account to accumulate and store financial data. Information in the accounts is updated periodically as transactions are recorded in journals and posted to the accounts.

The ability of the computer to store, retrieve, and process data allows it to accomplish the same thing as the double-entry system of accounting, but with considerably greater speed and accuracy.

Assume that the following information is presently contained in the general ledger of Code Corporation after the books have been closed on June 30, 19—.

	Debit	Credit
Cash	25,000	
Accounts receivable	40,000	
Merchandise inventory	70,000	
Plant and equipment	125,000	
Accumulated depreciation		36,000
Accounts payable		27,000
Common stock		100,000
Retained earnings		97,000
	260,000	260,000

The same data can be placed in a computer in the matrix form illustrated on page 141. Each block or cell in the matrix represents a specific location in the memory unit of the computer. Debit balances are located in the *column* of cells on the right side of the matrix and credit balances are located in the bottom *row* of cells.

One can record in the matrix by instructing the computer to enter amounts in the appropriate blocks or cells. For example, the acquisition of merchandise inventory on account would be entered in the cell where the merchandise inventory debit *row* and accounts payable credit *column* intersect. All amounts entered in this cell record a debit to merchandise inventory and a credit to accounts payable.

To illustrate, let us assume that the following transactions are the only transactions of Code Corporation on July 1, 19—: (a) the purchase of merchandise inventory on account for $500, (b) the receipt of $850 from a customer on account, and (c) the sale of merchandise costing $6,000 for $8,000 cash. The matrix appears as shown on page 142 after the transactions are entered. The retained earnings account has been credited for $8,000 sales revenue and debited for $6,000 cost of goods sold resulting from transaction (c).

The matrix can easily be expanded to include revenue and expense accounts of the firm. An additional row and column would be added for each item of revenue and expense. As the number of accounts increases, it obviously becomes difficult to present the matrix in the form shown on page 142. However, this is no problem for the computer so long as its memory unit has the capacity to accommodate the additional cells needed in the matrix each time a new account is added.

CODE CORPORATION
Accounting Matrix June 30, 19—

		Credits: Cash	Credits: Accounts Receivable	Credits: Merchandise Inventory	Credits: Plant and Equipment	Credits: Accumulated Depreciation	Credits: Accounts Payable	Credits: Common Stock	Credits: Retained Earnings	Totals of Debits	Beginning Debit Balances	Ending Debit Balances
Debits	Cash											25,000
Debits	Accounts Receivable											40,000
Debits	Merchandise Inventory											70,000
Debits	Plant and Equipment											125,000
Debits	Accumulated Depreciation											
Debits	Accounts Payable											
Debits	Common Stock											
Debits	Retained Earnings											
Totals of Credits												
Beginning Credit Balances												
Ending Credit Balances						36,000	27,000	100,000	97,000			260,000

Once the size of the matrix has been established for a specific firm, any transaction can be recorded within this framework. It is only necessary that the computer be instructed as to which cell is to be used to record the appropriate amount or amounts. Thus the matrix approach is applicable to any transaction, not just to those that may be described as repetitive or recurring.

The matrix approach should be viewed as another way of effecting the sequence of accounting procedures listed on the first page of Chapter 5 and commonly referred

CODE CORPORATION
Accounting Matrix   **July 1, 19—**

Debits \ Credits	Cash	Accounts Receivable	Merchandise Inventory	Plant and Equipment	Accumulated Depreciation	Accounts Payable	Common Stock	Retained Earnings	Totals of Debits	Beginning Debit Balances	Ending Debit Balances*
Cash		850						8,000	8,850	25,000	33,850
Accounts Receivable										40,000	39,150
Merchandise Inventory						500			500	70,000	64,500
Plant and Equipment										125,000	125,000
Accumulated Depreciation											
Accounts Payable											
Common Stock											
Retained Earnings			6,000						6,000		
Totals of Credits	850	6,000				500		8,000	15,350		
Beginning Credit Balances					36,000	27,000	100,000	97,000		260,000	
Ending Credit Balances**					36,000	27,500	100,000	99,000			262,500

*Beginning debit balance, plus total of debit row, minus total of credit column.
**Beginning credit balance, plus total of credit column, minus total of debit row.

to as the accounting cycle. Entries in the cells of the matrix are equivalent to the journalizing and posting steps in the cycle. Using the data in the matrix, the computer could prepare financial statements, close the accounts, and prepare an after-closing trial balance.

ASSIGNMENT

MATERIAL

QUESTIONS

1. List four different special journals and the type of transaction recorded in each.
2. What are two advantages of special journals?
3. Describe the relationship between the general ledger and a subsidiary ledger.
4. What is the purpose of a Sundry Accounts section in a special journal? Describe the posting procedure for items entered in the Sundry Accounts section.
5. Why may some amounts recorded in special journals have to be posted twice?
6. What is meant by "proving" the subsidiary ledgers?
7. List two advantages of maintaining controlling accounts in the general ledger.
8. What are the major advantages of using an electronic computer to process accounting data?
9. Describe two ways in which data can be prepared for processing by a computer.
10. What is a computer program?
11. List several possible accounting uses of the computer.
12. Describe the matrix approach to accounting.

SHORT EXERCISES

E6-1. The numbers below indicate the corresponding columns in the cash receipts and cash disbursements journals of Brevard Company:

Journal	Column Heading	Number
Cash Receipts	Cash debit	1
	Accounts Receivable credit	2
	Sales credit	3
	Sundry credit	4
Cash Disbursements	Cash credit	5
	Accounts Payable debit	6
	Merchandise Inventory debit	7
	Sundry debit	8

Indicate how the following transactions would be entered in the journals by designating the appropriate column numbers for the debits and credits.

(1) Payment to creditor on account.
(2) Payment of salaries.
(3) Collection from customer on account.
(4) Payment of insurance premium.
(5) Issuance of common stock for cash.
(6) Cash sale.
(7) Cash purchase of merchandise.

E6-2. Selected accounts from the ledger of Talbotton Company are presented below:

CASH

June	30		9,400		9,400
	30			8,250	1,150

ACCOUNTS RECEIVABLE

June	30		10,000		10,000
	30			7,000	3,000

MERCHANDISE INVENTORY

June	30		12,000		12,000
	30		3,000		15,000

PREPAID RENT

June	15		1,000		1,000

ACCOUNTS PAYABLE

June	30			12,500	12,500
	30		2,500		10,000

SALES

June	30			10,000	10,000
	30			2,300	12,300

OFFICE EXPENSE

June	4		500		500

SALARIES EXPENSE

June	14		900		900
	28		850		1,750

INTEREST REVENUE

June	10			100	100

Indicate the special journal from which each of the June postings was made. The company's merchandise purchases and sales are primarily on account.

E6-3. Thaxton Company began operations on February 1, 19+6. The firm's purchases journal shows the following for February:

Date		Creditor	Amount
February	2	B. Becholl	$ 500
	4	S. Spurlock	600
	7	L. Lowes	350
	12	A. Ashdown	400
	15	F. Frankfort	250
	20	A. Ashdown	700
	22	T. Towery	550
	28	L. Lowes	600
			$3,950

Cash payments were made to creditors as follows:

Date		Creditor	Amount
February	10	S. Spurlock	$ 600
	13	B. Becholl	400
	18	A. Ashdown	400
	27	F. Frankfort	250
			$1,650

Post the amounts to the accounts payable controlling account and the accounts payable subsidiary ledger, and prove the subsidiary ledger.

E6-4. The column headings listed below might appear in one or more special journals.

(1) Sundry debit.
(2) Merchandise Inventory debit.
(3) Accounts Payable debit.
(4) Accounts Receivable credit.
(5) Office Expense debit.

(6) Sundry credit.
(7) Accounts Payable credit.
(8) Cash credit.
(9) Accounts Receivable debit.
(10) Cash debit.

The company maintains subsidiary ledgers for accounts receivable and accounts payable. For each of the headings state the special journal or journals in which it would be found and whether or not the amounts entered in the column would be posted as a total, or separately, or both as a total and separately.

PROBLEMS

Problem A6-1. In addition to a two-column journal, Western Corporation keeps the following special journals to record its accounting transactions: sales journal, purchases journal, cash receipts journal, and cash disbursements journal. The special journals are designed as illustrated in the text.

The following transactions took place during July 19+3.

(1) Issued capital stock for cash, $7,500.
(2) Purchased merchandise from Akers Supply Company on account, $2,000.
(3) Sold goods to Thomas Kellert on account, $427.
(4) Paid four months' rent at $125 per month.

(5) Cash sales, $39.

(6) Sold merchandise to John Stanton on account, $750.

(7) Paid for rental of delivery truck, $8.

(8) Sold merchandise to Thomas Kellert on account, $933.

(9) Bought merchandise from Rivers Supply Corporation on account, $1,570.

(10) Paid Akers Supply Company for merchandise purchased in (2).

(11) Purchased merchandise for cash, $550.

(12) Sales salaries paid, $440.

(13) John Stanton paid his account. See (6).

(14) Sold merchandise to Martin Fulton on account, $550.

(15) Drivers' salaries paid, $275.

(16) Paid Rivers Supply Corporation the balance owed.

(17) Paid cash for a delivery truck, $2,750.

(18) Sold merchandise to Martin Fulton on account, $400.

(19) Sales salaries to date paid in cash, $360.

Required:

Designate the special journal in which each transaction would be entered. Use the following designations:

S—Sales; P—Purchases; CR—Cash Receipts; CD—Cash Disbursements.

Problem A6-2. All transactions affecting the cash account of Peerless Corporation for the month of October, 19+8, are presented below:

October   1—Purchased a parcel of land for $3,000.

          4—Received payment from J. Wells on account, $1,800.

          5—Paid truck expenses for the week, $78.

          6—Paid account of Ball Sales, Inc., $800.

        10—Cash sales, $2,780.

        12—Paid salaries of $1,000.

        13—Purchased equipment for cash, $1,400.

        15—Purchased merchandise for cash, $3,100.

        18—Sold the land purchased on October 1 for $3,000.

        19—Cash sales, $1,930.

        20—Received interest on note receivable, $50.

        24—Paid account of Walker Corporation, $475.

        28—Received payment from W. Jackson on account, $1,700.

        30—Purchased merchandise for cash, $1,200.

        31—Paid account of Houze, Inc., $950.

Required:

Record the transactions in the cash receipts journal and the cash disbursements journal.

Problem A6-3. Surbaugh Corporation's purchases and sales transactions for the month of February, 19+5, are presented below. All purchases and sales are on account.

February 2—Sale to Millman Supply, $355. Invoice No. 120.

          4—Sale to Lawson, Inc., $2,680. Invoice No. 121.

          8—Purchase of merchandise from Kintner Corporation, $4,600. Invoice dated February 7.

     S 9—Sale to Bangle Service Company, $2,792. Invoice No. 122.

     P 12—Purchase of office equipment from Atlas Sales Company, $570. Invoice dated February 12.

     P 13—Purchase of merchandise from T. F. Bloom, Inc., $2,984. Invoice dated February 12.

     S 17—Sale to Gossett Corporation, $3,420. Invoice No. 123.

     S 20—Sale to A. A. Wigley and Company, $1,715. Invoice No. 124.

     P 21—Purchase of merchandise from Gem Company, $1,950. Invoice dated February 19.

     S 22—Sale to Millman Supply, $940. Invoice No. 125.

     S 27—Sale to Gossett Corporation, $2,820. Invoice No. 126.

Required:

(a) Record the transactions in a sales journal and a purchases journal.

(b) Post the journals to the general ledger.

Problem A6-4. Brewster Corporation uses several special journals for recording its transactions. The following information is taken from the firm's special journals for the month of June, 19+2.

The firm uses a single-column sales journal, which totals $20,468 for the month. Sales were made to customers during the month as follows:

June 2—B.A. Jensen	$ 1,675
4—W.S. Rothrock	5,400
12—L.S. Mooney	7,243
20—W.S. Rothrock	6,150
	$20,468

A multi-column purchases journal is used to record all purchases on account. Column totals for the month are: Merchandise Inventory debit, $61,915; Office Expense debit, $500; Sundry debit, $3,750; and Accounts Payable credit, $66,165. The only item in the Sundry debit column is a purchase of store equipment on June 26.

Purchases for the month were made from the following creditors:

June 3—Arbor Suppliers	$19,265
13—Freemont Wholesalers	3,750
17—Somers Wholesale	16,293
20—Arbor Suppliers	3,500
25—Magley Office Supplies	500
28—Arbor Suppliers	22,857
	$66,165

Column totals taken from the cash receipts journal were: Cash debit, $36,766; Accounts Receivable credit, $13,225; Sales credit, $23,041; and Sundry credit, $500. The Sundry credit represented rent received on June 2 from a tenant in a building owned by the corporation.

Cash was received on account from the following customers in June:

June 16—W.S. Rothrock	$ 5,400
19—B.A. Jensen	1,675
25—W.S. Rothrock	1,900
26—L.S. Mooney	4,250
	$13,225

The cash disbursements journal had the following column totals for the month: Accounts Payable debit, $25,217; Sundry debit, $7,002; and Cash credit, $32,219.

Sundry debit items were:

June	2—Salaries	$1,562
	15—Taxes expense	340
	15—Salaries	1,748
	20—Advertising expense	352
	30—Dividends	3,000
		$7,002

Payments were made to the following creditors during the month.

June	20—Somers Wholesale	$ 5,000
	26—Arbor Suppliers	19,265
	26—Freemont Wholesalers	952
		$25,217

Required:

(a) Postings to all general ledger accounts for the month.

     Assume that all items posted from the special journals are from page 1 of the respective journals.

(b) Postings to the subsidiary accounts receivable and accounts payable ledgers.

(c) Prove the subsidiary ledgers.

Problem A6-5. Regional Sales Corporation closes its books monthly. The December 31, 19+1 after-closing trial balance is presented below.

REGIONAL SALES CORPORATION
After-Closing Trial Balance
December 31, 19+1

Cash	10,907	
Accounts receivable	1,212	
Notes receivable	7,200	
Interest receivable	142	
Merchandise inventory	1,157	
Prepaid rent	1,000	
Land	50,000	
Equipment	16,428	
Accumulated depreciation—Equipment		1,948
Accounts payable		2,375
Notes payable		8,000
Salaries payable		490
Taxes payable		156
Common stock		45,000
Retained earnings		30,077
	88,046	88,046

The subsidiary ledgers show the following detail as of December 31, 19+1:

Accounts receivable:
Milton Jones 972
Henry Druhan 240
   Total 1,212

Accounts payable:
Mart Wholesaling Corp. 2,375

January, 19+2 transactions are presented below.

January 2—Issued additional common stock for cash, $5,000.
           2—Gave Mart Wholesaling Corp. a 90-day note payable for the balance owed.
           3—Received payment for a $3,000 note receivable, plus interest of $30. The interest was part of the interest receivable as of December 31, 19+1.
           4—Sold merchandise to Peter Swanson on account, $327. Invoice No. 1017.
           5—Merchandise arrived from Mart Wholesaling Corp. Invoice date, January 3; amount, $1,559.
           6—Purchased merchandise for cash, $378.
           9—Peter Swanson remitted a check to settle his account.
           9—Cash sales were made in the amount of $264.
         10—Paid bi-weekly salary payroll, $943.
         10—Selling expenses paid in cash, $428.
         10—Paid the taxes owed on December 31, 19+1.
         11—Sold merchandise to Peter Swanson on account, $960. Invoice No. 1018.
         12—Cash sales, $375.
         13—Paid Mart Wholesaling Corp. invoice of the 3rd.
         15—Merchandise purchased from Bernard Supply Company received today. Invoice dated September 12; amount, $2,217.
         17—Paid $2,000 note payable due today plus interest of $20. (You may assume that the interest is applicable to 19+2.)
         19—Received payment from Peter Swanson in full.
         20—Sold merchandise on account to Henry Druhan, $1,129. Invoice No. 1019.
         21—Purchased merchandise from Mart Wholesaling Corp., $3,500. Invoice dated January 21.
         23—Received payment from Henry Druhan, $240.
         24—Paid Mart Wholesaling Corp. the balance of the account.
         25—Paid bi-weekly salary payroll, $1,015.
         26—Cash sales, $929.
         27—Purchased items on account from Office Sales and Service, $142. (Charge Office Expense.)
         29—Paid selling expenses, $43.
         29—Cash purchase of merchandise, $740.
         29—Sale of merchandise to Samuel Dodge, $626. Invoice No. 1020.
         30—Sold goods on account to Hyde and Smith, $1,524. Invoice No. 1021.
         30—Bought a parcel of land as an investment, paying $10,000 cash.

The following information pertains to month-end adjustments:

Depreciation on the equipment is $1,800 per year.
Additional interest receivable on notes amounts to $134 as of January 31, 19+2.
Accrued interest on notes payable amounts to $12.
Salaries owed at month-end amount to $370.
Rent on the building occupied by the company is $1,000 per month.
Cost of goods sold for the month is $3,681.

Required:

(a) Entries for the month in appropriate journals. The company uses the four special journals illustrated in the text, plus a two-column journal.
(b) Adjusting entries.
(c) Postings of all journals to general ledger accounts, using posting references.
(d) An adjusted trial balance.

Problem A6-6. The after-closing trial balance of New Bern Company, referred to in Problem B6-5, at the end of its first year of operation is presented below:

NEW BERN COMPANY
After-Closing Trial Balance
July 31, 19+7

Cash	14,312	
Accounts receivable	23,811	
Notes receivable	5,000	
Merchandise inventory	34,442	
Prepaid insurance	580	
Investments	4,000	
Land	5,000	
Buildings (net)	34,000	
Accounts payable		19,913
Notes payable		10,000
Salaries payable		740
Taxes payable		660
Mortgage payable		35,300
Common stock		40,000
Retained earnings		14,532
	121,145	121,145

The following transactions took place during the period August 1-7, 19+7:

August 1—Sold investments costing $2,000 for $2,500.
　　　1—Paid salaries accrued on July 31.
　　　3—Collected $2,300 from a customer on account.
　　　3—Cash sales of $1,711. Cost of goods sold, $1,010.
　　　4—Paid a creditor on account, $3,016.
　　　4—Sold merchandise on account for $3,820. Cost of the merchandise was $2,940.
　　　4—Paid a $5,000 note payable, plus interest of $75.
　　　5—Received payment from a customer on account, $1,319.
　　　5—Purchased merchandise on account, $5,704.
　　　6—Made a $500 mortgage payment, of which $102 represented interest expense.

Required:

(a) Enter the balances in the July 31, 19+7 after-closing trial balance in an accounting matrix similar to the one shown on page 142.

(b) Record the transactions for August 1–7, 19+7, in the matrix, using the retained earnings account to record all revenue and expense transactions. Key each entry in the matrix by placing the day of the month before the amount. Complete the matrix by showing the ending balances on August 7, 19+7.

Problem B6-1. The balance in the accounts receivable account of Allied Distributing Company on January 1, 19+1, is $86,015.

A schedule of the subsidiary accounts receivable ledger on the same date reveals the following:

Customer	Balance
Ellsworth Company	$15,612
Heckl, Inc.	22,000
Jablonski Corporation	9,806
Porter and Porter	27,733
Sickles Corporation	10,864
	$86,015

Page 12 of the firm's sales journal shows the following credit sales for the month:

January 2—Heckl, Inc.	$ 5,600
8—Porter and porter	8,010
13—Ellsworth Company	7,300
20—Heckl, Inc.	4,550
29—Favor Company	10,130
	$35,590

The information below is taken from the accounts receivable credit column of the company's Cash Receipts Journal in January (page 9):

January 5—Jablonski Corporation	$ 9,806
10—Porter and Porter	6,014
12—Heckl, Inc.	13,000
24—Sickles Corporation	8,545
	$37,365

Set up the required ledger accounts and enter the January 1, 19+1 balances therein.

Required:

(a) Postings to the accounts receivable controlling account.

(b) Postings to the subsidiary accounts receivable ledger.

(c) Prove the subsidiary ledger.

Problem B6-2. All transactions affecting the accounts payable account of Nationwide Company for the month of December, 19+7, are presented below.

December 3—Paid Martin Wholesaling Company invoice dated November 27, $575.

9—Purchased merchandise from Prowter, Inc., $4,675. Invoice dated December 7.

December 10—Purchased office supplies from Brownell Suppliers, $520. Invoice dated December 10. (Charge Office Expense)

13—Paid Stevens Manufacturing Company invoice of November 20, $2,000.

14—Purchased merchandise from Edgeworth Company, $2,337. Invoice dated December 13.

20—Paid Prowter, Inc., invoice dated December 7.

22—Paid Martin Wholesaling Company invoice of November 30, $1,385.

26—Purchased merchandise from Martin Wholesaling Company, $2,910. Invoice dated December 24.

30—Paid Brownell Suppliers invoice dated December 10.

30—Purchased store equipment from Gilroy, Incorporated, $868. Invoice dated December 29.

Required:

Enter the transactions in the purchases and cash disbursements journals.

Problem B6-3. Chico Corporation uses cash receipts and cash disbursements journals. The following cash transactions took place during November, 19+6.

November 1—Received rent from the occupants of office space rented by the firm, $4,300.

2—Paid salaries accrued on October 31, $6,432.

2—Received payment on account from Moeller Distributors, $1,306. Invoice dated October 10.

5—Paid Springer, Inc., invoice dated October 15, $924.

7—Purchased a parcel of land, $5,990.

8—Cash sales, $7,047.

10—Paid Hanson Agency for advertising, $319.

14—Paid Palm Company invoice dated November 5, $3,707.

16—Received payment on account from Toelke Company, $4,666. Invoice dated October 23.

17—Purchased a delivery truck from Metro Motors, $2,838.

18—Purchased merchandise for cash, $2,844.

18—Paid salaries, $3,593.

20—Received payment on account from Sandersville Manufacturing, Inc., $3,221. Invoice dated October 31.

23—Received payment on account from Christy and Associates, $1,572. Invoice dated November 5.

26—Paid First Trust Company interest on loan, $200.

27—Cash sales, $6,291.

29—Received payment on account from Toelke Company, $2,245. Invoice dated November 20.

30—Purchased merchandise for cash, $1,767.

Required:

Record the transactions in the cash receipts journal and the cash disbursements journal.

Problem B6-4. Durham Corporation was organized on May 1, 19+4. Summary information taken from the special journals of the corporation for May, 19+4, is presented below:

	Debit		Credit	
Accounts	Journal	Amount	Journal	Amount
Cash	CR1	$ 38,000	CD1	$ 27,906
Accounts receivable	S1	43,109	CR1	28,000
Merchandise inventory	P1	29,416		
Accounts payable	CD1	25,116	P1	34,716
Sales			S1	43,109
Office expense	P1	300		
Sundry	P1	5,000	CR1	10,000
	CD1	2,790		
		$143,731		$143,731

The detail contained in the sales journal is as follows:

Date	Customer	Amount
May 4	Jersey Company................................	$ 4,806
5	York Company	3,714
10	Carolina Company............................	2,500
14	York Company	6,904
17	Dakota Company.............................	10,079
24	Carolina Company............................	5,010
26	Maine Company	6,338
30	Jersey Company..............................	3,758
		$43,109

The information below is taken from the cash receipts journal:

Date	Customer	Amount
May 8	Jersey Company................................	$ 4,806
20	Dakota Company.............................	3,079
25	York Company	6,904
29	Carolina Company............................	7,510
31	Maine Company	5,701
		$28,000

Credits for May to Accounts Payable were:

Date	Creditor	Amount
May 1	Utah Company	$10,622
1	Vermont Company............................	5,000
1	Hampshire Company	300
4	Nevada Company.............................	5,100
15	Kentucky Company	6,706
21	Nevada Company.............................	6,988
		$34,716

Payments were made to creditors as follows:

Date	Creditor	Amount
May 10	Vermont Company	$ 5,000
11	Hampshire Company	300
20	Kentucky Company	6,706
22	Nevada Company.	5,100
28	Utah Company	8,010
		$25,116

An analysis of the sundry debits and credits is presented below:

Date	Description	Debit	Credit
May 1	Sold common stock		$10,000
1	Purchased office equipment	$5,000	
3	Paid rent	450	
15	Paid salaries	1,240	
30	Paid salaries	1,100	
		$7,790	$10,000

Required:

(a) General and subsidiary ledger accounts as they would appear after the journals had been posted. Show posting references.

(b) A trial balance.

(c) Prove the subsidiary ledgers.

Problem B6-5. New Bern Company began operations on August 1, 19+6, using the following general ledger accounts:

Chart of Accounts

1	Cash	40	Sales
3	Accounts Receivable	50	Cost of Goods Sold
4	Notes Receivable	60	Salaries Expense
6	Merchandise Inventory	61	Taxes Expense
7	Prepaid Insurance	62	Office Expense
8	Investments	63	Interest Expense
10	Land	70	Gain on Sale of Investment
11	Buildings		
15	Accounts Payable		
16	Notes Payable		
17	Salaries Payable		
18	Taxes Payable		
25	Mortgage Payable		
30	Common Stock		

Transactions for the month of August are presented below:

August 1—Issued common stock for cash, $40,000.

2—Merchandise was purchased on account from Beaufort Corp., $17,200.

2—Purchased land and buildings for $40,000, giving a mortgage for the amount. The land is estimated to have a value of $5,000.

August 5—Sold merchandise to Tarboro Company on account, $6,000. Invoice No. 1.

5—Purchased securities as an investment, $700 cash.

5—Office supplies were purchased on account from Burgaw, Inc., $172.

7—Sold merchandise for cash, $1,745.

8—Paid for the merchandise bought on the 2nd from Beaufort Corp.

8—Received payment in full from Tarboro Company.

9—Paid $550 for a three-year fire insurance policy.

10—Sold merchandise to Mayodan Company on account, $7,200. Invoice No. 2.

12—Purchased merchandise from Sylva Suppliers, Inc., on account. Invoice amount, $14,522.

13—Mayodan Company paid its account in full.

13—Sold merchandise to Newry, Inc., on account, $4,675. Invoice No. 3.

14—Sold merchandise to Mayodan Company on account, $1,362. Invoice No. 4.

16—Paid salaries of $1,350.

18—Sold merchandise to Gibsonville Sales Company on account, $5,540. Invoice No. 5.

18—Borrowed $14,000 at the bank, giving a note due one year from date.

18—Cash purchase of merchandise, $927.

20—Purchased merchandise from Glendale Company for $5,620.

22—Sold merchandise to Stevens Point Corporation on account, $1,128. Invoice No. 6.

23—Received partial payment of $980 from Gibsonville Sales Company.

25—Purchased merchandise from Sylva Suppliers, Inc., $4,352.

25—Received a 30-day note from Newry, Inc., in settlement of its account.

26—Sold the securities purchased August 5 for $900.

27—Paid Sylva Suppliers, Inc., half of their invoice of August 12.

29—Purchased securities for $1,700, cash.

30—Sold merchandise to Gibsonville Sales Company on account, $4,254. Invoice No. 7.

31—Cash sales, $542.

31—Paid mortgage installment of $500, of which $114 was interest expense.

31—Paid the semimonthly payroll, $1,400.

31—Purchased merchandise for cash, $2,010.

Required:

(a) Journal entries for the month, using the four special journals illustrated in the chapter, plus a two-column journal. Total and rule the journals.

(b) Indicate how the journals would be posted by placing posting references in the journals.

7

Monetary Assets–
Cash and Investments
in Securities

CASH

What is cash? In accounting usage, coin, paper money, bank balances, and other media of exchange such as checks, bank drafts, cashier's checks, and postal money orders are referred to as "cash." I.O.U.'s and postage stamps, sometimes found with the contents of a cash fund, are not cash. An I.O.U. is a receivable. Postage stamps represent a prepayment.

Although a business may have several cash accounts in its ledger, it is considered acceptable to combine the accounts for balance-sheet purposes, describing the combined accounts as "Cash on hand and in banks," or merely "Cash."

If some of the cash has been set aside for a special purpose or is otherwise not readily available for disbursement, such cash should be listed separately in the balance sheet.

As a general rule, cash is a current asset. There may be instances, however, where cash funds become so restricted or blocked that they should be excluded from the

Current Assets section of the balance sheet. Cash in an insolvent closed bank is an example.

Internal control. The objectives of a good system of internal control, as it relates to assets, may be summarized as follows:

(1) To safeguard the assets.
(2) To achieve more accurate accounting.

Those two objectives stand a better chance of being achieved if, whenever it is feasible, the custody of assets is entirely separated from the function of recording transactions affecting assets, and if the recording work is divided in such a way that the work of one person is verified by another. An irregularity would then require collusion.

In broad outline, a basic system of internal control with regard to cash must include the following:

(1) Establishment of a definite routine for accounting for cash transactions, with a division of labor that would automatically disclose errors and would require collusion to conceal a misappropriation of cash.
(2) Separation of the handling of cash from the recording function. Persons who handle cash receipts or make disbursements should have no access to the records, and those who record cash transactions should have no access to the cash.
(3) Separation of the activities associated with the disbursing of cash from those associated with the receiving of cash.
(4) Requirement that all cash received be deposited daily in the bank.
(5) Requirement that all disbursements be made by check.

The methods and procedures used to achieve internal control vary greatly in different organizations. The system described below is merely indicative of some of the methods and procedures in use.

Cash receipts. Some cash may be received *over the counter* as the proceeds of cash sales or as collections on account; cash may also come through the mail. Prenumbered invoices may be made out for all cash sales, and in that case it should be the duty of some person to see that the duplicates of cash sales invoices or tickets agree with the record of cash received, and that no invoices are missing and unaccounted for. Prenumbered receipts should be issued for all over-the-counter collections on account; if possible, those receipts should be issued by some person other than the one who receives the cash; and a third employee should compare the duplicates of the receipts with the cash record. All cash received over the counter should be recorded on a cash register, if possible. When this is done, all cash received over the counter should be counted and the total compared with the cash register tape by some person other than the one who collected the cash.

As noted above, the danger of misappropriations of cash is reduced if the system of internal control makes collusion necessary to conceal a theft of cash receipts. As to cash received *through the mail,* a system of internal control can be provided in which the perpetration and concealment of fraud would require the collusion of three people, whose records should be required to agree, as indicated below:

(1) All remittances received through the mail should go to an employee other than the cashier or bookkeeper for listing on an adding machine; this employee should also obtain the cash register readings so that his tape will include the total receipts for the day. After he has listed the mail receipts, he turns the cash over to the cashier and sends to the book-keeper any letters or documents relating to the remittances.

(2) The cashier prepares the deposit tickets and deposits the funds. Since all funds received should be deposited daily, the total of the deposit tickets for the day should equal the total of the adding machine tape prepared by the first employee. Some banks issue receipts for deposits; if the bank where a deposit is made does not do so, the cashier should prepare each deposit ticket in duplicate and request the receiving teller at the bank to receipt the duplicate; the cashier should present the bank's receipt or the duplicate deposit slip to the first employee for comparison with his tape.

(3) The bookkeeper records the cash receipts from information shown by the documents accompanying the remittances, cash register tapes, and other papers; the total recorded receipts for the day, as shown by the cash receipts journal, should equal the first employee's tape and the cashier's deposit.

With such a system of internal control, fraud cannot be practiced with the cash receipts and remain undetected without the collusion of three persons. The first employee has no access to the books and cannot falsify the records to conceal a misappropriation; he cannot expect to withhold funds received from debtors without detection, because the debtors will receive statements or letters from the credit department and will report their remittances.

If the cashier withholds any cash, his daily deposits will not agree with the first employee's list or with the bookkeeper's record of cash receipts made from the remittance letters and other sources of information. The bookkeeper, having no access to the cash, has no opportunity to misappropriate any of it, and therefore has no incentive to falsify his records unless he is participating in a three-party collusion.

Cash disbursements. Since all receipts are deposited daily in the bank, all disbursements must be made by check. The person authorized to sign checks should have no authority to make entries in any journal; thus a fraudulent disbursement by check could not be concealed without the collusion of two persons. The collusion of a third person can be made necessary by requiring that all checks shall be signed by one person and countersigned by another.

All checks should be prenumbered. All spoiled, mutilated, or voided checks should be preserved. Some companies even go so far as to require that such checks be recorded in their proper sequence in the cash disbursements record, without entry in the money column, but with a notation that the check is void.

Petty cash. In the discussion of the system of internal control on cash disbursements, the statement was made that all disbursements should be made by check. How is this possible when certain disbursements of trifling amounts, for carfares and postage, for instance, frequently must be made in cash? Although individual petty disbursements may not actually be made by check, their total can be covered by a check by operating a petty cash fund. The petty cash fund, sometimes called an "imprest fund," is operated as follows:

(1) Establishment of fund:

A check is drawn for a round amount ($10, $50, or such an amount as will provide for petty disbursements for a reasonable time) and cashed. The cash is held in the office for use in making petty disbursements. The establishment of a fund of $25 is recorded by debiting Petty Cash and crediting Cash.

(2) Disbursements from fund:

When expenditures are made, receipts or other memoranda are saved to show what the money was spent for.

(3) Replenishment of fund:

Whenever the petty cash expenditures have nearly exhausted the fund, it is necessary to replenish it. Assume that expenditures from the petty cash fund for transportation, advertising, office supplies, and delivery expense total $24.73. The fund is replenished by issuance of a check for that amount. The issuance of the check is recorded in the cash disbursements journal by the following debits and credit:

Transportation in	6.20	
Transportation out	7.35	
Advertising	8.00	
Office supplies	1.18	
Delivery expense	2.00	
Cash		24.73

The expense accounts are debited when the fund is replenished, and not when the petty disbursements are made. Thus, numerous small disbursements can be covered by one check.

It will be noted that, in the illustration, the only entry in the petty cash account is the one establishing the fund; other entries will be made in this account only if the established amount of the fund is increased or decreased because of a change in the amount of the fund needed.

The petty cash account is not debited for replenishments of the fund or credited for petty cash disbursements. The person in charge of the petty cash fund should always have cash or evidence of disbursements equal to the balance of the petty cash account.

As a general rule, all receipts or other memoranda supporting the petty cash disbursements must be presented by the petty cashier to a designated accounting officer for his review and approval. Such supporting memoranda should equal the replenishment check, and, after being marked "cancelled," to prevent their re-use, they are filed as support for the replenishment check.

The petty cash fund should always be replenished at the end of a period before the financial statements are prepared and the books are closed, so that the effect of expenditures from the petty cash fund will be reflected in the accounts of the period in which the expenditures are made.

Opening a bank account. When an account is opened at the bank, the persons authorized to draw checks against the account will be requested to sign cards furnished by the bank, to show the signatures to be used on checks.

These signature cards will be filed by the bank, so that a teller who may be unfamiliar with a depositor's signature can test the authenticity of a check by comparing the depositor's signature on the card with the signature on the check.

If the depositor is a corporation, the bank will request that the directors pass a resolution authorizing certain officers or employees of the corporation to sign checks, and that a copy of this resolution be filed with the bank.

Deposits. Deposits should be accompanied by deposit tickets which describe the items deposited. Deposit tickets are of various forms; an illustration appears on page 161.

Maintaining a record of the bank balance. Cash receipts and deposits are recorded in the cash receipts journal, and disbursements are recorded in the cash disbursements journal. At the end of the month, totals are posted from the two journals to the cash account* in the ledger, and the resulting balance in this account should show the balance in the bank.

But, during the month, how can one ascertain the balance in the bank? The record may be kept:

(1) On the stubs of the check book, or
(2) In a bank register.

A running record on the check book stub is shown on page 161.

If many checks are drawn, the computation of the bank balance after each deposit and each check is usually regarded as unnecessary. In some cases, unbound checks are used so that carbon copies can be prepared and handed to the bookkeeper for his information in recording disbursements. For either of these reasons, it may be expedient to eliminate the running record on the check book stubs and to keep a bank register which will not show the balance after *each* deposit and *each* check, but will show the balance at the end of each day.

The following is an illustration of a bank register:

BANK REGISTER

Date	FIRST NATIONAL BANK			FIRST STATE BANK		
	Deposits	Withdrawals	Balance	Deposits	Withdrawals	Balance
19— June 30			5,000 00			4,850 00
July 1	3,000 00	2,480 00	5,520 00	2,500 00	3,638 00	3,712 00
2	4,500 00	3,500 00	6,520 00	4,000 00	3,200 00	4,512 00

*The account title may be the name of a bank, but the account still is a cash account.

```
DEPOSITED WITH
ILLINOIS NATIONAL BANK
FOR ACCOUNT OF
_____
_____
_____
CHICAGO, ILLINOIS._____ . 19____
IN RECEIVING ITEMS FOR DEPOSIT OR COLLECTION, THIS BANK ACTS ONLY AS
DEPOSITOR'S COLLECTING AGENT AND ASSUMES NO RESPONSIBILITY BEYOND THE
EXERCISE OF DUE CARE. ALL ITEMS ARE CREDITED SUBJECT TO FINAL PAYMENT.

    PLEASE LIST EACH CHECK SEPARATELY

CURRENCY _____
SILVER _____
    CHECKS AS FOLLOWS:
_____|_____
_____|_____
_____|_____
_____|_____
_____|_____
_____|_____
_____|_____
_____|_____
_____|_____
_____|_____
             TOTAL, $ |
SEE THAT ALL CHECKS AND DRAFTS ARE ENDORSED
```

DEPOSIT TICKET

BALANCE BROUGHT FORWARD	8,503.75
DEPOSIT	
TOTAL	
CHECK NO.	93
DATE	July 17, 19—
PAYEE J. H. Guthrie	650.00
BALANCE	7,853.75
DEPOSIT 7/17/—	2,300.00
TOTAL	10,153.75
CHECK NO.	94
DATE	July 17, 19—
PAYEE F. L. Kenyon	400.00
BALANCE CARRIED FORWARD	9,753.75

CHECK BOOK STUB

This record is kept in following way:

Each day enter, in the Deposits columns of the bank register, the totals of the day's receipts (deposits) recorded in the Cash debit columns of the cash receipts journal.

Similarly, enter, in the Withdrawals columns of the bank register, the daily totals of the disbursements recorded in the Cash credit columns of the cash disbursements journal.

Compute the resulting daily bank balances and enter them in the Balance columns of the bank register.

The bank statement. Once a month the bank will render a statement to the depositor and return the checks which it has paid and charged to his account. The statement shows the balance at the beginning of the month, the deposits, the checks paid, other debits and credits during the month, and the balance at the end of the month. A simple illustration of such a statement is shown on page 162.

The symbols on the statement require some explanation:

N.S.F.—(Not sufficient funds)—On June 27 R. M. Walker Company received a check for $63.95 from Wm. Barnes; this check was included in the deposit of June 27. It was returned to The White National Bank because Barnes did not have a sufficient balance in his bank account to cover the check. The White National Bank therefore charged it back to R. M. Walker Company.

STATEMENT OF ACCOUNT WITH
THE WHITE NATIONAL BANK
CHICAGO, ILLINOIS

R. M. Walker Company
135 West State Street
Chicago, Illinois

CHECKS			DEPOSITS	DATE	BALANCES
				May 31, 19—	3,500.17
100.00 √			310.00 √	June 1, 19—	3,710.17
96.00				June 4, 19—	3,614.17
.10 Ex			175.00 √	June 5, 19—	3,789.07
75.00	150.50			June 6, 19—	3,563.57
			425.50 √	June 8, 19—	3,989.07
39.75				June 10, 19—	3,949.32
136.50				June 11, 19—	3,812.82
			136.75 √	June 12, 19—	3,949.57
84.20 √				June 13, 19—	3,865.37
164.19			216.80 √	June 15, 19—	3,917.98
7.25				June 18, 19—	3,910.73
			310.80 √	June 19, 19—	4,221.53
39.50				June 20, 19—	4,182.03
600.35				June 22, 19—	3,581.68
			165.00 √	June 24, 19—	3,746.68
13.75	19.50	123.80		June 26, 19—	3,589.63
.25 Col			138.20 √	June 27, 19—	3,727.58
76.35				June 29, 19—	3,651.23
12.60	63.95 N.S.F.				
109.11				June 30, 19—	3,465.57

CC—Certified Check Col—Collection charge
EC—Error Corrected P.S.—Payment stopped
DM—Debit Memo N.S.F.—Not Sufficient Funds
Ex—Exchange charge SC—Service Charge

**THE LAST AMOUNT
IN THIS COLUMN
IS YOUR BALANCE**

PLEASE EXAMINE. IF NO ERRORS ARE REPORTED WITHIN TEN DAYS, THE
ACCOUNT WILL BE CONSIDERED CORRECT.

BANK STATEMENT

When a returned check marked "N.S.F." is received from the bank,
an entry should be made crediting Cash and debiting the party
from whom the check was received. Such a check should not be
regarded as cash, even if it is redeposited, until it has been honored
by the drawer's bank, unless the payee's bank gives credit for it
at the time it is redeposited.

Ex.—On June 5 the bank charged $.10 exchange on a check included in the deposit of that date.

Col.—On June 27 the bank credited R. M. Walker Company with the proceeds of a note collected by the bank for the company's account, and charged a collection fee of $.25.

P.S.—(Payment stopped)—If R. M. Walker Company received and deposited with The White National Bank a check from a customer who, for some reason, stopped payment on the check, the customer's bank would refuse to pay it and would return it to The White National Bank, which would charge it back to the account of R. M. Walker Company.

S.C.—(Service charge)—Banks cannot profitably handle small accounts without making a service charge. The charge may be a fixed amount applicable to all accounts with balances averaging less than a certain minimum amount. Many banks base the service charge on a number of factors, such as the average balance of the account during the month, the number of deposits made, and the number of checks drawn.

When the bank renders the statement, it returns all paid checks to the depositor. Accompanying the statement and the canceled checks there will be debit memoranda for all charges to the depositor not represented by checks; these include charges for exchange, collection, and the check charged back (N.S.F.).

The check marks are discussed in the following section.

Reconciling the bank account. The balance shown by the bank statement rarely agrees with the balance shown by the depositor's books. Items may appear on the depositor's books which have not yet been recorded on the bank's books, such as:

Outstanding checks—not presented to and paid by the bank.

Deposits not yet received by the bank—perhaps in transit in the mails.

Negotiable instruments left with the bank and charged to the bank as a deposit, but taken by the bank for collection only and not credited to the depositor until collected.

Similarly, items may appear on the bank's books which have not yet been taken up on the depositor's books, such as:

Service charges.

Charges for collection and exchange.

Charges for checks returned N.S.F. Although the bank notifies the depositor immediately of such returned checks, and also of checks returned because payment has been stopped, entries may not be made immediately on the depositor's books.

If a company keeps funds on deposit in several banks, contra errors are sometimes made in the bank accounts on the depositor's books. For instance, checks drawn against one bank account may be recorded as disbursements from another bank, and deposits in one bank may be charged to another bank. Banks also occasionally make errors by charging or crediting one customer with another customer's checks or deposits, particularly if the customers' names are similar. For all these reasons, the bank statement should be reconciled as soon as possible after it has been received.

A bank reconciliation as of any given date shows the following:

- The balance of the bank account according to the depositor's books.
- Reconciling items—any charges or credits to the depositor recorded by the bank but not recorded by the depositor.
- The adjusted balance.

- The balance of the depositor's account according to the bank's books.
- Reconciling items—any charges or credits to the bank recorded by the depositor but not recorded by the bank.
- The adjusted balance.

If the two adjusted balances agree, the bank account is said to be reconciled.

Illustration. In order to reconcile a bank account, it is necessary to locate all of the reconciling items. This is done by comparing the bank statement with the depositor's books in order to discover those items that have not been recorded by both the bank and the depositor.

In this illustration, we shall reconcile the June bank statement of R. M. Walker Company (page 162) with the data recorded in its books.

The cash account in the ledger appears on the following page.

The posting references have been omitted from the cash account; they would refer to the source record from which the monthly totals of receipts and disbursements were obtained.

The detailed records maintained by R. M. Walker Company show the following cash transactions for June.

June Cash Receipts

Date	Explanation	Cash Receipts	Deposits
19—			
June 5	Cash sale.	175.00	175.00 √
8	Invoice, June 1, less 1%	297.00	
8	Invoice, May 5	128.50	425.50 √
12	Cash sale.	136.75	136.75 √
15	Invoice, June 8, less 1%	148.50	
15	Cash sale.	68.30	216.80 √
19	E. F. Watson note	250.00	
19	Cash sale.	60.80	310.80 √
24	Cash sale.	165.00	165.00 √
27	John Smith note	74.25	
27	Invoice, June 1	63.95	138.20 √
30	Cash sale.	60.50	60.50
		1,628.55	1,628.55

June Cash Disbursements

Date	Explanation	Check No.	Amount
19—			
June 1	Cash purchase	131	75.00 √
2	Invoice, May 28	132	150.50 √
3	Store rent for June	133	96.00 √
6	Invoice, June 4	134	136.50 √
9	Scales	135	39.75 √
13	Invoice, June 5	136	164.19 √
16	Invoice, June 6	137	39.50 √
17	Supplies	138	7.25 √
20	Invoice, June 12	139	600.35 √
24	Cash purchase	140	19.50 √
24	Freight on purchases	141	13.75 √
26	Invoice, June 20	142	123.80 √
28	Cash purchase	143	76.35 √
29	Cash purchase	144	12.60 √
29	Invoice, June 17	145	109.11 √
30	C. E. Whitely's salary	146	300.00
			1,964.15

CASH (The White National Bank) **Account No. 101**

19—					
May	31	Balance			3,625.97 Dr.
June	30		1,628.55		5,254.52 Dr.
	30			1,964.15	3,290.37 Dr.

STEPS IN THE RECONCILIATION PROCESS: The procedure of reconciling the bank account involves the following steps:

(1) Arrange in numerical order the paid checks returned from the bank.
(2) Refer to the reconciliation at the close of the preceding month; note the items which were outstanding at that date. The May 31st reconciliation appears below.

R. M. WALKER COMPANY
Bank Reconciliation
May 31, 19—

Balance, per books		$3,625.97
Balance, per bank statement		$3,500.17
Add deposit not credited by bank.......................		310.00 √
Total		$3,810.17
Deduct outstanding checks:		
129	$100.00 √	
130	84.20 √	184.20
Adjusted balance		$3,625.97

This reconciliation shows that $310 recorded by the company as a deposit in May had not been credited by the bank at the end of the month, and that checks for $100 and $84.20 were outstanding. Reference to the bank statement on page 162 shows that the deposit was credited by the bank on June 1, and that the checks were paid on June 1 and June 13. These items are now checked (√) on the May 31 reconciliation and on the June 30 bank statement.

(3) See whether the deposits shown by the company's records are in agreement with the entries in the Deposits column of the bank statement. Place check marks in the Deposits column of the company's record of cash receipts and in the Deposits column of the bank statement beside the items which are in agreement.

The unchecked deposits in the company's record represent deposits not taken up by the bank. By reference to the cash receipts record it will be noted that only one of the deposits is unchecked: the June 30 deposit of $60.50. This unchecked item is presumably a deposit in transit; observe that it is added to the balance per bank statement in the bank reconciliation below.

Any unchecked items in the Deposits column of the bank statement would represent credits by the bank not taken up by the depositor. It will be noted that there are no such unchecked items in the Deposits column of the bank statement.

(4) Compare the returned checks (which have been sorted in numerical order) with the entries in the cash disbursements record. Place a check mark in the company's cash disbursements record beside the entry for each check that has been returned by the bank.

Unchecked items are outstanding checks. By reference to page 165, it will be noted that only one item is unchecked: the $300 check drawn on June 30. The bank reconciliation following shows it as an adjustment of the balance per bank statement.

(5) Examine the bank statement for any items not recorded in the company's books; such items must be included in the bank reconciliation.

Charges by the bank shown by the bank statement that do not appear in the company's cash records are for:

Exchange	$ .10
Collection	.25
N.S.F. check returned	63.95

They are shown in the reconciliation as deductions from the balance per books.

(6) Prepare the reconciliation statement.

R. M. WALKER COMPANY
Bank Reconciliation
June 30, 19—

Balance, per books		$3,290.37
Deduct bank's charges not on the books:		
Exchange	$ .10	
Collection	.25	
N.S.F. check—Wm. Barnes	63.95	64.30
Adjusted balance		$3,226.07
Balance, per bank statement		$3,465.57
Add deposit not taken up by the bank		60.50
Total		$3,526.07
Deduct outstanding checks:		
No. 146		300.00
Adjusted balance (as above)		$3,226.07

Certified checks. An ordinary check is deducted from the drawer's account when the check is presented to the drawer's bank for payment. In contrast, a certified check is deducted from the drawer's account when it is certified by the drawer's bank. Therefore, outstanding certified checks need not be included in the list of outstanding checks in the bank reconciliation.

Adjustments after reconciliation. If the bank has made charges or credits to the company's account that have not been recorded on the company's books, and if the company recognizes these charges or credits as correct, adjustments should be made to bring them onto the company's books.

The illustrative bank reconciliation discloses the fact that the bank has made certain deductions from the depositor's account which have not been taken up on the depositor's books. To take up these items, the company should debit Collection and Exchange $.35, debit Accounts Receivable (Wm. Barnes) $63.95, and credit Cash $64.30.

Payroll bank account. If a company pays a large number of employees by check, it is desirable for it to open a special payroll bank account. At each pay date, a check on the regular bank account is drawn and deposited in the payroll bank account. Individual checks for the employees are then drawn on this special account, which is thus immediately exhausted. If the payroll account and the general account are kept in the same bank, different-colored checks should be used for the two accounts.

This procedure has several advantages. In the first place, the officer authorized to sign checks on the general bank account can be relieved of the work of signing numerous payroll checks; these can be signed by some other employee. In the second place, the general bank account can be reconciled without cluttering the reconciliation statement with all the outstanding payroll checks. And, in the third place, the labor of recording the payroll disbursements is reduced; instead of recording all payroll checks in the cash disbursements journal, check numbers may be entered in a payroll record.

Dividend bank account. If a company has a large number of stockholders, a special bank account may be used for the payment of dividends. A check for the total amount of the dividend is drawn and deposited in this special bank account. Checks payable to the individual stockholders are drawn on this account.

Bank overdrafts. A bank overdraft exists when checks written on the account exceed the account balance. An overdraft in a bank account should be shown in the balance sheet as a liability. This should be done even if there are balances in other banks that exceed the overdraft; the total of the available balances should be shown on the asset side of the balance sheet and the overdraft should be shown on the liability side.

INVESTMENTS IN SECURITIES

Cost of investments. The cost of an investment in bonds or stocks (although not a monetary asset, stocks are covered here because they are shown under the same balance sheet classification) includes the purchase price, brokerage, taxes, and other expenditures incident to acquisition.

If securities are purchased through a broker on margin (deposit with, or part payment to, the broker), the books and the balance sheet should reflect as an asset the full cost of the securities and not merely the margin deposit, and the unpaid balance should be shown as a liability.

Assume that a dividend was declared by a corporation on June 24, payable on July 10, to stockholders of record on June 30. If stock of this company was purchased after the declaration of the dividend and in time to have it recorded by the company in the name of the purchaser before the close of business on June 30, the purchaser would have the right to receive the dividend. Therefore, in recording the purchase, the purchaser should debit Dividends Receivable for the amount of the dividend to which he is entitled, and debit Investment in Stocks for the remainder of the cost.

If bonds are purchased between interest-payment dates, the purchaser pays the seller for the interest accrued from the last interest-payment date to the date of purchase; his entry should debit Bond Interest Receivable for the amount of the accrued interest, and Investment in Bonds for the remainder of the cost. Incidentally, bond prices are quoted as a percentage of the face value, i.e., 99 for a $100 bond means $99 and 99 for a $1,000 bond means $990.

Balance sheet classification and valuation. The balance sheet classification of an investment and its valuation at dates subsequent to acquisition depend generally on whether the investment presumably will be, or can be, within the limits of good management, disposed of to obtain funds for current needs.

INVESTMENTS CLASSIFIABLE AS CURRENT ASSETS: It has long been recognized as proper to classify investments as current assets if management intends to convert them into cash during a period in the operating cycle when cash requirements are high, and if there is a ready market for them either on an exchange or elsewhere. Accountants are now leaning toward the opinion that, even though management has no established intention to dispose of the securities in the near future, they can be classified as current if they are readily marketable and if they are not being held for purposes of control, to assist in establishing or maintaining good customer or supplier relationships, or for any other reason that would make their disposal inexpedient.

When marketable securities are classified as a current asset, there is an implied representation that they are being held as a reserve source of cash. Thus, if market value is materially below cost at a balance sheet date, there is a potential impairment of the reserve source of cash. This is considered to be of such importance as to require disclosure. The disclosure can be achieved in the following ways:

By adopting the lower of cost or market as the valuation basis, thus:

Marketable securities— at the lower of cost or market $50,000

Or by showing the market value parenthetically, thus:

Marketable securities— at cost (market value, $50,000) $52,500

Or in a footnote to the financial statements.

On the other hand, if the marketable securities have appreciated, disclosure is not required although it is recommended.

If the lower of cost or market is used, it is considered acceptable to apply the method by comparing the total cost and market for the entire group of securities classified as a current asset. In other words, an item-by-item comparison is not required. The valuation basis of investments classified as current should be disclosed in the balance sheet.

Because gains and losses on investments are reportable for income-tax purposes only in the year of disposal, it is advisable to maintain a record of their cost in the investment account. Therefore, market declines, if recorded, should not be recorded by credits to the investment account. The entry should be: debit Market Loss on Securities; credit the contra account Excess of Cost of Securities over Market Value. The investment may be shown in the balance sheet thus:

Stocks owned:
Cost $50,000
Excess of cost over market value 3,000
Market value $47,000

or merely thus:

Stocks owned—at the lower of cost or market $47,000

LONG-TERM INVESTMENTS: Long term investments are sometimes acquired in accordance with a financial policy looking to the accumulation of funds for such purposes as plant expansion or the liquidation of long-term indebtedness. Or, as noted above, they may be held for purposes of control or good customer or supplier relationships. Such investments in securities usually are shown in the balance sheet between Current Assets and Property, Plant, and Equipment, sometimes under a caption of Long-term Investments. Conservatism would suggest that serious declines in market value, with a probable inability to recover the cost of the investments, should be given recognition in the accounts. But the American Institute of Certified Public Accountants' 1966 edition of *Accounting Trends and Techniques* states that ". . . marketable securities, when shown in the noncurrent asset section of the balance sheet . . . are invariably valued at cost."

Revenue from investments. Bonds pay interest at the rate and on the dates shown on the bonds; for example, "6 per cent per annum; March 1 and September 1." Such revenue should be recorded in the period in which the interest is earned. Thus, end-of-period accrual entries should be made for any interest earned even though not collected unless the issuer has defaulted on his obligation to pay interest.

When bonds have been purchased between interest-payment dates, the first interest payment received by the new owner will cover a full interest-payment period even though he will have held the bonds for only a portion of the period. To determine the interest income of the new owner, any amount paid to the previous owner for accrued interest should be subtracted from the first interest collection. (Businessmen often use the term interest income as synonymous with interest revenue.)

Income from stocks takes the form of dividends. Dividends do not accrue, as interest does. Thus income does not arise from the ownership of stocks until a dividend is declared by the corporation's board of directors. It is customary to take up the income in the period in which the dividend is received.

Stock dividends are not properly regarded as income.

Amortization of premium on long-term investments. If the cost of a bond is in excess of its face value, the purchase is made "at a premium." When the bond matures, only the face amount (or par) will be collectible. The income on the bond during its remaining life is the amount of the interest collected minus the premium paid at purchase and not recovered at maturity. Because the aggregate income is less than the cash interest, it should be recognized that the true periodic interest income is at a rate *lower* than that printed on the bond. Therefore, a portion of the premium should be charged periodically against the interest collected. This charge should be offset by a credit to the bond investment account, thus gradually reducing the carrying value of the bond to its face value at maturity.

Assume that a $1,000 bond, bearing 6 per cent interest payable semiannually on June 30 and December 31, is purchased on January 1, 19+1 (two years before maturity), for $1,017.92. Although interest of $30 will be collected every six months, not all of this amount can be considered income; a portion of each $30 must be considered a repayment of premium. Because there are four interest periods, the premium may be written off by four semiannual entries of $17.92 ÷ 4, or $4.48. The entry to be made at each interest date would be:

Cash	30.00	
Investment in bonds (for amortization of premium)		4.48
Bond interest income		25.52

The interest collections and premium amortization may be scheduled as follows:

Schedule of Amortization
Two-Year 6 Per Cent Bond Bought for $1,017.92

Date	Debit Cash	Credit Investment in Bonds	Credit Interest Income	Carrying Value
January 1, 19+1				$1,017.92
June 30	$ 30.00	$ 4.48	$ 25.52	1,013.44
December 31	30.00	4.48	25.52	1,008.96
June 30, 19+2	30.00	4.48	25.52	1,004.48
December 31	30.00	4.48	25.52	1,000.00
	$120.00	$17.92	$102.08	

Note that the amortization of the premium gradually brings the carrying value of the bond down to its face value.

Amortization of discount on long-term investments. If the cost of a bond is less than its face value, the purchase is made "at a discount." When the bond matures, the face amount (or par) will be collectible. Thus the total income on a bond purchased at a discount, held to maturity, and collected at its face value is the total of the interest collections plus the discount; therefore, it appears proper to regard a portion of the discount as earned each period. Thus the true periodic interest income is at a rate *higher* than that printed on the bond.

Assume that a $1,000 bond, bearing 6 per cent interest payable semiannually on June 30 and December 31, is purchased on January 1, 19+1 (two years before maturity), for $982.80. The discount of $17.20 may be spread over the four periods in semiannual amounts of $4.30. The entry to be made at each interest date would be:

```
Cash . . . . . . . . . . . . . . . . . . . . . . . . . . . . . . . . . . .    30.00
    Investment in bonds (amortization of discount) . . . . . . . . . .     4.30
        Bond interest income . . . . . . . . . . . . . . . . . . . . . . .              34.30
```

The amortization may be scheduled as follows:

Schedule of Amortization
Two-Year 6 Per Cent Bond Bought for $982.80

Date	Debit Cash	Debit Investment in Bonds	Credit Interest Income	Carrying Value
January 1, 19+1				$ 982.80
June 30	$ 30.00	$ 4.30	$ 34.30	987.10
December 31	30.00	4.30	34.30	991.40
June 30, 19+2	30.00	4.30	34.30	995.70
December 31	30.00	4.30	34.30	1,000.00
	$120.00	$17.20	$137.20	

Thus, the amortization of the discount gradually brings the carrying value of the bond up to its face value, spreading the discount over the period between purchase and maturity as an addition to the bond interest income.

Amortization—short-term investments. Amortization procedures usually are applicable only to long-term investments in bonds. If bonds are purchased as short-term investments, with no prospect of holding them until maturity, the reason for an amortization procedure does not exist; an amortization procedure presupposes that the bonds will be held until maturity.

Sales of investment securities. If a stock investment carried at cost is sold, an entry similar to the following should be made:

Cash	54,000	
Investment in stocks		50,000
Gain on sale of stocks		4,000

But assume that an entry had been made some time in the past reducing the carrying value of the stock to $47,000 because of a decline in market value (see illustration on page 169), and that the entry had not been subsequently reversed. The entry for the sale would be:

Cash	54,000	
Excess of cost of stock over market value	3,000	
Investment in stocks		50,000
Correction of prior years' earnings		3,000
Gain on sale of stocks		4,000

Similar entries would be made for the sale of a bond at an interest-payment date. The credit to the investment in bonds account would be the amount of the balance of the account.

If bonds are sold between interest-payment dates, it is necessary first to record the interest accrued since the last interest-payment date before recording the sale, as shown below, assuming accrued interest of $200 on bonds costing $10,000.

Bond interest receivable	200	
Bond interest income		200
For interest accrued at date of sale.		

Then the sale of the bonds for $10,500 would be recorded as follows:

Cash	10,500	
Investment in bonds		10,000
Bond interest receivable		200
Gain on sale of bonds		300
To record sale of bonds.		

(If the bond was a long-term investment purchased at a premium or a discount, the premium or discount applicable to the fractional period since the last preceding interest date should be amortized. This is necessary in order to state correctly the interest income for the fractional period and the gain or loss on the sale.)

In the multiple-step form of the income statement, any gains or losses resulting from sales of securities are shown below net operating income.

ASSIGNMENT

MATERIAL

QUESTIONS

1. Which of the following items could properly be classified as *cash?*
   - (a) The balance in a bank account.
   - (b) Coin and currency on hand.
   - (c) Postage stamps on hand.
   - (d) Postal money orders.
   - (e) Checks received from customers.
   - (f) An employee's I.O.U.

2. Outline a basic system for the *internal control* of cash.

3. Describe the procedure for establishing a *petty cash* fund. Why is it necessary that the petty cash fund be replenished at the end of the accounting period?

4. List several items, other than deposits and cancelled checks, that might affect a depositor's bank balance.

5. What is the purpose of a bank reconciliation?

6. List the steps in the bank reconciliation process.

7. What is properly includible in the cost of an investment?

8. What is the difference between an investment that is classifiable as a current asset and one that represents a long-term investment?

9. Describe three ways of disclosing the fact that the market value of an investment is lower than its cost at a balance-sheet date.

10. How does the accounting for income from bond investments differ from the accounting for income from stock investments?

11. What takes place when a bond sells "at a premium" or "at a discount"?

12. Why are premium and discount amortization procedures not usually applied to short-term investments in bonds?

SHORT EXERCISES

E7-1. Listed below are several reconciling items which might appear in a bank reconciliation:

   (1) Bank service charges.
   (2) Checks written but still outstanding.

(3) Proceeds of a note collected by the bank but not entered on the books.
(4) A deposit in transit.
(5) A check erroneously charged against the account by the bank.
(6) A cancelled check recorded on the books for less than the amount of the check.
(7) A deposit erroneously credited to the account by the bank.
(8) A check deposited in the account but returned due to insufficient funds.

For each item state where it would appear in the reconciliation form by using the letters A, B, C, and D as follows:

A—Add to balance per books.
 B—Deduct from balance per books.
C—Add to balance per bank.
D—Deduct from balance per bank.

E7-2. Rochelle Company uses a petty cash fund in its operations. The following transactions took place in the order listed.

(1) Established the fund in the amount of $100.
(2) Disbursed $20 from the fund.
(3) Disbursed $10 from the fund.
(4) Replenished the fund by drawing a check for $30.
(5) Reduced the fund to $50.
(6) Disbursed $5 from the fund.
(7) Disbursed $10 from the fund.
(8) Replenished the fund by drawing a check for $15.
(9) Increased the fund to $75.

What is the balance in the petty cash fund immediately after each transaction? What is the balance in the petty cash account in the general ledger immediately after each transaction?

E7-3. The following data pertain to the marketable securities of Cusseta Company during $19+1$, the company's first year of operations.

(1) Purchased 100 shares of A Corporation stock at $12 per share, plus brokerage costs of $50.
(2) Purchased a $1,000 B Corporation bond at face, plus accrued interest of $15.
(3) Received a cash dividend of 50¢ per share on the A Corporation stock.
(4) Sold 50 shares of the A Corporation stock at $14 per share.
(5) Received interest of $25 on the B Corporation bond.
(6) Purchased 100 shares of C Company stock for $1,500.
(7) Received interest of $25 on the B Corporation bond.
(8) Sold 50 shares of the A Corporation stock for $10 per share.
(9) Received a cash dividend of 25¢ per share on the C Company stock.
(10) Interest receivable at year-end on the B Corporation bond amounts to $10.

What is the amount of each of the following for the year?

(a) Bond interest income.
(b) Dividend income.
(c) Gain or loss on sale of securities.

E7-4. Shannon, Inc., which closes its books on December 31, purchased fifty $1,000, 6%, 10-year bonds of Toccoa Corporation on January 1, 19+3, as a long-term investment. The bonds are dated January 1, 19+3, and interest is payable on January 1 and July 1.

    Present all entries pertaining to the bonds in 19+3, under each of the following assumptions: (a) purchase price is 103; (b) purchase price is 91.

PROBLEMS

Problem A7-1. The following transactions pertain to the petty cash account of Street Company for the accounting period ending June 30, 19+1.

    May 17—A check is drawn to establish a petty cash fund in the amount of $300.
        31—An examination reveals the following composition of the fund, which is replenished on this date:

Currency and coin	$214.03
Receipts for the following disbursements:	
Postage	18.75
Office supplies expense	24.02
Travel expense	13.76
Entertainment expense	29.44

    June 30—The following items are found in the fund on this date:

Currency and coin	$185.06
Receipts for the following disbursements:	
Postage	26.83
Office supplies expense	25.10
Telephone and telegraph	9.83
Travel expense	39.20
Miscellaneous expense	13.98

    The fund was replenished on June 30 and the amount was reduced to $200.
    Prepare journal entries to record the above information.

Problem A7-2. The following information pertains to the banking activities of Cobb Company with State National Bank during the month of September, 19+1.

    (1) The balance per ledger on September 1, 19+1, is $16,245.18.
    (2) Cash receipts for September per the cash journal are $45,634.92; checks during the month total $52,911.34.
    (3) The statement from the bank shows a balance of $6,652.02 at the end of the month.
    (4) Included in the returned checks is a memo stating that the check of M. Price has been returned marked N.S.F.; the amount is $876.47.
    (5) An examination of the checks reveals that the following are outstanding: No. 1593, $30.50; No. 1812, $110.38; No. 1962, $69.12; No. 2008, $117.39; No. 2009, $4.82; and No. 2010, $29.11.
    (6) The bank has deducted from the account, in error, a check of Sprott, Inc.; the amount of the check is $546.33.
    (7) There is a deposit of $2,100.30 in transit at the end of September.
    (8) The bookkeeper made an error in recording a check received from R. Mason; the amount recorded was $94.76; it should have been $947.60.

—OB   (9) A debit memo shows that service charges amounted to $7.80.

BALANCE
8,937.33

Required:

(a) A bank reconciliation as of September 30, 19+1.
(b) Any journal entries required as of September 30, 19+1.

Problem A7-3. The following selected account balances are taken from the books of Davidson Company as of February 28, 19+1.

	Balance	
	Debit	Credit
Cash on hand	$ 125	
Cash in bank—Citizens Bank		$300
Cash in bank—First National Bank	1,312	
Cash in bank—Bank of Monroe	4,806	
Petty cash	100	
Marketable securities—at cost (market value, $7,500)	8,306	
Excess of cost of marketable securities over market value ..		806
Investment in bonds of Company B—at cost and face		
(Bonds mature December 31, 19+5)	10,000	

State how each of the above items would be reported on Davidson Company's balance sheet on February 28, 19+1.

Problem A7-4. Collom Corporation made the following purchases of bonds during March, 19+2:

Purchase Date	Company	Face	Cost	Rate of Interest	Maturity Date	Last Interest Payment Date	
March 1	Zap Corp.	$ 6,000	103½	4%	July 1, 19+5	Jan. 1, 19+2	40 mo
10	Zip Corp.	10,000	96¾	6%	Nov. 1, 19+8	Nov. 1, 19+1	79 ³⁄
15	Zoom Corp.	8,000	93	4½%	July 1, 19+7	Jan. 1, 19+2	63 ½⁄₂
31	Zep Corp.	6,000	101¼	4¾%	Feb. 1, 19+7	Feb. 1, 19+2	

BOND INTEREST
INCOME.
C) 68.33
D) INTEREST
RECEIVABLE

Required:

(a) Journal entries to record the above purchases, assuming that the purchases represent long-term investments.
(b) All adjusting entries pertaining to the bondholdings on March 31, 19+2, assuming that the corporation closes its books on that date.

Problem A7-5. Clark Company purchased $10,000 of Winder Corporation 4½% bonds at 97 ½ plus accrued interest on February 1, 19+1. The bonds mature on October 1, 19+9, and interest is payable on April 1 and October 1.

On August 1, 19+3, Clark Company sold Winder Corporation bonds having a face value of $4,000 at 101 plus accrued interest.

Required:

(a) All entries for the years 19+1 and 19+2, assuming that Clark Company closes its books annually on December 31.
(b) The entry to record the sale of the bonds on August 1, 19+3.

Problem A7-6. Tucker, Inc., had the following transactions pertaining to purchases and sales to marketable securities in 19+1.

Jan. 10—Bought 40 shares of X stock for $155 per share.

Feb. 15—Bought 20 bonds of B, due January 1, 19+3, for 100 plus accrued interest at 3%. The bonds have a face value of $1,000 each, with interest payable January 1 and July 1.

   19—Bought 1,000 shares of Y stock for $7.95 per share; a dividend has been declared payable March 1 to stockholders of record February 25. The dividend is to be 75 cents per share.

Mar. 1—The dividend was received.

   10—Sold 24 shares of X stock for $162.50 per share.

May 4—Bought 75 shares of Z stock for $48.20 per share.

June 1—Sold 20 bonds of B for 98 plus accrued interest.

   30—The company's fiscal year ends on June 30. Stock quotations, as of June 30, were: X, $142.00; Y, $7.20; and Z, $39.50.

Sept. 6—Sold 50 shares of Z stock for $33 per share.

Required:

(a) All entries to record the above transactions.

(b) The presentation of the marketable securities account on the balance sheet as of June 30, 19+1.

Problem B7-1. Information concerning the petty cash fund of Martin Corporation, which closes its books on November 30, is presented below.

October 10—A petty cash fund of $100 is established.

October 31—Examination of the fund reveals the following composition:

Currency and coin	$ 7.30
Receipts for the following disbursements:	
Telephone and telegraph	10.67
Postage expense	15.20
Travel expense	24.07
Entertainment expense	9.38
Office supplies expense	23.38
Miscellaneous expense	10.00

The fund is replenished on this date and the amount is increased to $150.

November 30—The fund is composed of the following:

Currency and coin	$43.80
Receipts for the following disbursements:	
Travel expense	45.00
Postage expense	12.07
Office supplies expense	13.29
Entertainment expense	35.84

The fund is not replenished on this date.

Prepare journal entries to record the above information.

Problem B7-2. Boone Corporation opened a bank account with Citizens Trust Company on May 1, 19+1. The bank statement on page 178 was received at the end of May.

CITIZENS TRUST COMPANY

Checks		Deposits	Date 19+1	Balance
Balance brought forward				-0-
		7,280.14	May 1	7,280.14
259.12		279.18	May 2	7,300.20
42.30 N.S.F.		163.12	May 3	7,421.02
418.35		408.40	May 4	7,411.07
.75 Ex.		78.12	May 5	7,488.44
2.69		90.02	May 6	7,575.77
2.82 Col.		144.86	May 9	7,717.81
262.19	111.55	419.89	May 11	7,763.96
120.39		384.49	May 14	8,028.06
142.18		273.19	May 16	8,159.07
210.29		42.12	May 18	7,990.90
109.02	1.25 Ex.	90.15	May 20	7,970.78
69.80		29.30	May 22	7,930.28
135.14		272.44	May 25	8,067.58
		503.85	May 27	8,571.43
216.08			May 29	8,355.35

A summary of the May cash receipts and disbursements follows.

CASH RECEIPTS

Date	Receipts	Deposits
19+1		
May 1	29.18	
1	250.00	279.18
2	163.12	163.12
3	195.18	
3	26.62	
3	186.60	408.40
4	78.12	78.12
5	90.02	90.02
8	112.95	
8	31.91	144.86
10	419.89	419.89
12	265.03	
12	19.18	
12	100.28	384.49
15	273.19	273.19
17	42.12	42.12
19	86.03	
19	4.12	90.15
21	29.30	29.30
24	162.27	
24	110.17	272.44
26	503.85	503.85
28	90.49	
29	12.65	
30	102.87	206.01
	3,385.14	3,385.14

CASH DISBURSEMENTS

Date	Check No.	Amount
19+1		
May 1	101	259.12
2	102	418.35
2	103	262.19
3	104	110.03
4	105	111.55
4	106	2.69
6	107	100.35
7	108	120.39
10	109	142.18
11	110	210.29
13	111	124.15
17	112	69.80
18	113	135.14
20	114	109.02
26	115	147.18
27	116	216.08
29	117	57.33
		2,595.84

Required:

(a) A bank reconciliation as of May 31, 19+1.

(b) Any necessary journal entries, assuming that the cash journals have been ruled and posted for the month of May.

Problem B7-3. Cassada Corporation maintains a bank account with Union Banking Company. The following information pertains to the month of November, 19+1.

(1) The ledger shows a balance of $1,669.72 on November 30, 19+1.

(2) The bank statement shows a balance of $2,031.55 on November 30, 19+1.

(3) Cash totalling $527.38 has not been deposited in the bank.

(4) An examination of the returned checks reveals that the following have not cleared: No. 197, $13.65; No. 198, $105.09; No. 210, $86.10; No. 213, $303.80; and No. 214, $440.83.

(5) The bank statement shows $40.80 as the amount deducted for a certain check, while the check was made out for $40.08.

(6) During November J. A. Gillis, a customer, stopped payment of his check for $182.64.

(7) The bank collected a noninterest-bearing note for the company's account: face, $155; collection charges, $2.90.

(8) Interest charges on outstanding loans, deducted by the bank, amounted to $20.

(9) The bookkeeper recorded one of Cassada Corporation's checks in the amount of $321.92 as $312.92; the account was Gordon Supply Company.

(10) A certified check of $134.39, payable to Small Company, is included with the checks returned.

Required:

(a) A bank reconciliation as of November 30, 19+1.

(b) Any journal entries required as of November 30, 19+1.

Problem B7-4. The following long-term investments were made by Miller Corporation during 19+3:

April 30—$100,000 of 6%, 20-year bonds of Hancock Company purchased at 98½.
Interest is paid annually on January 1. The bonds were issued January
1, 19+3.

July   1—$80,000 of 4½%, 15-year bonds of Glasgow Corporation purchased at 103.
Interest is paid semiannually on April 1 and October 1. The bonds were
issued on October 1, 19+1.

Required:

(a) A schedule showing the total amount of interest that will be earned on each invest-
ment if held to maturity.
(b) All journal entries required for the years 19+3 and 19+4, assuming Miller Cor-
poration closes its books annually on December 31.

Problem B7-5. The following information relates to the bond investments of Glynn Company as of
December 31, 19+1, the end of the company's accounting period. Prepare amortization
schedules for each of the bond investments.

Bonds	No.	Face	Purchase Date	Cost	Interest Dates	Rate	Maturity
A Co.	10	$1,000	4/1/+1	102	2/1; 8/1	6%	8/1/+4
B Co.	12	1,000	10/1/+1	95	10/1	4%	10/1/+9

Monetary Assets–Receivables

ACCOUNTS RECEIVABLE

Accounts receivable in the balance sheet. The amount shown under the Current Assets caption as accounts receivable (without any further description) should include only amounts receivable on open account from customers. Accounts receivable from stockholders, officers, or employees should be shown separately in the balance sheet unless the receivables arose from sales and are collectible in accordance with the company's regular terms; accounts with such individuals for loans or other advances may be listed under the Current Assets caption if the terms of such receivables and the company's experience with them indicate that they will be collected as soon as ordinary current receivables; otherwise, they should be shown under the caption of Sundry Assets, thus:

Sundry assets:
    Amount receivable from officers and employees . . . . $xx,xxx

Sundry assets are reported on the balance sheet following long-term investments.
If goods are purchased from and sold to the same party, it is advisable to keep two accounts: one for the account receivable and the other for the account payable.

It is recommended that such receivables and payables not be offset when a balance sheet is prepared.

Trade discounts. Customers are frequently allowed deductions, known as trade discounts, from the list price of merchandise. Reasons for allowing such discounts are:

(a) To avoid frequent publication of catalogues; the prices can be changed merely by changing the discount rates.

(b) To allow dealers a deduction from an advertised retail price; this practice is followed, for instance, by publishers whose advertisements state the retail prices of their books, dealers being allowed a discount from the published, or list, price.

Trade discounts may be stated as a single rate or as a series of rates. For instance, assume that the list price is $2,000 and that trade discounts of 30 per cent and 10 per cent are allowed; the sales price is computed as follows:

List price	$2,000
First discount—30% of $2,000	600
Remainder after first discount	$1,400
Second discount—10% of $1,400	140
Sales price	$1,260

Or:

$$(100\% - 30\%, \text{ or } 70\%) - (10\% \text{ of } 70\%, \text{ or } 7\%) = 63\%.$$

$$63\% \text{ of } \$2,000 = \$1,260$$

No entries are made in the accounts for trade discounts; entries for sales are made at list price less trade discounts.

Cash discounts. Cash discounts are deductions allowed to customers to induce them to pay their bills within a definite time. Cash discount terms are stated in the following manner: 2/10; n/30 (read, 2% in 10 days; net* 30 days). This means that a 2 per cent discount will be allowed if the invoice is paid within 10 days from its date, and that the purchaser, by foregoing the discount, can postpone payment of the invoice until 30 days after its date.

Cash discounts are known as sales discounts to the seller and as purchase discounts to the purchaser. The seller records cash discounts as follows, assuming merchandise having an invoice price of $1,000 is sold under the terms of 2/10; n/30 and is paid for within the discount period:

Cash	980	
Sales discounts	20	
Accounts receivable		1,000

---

*The word "net" is a misnomer, because the gross amount of the invoice (*not the net amount*) is payable after ten days.

Because sales discounts reduce the amount received for sales, they are shown in the income statement contra to sales and not as an expense.

Returns and allowances. Customers, after receiving merchandise sold to them, may return the goods because they are not of the kind or quality ordered, or they may request and receive an allowance on the price. For the selling company such transactions reduce the revenue from sales of merchandise and are recorded as follows, assuming the return of merchandise that was sold for $200 and which has not been paid for:

Sales returns and allowances	200	
Accounts receivable		200

For the purchasing company such transactions reduce the cost of the goods acquired for resale.

The income statement treatment of the *contra* sales accounts just discussed is illustrated below.

Partial Income Statement

Sales		$40,560
Deduct:		
Sales returns and allowances	$200	
Sales discounts	640	840
Net sales		$39,720

There is a decided trend in modern accounting practice toward simplifying the income statement by omitting the sales deductions and starting with net sales. This is particularly true in the case of widely circulated statements.

Uncollectible accounts. It would be quite rare for a business to collect all of its accounts receivable; some losses are almost certain to occur. Therefore, if the balance sheet is to present fairly the financial position of the company, it should show the *net* amount that probably will be collected from the aggregate accounts receivable.

Moreover, the income statement for each period should include all losses and expenses applicable to the period. Losses from uncollectible accounts should, therefore, be deducted in the statement for the period in which the losses are incurred. In what period are bad debt losses incurred? Bad debt losses result from selling merchandise to customers who do not pay their accounts; such losses are, therefore, incurred in the period in which the sales are made. If goods were sold in 19— to customers whose accounts were found in 19+1 to be worthless, the loss was *incurred* in 19—. The loss was not incurred in 19+1; it was merely *discovered* in that year.

Thus it is evident that both the balance sheet and the income statement would be incorrect unless recognition were given to the probable losses on accounts receivable.

Assume that a firm has total accounts receivable of $13,000 as of December 31, 19—, the first year of operations, and it is estimated that $1,000 of this amount will not be collected. The following adjusting entry should be made at the end of 19—:

Bad debts expense	1,000	
Allowance for uncollectibles		1,000
Estimated loss on uncollectible accounts.		

Bad debts are usually classified as an operating expense in the income statement; however, some accountants advocate reporting them contra to sales, along with sales discounts and returns and allowances.

Nature of allowance account. The estimated loss from uncollectible accounts cannot be credited to Accounts Receivable, because this account should show the gross amount owed by all customers. Therefore, we credit Allowance for Uncollectibles (sometimes called Allowance for Doubtful Accounts), which is a contra account to Accounts Receivable. The balances of the two accounts are shown in the balance sheet as follows:

Accounts receivable $13,000
Less allowance for uncollectibles 1,000 $12,000

Writing off uncollectible accounts. After the adjusting journal entry shown above is posted, the ledger contains the following balances:

	Debit	Credit
Accounts receivable	$13,000	
Allowance for uncollectibles ...		$1,000

Let us now assume that it has been found impossible to collect $75 owed by P. K. Lane; this amount should be removed from the accounts receivable by the following journal entry:

Allowance for uncollectibles   75
    Accounts receivable (P. K. Lane)   75
    Amount owed by P. K. Lane found to be uncollectible.

It should be noted that the write-off is charged to the allowance account and not to Bad Debts Expense. If we debited the expense account when the *estimated* loss was recorded and later with *ascertained* losses, a double charge to expense would result.

Estimating bad debts. Two methods of estimating the adjustment for uncollectibles at the end of the accounting period are discussed below.

PERCENTAGE OF NET SALES: Assume that a ledger contains the following balances on December 31:

	Debit	Credit
Accounts receivable	$20,000	
Allowance for uncollectibles ...		$ 315
Sales		215,000
Sales returns and allowances ...	1,600	

Assume, further, that experience shows that the allowance account should be credited with a provision for bad debts equal to one-half of 1 per cent of the sales for the year less returns and allowances. The provision is computed as follows:

Sales	$125,000
Deduct sales returns and allowances	1,600
Net sales	$213,400

Provision $= \frac{1}{2}$ of 1% of $213,400 $= $1,067.

This amount is debited to Bad Debts Expense and credited to Allowance for Uncollectibles. The balance in the allowance account is now $315 + $1,067, or $1,382.

It should be noted that this approach is income-statement oriented. Emphasis is placed on determining the estimated portion of sales revenues which will ultimately prove to be uncollectible.

ESTIMATING PROBABLE COLLECTIBILITY OF ACCOUNTS: An alternative approach to estimating uncollectibles is balance-sheet oriented. Emphasis is placed on determining the net amount at which accounts receivable should be reported in the balance sheet. This is done by analyzing the accounts receivable to see if the balance in the Allowance for Uncollectibles is considered sufficient.

After the balance needed in the allowance account has been determined, that amount is compared with its existing balance. The bad debts expense for the period is the difference between the required balance and the existing balance. For example, suppose that management reviewed the accounts receivable, totaling $20,000 (see the preceding illustration), and decided that a $1,500 balance was required in the allowance account. The bad debts expense for the period would be computed as follows:

Balance required in allowance account	$1,500
Existing balance in allowance account	315
Amount to be debited to Bad Debts Expense and credited to Allowance	
for Uncollectibles	$1,185

The preparation of an aging schedule is one way of estimating the probable collectibility of the accounts. For example, experience may indicate that an allowance account balance of $4,460, as computed below, would be desirable, considering the age-distribution of the $77,000 of accounts receivable.

Age	Accounts Receivable Balances	Estimated Per Cent Uncollectible	Allowance Account Requirement
1–30 days old	$32,000	1	$ 320
31–60 days old	21,000	2	420
61–90 days old	14,000	8	1,120
91 days to 6 months old	8,000	20	1,600
Over 6 months old	2,000	50	1,000
Total accounts receivable	$77,000		
Total allowance account requirement			$4,460

However, supplementary information must also be considered; some accounts which are not old may be of doubtful collectibility, whereas accounts long past due may be collectible.

We may obtain the age-distribution by preparing a schedule of the accounts receivable on columnar paper, with columns headed to indicate various ages, such as *1 to 30 days, 31 to 60 days, 61 to 90 days, 91 days to 6 months,* and *Over 6 months.* The balance of each debtor's account is analyzed to determine the age of the component elements, and the aging schedule is completed as shown below:

Accounts Receivable Aging Schedule
November 30, 19—

Name	Total	1–30 Days	31–60 Days	61–90 Days	91 Days to Six Months	Over Six Months	Credit Balances
J. H. Boyce	775	525		250			
Fred Campbell	1,200		1,200				
G. C. Crane	800				800		
James Dawson	250					250	
Henry Edwards . . .							50
Williams Company	750				750		
Total debit balances	77,000	32,000	21,000	14,000	8,000	2,000	
Total credit balances							175

In addition to being useful in the computation of the allowance account requirements, data by age groups may be used by management to determine whether collections from customers are lagging. Such a trend would be revealed by a shift in the percentage relationships among the age groups, with the older balances making up a larger share of the total receivables than heretofore.

Bad debt recoveries. Suppose that an account receivable previously written off is collected. If subsequent developments indicate that the entry writing off the account was an error, the write-off should be reversed. To illustrate, assume that P. K. Lane's account in the amount of $75 had been written off. The reversing entry, at the time of the collection from Lane, will be as follows:

Accounts receivable (P.K. Lane)   75
    Allowance for uncollectibles   75
        To reverse entry writing off Lane's account.

The cash collection will then be recorded by an entry debiting Cash and crediting Accounts Receivable (P.K. Lane).

The proper treatment of partial collections on written-off accounts is somewhat more difficult to determine because it depends upon the probability of further collections. To illustrate, assume that, after Lane's account was written off, he paid $30. If this collection and other facts indicate that the account may be collected in full, the entries should be:

Accounts receivable (P.K. Lane)	75	
Allowance for uncollectibles		75
Cash	30	
Accounts receivable (P.K. Lane)		30

If no more collections are expected, the entries should be:

Accounts receivable (P.K. Lane)	30	
Allowance for uncollectibles		30
Cash	30	
Accounts receivable (P.K. Lane)		30

Allowance accounts for returns and allowances, cash discounts, and freight. A company that has total accounts receivable of $20,000 on December 31 has provided an allowance for uncollectibles of $1,000. This may be an adequate provision for bad debt losses, but it does not necessarily follow that the company will collect $19,000 from the accounts. Customers may demand credits for returned merchandise and allowances on defective goods; many of the debtors will take the cash discounts to which they are entitled; and, if the goods are sold on terms which require the customers to pay the freight but allow them to deduct such payments in remitting for the merchandise, deductions will be taken for such freight.

Theoretically, all these prospective deductions should be provided for by allowance accounts so that the accounts receivable will be stated in the balance sheet at the estimated net amount which will be collected after allowing for all such deductions. As a practical matter, however, such provisions are rarely made, primarily because the omission of such adjustments usually will have no significant effect on net income.

This might not be the case for the first year of a new business. Its accounts would show a full year's sales with something less than a full year's deductions from sales for discounts and returns and allowances. But in the second and succeeding years, since any deductions relating to prior years' sales are recorded when taken, the accounts for discounts and returns and allowances will show deductions covering a full period.

Hence, unless large fluctuations occurred in sales deductions, the failure to adjust for prospective returns and allowances and discounts affects the financial statements only in that accounts receivable will be stated at an amount slightly above their cash realizable value. Most accountants feel that this is not serious, since the amounts involved are so small. If, in a given case, it should develop that the amounts involved were significant, adjusting entries of the type indicated above could be recorded.

Discounts on returned sales. Assume that a customer buys merchandise for $1,000 subject to a 2 per cent discount, and that he pays the invoice within the discount period with a check for $980. Subsequently, he returns one-tenth of the goods, which had been billed to him at $100 and which were paid for at the net amount of $98. Should he receive credit for $100 or $98?

Although this is largely a matter of policy, it would seem that the credit should be $98 if he is to be reimbursed in cash, and $100 if the credit is to be traded out.

The reasoning may be made clearer if we assume that the entire shipment is returned. Allowing a credit of $1,000 to be repaid in cash would open the way to abuses of the cash discount privilege, whereas allowing a credit of only $980 payable in merchandise would cause the customer to lose the benefit of having paid his bill within the discount period.

Freight paid and discount taken by customer. It is assumed that a customer buys merchandise amounting to $1,000. The terms specify that he is to pay the freight, which amounts to $40, and deduct it in remitting for the merchandise; he is also allowed 2 per cent discount for cash within 10 days.

Should the 2 per cent discount be based on the $1,000 invoice, or on this amount less the $40 freight?

The discount should be based on the full amount of the invoice, because the customer is paying the freight for the seller, and he is entitled to a cash discount for the funds so used. The settlement should, therefore, be made as follows:

Invoice		$1,000
Deduct: Freight	$40	
Discount—2% of $1,000	20	60
Net amount of remittance		$ 940

Sales discounts on customers' partial payments. Suppose that a customer buys merchandise for $1,000 subject to terms of 2/10; n/30, that he is not able to pay the entire invoice, but sends a check for $588 in partial settlement within the ten-day discount period. Since the partial payment was made within the discount period, the seller may, as a matter of policy, allow the discount on the partial payment.

If the discount is granted on partial payments, the amount collected is the net amount, and therefore it is necessary to determine the amount of the gross obligation settled by the partial payment. This can be computed as follows:

$$\$588 \div .98 = \$600$$

In journal form, the collection would be recorded as follows:

Cash	588	
Sales discounts	12	
Accounts receivable		600
To record partial collection of an account receivable within the discount period.		

Accounts receivable from installment sales. An *installment sale* is a sales arrangement whereby the selling price is collected in periodic installments. A down payment usually is required. The uncollected balance may or may not be subject to interest. By mortgage or otherwise, the seller usually has the right to recover the sold property if the installments are not collected in accordance with the sales agreement. If repossession occurs, the repossessed property should be put back in the inventory at its value at the time of repossession and not at an amount equal to the uncollected balance in the installment account receivable.

> Installment receivables, if due in accordance with terms prevailing through-
> out an industry, are considered as current assets even though the collec-
> tion period may be quite lengthy.

Installment-basis accounting. If the installment-basis method is adopted for income-
measurement purposes, the gross margin on installment sales (sales minus cost of
installment sales) is taken into income as cash collections are received from the
installment customers. Thus, if a customer has paid 60 per cent of the sales price,
60 per cent of the gross margin arising from the installment sale is taken into income
and 40 per cent of the gross margin is deferred. In effect, each collection is regarded
as including gross margin and a return of cost in the same proportion that these
elements are included in the selling price. For instance, if an item costing $100 is
sold for $150, payable in ten equal installments, each collection of $15 would be
regarded as including a $10 return of cost and $5 of gross margin. The installment-
basis method is acceptable for income tax purposes. An accountant would consider
it acceptable for accounting purposes only if the method resulted in a better matching
of revenue and expense than would be achieved by taking the gross margin into
income in the period of sale.

Selling merchandise by the installment-sales method may complicate the matching
of revenue and expense for several reasons. In the first place, it may be more difficult
to estimate the losses from uncollectible accounts on installment sales than on ordi-
nary sales. In part this is due to the fact that the collection period often is much
longer under an installment-sales contract, hence there is additional uncertainty.
Also, installment receivables often are more vulnerable to collection delinquencies
should a slowdown in business activity occur than are the receivables of customers
who do not buy on the installment plan. Although the seller generally has the right
to repossess the property in case of nonpayment of installments, such right is not
always an adequate protection against loss because of the status of the property
as second-hand merchandise.

In the second place, installment sales involve more expenses in periods subsequent
to the period of sale than are usually incurred in connection with ordinary sales.
There are more collection and accounting costs. Also, the seller may find it necessary
to make repairs to the property before the sale price is completely collected because
the purchaser may otherwise refuse to make additional payments or to preserve the
value of the property which serves as security for the receivable. And, if the mer-
chandise is repossessed, costs may be incurred in reconditioning it for resale.

The above complications lend some appeal to installment-basis accounting. How-
ever, one can achieve a theoretically acceptable matching of revenue and expense
by taking the entire gross margin into income in the period of sale and making
adequate provisions in the same period for subsequent losses and expenses. When
experience indicates that reasonably accurate provisions can be made for the "after
costs," this alternative is preferred over the installment method for accounting
purposes.

NOTES AND ACCEPTANCES RECEIVABLE

Definition. The following definition is quoted from the Negotiable Instruments Act: "A negotiable promissory note within the meaning of this act is an unconditional promise in writing made by one person to another, signed by the maker, engaging to pay on demand or at a fixed or determinable future time a sum certain in money to order or bearer."

Maturity. Notes may be drawn to mature:

(1) On a date named in the note, thus: "On June 30, 19—, I promise to pay."
(2) On demand, thus: "On demand, I promise to pay."
(3) Upon the expiration of a stated period of time; the time may be stated in several ways, as indicated below.

    (a) Years, thus: "One year after date, I promise to pay."
        Such notes will mature in a subsequent year on the same day of the same month as the date of issue, except that notes issued on February 29, payable in a year having only 28 days in February, will mature on February 28.

    (b) Months, thus: "Three months after date, I promise to pay."
        Such notes will mature in a subsequent month on the same day of the month as the date of issue, except that: (1) notes dated on the 31st of a month and maturing in a month having only 30 days will mature on the 30th of the month; and (2) notes dated on the 29th, 30th, or 31st of a month and maturing in February will mature on the last day of February.

    (c) Days, thus: "Sixty days after date, I promise to pay."
        The method of determining the maturity of such notes is illustrated by the following computation of the maturity of a 60-day note dated December 15, 19+2:

Remaining days in December	16
Days in January	31
	47
Days in February	13 Maturity
	60

Entries for note receivable transactions. Notes are recorded in the notes receivable account at their face amount. Entries for note receivable transactions are described below.

ENTRIES FOR RECEIPT OF NOTES: The entries for the receipt of noninterest-bearing and interest-bearing notes are the same.

If a note is received for a cash loan, debit Notes Receivable and credit Cash.
If a note is received to settle, or apply on, an account receivable, debit Notes Receivable and credit Accounts Receivable.
If a note is received immediately for a sale, the entry *might be:* debit Notes Receivable and credit Sales. However, it is considered better practice to

make the two following entries, so that evidence of the transaction will appear in the customer's account: debit Accounts Receivable and credit Sales; debit Notes Receivable and credit Accounts Receivable.

ENTRIES FOR COLLECTION OF NOTES: The entries for the collection of notes depend on whether or not they are interest-bearing.

If the note does not bear interest, debit Cash and credit Notes Receivable.
If the note bears interest, debit Cash and credit Notes Receivable and Interest Revenue. If an end-of-period adjusting entry was made for accrued interest on the note, the amount of the accrual should be credited to Interest Receivable when the interest is collected, and the remainder should be credited to Interest Revenue.

ENTRIES IF NOTE IS DISHONORED: If the maker of a note does not pay it at maturity, the note is said to be *dishonored.* If the maker of the note is a customer, the dishonored note should be charged back to Accounts Receivable.

If the note does not bear interest, debit Accounts Receivable and credit Notes Receivable.
If the note bears interest, debit Accounts Receivable and credit Notes Receivable and Interest Revenue. The interest has been earned and the debtor owes the interest as well as the face of the note.

If, at the maturity of a note, we make a partial collection, only the uncollected portion should be charged back to Accounts Receivable, because the note was only partially dishonored.

ENTRIES FOR A RENEWAL NOTE: If a note is wholly or partially dishonored and a new note is received, the entry for the dishonor should be made as described above and the receipt of the new note should be recorded by debiting Notes Receivable and crediting Accounts Receivable.

Drafts. Instead of asking a debtor to give him a promissory note, a creditor may "draw a draft" on the debtor. Such a draft is illustrated below:

$100.00   *Chicago, Illinois,*   June 15,   *19--*

Thirty days after date   *Pay to the order of OURSELVES*

One Hundred-no/100 - *Dollars*

To   George Hill,

Freeport, Illinois.   *Peter Rowe*

DRAFT

Parties to a draft. The parties to a draft are:

The drawer—the person who draws and signs the draft.
The drawee—the person to whom the draft is addressed.
The payee—the person to whom the payment is to be made.

Although there are always three *parties* to a draft, only two *persons* may be involved. Thus, Peter Rowe is both the drawer and the payee of the illustrative draft. If Rowe had ordered Hill to pay Robinson, Rowe would have been the drawer, Hill the drawee, and Robinson the payee; such drafts are now rarely used.

Acceptance. The draft illustrated above should be presented to Hill to obtain his agreement to pay it at maturity. This agreement is called *acceptance* of the draft and is expressed in the manner illustrated below:

$100.00	Chicago, Illinois, _____ June 15, _____ 19--
Thirty days after date	Pay to the order of OURSELVES
One Hundred-no/100 -Dollars	
To_ George Hill,	
Freeport, Illinois.	_Peter Rowe_

Accepted George Hill

AN ACCEPTANCE

After a draft has been accepted, it is called an *acceptance.* Thus, the word *acceptance* has two meanings: the act of accepting, and an accepted draft.

Acceptances usually are payable a certain period after the date of the draft; thus a draft drawn on June 15, payable 30 days after date, will be due on July 15, regardless of the date on which it is accepted.

Accounting for acceptances. An accepted draft, like a promissory note, is a debtor's written agreement to pay a certain sum of money at a definite future date. Therefore, the accounting for acceptances receivable is the same as the accounting for notes receivable, previously described. Of course, no entry is made by the drawer at the time he draws the draft, because the drawee may refuse to accept.

Since a promissory note and an acceptance are similar in nature, it is customary to record both notes and acceptances in the notes receivable and notes payable accounts.

Uncollectible notes receivable. Possible losses on notes and acceptances receivable may be combined with the estimate of losses on accounts receivable. The debit to Bad Debts Expense covers estimated losses on both accounts and notes receivable. When a note is determined to be uncollectible, it should be written off against the allowance account. If the note came from a customer, it is customary to charge it back to Accounts Receivable before writing it off against the allowance account.

Discounting notes and acceptances receivable. Instead of borrowing money on its own note payable, a business may obtain funds by transferring to a bank any notes or acceptances receivable that the bank is willing to take. When a note or acceptance receivable is discounted at a bank, any difference between the carrying value of the instrument discounted (the carrying value includes the face of the instrument plus any recorded accrued interest thereon) and the cash proceeds is customarily recorded as interest. Thus, if the proceeds exceed the carrying value of the note or acceptance receivable, the difference is recorded as Interest Revenue. On the other hand, if the proceeds are less than the carrying value, the difference is recorded as Interest Expense. However, it is also acceptable to use a special account for the difference, as follows:

> Gain from Discounting Notes Receivable
> (This account is credited when the proceeds are greater than the carrying value of the negotiable instrument discounted.)
> Loss from Discounting Notes Receivable
> (This account is debited when the proceeds are less than the carrying value of the negotiable instrument discounted.)

A business obtaining funds in this way usually assumes an obligation to pay the note or acceptance if the party primarily liable on the paper fails to do so. If, at a balance sheet date, any such discounted receivables have not matured, a balance sheet footnote should disclose the contingent liability, thus:

Note: On December 31, 19—, the company was contingently liable on notes receivable discounted in the amount of $15,000.

ASSIGNMENT

MATERIAL

QUESTIONS

1. What amounts are properly includible as accounts receivable in the balance sheet?
2. What are cash discounts? How are cash discounts accounted for in the financial statements?
3. Why should estimated uncollectible accounts be recognized prior to the time they actually prove to be uncollectible?
4. Describe the procedure for writing off an uncollectible account.
5. There are two methods for estimating the adjustment for uncollectible accounts. Name the methods and explain the difference between them.
6. What is an aging schedule? How is it used by the accountant?
7. Describe the procedure for recording bad debt recoveries.
8. What is meant by the installment basis of accounting for installment sales? What is an alternative method of accounting for installment sales?
9. What is a promissory note?
10. When is a note said to be dishonored? How is a customer's dishonored note accounted for?
11. What would be the due date for a 90-day note dated March 20? What would be the due date of the note if it were payable three months after date?
12. Describe the procedure involved in accounting for the discounting of notes and acceptances receivable.

SHORT EXERCISES

E8-1. The accounts on page 195 pertain to Ellijay Company for the years 19+1 and 19+2.

Give the following amounts for both 19+1 and 19+2:

(a) Bad debts expense reported on the income statement.
(b) Worthless accounts actually written off.
(c) Net accounts receivable reported on the balance sheet at the end of the year.

ACCOUNTS RECEIVABLE

19+1				
Jan. 1	Balance			12,000 Dr.
July 10			800	
Dec. 31		26,000	22,000	
19+2				
May 3			600	
Aug. 18			400	
Dec. 6			300	
Dec. 31		34,000	29,000	

ALLOWANCE FOR UNCOLLECTIBLES

19+1				
Jan. 1	Balance			1,000 Cr.
July 10		800		
Dec. 31			1,100	
19+2				
May 3		600		
Aug. 18		400		
Dec. 6		300		
Dec. 31			1,500	

E8-2. From the following selected accounts of Cedartown Corporation, prepare an income statement in good form for the year ended June 30, 19+9.

Selling expense	$ 4,300
Cash	8,100
Allowance for uncollectibles	500
Sales	53,000
Accounts receivable	12,400
Accounts payable	9,700
Sales returns and allowances	450
Office expense	3,300
Cost of goods sold	39,000
Merchandise inventory	11,200
Bad debts expense	800
Rent expense	1,200
Depreciation expense—Equipment	2,000
Sales discounts	1,400

E8-3. The ledger of Carollen Company, which closes its books on December 31, contained the following balances, before adjustment, on December 31, 19+6: Accounts Receivable, $15,000 debit; Allowance for Uncollectibles, $100 debit. It is estimated that $800 of the accounts will ultimately prove to be uncollectible.

On January 15, 19+7, the $300 account of Cory Donald is written off as uncollectible. On August 20, 19+7, Donald made a $200 payment on the account and is expected to pay the balance by September 30, 19+7.

Present all entries needed to record the information above.

E8-4. Demorest Corporation had the following note transactions during 19+2:

(1) Received a note from customer A in settlement of a $500 account receivable.

(2) Received payment of $1,000 plus interest of $10 on a note received in 19+1. Half of the interest was applicable to 19+1.

(3) Received a note from customer B in settlement of a $400 account receivable.

(4) The note of customer A matures, with interest of $25. The maker dishonors the note.

(5) Customer C gives the corporation a $700 note in settlement of an account receivable.

(6) Customer B pays his note plus interest of $12.

(7) Interest earned on the note of customer C is $14 on December 31, 19+2.

What is the amount to be reported for each of the following on the financial statements prepared at the end of 19+2?

(a) Notes receivable.

(b) Interest receivable.

(c) Interest revenue.

PROBLEMS

Problem A8-1. The following amounts are taken from the trial balance of Vincent Company on December 31, 19+1.

	Debit	Credit
Accounts receivable	90,000	
Allowance for uncollectibles		400
Sales		150,000
Sales returns and allowances	2,300	
Sales discounts	4,700	

(a) Assuming that the firm estimates bad debts to be 1% of net sales, write the adjusting entry required as of December 31, 19+1.

(b) Assuming that the firm ages the accounts receivable and estimates that $2,000 of the total will ultimately prove to be uncollectible, write the adjusting entry required as of December 31, 19+1.

(c) The $500 account of customer A proves to be worthless on January 15, 19+2. Show the entry to write the account off the books.

Problem A8-2. The following information pertains to notes received from customers by Suggs Company during 19+1.

Date of Note	Face Amount	Rate of Interest	Time Period
(1) March 22, 19+1	$200	4%	90 days
(2) April 5, 19+1	300	3%	2 months
(3) June 8, 19+1	150	$4\frac{1}{2}\%$	3 months
(4) September 28, 19+1	400	5%	120 days
(5) November 17, 19+1	250	4%	60 days

Determine the due date and the total amount that will have to be paid at maturity for each note.

Problem A8-3. Below are listed certain selected transactions of Fortenberry Company for the month of September, 19+1.

(1) A collection of $392 was received within the discount period in satisfaction of a $400 account receivable.

(2) Subsequently the customer in (1) returned one-fourth of the merchandise and directed that his account be credited.

(3) A credit of $50 was given for returned merchandise, which had originally been delivered to the customer last year. Fortenberry Company uses the following account: Allowance for Expected Returns.

(4) A $500 cash loan was granted to an employee.

(5) The company paid $25 to a customer to eliminate his credit balance in the subsidiary ledger.

(6) The account of C. A. Janis in the amount of $450 was considered uncollectible and was written off.

(7) A request was received from a supplier that his bill of $70, which has been recorded by a credit to Accounts Payable, be offset against the supplier's account with Fortenberry Company.

(8) Fortenberry Company paid $700 to a bank because a note previously discounted with the bank had been dishonored. The maker of the note was a customer of Fortenberry Company.

(9) The company accepted a draft covering a shipment previously recorded by a $750 credit to Accounts Payable.

(10) The company accepted $150 from C. A. Janis and marked his overdue account as paid.

(11) A 6%, 60-day, $1,000 note held by Fortenberry Company was dishonored. The note was received from a customer earlier in this fiscal period.

(12) A 4%, 90-day, $1,000 note was collected on its maturity date, September 30.

The company closes its books on August 31.
Prepare journal entries for the above transactions, omitting explanations.

Problem A8-4. The following transactions of Duncan Corporation occurred during the month of March, 19+1.

March 3—Sold goods to Roger Parker on account, $3,000.
　　　 8—Sold goods to S. Babcock on account, $1,413.
　　　 11—Sold goods to Warner and Darrow on account, $725.
　　　 14—Issued a credit memo for goods returned by S. Babcock, $160.
　　　 17—Received a check from S. Babcock, $800.
　　　 21—Received a check from Warner and Darrow for $725.
　　　 25—Sold goods to Roger Parker on account, $629.
　　　 30—Issued a credit memo for goods returned by Roger Parker, $138.
　　　 30—Issued a credit memo for goods returned by Warner and Darrow, $210.

Required:

(a) Journal entries for the above transactions. Omit explanations.

(b) Subsidiary ledger accounts (omit posting references).

(c) A schedule of accounts receivable as of March 31, 19+1.

Problem A8-5. Sparks Corporation had the following transactions during October and November of 19+1.

October   18—Sold goods to Dougherty Company for $820, freight charges to be paid by the customer. Terms, 3/10; n/30.

23—Sold goods to Floyd Corporation for $543. Terms, 3/10; n/30.

24—Sold goods to Bixler, Inc., for $1,230. Terms, 3/10; n/30.

26—Floyd Corporation returned goods with an invoice price of $100. A credit memo was issued.

27—Received a check from Dougherty Company, accompanied by a paid freight bill for $36.50, in payment of the goods purchased on October 18.

November 6—Received a check from Bixler, Inc., for $800 to apply on account. It is the company's policy to allow discounts on customers' partial payments.

9—Received a check from Floyd Corporation for payment in full.

10—Sold goods to Lawrence and Associates, $630. Terms, 3/10; n/30.

12—A noninterest-bearing note receivable for $590 from Mastin Company, a customer, is dishonored and is written off as uncollectible.

18—Received a check from Lawrence and Associates in settlement of the November 10 transaction.

19—Received $300 from Linson Company, a customer whose account had been written off. A notification enclosed stated that the entire amount originally due, $620, is collectible.

20—Lawrence and Associates returned one-fourth of the shipment of November 10. A credit memo was issued.

22—Since the entry for the return by Lawrence and Associates created a credit balance in the account, Sparks Corporation issued a check covering the return.

Prepare general journal entries to record the above transactions.

Problem A8-6. The accounts on page 199 were on the books of Gillis Corporation on February 28, 19+2, the end of the firm's accounting period.

The company provides for doubtful accounts on the basis of the age of the receivables, as follows:

1—30 days. 1%
31—60 days. 5
61—90 days. 12
91 days to 6 months 30
Over 6 months. 50

There is a balance of $1,203.13 in the allowance for uncollectibles account on February 28, 19+2.

Required:

(a) An aging schedule.
(b) Computation of the required balance in the allowance for uncollectibles account on February 28, 19+2.
(c) The adjusting entry to adjust the allowance account.

ACCOUNTS RECEIVABLE LEDGER
R. Franklin

19+1							
Sept.	16			S 3	2,230		2,230
Oct.	9			S 4	4,920		7,150
	22			CR 9		2,230	4,920
Dec.	3			S 6	2,015		6,935
	16			S 6	2,906		9,841
19+2							
Jan.	6			CR12		2,906	6,935
Feb.	10			S 8	595		7,530
	22	Return, 2/10 sale		J 5		89	7,441

L. Moon

19+1							
Aug.	8			S 2	850		850
Dec.	14	Return		J 3		124	726
19+2							
Jan.	10			S 7	845		1,571
	17			S 7	211		1,782
Feb.	10			CR13		845	937

G. Willis

19+1							
Oct.	17			S 4	880		880
	24			CR 9		75	805
Dec.	3			S 6	428		1,233
19+2							
Jan.	17			S 7	283		1,516
Feb.	21	Note		J 5	.	428	1,088

C. Zachary

19+1							
June	8			S50	1,450		1,450
Sept.	12			S 3	314		1,764
	19			CR 8		1,250	514
	28			CR 8		314	200
Dec.	4			S 6	1,076		1,276
	6			CR11		538	738
19+2							
Feb.	10			S 8	567		1,305

Problem B8-1. Warden Company made the following sales during the month of January, 19+1.

Date	List Price	Trade Discounts	Credit Terms	Date of Payment
January 3	$500	30%	2/10; n/60	January 10
10	475	20%; 10%	2/10; n/60	January 19
16	380	15%; 10%	n/60	March 10
24	398	20%	2/10; n/30	February 20
30	440	none	3/10; n/60	February 8

Compute the amount required to pay each invoice on the date of payment.

Problem B8-2. The trial balance of Hall Company contains the following account balances on December 31, 19+1, the end of the firm's accounting period.

	Debit	Credit
Accounts receivable	60,000	
Allowance for uncollectibles		4,000
Sales		400,000
Sales returns and allowances	2,100	
Sales discounts..............................	5,600	

Prepare the adjusting entry at the end of 19+1 under each of the following assumptions:

(a) It is decided that the balance in the allowance account should be 10% of the total accounts receivable.
(b) An aging of the receivables indicates that $7,000 will ultimately prove to be uncollectible.
(c) It is estimated that 1½% of net sales will prove to be uncollectible.

Problem B8-3. The following information was taken from the ledger of Hayes, Inc., on June 30, 19+2, the end of the firm's accounting period. Adjustments have not been recorded for the period.

Accounts receivable .... $39,000 Debit balance
Allowance for uncollectibles .... 435 Debit balance

An aging of the accounts receivable indicates that accounts totaling $1,200 probably will prove to be uncollectible.

Summary information for the year ending June 30, 19+3, is as follows:

(1) Total sales were $280,000. Eighty per cent of the company's sales were on account.
(2) Uncollectible accounts written off totaled $1,490.
(3) Customers paid $272,000 on their accounts, including $250 that had been written off during the year as uncollectible.

It is estimated that accounts totaling $1,780 on June 30, 19+3, will prove to be uncollectible.

Prepare:

(a) The adjusting entry for uncollectible accounts as of June 30, 19+2.
(b) Entries to record the data for the year ending June 30, 19+3.
(c) The adjusting entry for uncollectible accounts as of June 30, 19+3.

Problem B8-4. Selected transactions of Deese Company for August, 19+1, are listed below.

(1) A 6% note in the amount of $1,500 is received from a customer whose account is past due. The note matures in 90 days.
(2) The above note is dishonored.
(3) Sold goods to Mickle Corporation for $800, freight charges to be paid by the customer. Terms, 3/10; n/30.
(4) Received a check for $1,455 to apply on account. The terms were 3/10; n/30, and the partial payment was received within the discount period. It is the corporation's policy to allow discounts on customers' partial payments.
(5) Cash is received from a customer to cover a $350 account previously written off as uncollectible.

(6) A cash refund is paid to a customer who returned one-half of the goods purchased under the following terms: Total invoice, $1,200; terms, 3/10; n/30. He had paid the invoice within the discount period.

(7) Received a check from Mickle Corporation within the discount period, accompanied by a paid freight bill for $50 which had been deducted, in payment of the sale in (3) above.

(8) Provision is made at year-end for prospective returns and allowances in the amount of $500.

(9) A $100 credit is granted for returned merchandise. The sale was made in the preceding period.

Problem B8-5. As of February 28, 19+2, information concerning the accounts receivable of Klindworth Company was as follows.

ACCOUNTS RECEIVABLE LEDGER
B. Arndt

19+1							
Dec.	4			S10	320		320
	20	Note		J 6		100	220
19+2							
Feb.	10			S12	400		620

R. Drake

19+1							
Nov.	3			S 9	75		75
	15			CR20		75	—
Dec.	8			S10	212		212
	10	Return		J 6		40	172
	12			S10	89		261
	15			CR21		172	89
19+2							
Jan.	9			S11	62		151
	15			CR22		62	89
	20			S11	214		303
	31			CR22		107	196

J. Messick

19+1							
July	8			S 5	246		246
Oct.	8			S 8	317		563
	12			S 8	490		1,053
Nov.	9			CR20		807	246
Dec.	8			S10	517		763
19+2							
Jan.	3			CR22		517	246
	11			S11	203		449
	15	Return on 1/11 sale		J 7		45	404
Feb.	1			S12	710		1,114

S. Pelham

19+1						
May	5		S 3	95		95
Sept.	15		S 7	212		307
Oct.	3		S 8	614		921
Nov.	1		CR20		614	307
Dec.	10		S10	530		837
	15	Return on 12/10 sale	J 6		57	780
19+2						
Jan.	5	Note, applicable to 12/10 sale	J 7		400	380

R. Tolliver

19+2						
Jan.	10		S11	472		472
	20	Note receivable	J7		200	272
	29		S11	409		681
Feb.	10		CR23		409	272
	15		S12	950		1,222
	22	Partial collection of 2/15 sale	CR23		650	572

J. Wallace

19+1						
Nov.	3		S 9	1,218		1,218
Dec.	4		CR21		1,218	—
19+2						
Jan.	8		S11	550		550
	15		CR22		200	350
Feb.	10	Return	J 8		462	112 Cr.

The company decided to provide for doubtful accounts as follows:

1—30 days.	2%
31—60 days.	5
61—90 days.	20
91 days to 6 months	35
Over 6 months.	80

In addition, the management wishes to provide for various amounts that probably will not be collected as a result of expected returns, discounts, and freight, as follows:

Total expected returns are estimated to be 7% of sales for the year; there are returns of $3,987 to date on the sales of the current fiscal year.

Total expected discounts are estimated to be 3% of sales for the year; there are discounts of $2,220.93 to date on the sales of the current fiscal year.

An analysis of the freight charges reveals that an additional $755.50 should be provided for expected deductions.

Sales for the fiscal year ended February 28, 19+2, were $81,904. The balance in the Allowance for Uncollectibles as of February 28, 19+2, is $239.14.

Prepare (a) an aging schedule; (b) the computation of the requirement for uncollectibles; (c) the computations of the current provisions for uncollectibles, expected returns, discounts, and freight deductions; and (d) related adjusting journal entries.

9

Inventory Costing and Control

Inventory accounting methods. There are two methods of accounting for inventories and, therefore, the cost of goods sold. They are:

Perpetual inventory method.
Periodic inventory method.

The basic characteristic of the perpetual inventory method is that it results in a running record of the inventory on hand. Changes in the inventory are recorded, as they occur, by debits and credits in the inventory account. Thus, *incoming* merchandise is recorded at cost by a debit to the inventory account. When merchandise is sold or returned to the supplier for some reason, and thus becomes *outgoing* merchandise, the inventory account is credited to record, at cost, the reduction of the asset. The offsetting debit is to Cost of Goods Sold when the merchandise is sold and to Accounts Payable when the merchandise is returned to the supplier.

Because, under the perpetual method, the cost of all merchandise purchased is debited to the inventory account and the cost of all goods sold or returned is credited to the inventory account, the inventory account balance should indicate the cost of goods on hand at the end of the period, provided that no merchandise has been lost or stolen.

Detailed perpetual inventory records. In most instances where the perpetual inventory method is in use, a *subsidiary record* in terms of quantities is maintained for each of the various types of goods held for sale. Cost data may also be included. Such a supplementary record is illustrated below.

	INVENTORY CARD					
DESCRIPTION	Room Air Conditioners					
	QUANTITIES			DOLLARS		
DATE	PURCHASED	SOLD	BALANCE	DEBIT	CREDIT	BALANCE
19--						
April 1			4			$1,200
3	10		14	$3,000		4,200
18		9	5		$2,700	1,500

As a check on the accuracy of these detailed or subsidiary records, it is advisable and customary to make counts of the physical inventory from time to time. Many concerns count portions of the inventory throughout the year and take a complete inventory annually.

When subsidiary records are maintained their purpose is to provide a record in greater detail than that supplied by a ledger account. Presumably, such details are useful to those managing the business or the subsidiary record would not be maintained. Subsidiary records are not part of the ledger, but the data recorded therein should tie in with the balance shown in the related ledger account. For example, assume that a business carries ten different kinds of merchandise in its inventory and that it maintains in addition to the inventory account in the ledger a subsidiary record which accounts for the changes in the inventory by kind of merchandise. Thus there would be an inventory card (subsidiary record) for each kind of merchandise; the total of the balances shown in the inventory cards should be in agreement with the inventory account balance in the general ledger, as illustrated below.

Balances per inventory cards:

Merchandise type 1	$ 100
2	200
3	300
4	400
5	500
6	400
7	300
8	200
9	100
10	1,000
Total per subsidiary record	$3,500
Balance per inventory account in the general ledger	$3,500

Periodic inventory method. Under the periodic inventory method, no running record of the inventory on hand is maintained. Incoming merchandise is recorded in a separate account; the usual account title is "Purchases." Also, no entry for the cost of goods sold is made at the time of the sale. Inventory amounts are determined periodically by making a physical count of the merchandise on hand. The accountant then makes use of an adjusting entry to have the accounts show the cost of goods sold for the period and the inventory balance as of the end of the period.

COST OF GOODS SOLD: Under the periodic inventory method the cost of goods sold is determined by the computation shown below. The amounts conform to the data used in the inventory card shown on page 204.

Computation		Source of Data
Inventory of merchandise at beginning of period		
(4 units at $300)	$1,200	Inventory account
Purchases during period (10 units at $300)	3,000	Purchases account
Cost of merchandise available for sale	$4,200	
Deduct inventory on hand at end of period		(a) For the quantity on hand: physical count.
(5 units at $300)	1,500	
		(b) For the cost information: business documents.
Cost of goods sold during period	$2,700	

END-OF-PERIOD ADJUSTING ENTRY: As indicated by the above cost-of-goods-sold computation, the cost of merchandise that was available for sale equals the total of the following ledger account balances:

Inventory (before adjustment this account balance shows the inventory which was on hand at the beginning of the period)	$1,200
Purchases	3,000
Amount that was available for sale	$4,200

An end-of-period adjusting entry can be used to apportion (regroup or reclassify) the amount that was available for sale, so that the ledger will show the following:

(1) Ending inventory—Unexpired cost (asset)	$1,500
(2) Cost of goods sold—Expired cost (expense)	2,700
Amount that was available for sale	$4,200

The adjusting entry applicable to the data used in the illustration, which would be dated as of April 30th, is as follows:

JOURNAL

19—					
Apr.	30	Inventory (ending)	1,500		
		Cost of goods sold	2,700		
		Inventory (beginning)		1,200	
		Purchases		3,000	
		To adjust the inventory account to show the end-of-period inventory and to place the cost of goods sold in a separate account.			

Inventory methods contrasted. The contrasting features of the two inventory methods can be seen in the following illustration based on the data shown in the Inventory Card.

Beginning inventory—4 units	$1,200
A purchase during the period—10 units	3,000
A sale during the period—9 units:	
Selling price	3,600
Cost of units sold	2,700
Ending inventory—5 units	1,500

Periodic Method   Perpetual Method

Beginning inventory:

Inventory			Inventory	
1,200			1,200	

Purchase:

Purchases 3,000			Inventory 3,000	
Accounts payable	3,000		Accounts payable	3,000

Sale:

Accounts receivable 3,600			Accounts receivable 3,600	
Sales	3,600		Sales	3,600

Adjusting entry under the periodic method—ending inventory determined by physical count:

Inventory 1,500	
Cost of goods sold 2,700	
Inventory	1,200
Purchases	3,000

Cost of goods sold 2,700	
Inventory	2,700

Content of inventory. The inventory should include all goods to which the company holds title, wherever they may be located.

If a business has received a sales order but is holding the goods for future delivery, it is important to determine whether title has passed. The mere fact that the goods have been segregated from other merchandise may or may not mean that title has passed to the customer. If title has passed, an entry for the sale should have been made and the goods should be excluded from the inventory; if title has not passed, no sales entry should have been made and the goods should be included in the inventory.

On the other hand, goods which have been ordered but not received by the purchaser at his inventory date may properly belong in the purchaser's inventory. If the goods are in transit, the general rule as to passing of title is as follows:

If the goods were shipped f.o.b. destination and have not arrived at the destination, they belong to the seller.

F.o.b. destination means "free on board cars (or other means of transportation) at destination." Under these terms the seller bears the transportation charges.

If the goods were shipped f.o.b. shipping point, they belong to the purchaser. F.o.b. shipping point means that the seller delivers the merchandise to the carrier, but the purchaser bears the transportation charges.

If title has passed and the goods are included in the inventory, an entry for the purchase should have been made.

A *consignment* is a shipment of merchandise from the owner (called the *consignor*) to another party (called the *consignee*) who attempts to sell the goods as an agent for the consignor. The consignor should not record consignments as sales, and the consignee should not record them as purchases, because there is no change in the ownership of the goods. Because the consignor has not made a sale, he should not take up any profit at the time of making the consignment; no sales entry should be made until a sale is reported by the consignee. Any unsold goods in the hands of the consignee at the end of the accounting period should be included in the consignor's inventory at cost plus consignment expenditures applicable to the unsold goods.

Cost of goods available for sale. The several elements that make up the cost of merchandise acquired for resale are included in the following tabulation.

Inventory—beginning of period			$ 7,000
Purchases (Invoice cost of goods purchased)		$30,000	
Add transportation in		1,000	
Total		$31,000	
Deduct:			
Purchase returns and allowances	$700		
Purchase discounts	500	1,200	29,800
Cost of goods available for sale			$36,800

When the periodic inventory method is in use, separate accounts are used for the items included in the above tabulation. The debit-credit plan for the separate accounts illustrated is indicated by the following journal entries based on the above data.

Purchases	30,000	
Accounts payable		30,000
Purchases for the period on account.		
Terms: 2/10; n/30.		
Transportation in	1,000	
Cash		1,000
Payment for transportation charges on goods purchased.		
Accounts payable	700	
Purchase returns and allowances		700
Purchase returns (and/or allowances) for the period.		
Accounts payable	25,000	
Purchase discounts		500
Cash		24,500
Payments on accounts within the discount period.		

When the perpetual inventory method is in use, such items are debited and credited to the inventory account, as indicated in the following ledger account.

INVENTORY

Beginning inventory...............	7,000		7,000 dr.
Purchases.....................	30,000		37,000 dr.
Transportation in.................	1,000		38,000 dr.
Purchase returns and allowances		700	37,300 dr.
Purchase discounts...............		500	36,800 dr.

Inventory determination. There are basically two steps involved in the determination of the amount at which the inventory is stated in the accounts and in the financial statements. These are:

(1) Determination of quantities.
(2) Determination of dollar amounts.

The selection of dollar amounts to be used involves a choice among several acceptable bases, some of which are widely applicable, while others are considered acceptable only under special circumstances. The two bases most widely applicable are:

(1) Cost.
(2) Lower of cost or market.

Cost. Cost of merchandise or materials purchased includes not only the purchase price but also any additional costs necessary to put the goods into condition for sale. These incidental costs include duties, freight, cartage, storage, insurance while the goods are being transported or stored, and costs incurred during any aging period.

Incidental costs frequently are omitted for inventory-costing purposes. Such omission is sanctioned by accountants if the incidental costs are immaterial in amount and if the effect of their exclusion on the financial statements is negligible.

From a theoretical standpoint, purchase discounts are unquestionably cost reductions. However, as a general rule, it is impractical to attempt to relate discounts taken to the merchandise on hand. Furthermore, the amount involved is relatively small. Therefore, it does not seem reasonable for accountants to insist that purchase discounts be given consideration when unit costs are determined for inventory-costing purposes.

Inventory cost selection. It is a readily observable fact that prices change. Therefore, identical goods may be acquired at different costs. Consequently, accountants are faced with the problem of determining which costs apply to the goods that have been sold, and which costs apply to the goods that remain in the inventory.

Several of the more widely used methods of selecting the costs which are to be regarded as applicable to the goods in the inventory are discussed in the following paragraphs.

For purposes of illustration, assume the following facts.

	Units	Unit Cost	Total
Beginning inventory	2	$10	$20
First purchase	1	11	11
Second purchase	1	10	10
Third purchase	1	12	12
Fourth purchase.	1	13	13
Cost of goods available for sale			$66
Total quantity available for sale	6		
Sold during the period	4		
Ending inventory	2		

Specific identification. If the goods on hand can be identified as pertaining to specific purchases, they may be inventoried at the costs shown by the related invoices. Assume, for instance, that the two units in the ending inventory can be identified as having been acquired by the second and fourth purchases; the cost for inventory purposes would be:

Units	Unit Cost	Total
1	$10	$10
1	13	13
Ending inventory		$23

Specific identification is not practical where each unit or lot is indistinguishable from another; the bookkeeping would be too costly. Also, the method has the disadvantage of being susceptible to schemes devised to manipulate earnings. A dishonest manager could select low-cost items to include in cost of goods sold, or claim that the low-cost items were sold even though higher-cost items were actually sold, to increase reported net income.

Weighted-average method. The cost of the goods available for sale is divided by the total units available for sale. The resulting average unit cost is used for pricing the ending inventory. The computation is illustrated below.

Cost of goods available for sale	$66
Total units available for sale	6
Average unit cost	$11
Ending inventory, $11 × 2	$22

The costs determined by the weighted-average method are affected by purchases early in the period as well as toward the end of the period; therefore, on a rising market, the weighted-average unit cost will be less than current unit cost, and, on a falling market, the weighted-average unit cost will be in excess of the current cost.

First-in, first-out method. This method is based on the assumption that the first goods purchased are the first to be sold, and that the goods which remain are of the last purchases. This method, referred to as the *fifo* (initial letters of *first-in, first-out*) method, is probably the one most commonly used. Applying this method to the facts used for illustrative purposes, the two units in the ending inventory would be regarded as having been acquired by the last two purchases and would be priced as follows:

Units	Unit Cost	Total
1	$12	$12
1	13	13
Ending inventory		$25

The assumption that the older stock is usually the first to be disposed of is generally in accordance with good merchandising policy. There are, of course, cases in practice where the assumption does not square with the facts; for instance, the first coal dumped on a dealer's pile will be the last sold.

This method has also been considered desirable because it produces an inventory valuation which is in conformity with price trends; because the inventory is assumed to consist of the most recent purchases and is costed at the most recent costs, the pricing follows the trend of the market.

Last-in, first-out method. Under this method, referred to as the *lifo* method, the oldest costs are assumed to be applicable to the goods on hand. In the case assumed here, the two units in the ending inventory would be costed at the unit cost used in costing the two units in the beginning inventory. Thus, the ending inventory would be computed as follows:

Units	Unit Cost	Total
2	$10	$20

If the ending inventory had been composed of three units, the third unit would be costed under *lifo* by using the unit cost applicable to the first purchase. Thus, an ending inventory of three units would total $31 under *lifo*. Graphically, the beginning and ending inventories under *lifo* can be shown as follows:

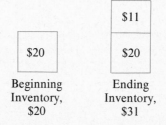

If, one year hence, the ending inventory should again consist of two units, the $11 unit would be dropped, since it was the last one added to the inventory, and the two units would be costed at $10 each for *lifo* inventory purposes.

Fifo—lifo and income results. The choice between *lifo* and *fifo* will have an effect on the amounts shown in a company's income statements for the cost of goods sold. This, in turn, will affect the gross margin and net income figures. To illustrate the point by a simple, and rather arbitrary, example, let us assume that a company sells one unit of a commodity each year. At the beginning of the first year it purchased one unit for $1 and marked it to sell for $1.50, because a gross margin of $.50 was considered necessary to cover expenses and leave a reasonable net income. Before any sale was made in the first year, the company purchased a second unit for $1.10 and raised its selling price of the commodity to $1.60—a price that will provide for replacing the merchandise and $.50 additional.

Assuming that one unit is subsequently sold for $1.60:

By the *fifo* method, the cost of goods sold and gross margin would be computed thus:

Sale	$1.60
Cost of unit sold	1.00
Gross margin	$ .60

and the ending inventory would be costed at $1.10.

By the *lifo* method, the cost of goods sold and gross margin would be computed thus:

Sale	$1.60
Cost of unit sold	1.10
Gross margin	$ .50

and the ending inventory would be costed at $1.00.

Suppose that two separate companies were involved in the above case, one using *fifo* and the other *lifo*. Actually, the companies would be in the same position; each would have sold one unit and have one unit remaining in the inventory, but their financial statements would not be identical.

Those favoring the *lifo* method think of the expression "last-in, first-out" as not necessarily referring to an assumption regarding the flow of goods, but rather to an assumption regarding the flow of costs. The advocates of *lifo* maintain that, during periods of changing costs and selling prices, more meaningful income statements are produced if relatively "current" costs are assigned to cost of sales; this, in their opinion, would achieve a better matching of costs and revenues.

Lower of cost or market. Under the "lower-of-cost-or-market" basis for determining the dollar amount of inventories, cost is used except under certain conditions, described later, where market is lower than cost. The term "market," as used here, means current replacement cost.

In making the necessary comparisons to see whether market is lower than cost, the accountant may refer to some of the following sources for information regarding market prices: current catalogues or other price lists; recent invoices; market price quotations as published in newspapers or trade journals; specific quotations furnished by suppliers for this purpose; current contracts for the purchase of like goods.

In the use of market prices for purposes of comparison with cost, if prices vary for different quantities, the accountant should use, for inventory purposes, the price for the quantity typically purchased by the business.

Application of cost or market. There are three ways of applying the cost-or-market method:

(1) By comparing the cost and market for each item in the inventory and using the lower figure in each instance.

DETERMINATION OF LOWER OF COST OR MARKET—
ITEM-BY-ITEM METHOD

| | | Unit Price | | Extension at Lower of Cost or Market |
	Quantity	Cost	Market	
Men's department:				
Suits	200	$40	$37	$ 7,400
Coats	100	31	35	3,100
Ladies' department:				
Dresses	300	10	12	3,000
Coats	80	30	32	2,400
Inventory at lower of cost or market				$15,900

(2) By comparing the total cost and market for major inventory categories and using the lower figure for each category.

DETERMINATION OF LOWER OF COST OR MARKET—
CATEGORY METHOD

| | | Unit Price | | Extended | | Lower of Cost or Market |
	Quantity	Cost	Market	Cost	Market	
Men's department:						
Suits	200	$40	$37	$ 8,000	$ 7,400	
Coats	100	31	35	3,100	3,500	
Total				$11,100	$10,900	$10,900
Ladies' department:						
Dresses	300	10	12	$ 3,000	$ 3,600	
Coats	80	30	32	2,400	2,560	
Total				$ 5,400	$ 6,160	5,400
Inventory at lower of cost or market						$16,300

(3) By comparing the total cost and market for the entire inventory, and using the lower figure.

DETERMINATION OF LOWER OF COST OR MARKET— TOTAL INVENTORY METHOD

	Quantity	Unit Price		Extended		Lower of Cost or Market
		Cost	Market	Cost	Market	
Men's department:						
Suits	200	$40	$37	$ 8,000	$ 7,400	
Coats	100	31	35	3,100	3,500	
Ladies' department:						
Dresses	300	10	12	3,000	3,600	
Coats	80	30	32	2,400	2,560	
Total				$16,500	$17,060	
Inventory at lower of cost or market						$16,500

For many years it was considered imperative to use the item-by-item method; the category and total inventory methods are now regarded as acceptable alternatives. However, the alternative adopted must be used consistently through the years. This consistency requirement applies to inventory methods generally and is not limited to the cost-or-market method.

Recent modifications. The lower-of-cost-or-market basis of inventory valuation was adopted as one of the earliest applications of an old rule of accounting conservatism often stated as follows: Anticipate no profit and provide for all possible losses. In the days when primary emphasis was placed on balance sheet conservatism, the cost-or-market rule required that inventories be costed at market whenever market was less than cost, regardless of whether the downward trend in replacement costs had been accompanied, or would probably be followed, by a decrease in selling prices. It was merely presumed that, when market purchase prices decreased, a loss of realizable value in the inventory was inevitable; this presumptive loss was "provided for" by reducing the inventory valuation to the market replacement cost.

With the increasing emphasis on the income statement and the proper matching of revenue and related expense, accountants came to realize that decreases in replacement costs are not always and inevitably accompanied by decreases in selling prices, and that, when decreases in selling prices do occur, they may be proportionately less or greater than the decreases in replacement costs. Therefore, the old cost-or-market rule was modified somewhat to lessen its reliance on replacement cost (market). The general principles now governing the application of the cost-or-market rule may be stated as follows:

Inventories may be valued at cost, even though replacement cost is lower, if it appears probable that the inventory can be disposed of at a normal profit —that is, if there has been no decline, and there is no prospect of a decline, in selling prices.

If there is an actual or prospective decline in selling prices so that, when the inventory on hand is sold, realization of a normal profit is unlikely, an amount lower than cost should be used for inventory costing. However, such lower amount may not coincide with replacement cost; the proper lower amount will be based on one of the following:

(1) The estimated net proceeds realizable from the sale of the inventory; that is, estimated cash inflow from the sale of the goods on hand minus estimated cash outflow that would be incurred to sell such goods.

(2) The estimated inventory valuation that will result in a normal profit from the sale of the inventory. In other words, the amount a merchant would be willing to pay to replace the inventory because at that price he could expect to realize a normal profit from its sale under existing business conditions. (This amount will always be less than the estimated net realizable proceeds because of the profit element.)

(3) The replacement cost of the inventory.

The following guidelines are used to select from the above three alternatives the appropriate lower-than-cost amount for inventory valuation:

> If replacement cost is above the net realizable proceeds, use the latter.
>
> If replacement cost is below the inventory valuation that will result in a normal profit, use the latter.
>
> If replacement cost is below net realizable proceeds but above the inventory valuation that will result in a normal profit, use replacement cost.

Four examples of lower-of-cost-or-market inventory costing are presented below. The amount circled is the proper basis for inventory costing under each of the four assumed cases.

	Dollars per Unit			
	Case			
	1	2	3	4
Cost.	(8)	8	8	8
Net realizable proceeds	9	(6)	7	8
Inventory valuation that will result in normal profit	8	5	(6)	6
Replacement cost	7	7	5	(7)

Effect of cost-or-market rule on gross margin. Although the cost-or-market rule is a conservative one and is generally accepted, the application of the rule distorts the gross margin of a period in which lower-than-cost figures are used for inventory-costing purposes.

To illustrate, assume that a company buys goods at a cost of $10,000 and sells one-half of them for $7,500. The gross margin on the goods sold may be determined as follows:

Sales		$7,500
Cost of goods sold (½ of $10,000)		5,000
Gross margin on sales.		$2,500

But assume that the inventory valuation of the remaining half at the lower of cost or market is only $4,000. The income statement would usually be prepared in the following manner.

Sales		$7,500
Cost of goods sold:		
Purchases	$10,000	
Less inventory at end of period	4,000	6,000
Gross margin on sales.		$1,500

A more comprehensive statement of facts would be:

Sales		$7,500
Cost of goods sold:		
Purchases	$10,000	
Less inventory—at cost	5,000	5,000
Gross margin on sales.		$2,500
Less decline in replacement cost of inventory		1,000
Gross margin less inventory adjustment		$1,500

Of course, to prepare a statement in the latter form illustrated, it would be necessary to compute an aggregate inventory valuation at both cost ($5,000) and the lower of cost or market ($4,000) in order to determine the amount of reduction.

It should also be pointed out that some accountants believe that the lower-of-cost-or-market rule is inconsistent. That is, decreases in replacement cost are given some consideration, but increases in replacement cost are ignored.

Basis should be disclosed. Either in the balance sheet itself or in comments or footnotes accompanying the balance sheet, the basis of the inventory should be stated.

Two examples of such disclosure are presented below:

Inventory, at cost, on a last-in, first-out basis.	$123,600
Inventories, on a first-in, first-out basis, at the lower of cost or market	$321,400

Importance of accuracy in inventory determination. If the inventory is misstated, both the balance sheet and the income statement will be affected. For example, if the December 31, 19+1 inventory is overstated $5,000, then *both* current assets and the net income before income tax will be overstated $5,000. The effect on the income statement can be seen from the following illustration, in which two income statements are presented. In the first the correct ending inventory, $30,000, is used; in the second the ending inventory is overstated $5,000.

DEUCE COMPANY
Income Statement
For the Year Ended December 31, 19+1

	Correct Ending Inventory		Incorrect (Overstated) Ending Inventory	
Sales	$100,000		$100,000	
Cost of goods sold:				
Beginning inventory, 12/31/19—	$20,000		$20,000	
Purchases	70,000		70,000	
Total	$90,000		$90,000	
Deduct ending inventory, 12/31/19+1	30,000	60,000	35,000	55,000
Gross margin		$ 40,000		$ 45,000
Operating expenses		25,000		25,000
Net income before income tax		$ 15,000		$ 20,000

If it is assumed that the corporate income tax rate is 30 per cent, the effect on net income from the $5,000 ending inventory overstatement is $3,500, thus:

Income Statement—Concluded

Net income before income tax—per above	$ 15,000	$ 20,000
Income tax	4,500	6,000
Net income	$ 10,500	$ 14,000

Because the ending inventory of one year is the beginning inventory of the next year, a misstatement of an inventory will affect two income statements—the statement for the year in which the inventory error occurred, and the statement for the following year. This can be demonstrated by continuing the preceding illustration through 19+2. It is assumed that the correct inventory for December 31, 19+2, is $25,000.

DEUCE COMPANY
Income Statement
For the Year Ended December 31, 19+2

	Correct Beginning Inventory		Incorrect (Overstated) Beginning Inventory	
Sales	$110,000		$110,000	
Cost of goods sold:				
Beginning inventory, 12/31/19+1	$30,000		$ 35,000	
Purchases	65,000		65,000	
Total	$95,000		$100,000	
Deduct ending inventory, 12/31/19+2	25,000	70,000	25,000	75,000
Gross margin		$ 40,000		$ 35,000
Operating expenses		27,000		27,000
Net income before income tax		$ 13,000		$ 8,000
Income tax		3,900		2,400
Net income		$ 9,100		$ 5,600

If the annual net income figures shown above are added to arrive at net income for the two-year period, it will be seen that the net income figure for the two-year period is unaffected by the inventory error.

| | Net Income Computed With | | |
Year	Correct Inventories	An Inventory Error	Error in Net Income
19+1...................	$10,500	$14,000	$3,500 over
19+2...................	9,100	5,600	3,500 under
Total.................	$19,600	$19,600	-0-

Although an inventory overstatement causes an overstatement of net income in the first year, it causes an offsetting understatement of net income in the second year. Thus, inventory errors are counterbalancing over a two-year period. The net income is misstated in each of the two years, but it is not misstated in the aggregate.

If the December 31, 19+1 inventory had been understated instead of overstated, the opposite results would have occurred; the 19+1 net income would have been understated and the 19+2 net income would have been overstated.

The above observations are summarized below:

If the ENDING inventory is:	Net income for the period will be:
Overstated	Overstated
Understated	Understated

If the BEGINNING inventory is:	Net income for the period will be:
Overstated	Understated
Understated	Overstated

Obsolete and damaged merchandise. Regardless of the inventory basis adopted, merchandise that has become obsolete or damaged should be excluded entirely from the inventory if it is unsalable. If it can be sold at a reduced price, a conservative estimate of realizable value may be assigned to it. Thus the loss on goods remaining unsold which have been damaged or have become obsolete is taken in the period when the loss developed, not in the period in which the goods are sold.

Retail inventory method. As its name suggests, the "retail" method of inventory costing is frequently used in department and other retail stores; it is suitable for use by wholesalers also. To apply the retail method, it is necessary to maintain records of:

Purchases (and any returns thereof)—at both cost and selling price.
Sales (and any returns thereof)—at selling price.

With this information it is possible to determine a ratio of cost to selling price, the uses of which are described below:

(1) To prepare an estimate of the inventory for interim financial statements without taking a physical inventory; the procedure is illustrated as follows:

	Cost	Selling Price
Inventory at beginning of period	$ 10,000	$ 15,000
Purchases during the period	109,000	188,000
Transportation in	3,000	
Deduct purchase returns	2,000*	3,000*
Totals	$120,000	$200,000

(Ratio of cost to selling price = 60%)

	Selling Price
Sales	180,000
Estimated inventory at selling price	$ 20,000

Estimated inventory under the retail method of inventory valuation—60% of $20,000 equals	$ 12,000

(2) To permit costing a physical inventory at marked selling prices and reducing the selling price valuation by applying the ratio of cost to selling price, as follows:

Determining ratio of cost to selling price:

	Cost	Selling Price
Inventory at beginning of period	$ 22,000	$ 40,000
Purchases (none returned)	169,000	260,000
Transportation in	4,000	
Totals	$195,000	$300,000

(Ratio of cost to selling price = 65%)

Applying cost ratio to ending inventory:

Physical inventory priced at marked selling prices	$ 50,000
Ratio of cost to selling price—See above	65%
Ending inventory for financial statements	$ 32,500

Using selling prices when compiling the physical inventory reduces the clerical work considerably because it eliminates the work of referring to invoices for cost data and dealing with the problem created by the fact that identical merchandise may have been acquired at several different cost figures and possibly from different suppliers.

Gross profit method of estimating inventories. It is sometimes desired to estimate an inventory. Perhaps it is desired to prepare financial statements without taking a physical inventory, or to estimate the cost of an inventory which has been destroyed by fire. The gross profit method is frequently used for such purposes.

To illustrate this method, assume that the goods on hand June 30, 19+2, were destroyed by fire; no physical inventory had been taken since December 31, 19+1. The books showed the following balances at the date of the fire:

	Debit	Credit
Sales		$90,000
Sales returns and allowances	$ 700	
Inventory, December 31, 19+1	20,000	
Purchases	65,000	
Purchase returns and allowances		1,000
Transportation in	800	

Assume, further, that the company's records show that in prior years it made a gross margin (profit) of approximately 25 per cent of net sales. Therefore, if it may be assumed that the same rate of gross profit was realized during the six months preceding the fire, the inventory at the date of the fire can be estimated as follows:

Inventory, December 31, 19+1		$20,000
Add net purchases:		
Purchases	$65,000	
Transportation in	800	
Total	$65,800	
Less purchase returns and allowances..............	1,000	64,800
Total goods available for sale		$84,800
Less estimated cost of goods sold:		
Gross sales	$90,000	
Less sales returns and allowances	700	
Net sales	$89,300	
Less estimated gross margin—25% of $89,300	22,325	66,975
Estimated inventory, June 30, 19+2		$17,825

ASSIGNMENT

MATERIAL

QUESTIONS

1. Describe two inventory accounting methods.
2. What is the purpose of maintaining detailed subsidiary perpetual inventory records?
3. How is the cost of goods sold determined under the periodic inventory method?
4. What is consignment merchandise? When should the consignor recognize profit on consignment merchandise?
5. What items enter into the determination of cost of goods available for sale?
6. Describe the two most widely used bases for determining the dollar amount at which the inventory is stated.
7. How is inventory costed under each of the following methods?
   (a) Specific identification.
   (b) Weighted-average method.
   (c) First-in, first-out method.
   (d) Last-in, first-out method.
8. How will the choice between the *fifo* and *lifo* costing methods affect net income in a period in which all purchases are made at the same per-unit price as the cost of the beginning inventory? What will be the effect in a period of constantly rising prices?
9. Describe the "lower of cost or market" basis for determining the dollar amount of inventories. What are three ways in which it can be applied?
10. Under what circumstances might the lower-of-cost-or-market rule distort the gross margin?
11. How should obsolete and damaged merchandise be accounted for?
12. Describe the retail inventory method. What are two situations in which it may be used to estimate inventories?

SHORT EXERCISES

E9-1. From the following information, taken from the records of Aragon Company, compute the cost of goods available for sale. The company uses the periodic inventory method.

Sales	$42,000
Cash	14,000
Transportation in	1,200
Accounts payable	13,500
Purchases	55,000
Sales discounts.	1,700
Purchase discounts	1,950
Merchandise inventory	16,000
Purchase returns and allowances	1,450
Sales returns and allowances	1,300

E9-2. Saluda Corporation had the following transactions pertaining to its inventory during January, 19+3:

January	1	Balance, 100 units at $5 each.
	4	Purchased 100 units at $6 each.
	6	Sold 45 units at $12 each.
	10	Purchased 100 units at $7 each.
	18	Sold 60 units at $14 each.
	25	Sold 50 units at $14 each.

The company uses perpetual inventory procedures. Compute the following under both the first-in, first-out and last-in, first-out costing methods:

(a) Inventory reported on the balance sheet as of January 31, 19+3.

(b) Cost of goods sold for the month.

E9-3. The following data pertain to Lenoir Corporation for the year ended December 31, 19+3:

Beginning inventory	$16,000
Purchases	59,000
Transportation in	2,400
Purchase returns and allowances	2,100
Purchase discounts	1,400
Cost of goods sold	52,000

How would the information above be reflected in the unadjusted trial balance of the corporation at the end of the year under each of the following assumptions: (a) Periodic inventory procedures are used; (b) Perpetual inventory procedures are used.

E9-4. The following inventory errors were made on the records of Longhurst Company during the period 19+1 to 19+5. None of the errors was discovered until early in 19+6.

Date	Ending Inventory Error
December 31, 19+1	$1,000 understatement
December 31, 19+2	200 overstatement
December 31, 19+3	500 overstatement
December 31, 19+4	800 understatement
December 31, 19+5	1,500 understatement

What is the amount by which the net income for each of the five years is misstated?

E9-5. Holly Company had an inventory of $20,000 on June 1, 19+7. The following data are taken from the records for June:

Sales	$40,000
Sales returns and allowances	1,700
Sales discounts	1,100
Purchases	50,000
Purchase returns and allowances	600
Purchase discounts	900

In the past, the company's gross margin has averaged 30 per cent of net sales. Compute the estimated inventory on June 30, 19+7.

PROBLEMS

Problem A9-1. Bagemore Company had a beginning inventory of 100 units of item Y-12, costing $1.85 per unit, on April 1, 19+1. During the month the following purchases were made:

	Quantity	Unit Cost	LIFO
April 5	80	$1.95	
12	100	1.98	
20	90	2.05	
24	125	2.10	FIFO

A count of the inventory on April 30, 19+1, revealed that there were 130 units on hand. Determine the ending inventory by each of the following costing methods:
   (a) Weighted average. *UNIT COST $1.99 = $258.70 inventory value.*
   (b) First-in, first-out. *$272.75*
   (c) Last-in, first-out. *$243.50*

Problem A9-2. Fears Company had the following transactions pertaining to an item of inventory during August, 19+1:

August 1	......	Beginning inventory, 60 units at $20 each
9	......	Sold 40 units at $39 each
20	......	Purchased 90 units at $21 each
26	......	Sold 35 units at $41 each

(a) Compute the August 31, 19+1 inventory, assuming that perpetual inventory procedures are used, by each of the following costing methods:
   (1) First-in, first-out.
   (2) Last-in, first-out.
(b) Assuming the use of the *fifo* costing method, record the sale of August 26 under each of the following:
   (1) Periodic inventory procedures.
   (2) Perpetual inventory procedures.

Problem A9-3. The information on the following page is taken from the records of Alford Corporation for the year 19+1.

   Required:

   (a) Compute the following for the year:
      (1) Cost of goods sold.
      (2) Gross margin.
      (3) Net income.

(b) Assuming the use of the lower-of-cost-or-market rule, compute net income when:
  (1) Market value of the ending inventory is $19,700.
  (2) Market value of the ending inventory is $23,400.

Sales	$250,000
Purchases	185,000
Purchase returns and allowances	8,000
Purchase discounts	7,000
Transportation in	1,200
Beginning inventory	25,000
Ending inventory	22,500
Other expenses	47,000

Problem A 9-4. Chatham Appliance Outlet maintains two departments. On May 31, 19+3, the inventory by departments was as follows:

		Unit Price	
	Quantity	Cost	Market
Main salesroom:			
Refrigerators	90	$210	$230
Dryers.	105	100	100
Dishwashers	80	75	95
Automatic washers	70	160	145
Bargain basement:			
Refrigerators	12	155	165
Dryers.	22	60	70
Dishwashers	35	50	45
Automatic washers	50	120	115

Compute the ending inventory, using the lower of cost or market, applying the method to:

(a) Each item in the inventory; (b) The inventory in each department; (c) The entire inventory.

Problem A 9-5. The management of Gardner's Department Store has become concerned about the suspected theft of merchandise from Department B, over which a single clerk has exclusive control. A surprise inventory count in the department on May 15, 19+4, revealed an inventory with a retail value of $14,200.

The company's fiscal period ends on March 31, and its records contain the following information concerning Department B for the period from March 31 to May 15:

		Selling
	Cost	Price
Inventory, March 31, 19+4	$8,400	$12,260
Purchases	6,170	8,220
Sales		5,600
Transportation in	169	
Purchase returns and allowances	195	280

Compute the loss to the company, at cost, due to the employee's theft during the period March 31 to May 15.

Problem A 9-6. The after-closing trial balance of Hardy Corporation as of December 31, 19+1, included the following:

Inventory—Product A	$ 8,100
Inventory—Product B	7,900
Retained earnings..................................	12,000

An audit of the inventory accounts and procedures of the company reveals the following data:

(1) Purchases of 400 units of Product A on November 30, costing $9 each, in transit on December 31, 19+1, were not included in the closing inventory, although the invoice from the vendor had been entered in the purchases journal. The goods were shipped f.o.b. Hardy Corporation's plant.

(2) 150 units of Product A were sold to Hawk Company and the sale was recorded. Hawk Company requested that delivery be postponed until January 15, 19+2. The cost of these goods was included in the Product A inventory on December 31, 19+1, although title had passed to Hawk Company.

(3) The purchases journal also included a purchase of 50 units of Product B at $15 each which were in transit on December 31, 19+1, and not included in the closing inventory. These goods had been shipped f.o.b. shipping point.

(4) Another group of 50 units of Product B had also been excluded from the ending inventory because they were not on hand when the inventory count was made. These units were shipped to Hurt Wholesalers on consignment, and, as of December 31, 19+1, had not been sold by the consignee.

(5) The company uses the *fifo* inventory valuation method. The accountant had computed the ending inventory, using the following data:

PRODUCT A

			Quantity	Price	Total
Jan.	1	Inventory................	1,000	$10	$10,000
Feb.	15	Purchase	300	11	3,300
Apr.	1	Purchase	200	12	2,400
	28	Purchase	200	12	2,400
June	5	Purchase	250	11	2,750
Aug.	1	Purchase	350	9	3,150
Oct.	1	Purchase	300	8	2,400
Nov.	30	Purchase	400	9	3,600
		Totals	3,000		$30,000
Dec.	31	Inventory................	900		

PRODUCT B

Jan.	1	Inventory................	400	$14	$ 5,600
	20	Purchase	100	15	1,500
Mar.	25	Purchase	120	16	1,920
May	30	Purchase	150	16	2,400
July	15	Purchase	110	17	1,870
Sept.	10	Purchase	90	18	1,620
Nov.	1	Purchase	130	17	2,210
Dec.	15	Purchase	80	19	1,520
		Totals	1,180		$18,640
Dec.	31	Inventory................	550		

His computations were as follows:

$$\text{Product A: } \underline{\underline{900}} \times \$\ 9 = \underline{\$8,100}$$

$$\text{Product B: } \begin{array}{rr} 400 \times \$14 = & \$5,600 \\ 100 \times \$15 = & 1,500 \\ \underline{50} \times \$16 = & \underline{\ \ 800} \\ \underline{\underline{550}} & \underline{\underline{\$7,900}} \end{array}$$

(a) Compute the correct inventory balances as of December 31, 19+1.
(b) Compute the correct retained earnings balance at December 31, 19+1.

Problem B9-1. Certain information concerning the ending inventory of Cobb Company is presented below. Using the lower-of-cost-or-market basis, select the appropriate amount at which each item should be included in the inventory. State the reason why each figure chosen is the appropriate one.

Item	Cost	Net Realizable Proceeds	Inventory Valuation That Will Result in Normal Profit	Replacement Cost
A	$1.82	$1.92	$1.83	$1.86
B	1.95	1.92	1.83	1.90
C	1.95	1.92	1.83	1.80
D	1.78	1.92	1.83	1.75
E	1.94	1.92	1.83	1.93

Problem B9-2. Gillam Company's beginning inventory and purchases for the month of June, 19+3, were as follows:

	Units	Unit Cost
June 1 Beginning inventory	500	$50
4	1,500	55
9	1,000	57
15	2,500	56
26	2,000	60

A periodic inventory was taken on June 30, 19+3, and 1,300 units were on hand. Compute the ending inventory under each of the following costing methods:

(a) Weighted average.
(b) First-in, first-out.
(c) Last-in, first-out.

Problem B9-3. Carroll Company's beginning inventory on January 1, 19+2, consisted of 10,000 units costing $2.30 per unit. Purchases for the six-month period ending June 30, 19+2, were as follows:

	Quantity	Total Cost
January 15	7,000	$15,400
March 1	9,000	20,880
April 15	5,000	12,000
May 5	8,000	19,200
May 26	5,000	12,500
June 20	6,000	14,400
	40,000	$94,380

The inventory on June 30, 19+2, consisted of 14,000 units. All sales during the period were made at a price of $4 per unit.

Assuming the use of the periodic inventory procedure, prepare a partial income statement showing the gross margin on sales, using each of the following costing methods:

(a) Weighted average. (Compute to the nearest cent.)
(b) First-in, first-out.
(c) Last-in, first-out.

Problem B9-4. The following amounts are found on the books of Brothers Company on January 31, 19+2:

	Cost	Selling Price
Inventory, December 31, 19+1	$14,555	$21,900
Purchases	47,500	72,060
Sales		70,460
Transportation in	205	
Purchase returns and allowances	300	460
Sales returns and allowances		2,550

Using the retail inventory method, compute the estimated inventory as of January 31, 19+2. Carry per cents to two decimal places and round all dollar amounts to the nearest dollar.

Problem B9-5. A fire destroyed the entire inventory of Jenkins Wholesalers during the night of September 10, 19+1. Although most of the accounting records were destroyed, sufficient information was recovered to compute the following balances:

As of June 30, 19+1, the end of the company's accounting period, the inventory was valued at $12,600.

As of September 10, 19+1:

Purchases	$ 7,680
Purchase returns and allowances	110
Transportation in	128
Sales	18,440

One of the items recovered from the fire was a copy of a condensed income statement for the preceding year.

JENKINS WHOLESALERS
Condensed Income Statement
For the Year Ended June 30, 19+1

Sales		$94,000
Cost of goods sold		54,520
Gross margin		$39,480
Deduct:		
Selling expenses	$19,200	
Administrative expenses	9,210	28,410
Net income before income taxes		$11,070
Income taxes		5,314
Net income		$ 5,756

Compute the cost of the inventory destroyed by the fire. Round amounts to the nearest dollar.

10

Long-lived Assets

Definitions. Assets with a relatively long life used in the operation of the business and not intended for sale are the topic of this chapter. A building used as a factory is such an asset; it normally will have a relatively long life; it is used in the operation of the business, and it is not intended for sale. A factory building no longer in use is not so classified because it is not used in operations. Land held as a prospective factory site is also excluded; it meets the long-life test and is not for sale, but it is not used in operations.

Such assets, often referred to as fixed assets, may be either tangible or intangible. An asset is tangible if it has physical substance, like a building or a machine. An asset is intangible if, like a patent or a copyright, its value resides not in any physical properties but in the rights which its possession confers upon its owner.

Cost and expense. Most long-lived assets have a limited useful life. The cost of such an asset (less any scrap or residual value which may be realizable at the end of the asset's usefulness) should be charged off gradually against revenue during the period (known or estimated) of its useful life. The words most commonly used to describe such systematic assignment of asset costs to expense are:

Depreciation, which is the systematic assignment of the cost of tangible assets other than natural resources to expense.

Depletion, which is the systematic assignment of the cost of natural resources
to expense.

Amortization, which is the systematic assignment of the cost of intangible assets
to expense.

Classification. Long-lived assets may be classified, with respect to the nature and type of
cost assignment to which they are subject, as follows:

(A) Tangible:
   (1) Property, plant, and equipment.
      (a) Subject to depreciation.
          Examples: Buildings, machinery, tools and equipment, delivery
                      equipment, furniture and fixtures.
      (b) Not subject to depreciation.
          Example: Land.
   (2) Natural resources, subject to depletion.
      Examples: Timber tracts, mines, oil wells.
(B) Intangible:
   (1) Normally subject to amortization.
      Examples: Patents, copyrights, franchises, leasehold improvements.
   (2) Not normally subject to amortization.
      Examples: Goodwill, trademarks.

These various classes will be discussed in the order in which they are mentioned
in the foregoing classification.

Valuation. Long-lived assets usually are carried in the accounts on one of the following bases
of valuation:

Cost.
Cost less depreciation, depletion, or amortization.

Prior to 1940, it was not an uncommon practice for companies to write up their
fixed assets, that is, their long-lived assets, to appraised values. The offsetting credit
was shown as an element of the stockholders' equity. Various account titles were
given to the credit-balance account; those most appropriate clearly indicated the
source of the credit balance and that the amount represented an unrealized incre-
ment.

In 1940 the Institute's Committee on Accounting Procedure issued a bulletin con-
taining the following statement: "Accounting for fixed assets should normally be
based on cost, and any attempt to make property accounts in general reflect current
values is both impracticable and inexpedient." As a consequence of the issuance
of this bulletin, the writing up of fixed assets to appraised values is now regarded
by the accounting profession as an improper practice.

It may be noted, however, that some theoretical interest continues to exist regard-
ing the potential merits of appraisal data. At times cost information may fail rather
significantly in communicating a reasonable indication of the current values of a
company's assets. This limits the usefulness of financial statements. However, there

is no objection to the disclosure of such data as supplementary information. But it is quite a different matter when advocates of appraisal information urge that it replace cost data. It has yet to be established that appraisal data can meet the tests of verifiability, objectivity, and uniformity expected of accounting information. At the date of this writing, generally accepted accounting principles do not support the substitution of appraisal data in the accounts.

Determination of cost. As a general statement, it can be said that the cost of an asset is measured by, and is equal to, the cash value of the consideration parted with when acquiring the asset. As applied to acquisitions of property, plant, and equipment, cost includes all expenditures made in acquiring the asset and putting it into a place and condition in which it can be used as intended in the operating activities of the business. Thus the cost of machinery includes such items as freight and installation costs in addition to its invoice price.

Separate accounts should be kept for land and buildings, because the buildings are subject to depreciation whereas the land is not. If land and a building thereon are purchased for a lump-sum price, an appraisal may be necessary to provide a basis for dividing the cost between the land and the building. For instance, assume that land and a building are purchased at a lump-sum price of $50,000. An apportionment of the cost on an appraisal basis may be made as follows:

	Appraisal Valuation	Fraction	Cost Apportionment
Land	$15,000	1/4	$12,500
Building	45,000	3/4	37,500
Total	$60,000		$50,000

If, in order to obtain a desired building site, it is necessary to acquire land that has an unsuitable building thereon, the land account should be charged with the entire purchase price. Under such circumstances it will be necessary to demolish or remove the unsuitable building. Any costs incurred in this connection should also be charged to the land account, because the costs were incurred to make the site suitable for building purposes. Any amounts received as salvage from the disposal of the building should be credited to the land account.

The cost of land purchased without improvements includes the purchase price, broker's commission, fees for examining and recording title, surveying, draining, clearing (less salvage), and landscaping. Any interest accrued at the date of purchase on mortgages or other encumbrances and paid by the purchaser and any accrued taxes paid by the purchaser are part of the cost of the land. If land and improvements are purchased, the broker's commission and any accrued interest or tax costs should be apportioned between the land and the buildings.

Expenditures for land improvements may be charged to the land account if the expenditures result in the addition of costs which are not subject to depreciation. If depreciation must be considered in relation to such expenditures, an account for Land Improvements should be opened. Such an account would be charged with expenditures for fences, water systems, sidewalks, and paving. Special assessments for local improvements which benefit the property may be charged to the land account.

When a building has been purchased, any renovating or remodeling costs incurred to put it in a condition suitable for its intended use should be charged to the building account. Any costs for subsequent improvements, in contrast to mere repairs, should also be debited to the building account.

The cost of a building constructed includes the payments to contractors, fees for permits and licenses, architects' fees, superintendents' salaries, and insurance and similar expenditures during the construction period. It is considered permissible to charge the building account with interest costs incurred during the construction period on money borrowed for the payment of construction costs.

If a machine or other fixed asset is constructed by a company for its own use, it should be recorded at cost, and not at some higher price which it might have been necessary to pay if the asset had been purchased from outsiders.

Depreciation. Plant and equipment do not last forever. They either wear out or become obsolete. The wearing out of a depreciable asset is characterized by physical deterioration caused by use or by the action of the elements. The nature of obsolescence is indicated by the following illustrations.

> A company owns a hand machine capable of making 100 articles a day. The business has grown so that 1,000 articles must be made each day. Instead of buying nine more hand machines, it may be better to dispose of the one machine owned and buy a power machine capable of making 1,000 units a day. If so, the hand machine is obsolete.
>
> The operation of the power machine requires the services of five men. A new automatic machine has been invented. Because of the saving in labor, it may be economical business management to dispose of the recently acquired power machine and purchase the new automatic machine. If so, the power machine is obsolete.
>
> The new automatic machine is capable of producing only one product. The market for this product suddenly ceases. The automatic machine is obsolete.

Whether the usefulness of a plant fixed asset is terminated by physical deterioration or by obsolescence, it is the objective of depreciation accounting to spread the cost of the asset over the years of its usefulness in a systematic and sensible manner. This notion of depreciation is supported by the following definition proposed by the Committee on Terminology of the American Institute of Certified Public Accountants: "*Depreciation accounting* is a system of accounting which aims to distribute the cost or other basic value of tangible capital assets, less salvage (if any), over the estimated useful life of the unit . . . in a systematic and rational manner. It is a process of allocation, not of valuation." It is important to stress the fact that depreciation, in the accounting sense, does not consist of measuring the effects of wear and tear. It is a systematic cost-assignment procedure, determined primarily by the use-life expectancy of assets.

Long-lived assets are, of course, subject to changes in market value, but accountants do not consider it necessary to record such changes, because such assets are not intended for sale. The market values may be up today and down tomorrow; such fluctuations in value may be ignored because the value of property, plant, and equipment to a business normally lies in usefulness rather than marketability.

Computing depreciation. There are numerous methods of estimating periodic depreciation charges. Three methods are discussed in this chapter. Other methods are discussed in Finney and Miller's *Principles of Accounting, Intermediate.*

The illustrations which follow are based on the following assumed data:

Cost of asset $3,900
Estimated residual or scrap value—amount which it is estimated can be
    realized from the asset when it is no longer usable to the business   300
Total depreciation to be charged to expense during the total useful
    life of the asset $3,600

Estimated useful life . . . . 8 years

Estimates of useful life may be based on the past experience of a business with assets of the same type, or experience data may be obtained from manufacturers or trade associations. Prior to 1962, probably the most widely used reference source reporting on commonly accepted estimates of useful life for various assets was *Bulletin F,* published by the Internal Revenue Service. In 1962, a new manual was issued; its official title: *Revenue Procedure 62-21.* Instead of the thousands of individual items listed by *Bulletin F,* the new book uses 75 broad groupings. Generally a single industry classification covers all the production machinery and equipment used in the industry. However, some assets like motorcars, trucks, and office machines are listed separately with suggested useful lives applicable to all industries.

STRAIGHT-LINE METHOD: Giving consideration to all of the preceding assumed data, the accountant would compute the annual depreciation charge by the straight-line method as follows:

$$\$3,600 \div 8 = \$450$$

The tabulation below shows the accumulation of depreciation over the years.

TABLE OF DEPRECIATION
Straight-line Method

Year	Debit Depreciation	Credit Accumulated Depreciation	Total Accumulated Depreciation	Book Value
				$3,900
1.	$ 450	$ 450	$ 450	3,450
2.	450	450	900	3,000
3.	450	450	1,350	2,550
4.	450	450	1,800	2,100
5.	450	450	2,250	1,650
6.	450	450	2,700	1,200
7.	450	450	3,150	750
8.	450	450	3,600	300
	$3,600	$3,600		

SUM OF YEARS' DIGITS METHOD: The sum of years' digits method produces a diminishing annual charge to depreciation expense. It is a device for obtaining a larger depreciation charge during the early years of the asset's life than during the later years. Subject to certain limitations, it is acceptable for income tax purposes. The procedure is described below:

Add the numbers representing the periods of life: In the illustration,
$1 + 2 + 3 + 4 + 5 + 7 + 8 = 36$.

Use the sum thus obtained as a denominator.

Use as numerators the same numbers taken in inverse order: Thus, 8/36, 7/36, and so forth.

Multiply the total to be depreciated (cost minus scrap value) by the fractions thus produced.

The following tabulation shows the accumulation of depreciation.

TABLE OF DEPRECIATION
Sum of Years' Digits Method

Year	Fractions Used for Computations	Debit Depreciation	Credit Accumulated Depreciation	Total Accumulated Depreciation	Book Value
					$3,900
1........	8/36 (of $3,600)	$ 800	$ 800	$ 800	3,100
2........	7/36	700	700	1,500	2,400
3........	6/36	600	600	2,100	1,800
4........	5/36	500	500	2,600	1,300
5........	4/36	400	400	3,000	900
6........	3/36	300	300	3,300	600
7........	2/36	200	200	3,500	400
8........	1/36	100	100	3,600	300
		$3,600	$3,600		

DECLINING-BALANCE METHOD: Under this method a fixed or uniform rate is applied to the undepreciated cost of the asset. More specifically, the depreciation rate is applied at the end of the first period to cost and thereafter to the book value at the beginning of each successive period, as shown by the following table, which is based on a depreciation rate of 25%.

TABLE OF DEPRECIATION
Declining-Balance Method
Rate: 25%

Year	Debit Depreciation	Credit Accumulated Depreciation	Total Accumulated Depreciation	Book Value
				$3,900
1 (25% of $3,900)	$975	$975	$ 975	2,925
2 (25% of $2,925)	731	731	1,706	2,194
3 (25% of $2,194)	549	549	2,255	1,645
4 (25% of $1,645)	411	411	2,666	1,234
5 (25% of $1,234)	309	309	2,975	925
6 (25% of $ 925)	231	231	3,206	694
7 (25% of $ 694)	174	174	3,380	520
8 (25% of $ 520)	130	130	3,510	390

As a practical matter, the rate used is often based on what is permissible for income tax purposes. The law and regulations in effect at the time of this writing permit, for the declining-balance method, the use of a depreciation rate not exceeding twice that acceptable as a straight-line rate. The regulations also provide that scrap value need not be taken into account. Thus, if it is acceptable to use $12\frac{1}{2}\%$ as a straight-line rate (this would agree with the eight-year use life being used in the illustrations; the rate is computed by dividing one by the number of years of useful life—in this case $1 \div 8 = 12\frac{1}{2}\%$), a rate up to 25% ($2 \times 12\frac{1}{2}\%$) is acceptable for the declining-balance method.

When the declining-balance method is being used, depreciation should not be continued when the result would be to reduce the book value below the estimated scrap value. To reach scrap value, the depreciation charge for the last year of useful life would be modified as needed from that shown in the Table of Depreciation.

Depreciation for fractional periods. If assets subject to depreciation are acquired during an accounting period, depreciation must be computed and recorded for a fractional period. Since depreciation is an estimate, it seems unnecessary to compute fractional-period depreciation in terms of days. Depreciation is not that precise. As a general rule, fractional-period depreciation is computed in terms of months or fractions of months. This procedure is illustrated below, where it is assumed that the company closes its books annually on December 31.

	Delivery Equipment	Office Machine
Date asset acquired	March 31	September 17 (treated as Sept. 15 for fractional-period purposes)
Cost of asset	$4,000	$1,200
Depreciation rate per annum	20%	10%
Annual charge for depreciation	$ 800	$ 120
Months asset was in use first year	9	$3\frac{1}{2}$ (7 half-months)
Fraction of year	9/12	7/24
Depreciation charge applicable to first accounting period .	$ 600	$ 35

Ignoring residual value. Theoretically, the depreciation provisions should be based on cost less residual value, as in the preceding illustrations. As a practical matter, the scrap value is often (perhaps usually) ignored and the depreciation provisions are based on total cost. This procedure is probably justified because depreciation allowances are at best mere estimates; unless estimated residual values are material in amount, they may be ignored.

Recording depreciation. One may record depreciation by:

Debiting a depreciation account, which is an operating expense account.
Crediting either:
An accumulated depreciation account, which will have a credit balance to be deducted in the balance sheet from the asset account; or

The asset account. This is called *writing down* the asset. This method usually is not desirable for two reasons:

First, if depreciation is credited to the asset account, the cost of the fixed asset will be lost sight of.

Second, the provision for depreciation is only an estimate; by crediting it to an accumulated depreciation account, the amount of depreciation provided can be shown in the balance sheet, where interested parties can get information on which to base their own opinions as to the adequacy of the provision.

Depreciation vs. provision for replacement. The nature of depreciation accounting is often misunderstood. The misunderstanding arises from a tendency to assume that depreciation entries somehow produce funds for the replacement of depreciable assets; this false assumption may have been caused by a misunderstanding of the expression "provision for depreciation" frequently used by accountants.

Depreciation entries merely charge operations, during a series of periods, with the cost of an asset previously acquired. Depreciation entries as such in no way affect the cash account. If it is desired to provide a fund for the replacement of depreciable assets, cash may be set aside in a special bank account or invested in securities to be held until money is required for replacement purposes. The creation of such a replacement fund is very unusual, because management usually believes that the cash can be more profitably used to finance regular business operations.

Expenditures during ownership. An expenditure is the payment, or the incurring of an obligation to make a future payment, for a benefit received. Expenditures incident to the ownership of property, plant, and equipment are of two classes:

Those that should be capitalized—recorded by increasing the book value of the assets. In most cases, this is done by a debit to the asset account; in some cases, it is done by a debit to the accumulated depreciation account.

Those that should be expensed—recorded by charges to appropriate expense accounts.

A careful distinction must be made between capitalizing and expensing if a correct accounting for long-lived assets and for net income is to be maintained. If an expenditure that should be capitalized is charged to an expense account, the book value of some asset is understated, and the owners' equity and the net income for the current period also are understated. On the other hand, if an expenditure that should be expensed is charged to an asset account, the book value of the asset is overstated and the owners' equity and the net income for the current period also are overstated.

In general, expenditures that are capitalized are those undertaken to make some asset more valuable for its intended use or to extend its useful life. However, it is not always easy to determine whether a given expenditure should be capitalized or expensed. The proper treatment of some of the more common types of expenditures is indicated on the opposite page.

Disposal of depreciable assets. If a depreciable asset is disposed of during the year and it is the accounting policy to record depreciation for fractional periods, an entry is

Particulars	Expenditures Expensed	Expenditures Capitalized	
		Book Value of Assets Increased by Charges to	
	Expense Accounts	Asset Account	Accumulated Depreciation Account
Acquisition cost: A company purchased three second-hand machines; charge the asset account		$3,000	
Expenditures to make good depreciation which took place prior to acquisition: Before the machines were put into use, they were thoroughly overhauled. This was a capital expenditure		400	
Installation cost: This is a capital expenditure		50	
Betterment: Additional accessories were purchased for use with the machines; this expenditure is chargeable to the asset account		75	
Ordinary repair: At the end of the first month of operations, a repair bill was paid; this was a revenue expenditure or expense	$18		
Extraordinary repair: After three years of use, the machines were again thoroughly reconditioned at a cost of $400. Such reconditioning had not been anticipated when the useful life of the machines was established. This was capitalized because it made good some of the depreciation subsequent to acquisition and thus extended the useful life of the asset; it is customarily recorded by a charge to the accumulated depreciation account			$400

Reinstallation expense:
The first cost of installing machinery in a factory is a proper charge to the asset account. If machinery is rearranged in the factory for the purpose of improving the routing or otherwise reducing the time and cost of production, a question arises with respect to the proper treatment of the reinstallation expense. Presumably, the cost of one installation will already have been charged to the machinery account. Theoretically, therefore, the cost, or the undepreciated remainder of the cost, of the first installation should be removed from the accounts (by crediting the fixed asset with the original cost and debiting the accumulated depreciation account with the accumulated depreciation thereon), and the reinstallation cost should be capitalized by charge to the machinery account.

required debiting depreciation and crediting accumulated depreciation for depreciation from the date of the last preceding depreciation provision to the date of disposal.

To record the disposal, an entry should be made debiting Cash for the amount received, debiting the accumulated depreciation account with the depreciation provided against the asset, crediting the asset account with the cost of the asset, and debiting or crediting an account to show the loss or gain on the disposal.

Three illustrations follow; it is assumed that any required entries for fractional-period depreciation have been made.

(1) Selling price equal to book value:

Assume that, at the date of disposal of a machine, the asset and accumulated depreciation accounts had the following balances:

	Debit	Credit
Machinery	$2,500	
Accumulated depreciation—Machinery...............		$2,200

The asset had a book value of $300 and was sold for $300. The entry to record the sale is:

Cash	300	
Accumulated depreciation—Machinery...............	2,200	
Machinery		2,500

To record the sale of machinery, relieving the accounts of the cost and accumulated depreciation.

(2) Selling price less than book value:

Assume that the accounts had the following balances:

	Debit	Credit
Machinery	$2,500	
Accumulated depreciation—Machinery...............		$1,760

The asset had a book value of $740 and was sold for $400; hence there was a loss of $340. The entry to record the sale is:

Cash	400	
Loss on disposal of machinery	340	
Accumulated depreciation—Machinery...............	1,760	
Machinery		2,500

To record the sale of machinery.

(3) Selling price more than book value:

Assume that the accounts had balances as below:

	Debit	Credit
Machinery	$2,500	
Accumulated depreciation—Machinery...............		$2,200

The asset had a book value of $300 and was sold for $500; hence there was a gain of $200. The entry to record the sale of the machine at a gain of $200 is:

Cash	500	
Accumulated depreciation—Machinery...............	2,200	
Machinery		2,500
Gain on disposal of machinery		200

To record the sale of machinery.

Trade-ins. The preceding paragraphs dealt with disposals of depreciable assets by sale. However, it is not uncommon for a business to dispose of depreciable assets by trading them in on new assets. It is considered acceptable to account for trade-ins by treating the trade-in allowance as though it were the selling price of the old asset. Thus, the difference between the trade-in allowance and the book value of the asset being traded in, after depreciation to the date of disposal has been recorded, is the gain or loss on disposal.

This approach to trade-ins is illustrated by the following data:

	Case A	Case B
Old asset:		
Cost	$5,000	$5,000
Accumulated depreciation	3,000	3,000
Book value	2,000	2,000
Trade-in allowance	2,300	1,800
List price of new asset	6,000	6,000
Cash payment	3,700	4,200

Entries

	Case A	Case B
Asset account (new asset)	6,000	6,000
Accumulated depreciation	3,000	3,000
Loss on disposal of old asset		200
Gain on disposal of old asset	300	
Asset account (old asset)	5,000	5,000
Cash	3,700	4,200
To record exchange of assets.		

Under this approach, the new asset is set up in the accounts at its list or advertised price. It seems relevant to inquire whether this practice will always satisfy the general rule that, initially, depreciable assets should be recorded at their cost. As noted earlier, cost is equal to the cash value of the consideration parted with; that is, the cash paid and the amount that could be obtained by a sale of the old asset. Referring to the two preceding cases, and assuming that, in each case, the old asset could be disposed of for $1,750, the facts to be recorded would be:

	Case A	Case B
Cost of new asset:		
Cash payment	$3,700	$4,200
Cash value of old asset	1,750	1,750
Total	$5,450	$5,950
Loss on disposal of old asset:		
Cost	$5,000	$5,000
Accumulated depreciation	3,000	3,000
Book value	$2,000	$2,000
Cash value	1,750	1,750
Loss on disposal of old asset	$ 250	$ 250

Entries

	Case A	Case B
Asset account (new asset)	5,450	5,950
Accumulated depreciation	3,000	3,000
Loss on disposal of old asset	250	250
Asset account (old asset)	5,000	5,000
Cash	3,700	4,200

For income tax purposes, no recognition is given to gains or losses resulting from trading in one asset as part payment for another. Under the tax rule, the cost of the new asset, for purposes of computing depreciation and the gain or loss on subsequent disposal, is the sum of the book value of the old asset plus the additional expenditure made in acquiring the new asset. On this basis, the entry to record the exchange of assets in cases A and B would be as shown below.

	Case A	Case B
Asset account (new asset)	5,700	6,200
Accumulated depreciation	3,000	3,000
Asset account (old asset)	5,000	5,000
Cash	3,700	4,200

Observe that the $500 difference in the debit to the asset account under the two alternatives is due to the difference in the trade-in allowance. Many accountants, as a matter of convenience, prefer to follow the tax rule in the accounts.

Unit and group bases of depreciation accounting. In the discussion thus far it has been assumed that the accountant, in his attempts to compute and account for depreciation, approaches the problem by considering each asset as a separate unit. Thus the estimated useful life or depreciation rate selected is one believed to be specifically applicable to the unit of property being depreciated. Accumulated depreciation is related to each unit and, if an asset is retired, the accumulated depreciation related to that particular asset is removed from the accounts when the cost of the asset is removed. It is not uncommon for gains and losses on disposals to arise under this general plan of depreciation accounting.

In contrast, depreciation may be computed on a group basis. Under such a plan, each asset group is depreciated on the basis of an average useful life representative of the entire group. Justification for the use of a group basis does not exist unless a business owns a relatively large number of assets that can be identified as belonging to a class. Examples of acceptable asset classes include hotel furniture, telephone poles, and typewriters.

Under this plan, accumulated depreciation is not associated with individual assets. When assets are disposed of or retired, the cost less salvage is charged against the accumulated depreciation account, and no loss or gain is recognized. This procedure is based on a presumption, which should be supported by past experience, that any underdepreciation on assets retired early will be offset by overprovisions of depreciation on assets which prove to have a longer life than estimated.

Depreciation program revisions. After an asset has been in use for some time, it may be found that too much or too little depreciation has been provided. Such a condition may be due to an error in estimating the life of the asset or to an incorrect estimate of the residual value. In any event, it would be incorrect to continue with the existing depreciation program under such circumstances unless, of course, the amount involved is so small that it can be ignored on practical grounds. If a change is warranted, either of the following alternatives is acceptable:

(1) Adjust the accumulated depreciation account to the amount which it would have contained if depreciation had originally been based on the estimates which now seem correct, and base subsequent depreciation charges on the revised estimates.

Data for example:

Asset cost $9,000

Estimated scrap value . . . .   -0-
Estimated useful life—10 years.
Depreciation entries to date:

Year 1	$ 900
2	900
3	900
4	900
5	900
6	900
Accumulated depreciation at the end of 6th year	$5,400

At the beginning of the seventh year, it is established that the asset will probably last six more years (revised useful life = 12 years).

Computation of correction of accumulated depreciation:

Depreciation recorded during the first six years $5,400
Revised annual charge for depreciation:
  $9,000 ÷ 12 = $750.
Revised depreciation for the first six years:
  $750 × 6 = ...   4,500
Amount of adjustment . . . . $ 900

Entry to adjust the accumulated depreciation account:

Accumulated depreciation 900
    Correction of prior years' depreciation (shown in the income
        statement)   900
    To adjust the accumulated depreciation account to conform to the
    revised estimate of useful life.

Entry for depreciation for seventh and subsequent years:

Depreciation expense 750
    Accumulated depreciation   750
    Depreciation for the year.

(2) Spread the undepreciated amount over the remaining useful life of the asset by revised depreciation provisions, without changing the current balance in the accumulated depreciation account.

Data for example:

Same conditions as in (1).

Computation of depreciation provision for the seventh and subsequent years:

Undepreciated cost:
Cost $9,000
Accumulated depreciation 5,400 $3,600

Revised remaining useful life—6 years.
Revised annual depreciation provision . . . . $ 600

Entry for depreciation for seventh and subsequent years:

Depreciation expense   600
   Accumulated depreciation   600
Depreciation for the year.

The above illustration dealt with overdepreciation. If underdepreciation is discovered, the changes will be as follows:

For alternative (1):
   The accumulated depreciation account is credited for the amount of the underdepreciation, and Correction of Prior Years' Depreciation is debited.
   The subsequent provisions for depreciation will be larger than the former annual provisions.
For alternative (2):
   The subsequent provisions for depreciation will be larger than the former annual provisions.

The second alternative is found more commonly in practice, possibly for the following reasons:

(a) One reason was well expressed by the Committee on Accounting Procedure in its *Bulletin 27:* "Under most circumstances, costs once identified and absorbed through amortization or depreciation charges are not considered to be subject to further accounting, and corrections of estimates affecting the allocations are commonly reflected in revised charges during the remaining life of the property."
(b) Alternative (1) is not acceptable for federal income tax purposes.
(c) Particularly if the difference between the former annual depreciation provision and the new annual depreciation provision is not large in relation to average net income, accountants are inclined to avoid an adjustment

for the accumulated error resulting from past depreciation entries, since their effect on reported net income was immaterial. The approximate character of depreciation accounting does not seem to require such a precise treatment.

Natural resources—Valuation. Natural resources, such as timber tracts, mines, and oil wells, should be carried in the asset accounts at cost. Such assets are sometimes called *wasting assets.* As the resource is converted, a portion of its cost is removed from the asset account and assigned to an inventory account as part of the cost of the product obtained from the natural resource, thereby reducing the book value of the natural resource. Such cost transfers give recognition to depletion.

Development expenditures, such as those made for the removal of surface earth for strip-mining operations, which do not result in the acquisition of separate tangible assets, may be charged to the wasting asset account. Depreciable assets acquired for use in the conversion of a wasting asset should be recorded in separate accounts; they should be depreciated in amounts proportionate to the depletion, if the assets will render service throughout the entire life of the wasting asset; they should be depreciated over a shorter period if their useful lives will expire before the wasting asset is completely depleted.

Depletion. To compute per-unit depletion, the cost of the wasting asset is divided by the estimated number of units (tons, barrels, thousand feet, and so forth) in the asset. To compute the depletion for any period, then, the unit rate is multiplied by the number of units converted during the period.

To illustrate, assume that $90,000 was paid for a mine which was estimated to contain 300,000 tons of available deposit. The unit depletion is $90,000 ÷ 300,000, or $.30. If 60,000 tons are mined during a given year, the depletion is $.30 × 60,000, or $18,000, and is recorded as follows:

Inventory	18,000	
Accumulated depletion		18,000

For purposes of income determination, the amount thus entered in the inventory account is transferred to expense via cost of goods sold as the resources are sold. If some of the units converted are unsold at year end, the depletion related to such units should remain in the inventory account.

The credit balance in an accumulated depletion account should be deducted in the balance sheet from the asset being depleted.

INTANGIBLE ASSETS NORMALLY SUBJECT TO AMORTIZATION

Reason for amortization. Some intangible assets are subject to amortization because their lives are limited by law, regulation, contract, or the nature of the asset. Examples are patents, copyrights, franchises for limited periods, leaseholds, and leasehold improvements. It should be understood that the period fixed by law, regulation, or contract is the maximum period of life, and that the usefulness of such assets may cease prior to the expiration of that period; in such instances, the shorter useful life should be the period on which the amortization is based.

If the original estimate of useful life is subsequently regarded as incorrect, the accountant may either (1) adjust the book value of the asset to the amount which would be reflected by the accounts if amortization had originally been based on the estimates which now seem correct, and base the subsequent amortization on the revised useful life, or (2) spread the unamortized balance over the remaining useful life, as revised. These are the same alternatives that were discussed in connection with depreciation revisions, on pages 239–240.

Patents. If a patent is acquired by purchase, its cost is the purchase price. If it is obtained by the inventor, its cost is the total of the outlays for experiments and costs of constructing working models and obtaining the patent, including drawings, attorney's fees, and filing costs. Because a patent has no proven value until it has stood the test of an infringement suit, the cost of a successful suit may be charged to the patents account. If the suit is unsuccessful, and the patent is thereby proved to be valueless, the cost of the suit and the cost of the patent should be written off.

A patent is issued for 17 years, and its cost should be amortized over that period, unless it was acquired after the expiration of a portion of the 17-year period, in which case it should be written off over its remaining life. If there is a probability that the patented device or the product of the device will become obsolete before the expiration of the patent, conservatism would suggest writing off the patent during a period shorter than its legal life.

Even though a patent may give its owner a monopoly which enables him to develop his business to a point where, after the expiration of the patent, competitors will find it extremely difficult to enter the field and overcome the handicap, the patent should be amortized.

Copyrights. A copyright gives its owner the exclusive right to produce and sell reading matter and works of art. The fee for obtaining a copyright is only a nominal amount, too small to justify an accounting procedure of capitalization and amortization. Costs sufficient in amount to justify such an accounting procedure may be incurred, however, when copyrights are purchased.

Copyrights are issued for 28 years with a possibility of renewal for an additional 28 years. However, publications rarely have an active market for a period as long as 28 years, and it usually is regarded as advisable to write off copyright costs over a much shorter period.

Franchises. Franchises should not be recorded in the books unless a payment was made in obtaining them. Franchises are sometimes perpetual, in which case their cost need not be amortized; usually they are granted for a definite period of time, in which case their cost should be amortized over that period.

Leasehold improvements. Leases of real estate for long periods frequently provide that the lessee (the party who acquired the right to occupy the property) shall pay the cost of any alterations or improvements which he may desire, such as new fronts, partitions, and built-in shelving. Such alterations and improvements become a part of the real estate and revert to the owner of the real estate at the expiration of the lease; all that the lessee obtains by the expenditure is the intangible right to benefit by the improvements during the life of the lease. The lessee should therefore charge such expenditures to a leasehold improvements account; the cost should be amortized over the life of the lease or the expected useful life of the improvements, whichever is shorter, by journal entries charging Rent and crediting Leasehold Improvements. The rent account is also charged with the cash payment for rent. Or the amortization may be debited to Amortization—Leasehold Improvements.

INTANGIBLE ASSETS NOT NORMALLY SUBJECT TO AMORTIZATION

Some intangible assets are not normally subject to amortization because they are assumed to have an unlimited useful life. Examples are trademarks, trade names, secret processes and formulas, and goodwill.

Such assets may be carried indefinitely at cost if there is no reason to believe that their useful lives will terminate so long as the business continues to be a going concern. However, their amortization or complete write-off may be proper under several conditions. First, at the time of its acquisition there may be good reason to believe that the asset will not have an unlimited life, even though there is no conclusive evidence to that effect; in such instances, periodic amortization charges may be made against revenue. Second, at some date subsequent to acquisition, the asset may be found to be valueless, in which case it should be written off; or conditions may have developed which indicate that the life of the asset will terminate, in which case its cost may be amortized over the estimated remaining life; or a portion of the cost may be charged off immediately (as representing amortization for prior periods) and the remainder may be amortized over the estimated remaining life.

Trademarks. The right to the use of a trademark may be protected by registry; the right does not terminate at the end of a definite period, and trademarks are, therefore, normally carried indefinitely in the accounts at cost, without amortization.

Goodwill. The following statement, intended to indicate the nature of goodwill, is quoted from a court decision:

"When an individual or a firm or a corporation has gone on for an unbroken series of years conducting a particular business, and has been so scrupulous in fulfilling every obligation, so careful in maintaining the standard of the goods dealt in, so absolutely fair and honest in all business dealings that customers of the concern have become convinced that their experience in the future will be as satisfactory as it has been in the past, while such customers' good report of their own experience tends continually to bring new customers to the concern, there has been produced an element of value quite as important as—in some cases, perhaps, far more important than—the plant or machinery with which the business is carried on. That it is property is abundantly settled by authority, and, indeed, is not disputed. That in some cases it may be very valuable property is manifest. The individual who has created it by years of hard

work and fair business dealing usually experiences no difficulty in finding
men willing to pay him for it if he be willing to sell it to them."

This quotation is interesting because it indicates some of the ways in which
goodwill may be created. However, it does not adequately indicate the nature of
goodwill for two reasons.

In the first place, it implies that goodwill is produced only by satisfactory customer
relations; but because goodwill is dependent upon earnings, and because many
things other than customer satisfaction contribute to earnings, there are many sources
of goodwill. Some of these sources are: location; manufacturing efficiency; satisfac-
tory relations between the employees and the management, which contribute to
earnings through effective employee service and the reduction of losses from labor
turnover; adequate sources of capital and a credit standing which is reflected in low
money costs; advertising; monopolistic privileges; and, in general, good business
management.

In the second place, in laying the emphasis on customer relations, the quotation
fails to put the emphasis where it really belongs: on the relation between earnings
and assets. A company may be scrupulous, fair, and honest, and its good repute
may tend continually to attract new customers, and yet the company may have no
goodwill. The existence of goodwill depends upon the amount of the earnings.

The meanings of three terms, as used in the following discussion of goodwill,
are stated below:

Investment—The assets of a business exclusive of any goodwill.

Basic rate of income—The rate of net income on the investment which, for
the particular industry, may be agreed upon by the purchaser and seller
as the rate which a new enterprise entering the field might reasonably be
expected to earn.

Excess earnings—The amount by which the earnings of a business exceed
earnings on the investment at the basic rate of income.

Goodwill may be defined as the value of the excess earnings. Let us assume the
following conditions:

	Company A	Company B
Investment	$100,000	$100,000
Basic rate of income	10%	10%
Net income earned	$ 10,000	$ 15,000
Income on investment at basic rate	10,000	10,000
Excess earnings	$ —	$ 5,000

The excess earnings of Company B indicate that it has a goodwill; Company A
apparently has no goodwill because it has no excess earnings.

Methods of computing goodwill. The price to be paid for goodwill in connection with the
sale of a business may be an amount arbitrarily agreed upon by the purchaser and
seller, without formal computation. On the other hand, it may be computed on the

basis of past or anticipated earnings of the business. When the purchaser of a business pays a price for goodwill, he is not paying for the excess earnings of the past, but for probable excess earnings of the future. The accomplishments of the past, however, may furnish the best available evidence of the probable accomplishments in the future. But when past earnings data are used as a basis for an estimation of future excess earnings, all extraneous and nonoperating gains and losses should be excluded. Also, allowance should be made for anticipated changes in revenue and expense, such as higher wage rates, because of their impact on future earnings. Three goodwill valuation bases are illustrated below.

(1) Some multiple of the average past annual earnings, after adjustment for unusual and nonrecurring items and anticipated changes affecting future revenue and expense. For instance, assume that the average adjusted earnings for five years prior to the sale of the business have been $10,000, and that the goodwill is to be valued at twice the average earnings; the goodwill will be valued at $20,000. The price so computed is said to be "two years' purchase" of the average annual earnings.

This method is illogical because it fails to give recognition to the fact that goodwill is dependent upon the existence of excess earnings. Recognition is given to this fact in the two following bases of goodwill valuation.

(2) Some multiple of the average past earnings, as adjusted, in excess of a return at an agreed rate on the average investment. For instance, assume average annual earnings for five years of $10,000, an average investment of $100,000, and an agreement to pay three years' purchase of the average earnings in excess of 8 per cent on the average investment. The goodwill computation would be:

Average earnings, as adjusted	$10,000
Less 8% on average investment	8,000
Excess	$ 2,000
Multiply by number of years' purchase	3
Goodwill	$ 6,000

(3) The capitalized value of excess earnings. For instance, assuming the same facts as in (2) with respect to average income and investment, and assuming an agreement to compute goodwill by capitalizing, at 10 per cent, the average annual adjusted earnings in excess of 8 per cent on the average investment, we would compute the goodwill as follows:

Average earnings, as adjusted	$10,000
Less 8% on average investment	8,000
Excess to be capitalized	$ 2,000

Capitalized value . . . . $2,000 ÷ .10 = $20,000

Proper book value of goodwill. A goodwill account can properly appear on the books only if the goodwill was specifically paid for. The management of a business may believe that it has created goodwill by advertising expenditures or otherwise, and may desire to charge such items to a goodwill account. Accountants do not approve of such charges to goodwill because of the practical impossibility of identifying specific expenditures as representing the cost of goodwill.

It is usually considered good accounting to carry goodwill as an asset indefinitely at its cost. However, because the price paid for goodwill is generally based on a belief that "excess earnings" will be realized, what should the accountant do with the goodwill account if "excess earnings" fail to materialize?

As a general rule, accountants do not favor perpetuating an asset balance when there is no underlying value in support of the asset. And, where an accountant has convincing evidence that an asset is significantly overstated, such overstatement should be removed from the accounts.

As a practical matter, there is no way of determining the "life" of goodwill. Many accountants believe that it is unlikely that goodwill will last over the entire life of an enterprise. For this reason, it is considered acceptable to amortize goodwill over a reasonable period of time.

Organization costs. The organization of a corporation involves expenditures for attorneys' fees, the fee paid to the state at the time of incorporation, and other costs.

Organization costs have sometimes been regarded as a sheer loss, to be written off as soon as possible. Such an attitude is illogical. The very existence of a corporation is dependent upon the incurring of organization costs; they benefit the business during its entire existence. Management is entirely justified, from the standpoint of acceptable accounting principles, in regarding such costs as an intangible asset to be shown indefinitely in the balance sheet as Organization Costs.

ASSIGNMENT
MATERIAL

QUESTIONS

1. Define the following terms:
   (a) Depreciation.
   (b) Depletion.
   (c) Amortization.
2. Describe a classification system for long-lived assets.
3. How is the cost of an asset determined?
4. How should expenditures for land improvements be treated?
5. What is the difference between depreciation and obsolescence?
6. What is the relationship between depreciation and the replacement of assets?
7. Distinguish between the unit and group bases of depreciation accounting.
8. Describe two ways of accounting for changes in depreciation programs.
9. Name several intangible assets which are normally subject to amortization. What rule should be followed in determining the period over which they should be amortized?
10. How should intangible assets not normally subject to amortization be accounted for?
11. What is the relationship between goodwill and the earnings of a firm?
12. Describe three ways in which goodwill may be computed.

SHORT EXERCISES

E10-1. Richway Company acquired an asset on January 1, 19+1, at a cost of $15,000. The asset has an estimated useful life of 10 years and an estimated salvage value of $1,000. Compute the depreciation for each of the first two years, assuming the following depreciation methods: (a) straight-line; (b) sum of years' digits; and (c) declining-balance at twice the straight-line rate. Round all amounts to the nearest dollar.

E10-2. Scranton Corporation purchased a machine on January 1, 19+1, at a cost of $5,100. The estimated life was 10 years and the estimated salvage value was $100. On January 1, 19+4, it was estimated that the remaining life of the machine was four years. (The accumulated depreciation account is to be adjusted.) The asset was sold for $300 cash on January 1, 19+7.

Compute the following, using the straight-line method:

(a) Depreciation for 19+1.
(b) Depreciation for 19+4.
(c) Gain or loss on disposal of the machine.

E10-3. Bethune Company acquired a building with an estimated life of 50 years and zero salvage value on June 1, 19+1, at a cost of $50,000. On January 1, 19+2, a new wing costing $19,800 was added to the building. On January 1, 19+3, the entire building was painted at a cost of $2,500.

Show how the building account and its related accumulated depreciation account would appear for the period June 1, 19+1, to December 31, 19+3, assuming the firm closes its books on December 31.

E10-4. Through December 31, 19+3, accumulated depreciation of $8,000 has been recorded on a machine with an original cost of $12,000. Record the disposal of the asset on that date under each of the following assumptions:

(a) The asset is sold for $5,000 cash.
(b) The asset is junked, with no proceeds.
(c) The asset, which has a cash value of $5,000, is traded for a new asset. A trade-in allowance of $4,500 is received on the old asset and cash of $10,000 is paid. Any gain or loss on disposal is to be recognized.
(d) The conditions are the same as in part (c) except that the income tax rule is to be followed.

E10-5. The following asset accounts were originally debited on January 1, 19+1, for the amounts shown. All amounts represent cash payments.

Patents (The patent is expected to have value during its entire legal life, 12 years of which had expired when purchased)	$ 5,000
Copyright (Its useful life is expected to be one-half its legal life of 28 years)	10,000
Leasehold improvements (The improvements have a ten-year life. The lease expires on December 31, 19+5)	6,000
Goodwill (It was decided at the time of purchase that the goodwill should be amortized over five years)	20,000
Organization costs	3,000

At what amount should each of the items be reported on the balance sheet at December 31, 19+3?

PROBLEMS

Problem A10-1. Muscogee Company acquired land, on which a building was located, for $100,000. In order to construct a new plant on the site, the existing building was demolished. Demolition costs totaled $4,300, and materials from the old building were sold for $1,900. The following costs were incurred during construction of the new building:

Contract price paid to contractor.	$475,000
Fees paid to architect	4,350
Real estate taxes (Building, $1,000; Land, $450)	1,450

Grading costs to prepare site for new building.	$ 6,000
Building permit	200
Landscaping	3,100
Surfacing of parking lot.	4,000
Installation of outside lighting for parking lot	1,600
Construction of fence around parking lot	2,900
Interest on money borrowed for payments to contractor	1,000

Record the information above in appropriate general ledger accounts.

Problem A10-2. Dublin Company acquired the following assets on January 1, 19+3:

	A	B	C
Cost.	$12,000	$18,000	$16,000
Scrap value	2,000	None	1,000
Estimated life	6 years	10 years	5 years

Compute the depreciation to be recorded for each asset for the years ending December 31,
19+3 and 19+4, under each of the following depreciation methods:

(a) Straight-line.
(b) Sum of years' digits.
(c) Declining balance at twice the straight-line rate.
Round all amounts to the nearest dollar.

Problem A10-3. Bambridge Corporation made the following equipment acquisitions and dispositions.

Date Acquired	Cost	Estimated Scrap Value	Estimated Useful Life	Depreciation Method	Disposal Date	Disposal Details
(a) 7/1/+1	$1,350	$350	5 years	Straight-line	12/31/+2	Traded in on (b)
(b) 12/31/+2	$600 plus trade in	$250	8 years	Declining balance— (25%)	1/3/+5	Sold for $850
(c) 1/2/+2	$1,800	-0-	5 years	Sum of years' digits	10/1/+4	Traded in on (d)
(d) 10/1/+4	$925 plus trade in	$195	4 years	Straight-line	12/31/+8	Sold as scrap for $200

Required:

(a) Entries to record the purchases of the assets.
(b) Entries to record the depreciation for each asset at the end of each of the first
two accounting periods, assuming the company is on a calendar-year basis.
(c) Entries to record the disposals of the assets under the income tax rule.

Problem A10-4. Wolff Oil Company acquired property containing oil reserves for a total of $500,000
on January 1, 19+6. It was estimated that the reserves amounted to 75,000 barrels of oil
and that the land would have a value of $10,000 after removal of the oil.

Additional expenditures were made of $80,000 for development costs and $150,000 for
equipment. The equipment will be abandoned when the reserves are depleted.

Production during the first year was 12,000 barrels of oil.

Prepare journal entries to record the above information.

Problem A10-5. LaGrange Company purchased a machine for $10,000 on July 1, 19+1. It was estimated at that time that the useful life would be 10 years and salvage value would be $500. Transportation charges of $200 were paid to have the asset delivered and $400 was invested in a special foundation.

On January 1, 19+6, LaGrange Company paid $2,445 for a major overhaul of the machine. It was then estimated that the remaining life after the overhaul would be 8 years and that the asset would be worthless at the end of that time.

Required:

Journal entries for the following, assuming the straight-line method is used to depreciate the asset:

(a) Purchase of the asset on July 1, 19+1.
(b) The adjustment for depreciation expense on December 31, 19+1, and December 31, 19+2.
(c) The adjustment for depreciation expense on December 31, 19+6, assuming that no adjustment is to be made to the accumulated depreciation account.
(d) The sale of the asset on July 1, 19+7, for $1,400 cash.

[handwritten: JAN 1, 19+6 / DEBIT mach, CREDIT a / Cash For 2,445]

Problem A10-6. An examination of the depreciable asset records of Scott Company on January 4, 19+6, reveals the following information pertaining to equipment items:

	Asset A	Asset B
Date acquired	January 1, 19+1	July 1, 19+3
Estimated life	10 years	10 years
Cost	$16,000	$20,000
Estimated scrap value	2,000	4,000
Annual depreciation:		
19+1	1,600	
19+2	1,440	
19+3	648	1,000
19+4		1,900
19+5		1,710

Asset A was traded in on asset B on July 1, 19+3, and the following journal entry was recorded at that time:

July 1	Equipment (Asset B)	20,000	
	Accumulated depreciation—Equipment	3,688	
	Gain on disposal of equipment		5,188
	Cash		2,500
	Equipment (Asset A)		16,000

Trade in of Asset A for Asset B plus cash. (Cash value of Asset A, $13,000; list price of Asset B, $20,000.)

The company uses the straight-line method of depreciation and normally records new assets involving a trade at the sum of the cash paid plus the actual cash value of the old asset.

Required:

(a) Depreciation schedules for both assets A and B based on the above information.
(b) The journal entry necessary to correct the accounts as of December 31, 19+5.

Problem B10-1. Selected information concerning long-lived asset acquisitions of Tidwell Corporation during 19+5, its first year of operations, is presented below.

January 17—Occupied a new building costing $100,000 and having an estimated life of 50 years. Took delivery on machinery costing $75,000 and having an estimated useful life of 10 years.

February 8—Acquired five trucks costing $2,500 each and having an estimated life of 4 years.

July 27—A machine having an original cost of $8,000 is traded for a new machine. The new machine is recorded at a cost of $10,000 and is expected to have a 10-year life.

November 11—One of the trucks is sold for $1,800 cash.

Assuming that the company uses the unit basis of depreciation accounting and the straight-line method of computing depreciation, determine the depreciation applicable to the building, machinery, and trucks for the year ending December 31, 19+5. Round amounts to the nearest dollar.

Problem B10-2. In 19+1, Block Coal Company paid $10,000,000 for property which was estimated to contain 800,000 tons of coal. It was estimated that the land would have a value of $100,000 after depletion of the coal reserves.

The following quantities were mined during the first three years:

19+1	42,000 tons
19+2	73,000 tons
19+3	66,000 tons

Early in 19+4, adjoining property containing an estimated 60,000 tons of coal was purchased for $811,000. It was estimated this additional property would have a value of $25,000 after the coal had been removed. In 19+4, 59,000 tons of coal were mined.

Compute the depletion charges for each of the four years.

Problem B10-3. The following data pertain to certain equipment belonging to Troup Company.

Asset	Date Acquired	Cost	Estimated Useful Life	Estimated Salvage
A	July 1, 19+1	$3,000	6 years	-0-
B	Jan. 1, 19+2	4,000	4 years	$400
C	May 1, 19+3	5,600	4 years	800

Information concerning the disposal of the assets during the year 19+5 is given below.

Asset	Date Traded	List Price of New Asset	Allowance on Old Asset	Cash Value of Old Asset
A	Jan. 1, 19+5	$3,200	$1,400	$1,200
B	Oct. 1, 19+5	4,175	525	450
C	Dec. 31, 19+5	5,000	1,450	1,425

All assets are being depreciated by the straight-line method.

Required:

(a) The entry to record the trade of Asset A, assuming that the income tax method is followed.

(*Continued on page 252.*)

(b) The entry to record the trade of Asset B, assuming that the cash value of the old asset is recognized.

(c) The entry to record the trade of Asset C, assuming that the new asset is recorded at its list price.

Problem B10-4. Condensed financial statement information for Klondike Corporation for the past three years is presented below.

	December 31,		
	19+1	19+2	19+3
Tangible assets	$500,000	$518,000	$525,000
Total assets	$500,000	$518,000	$525,000
Liabilities	$ 48,000	$ 54,000	$ 65,000
Common stock	300,000	300,000	300,000
Retained earnings	152,000	164,000	160,000
Total liabilities and stockholders' equity	$500,000	$518,000	$525,000
Net income	$ 42,000	$ 54,000	$ 56,000

The company has been sold and the sales agreement calls for the computation of goodwill by capitalizing, at 10 per cent, the average annual earnings in excess of 7 per cent on the average investment for the past three years.

Compute the amount to be paid for the goodwill.

Problem B10-5. Habersham Corporation acquired a machine on January 1, 19+1, at an invoice price of $15,000. Additional amounts were paid for transportation, $250, and installation, $350. It was estimated that the machine would have a useful life of 8 years and no salvage value. The company used the declining-balance method at twice the straight-line rate to compute depreciation.

On January 1, 19+3, the company reexamined its estimates of useful lives and salvage values, and decided that the remaining life of this machine was 4 years from that date, and that it had a salvage value of $500.

On January 1, 19+6, $4,000 was paid for a major overhaul of the machine, and it was estimated that the overhaul would result in a total useful life of 7 years and a salvage value of $2,000 for the asset.

Required:

(a) The entry to record annual depreciation on December 31, 19+3, assuming that the accumulated depreciation account is to be adjusted.

(b) The entry to record annual depreciation on December 31, 19+6, assuming that the accumulated depreciation account is not adjusted.

(c) Computation of the gain or loss on disposal if the asset is sold for $3,000 on July 1, 19+7.

Liabilities

Classes of liabilities. Amounts shown in a balance sheet as liabilities may be classified as follows:

(1) Money obligations:
    (a) Long-term, such as bonds and mortgages payable.
    (b) Short-term, such as accounts and notes payable.
(2) Performance obligations, such as revenue received in advance and provisions for future free service.

Account balances representing performance obligations are usually the result of a proper matching of revenue and expense for a period. The portion of revenue collected in advance that has not been earned at the end of the accounting period remains in an unearned revenue account, where it represents an obligation to be satisfied, not by the payment of money, but by the rendering of service or the delivery of merchandise.

A proper matching of revenue and expense requires that, in the period when revenues are reported in the income statement, the debits against such revenues include the costs already incurred and estimated applicable future costs such as those to be incurred in rendering free repair service or in the fulfillment of guarantees.

The debits for future costs are offset by credits to allowance accounts, such as Allowance for Product Service Costs.

In this chapter we are concerned primarily with money obligations.

Long- and short-term liabilities. The accepted rules for distinguishing between long-term and short-term money obligations were stated in Chapter 2.

A special problem arises when long-term liabilities approach their maturity and are due within, say, a year. Should they be included among the current liabilities although in preceding balance sheets they have been classed as long-term liabilities? The proximity of the maturity date probably should not be the sole determining factor. If a maturing issue of bonds is to be paid from the proceeds of another issue of long-term securities, it is proper to continue to classify it as a long-term liability.

Sources of corporate funds. When a corporation finds it necessary or desirable to raise additional funds, it may borrow them on a short-term note, on a long-term mortgage note, or on bonds, or it may issue additional stock. It usually is regarded as good business management to borrow on short-term notes only if the funds are needed for current operations and the current operations presumably will produce the cash with which to repay the loan. If the funds are to be used for plant additions or permanent investments, they usually should be obtained by issuance of either stocks or bonds.

Stocks and bonds—advantages and disadvantages. For the corporate borrower, bond issues have certain advantages over stock issues:

(1) Bondholders have no vote; therefore, the stockholders do not have to share the management with them.

(2) The money cost may be lower. If common stock is issued, the contributors of new capital will share pro rata with the old common stockholders in dividends and retained earnings. If preferred stock is issued, it may be participating, in which case the dividends may be greatly in excess of reasonable interest on bonds; or it may be nonparticipating, in which case it usually is necessary to give the preferred stock a dividend rate higher than the interest rate at which bonds could be sold, because bonds are a positive and usually a secured liability with a definite maturity, and also because bond interest is payable unconditionally, whereas the payment of preferred dividends is dependent upon earnings and the existence of retained earnings.

(3) The fact that bond interest is deductible as an expense in the computation of income taxes, whereas dividends are not, is frequently a deciding factor in the choice of securities to be issued and has sometimes even influenced corporations to convert preferred stock into bonds.

On the other hand, if interest and principal payments on a bond issue are not made when due, the bondholders may institute foreclosure proceedings and the borrowing company may lose some of its property, plant, and equipment which are essential to its operations, and may even be forced into liquidation with a consequent loss which may leave a very small equity for the stockholders.

LONG-TERM LIABILITIES

Mortgage notes and bonds. If all the desired long-term funds can be borrowed from one lender, the borrower may issue a note and a mortgage; the note will recite the terms of the obligation (date, maturity, interest rate, and so forth) and the mortgage will effect a pledge of certain property as security. A mortgage originally was a conveyance of property from a debtor to a creditor or his representative, subject to the proviso that, if the debtor met his obligation, the conveyance would be nullified. In most states the form of the mortgage has been changed to give it the status of a lien instead of a conveyance or transfer of title.

If it is impossible to obtain the funds from one lender, an issue of bonds may be offered to the public. Because the bonds may be held by many people, who are not known at the time of arranging for the issue and who will change with each transfer of a bond from one holder to another, the lenders cannot be named in the mortgage. Therefore, the borrower selects a trustee, usually a bank or a trust company, to act as a representative of the bondholders; and a mortgage, or deed of trust, relating to the pledged property is executed in favor of the trustee as agent for the bondholders. This trustee is called the *trustee under the mortgage.*

Because long-term borrowings by corporations are usually represented by bonds, this chapter will deal specifically with bonds. However, except as indicated above, long-term mortgage notes are essentially of the same nature as secured bonds. Therefore, what is said with respect to secured bonds generally applies also to long-term mortgage notes.

Classes of bonds. It is impossible to discuss all the different kinds of bonds which have been devised for use in corporate financing. Some of the more common forms are:

(1) Secured bonds. These differ as to the nature of the property that is pledged as security. Three classes of secured bonds are in common use:
  (a) Real estate mortgage bonds, secured by mortgages on land, or on land and buildings.
  (b) Chattel mortgage bonds, secured by mortgages on tangible personal property, such as machinery and equipment of various kinds.
  (c) Collateral trust bonds, secured by a pledge of stocks, bonds, or other negotiable instruments.
(2) Unsecured bonds, sometimes called *debentures.* Because they are not secured by a pledge of any specific property, their marketability depends upon the general credit of the borrower.

Bonds of any of the classes mentioned above may be convertible; that is, their holders may have the right to exchange them for the issuing company's stock—usually common stock. The bond stipulates the terms on which the exchange can be made; that is par for par; or par and accrued interest for the bonds; or a specified number of shares of stock per bond; or some other arrangement. Such bonds give the holder a more assured income during the development period of the issuing company than he might have as a stockholder, with a right to become a stockholder if the business proves to be successful.

Bonds may be secured by first, second, or even third mortgages on the same property. If the obligations are not met, and foreclosure ensues, the proceeds from the disposal of the mortgaged property must go first to the satisfaction of the first-mortgage bondholders, any residue to the satisfaction of the second-mortgage bondholders, and so on.

Recording the bond issue. A separate liability account should be kept with each bond issue. The balance sheet should show the nature of each bond issue, for example, "First Mortgage, 6% Real Estate Bonds Payable, 1995."

The mortgage, or trust deed, states the amount of bonds than can be issued. Each bond is signed by the trustee under the mortgage to indicate that it is secured by the mortgage; this is called *authentication by the trustee.*

Very frequently the amount of bonds immediately authenticated by the trustee and issued by the borrowing company is less than the total issue provided for under the trust deed. The amount of bonds that can be issued may be shown by a memorandum notation in the bond account, and the face amount of the bonds issued is shown by a credit entry in the account. To illustrate, assume that a company's real estate is ample in value to secure an issue of $100,000 of first-mortgage bonds. Only $60,000 of funds are immediately required, but there may be future requirements for $40,000 more. If the trust deed were drawn to secure an issue of only $60,000, a subsequent loan of $40,000 could be secured only by a second mortgage; a second-mortgage issue, being less desirable, might require a higher interest rate and might be difficult to market. In anticipation of its future requirements, the company may authorize a total first-mortgage bond issue of $100,000, drawing a trust deed as security for a loan of that amount. If $100,000 of bonds are authenticated, but only $60,000 are issued, the entry for the issuance will be:

```
Cash . . . . . . . . . . . . . . . . . . . . . . . . . . . . . . . . . . . . . . . . .  60,000
      First-mortgage, 6% real estate bonds payable, 1995 . . . . .        60,000
      To record the issuance of $60,000 face value of bonds.
```

The facts with respect to authorized, unissued, and issued bonds may be shown in the balance sheet as follows:

```
Long-term liabilities:
  First-mortgage, 6% real estate bonds payable, due
    March 1, 1995:
      Authorized . . . . . . . . . . . . . . . . . . . . . . . . . . . . . .  $100,000
      Less unissued . . . . . . . . . . . . . . . . . . . . . . . . . . . .     40,000 $60,000
```

Or thus:

```
Long-term liabilities:
  First-mortgage, 6% real estate bonds payable, due March 1, 1995;
    authorized, $100,000; issued . . . . . . . . . . . . . . . . . . . . . . . .  $60,000
```

The amount of unissued bonds should be indicated in the balance sheet, because the bondholders have a right to know that $40,000 of additional bonds can be issued under the same trust deed which secures their bonds. Thus, if the real estate is carried in the balance sheet at $150,000, the holders of the $60,000 of issued bonds would be interested in knowing that an additional $40,000 of bonds could be issued. On the basis of the issued bonds only, the ratio of security (at book value) to debt is 150 to 60; but on the basis of the total authorized issue, the ratio is only 150 to 100.

Issuances between interest dates. Most bonds provide for the payment of interest semiannually. The interest-payment dates are printed on the bonds; for example, March 1 and September 1, or June 1 and December 1.

Bonds are often issued between the interest dates specified on the bonds, in which case the purchaser usually is required to pay for the interest that has accrued from the previous interest-payment date specified on the bonds to the issuance date. Of course, such payment for accrued interest is returned to the investor as a part of the first interest payment. To illustrate, assume that $10,000 of 6 per cent bonds are issued two months after the specified interest date, at face plus accrued interest; the entry will be:

Cash	10,100	
Bonds payable		10,000
Bond interest payable ($10,000 $\times$ .06 $\times$ $\frac{2}{12}$)		100
Issuance of bonds at face plus accrued interest.		

The entry when the semiannual interest is paid four months later will be:

Bond interest payable	100	
Bond interest expense ($10,000 $\times$ .06 $\times$ $\frac{4}{12}$)	200	
Cash ($10,000 $\times$ .06 $\times$ $\frac{6}{12}$)		300
Payment of semiannual interest.		

Payment of interest. The method of paying bond interest depends upon whether interest checks are issued to the bondholders or whether the bonds have interest coupons attached which are clipped by the holders and presented for collection.

(1) If checks are issued and the number of bondholders is large, it is advisable to draw a check for the entire amount of the bond interest and deposit it in a special bond-interest bank account. The entry would be:

The X Bank—Bond interest account	6,000	
Cash		6,000
Deposit of funds in special account for payment of bond interest.		

This procedure has the advantage of simplifying the reconciliation of the principal bank account; also, the chief disbursing officer can be relieved of the task of signing, or being responsible for, a large number of interest checks by delegating such work to a subordinate.

Separate checks will then be drawn on the bond interest account, the total of the checks being debited to Bond Interest Expense and credited to the special bank account.

(2) If the bonds are coupon bonds, the bondholder usually deposits the coupons in his own bank account as they come due, and his bank presents them for collection. The coupons usually designate a bank at which collection can be made; when the semiannual interest is due, the company deposits the total amount of the interest in a special account at the bank where the coupons are payable; when coupons are presented for payment, the bank pays them and charges the amount to the company's account. The issuing company's entries are:

On or before the date when interest is payable:

```
The X Bank—Bond interest account ................... 6,000
    Cash .........................................        6,000
    Transfer of funds to special account for payment of bond interest.
```

On the date when the interest is payable:

```
Bond interest expense ............................. 6,000
    Bond interest payable .........................        6,000
    Expense and liability for six months' bond interest.
```

At the end of the month or at any other date when the bank has reported the amount of coupons paid:

```
Bond interest payable ............................. 5,700
    The X Bank—Bond interest account ..............        5,700
    Amount of interest coupons presented to and paid by the bank.
```

Because some bondholders may be dilatory in presenting coupons for payment, balances may remain in the special bank account and in the bond interest payable account. The cash shown in the balance sheet should include any balance in the special bank account, and the balance sheet should show as a liability any balance in the bond interest payable account; the mere deposit of funds in a special bank account to be used for the payment of bond interest does not constitute payment of the liability. It would be improper to offset the special bank account and the liability account as though the liability for interest had been satisfied.

Bond discount. If the interest rate specified on a given bond issue is lower than the market rate for bonds of a similar nature (for instance, similar in the nature of the borrower's business and credit standing, in the nature of the borrower's security, or in the amount of its earnings), it may be impossible to obtain the face amount of the bonds. Let us assume, by way of illustration, that a five-year, 5 per cent bond issue of $100,000 is disposed of for a net amount of $99,000. Issuance of the bonds will be recorded by the following entry:

```
Cash .............................................. 99,000
Bond discount ..................................... 1,000
    Bonds payable .................................        100,000
    Issuance of bonds at 99.
```

Amortization of bond discount. In the preceding illustration, $99,000 was received, but $100,000 must be repaid. The $1,000 excess of the amount to be paid over the amount received is an expense to be spread over the life of the bonds. The total interest cost over the life of the bonds includes the discount as well as the semiannual interest payments.

The bond discount account should be written off to Bond Interest Expense in periodic installments. If an interest-payment date coincides with the close of the company's accounting year, the write-off usually is made in equal amounts each six months, at the semiannual interest-payment dates. Since there will be ten semi-annual interest payments during the five-year life of the bonds, the discount may be written off in ten equal installments of $100. The charges to Bond Interest Expense every six months will appear as in the following entries:

Bond interest expense ($100,000 × .05 × ⁶/₁₂)	2,500	
Cash		2,500
Payment of semiannual interest.		

Bond interest expense	100	
Bond discount (¹/₁₀ of $1,000)		100
To amortize ¹/₁₀ of the discount.		

Such semiannual amortizations will completely write off the bond discount account at the end of the fifth year, and will produce equal total semiannual charges to Bond Interest Expense.

Or, the two entries may be combined, as follows:

Bond interest expense	2,600	
Cash		2,500
Bond discount		100
Semiannual bond interest.		

The following amortization schedule shows that the total interest for the life of the bond issue equals the semiannual cash disbursements for interest plus the bond discount, and that the amortization process succeeds in reducing the balance in the bond discount account to zero by the time the bonds mature.

Schedule of Bond Interest and Discount Amortization

Semiannual Periods	Debit Bond Interest Expense	Credit Cash	Bond Discount	Unamortized Bond Discount
				$1,000
1	$ 2,600	$ 2,500	$ 100	900
2	2,600	2,500	100	800
3	2,600	2,500	100	700
4	2,600	2,500	100	600
5	2,600	2,500	100	500
6	2,600	2,500	100	400
7	2,600	2,500	100	300
8	2,600	2,500	100	200
9	2,600	2,500	100	100
10	2,600	2,500	100	-0-
	$26,000	$25,000	$1,000	

If a semiannual interest-payment date does not coincide with the end of the issuing company's accounting period, an adjusting entry will be required for the accrued interest, and another entry will be required to amortize the portion of the discount applicable to the period between the last preceding interest date and the end of the accounting period. For example, referring to the preceding illustration, assume that interest was paid and an amortization entry was made on September 30, and that the issuing company's accounting year ends on December 31. The following entries will be required on December 31.

```
Bond interest expense ($100,000 × .05 × 3/12) . . . . . . . . . . . .  1,250
    Bond interest payable . . . . . . . . . . . . . . . . . . . . . . . .         1,250
    Accrued interest for three months.

Bond interest expense . . . . . . . . . . . . . . . . . . . . . . . . . .     50
    Bond discount ($100 × ½) . . . . . . . . . . . . . . . . . . . . .             50
    Amortization of discount for three months.
```

Bond premium. If the interest rate specified on a given bond issue is higher than the market rate for bonds of a similar nature, the proceeds from issuance may exceed the face amount of the bonds because of the attractive bond interest rate. That is, the bonds may be issued at a premium. If bonds are issued at a premium, the premium reduces the interest expense. For instance, if the bonds mentioned in the preceding illustration were issued for $101,000, the $1,000 premium received when the bonds were issued would not have to be repaid at their maturity, and should therefore be offset against the interest payments to determine the net cost of the use of the money.

The entry at the time of the issuance of the bonds would be as follows:

```
Cash . . . . . . . . . . . . . . . . . . . . . . . . . . . . . . . . . . . 101,000
    Bonds payable . . . . . . . . . . . . . . . . . . . . . . . . . . .         100,000
    Bond premium . . . . . . . . . . . . . . . . . . . . . . . . . . .           1,000
    Issuance of bonds at 101.
```

The payment of the bond interest and the amortization of the bond premium in equal semiannual installments would be recorded by the entries shown below.

```
Bond interest expense ($100,000 × .05 × 3/12) . . . . . . . . . . . .  2,500
    Cash . . . . . . . . . . . . . . . . . . . . . . . . . . . . . . . . . . .       2,500
    Payment of semiannual interest.

Bond premium (1/10 of $1,000) . . . . . . . . . . . . . . . . . . . . .     100
    Bond interest expense . . . . . . . . . . . . . . . . . . . . . . . .           100
    Amortization of bond premium.
```

If an interest-payment date does not coincide with the end of the issuing company's accounting period, end-of-period entries should be made for the accrued interest and for the amortization of premium for the fractional period.

Bond premium and discount in the balance sheet. It has long been regarded as correct accounting procedure to show unamortized bond discount under a Deferred Charges caption at the bottom of the asset side of the balance sheet, and unamortized bond premium on the liability side under a caption of Deferred Credits, between the long-term liabilities and the stockholders' equity. For instance, assume that a trial balance contained the following balances:

First-mortgage, 6% real estate bonds, 1995	100,000
First-mortgage equipment bonds, 5½%, 1990	50,000
Premium on first-mortgage real estate bonds	3,000
Discount on first-mortgage equipment bonds 1,800	

The customary presentation of these facts in the balance sheet is:

Assets

Deferred charges:
Discount on first-mortgage equipment bonds . . . . $ 1,800

Equities

Long-term liabilities:
First-mortgage, 6% real estate bonds, 1995 . . . . $100,000
First-mortgage equipment bonds, 5½%, 1990   50,000
   Total long-term liabilities. $150,000

Deferred credits:
Premium on first-mortgage real estate bonds 3,000

There has been some agitation in accounting literature in favor of showing unamortized premium as an addition to, and unamortized discount as a deduction from, the face amount of the bonds, thus:

Equities

Long-term liabilities:
First-mortgage, 6% real estate bonds, 1995 . . . . $100,000
  Add unamortized premium 3,000 $103,000
First-mortgage equipment bonds, 5½%, 1990 . . . . $ 50,000
  Deduct unamortized discount   1,800   48,200

This procedure has not been generally adopted by the accounting profession even though it has much authoritative support in its favor.

Retirement of bonds. Bonds may be retired:

(1) In total at maturity:
  (a) By payment from the company's general funds, or from the proceeds of a refunding operation in which new securities are issued.
  (b) Through the operation of a sinking fund.
(2) In installments:
  (a) Bonds may be issued payable in installments; these are called *serial bonds.*

(b) A call privilege, stated in the terms of issuance, may give the company the right to retire, before maturity, specified bonds or bonds determined by lot. (The call privilege may be made applicable to the entire issue.)

(c) Bonds may be retired periodically through the operation of a sinking fund.

Serial bonds. As an illustration of serial bonds, assume that $100,000 is borrowed; nothing is to be paid off during the first five years; at the end of the sixth year and each year thereafter, $20,000 is to be paid, so that the bonds will be retired serially by the end of the tenth year. Each retirement is recorded by a debit to Bonds Payable and a credit to Cash.

AMORTIZATION OF PREMIUM OR DISCOUNT ON SERIAL BONDS: Premium or discount on serial bonds may be amortized by the "bonds outstanding" method. The following illustration of the procedure is based on the facts assumed in the preceding section, with the further assumption that the bonds were issued at a discount of $4,000.

SCHEDULE OF DISCOUNT AMORTIZATION
Bonds Outstanding Method

During Year	Bonds Outstanding	Fraction of Total	Discount Amortization
1	$100,000	10/80 (100,000/800,000)	$ 500 (10/80 of $4,000)
2	100,000	10/80	500
3	100,000	10/80	500
4	100,000	10/80	500
5	100,000	10/80	500
6	100,000	10/80	500
7	80,000	8/80	400
8	60,000	6/80	300
9	40,000	4/80	200
10	20,000	2/80	100
	$800,000	80/80	$4,000

To compute the fractions of total, the amounts of bonds outstanding each year were divided by the $800,000 total. To determine the discount amortizations, the $4,000 discount was multiplied by the fractions of total.

Sinking funds. If bonds are to be retired at maturity or periodically through the operation of a sinking fund, the borrowing company agrees, as one of the terms of the bond agreement, to make periodic deposits with a sinking fund trustee, who may or may not also be the trustee under the mortgage. When deposits are made with the trustee, the company debits Sinking Fund and credits Cash. The trustee generally invests such deposits in securities; any income therefrom increases the fund.

In recent years there has been an increasing tendency to use a sinking fund procedure for the periodic retirement of bonds through the exercise of a call privilege. The sinking fund trustee may call the bonds by lot, or in accordance with any other arrangement set forth in the indenture. Usually the call price is above face—with the call premium declining as the maturity date approaches. Any gain or loss on retirement, after any unamortized issuance discount or premium applicable to the retired bonds has been written off, should be recorded on the company's books as shown below. It is assumed that the retirement premium was $500, that $100,000 of bonds were outstanding, and that the unamortized bond premium as of the retirement date was $2,000; thus 10 per cent of the bonds were being retired.

```
Bonds payable (1⁄10 of outstanding bonds). . . . . . . . . . . . . . 10,000
Bond premium (1⁄10 of unamortized issuance premium) . . . . . .    200
Loss on bond retirement . . . . . . . . . . . . . . . . . . . . . . . . . . .    300
     Sinking fund . . . . . . . . . . . . . . . . . . . . . . . . . . . . . .         10,500
```

A sinking fund is properly shown in the balance sheet under the Long-term Investments caption.

Convertible bonds. Bonds sometimes contain a provision entitling their holders to convert them into other securities of the issuing company, such as capital stock. When such a conversion is made, consideration must be given to the terms of the conversion as set forth in the bond indenture. Such terms will indicate the kind and quantity of securities to be received in exchange and the disposition to be accorded accrued interest on the bonds, should the conversion occur between interest dates. At the time of conversion, any unamortized premium or discount on the converted bonds should be removed from the accounts.

Assume that $10,000 of bonds are converted into 200 shares of no-par common stock; that the stock has a stated value of $40 per share; that there is unamortized discount of $300 applicable to the converted bonds at the conversion date; and that there is no accrued interest. The entry for the conversion is:

```
Bonds payable . . . . . . . . . . . . . . . . . . . . . . . . . . . . . . . . 10,000
Bond discount  . . . . . . . . . . . . . . . . . . . . . . . . . . . . . .           300
Common stock . . . . . . . . . . . . . . . . . . . . . . . . . . . . . . .         8,000
Capital in excess of stated value— Common stock . . . . . . . .         1,700
```

The credit to the capital-in-excess account is based on the theory that, because the cancellation of the liability on the bonds constitutes payment for the stock, the amount at which the liability is carried in the accounts is the amount received for the stock. The excess of the amount thus received over the stated value of the stock is a proper credit to paid-in capital.

Bond restrictions on dividends. As a protection to bondholders, the borrowing company may agree to certain limitations on the payment of dividends. For instance, it may agree that dividends shall not reduce the working capital or the stockholders' equity below the amounts existing at the date of issuance of the bonds. Such restrictions should be shown in balance sheet footnotes, or parenthetically in the balance sheet, thus:

```
Stockholders' equity:
  Capital stock . . . . . . . . . . . . . . . . . . . . . . . . . . . . . . . $100,000
  Retained earnings (of which $40,000 is not available for
    dividends because of restrictions in the bond inden-
    ture) . . . . . . . . . . . . . . . . . . . . . . . . . . . . . . . . . . . . .   65,000  $165,000
```

CURRENT LIABILITIES

Inclusion of all liabilities. The most important matter in connection with current liabilities is to see that all such liabilities are included in the balance sheet. Some of the liabilities susceptible to being overlooked are listed here:

(1) Accounts payable for purchases. There is normally some delay between receipt of the merchandise and recording of the purchase. At the end of any period for which financial statements are prepared, it is highly important that all purchases of goods to which title has passed be recorded before the statements are prepared.

(2) Miscellaneous liabilities for services rendered to the firm before the close of the period but not billed until the succeeding period.

(3) Accrued liabilities for wages, interest, taxes, employees' bonuses, and so forth.

(4) Dividends which have been declared and thus represent a liability, but which have not been recorded.

(5) Unpaid installments on purchases of assets.

(6) Unearned revenues.

Recording purchase liabilities net. Under the method of recording purchase discounts previously explained in this text, purchases and the liabilities therefor were recorded gross, and any discounts taken were credited to Purchase Discounts.

For example, assume that goods are purchased at a list price of $1,000, and with terms of 2/10; n/30. The purchase would be recorded thus:

Purchases	1,000	
Accounts payable*		1,000

If the bill was paid within the discount period, the payment would be recorded thus:

Accounts payable	1,000	
Purchase discounts		20
Cash		980

The foregoing procedure shows the amount of discount *taken.* The accounts do not show the amount of the discount *lost* by failure to pay bills within the discount period. An alternative method of recording purchases and purchase discounts to disclose this important information is illustrated below:

The purchase is recorded at the *net* price:

Purchases	980	
Accounts payable		980

If the bill is paid within the discount period, the payment is recorded thus:

Accounts payable	980	
Cash		980

---

*In this and subsequent entries in this illustration, an account in the subsidiary ledger should also be debited or credited.

If the bill is paid after the discount period has expired, the following entry is made:

Accounts payable   980
Discounts lost   20
  Cash   1,000

At the end of each period for which statements are prepared, an adjusting entry debiting Discounts Lost and crediting Accounts Payable should be made for the discount on all invoices for which the discount period has expired.

DISCUSSION OF THE METHOD: The method of recording purchases and purchase discounts lost, just described, is commonly known as the "net price" procedure. Many accountants favor the net price procedure for three reasons: (1) it discloses very significant information for management purposes—namely, the amount of discount lost; (2) it records purchases at the price that will secure the goods; and (3) it results in presenting liabilities more nearly in terms of the amounts that will be expended for their settlement; if most invoices are paid before the discount period expires, the recording of purchases and liabilities in terms of gross invoice price tends to overstate the liabilities by the amount of the purchase discounts on unpaid invoices. But, since the net price procedure is unusual, if it is followed the balance sheet should indicate parenthetically that the liability on accounts payable is stated net of available discounts.

There is some difference of opinion regarding the proper position of the Discounts Lost account in the income statement. Many accountants believe that, as a matter of theory, the net price is the correct measure of cost. Following this theory, they would show the discounts lost in the income statement as an administrative expense, since, presumably, it is the responsibility of the administrative officers to see that obligations of the business are paid within the discount period.

Other accountants believe that cost is equal to the entire amount paid for an item. Under this theory, the balance of the Discounts Lost account is added to the purchases.

Notes payable. Entries for notes payable transactions are described below. The student is already familiar with some of them.

ISSUANCE OF A NOTE: The issuance of a note is recorded by a debit to Cash or Accounts Payable and a credit to Notes Payable.

DISCOUNTING OF A NOTE: When a note payable is issued to a bank for a loan, the interest may be payable at maturity or deducted in advance; in the latter case, the note is said to be discounted. For instance, assume that we give a bank a 60-day note for $1,000, and that the bank charges discount at the rate of 6 per cent per year. The discount is $10, and the proceeds are $990.

If the note matures before the end of the accounting period, debit Cash $990, debit Interest Expense $10, and credit Notes Payable $1,000.

If the note matures after the end of the accounting period, Prepaid Interest (instead of Interest Expense) should be debited. At the end of the accounting period an adjusting entry will be required to transfer the expense-incurred portion from Prepaid Interest to Interest Expense.

PAYMENT OF A NOTE: The payment of a note is recorded by a debit to Notes Payable (and usually a debit to Interest Expense) and a credit to Cash. If an end-of-period adjusting entry was made for accrued interest, the amount of the recorded accrual should be debited to Interest Payable when the interest is paid, and the remainder should be debited to Interest Expense.

CONTINGENT LIABILITIES

A contingent liability exists when there is no present debt but when a liability may develop, usually as the result of an action or default by an outsider. For instance, if a note receivable is endorsed and thus transferred to another, no immediate liability is created; however, a contingent liability exists because the maker of the note may default and the endorser may be required to make payment. Other examples are pending lawsuits in which the company is defendant, disputed claims for additional income tax payments, and contingencies related to renegotiations of government contracts.

If there is little probability that a liability and an accompanying loss or expense will develop, it is sufficient to disclose the contingent liability by a balance sheet footnote. If a liability and an accompanying loss or expense are likely to develop, a liability account (for instance, Provision for Possible Additional Income Taxes) may be credited, with (usually) an offsetting debit to an expense account. As indicated on pages 347–348 (in the discussion of clean surplus and current operating concepts), circumstances might justify a charge to Retained Earnings.

ASSIGNMENT
MATERIAL

QUESTIONS

1. To a corporation, what are the advantages of a bond issue over a stock issue?
2. Describe three types of secured bonds.
3. A corporation has authorized a bond issue totaling $50,000, of which $40,000 worth have been issued. Show two ways in which these facts might be reported in the firm's balance sheet.
4. How is bond interest recorded when bonds are issued between interest-payment dates?
5. Describe two methods of paying interest to bondholders.
6. What effect does the issuance of bonds at a premium have on the cost of the money to the issuing corporation?
7. Describe two ways in which unamortized bond discount may be shown in the balance sheet.
8. What is a bond sinking fund? How should it be reported on the balance sheet?
9. Under what circumstances might the conversion of bonds result in credits to capital accounts in excess of the par or stated value of the stock issued? What is the rationale underlying such a credit?
10. A corporation which issues bonds may sometimes be restricted as to the dividend payments that can be made while the bonds are outstanding. What are two ways of reporting such a restriction in the balance sheet?
11. What are the arguments in favor of the "net price" procedure for recording purchases?
12. What is a contingent liability? How should such liabilities be reported in the financial statements?

SHORT EXERCISES

E11-1. Canton Corporation is authorized to issue $50,000 of 6%, 10-year bonds dated January 1, 19+1. Interest is payable January 1 and July 1. Compute the total amount of cash received at the time of sale in each of the following cases:

(a) The bonds are sold at 100 on January 1, 19+1.
(b) The bonds are sold at 105 on April 1, 19+1.
(c) The bonds are sold at 97 on May 1, 19+1.
(d) The bonds are sold at 100 on October 1, 19+1.

E11-2. On July 1, 19+4, Albemarle Company, which closes its books on December 31, issued $20,000 of 5%, 20-year bonds at 102. The bonds are dated July 1, 19+4, and interest is payable on January 1 and July 1. Present all entries pertaining to the bond issue for the period July 1, 19+4, to July 1, 19+5.

E11-3. Corporations A and B each sold a 10-year, $100,000 bond issue during 19+8. Data pertaining to the issues are given below:

Corporation	Date of Bonds	Date of Issue	Interest Rate	Interest Payment Dates	Selling Price
A	January 1, 19+8	January 1, 19+8	6%	1/1; 7/1	101
B	March 1, 19+8	March 1, 19+8	4½%	3/1; 9/1	97

The corporations close their books on December 31.
For each corporation, compute the following for 19+8:

(a) Interest paid.
(b) Interest expense.
(c) Interest payable at the end of the year.

E11-4. Zolite, Inc., began operations on January 1, 19+7. Summary data concerning purchases and payments on account during the year are presented below:

Purchases on account (gross)	$95,000
Payments on account (gross)...........................	81,000
Purchase discounts taken	1,900
Purchase discounts not taken on payments made	400
Purchase discounts lost on amounts not yet paid	100
Purchase discounts which could be taken on amounts not yet paid .	600

What would be the adjusted balance in the following accounts at December 31, 19+7, under the net method of recording purchases?

Accounts payable.
Purchases.
Discounts lost.

PROBLEMS

Problem A11-1. On July 1, 19+1, Austin Corporation issued $100,000 of 4 per cent, 10-year sinking fund bonds at 101. The bonds are callable at the option of the sinking fund trustee. Interest is payable annually on July 1.

On October 1, 19+5, the trustee called one-fourth of the bond issue at a call price of 103.

(a) Show all entries pertaining to the bond issue during the accounting period ending December 31, 19+1.
(b) Compute the gain or loss on retirement of the bonds called on October 1, 19+5.

Problem A11-2. On January 1, 19+1, Millvion Corporation issued $500,000 of 4 per cent bonds at 104. The bonds are dated January 1, 19+1, and mature in 5 years. Coupons are dated January 1 and July 1.

(a) Show the entry to record the sale of the bonds.

(b) Prepare a schedule of bond interest expense and premium amortization.

Problem A11-3. The following information pertains to the merchandise purchases of Angiers Company during March, 19+4.

Date of Purchase	Gross Amount	Terms	Date Paid
March 1	$ 600	2/10; n/30	March 12
5	1,000	3/10; n/45	14
8	100	2/10; n/30	20
15	2,000	2/15; n/30	20
23	1,000	2/10; n/30	30

Post the above information in T-accounts, assuming that the company uses the net-price procedure for recording purchases.

Problem A11-4. Suffolk Corporation issued 10-year, 6 per cent serial bonds having a face value of $100,000 on January 1, 19+1, at 105½. Interest is payable annually on January 1.

The bonds are to be retired in ten equal payments of $10,000 beginning on January 1, 19+2.

Required:

(a) A schedule of premium amortization using the bonds-outstanding method.

(b) All entries pertaining to the bond issue during the accounting period ending December 31, 19+5.

Problem A11-5. Portland Corporation is authorized to issue $200,000 of 8-year, 6 per cent bonds dated *(AUTHORIZE)* March 1, 19+3. Interest is payable on March 1 and September 1. The entire issue is sold on July 1, 19+3, at 96 plus accrued interest.

DEBIT
BOND INTEREST
PAYABLE

Required:

(a) All entries pertaining to the bond issue through December 31, 19+3, the close of the company's accounting period.

(b) All entries pertaining to the bond issue during the year ending December 31, 19+4.

Problem A11-6. The following selected information is taken from the trial balances of Maloy Corporation.

Trial Balance Data

	Adjusted		Unadjusted
Debits	12/31/+1	12/31/+2	12/31/+3
Bond interest expense	$ 1,800	$ 10,800	$ 7,200
Loss on bond retirement	-0-	-0-	1,000
Credits			
Bond interest payable	4,000	4,000	-0-
Bonds payable (Issued 11/1/+1)	200,000	200,000	180,000
Bond premium	17,600	16,400	15,600

The data in the adjusted trial balance columns are correct. The bonds were issued between interest-payment dates. On September 1, 19+3, the company retired $20,000 of bonds by a disbursement of $21,000.

(a) Compute the price at which the bonds were issued on November 1, 19+1.

(b) Prepare the journal entry to record the issuance of the bonds on November 1, 19+1.

(c) Show any adjusting or correcting entries required as of December 31, 19+3.

Problem B11-1. Information concerning five different bond issues of Bedford Corporation is presented below. Compute the amount of the bond interest expense for the year of issue for each bond issue, assuming that the issuing corporation closes its books annually on December 31.

Date of Bonds	Date Issued	Face Amount	Interest Rate	Life	Interest Payment Dates	Selling Price
(1) 1/1/+2	1/1/+2	$100,000	3%	10 years	1/1; 7/1	101
(2) 1/1/+4	5/1/+4	200,000	6%	10 years	1/1; 7/1	98
(3) 10/1/+4	1/1/+5	150,000	6%	20 years	10/1; 4/1	95
(4) 7/1/+5	3/1/+6	500,000	5%	12 years	7/1	104
(5) 3/1/+6	12/1/+6	300,000	4%	15 years	3/1; 9/1	100

Problem B11-2. Somerset Corporation, which closes its books annually on December 31, issued 6 per cent, 20-year debenture bonds having a face value of $500,000 on January 1, 19+1, for $480,000. Interest is payable on January 1 and July 1.

Required:

(a) All entries pertaining to the bonds during the year ending December 31, 19+1.

(b) All entries pertaining to the bonds during the year ending December 31, 19+5.

(c) The entry to record the payment of the bonds at maturity.

Problem B11-3. Spartan Corporation issued 6 per cent, 10-year coupon bonds having a face value of $100,000 at a price of 100 on January 1, 19+4. Interest is payable on January 1 and July 1.

The corporation uses a special bond interest bank account and makes deposits to the account on the day preceding interest-payment dates. During the years 19+4 and 19+5, the bank reported the following concerning the amount of coupons paid:

July 31, 19+4	$2,850
January 31, 19+5.	2,925
July 31, 19+5	2,880

Required:

(a) All entries pertaining to the bond issue for the years 19+4 and 19+5, assuming that the firm closes its books annually on December 31.

(b) The balance in the special bank account on July 31, 19+5.

Problem B11-4. On November 1, 19+2, Sterling Corporation issued 10-year, 5 per cent convertible bonds having a face value of $200,000 at 97½. Interest is payable on May 1 and November 1. The corporation closes its books annually on December 31.

Bondholders may convert their holdings into Sterling Corporation common stock any time after November 1, 19+3, at the rate of one $1,000 bond for 16 shares of the company's $50 par value common stock. One-fourth of the bond issue is converted on November 1, 19+4. Another conversion on November 1, 19+7, involves one-half of the original issue.

Required:

(a) Computation of the carrying value of the bonds converted on November 1, 19+4, and November 1, 19+7.

(b) The entries on November 1, 19+4, and November 1, 19+7, to record the conversions.

Problem B11-5. The December 31, 19+6 trial balance of Hensler Company is presented below.

HENSLER COMPANY
Trial Balance
December 31, 19+6

Cash	5,150	
Inventory	43,400	
Sinking fund	44,000	
Land	76,000	
Accounts payable, all at net of discount		14,720
Notes payable		1,980
Bond premium		1,200
Bonds payable, 6%, due October 1, 19+9		50,000
Common stock		50,000
Retained earnings		36,740
Sales		198,500
Cost of goods sold	123,720	
Selling expenses	30,630	
Discounts lost	180	
Administrative expenses	28,110	
Bond interest expense	1,950	
	353,140	353,140

When the semiannual bond interest was paid on October 1, 19+6, the bond premium account was correctly debited for $200. There have been no entries in the account since that date.

A 2 per cent discount has been lost on accounts payable carried at a net amount of $2,156.

On November 1, 19+6, the company received $1,980 as proceeds of a loan from State National Bank. The company gave the bank a $2,000 two-month note due January 1, 19+7.

Show all adjusting entries needed as of December 31, 19+6.

12

Stockholders' Equity

The corporation. Probably the most famous definition of the corporation is the one given in 1819 by Chief Justice Marshall in the Dartmouth College case decision, in which he described a corporation as "an artificial being, invisible, intangible, and existing only in contemplation of law."

This definition emphasizes the basic characteristic of the corporation—its separate legal entity. It is not a group of separate persons, as is the case with a partnership; it is itself a legal "person." It can make contracts in its own name; it can sue and be sued, even by its own stockholders; and it can own real estate. Within the limits of its charter, it can perform any business act which could be performed by a natural person.

Because a corporation is a legal entity, a stockholder usually is not liable for its debts unless his shares have a par value and were issued at a discount, and even under such circumstances he is liable only for the amount of the discount. Stockholders of certain classes of corporations, such as banks organized under the laws of some of the states, may have a personal liability in an amount not in excess of the par value of their shares. Although relief from personal liability is an advantage to the stockholders, it sometimes operates to the disadvantage of the corporation by limiting its borrowing power: banks sometimes refuse to lend money to a corporation unless stockholders of means endorse the notes.

The separate legal entity of a corporation gives it a continuity of life. A partnership is dissolved by the death, insanity, insolvency, or withdrawal of a partner; therefore, the continued life of a partnership is constantly in jeopardy. A corporation can be dissolved only by agreement of the stockholders, by forfeiture of the charter to the state, by judicial decree, or by the expiration of the period stated in the charter. A charter may give a corporation an unlimited life; if the life is limited by the charter, a renewal usually can be obtained.

Continuity of corporate life, notwithstanding changes in ownership, is brought about by the issuance of transferable shares. Transferability of interest gives a stockholder several advantages not enjoyed by a partner. (1) A partner cannot withdraw from a partnership or sell his interest without the consent of the other partners; if he undertakes to do so without their consent, he renders himself liable to a suit for damages. Unless there is an agreement among the stockholders to the contrary, a stockholder may sell his stock to any willing purchaser whenever he desires to do so; the consent of the other stockholders is not required. (2) If a partner dies, his heirs have a right to be paid the amount of his capital interest, but they have no right to enter the business as partners without the consent of the other partners. If a stockholder dies, his stock passes to his heirs, who thus acquire an interest in the business. (3) A stockholder can pledge his stock as collateral to a loan; a partner cannot easily pledge his partnership interest. Therefore, a stockholder is in a better position than is a partner to borrow needed funds.

These characteristics of the corporation make it an attractive form of business organization even for small enterprises. In large businesses, in which the capital requirements make it necessary to obtain funds from many investors, the adoption of the corporate form is virtually imperative. A partnership with hundreds of partners, subject to termination upon the death of any one of them, would be in an intolerable chaos of repeated dissolution and reorganization; the orderly conduct of business would be impossible, and capital could not be attracted.

On the other hand, the corporation has certain disadvantages, the chief of which are mentioned below.

Corporations are required to pay income taxes, and the stockholders are required to pay income taxes on dividends received in excess of an amount stated by the Internal Revenue Code. This "double taxation" has induced a number of small corporations to reorganize as partnerships.

The state requires the payment of a fee at the time the corporation is organized and may impose an annual franchise tax for the privilege of continuing operations. Numerous reports, not required of partnerships, must be submitted to the state of incorporation and to other states where business is transacted.

A corporation has a right to conduct only the kind of business authorized in its charter; to engage in other lines of business, it must obtain an amendment of its charter.

Each state regards corporations organized in other states as *foreign* corporations. If a corporation desires to do business in states other than the one from which it obtained its charter, it may be required to obtain licenses from those states and pay a license fee to each of them. Failure to obtain such licenses may result in losses of far greater amount than the fees. For instance, a state may refuse unlicensed foreign corporations the privilege of bringing actions in its courts, and heavy losses may be incurred because of the inability to enforce claims by actions at law.

Restrictions of various kinds are placed upon corporations by the states. In some states a corporation cannot own the stock of another corporation; in some states, it cannot own its own stock; in some states, its liabilities cannot exceed a certain percentage of its capital stock. Also, corporations frequently are prohibited from owning more real estate than they require for business uses.

Organization of a corporation. The organization of a corporation is governed by the laws of the respective states. The procedure differs in the various states and normally the services of an attorney should be used to be certain that the applicable laws are complied with.

In general the following steps are involved:

(1) An application, signed by a required number of incorporators, is filed with a designated state officer. The application states, among other things:
   (a) The name of the corporation.
   (b) The nature of the business which it is desired to conduct.
   (c) The amount of the authorized capital stock, and the number of shares into which it is to be divided.
   (d) The names and addresses of the original subscribers to the stock.
   (e) The assets paid into the corporation by those original subscribers.
(2) If the application is approved, a charter (which is often the approved application itself) is received from the state officer with whom the application was originally filed. This charter evidences the fact that the corporation has been organized and is authorized to conduct business.
(3) A meeting of the incorporators (or stockholders) is held for the purpose (among other things) of electing directors.
(4) A meeting of the directors is held, and officers are elected.
(5) Capital stock certificates are issued.

Corporate management. If a business is organized as a corporation, the stockholders are its owners, but they have no authority to transact its business. The stockholders elect directors, to whom the general management of the business is committed. In most states a person cannot serve as a director of a corporation unless he is one of its stockholders.

Although the directors are charged with responsibility for the general management of the business, their duties are to a considerable extent supervisory, since most of the work of management is performed by officers elected by them. The officers usually include a president, a vice-president, a secretary, and a treasurer. Sometimes one individual holds more than one office; for instance, one person may be secretary and treasurer. On the other hand, there may be several vice-presidents, an assistant secretary, and an assistant treasurer. The president usually is the ranking officer, but in some corporations there is an officer called the "chairman of the board," whose rank is superior to that of the president. The secretary is the official custodian of the corporate records and seal. The treasurer is the chief financial officer.

Transfer agent and registrar. Large corporations, particularly those whose stock is listed on a stock exchange, may (either by requirement of the stock exchange or voluntarily) engage a transfer agent and a registrar to perform the duties incident to the issuance and transfer of shares and the keeping of records showing the names and addresses of stockholders and the number of shares owned by each stockholder. A bank or trust company usually is engaged to perform the duties of transfer agent. Another bank or trust company is engaged to perform the duties of registrar.

The employment of a transfer agent and a registrar serves as a safeguard to the stockholders. When certificates are to be transferred, they are delivered to the transfer agent, who cancels the old certificates, signs the new certificates, and passes them to the registrar, who also signs them. Records of the stockholders are kept by the transfer agent. The registrar's chief function is to act as a control against any possible overissuance of stock, and for this purpose the registrar maintains a record showing the aggregate number of shares outstanding.

Minute book. A record of all the actions taken by the stockholders and directors at their meetings is kept by the secretary of the company in a minute book. This book does not contain debit and credit entries; it contains a record of events written in narrative form, or in the form of resolutions.

The minute book contains information which may be required by the company's accountant for purposes of making entries in the books, and by the public accountants when they audit the company's accounts. For instance, reference to the minutes may be necessary to validate the stated value of no-par stock, the amounts of officers' salaries, the valuations assigned to noncash assets acquired for stock, and liabilities for dividends.

The minute book usually contains a copy of the company's by-laws. The rights and duties of the stockholders, directors, and officers are in general governed by the state corporation law; in many particulars, however, they are stipulated by the corporation's own by-laws. The by-laws contain other stipulations with respect to the management of the corporation, such as the dates on which the regular meetings of the stockholders and directors shall be held, the formalities to be complied with in calling special meetings, and any transactions (such as the issuance of new stock with special privileges) that require the approval of the stockholders. The by-laws are usually passed by the stockholders, but in some states they may be passed or amended by the board of directors.

Elements of stockholders' equity. Corporate accounts need not differ from the accounts of other types of business organization except in the manner of displaying the elements of the owners' equity. In accounting for the elements of stockholders' equity of a corporation, the emphasis is placed on *source:* how much of the stockholders' equity is traceable to:

> Investments by stockholders.
> Gifts—such as the gift of a plant to a company to induce it to locate in the donor city.
> Earnings.

Accounting for these matters is discussed on the following pages.

Capital stock. Stockholder investments in a corporation are represented by shares of capital stock. The two principal classes of stock are common and preferred. Capital stock may have a par value or be without par value.

Par value stock. The par value of a share of stock is a purely arbitrary amount and is in no way related to the market value of the stock. Par value per share can be any amount the organizers wish it to be. Three possibilities for a corporation organized with an authorized capital of $100,000 are:

Par Value per Share		Number of Shares		Total Authorized Capital
$1,000	×	100	=	$100,000
100	×	1,000	=	100,000
10	×	10,000	=	100,000

The primary accounting significance of par value is that it determines the amount credited to the capital stock account upon issuance of the stock. It may also have implications for the determination of legal capital, a concept discussed in greater detail in the next chapter.

At one time all states required that stock have a par value. This led to abuses by some promoters who found the public unable to resist buying stock at an amount below its par value. For many people there is an inevitable attraction about a $100 par value share of stock being offered for $50, even though the par value is completely unrelated to market value. Under the laws of some states, if par value stock was issued for an amount below par (that is, at a discount), the corporation's creditors could hold the stockholder liable for the difference in the event the firm should later encounter financial difficulty. However, such laws were ineffective in preventing abuses, particularly when stock was issued for noncash assets.

No-par stock. The abuses of par value led, in 1912, to the enactment of the first American law permitting the issuance of stock without par value, called no-par stock, by the State of New York. It was felt that the no-par designation might result in a closer inspection of the assets and earnings of a corporation by prospective investors. Another advantage of no-par stock was that it eliminated the potential liability for the issuance discount.

Authorized stock. The kind of stock, its basic features, and the number of shares authorized are recorded directly in the ledger, as follows:

Common Stock			
(Authorized issue, 10,000 shares of $10 par value.)			

Recording the issuance of par value shares. In the case of par value stock, the stock account is always credited with the par value of shares issued, regardless of the issuance price of the shares.

Using the preceding stock authorization data, if 5,000 shares of common stock are issued at par, the entry for the issuance is:

Cash   50,000
       Common stock   50,000
      Issuance of 5,000 authorized shares at their par value of $10.

When this entry is posted, the common stock account will appear as follows:

Common Stock

		(Authorized issue, 10,000 shares of $10 par value.)			
Date			1	50,000	50,000 Cr.

If stock is issued for more than par value, the excess may be credited to a "premium on common stock" account, or preferably to an account called Capital in Excess of Par Value—From Stock Issuances (with the class of stock included in the title). The entry below illustrates a case where 4,000 shares of $10 par value common stock are issued for $11 per share.

Cash   44,000
      Common stock   40,000
      Capital in excess of par value—From common stock
        issuances   4,000
     Issuance of 4,000 authorized shares at a premium of $1
     per share

Stock may be issued at a premium at the time of the organization of the corporation. Stock premiums are probably more common, however, when additional shares are issued at a subsequent date. For instance, assume that a company with 1,000 outstanding shares of capital stock with a total par value of $100,000 has been successful in its operations and has accumulated, over several years, retained earnings of $50,000, thus giving the stock a book value of $150 per share. It might not be fair to the old stockholders to allow new stockholders to acquire stock at par. Moreover, because of the book value of the outstanding stock and the company's earnings record and prospects, its stock might be so attractive that investors would willingly pay a premium to obtain it.

Stock is rarely issued at a discount; that is, for less than par. In many states the issuance of stock at a discount is illegal. In states where it is legal, a discount may be allowed as an inducement to prospective investors. However, such an inducement is of doubtful value because, if stock is issued at a discount and the company becomes unable to pay its debts, the holders of such stock at the time of the corporation's insolvency (whether they be the original subscribers or subsequent transferees) may be held personally liable to the corporation's creditors for amounts equal to the original discount on the shares which they hold.

Stock premium in the balance sheet. The balance of the account credited with stock premiums should be shown in the Stockholders' Equity section of the balance sheet in the manner illustrated below:

> Stockholders' equity:
> Common stock—$10 par value; authorized, 10,000 shares;
>   issued, 9,000 shares. $90,000
> Capital in excess of par value—From common stock
>   issuances. 4,000 $94,000
> Retained earnings   25,000

Recording the issuance of no-par stock. The methods just described for recording issuances of par value stock can be used for recording issuances of no-par stock. But, in the absence of a par, this question arises: At what amount should the shares be recorded in the capital stock accounts? The answer depends on the law of the state of incorporation and on any resolution which the directors, with the permission of the law, may have passed.

The laws of some states require that the entire amount received for no-par stock shall (like the par of par value shares) be regarded as stated, or legal, capital, not to be impaired by distributions to stockholders; if a corporation is organized in a state with such a law, the entire amount received for its no-par stock should be credited to a capital stock account.

Some states allow a corporation's directors to establish a stated value for the company's no-par shares. If the directors elect to take no action establishing a stated value, the entire proceeds of the issuance of no-par shares should be credited to a capital stock account. However, when a stated value has been established, that amount should be credited to a capital stock account for each share issued.

The amount established as the stated value may be less than that received for such shares. What account should be credited for the proceeds in excess of the stated value? A paid-in surplus account has been used for this purpose, but the American Institute of Certified Public Accountants has recommended the discontinuance of the term "surplus" in the title of any account showing an element of the stockholders' equity. Compliance with the recommendation is rapidly increasing. In line with the recommendation, the excess over stated value could be credited to the account Capital in Excess of Stated Value—From Stock Issuances.

Basis of illustrations. In the following illustrations of entries recording the issuance of no-par stock, it is assumed that the corporation is authorized to issue 1,000 shares of no-par value common stock. The authorization is recorded by a memorandum notation in the common stock account, in the manner previously illustrated.

FIRST ILLUSTRATION: In this illustration it is assumed that the corporation was organized in a state which requires that the entire proceeds of the issuance of shares be regarded as stated capital, and that all of the authorized shares were issued at $60 per share. The entry to record the issuance is:

> Cash 60,000
>   Common stock   60,000
>   Issuance of 1,000 authorized shares at $60 per share.

SECOND ILLUSTRATION: It is again assumed that all of the authorized stock was issued for $60,000, that the laws of the state of incorporation permitted the company to credit Common Stock with an amount less than the total issuance proceeds, and that the directors established a $50 stated value for the shares. The entry to record the issuance is:

Cash	60,000	
Common stock		50,000
Capital in excess of stated value—From common stock issu-		
ances		10,000
Issuance of 1,000 shares at $60 per share. Stated value of $50 per share established by the directors.		

Paid-in capital in the balance sheet. If only a portion of the proceeds of no-par stock is credited to a capital stock account, the facts may be shown in the balance sheet like this:

Stockholders' equity:		
Common stock—No par value; authorized and issued, 1,000		
shares at stated value	$50,000	
Capital in excess of stated value—From common stock		
issuances	10,000	$60,000
Retained earnings		15,000

Stock subscriptions. There may be some interval between the date when stock subscriptions are received and the date when the cash is received and the stock is issued. The illustrations that follow show the accounts which are used to record the subscriptions and subsequent payments by the subscribers.

PAR VALUE STOCK: Assume that a corporation has been authorized to issue 1,000 shares of $100 par value common stock. Subscriptions for 750 shares at $110 per share are recorded as follows:

Subscriptions receivable	82,500	
Common stock subscribed		75,000
Capital in excess of par value—From common stock		
issuances		7,500
Subscriptions for 750 authorized shares at $110 per share.		

When payment is received the following entries are made:

Cash	82,500	
Subscriptions receivable		82,500
Collection of subscriptions in full.		
Common stock subscribed	75,000	
Common stock		75,000
Issuance of 750 shares after full payment of subscriptions.		

NO-PAR STOCK: Assume the same facts as in the previous illustration except that the stock has no par value. Subscriptions for 750 shares at $110 per share are recorded as follows:

Subscriptions receivable	82,500	
Common stock subscribed		82,500
Subscriptions for 750 authorized shares at $110 per share.		

It should be noted that the total amount to be paid by the subscribers is credited to the common stock subscribed account.

When the subscriptions are collected, the following entries are made:

Cash 82,500
    Subscriptions receivable   82,500
    Collection of subscriptions in full.

Common stock subscribed 82,500
    Common stock   82,500
    Issuance of 750 shares after full payment of subscriptions.

If the no-par stock had a stated value of $50 per share, only the stated value of the stock subscribed would be credited to the common stock subscribed account, as shown below:

Subscriptions receivable 82,500
    Common stock subscribed   37,500
    Capital in excess of stated value—From common stock is-
    suances   45,000
    Subscriptions for 750 shares at $110 per share. Stated value
    of $50 per share established by the directors.

Uncollected balances of subscriptions for capital stock. If it is expected that uncollected balances of stock subscriptions will be collected in the near future, they may be shown in the balance sheet under the Current Assets caption, but they should be distinctively labeled and not combined with accounts receivable from customers.

If there is no immediate intention to call on the subscribers for the uncollected balances arising from their stock subscriptions, the receivables may still be shown on the asset side of the balance sheet, but not under the Current Assets caption.

The common stock subscribed account would be reported as part of stockholders' equity if a balance sheet was prepared before the stock was issued.

Stock issued for property. When capital stock is issued for property other than cash, a valuation problem may arise. If 1,000 shares of $25 par value stock are issued for a piece of property, it does not follow that $25,000, the aggregate par value of the shares issued, is the proper amount to use in recording the transaction. In accounting, the rule is that property should be recorded initially at cost. The problem is, how is cost measured when shares of stock are issued to make payment?

Under such circumstances, cost may be estimated by reference to market values. For example, suppose that the stock being issued for property is actively purchased and sold by investors through an established stock exchange. If recent stock transactions show that the shares are currently worth $80 per share, it would be reasonable to deduce that property acquired for 1,000 shares of stock "cost" the corporation $80,000. As an alternative, the accountant might use, as an indication of the price being paid for the property, the per-share amount at which stock of the same class was issued recently for cash.

If there are no data available regarding the value of the shares issued, the accountant will look for evidence indicative of the current value of the property acquired.

Perhaps there have been recent cash sales of identical or similar property. In some instances the appraised value of the property may be relevant.

To summarize, the accountant will settle on a figure for accounting purposes by using the value of the shares issued or the value of the asset acquired, whichever is the better indicator under the circumstances of the amount "paid" for the property.

Three illustrations follow.

Data:

A corporation acquires land for 1,000 shares of $50 par value common stock.

The common stock is actively traded on a national stock exchange; recent transactions were completed at $65 per share.

There is no recent information regarding the value of the land.

Entry:

Land	65,000	
Common stock		50,000
Capital in excess of par value—From common stock issuances		15,000
Acquisition of land for 1,000 shares of common stock.		

Data:

A corporation acquires a patent in exchange for 1,000 shares of no-par common stock, no stated value.

The common stock is not listed on any stock exchange.

Several days ago, 1,500 shares were issued for $10 per share.

There is only meager information regarding the value of the patent.

Entry:

Patent	10,000	
Common stock		10,000
Acquisition of patent for 1,000 shares of common stock.		

Data:

A corporation acquires land in exchange for 500 shares of common stock having a stated value of $20 per share.

No shares have been issued for five years and there is no established market for the outstanding shares.

During recent weeks similar plots of land have been sold to other businesses for $12,500, cash.

Entry:

Land	12,500	
Common stock		10,000
Capital in excess of stated value—From common stock issuances		2,500
Acquisition of land for 500 shares of common stock.		

It should be mentioned that the law allows the directors of a corporation to set a valuation for accounting purposes on property acquired by the issuance of shares of stock. If the directors have exercised their prerogative in this matter, the accountant will record the property at the valuation ordered by the board of directors.

Classes of stock. Shares of stock entitle their holders to four basic rights, namely:

(1) To share in the management; that is, to vote at the stockholders' meetings.
(2) To share in the earnings; that is, to receive dividends when they are declared by the directors.
(3) To share in the distribution of the assets of the corporation if it is dissolved.
(4) To subscribe to any additional issues of stock of the class held. This is known as the *pre-emptive right.*

If there is only one class of stock, these four fundamental rights are enjoyed proportionately, share and share alike, by all stockholders.

If there are two or more classes of stock, one class may enjoy more than its proportionate share of some right, or may have some right curtailed. Thus preferred stock may enjoy special preferences in the matter of dividends or in the distribution of assets in liquidation; on the other hand, the preferred stockholders may have no right to vote, or may have a right to vote only under certain conditions, such as the failure of the corporation to pay preferred dividends for a stated period of time.

Stock preferred as to dividends. Stock which is preferred as to dividends entitles its holders to a dividend at a stipulated rate on par, or to a stipulated amount per share in the case of no-par stock, before any dividend is paid on the common stock. Stockholders have no right to dividends unless the directors declare them. Directors may decline to declare dividends on preferred as well as common stock on the ground that the funds are needed in the business; the stockholders then have no recourse except to elect a board that will pay dividends, or to bring action in the courts in the hope of proving that the retention of the funds is not justifiable.

CUMULATIVE AND NONCUMULATIVE STOCK: Stock which is preferred as to dividends may be:

(a) Cumulative, in which case all dividends in arrears on preferred stock must be paid before dividends can be paid on the common stock.
    To illustrate, assume $100,000 par value of 6% cumulative preferred stock, $100,000 par value of common stock, and retained earnings of $30,000; no dividends have been paid on the preferred stock for four years—three prior years and the current year. Since the preferred stock is cumulative, the preferred stockholders are entitled to dividends of $24,000 before any dividends can be paid to the common stockholders.
(b) Noncumulative, in which case dividends omitted in any year are lost forever.
    Noncumulative preferred stock is not a desirable investment because of the danger that dividends may be lost. This is particularly true if the preferred stock is nonvoting, or if the voting power of the common stock exceeds that of the preferred stock and the directors are elected by the common stockholders.

PARTICIPATING AND NONPARTICIPATING STOCK: Stock which is preferred as to dividends may be:

(*a*) Fully participating, or entitled to dividends at as high a rate as the dividends paid on the common stock.

To illustrate, assume $100,000 par value of 6% fully participating preferred stock, $200,000 par value of common stock, and retained earnings of $27,000.

The preferred stock is entitled to a 6% dividend, or $6,000.

A 6% dividend (or $12,000) may then be paid to the common stockholders without any additional dividend payment being made to the preferred stockholders.

But if a 9% dividend ($18,000) instead of a 6% dividend is paid to the common stockholders, an extra 3% must be paid to the preferred stockholders.

(*b*) Partially participating, or entitled to participate with the common stock, but only to a limited degree. For instance, the preferred may carry a 6% preference rate, with a right to participate to a total of 8%.

(*c*) Nonparticipating, or entitled to receive its stipulated preferred dividend but no more, regardless of the rate paid on the common stock.

RIGHTS UNDER VARIOUS CONDITIONS OF PREFERENCE: If the preferred stock is noncumulative and nonparticipating, its holders have a right to only the stipulated rate of return, regardless of the earnings; and if a dividend is not paid in one year, the right to it is forever lost. On the other hand, if the stock is participating and cumulative, the preferred stockholders will receive as high a rate of dividend as the common stockholders receive, and the preferred dividend for every year must be paid before anything can be paid to the common stockholders.

If a corporation is successful, and its preferred stock is nonparticipating, the common stockholders may receive larger dividends than those paid to the preferred stockholders. As a consequence, the common stock may have a much higher market value than the preferred stock.

Stock preferred as to assets. In the event of dissolution and liquidation, stock that is preferred as to assets is entitled to payment in full (the par value of par stock or a stated liquidation value for no-par stock) before any distribution is made on the common stock.

To illustrate, assume $100,000 par value of preferred stock, $100,000 par value of common stock, and assets of only $150,000 after all liabilities are paid. If the preferred stock is preferred as to assets, $100,000 should be paid to the preferred stockholders and only $50,000 to the common stockholders. If the preferred stock is not preferred as to assets, the assets should be divided between the common and the preferred stockholders in the ratio of the par value of the two classes of stock—that is, equally.

The preference as to assets may extend only to the par of the stock, or the preferred stockholders may have a right to receive par and all dividends in arrears. Just what the preferred stockholders' rights are must be determined in each case by reference to the stock certificate or the charter.

The fact that stock is preferred as to dividends does not make it preferred as to assets also, nor is stock which is preferred as to assets necessarily preferred as to dividends also.

Convertible preferred stock. Preferred stock may be convertible into shares of common stock of the issuing corporation. If it is, the conversion ratio will be stated in the certificate. The ratio may change with the passage of time. Sometimes the terms specified give the corporation the right to call (redeem) the entire issue at a predetermined price per share.

The principal appeal of convertible preferred is the conversion feature, which enables the holder to switch to common shares whenever such an action would be to the stockholder's advantage. For example, a good earnings record and bright prospects of the corporation together with a high common stock dividend rate may well make the holding of common shares more lucrative than the retention of the convertible preferred with its fixed dividend rate.

Whenever conversion occurs, the amount of stockholders' equity identifiable with the preferred should be transferred from the preferred stock and related capital-in-excess accounts, if any, to the common stock and related capital-in-excess accounts. To illustrate, assume that one-fourth of the following preferred shares, or 5,000 shares, are converted into 12,500 shares of common stock with a stated value of $5 per share.

Outstanding convertible preferred before conversion:
Convertible preferred stock—$1 cumulative, nonparticipating; $10
    stated value; authorized and issued, 20,000 shares; callable at $20
    per share $200,000
Capital in excess of stated value—From convertible preferred
    stock issuances 100,000

The accounting entry for the conversion will need to transfer one-fourth of the balance in the preferred stock account out of that account. Apparently the preferred stock was issued for more than its stated value, so one-fourth of the capital-in-excess account balance should also be transferred. In effect, $75,000 ($\frac{1}{4}$ of $300,000) of the stockholders' equity must be transferred from preferred stock accounts to common stock accounts.

Entry for conversion:

Convertible preferred stock 50,000
Capital in excess of stated value—From convertible preferred
    stock issuances 25,000
    Common stock (12,500 shares at $5) 62,500
    Capital in excess of stated value—From common stock
        issuances 12,500
    Conversion of 5,000 shares of $10 stated value convert-
    ible preferred for 12,500 shares of $5 stated value common.

Now assume that the remaining outstanding convertible preferred shares, which number 15,000, are called by the corporation at the $20 per-share call price.

Entry for call of convertible preferred:

Convertible preferred stock 150,000
Capital in excess of stated value—From convertible preferred
   stock issuances 75,000
Retained earnings. 75,000
     Cash   300,000
     Call of 15,000 shares of convertible preferred at the $20
     per-share call price.

Observe that the amount by which the cash payment exceeded the paid-in capital identified with the convertible preferred ($150,000 plus $75,000) was charged to Retained Earnings. In essence, a portion of the corporation's retained earnings was distributed to the convertible preferred shareholders.

If the cash payment had been less than the paid-in capital identified with the called preferred stock, the difference would have been credited to a special paid-in capital account, as follows (where it is assumed that the call price is $12 per share):

Convertible preferred stock 150,000
Capital in excess of stated value—From convertible preferred
   stock issuances 75,000
     Cash   180,000
     Paid-in capital—From call of preferred shares   45,000
     Call of 15,000 shares of convertible preferred at the $12
     per-share call price.

Reasons for classes of stock. Different classes of stock with differing rights have been devised to meet the desires of management and to make the shares sufficiently attractive to investors.

One reason for issuing preferred stock might be to obtain control of a corporation. Assume that the prospective buyers of a going concern have the opportunity to purchase the business for $500,000, but have only $250,000 available. They decide to organize a corporation to acquire the business. If they obtain a charter which authorizes the corporation to issue only common stock, they would not have control, because outsiders could purchase half of the stock and have equal voting rights with them. They decide to issue $250,000 par value of common stock, which they purchase, giving them complete control of the voting stock of the firm, and $250,000 par value of nonvoting preferred stock.

Another reason for issuing preferred stock is to obtain financial leverage. This involves the use of funds bearing a limited return to finance a portion of the firm's assets. For example, if money can be obtained at a cost of 6 per cent per year and invested to earn 10 per cent per year, the difference, which is favorable in this case, has the effect of increasing the rate of return to the common stockholders.

Using the above example, assume that the firm is expected to earn $50,000 per year and that the buyers are able to sell $250,000 of 6 per cent cumulative preferred stock. The effect of the sale of preferred stock on the rate of return earned by the common stockholders is shown on the following page.

	Sale of Common Stock Only	Sale of Preferred and Common Stock
Net income	$50,000	$50,000
Less:		
Preferred dividend ($250,000 × 6%) . .	-0-	15,000
Net income to common stockholders . . .	$50,000	$35,000
Investment of common stockholders . . .	$500,000	$250,000
Rate of return to common stockholders .	10%	14%

In this case, the common stockholders increase the rate of return on their investment by using some preferred stock financing. The proceeds of the preferred stock issue are invested to earn 10 per cent, but only 6 per cent has to be paid to the preferred stockholders.

Accounting for various classes of stock. The methods of recording the issuance of preferred stock are the same as for common stock. If several classes of stock are issued, the account title for each class should clearly indicate its nature. If there are two classes of stock, the amounts thereof should be shown separately in the balance sheet, and the special rights of the preferred stock should be described briefly. The balance sheet presentation of the facts may, therefore, be as follows:

```
Stockholders equity:
  Capital stock:
    Preferred, 6% participating, cumulative; par
      value, $100; authorized and issued, 1,000
      shares . . . . . . . . . . . . . . . . . . . . . . . $100,000
    Common, no par value; stated value, $10;
      authorized and issued, 10,000 shares . . . .  100,000 $200,000
  Capital in excess of par or stated value—From
    stock issuances:
    Preferred stock . . . . . . . . . . . . . . . . . . $  2,000
    Common stock . . . . . . . . . . . . . . . . .   10,000   12,000 $212,000
  Retained earnings . . . . . . . . . . . . . . . . . . . . . . . . . . . . .  75,000
  Total . . . . . . . . . . . . . . . . . . . . . . . . . . . . . . . . . . . . . . . $287,000
```

ASSIGNMENT
MATERIAL

QUESTIONS

1. Describe the basic characteristics of a corporation.
2. Outline the steps involved in the organization of a corporation.
3. Discuss the significance of the par value of a share of stock.
4. Illustrate the procedure involved in recording the sale of par value stock at a price in excess of par value.
5. Describe two ways in which the sale of no-par stock may be recorded.
6. What is the relationship between the common stock account and the common stock subscribed account?
7. What is the proper balance sheet treatment of the subscriptions receivable and common stock subscribed accounts?
8. Describe the nature of the problem which may arise when capital stock is issued for property other than cash. How does the accountant solve this problem?
9. List the four basic rights of stockholders.
10. Describe the following features of preferred stock;
    (a) Preferred as to dividends.
    (b) Cumulative preferred stock.
    (c) Participating preferred stock.
    (d) Convertible preferred stock.
    (e) Preferred as to assets.
11. What is the general rule to be followed in accounting for the conversion of preferred stock into common stock?

SHORT EXERCISES

E12-1. New Holland Company is authorized to issue 10,000 shares of $5 par value common stock. Present the Stockholders' Equity section of the firm's balance sheet immediately after each of the following unrelated transactions:

(a) The sale of 5,000 shares for cash at $7 per share.
(b) The entire issue is subscribed at $10 per share, and half of the subscribers pay their accounts in full.
(c) The entire issue is sold for cash at $6 per share.

E12-2. Present the Stockholders' Equity section of the balance sheet after each of the transactions in Exercise 1, assuming that the New Holland Company stock is no-par stock.

E12-3. The following transactions pertain to the sale of no-par common stock, having a stated value of $5 per share, by Remerton Company:

(1) Received subscriptions for 2,000 shares at $12 per share.
(2) Received payment of one-half of the amount owed by all subscribers.
(3) Subscribers for 1,000 shares paid their accounts in full.
(4) Received subscriptions for 3,000 shares at $15 per share.

Present entries to record the information above. Omit explanations.

E12-4. Buena Vista Corporation has 2,000 shares of $100 par value preferred stock outstanding. The stock was originally issued at a price of $105 per share. Present entries to record the following on August 1, 19+4:

(a) Conversion of 1,000 of the preferred shares into 8,000 shares of the company's $10 par value common stock.
(b) Call of the remaining shares by the company at a price of $107 per share. The retained earnings balance is $100,000 on August 1, 19+4.

E12-5. On April 1, 19+6, the date of organization, Baxley Company acquired a tract of land in exchange for 700 shares of its $10 par value common stock. The best information available indicated the land was worth $9,500 at the time. A second tract was acquired on August 15, 19+6, in exchange for 1,000 shares of stock. The corporation had sold 500 shares of stock on August 13, 19+6, for $18 per share.

Assuming that there were no other transactions during the period, prepare a balance sheet for the company as of August 15, 19+6.

PROBLEMS

Problem A12-1. Bannes Corporation has an authorized capital of 20,000 shares of common stock. The entire issue is to be sold at $20 per share.

Required:

The entry to record the sale of the stock under each of the following assumptions:

(a) The par value of the stock is $20 per share.
(b) The par value of the stock is $10 per share.
(c) The stock has no par value.
(d) The stock is no-par stock with a stated value of $15 per share.
(e) The par value of the stock is $5 per share.

Problem A12-2. Talton Corporation was organized on October 1, 19+2, and was authorized to issue 100,000 shares of $10 par value common stock. The company issued the following stock during the month of October:

October   2—Forty thousand shares for cash at $10 per share.
            14—Ten thousand shares in exchange for land valued at $25,000, a building worth $75,000, and $25,000 cash.
            26—Twenty thousand shares for cash at $14 per share.

Prepare the Stockholders' Equity section of Talton Corporation's balance sheet as of October 31, 19+2, assuming earnings of $15,300 for the month and no dividend payments.

Problem A12-3. Levitt Corporation was authorized to issue 10,000 shares each of the following classes of stock:

> 4% preferred stock, $25 par value.
> Common stock, $10 stated value.

The following transactions occurred during the month of November 19+3:

> November 2—One thousand shares of common stock were issued for cash at $10 per share.
> 8—Five hundred shares of preferred stock were issued for $25 per share.
> 12—Twenty-five shares of preferred stock were issued to an attorney for services rendered in organizing the corporation. The attorney purchased an additional 50 shares for $28 per share.
> 15—Two thousand shares of common stock were issued at $12 per share.
> 16—Seven hundred shares of common stock were issued in exchange for a tract of land.

Show the journal entries to record the above information.

Problem A12-4. Nettles Corporation was organized on July 1, 19+8, with authorized capital of 10,000 shares of no-par common stock. In order to comply with state laws, a stated value of $50 per share has been assigned to the stock.

The following transactions occurred during the month of July, 19+8:

> July 15—One thousand shares were issued at $52 per share.
> 20—Eight hundred shares were issued at $55 per share.
> 24—Paid legal fees of $2,500 incurred in organizing the firm.
> 27—Received subscriptions for 1,500 shares at $56. The subscribers paid for 20% of their subscriptions.

Required:

> (a) Journal entries for the transactions.
> (b) The Stockholders' Equity section of the firm's balance sheet as of July 31, 19+8, assuming no retained earnings.

Problem A12-5. Kingman Company was organized on January 1, 19+4, with an authorized capital consisting of 5,000 shares of $50 par value, 6 per cent preferred stock and 10,000 shares of $25 par value common stock. The preferred stock is convertible into common stock at any time at the rate of 2 shares of preferred for 5 shares of common.

The company issued 3,000 shares of preferred stock for cash at $65 on January 10, 19+4. On the same date, 5,000 shares of common stock were issued at a price of $30 per share. One-third of the preferred shares was converted on July 31, 19+7, the end of the company's accounting period.

Required:

> (a) Appropriate stockholders' equity ledger accounts for the company just prior to conversion, assuming a retained earnings balance of $68,000.

(b) The journal entry to record conversion of the preferred shares.

(c) The journal entry required on August 1, 19+7, assuming that the remaining shares of the preferred stock are called at a price of $75 per share.

Problem A12-6. The following information is taken from the ledger of Golden Company as of December 31, 19+7.

Cash	$ 52,765
Accounts receivable	27,436
Land (Cost, $15,000)	23,000
Building	175,000
Common stock subscriptions receivable	10,000
Organization costs	3,250
Capital in excess of par value—From preferred stock issuances	14,000
Common stock	100,000
Bonds payable	50,000
Preferred stock	50,000
Bond discount	4,000
Allowance for uncollectibles	900
Accumulated depreciation—Building	20,000
Retained earnings	?
Capital in excess of par value—From common stock issuances	43,200
Inventory	28,700
Accounts payable	17,612
Common stock subscribed	8,000
Bond interest payable	1,500

The company is authorized to issue 5,000 shares of 6 per cent cumulative preferred stock and 10,000 shares of $25 par value common stock. As of December 31, 19+7, 500 shares of preferred stock and 4,000 shares of common stock have been issued. An additional 320 shares of common stock have been subscribed.

Prepare a classified balance sheet as of December 31, 19+7, following proper accounting practices.

Problem B12-1. Struble Corporation was organized on January 1, 19+2, with its authorized capital consisting of 2,000 shares of common stock. All of the 2,000 shares were sold for $90 per share on January 15, 19+2.

Show the journal entry to record the sale of the stock under each of the following assumptions:

(a) Authorization had been obtained for 2,000 shares of no-par stock, and the company was organized in a state in which the laws require that the entire amount received for no-par shares shall be legal capital.

(b) Authorization had been obtained for 2,000 shares of no-par stock. The company was organized in a state in which the laws require that a stated value be assigned to no-par stock. The directors have voted to assign a stated value of $80 per share.

(c) Authorization has been obtained for 2,000 shares of $50 par value stock.

Problem B12-2. Kirbs Corporation was organized on May 1, 19+4, with authorized capital as follows:

3,000 shares of 5% cumulative preferred stock, $100 par value.
25,000 shares of common stock, $100 par value.

During the month of May, 19+4, the following transactions occurred:

May 3—Sold 500 shares of preferred stock for cash at $104 per share.
     12—Sold 2,500 shares of common stock for cash at $110 per share.
     17—Received subscriptions for 2,500 shares of common stock at $112 per share.
     27—Subscribers to 2,000 shares paid their subscriptions in full and the stock
         certificates were issued.
     31—Subscribers to the remaining 500 shares paid half of the balance owed.

Required:

(a) Journal entries to record the stock transactions.
(b) A balance sheet as of May 31, 19+4, assuming that the transactions above are
    the only ones for the month.

Problem B12-3. Graham Corporation was organized early in January, 19+7. Authorization was ob-
tained to issue 10,000 shares of $10 par value common stock. The following transactions
took place during the month of January:

January 10—Subscriptions were received for 2,500 shares at $10 per share.
        13—The subscriptions received January 10 were collected in full and stock
            certificates were issued.
        20—Subscriptions were received for 3,000 shares at $14 per share.
        23—The subscriptions received January 20 were collected in full and stock
            certificates were issued.
        26—Subscriptions were taken for 2,000 shares at $15 per share.
        30—Subscriptions received January 26 for 500 shares were collected in full
            and $4,500 cash was received from other subscribers of that date.

Required:

(a) Journal entries for the stock transactions.
(b) Postings to the following general ledger accounts:
    Subscriptions Receivable
    Common Stock
    Common Stock Subscribed
    Capital in Excess of Par Value—From Common Stock Issuances
(c) The Stockholders' Equity section of the January 31, 19+7 balance sheet.

Problem B12-4. The stockholders' equity of Patton Company consists of $100,000 of $25 par value
common stock, all of which was sold for cash at $25 per share. The management of the
firm is considering the following alternatives for obtaining additional financing of $50,000:

(a) Sale of $25 par value common stock at par.
(b) Sale of 5 per cent cumulative preferred stock at par.

Required:

(a) Computation of the rate of return to common stockholders under each alternative,
    assuming an annual income of $18,000.
(b) The same computations, assuming an income of $6,000 annually.

Problem B12-5. The charter of Weber Corporation authorized 50,000 shares of no-par common stock
and 30,000 shares of $50 par value, 6 per cent cumulative preferred stock. The following
stock transactions have taken place since the date of organization:

March 1, 19+2—Sold 20,000 shares of common stock at $12 per share.
August 1, 19+2—Sold 10,000 shares of preferred stock at $53 per share.
December 31, 19+2—Sold 5,000 shares of common stock at $18 per share.

Required:

(a) Journal entries to record the stock transactions.
(b) Preparation of the Stockholders' Equity section of the firm's balance sheet as of December 31, 19+2, assuming retained earnings of $48,000.
(c) The entry to record the calling of all the preferred stock at $60 per share on December 31, 19+4, assuming a retained earnings balance of $110,000.

Problem B12-6. Albert Alvis, Benny Baker, and Clyde Coats organized Sunset Corporation on January 1, 19+1, with authorized capital of 5,000 shares of $100 par value common stock.

On January 1, the organizers subscribed to stock at $105 per share as follows: Alvis, 1,000 shares; Baker, 1,200 shares; and Coats, 900 shares.

On January 10, Alvis transferred land having a value of $30,000 and a building valued at $60,000 to the corporation in partial payment of his subscription.

On January 12, 500 shares of common stock were sold to Danny Davis for cash at $110 per share.

Edward Earnest transferred a patent to the corporation on January 14, receiving in exchange 1,000 shares of common stock. Virtually nothing is known about the value of the patent.

A local attorney rendered a bill on January 23 for legal fees incurred in the organization of the firm. The attorney accepted 50 shares of stock in full payment and the certificate was issued.

On January 31, the balance was collected on all subscriptions and stock certificates were issued. No other transactions occurred this month.

Required:

(a) Journal entries for the January transactions.
(b) Postings of the transactions to ledger accounts.
(c) A classified balance sheet as of January 31, 19+1.

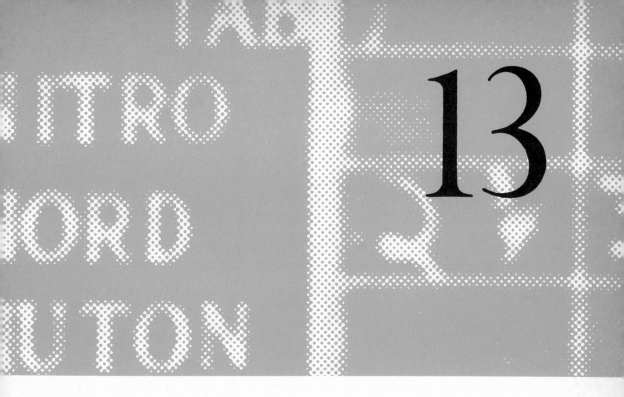

Stockholders' Equity (Concluded)

Terminology. The following terms are used in reference to capital stock.

PAR VALUE: This is a nominal value, printed on the certificate. For instance, if a corporation is authorized to issue $100,000 of capital stock, represented by 1,000 shares, the par value of each share is $100. When a dividend rate is stated in connection with par value stock, such as 6% preferred stock with a $25 par value, the rate is applied to the par value.

BOOK VALUE: To determine the book value of a share of stock of a certain class, divide the stockholders' equity applicable to the class by the number of shares of the class outstanding.

For instance, if a corporation has 1,000 shares of common stock (and no preferred stock) outstanding, and its balance sheet shows:

Capital stock	$100,000
Retained earnings.	30,000
Total	$130,000

the book value of each share is $130,000 ÷ 1,000, or $130.

If there is preferred stock outstanding, the preferred stockholders' interest in the retained earnings will depend upon whether the stock is participating, and also upon whether the preferred stock is cumulative and whether there are preferred dividends in arrears.

Generally, book value is a poor indicator of what a share of stock is worth. Unless all of the corporation's assets are stated in the accounts at their present value, the stockholders' equity, being the remainder after subtracting the liabilities from the assets (Assets − Liabilities = Stockholders' Equity), will not indicate the value of the company's outstanding capital stock.

MARKET VALUE: This is the price at which a share of stock can be sold. It depends partly on the book value of the stock and partly on the corporation's earnings record and the prospects of future earnings and dividends.

LIQUIDATION VALUE: This is the amount which a stockholder will be entitled to receive if the corporation goes out of business, disposes of its assets, pays its liabilities, and distributes the residue among its stockholders. If common stock only is outstanding, its liquidation value will depend only on the amount available for distribution to the stockholders after the realization of the assets and the payment of liabilities and liquidation expenses. If common and preferred stocks are outstanding, the liquidation values of both classes will also depend upon whether the preferred stock is preferred as to assets and whether the preferred stockholders are entitled to any dividends in arrears.

REDEMPTION VALUE: Corporations sometimes issue preferred stock with a right to redeem it. The redemption or call price may be stated in terms such as: *par, par and dividends in arrears,* or *par and a premium of $5 per share.*

STATED CAPITAL: Among the advantages of the corporate form of business organization is that of limited liability: the stockholders are not personally liable for the debts of the corporation. Since the law gives stockholders this protection, it is only fair that creditors should be given some assurance that the corporation will not make payments to its stockholders, either as dividends or for the acquisition or retirement of stock, which will reduce the stockholders' equity below a stipulated amount.

Originally the corporation laws placed restrictions only on dividends. More recently it has been recognized that the protection of creditors is inadequate unless, in addition to a restriction on dividends, there is a restriction on the amount which can be paid to stockholders for the acquisition or retirement of their stock.

For the reasons indicated above, a definition of stated capital has been included in the laws of many states. Unfortunately, the concepts of stated capital are not uniform in all states. In some, the stated capital includes the total amount received for par or no-par shares issued, including any amount credited to an account other than Capital Stock. In other states, the stated capital is measured by the par value of par shares or, with respect to no-par shares, the amount per share which the directors elect to credit to a capital stock account. In some states, the amount which the directors elect to establish as stated capital per share cannot be less than a minimum fixed by law.

Since it has come to be realized that a restriction as to dividends is only a partial protection to creditors, many state statutes prescribe that the stated or legal capital must not be impaired either by the payment of dividends or by disbursements for the acquisition or retirement of shares.

Legality of dividends. Under what conditions does a company have a legal right to declare a dividend? It is difficult to state general rules; they would be subject to exceptions because the laws of the various states differ in their regulations. In general, but subject to restrictions mentioned below, it may be said that a corporation has a right to pay a dividend if it has retained earnings that were produced by either operations or extraneous transactions, but dividends must not reduce the stockholders' equity below the amount of the stated or legal capital.

The opinion has sometimes been expressed that dividends should be paid only from funds generated by the retention of earnings. This may be incorrect, depending on the law of the state of incorporation. It probably would be better to say that stockholders should have a right to assume that dividends come from retained earnings, and that, if they come from any other source, disclosure should be made to the stockholders. There have been instances in which a corporation has charged dividends to an account that was credited with the excess of the issuance proceeds of stock over the par or stated value thereof, thus merely giving back to the stockholders a portion of their investment but giving the impression that they are receiving dividends out of earnings.

Dividend restrictions. Dividend restrictions may result from:

    (A) Contracts:

        (1) With creditors.

            Bond indentures may place a limitation on the amount of dividends that can be paid while the bonds are outstanding.

        (2) With preferred stockholders.

            If, under the terms of issuance, the preferred stock of a company is to be retired (periodically or otherwise) out of funds provided by earnings, the charter provisions for the retirement of the preferred stock may place a limitation on dividends to the holders of common stock while any of the preferred stock is outstanding.

        Such restrictions are intended to safeguard the bondholders or preferred stockholders by preventing an impairment of working capital. If part of the funds produced by operations were used for the retirement of bonds or stock and, in addition, dividends were paid to the full amount of the net income, the working capital might be depleted to the point where operations would be hampered and the corporation's stability weakened.

    (B) Law:

        Mention has previously been made of the fact that many state statutes prescribe that the total of dividends and disbursements for the acquisition of a company's own shares must not impair the stated capital. As a result, a portion of the retained earnings equal to the cost of the stock acquired becomes unavailable for dividend charges.

(C) Voluntary action by the directors:

    (1) To indicate that dividends will be limited in order to permit the accumulation of funds for general purposes or for some specific purpose, such as the acquisition of additional equipment.

    (2) To indicate the existence of a contingency that might result in a loss, but a loss so problematical and so impossible of reasonable estimate that a charge therefor against current earnings or retained earnings at this time would be unwarranted.

In the past, dividend restrictions such as those mentioned above frequently were recorded by journal entries making transfers from the retained earnings account to "restricted" or "appropriated" retained earnings accounts, which were shown in the Stockholders' Equity section of the balance sheet. No charges could properly be made against such accounts except to restore all or portions of their balances to the retained earnings account.

More recently it has come to be recognized that better disclosure can be made: By parenthetical comments in the balance sheet, such as:

> Retained earnings (of which $15,000 is not available for dividend charges because of restrictions in the bond indenture) $90,000

Or by footnotes below the balance sheet totals, such as:

> Note—The company is defendant in a suit alleging patent infringement. The company's management and counsel are of the opinion that the allegation is unwarranted.

(Footnotes to the financial statements are regarded by accountants as being part of the statements.)

A balance sheet procedure for showing a dividend restriction resulting from the purchase of a company's own stock is shown on page 304.

Financial policy with respect to dividends. In making their decisions with respect to the amounts of dividend payments, directors give consideration not only to the amount legally available for the payment of dividends but also to matters of financial policy. A dividend payment may be undesirable because the available cash is inadequate; but, if there is only a temporary shortage of cash, the directors may consider it advisable to borrow money for dividend purposes in order to maintain a continuity of dividend payments. Even when adequate cash is available, the directors may consider it advisable to pay no dividends, or to pay dividends of only limited amounts, in order to conserve the funds for expansion of the business.

Significant dates applicable to dividends, and related entries. For corporations with only a few stockholders and with infrequent transfers of shares, it may be practicable to declare and pay a dividend on the same day. But for large corporations with many stockholders and frequent transfers of shares, such a procedure would be impracticable. Under such conditions there are three significant dates applicable to dividends: the date of declaration, the date of record, and the date of payment.

DATE OF DECLARATION: On the date when the dividend is declared, and a liability therefore created, the following entry is made:

```
Dividends (contra to retained earnings) . . . . . . . . . . . . . .   100,000
    Dividends payable . . . . . . . . . . . . . . . . . . . . . . . .              100,000
    To record the declaration of a dividend.
```

DATE OF RECORD: The directors' resolution authorizing the payment of a dividend states a date as of which the corporation, by an examination of its stock records, will determine the "stockholders of record." For instance, a dividend may be declared on January 5, payable on January 30 to stockholders of record on January 20. If stock is purchased after the dividend declaration date but in time to have the change in ownership recorded by the date of record, the *purchaser* obtains the right to the dividend. When there is no longer sufficient time to record the change in ownership before the date of record, the stock is sold "ex-dividend"—that is, the *seller* is entitled to the dividend.

No entry need be made by the company on the date of record.

DATE OF PAYMENT: A period of time is usually required between the date of record and the date of payment because of the work involved in the determination of the stockholders of record and the preparation of the dividend checks. When the checks are mailed, thus removing the liability, the following entry is made:

```
Dividends payable . . . . . . . . . . . . . . . . . . . . . . . . . .   100,000
    Cash . . . . . . . . . . . . . . . . . . . . . . . . . . . . . . . .              100,000
    Payment, to stockholders of record on January 20, of dividend
    declared on January 5.
```

Unpaid declared dividends. After a dividend has been legally declared and notice of the declaration has been given to the stockholders, by publication or otherwise, the unpaid dividend ranks as a liability and should be shown as such in the balance sheet, usually under the Current Liabilities caption. The directors may rescind the declaration of a dividend, but they can do so only if no notice of the declaration has been given to the shareholders.

Dividends in arrears on preferred stock. Since even a preferred stockholder has no right to a dividend until it is declared, preferred dividends do not accrue; no entry for them should be made until the date of declaration.

But if dividends on cumulative preferred stock are in arrears, there is an obligation to pay these arrearages before dividends are paid to the common stockholders. The amount of the cumulative dividends in arrears should, therefore, be shown in the balance sheet. This is usually done in a footnote below the balance sheet totals, thus:

Note: Cumulative dividends on preferred stock were in arrears on (the balance sheet date) in the amount of $12,000.

Cash dividends and retained earnings. One prerequisite to any dividend payment is that sufficient cash be available. Some stockholders may equate the amount of retained earnings reported on the balance sheet with cash. However, there is no direct relationship between the amounts. Retained earnings are a part of the stockholders' equity in the assets of the firm, and cash is only one of many forms the assets may take.

For example, assume that a corporation has the following balance sheet:

Cash	$100,000	Common stock	$ 50,000
		Retained earnings	50,000
	$100,000		$100,000

If the firm purchases a building for $95,000 cash, the balance sheet will be:

Cash	$ 5,000	Common stock	$ 50,000
Building	95,000	Retained earnings	50,000
	$100,000		$100,000

Retained earnings are still $50,000, but only $5,000 is available for dividends.

Stock dividends. Dividends are sometimes paid in capital stock instead of in cash. Usually the dividend distribution is in common stock to holders of common stock.

To illustrate, assume that a company has 10,000 authorized shares of common stock of $10 par value, of which 6,000 shares are outstanding; also assume that a 10 per cent stock dividend (600 shares) is declared and immediately issued. The Committee on Accounting Procedure of the American Institute of Certified Public Accountants has taken the position that, when the shares issued as a dividend are less than about 20 per cent of the shares previously outstanding, an amount equal to the fair value of the shares issued should be capitalized by transfer from retained earnings. Assuming that the shares issued in this illustration have a fair value of $12 each, the entry to record the distribution of the stock dividend is:

Stock dividends (to be closed to Retained Earnings) 7,200
    Common stock 6,000
    Capital in excess of par value—From stock dividends 1,200
    Issuance of a 10% dividend: 600 shares of $10 par value stock
    having a fair value of $12 each.

Assume that the stock was without par value and that it had been given a stated value of $7.50 per share; the entry would be:

Stock dividends (to be closed to Retained Earnings) 7,200
    Common stock 4,500
    Capital in excess of stated value—From stock dividends . . . 2,700
    Issuance of a 10% dividend: 600 shares of no-par stock (stated
    value, $7.50 per share) having a fair value of $12 each.

Stock splits. A stock split should be distinguished from a stock dividend. A stock split occurs when a corporation, after obtaining the required approval of its board of directors and stockholders, issues additional shares based on some multiple of the outstanding shares held by existing stockholders prior to the split. For example, after a 2-for-1 stock split, every stockholder would hold twice as many shares.

The increase in the number of shares is accompanied by a proportionate reduction in the par or stated value of the class of stock being split. To expand on the above example of a 2-for-1 stock split, assume that the stock being split had a stated value of $10 per share. The stated value would be changed to $5 per share. Consequently, a stock split does not cause any changes in the dollar balances of the stockholders' equity accounts. To illustrate:

Account balances *before* stock split:

Stockholders' equity:		
Common stock, $10 stated value; 100,000 shares issued and outstanding	$1,000,000	
Capital in excess of stated value—From stock issuances	200,000	$1,200,000
Retained earnings		600,000
		$1,800,000

Account balances *after* a 2-for-1 stock split; stated value reduced by one-half, to $5 per share:

Stockholders' equity:		
Common stock, $5 stated value; 200,000 shares issued and outstanding	$1,000,000	
Capital in excess of stated value—From stock issuances	200,000	$1,200,000
Retained earnings		600,000
		$1,800,000

No debit-credit entry need be made in the accounts for a stock split. Of course, the title of the common stock account should be revised to indicate the new stated value. Also, the company's records should show the new number of shares outstanding. Such revisions can be made by suitable notations in the ledger and supporting records, or the following journal entry can be made to accomplish the same purpose:

Common stock, $10 stated value	1,000,000	
Common stock, $5 stated value		1,000,000
Reduction in stated value and increase in outstanding shares from 100,000 to 200,000 as a result of a 2-for-1 stock split.		

Since a stock split does not result in any changes in account balances or changes in the proportionate holdings of the individual stockholders (if a stockholder owned 5 per cent of the outstanding shares before a stock split he would continue to own 5 per cent of the outstanding shares after a stock split), why does a corporation split its stock? The reasons relate to such matters as the level of market price of the company's stock and the extent of distribution of stock ownership desired by the company's management. To elaborate, suppose that a company's stock has a market value of $300 per share. If the company made a 5-for-1 stock split, the market value would drop to about one-fifth of its former value, or $60 per share. Experience indicates that the new price level will attract additional investors. The commission charged by stockbrokers for the purchase of shares of stock is less per share for a round lot of 100 shares than for an odd lot of less than 100 shares. The actions of investors support the following generalization: Investors are more inclined to purchase 100 shares of $60 stock than 20 shares of $300 stock.

The following list of questions and answers should help differentiate stock dividends and stock splits.

	Stock Dividends	Stock Splits
Will the action:		
Change the number of shares outstanding?	Yes	Yes
Change the per cent of stock ownership among the company's stockholders?	No	No
Alter the par or stated value of the capital stock?	No	Yes
Result in income to the stockholders?	No	No
Alter the retained earnings balance?	Yes (reduce it)	No
Alter the capital stock account balance?	Yes (increase it)	No
Change the dollar balance of the Stockholders' Equity section of the balance sheet?	No	No

Treasury stock. Treasury stock is a corporation's own stock which has been issued, reacquired, and not canceled in accordance with a formal procedure specified by law. It will be noted that there are three important elements in this definition:

(1)   Treasury stock must be the company's own stock; holdings of the stocks of other companies are not treasury stock.

(2)   The stock must have been issued.

(3)   The stock, although reacquired, must not have been canceled. Cancellation of stock is brought about by a procedure prescribed by law, and places the stock in the status of unissued, or sometimes even unauthorized, shares.

Treasury stock is not an asset. Although treasury shares may have a ready marketability and may again become outstanding, it seems obvious that treasury stock, like unissued stock, is not an asset but is merely a possible source of additional funds.

Although treasury stock has been shown in balance sheets as an asset (sometimes even combined with securities which *are* assets, under some title such as "Government Bonds and Other Securities"), accountants now generally recognize that the acquisition of treasury stock causes a reduction in the stockholders' equity.

Treasury stock in the balance sheet. Since the acquisition of treasury stock causes a reduction of the stockholders' equity to the extent of the cost of the stock, the cost should be shown as a deduction in the Stockholders' Equity section of the balance sheet. There are several ways of showing the deduction; the method illustrated below is generally regarded as acceptable provided the corporation was organized in a state where the holding of treasury stock does not impose a restriction on dividends. (Balance sheet presentations when dividend restrictions exist are shown later.) The illustration is based on the following facts with respect to the capital stock:

The authorized issue is 1,000 shares of $100 par value common.
All the authorized stock has been issued.
The corporation has reacquired 100 shares at a cost of $12,000.

The distinction between "issued" and "outstanding" should be noted. All of the 1,000 shares have been issued, and are so shown. The number of outstanding shares is not stated directly in the balance sheet, but can be easily determined; there are 900 outstanding, the difference between the issued shares and the treasury shares.

Stockholders' equity:
Common stock—$100 par value; authorized and issued,
    1,000 shares, of which 100 shares are in the treasury . $100,000
Retained earnings   25,000
Total $125,000
Deduct cost of treasury stock 12,000 $113,000

Incidentally, corporations do not pay dividends on treasury stock. Continuing with the above illustration, should the board of directors authorize the payment of a cash dividend of $1 per share, the dividend payment would amount to $900 ($1 × 900 [shares outstanding]).

If a company originally issued its stock at more than par or stated value, the facts may be shown in the balance sheet in this manner:

Stockholders' equity:
Common stock—$100 par value; authorized and
    issued, 1,000 shares, of which 100 shares are
    in the treasury $100,000
Capital in excess of par value—From common
    stock issuances 10,000 $110,000
Retained earnings   25,000
Total $135,000
Deduct cost of treasury stock 12,000 $123,000

If treasury stock is acquired by donation, there is no cost to deduct; the facts may be shown as follows:

Stockholders' equity:
Common stock—$100 par value; authorized and issued,
    1,000 shares, of which 100 shares, acquired by dona-
    tion, are in the treasury $100,000
Retained earnings 25,000 $125,000

Recording treasury stock acquisitions—cost basis. As indicated above, the cost of treasury stock may properly be shown in the balance sheet as a deduction in the Stockholders' Equity section. To provide the information for this balance sheet presentation, it is considered proper to debit the treasury stock account with the cost of the stock acquired. If this procedure is adopted, an acquisition of treasury stock is recorded as follows:

```
Treasury stock ................................  12,000
     Cash  ......................................              12,000
     To record the acquisition of 100 shares of $100 par value
     stock at a cost of $12,000.
```

An entry of this nature should be made regardless of whether the shares have a par value or are without par value, and regardless of the amount which was received for the shares when they were issued. The treasury stock account title should indicate the nature of the stock if there is more than one class of issued stock. If the company has only one class of stock, the account title may be merely Treasury Stock; otherwise, it might be Treasury Stock—Preferred, or Treasury Stock—Common, or Treasury Stock—Common—No Par Value.

As noted, stockholders sometimes donate shares to the company; this may be done because the company needs working capital and the stockholders do not wish to invest additional funds; they, therefore, donate portions of their stock, which possibly can be used to obtain additional funds. Since donated shares are acquired without cost, no debit and credit entries are made to record the acquisition. A memorandum notation is made in the treasury stock account, as shown below:

Treasury Stock

Date		50 shares donated						

Disposal of treasury shares—cost basis. When treasury stock is disposed of, the treasury stock account should be credited with the acquisition price. Entries under various conditions are shown below.

DISPOSAL AT COST: Assume that the treasury stock acquired for $12,000 is disposed of for $12,000; the entry is:

```
Cash ........................................  12,000
     Treasury stock .............................              12,000
```

DISPOSAL AT A PRICE IN EXCESS OF COST: Assume that the shares brought $13,500; the entry is:

```
Cash ........................................  13,500
     Treasury stock .............................              12,000
     Capital in excess of par value—From treasury stock trans-
         actions .................................               1,500
```

DISPOSAL AT A PRICE LESS THAN COST: The method of recording disposals of treasury stock at a price less than the original cost depends on the law of the state of incorporation and the stockholders' equity accounts on the company's books. Assume that shares acquired for $12,000 brought only $11,500. If treasury stock of the same class had previously been disposed of at more than cost, the entry for the present disposal might be:

Cash	11,500	
Capital in excess of par value—From treasury stock transactions	500	
Treasury stock		12,000

In the absence of any such applicable "capital in excess" accounts, the charge should be made to Retained Earnings, thus:

Cash	11,500	
Retained earnings	500	
Treasury stock		12,000

DISPOSAL OF DONATED SHARES: The entire proceeds from the disposal of donated treasury stock should be credited to Capital in Excess of Par Value—From Treasury Stock Transactions.

Recommended departure from the cost basis. The procedure recommended by committees of the American Accounting Association to account for treasury stock transactions is indicated by the following quotation from *Accounting Concepts and Standards Underlying Corporate Financial Statements:*

"An outlay by a corporation for shares of its own stock should be treated as a reduction of paid-in capital up to the pro-rata amount represented by the acquired shares, whether or not such shares are reissuable. If the outlay for the reacquired shares exceeds the pro-rata reduction in paid-in capital, the excess should be treated as a distribution of retained income. The reissue of acquired shares should be accounted for in the same manner as an original issue of corporate shares."

As an illustration of the recommended procedure, let us assume that a company's no-par stock was originally issued at $80 per share, of which $75 was credited to Capital Stock and $5 was credited to Capital in Excess of Stated Value—From Stock Issuances. Also assume that a share of treasury stock is acquired at a cost of $85. If the recommended procedure is used, the entry is:

Treasury stock (Amount originally credited to Capital Stock)	75	
Capital in excess of stated value—From stock issuances (Per-share amount originally credited to this account)	5	
Retained earnings	5	
Cash		85

It is believed that this procedure is followed much less frequently than the cost-basis procedure.

Dividend restrictions resulting from treasury stock acquisitions. Assume that a company has issued capital stock of $100,000 par value and has retained earnings of $25,000, but that it is holding treasury stock which it acquired at a cost of $12,000. Assume also that the law of the state of incorporation provides that dividend payments and treasury stock acquisitions, together, must not impair the stated capital—which, in this illustration, is assumed to be par value of the issued shares, including the treasury shares. In effect, this means that a $12,000 portion of the retained earnings is restricted* so long as the treasury stock is retained, and that, so long as this restriction exists, dividends and disbursements for additional treasury stock acquisitions must not, together, exceed the $13,000 unrestricted retained earnings. The balance sheet should be prepared in such a way as to disclose this restriction. The following Stockholders' Equity section of the balance sheet illustrates a method of making the disclosure.

```
Stockholders' equity:
  Common stock—$100 par value; authorized and issued,
    1,000 shares, of which 100 shares are in the treasury . . . . . . . .   $100,000
  Retained earnings:
    Not available for dividend charges—Equal to cost of
      treasury stock . . . . . . . . . . . . . . . . . . . . . . . . .   $12,000
    Free  . . . . . . . . . . . . . . . . . . . . . . . . . . . . . .    13,000    25,000
  Total . . . . . . . . . . . . . . . . . . . . . . . . . . . . . . . . . . .   $125,000
  Deduct cost of treasury stock . . . . . . . . . . . . . . . . . . . . .     12,000
  Stockholders' equity . . . . . . . . . . . . . . . . . . . . . . . . .   $113,000
```

Reporting stockholders' equity by sources. Stockholders' equity accounts are generally presented in the balance sheet so as to show the major sources of the equity. Basically there are two sources:

Paid-in capital. This includes all amounts invested in the corporation by the stockholders in exchange for shares of stock.

Retained earnings. The portion of the earnings of the firm which has been kept within the firm. This would be the sum of all earnings since organization, reduced by losses and dividends.

The following illustration shows the balance sheet treatment of various matters affecting the stockholders' equity.

---

*The state laws differ with respect to the effect of a treasury stock acquisition on retained earnings. In at least one state, the retained earnings are reduced; more commonly, they are merely restricted.

Stockholders' equity:
Capital stock:

Preferred stock—6% cumulative, participating; par value, $100; authorized and issued, 1,000 shares	$100,000		
Common stock—No par value; stated value, $10; authorized and issued, 10,000 shares, of which 500 shares are in the treasury	100,000	$200,000	
Capital in excess of par or stated value:			
From preferred stock issuances	$ 5,000		
From common stock issuances	27,000		
From treasury stock transactions	2,000		
From stock dividends	3,000	37,000	$237,000
Retained earnings:			
Not available for dividend charges—Equal to cost of treasury stock	$ 7,500		
Free	132,000	139,500	
Total			$376,500
Deduct cost of treasury stock			7,500
Stockholders' equity			$369,000

Instead of detailing the four elements of Capital in Excess of Par or Stated Value, a balance sheet might show merely:

Capital in excess of par or stated value 37,000

Charges to "capital in excess" accounts. Accounts such as those shown in the foregoing illustrative Stockholders' Equity section under the caption "Capital in excess of par or stated value" should never be charged with asset write-downs and losses that normally would be charged to income or retained earnings. Following are two illustrations of the application of the rule. If the allowance for uncollectible accounts is inadequate, it should not be increased by an offsetting debit to such an account; nor should such an account be charged with write-downs of long-lived assets.

Donated capital. Donated capital results from gifts of assets to a corporation. A common example was mentioned earlier, namely, the gift of a plant to induce a business to locate in the donor city.

Donated assets are recorded at their estimated value, with the credit to Donated Capital. The donated capital account is shown in the balance sheet under the Stockholders' Equity caption. It is usually listed separately just above retained earnings.

Appraisal increments. Prior to 1940, it was not an uncommon practice for companies to write up their long-lived assets to appraised values. The offsetting credit was shown as an element of the stockholders' equity. Various account titles were given to the credit-balance account; those most appropriate clearly indicated the source of the credit balance and that the amount represented an unrealized increment.

As noted in Chapter 10, the writing up of long-lived assets to appraised values is now regarded by the accounting profession as an improper practice. It follows that a credit balance denoting an unrealized increment from the writing up of long-lived assets is not a proper element of stockholders' equity.

ASSIGNMENT
MATERIAL

QUESTIONS

1. How is the book value of a share of stock determined? Why is book value generally a poor indicator of the worth of a share of stock?
2. What are two ways in which state laws define stated capital? What is the significance of stated capital?
3. Generally, when may a corporation legally declare a dividend?
4. Discuss three situations in which dividends may be restricted.
5. What factors influence a corporation's dividend policy?
6. What are three significant dates pertaining to dividends? Show by example the entries, if any, which are required on each date.
7. Describe the proper accounting treatment of a stock dividend.
8. What is the difference between a stock split and a stock dividend?
9. Why might a corporation wish to effect a stock split?
10. Define treasury stock. How should treasury stock be reported in the financial statements?
11. Describe two methods of accounting for the acquisition of treasury stock.
12. What are the two major sources of stockholders' equity?

SHORT EXERCISES

E13-1. The stockholders' equity of McQueen Corporation consists of the following on December 31, 19+8:

Preferred stock (5%, $100 par)	$ 50,000
Common stock ($25 par)	80,000
Capital in excess of par—From common stock issuances	16,000
Retained earnings	20,000
Total	$166,000

Dividends were last paid on the preferred stock for the year ended December 31, 19+6. Compute the book value per share of the preferred and common stock, assuming: (a) that the preferred stock is noncumulative; (b) that the preferred stock is cumulative.

E13-2. Knoxville Company has 5,000 shares of 6%, $50 par value preferred stock and 10,000 shares of no-par value common stock outstanding. Present entries for the following dividend transactions which took place during 19+5. Omit explanations.

  (1) Paid the annual cash dividend on the preferred stock. The dividend was declared on December 15, 19+4.
  (2) Declared a cash dividend of $1 per share on the common stock.
  (3) Paid the common stock dividend.
  (4) Declared and issued a 10 per cent stock dividend on the common stock. The fair value of the stock issued is $18 per share.

E13-3. The stockholders' equity of Swansea Corporation consists of the following:

Common stock ($10 par)	$50,000	
Capital in excess of par—From common stock issuances	25,000	
Retained earnings	60,000	$135,000

Present the Stockholders' Equity section of the firm's balance sheet after the declaration and issuance of a 5 per cent stock dividend. The fair value of the common stock is $20 per share.

E13-4. Using the data in Exercise 3, present the Stockholders' Equity section after a 2-for-1 stock split rather than a 5 per cent stock dividend.

E13-5. Kershaw Corporation acquired 600 shares of its own $25 par value common stock at a total cost of $18,000, using the cost basis to record the acquisition. Journalize the following sales of the stock: (a) 300 shares at $32 per share; (b) 200 shares at $35 per share; (c) 100 shares at $27 per share.

PROBLEMS

Problem A13-1. Haslem Corporation had 1,000 shares of 5% cumulative $50 par value preferred stock and 10,000 shares of $25 par value common stock outstanding on July 1, 19+6. The following transactions took place during the month of July.

  July 2—Declared a cash dividend of $.50 per share on the preferred stock.
       5—Declared a 10 per cent stock dividend on the common stock. Fair value at the time was $27 per share.
      13—Acquired 500 shares of common stock for $12,500. (The company records treasury stock acquisitions at cost.)
      20—Sold 200 shares of treasury stock at $26 per share.
      22—Sold 300 shares of treasury stock for $7,500.
      31—Paid the cash dividend declared on July 2.

  Show the journal entries required to record the transactions.

Problem A13-2. Summerville Company has 3,000 shares of $100 par value, 5 per cent preferred stock and 8,000 shares of $50 par value common stock outstanding. The company paid dividends during a three-year period as follows:

19+2	$ 6,000
19+3	28,000
19+4	42,000

Compute the total dividends paid to each class of stock for the three-year period under each of the following assumptions:

(a) The preferred stock is noncumulative and nonparticipating.
(b) The preferred stock is cumulative and nonparticipating.
(c) The preferred stock is cumulative and fully participating.

Problem A13-3. The following information pertains to Maris Corporation as of December 31, 19+4:

Preferred stock—6% cumulative; par value, $100; 1,500 shares authorized	$150,000
Common stock—Par value, $10; 20,000 shares authorized	200,000
Retained earnings	40,000
Capital in excess of par value—From treasury stock transactions	10,000
Donated capital	20,000
Capital in excess of par value—From common stock issuances	15,000

Dividends have been paid on the preferred stock through December 31, 19+2.

Required:

(a) The Stockholders' Equity section of the balance sheet as of December 31, 19+4.
(b) Computation of book value per share for each class of stock as of December 31, 19+4.

Problem A13-4. Partial balance sheets of Ponder Corporation are presented below. (a) Prepare journal entries to reflect the transactions affecting stockholders' equity during the year. Assume any stock subscriptions are paid in full immediately upon subscription.

(b) Compute the net income for 19+4, assuming no cash dividends were paid.

PONDER CORPORATION
Partial Balance Sheet
December 31, 19+3

Stockholders' equity:		
Common stock—No par; stated value, $20; authorized, 6,000 shares; issued, 4,000 shares		$ 80,000
Capital in excess of stated value—From common stock issuances		16,000
Total		$ 96,000
Retained earnings		55,000
Total stockholders' equity		$151,000

PONDER CORPORATION
Partial Balance Sheet
December 31, 19+4

Stockholders' equity:		
Common stock—No par; stated value, $20; authorized, 6,000 shares; issued, 5,480 shares, of which 200 shares are in the treasury		$109,600
Capital in excess of stated value:		
From common stock issuances	$26,000	
From stock dividends	2,400	28,400
Total		$138,000
Retained earnings		63,500
Total		$201,500
Deduct cost of treasury stock		7,000
Total stockholders' equity		$194,500

The treasury stock was acquired prior to the issuance of 480 shares as a stock dividend.

Problem A 13-5. Fisher Company was organized on January 1, 19+1, with authorized capital of 10,000 shares of no-par common stock. A stated value of $10 per share was assigned to the stock. The following selected transactions occurred in the order listed over a period of several years:

   (1) Issued 2,000 shares of stock at $10 per share.
   (2) Issued 2,000 shares of stock at $12 per share.
   (3) Acquired 500 shares of treasury stock at $14 per share.
   (4) Paid a cash dividend of $1 per share.
   (5) Sold 300 shares of treasury stock at $15 per share.
   (6) Paid a cash dividend of $1 per share.
   (7) Sold 200 shares of treasury stock at $19 per share.
   (8) Paid a 10 per cent stock dividend. Fair value of the stock at the time was $19 per share.
   (9) Paid a cash dividend of $1.25 per share.
  (10) Split the stock 2-for-1.
  (11) Paid a cash dividend of $1 per share.
  (12) Paid a 5 per cent stock dividend. Fair value of the stock at this time was $11 per share.
  (13) Acquired 1,000 shares of treasury stock at $15 per share.
  (14) Sold 300 shares of treasury stock at $16 per share.

The company uses the cost basis to account for its treasury stock transactions.

Required:

  (a) Journal entries to record the transactions. Omit explanations.
  (b) The Stockholders' Equity section of the balance sheet as of December 31, 19+8, the end of the period covered by the above transactions. Retained earnings on this date totaled $67,000. The company was organized in a state where treasury stock acquisitions must not impair stated capital.

Problem A 13-6. The information below is taken from the general ledger of Alpine Corporation on June 30, 19+7.

Cash	$ 12,500
Accounts receivable	28,543
Land	25,000
Building	200,000
Treasury stock—Preferred	9,900
Treasury stock—Common	5,700
Organization costs	3,500
Capital in excess of par value—From common stock issuances	14,000
Common stock subscribed	10,000
Common stock	95,000
Subscriptions receivable—Common	8,000
Dividends payable	1,800
Preferred stock	60,000
Subscriptions receivable—Preferred	12,500
Preferred stock subscribed	30,000
Allowance for uncollectibles	1,200
Accumulated depreciation—Building	15,000
Retained earnings	68,343
Capital in excess of par value—From treasury stock transactions	5,800
Merchandise inventory	16,500
Accounts payable	21,000

The company was authorized to issue 2,000 shares of 5 per cent cumulative participating preferred stock with a par value of $100, and 3,000 shares of $50 par value common stock. It has issued 600 shares of preferred and 1,900 shares of common. Shares subscribed for but not issued consist of 300 preferred and 200 common, and the subscriptions are due in the near future.

The company holds 90 shares of preferred and 100 shares of common in the treasury, both classes being carried at cost. The company is organized in a state where treasury stock acquisitions must not impair the stated capital.

Prepare a classified balance sheet as of June 30, 19+7.

Problem B13-1. Bryant Corporation has authorized capital of 10,000 shares of $10 par value common stock. There were 5,000 shares outstanding on October 1, 19+3, all having been sold at a price of $12 per share.

The following transactions took place during the month of October.

October 3—Acquired 500 shares of treasury stock at $18 per share.
           10—Sold 200 shares of treasury stock for $20 per share.
           12—Received 300 shares of the company's stock as a donation.
           18—Sold the donated treasury stock for $21 per share.
           26—Sold 300 shares of treasury stock for $20 per share.

Show the journal entries to record the transactions, using the cost basis.

Problem B13-2. Foushee Company acquired 1,000 shares of its no-par common stock on August 2, 19+2, at a price of $30 per share. The stock has a stated value of $25 per share. Of the 50,000 shares authorized, 25,000 shares were originally sold for $28 per share.

The treasury stock, which was recorded at cost, was disposed of as follows:

September 3, 19+2 . . . . .300 shares for $30 per share.
December 12, 19+2 . . . . .300 shares for $33 per share.
January 8, 19+3 . . . . .400 shares for $28 per share.

Required:

(a) Journal entries to record the acquisition and subsequent sale of the treasury stock.
(b) The Stockholders' Equity section of the company's balance sheet as of December 31, 19+2, assuming a retained earnings balance of $45,000. The company was organized in a state where treasury stock acquisitions must not impair stated capital.

Problem B13-3. Dunlap Corporation was organized on January 1, 19+4, with an authorized capital of 1,000 shares of 6 per cent, $100 par value cumulative preferred stock and 5,000 shares of $50 par value common stock.

As of December 31, 19+8, the company had issued the following stock:

January 1, 19+4 . . . . .2,500 shares of common at $50 per share.
January 11, 19+4. . . . . .500 shares of preferred at $110 per share.
January 1, 19+6 . . . . .250 shares of common issued as a stock dividend.
January 1, 19+6 . . . . .1,250 shares of common at $58 per share.

During the period from January 1, 19+4, to December 31, 19+8, the corporation reported earnings and paid cash dividends as follows:

For Year Ended:	Net Income or (Loss)	Preferred Dividends	Common Dividends
December 31, 19+4...............	$ 5,000	$2,000	
December 31, 19+5...............	15,000	2,000	
December 31, 19+6...............	30,000	5,000	$ 3,000
December 31, 19+7...............	(18,000)	3,000	10,000
December 31, 19+8...............	21,500		

Compute the book value per share for each class of stock as of December 31, 19+8.

Problem B13-4. The outstanding stock of Appling Corporation on December 31, 19+3, consists of 10,000 shares of $25 par value common stock and 5,000 shares of $50 par value, 6 per cent preferred stock. Cash dividends totaling $50,000 are to be paid on stock outstanding on this date.

Compute the allocation of the total dividends between the common and preferred stock under each of the following assumptions:

(a) The preferred stock is cumulative and dividends have been paid to December 31, 19+2.
(b) The preferred stock is cumulative and dividends have been paid to December 31, 19+1.
(c) The preferred stock is noncumulative and dividends have been paid to December 31, 19+1.
(d) The preferred stock is cumulative and fully participating. Preferred stock dividends have been paid to December 31, 19+2.

Problem B13-5. Emerson Corporation, whose accounting period ends on December 31, has an authorized capital of 10,000 shares of $40 par value common stock. On August 31, 19+6, the following account balances were taken from the firm's ledger:

Common stock	$160,000
Capital in excess of par value—From common stock issuances	40,000
Retained earnings.................................	60,000

The company had net income of $2,000 per month throughout the period covered by the following dividend transactions:

On September 20, 19+6, the directors declared a dividend of $.50 per share, to be paid in cash on October 10, 19+6, to stockholders of record on September 28, 19+6.
A 10 per cent stock dividend was issued on July 10, 19+7. Fair value of the shares was $60 per share.
Another cash dividend of $.50 per share was declared by the directors on September 20, 19+7, to be paid on October 10, to stockholders of record on September 28. One-half of the dividend was to be charged to Capital in Excess of Par Value— From Common Stock Issuances, which was permissible under the laws of the state in which the company was incorporated.

Show the journal entries to record the dividend transactions and the related closing entries on December 31, 19+6, and December 31, 19+7.

Problem B13-6. The December 31, 19+7 balance sheet of Casse Corporation presented the Stockholders' Equity section as follows:

Stockholders' equity:
Capital stock:
7% cumulative preferred—3,000 shares authorized; 1,000 shares
issued; par value, $100 . . . . $105,000
No-par common—20,000 shares issued; 3,000 shares held in treasury; 25,000 shares authorized; stated value, $20   331,000
Retained earnings:
Capital in excess of par value—From common stock issuances .   60,000
Operating income (see Note A).   136,000
                                                                      $632,000

Note A: In view of a planned future purchase to reduce the number of preferred shares outstanding, the directors have earmarked $50,000 of accumulated earnings as not available for dividend purposes.

The common stock has been issued at various dates. Collections from shares issued have been: 15,000 shares at $22 per share, and 5,000 shares at $26 each.

There are no subscriptions receivable as of December 31.

The 3,000 shares of common stock held in the treasury were purchased recently at $23 per share. The company is organized in a state where treasury stock acquisitions must not impair the stated capital.

The preferred stock was issued on January 1, 19+5. To date no dividends have been declared on this stock.

Prepare the Stockholders' Equity section of the balance sheet in a more acceptable form.

14

Other Forms
of Business Organization

The three principal forms of business organization are: (1) individual proprietorship, (2) partnership, and (3) corporation. Previous chapters have assumed the corporate form of organization. It is only in the accounting for owners' equity that the records of the individual proprietorship and the partnership necessarily differ from those of a corporation.

INDIVIDUAL PROPRIETORSHIPS

Capital and drawing accounts. In place of the capital stock, retained earnings, and dividends accounts kept by a corporation, the books of an individual proprietorship include a capital account and a drawing account.

The capital account is credited with the proprietor's original investment and with any additional investments; it is credited with the net income or debited with the net loss for the period.

A drawing account is generally kept in addition to the capital account, although all changes in a proprietor's equity could be, and sometimes are, recorded in his capital account.

When a drawing account is kept, it is debited with:

(a) Withdrawals of cash or other business assets.

When a proprietor takes merchandise for his own use, it is customary to charge him for it at cost. Debiting the proprietor at sales price and crediting the sales account would be illogical; a withdrawal of merchandise is not a sale. The debit to the proprietor's drawing account is offset by a credit to Purchases or Inventory, depending on the inventory method in use.

(b) Disbursements of business cash for the personal benefit of the proprietor—as, for instance, a payment for fuel used in heating his home.

When the books are closed at the end of the period, the balance of the drawing account is transferred to the capital account.

Typical entries in both kinds of accounts are shown here:

JAMES WHITE, CAPITAL

19—						
Jan.	1	Investment	CR 1		7,500	7,500 Cr.
Feb.	15	Additional investment	CR 2		1,500	9,000 Cr.

JAMES WHITE, DRAWINGS

19—					
Mar.	25		CD 3	900	900 Dr.
July	8		CD 7	400	1,300 Dr.
Sept.	5		CD 9	750	2,050 Dr.
Dec.	17		CD12	600	2,650 Dr.

Closing the books. The procedure of closing the revenue and expense accounts is the same for an individual proprietorship as for a corporation except that the net income or net loss, as the case may be, is transferred to the proprietor's capital account instead of to a retained earnings account. A retained earnings account will not be found in the books of proprietorships or partnerships.

The closing of the revenue and expense accounts is illustrated by the following entry which is based on the data shown in the income statement of James White on page 315.

Sales	48,000	
Sales returns and allowances		1,000
Cost of goods sold		30,500
Operating expenses		12,000
James White, capital		4,500

To close the revenue and expense accounts and transfer the net income to the proprietor's capital account.

To complete the closing procedure, the balance of the drawing account is transferred to the capital account by the following entry:

James White, capital	2,650	
James White, drawings		2,650

To close the drawing account.

Working papers and statements. Instead of a pair of Retained Earnings columns, the working papers for an individual proprietorship contain a pair of Capital columns. Otherwise there is no difference.

The arrangement of data in the income statement of an individual proprietorship does not differ from that of a corporation in the same line of business. An income statement for an individual proprietorship is shown below.

JAMES WHITE
Income Statement
For the Year Ended December 31, 19—

Sales		$48,000
Sales returns and allowances		1,000
Net sales		$47,000
Cost of goods sold	$30,500	
Operating expenses	12,000	42,500
Net income		$ 4,500

Note that no income tax is shown in this income statement. In contrast to a corporation, a business conducted as an individual proprietorship is not regarded as a separate entity for the purpose of income taxation. In his individual tax return, the proprietor reports his taxable income or his loss from his business and all other sources. Since graduated rates are applied to the total, the tax on his business income is affected by matters outside the business. Therefore, an income statement showing taxes that would be assessed on business income without consideration of the tax-rate effect of other income and losses might be very misleading.

Instead of the statement of retained earnings prepared for a corporation, a statement of the proprietor's capital is prepared.

JAMES WHITE
Statement of Proprietor's Capital
For the Year Ended December 31, 19—

Investment, January 1, 19—		$ 7,500
Add:		
Additional investment	$1,500	
Net income for the year	4,500	6,000
Total		$13,500
Deduct withdrawals		2,650
Balance, December 31, 19—		$10,850

The investment at the beginning of the year and the additional investment during the year were determined from the capital account.

The balance sheets of an individual proprietorship and a corporation do not necessarily differ except in the owners' equity section. The balance sheet of an individual proprietorship shows the proprietor's capital in one amount, whereas the balance sheet of a corporation shows the capital stock and retained earnings.

JAMES WHITE
Balance Sheet
December 31, 19—

Assets		Equities	
Current assets:		Current liabilities:	
Cash	$ 3,850	Accounts payable	$ 6,000
Accounts receivable	9,000	Notes payable	2,000
Notes receivable	2,000	Total current liabilities	$ 8,000
Merchandise inventory	4,000		
		Proprietor's equity:	
		James White, capital	10,850
	$18,850		$18,850

PARTNERSHIPS

Nature of a partnership. "A partnership," as defined by the Uniform Partnership Act, "is an association of two or more persons to carry on, as co-owners, a business for profit."

The partnership and the corporation are the two most common forms of organization by which two or more persons can join in a business enterprise. The partnership form is usually found among comparatively small businesses requiring no more capital than can be contributed by a few partners; or in professional practices, such as law, medicine, and accounting, in which the relations of the firm to its clientele should involve a personal responsibility.

The partnership relation is created by a contract. The contract may be oral, but it is much better to have it in writing, because partners have been known to forget the features of oral agreements which prove ultimately to be to their disadvantage. A partnership contract is sometimes called *the partnership agreement* and sometimes *the articles of partnership.* Some of the more important matters that should be covered by the partnership contract are listed below.

(1) The names of the partners and the name of the partnership.
(2) The date when the contract becomes effective.
(3) The nature of the business.
(4) The place where operations are to be conducted.
(5) The amount of capital to be contributed by each partner and the assets to be invested and the valuations to be placed on them.
(6) The rights and duties of the partners.
(7) The dates when the books are to be closed and the profits ascertained and divided.
(8) The portion of the net income to be allowed to each partner.
(9) The drawings to be allowed each partner and the penalties, if any, to be imposed because of excess withdrawals.
(10) The length of time during which the partnership is to continue.
(11) The conditions under which a partner may withdraw or may be compelled to withdraw; the bases for the determination of his equity in the event

of withdrawal; and agreements regarding the payment of his equity in full or in installments.

(12) Procedures in the event of the death of a partner.

(13) Provision for arbitration in the event of disputes.

(14) The rights and duties of the partners in the event of dissolution.

Some of the significant characteristics of the partnership form of business organization are briefly discussed below and on the following page. For a comprehensive treatment of these matters, a text on the law of partnerships should be consulted.

NO SEPARATE LEGAL ENTITY: Although the accountant treats a partnership as a separate entity for accounting purposes, it has no *legal* status as an entity. The assets are owned, and the liabilities are owed, by the partners collectively. However, this common-law concept of the partnership has been somewhat modified by the Uniform Partnership Act, which, for instance, enables a partnership to hold real and personal property in its own name. The Uniform Partnership Act has not been adopted by all of the states.

MUTUAL AGENCY: Each partner is an agent for all of the other partners in matters coming within the scope of partnership activities. Therefore, outsiders have a right to assume that the partnership is bound by the acts of any partner relative to its affairs.

UNLIMITED LIABILITY: Usually each partner is individually liable for all of the debts of a partnership incurred during his membership in the firm; he may assume a liability for debts incurred before his admission to the partnership; and, unless proper notice of withdrawal is given to the public, he may be liable for partnership debts incurred after his retirement. If a partner pays partnership debts from his personal assets, he is entitled to reimbursement from the other partners.

Limited partnerships are permissible in some states. A limited partner has no personal liability to creditors, but he must maintain his investment at an amount at least equal to that contributed at the time of organization. There must be at least one general partner who is liable to creditors for debts which cannot be paid from firm assets.

LIMITED RIGHT TO DISPOSE OF INTEREST: A partner has a legal right to assign his partnership interest to another person, although he may be subject to a suit for damages for any loss incurred by his partners as a consequence of such an assignment. But he cannot compel the other partners to accept the assignee as a partner.

DIVISION OF INCOME: Partnership income may be divided among the partners in any manner to which they agree. Consequently, the division of income is more flexible in a partnership than in a corporation.

WITHDRAWAL OF ASSETS: Because the stockholders of a corporation generally have no personal liability for corporate debts, the law places limitations on the amounts of dividend payments or other asset distributions which may be made to corporate stockholders. There are no similar legal restrictions on partners' withdrawals of cash or other assets; however, the partners may make agreements among themselves placing limitations on the amounts which they may withdraw.

EFFECT OF PARTNER'S DEATH: Unless the partnership agreement provides otherwise, the death of a partner automatically dissolves the partnership of which he was a member. His heirs have a right to be paid the amount of his partnership interest, but they have no right (except by consent of the other partner or partners) to succeed him as members of the firm.

Capital and drawing accounts. The capital and drawing accounts of a partnership are similar to those of an individual proprietorship. The following accounts are illustrative:

D. E. SNYDER, CAPITAL

19—						
Jan.	1	Investment	CR 1		9,000	9,000 Cr.
June	1	Additional investment	CR10		1,000	10,000 Cr.

D. E. SNYDER, DRAWINGS

19—						
Apr.	15		CD 5	200		200 Dr.
Oct.	20		CD14	800		1,000 Dr.

J. O. LONG, CAPITAL

19—						
Jan.	1	Investment	CR 1		15,000	15,000 Cr.
July	1	Additional investment	CR11		4,000	19,000 Cr.

J. O. LONG, DRAWINGS

19—						
Mar.	10		CD 4	500		500 Dr.
Nov.	5		CD15	700		1,200 Dr.

Loan accounts. A partnership may be in need of funds, which a partner is able to supply but which he is willing to provide for a short time only. In such instances the credit to the partner may be made in a loan account. Such loans should not be shown in the balance sheet as part of the partners' equity; they should be shown among the liabilities, but clearly distinguished from liabilities to outsiders.

On the other hand, a partner may wish to make a temporary withdrawal of funds in the form of a loan. A loan receivable account will then appear on the partnership books. Such a loan should be shown separately from receivables from outsiders in the balance sheet.

Opening the books. If all capital contributions are in the form of cash, no problems arise; the cash account is debited and each partner's capital account is credited.

If noncash assets are invested, it is extremely important that they be recorded at their *fair values* at the date of the investment. Assume, for instance, that a partner invests land and a building which he is carrying on his books at $40,000, which was the cost to him less depreciation. At the date when he invests this property in the partnership, it is worth $50,000. If the property were recorded on the partnership books at $40,000 and later sold for $50,000, all of the partners would share in the gain; this would not be fair to the partner who invested the property and who should have received a $50,000 credit for it.

If any liabilities of a partner are assumed by the partnership, they should, of course, be credited to liability accounts, and the partner's capital account should be credited with the net investment; that is, the difference between the assets and the liabilities.

GOODWILL: If a partner's investment consists of a going business, it may be equitable to give the partner a capital credit for the goodwill of the business. A business may have goodwill if it has exceptionally good earnings. The valuation of the goodwill is a matter of agreement among the partners, and should be based on the probable future amount of earnings attributable to the business brought in by the partner. The amount, if any, agreed upon should be debited to a goodwill account, with an offsetting credit to the partner's capital account.

The profit and loss ratio. The ratio in which partners divide their net income or net loss is called the *profit and loss ratio*. If partners make no agreement regarding the division of income and losses, the law assumes an agreement to divide them equally. If partners make an agreement regarding the division of income, without any mention of losses, the agreed method for the division of income applies also to the division of losses.

Closing the books. Closing entries for a partnership are shown below. The data agree with the financial statements of Snyder and Long. It is assumed that the net income is divided equally.

Sales	90,000	
Sales discounts		200
Cost of goods sold		54,300
Operating expenses		27,500
D. E. Snyder, capital		4,000
J. O. Long, capital		4,000
To close the revenue and expense accounts and transfer the net income to the partners' capital accounts.		
D. E. Snyder, capital	1,000	
D. E. Snyder, drawings		1,000
To close the drawing account.		
J. O. Long, capital	1,200	
J. O. Long, drawings		1,200
To close the drawing account.		

Working papers and statements. The working papers of a partnership contain a pair of capital columns for each partner in place of columns for retained earnings.

INCOME STATEMENT: The income statement of a partnership is similar to that of an individual proprietorship or a corporation in the same line of business.

SNYDER AND LONG
Income Statement
For the Year Ended December 31, 19—

Sales		$90,000
Sales discounts		200
Net sales		$89,800
Cost of goods sold	$54,300	
Operating expenses	27,500	81,800
Net income		$ 8,000

This statement does not show any deduction for income taxes. A partnership, as such, does not ordinarily pay any federal income tax, but it is required to file an information return showing the results of its operations and each partner's share of the net income or net loss. Each partner is subject to income tax on his share of the partnership net income.

STATEMENT OF PARTNERS' CAPITALS: In order to prepare the following statement, it was necessary to refer to the capital accounts to determine the investments at the beginning of the year and the additional investments during the year.

SNYDER AND LONG
Statement of Partners' Capitals
For the Year Ended December 31, 19—

	D. E. Snyder	J. O. Long	Total
Investments, January 1, 19—	$ 9,000	$15,000	$24,000
Add:			
Additional investments	1,000	4,000	5,000
Net income for the year	4,000	4,000	8,000
Totals	$14,000	$23,000	$37,000
Deduct withdrawals	1,000	1,200	2,200
Balances, December 31, 19—	$13,000	$21,800	$34,800

BALANCE SHEET: The balance sheet of a partnership usually shows the capital of each partner, with a reference to the statement of partners' capitals, where details can be found.

SNYDER AND LONG
Balance Sheet
December 31, 19—

Assets

Current assets:		
Cash		$14,800
Accounts receivable		18,000
Merchandise inventory		5,000
		$37,800

Equities

Current liabilities:
  Accounts payable . . . . $ 3,000

Partners' equity:
  D. E. Snyder, capital $13,000
  J. O. Long, capital.   21,800   34,800
                                                                                       $37,800

Other methods of dividing earnings and losses. Some of the factors which may be given consideration in the determination of an equitable division of partnership earnings are:

The relative amounts of capital provided by the partners.
The relative values of the services rendered by the partners.
  These may differ because of differences in business ability and/or in time devoted to partnership affairs.
Various matters, such as seniority, business contacts, earnings potential of a going business contributed by a partner, and the degree of risk-taking. The degree of risk-taking depends on the dangers of loss and the relative amounts of the partners' capitals, as well as their outside assets to which the firm creditors may have recourse for the payment of partnership debts.

Various methods of dividing partnership earnings and losses are shown below.

Basis of illustrations. Let us assume, for example, that the capital accounts of two partners appear as follows:

J. L. LANE, CAPITAL

19+1							
Jan.	1			CR 1		10,000	10,000 Cr.
June	1			CD 6	500		9,500 Cr.
Aug.	1			CR 8		2,000	11,500 Cr.
Nov.	1			CD11	1,500		10,000 Cr.

D. K. BURTON, CAPITAL

19+1							
Jan.	1			CR 1		20,000	20,000 Cr.
Apr.	1			CD 4	1,000		19,000 Cr.
July	1			CR 7		2,000	21,000 Cr.
Dec.	1			CD12	2,000		19,000 Cr.

The debits in the capital accounts record withdrawals in excess of the agreed monthly drawing amounts. Drawings equal to the agreed monthly amounts are debited to the drawings accounts. In the absence of any agreement about the amounts of withdrawals, all drawings are debited to the drawings accounts.
The amount of net income for the year is $12,000.
  (1) Divisions in a fractional ratio. The equal division of the net income to Snyder and Long on page 320 is an illustration of a division in a frac-

tional ratio. Partners, after consideration of the determinants of an equitable division of earnings, may agree to any fractional ratio.

(2) Divisions in a capital ratio. If the capital investments are the major source of income and the other determinants of an equitable division of earnings are not pertinent, the net income may be divided in a capital ratio. Two illustrations are given below.

DIVISION IN RATIO OF CAPITALS AT BEGINNING OF PERIOD: The capital accounts on page 321 show the following balances on January 1:

J. L. Lane. $10,000
D. K. Burton. 20,000

The net income division on this basis is shown below:

Partner	Capitals at Beginning	Fraction	Amount
Lane	$10,000	$\frac{1}{3}$	$ 4,000
Burton	20,000	$\frac{2}{3}$	8,000
Total	$30,000		$12,000

DIVISION IN RATIO OF CAPITALS AT END OF PERIOD: As an inducement for partners to refrain from making withdrawals of substantial amounts during the period for which income is being divided, and to encourage them to invest additional capital as needed, it may be preferable to divide the net income in the ratio of the capitals at the end of the period, thus:

Partner	Capitals at End	Fraction	Amount
Lane	$10,000	$\frac{10}{29}$	$ 4,138
Burton	19,000	$\frac{19}{29}$	7,862
Total	$29,000		$12,000

(3) Interest on capitals; remainder in fractional ratio. Suppose that the partners agree that *some* consideration should be given to capital investments, but that consideration should also be given to other determinants of an equitable division of the net income. Therefore, they agree to divide a portion of the net income in the capital ratio by allowing 6% interest on the capitals, and to divide the remainder in some other fractional ratio—say, equally. The interest may be computed on the capitals at the beginning or at the end of the year, as agreed; in the following tabulation, the interest is computed on opening capitals.

	J. L. Lane	D. K. Burton	Total
Interest on opening capitals:			
6% on $10,000	$ 600		
6% on $20,000		$1,200	
Total			$ 1,800
Remainder equally	5,100	5,100	10,200
Totals	$5,700	$6,300	$12,000

(4) Salaries to partners, and remainder in a fractional ratio. Partners may agree to make a partial division of the net income in the form of salaries in order to give recognition to the difference in the value of their services. The remaining net income may be divided equally or in any other ratio to which the partners agree. One illustration will be sufficient: salaries and an equal division of the remainder.

Assume that Lane is allowed a salary of $3,600 a year and Burton is allowed a salary of $4,800. The following distribution will be made:

	J. L. Lane	D. K. Burton	Total
Salaries	$3,600	$4,800	$ 8,400
Remainder equally	1,800	1,800	3,600
Totals	$5,400	$6,600	$12,000

(5) Salaries, interest, and remainder in a fractional ratio. Assume that Lane and Burton agree to make the following income division:

Salaries:
Lane. $3,600
Burton 4,800
Interest on capitals—6% on January 1 balances.
Remainder equally.

	J. L. Lane	D. K. Burton	Total
Salaries	$3,600	$4,800	$ 8,400
Interest on opening capitals:			
Lane—6% of $10,000	600		
Burton—6% of $20,000		1,200	
Total			1,800
Remainder equally	900	900	1,800
Totals	$5,100	$6,900	$12,000

Interest on partners' capitals and salaries to partners are not expenses but are divisions of net income; therefore, they do not enter into the computation of the net income shown by the income statement, but are shown in the statement of partners' capitals.

Salaries and interest in excess of net income. The salaries and interest in the preceding illustration totaled $10,200. Suppose that the net income had been only $9,000; how should it have been divided? Such a situation does not void the provisions of the partnership agreement. Therefore, the partners must be allowed the salaries and interest agreed upon. After this has been done the total credits allowed the partners will be greater than the net income. Because the partners agreed to an equal division of any income after salaries and interest, the $1,200 balance, which is negative in this case ($9,000 minus $10,200), is divided equally between Lane and Burton. This is illustrated on the next page.

	J. L. Lane	D. K. Burton	Total
Credits:			
Salaries	$3,600	$4,800	$ 8,400
Interest on capitals	600	1,200	1,800
Total credits	$4,200	$6,000	$10,200
Less debit for remainder	600	600	1,200
Distribution of net income	$3,600	$5,400	$ 9,000

Liquidation of a partnership. A partnership is liquidated when the business is discontinued or the assets (or net assets) are transferred to other parties. The balance sheet of a partnership about to liquidate appears below.

A AND B
Balance Sheet
October 31, 19—

Assets			Equities	
Cash		$ 5,000	Accounts payable	$ 9,000
Accounts receivable	$25,000		A, capital	30,000
Less allowance for			B, capital	20,000
uncollectibles	1,000	24,000		
Inventory		30,000		
		$59,000		$59,000

Disposal of assets. Assume that X desires to acquire the business of A and B, and that the partners sell their inventory and accounts receivable to X for $52,000. A and B retain the $5,000 of cash shown in the foregoing balance sheet and are to pay the $9,000 of accounts payable. The sale of the inventory and receivables will be recorded as follows:

X	52,000	
Loss on sale of business	2,000	
Allowance for uncollectibles	1,000	
Inventory		30,000
Accounts receivable		25,000
To record the sale of the assets to X.		
Cash	52,000	
X		52,000
To record collection for assets sold.		

Division of the gain or loss. Any gain or loss on the disposal of the assets should always be divided between the partners before any cash distribution is made to them, because the amounts of cash to which the partners are entitled cannot be determined until their shares of the gain or loss have been credited or charged to them. The gain or loss should be divided between the partners in their profit and loss ratio. Assuming that A and B share earnings equally, the $2,000 loss on the sale of the assets to X will be divided by the following entry:

A, capital	1,000	
B, capital	1,000	
Loss on sale of business		2,000

Distribution of cash. After the disposal of the inventory and the receivables, the collection of the cash, and the division of the loss between the partners, the balance sheet of the firm is as shown below.

A AND B
Balance Sheet
November 3, 19—

Assets		Equities	
Cash	$57,000	Accounts payable	$ 9,000
		A, capital	29,000
		B, capital	19,000
	$57,000		$57,000

The distribution of cash should be made in the following order:

(1) In payment of liabilities to outside creditors:

Accounts payable	9,000	
Cash		9,000

(2) In payment of partners' capitals:

A, capital	29,000	
B, capital	19,000	
Cash		48,000

Partner with a debit balance. It sometimes happens that a partner has a debit balance in his capital account as a result of operating losses, drawings, and losses on the disposal of assets during liquidation. Two illustrative cases are presented.

Case 1. Assume that, after the sale of all assets and the payment of liabilities, the trial balance of a partnership shows the following balances:

Cash	20,000	
M, capital	5,000	
N, capital		25,000
	25,000	25,000

The entire cash balance should be paid to N; this payment would reduce his capital credit to $5,000. He has a right to collect $5,000 from M.

Case 2. In this case it is assumed that, after the sale of all assets and the payment of all liabilities, a partnership's trial balance appears as follows:

Cash	20,000	
R, capital	5,000	
S, capital		15,000
T, capital		10,000
	25,000	25,000

The profit-and-loss-sharing arrangement was as follows: R, 20%; S, 40%; T, 40%. R should pay $5,000 cash into the partnership to make good the debit balance in his capital account; if he does so, there will be $25,000 cash on hand, which will be sufficient to pay S and T in full.

But suppose that it is desired to distribute the $20,000 of cash on hand to S and T before it is known whether or not R will be able to pay in the $5,000. In determining how to divide the cash between S and T, we should remember that, if R fails to pay in the $5,000, this loss will have to be borne by S and T in their profit and loss ratio. In the past, S and T each had a 40 per cent share in the net income or net loss; that is to say, their shares were equal. Therefore, if R should fail to pay in the $5,000, S and T would share the loss equally. Accordingly, they should be paid amounts that will reduce their capital balances to $2,500 each, thus leaving each of these partners with a capital balance sufficient to absorb his share of the loss if R fails to pay in the $5,000. The entry to record the payment is:

S, capital	12,500	
T, capital	7,500	
Cash		20,000
To record the distribution of cash to S and T.		

The resulting trial balance will be:

R, capital	5,000	
S, capital		2,500
T, capital		2,500
	5,000	5,000

Incorporation of a partnership. Partners may decide to organize a corporation to take over the operation of the partnership. In such a case, the partnership books may be retained for use by the corporation or the partnership books may be closed and new books opened for the corporation.

Assume that the December 31, 19— after-closing trial balance of the Able and Baker partnership appears as follows:

ABLE AND BAKER
After-Closing Trial Balance
December 31, 19—

Cash	200	
Accounts receivable	2,100	
Allowance for uncollectibles		200
Merchandise inventory	5,900	
Land	12,000	
Building	22,500	
Accumulated depreciation		6,500
Accounts payable		1,000
Notes payable		600
Able, capital		16,000
Baker, capital		18,400
	42,700	42,700

On this date the partners decide to incorporate with an authorized capital of 5,000 shares of $10 par value common stock, of which 3,700 shares will be issued to the partners for their present interests.

PARTNERSHIP BOOKS RETAINED: As a preliminary step it may be necessary to adjust certain accounts on the partnership books in order to reflect the amounts agreed upon for the purpose of transfer to the corporation. The net effect of such adjustments is carried to the partners' capital accounts in the profit and loss ratio.

Assume that Able and Baker agree that the assets of the partnership should be taken over by the corporation at the following amounts:

Cash	$ 200
Accounts receivable	1,800
Merchandise inventory	5,900
Land	14,200
Building	16,500

The following entries are required to give effect to the above agreement.

Land	2,200	
Accumulated depreciation [(22,500 − 6,500) − 16,500]	500	
Allowance for uncollectibles		100
Capital adjustment account		2,600
Adjustment of accounts prior to incorporation.		

Capital adjustment account	2,600	
Able, capital		1,300
Baker, capital		1,300
Division of the net result of asset adjustments made prior to incorporation.		

To make the change from the partnership form of organization to the corporate form, the partners' capital accounts are debited to close them, and a capital stock account is credited for the shares issued to the partners. If the sum of the partners' capital account balances exceeds the par or stated value of the shares issued to the partners in exchange for the net assets of the partnership, a paid-in capital account will be credited.

The entry for the issuance of the shares to Able and Baker is:

Able, capital (16,000 + 1,300)	17,300	
Baker, capital (18,400 + 1,300)	19,700	
Common stock ($10 × 3,700)		37,000
Issuance of 3,700 shares of stock to Able and Baker.		

NEW BOOKS OPENED FOR THE CORPORATION: If the partnership books are to be closed and new books opened for the corporation, the following entries should be made:

(1) Adjusting entries to bring the account balances into conformity with agreed-upon transfer values.

(2) Entries to record the effect of the adjustments on the partners' capital accounts.

(3) Entries to close the asset and liability accounts taken over by the corporation and to record the capital stock received in exchange.

(4) Entries to distribute the capital stock of the corporation to the partners, which entries will close the partners' capital accounts.

ASSIGNMENT
MATERIAL

QUESTIONS

1. Name the three principal forms of business organization.
2. Describe the use of a drawing account on the books of a proprietorship or a partnership.
3. What information is reported in a statement of proprietor's capital?
4. Define a partnership. How is a partnership created?
5. How does the legal status of a partnership differ from that of a corporation?
6. What is the profit and loss ratio? How is the ratio determined?
7. Describe the closing procedure for the books of a partnership.
8. List several factors that may be considered in the division of partnership earnings.
9. How are gains and losses resulting from the liquidation of a partnership divided among the partners? Why should such gains and losses be divided before cash payments are made to the partners?
10. How does a debit balance in the capital account of a partner affect the liquidation of a partnership?
11. Describe two alternatives which may be used to account for the incorporation of a partnership.
12. What is meant by the unlimited liability characteristic of a partnership?

SHORT EXERCISES

E14-1. Present the equity section of the balance sheet immediately after the organization of the following business firms:

(a) Bill Blue begins operation as an individual proprietor by transferring assets totaling $100,000 to the proprietorship.
(b) Bill Blue and Bob Black form a partnership by investing $60,000 and $40,000, respectively.
(c) Bill Blue and Bob Black organize a corporation, with each of the organizers acquiring $50,000 of common stock at par.

E14-2. Ben Beacon and Dan Deacon formed a partnership on January 1, 19+7, investing $45,000 and $15,000, respectively. They agreed to share profits and losses in a 60:40 ratio. On July 30, 19+7, the partners each withdrew $10,000 from the firm. Deacon invested an additional $15,000 on August 15, 19+7. Assuming the first year's profit is $5,000, present the partners' capital and drawing accounts after the books have been closed.

E14-3. Using the data in Exercise 2, prepare a statement of partners' capitals for the year ended December 31, 19+7.

E14-4. The partnership agreement of Derrick Scoville and Jarrett Ison states that profits will be divided as follows: (a) salaries of $5,000 each; (b) interest at 5 per cent on beginning capital balances; and (c) remainder to be shared equally. Scoville and Ison had capital balances on January 1, 19+9, of $14,000 and $17,000, respectively. Compute the allocation of (a) a $22,000 profit for the year; (b) a $7,000 profit for the year.

E14-5. Jackson, Kitteridge, and Lamone, who share profits and losses in a 4:2:2 ratio, are in the process of liquidating their partnership. Present journal entries for the distribution of cash assuming the following trial balance data:

Cash	$20,000	
Accounts payable		$ 4,000
Jackson, capital		12,000
Kitteridge, capital		10,000
Lamone, capital	6,000	
	$26,000	$26,000

PROBLEMS

Problem A14-1. Ted Barton began operations as an individual proprietor on March 3, 19+1. The following selected transactions took place between then and December 31, 19+1:

March 3 . . . . . Invested cash of $10,000 and a building having a value of $20,000.

June 10 . . . . . Invested an additional $10,000 cash.

August 31 . . . . Withdrew $2,000 cash and inventory having a selling price of $500. The inventory cost $300.

November 15 . Proprietorship cash was used to pay $800 of medical expenses incurred by Barton.

December 20 . Withdrew $1,000 cash.

Required:

(a) Journal entries to record the transactions.

(b) Postings to Barton's capital and drawing accounts. Omit posting references.

Problem A14-2. The December 31, 19+2 adjusted trial balance of F. R. Todd, an individual proprietor, is presented below:

F. R. TODD
Adjusted Trial Balance
December 31, 19+2

Cash	10,700	
Accounts receivable	17,690	
Merchandise inventory, December 31, 19+2	17,316	
Building	50,000	
Accumulated depreciation—Building		1,360
Accounts payable		5,124
Notes payable		3,000
F.R. Todd, capital		75,000
F.R. Todd, drawings	9,400	
Sales		162,000
Cost of goods sold	122,200	
Operating expenses	19,628	
Interest revenue		450
	246,934	246,934

Required:

    (a) A statement of proprietor's capital for the year ended December 31, 19+2, assuming an additional investment of $15,000 by Todd on May 10, 19+2.

    (b) A balance sheet as of December 31, 19+2.

    (c) Closing entries.

Problem A14-3. Earl Daley and Dan Earley decide to form the D and E partnership by combining the operations of their individual proprietorships as of July 1, 19+7.

    The after-closing trial balances of the proprietorships on this date are presented below.

EARL DALEY
After-Closing Trial Balance
July 1, 19+7

Cash	10,000	
Accounts receivable	14,320	
Allowance for uncollectibles		1,025
Merchandise inventory	15,760	
Accounts payable		6,380
Notes payable		15,000
Earl Daley, capital		17,675
	40,080	40,080

DAN EARLEY
After-Closing Trial Balance
July 1, 19+7

Cash	2,005	
Merchandise inventory	10,420	
Land	12,000	
Building	30,000	
Accumulated depreciation—Building		18,500
Accounts payable		4,940
Dan Earley, capital		30,985
	54,425	54,425

An analysis of the assets of the proprietorships reveals that Daley's accounts receivable have a net value of $12,200. His inventory is to be valued at $16,000, and Earley's at $8,300. The building and land have values of $20,000 and $15,000, respectively.

Required:

> (a) Journal entries on the partnership books to record the investments of Daley and Earley. The accounts receivable and building are to be recorded at their net values.
>
> (b) A balance sheet for the partnership as of July 1, 19+7, immediately after organization.

Problem A14-4. Rogers, Radford, and Powell are in the process of liquidating their partnership. All assets have been sold except the equipment, but no cash has yet been paid to the partners during the liquidation process.

A trial balance taken on March 1, 19+2, is presented below.

ROGERS, RADFORD, AND POWELL
Trial Balance
March 1, 19+2

Cash	60,000	
Equipment	105,000	
Accumulated depreciation—Equipment		40,000
Accounts payable		33,000
Rogers, capital		45,000
Radford, capital		35,000
Powell, capital		12,000
	165,000	165,000

Required:

Computation of the cash distribution under each of the following assumptions:

> (a) The equipment is sold for $80,000.
> (b) The equipment is sold for $35,000.
> (c) The equipment is sold for $20,000.

Problem A14-5. Tabb, Adkerson, and Allison decide to liquidate their partnership on January 1, 19+6. The after-closing trial balance of the firm as of that date is presented below.

TABB, ADKERSON, AND ALLISON
After-Closing Trial Balance
January 1, 19+6

Cash	8,000	
Accounts receivable	37,000	
Allowance for uncollectibles		3,000
Merchandise inventory	45,000	
Equipment	50,000	
Accumulated depreciation—Equipment		24,000
Accounts payable		43,000
Tabb, capital		30,000
Adkerson, capital		15,000
Allison, capital		25,000
	140,000	140,000

The partners share profits and losses as follows: Tabb, 40%; Adkerson, 30%; and Allison, 30%.

On January 1, 19+6, the assets were sold for the following cash amounts: accounts receivable, $29,000; inventory, $42,000; and equipment, $25,000.

Required:

All entries to record liquidation of the partnership.

Problem A14-6. Ben Snead and Hal Harris formed a partnership on January 1, 19+3. The capital and drawing accounts of the partners appeared as follows at the end of the first year of operation prior to closing the books.

BEN SNEAD, CAPITAL

19+3						
Jan.	1		CR 1		12,500	12,500 Cr.
June	1		CD12	5,000		7,500 Cr.
Dec.	31		CR16		10,000	17,500 Cr.

BEN SNEAD, DRAWINGS

19+3						
June	30		CD15	3,000		3,000 Dr.
Dec.	31		CD34	3,000		6,000 Dr.

HAL HARRIS, CAPITAL

19+3						
Jan.	1		CR 1		18,000	18,000 Cr.
July	1		CR 9		10,000	28,000 Cr.

HAL HARRIS, DRAWINGS

19+3						
June	30		CD15	4,000		4,000 Dr.
Dec.	31		CD34	4,000		8,000 Dr.

The net income for the year was $20,225. According to the partnership agreement, net income is to be divided as follows:

(1) Salaries to $6,000 to Snead and $8,000 to Harris.
(2) Interest at the rate of 7 per cent on beginning capital balances.
(3) Remainder divided equally.

Required:

(a) Computation of each partner's share of net income for the year.
(b) Posting of all closing entries to the partners' capital and drawing accounts.

Problem A14-7. The income statement of the ABC partnership showed a net income of $25,000 for the year ended December 31, 19+4.

A's capital account balance was $22,000 during the entire year. B's capital account had a balance of $16,000 on December 31, 19+4. This included an investment of $5,000 made on August 1, 19+4. C's ending capital balance was $10,000. His capital account had been debited for a withdrawal of $2,000 on June 30, 19+4.

Required:

(a) Schedules showing the division of net income under each of the following arrangements:

 (1) B is to be allowed a salary of $6,000. The remainder is to be divided: A, 40%; B, 20%; and C, 40%.
 (2) A salary of $5,000 is to be allowed each partner. Interest at 6 per cent is to be allowed on beginning capitals. The remainder is to be divided in a 2–1–1 ratio.
 (3) A is to be allowed interest at 8 per cent on his beginning capital. The remainder is to be divided in a 2–4–4 ratio.

(b) Schedules showing the division of net income under each of the arrangements in part (a), assuming a net loss of $5,000 for the year.

Problem B14-1. The following information is taken from the adjusted trial balance of Harry Sloan, an individual proprietor, as of June 30, 19+5.

Accounts payable	$25,450
Accumulated depreciation—Equipment	6,600
Cash	11,800
Equipment	27,000
General expenses	6,240
Merchandise inventory, June 30, 19+5	10,540
Accounts receivable	15,500
Cost of goods sold	48,830
Sales	68,280
Sales returns and allowances	2,200
Selling expenses	12,020
Harry Sloan, capital	53,300
Harry Sloan, drawings	19,500

The only change in the proprietor's capital account during the year was an additional investment of $8,500 on March 15.

Required:

(a) An income statement for the year ended June 30, 19+5.
(b) A statement of proprietor's capital for the year ended June 30, 19+5.
(c) A balance sheet as of June 30, 19+5.

Problem B14-2. The December 31, 19+8 adjusted trial balance of Washington and Langley, a partnership, is presented below.

WASHINGTON AND LANGLEY
Adjusted Trial Balance
December 31, 19+8

Cash	10,590	
Accounts receivable	17,385	
Merchandise inventory, December 31, 19+8	42,565	
Equipment	99,000	
Accumulated depreciation—Equipment		35,400
Accounts payable		60,450
Notes payable		5,000
Loans payable (N. Langley)		7,000
R. Washington, capital		40,000
N. Langley, capital		28,000
R. Washington, drawings	5,200	
N. Langley, drawings	5,900	
Sales		298,910
Sales returns and allowances	3,625	
Cost of goods sold	269,515	
Selling expenses	17,150	
Office expenses	3,830	
	474,760	474,760

Partnership profits and losses are shared equally. The only changes in the partners' capital accounts during the year were additional investments of $10,000 by Langley on May 15 and of $5,000 by Washington on October 1.

The loan is to be repaid to N. Langley on July 1, 19+9.

Required:

(a) A statement of partners' capitals for the year.
(b) A balance sheet as of December 31, 19+8.

Problem B14-3. Lemmonds and Moody, who share profits and losses equally, decide to liquidate their partnership on May 1, 19+9. Certain assets of the business are sold to Hartwell Corporation on the following basis:

Merchandise inventory	$25,000
Land	3,600
Accounts receivable	38,500

Lemmonds and Moody are to keep the cash and pay all debts.

LEMMONDS AND MOODY
After-Closing Trial Balance
May 1, 19+9

Cash	3,000	
Accounts receivable	42,000	
Merchandise inventory	20,000	
Land	4,000	
Accounts payable		7,000
Loans payable (H. Moody)		10,000
B. Lemmonds, capital		35,000
H. Moody, capital		17,000
	69,000	69,000

Required:

Entries to close the books of the partnership, assuming that cash is received from Hartwell Corporation and that all cash is distributed.

Problem B14-4. The capital accounts of Deacon, Enloe, and Farrow for the year 19+1 are presented below. The accounts show investments and drawings in excess of agreed amounts for the year.

B. C. DEACON, CAPITAL

19+1						
Jan.	1	Balance				27,000 Cr.
Mar.	31				1,000	26,000 Cr.

C. D. ENLOE, CAPITAL

19+1						
Jan.	1	Balance				40,000 Cr.
May	15				5,000	45,000 Cr.
Aug.	31			250		44,750 Cr.
Sept.	30			750		44,000 Cr.

D. E. FARROW, CAPITAL

19+1						
Jan.	1	Balance				26,000 Cr.
Sept.	4				4,000	30,000 Cr.

Net income for the year was $13,800.

Required:

Computation of each partner's share of the income under each of the following arrangements.

    (a) The first $6,600 is to be divided equally, the remainder 1:2:1.

    (b) Each partner is to be allowed a salary of $4,200, the remainder divided equally.

    (c) The net income is to be divided in the ratio of partners' capitals at year end.

(Continued)

(d) Salaries are to be allowed as follows: Deacon, $5,000; Enloe, $4,600; and Farrow, $6,000; the remainder to be divided equally.

(e) Interest at 6% is to be allowed on capitals at the beginning of the year, salaries of $3,000 each are to be paid, and the remainder divided 3:2:1.

Problem B14-5. Jarvis and Kingston have been operating as a partnership for some time, sharing profits and losses in a 60:40 ratio. On July 1, 19+3, they decide to incorporate as Ja-Ka Corporation. The after-closing trial balance of the partnership on that date appears below.

JARVIS AND KINGSTON
After-Closing Trial Balance
July 1, 19+3

Cash	4,546	
Accounts receivable	9,404	
Allowance for uncollectibles		300
Merchandise inventory	5,000	
Furniture and fixtures	2,200	
Accumulated depreciation—Furniture and fixtures		330
Land	20,000	
Goodwill	10,000	
Accounts payable		3,800
Notes payable		5,000
J. A. Jarvis, capital		24,000
A. J. Kingston, capital		17,720
	51,150	51,150

An examination of the assets reveals that the merchandise inventory is worth only $4,500. The land is appraised at a current value of $25,000. It is decided that the goodwill is not to be carried forward to the corporation.

A new set of books is to be opened for Ja-Ka Corporation, which has an authorized capital of 10,000 shares of $10 par value common stock.

Required:

All entries to close the partnership books.

Problem B14-6. S. T. Hokins has been operating his business as a sole proprietor for some time. The following information is taken from his ledger as of March 31, 19+2.

Cash	$10,000
Accounts receivable	28,000
Merchandise inventory	70,000
Patent	14,000
Accounts payable	58,000
Notes payable (due July 1, 19+3)	20,000
S.T. Hokins, capital	44,000

On March 31, 19+2, it was agreed that A. L. Ingram would join Hokins in a partnership. Ingram was to invest the following:

Goodwill	$14,000
Land	6,000
Building	50,000

The building had an estimated useful life of 50 years as of March 31, 19+2.

The partnership was also to assume Ingram's accounts payable of $6,000, giving Ingram beginning capital of $64,000.

It was also agreed that certain assets of Hokins would be recorded on the partnership books at the following amounts: accounts receivable, $26,000; merchandise inventory, $71,000; and patent, $5,000. The patent is to be amortized over a 10-year period. A new set of books is to be opened for the partnership.

During its first year of operations, the partnership earned a net income of $77,500, which was divided equally. Each partner withdrew $15,000 in cash, leaving a cash balance of $25,000 in the partnership bank account as of March 31, 19+3. Changes other than in cash were as follows:

> $ 8,000 increase in inventory
> 38,000 increase in accounts receivable
> 12,000 increase in accounts payable

L. R. Justice joined the partnership on March 31, 19+3, under the following terms:

Inventory is to be valued at . . . . $ 90,000
Justice is to invest cash of   100,000

Required:

(a) Entries to record the formation of the partnership on March 31, 19+2.
(b) Entries to record the admission of Justice to the partnership on March 31, 19+3.
(c) The balance sheet of the Hokins, Ingram, and Justice partnership on March 31, 19+3.

15

Accounting Principles

Usefulness of accounting data. Accounting data serve the needs of businessmen and others who are interested in the results of operations and in the financial position of a business.

In order to conduct the routine operations of a business, management requires records showing the assets, liabilities, revenues, expenses, and the elements of the owners' equity. Supplementary detailed records are required for various purposes. For example, records are required for payroll tax purposes; property records enable the management to keep track of the location and condition of numerous items of property, plant, and equipment; records showing the names and addresses of stockholders are needed for making dividend payments.

Accounting data are also useful to management in making policy decisions. Should the physical plant be expanded? If so, where should the new plant be located? Should a new product be introduced? Should selling prices be changed? Should an employee retirement program be started, or the old one revised? Decisions on such matters usually are not made without reference to accounting data. The more accounting information relevant to management problems that is available for management's use, the better are the chances for excellent decisions.

Accounting data are of use also to grantors of credit, such as banks and suppliers. What are the borrower's earnings prospects? What is its debt-paying ability? What is the record of past performance in debt payment? These are pertinent questions. Although accounting data cannot be expected to be the only determining factor in the granting or refusal of credit in all cases, such information usually affects the decision.

In a similar fashion, accounting information may serve the needs of stockholders, governmental agencies, labor unions, and possible investors. These groups are often interested in the effectiveness of the operating activities of a business, as shown by its earnings data, and in its financial position.

Need for accounting principles. The preceding comments indicate that those served by accounting may be divided into two major categories and identified as:

(1) "Insiders"—that is, management.

The function of management includes planning, controlling, decision-making, and reporting. It is difficult to specify the kinds of accounting and other data needed by management. Much depends on the particular problem or task facing management. For some purposes, net income data may be relevant. For other purposes, a comparison of estimated cash receipts and disbursements may be pertinent. For some decisions, certain expenses probably should be ignored; for example, departmental expenses beyond the control of a department head should be ignored when his performance is being evaluated. When considering accounting data in relation to the needs of insiders, such words as *pertinence* and *flexibility* come to mind. In other words, there probably can be no widespread agreement about the kinds of accounting data that must in all cases be considered and how the information should be compiled for managerial uses.

(2) "Outsiders"—such as stockholders and creditors.

The responsibility of management to account to outsiders is well established in the American business scene. Outsiders want to know whether a particular business is profitable and whether its financial position is improving. There is considerable interest in a company's rate of growth and in the performance of management. Such matters call for measurement and reporting procedures that will communicate effectively to those outsiders having an interest in the affairs of any given business. When considering accounting data in relation to the needs of outsiders, such words as *reasonable comparability* and *uniformity* come to mind.

It is the accountability function that creates the clearest need for accounting principles. The accountant must have some "principles" or "guidelines" for a task of such dimensions as that of accounting to outsiders. Unless there exist some generally accepted concepts regarding the nature and measurement of assets, liabilities, revenues, and expenses and some widely supported standards of disclosure and reporting, the usefulness of financial statements as reports to outsiders will not be maximized. There can be no widespread understanding of and reliance on financial statements unless they have been prepared in conformity with generally accepted principles. The necessity of some common agreement on accounting matters becomes apparent when we contemplate the chaotic condition that would prevail if every businessman or every accountant could follow his own definitions of "revenue" and "expense" in preparing reports for outsiders.

The nature of accounting principles. It would be incorrect to suggest that accounting principles are a body of basic laws like those found in physics or chemistry. Accounting principles are more properly associated with such terms as *concepts, conventions,* and *standards.* It is important to stress the fact that accounting principles are man-made, in contrast to natural law.

Accounting principles are constantly evolving, being influenced by many things: business practices; the needs of statement users; legislation and governmental regulation; the opinions and actions of stockholders, creditors, labor unions, and management; and the logical reasoning of accountants. The sum total of such influences finds its expression first in accounting theory. Some theories are rejected; some are accepted. General acceptance of an accounting theory is essential to raise it to the authoritative status of an accounting principle. Such acceptance is unlikely if application of the principle being advocated is impracticable, or if users of financial statements believe that the accounting data resulting from its application lack usefulness or meaningfulness.

Standards and the accounting process. Objectivity, conservatism, and consistency characterize the accounting process. Accountants believe that adherence to these standards contributes to the usefulness of accounting data. In fact, such standards have an overriding effect on accounting principles. Each of these is discussed below.

OBJECTIVITY: Changes in account balances must be supported by adequate evidence. Accounting entries based on mere whim or fancy would not be tolerated by an accountant. Likewise, an entry writing up an asset merely because management was of the opinion that the asset was worth more than it cost when acquired by the business would not be acceptable to an accountant. There must be adequate objective support for the dollar amounts recorded in the accounts and shown in the financial statements.

The accountant makes use of various kinds of evidence to support entries made in the accounts. Legal contracts, bills of sale, canceled checks, employee time cards, market prices (used in applying the lower-of-cost-or-market inventory method), and formal actions taken by the board of directors are examples. Evidence may range in quality from that which is subjective—such as someone's opinion about something—to that which is objective—as for example a completed transaction with a customer. There are many gradations of evidence and often more than a single kind of evidence relating to accounting entries. The best evidence in the eyes of the accountant is that which is most objective, that is, that which is least influenced by personal opinion and judgment. It is neither desirable nor possible to remove judgment and opinion from the accounting process, but judgment and opinion should not prevail in the face of more convincing, more objective evidence. An accountant is expected to evaluate the various kinds of support for accounting entries, rejecting those lacking sufficient objectivity to justify an accounting entry.

In short, accounting data should be verifiable and free from bias. Confidence in financial statements would be seriously undermined if accounting principles failed to give adequate recognition to the need for convincing support for the dollar amounts shown in financial statements. This aspect of accounting is noticeable in many of the principles found in present-day accounting practices.

CONSERVATISM: Conservatism is particularly applicable when matters of opinion or estimates are involved, accountants believing that it is commendable, when in doubt, to understate net income and owners' equity rather than to overstate them. The doctrine of conservatism found expression in the oft-repeated tenet: "Anticipate no profit and provide for all possible losses."

Accountants can cite ample evidence that businessmen are inclined to be optimistic. Unless accounting conservatism were applied, assets would in many cases be overstated or liabilities understated, with the result that bankers, other creditors, and investors might be misled. Provisions for uncollectible accounts, for example, are a matter of estimate, and most accountants would rather overstate, slightly, than understate the allowance for uncollectibles. The consequences of understated assets and net income, do not seem so serious as the effects of an overstatement.

Balance sheet conservatism was once considered to be the accounting rule that outranked all other rules. There is now a tendency to question the three time-honored beliefs that balance sheet conservatism outweighs all other considerations, that a conservative balance sheet is a good balance sheet for all purposes, and that balance sheet conservatism automatically produces a proper statement of operations. Accountants are increasingly aware that adherence to the doctrine of balance sheet conservatism may result in income statements that are:

(a) Incorrect.

It may be conservative from the balance sheet standpoint to charge expense accounts with expenditures that would more properly be charged to long-lived asset accounts, or to make excessive allowances for depreciation and uncollectible accounts, but then the net income is misstated.

(b) And sometimes unconservative.

For instance, assume that excessive depreciation allowances are made, with the result that certain depreciable assets are fully depreciated before the end of their useful lives. The periods in which such assets are used after they have been fully depreciated are relieved of charges for depreciation expense; the net income for such periods is overstated and the income statements are unconservative.

Conservatism can scarcely be regarded as a virtue if, as its consequence, balance sheets and income statements do not fairly present the financial position and the results of operations.

CONSISTENCY: Another important feature of accounting is consistency of method. Accounting is not composed of a set of rules which prescribe the "one way" that things can be done. For example, there are several methods of computing periodic depreciation. The accountant should seek to apply the method best suited for each particular case, and it is of prime importance that the method selected be applied consistently year after year. If the accountant continually changed the method of accounting for certain assets or expenses, each method might be acceptable but successive financial statements would not be comparable. For example, by changing depreciation methods, the net income could be altered, perhaps significantly. A statement user might be misled and think that earnings had improved, whereas in reality the increase was the result of a change in accounting method. Changes in net income reported in successive statements should be traceable to changes in business conditions or management effectiveness, and not merely to changes in accounting methods. Consistency of method, then, is indeed an important element in the accounting process.

The emphasis on consistency does not mean that accounting methods once adopted must never be changed. If an accountant believes that a change to another generally accepted method of accounting would more fairly reflect the results of operations and the financial position of the business, the change may be made. However, adequate disclosure is required. For example, if the method of computing depreciation is changed at the beginning of 1970, the accountant would compute depreciation for 1970 by both the old and the new methods. The amount computed under the new method would be recorded in the books and reported in the statements. A footnote would be appended to the financial statements for 1970 describing the change in depreciation method; if the difference between the amounts computed by the two methods was significant, the effect on net income should be stated.

Principles and procedures contrasted. When accounting principles are set forth broadly, their generality necessarily limits their usefulness in solving specific accounting problems. Nevertheless, a statement of broad principles has potential value in that it provides a frame of reference for testing the compatibility and merits of more narrow principles.

Although accountants are not agreed on a specific set of broad principles, the following is illustrative of broad accounting principles:

Account for all assets, equities, revenues, and expenses of the enterprise (entity) for which money measurements can be made, provided that such measurements will satisfy the standards of verifiability and freedom from bias.

Maintain a record of all transactions and events that result in measurable changes to the assets and equities of the enterprise.

Differentiate between those resource inflows resulting from the pursuit of revenue-generating activity and those resulting from capital-raising activity.

Differentiate between those resource outflows and utilizations made for income-producing purposes and those made for the settlement (or reduction) of equity claims.

Relate all revenues and expenses to time periods.

Adopt reporting practices that will permit meaningful comparisons over time and among enterprises.

Classify the assets, equities, revenues, and expenses to disclose significant simi-
larities, dissimilarities, and interrelationships, and such other relevant mat-
ters as the source and the kind of equity claim.

Report the results of the accounting process with sufficient detail and disclo-
sures so that the report will achieve its purpose.

The following are illustrative of more specific, narrow principles. They and other
such principles found throughout this text seem compatible with the broad principles
listed above:

Do not carry assets at amounts in excess of realizable values.

Nonrecurring and extraordinary gains and losses should be given recognition
in the period they occur, but should be shown separately from the revenues
and expenses resulting from ordinary and usual operations.

Accumulated depreciation should be shown as a deduction from the deprecia-
ble asset.

Procedures are adopted to apply principles. The following are illustrative of
accounting procedures:

The first-in, first-out and last-in, first-out inventory methods are ways to apply
the cost principle to inventory valuation.

The straight-line and sum of years' digits depreciation methods are ways to
relate expense to time periods.

To estimate uncollectible accounts receivable as a percentage of sales, based
on past experience, follows the principle that assets should not be carried
in the accounts at amounts in excess of realizable values.

The student will soon discover that accountants often use the terms "principles"
and "procedures" more or less interchangeably. Such usage may be due to careless-
ness; it also indicates, however, that sometimes it is difficult to sort out and identify
separately the procedural part of an accounting method.

To apply accounting principles often requires good judgment. To achieve effective
financial reporting by the application of accounting principles to data resulting from
business transactions, the accountant must consider such important matters as objec-
tivity, usefulness, and feasibility. He strives to maximize objectivity and usefulness
without losing sight of feasibility. Necessarily some trade-off among these variables
is to be expected in practical situations. How much trade-off and when permissible
are matters of judgment.

For instance, under certain conditions more effective financial reporting may be
achieved if the objectivity standard is relaxed a bit to permit a greater usage of
estimates. To be more specific, the financial statements of a business on the brink
of bankruptcy may be more meaningful if estimates of realizable values for plant
and equipment are substituted for historical cost less depreciation. Or, for a more
theoretical example, in periods of inflation, estimates of replacement cost for plant
and equipment might sensibly be substituted for historical cost. To decide when such
shifts in reporting practices are justified, that is, when the accountant might properly

trade-off some objectivity for a prospective gain in usefulness, requires the exercise of judgment.

Feasibility becomes a matter of concern to the accountant in certain situations. For example, to develop data on replacement costs for a large steel-producing company might prove to be so complicated and expensive that the accountant might well conclude that the prospective added usefulness was not worth it. In other words, the cost of accumulating and processing information of the type believed to possess superior meaningfulness could be excessive. The accountant is justified when he sacrifices a little usefulness to save considerable expense. He should not sacrifice great usefulness for a small saving. Determining the point where some further loss of usefulness should not be tolerated on grounds of savings requires the exercise of judgment.

The role of historical cost. The financial statements developed and illustrated in the preceding chapters are the end product of an accounting process based *primarily* on *historical cost*. To a limited extent accountants make use of other data, generally either replacement costs or estimated realizable values. Such departures from historical cost are considered acceptable when historical data clearly fail to provide useful financial information, when complexity forces the use of estimates, or when conservatism dictates the use of lower-than-historical cost data.

In general, accountants give relatively little attention to present (actual) values when preparing conventional financial statements. They acknowledge the usefulness of value data, but question whether the level of objectivity attainable would be satisfactory should current value be adopted as the basis for the accounting process. Even so, market values are used in a limited way because under certain circumstances market values can be determined with greater confidence than cost. For instance, agricultural products and precious metals are commonly inventoried by the producer at market less cost of disposal because of the difficulty of computing the cost to grow or mine a unit of product. Another factor lending support to the use of market values is that farm products and precious metals can be disposed of without any marketing effort. The gold miner can sell all the gold he mines. Perhaps the market price won't please the producer, but there is no uncertainty about the marketability of the inventory. The same assurance does not prevail in most other businesses.

Also, it should be remembered that historical cost is used for financial reporting to those outside the firm; however, management is not bound to use historical cost data for its own decision-making purposes. Management uses whatever accounting data are relevant to a particular financial problem; such data may or may not be based on historical costs.

Should the time come when value data generally can be determined with greater objectivity and more feasibility than at present, greater reliance no doubt will be placed on value data by accountants and businessmen.

Revenue recognition. It follows from the above discussion that the accountants' concept of income is not based on mere changes in value. Cost is continued as the valuation basis until realization occurs. Only at that time can income (profit) be reported as earned. Specifically, an increase in the value of inventory would not justify the reporting of income.

Revenue recognition was discussed earlier (Chapter 3). It is the point at which a conversion takes place—an exchange of one asset for another—and it is the point at which the amount of revenue is, in the normal case, objectively determinable. Another condition sometimes associated with the recognition of revenue is that the earnings process must be completed or virtually completed.

However, the revenue-recognition test is relaxed somewhat when the nature of the business is such that the usefulness of financial statements would be restricted if income could be reported only if realized. Consider the case of a business working under a long-term contract to build an aircraft carrier or a huge dam. Several years might be required to complete the contract and deliver the product. It would be unrealistic if accounting principles provided for no exceptions and required that all of the income from such a long-term contract be reported in the year of contract completion because only then would the realization test be satisfied. A better solution, and one which is permitted by generally accepted accounting principles, permits the income to be spread over the entire contract period and a share of the total income to be allotted to each year involved, based on the percentage of work completed.

Another exception to the conventional revenue-recognition rules is the installment-basis method of accounting. As noted in Chapter 8, by this method the gross margin is taken into income as cash collections are received from the installment customers. An accountant would consider this method acceptable only if it resulted in a better matching of revenue and expense than would be achieved if the gross margin were taken into income in the period of sale.

It should be apparent that unrealized appreciation is not income in the accounting sense. Until the appreciated asset is sold for more than its cost, there is only potential income.

Income versus savings. A saving, but not income, results from manufacturing an asset at a cost less than the price at which it could have been purchased. To regard such savings as income would not be compatible with the accountants' approach to revenue recognition, which requires an exchange or conversion before income is realized.

Companies which construct depreciable assets for their own use at a cost less than the market purchase price sometimes desire to record such assets at a theoretical purchase price and take up a "profit." The manufacture of plant and equipment may increase the future income by reducing future depreciation charges, but a present saving with a prospect of increased future income should not be confused with realized income.

Ultimate income from sales of merchandise may be increased by the manufacture of goods instead of their purchase; but no income should be regarded as realized until the goods are sold.

Guidelines for recurring transactions. The greater part of the accountant's task is concerned with the measurement of revenues and expenses for relatively short periods of time. And the bulk of the transactions that affect revenue and expense occur over and over again, in contrast to what might be termed unusual and nonrecurring transactions. When analyzing recurring transactions in order to account for their consequences in a manner that is consistent with the broad principles set forth earlier, practicing accountants often rely on the following guidelines.*

Record the effect on net income of transactions and events in the period in which they arise unless there is justification for recording them in some other period or periods.

Where a direct relationship between the two exists, match expenses with revenues.

When there is justification for allocating amounts affecting net income to two or more years, but there is no direct basis for measuring how much should be associated with each year, use an allocation method that is systematic and rational.

From among systematic and rational methods, use that which tends to minimize distortions of periodic net income.†

Concerning the last guideline, some accountants apply it with caution to make certain that the method adopted will not conflict with the following well-established principle: Avoid approval of any accounting policy which has as its primary purpose the artificial smoothing of net income over time.

Alternative accounting methods. In view of the variety and complexity of conditions facing business enterprises today, it should come as no surprise that whenever the accountant needs to allocate amounts affecting net income to two or more years (third guideline above), there will be differences of opinion regarding the best method by which to accomplish such allocation. As a consequence, a considerable number of alternative accounting methods have been developed and, through usage, have become established as acceptable. Perhaps the most striking examples of this condition can be found, as we have learned from the preceding chapters, among the various inventory and depreciation methods.

Each alternative method which has acquired acceptability has the same purpose as all the others, namely, to make systematic and rational allocations over time in a manner not in conflict with generally accepted accounting principles. Furthermore, sufficient differences peculiar to the operating conditions of a particular business can usually be cited in support of the method in use. In other words, the methods chosen have not been selected frivolously or casually. In each instance the method will have been adopted after careful study of the alternatives.

Whether the existence of alternative methods impairs the comparability of financial statements is a matter about which there is also much difference of opinion—even controversy. Many accountants believe that as long as the method adopted

---

*These guidelines are discussed in Chapter V of *Corporate Financial Reporting in a Competitive Economy,* by Herman W. Bevis, © 1965 by Collier-Macmillan Canada, Ltd., Toronto.

†These guidelines are compatible with the approaches to the measurement of cost expirations discussed on pages 60 and 61.

is compatible with the broad principles of accounting and is consistently applied year after year, it will be possible for the users of financial statements to make meaningful comparisons over time and among enterprises. Such belief, though sincere, seems to be founded more on intuition and judgment than on empirical data. Therefore, it would seem to be wise policy for accountants to reduce the number of equally acceptable alternative methods, particularly in those cases in which there is an absence of convincing evidence that the underlying circumstances are sufficiently different to justify a method different from that used by other companies in the same industry.

Although accountants have expressed great interest in reducing the number of acceptable alternative methods and accelerating the process whereby the superiority of one method over alternatives becomes known, very little "reduction" has occurred. In the final analysis, the usefulness of financial statements is enhanced if they permit the making of meaningful comparisons between companies. Regrettably, the area of acceptable alternatives is so extensive at present that efforts to make comparisons will as likely prove misleading as informative.

Unusual and nonrecurring items. For many years accountants have held conflicting opinions regarding the proper accounting for unusual and nonrecurring items. According to one school of thought, the income statement should show only the results of *regular operations* for the *current period;* any corrections of earnings of prior periods and any extraordinary, unusual, or nonrecurring gains and losses, such as those resulting from the disposal of fixed assets or discontinuance of a product line, should be shown in the statement of retained earnings. Statements prepared in this manner were said to be in accordance with the *current operating concept* of net income.

The contrary opinion, known as the *all-inclusive* (or *clean surplus*) *concept,* favored showing corrections of prior-period earnings and extraordinary gains and losses in the income statement, suitably described and classified so that their impact on net income would be disclosed.

Some of the arguments presented by the two schools of thought are briefly stated below.

CURRENT OPERATING CONCEPT: The proponents of the current operating concept of net income support their position by the following arguments:

Investors are more interested in the net income of a business than in any other figure shown by the annual statements. And the net income in which they are interested is that which resulted from normal operating transactions. If extraneous gains and losses and corrections of the reported net income of prior periods are included, it is difficult to determine the trend of a company's operations.

If the stated net income of one year is affected by a material correction of the net income of a prior year, the error is compounded—the current year's net income is overstated or understated to the extent that the net income of the past was understated or overstated. Indicated trends are therefore misleading.

ALL-INCLUSIVE CONCEPT: The proponents of the all-inclusive concept present the following arguments:

The total of the amounts shown as net income in the statements for a series of years should be the aggregate net income for those years; this will not be the case if corrections of the reported net income of prior periods are shown in the statement of retained earnings.

When an accountant charges retained earnings with a loss because he considers it extraordinary or extraneous, he implies that it is nonrecurring. But a study of business history indicates that such losses do recur.

The line of demarcation between operating items and extraordinary and extraneous items is not clear-cut and is often a matter of opinion. Studies of annual reports have shown many inconsistencies in classifications between income and retained earnings made by different companies, and by the same company in different years. Wide variations in net income can be caused by such inconsistencies.

Many so-called extraordinary or extraneous charges and credits are closely related to operations—not to the operations of a single year, but to those of a series of years.

They may be regarded as corrections of the stated net income of a number of prior years; for instance, a gain or loss on the disposal of a depreciable asset may be regarded as a correction of prior years' charges for depreciation resulting from such causes as an error in estimating the useful life of the asset.

Or extraordinary charges may relieve future periods of operating charges which otherwise would be required; this is the case when long-lived assets are written down or written off and future years are thereby relieved of depreciation charges that otherwise would be required.

Action by Accounting Principles Board. Early in 1967, the Accounting Principles Board, in an effort to resolve the controversy concerning the accounting for extraordinary items and prior-period adjustments, issued an opinion (No. 9) devoted to this matter. The position taken was somewhat between the two schools of thought described above, but closer to the all-inclusive concept. Specifically, the opinion took the position that the income statement should show all items of profit and loss recognized during the period with the sole exception of prior-period adjustments, with extraordinary items to be segregated from the results of ordinary operations and shown separately in the income statement.

With respect to prior-period adjustments, the Board concluded that those rare items which relate directly to the operations of a specific prior period or periods, and which are material, should be shown in the statement of retained earnings as adjustments of the beginning-of-period balance of retained earnings. Such adjustments, which are excluded in the determination of net income, are limited to those material items which: "(a) can be specifically identified with and directly related to the business activities of particular prior periods, and (b) are not attributable to economic events occurring subsequent to the date of the financial statements for the prior period, and (c) depend primarily on determinations by persons other than management and (d) were not susceptible of reasonable estimation prior to such determination."

As noted above, any extraordinary items, in contrast to prior-period adjustments, should be set forth in the income statement, but separated in such a way that both the income before extraordinary items and the net income (which is the amount remaining after the extraordinary items have been added or deducted) are disclosed. The Board listed the following as examples of extraordinary items: "... material gains or losses (or provisions for losses) from (a) the sale or abandonment of a plant or a significant segment of the business, (b) the sale of an investment not acquired for resale, (c) the write-off of goodwill due to unusual events or developments within the period, (d) the condemnation or expropriation of properties and (e) a major devaluation of a foreign currency." Such items are not expected to recur frequently and would not be considered as recurring factors in any evaluation of the ordinary operating processes of a business.

To clarify further its concept of extraordinary items, the Board states as follows: "Certain gains or losses (or provisions for losses), regardless of size, do not constitute extraordinary items (or prior period adjustments) because they are of a character typical of the customary business activities of the entity. Examples include (a) write-downs of receivables, inventories, and research and development costs, (b) adjustments of accrued contract prices and (c) gains or losses from fluctuations of foreign exchange."

Net-of-tax treatment. It is possible that extraordinary items and prior-period adjustments will affect a company's income tax liability by being includible or deductible in the computation of taxable income. In those cases in which an extraordinary item or prior-period adjustment affects the income tax liability for the current year, it is preferred practice to associate the tax effect with the extraordinary item or prior-period adjustment. That is, the change in the income tax liability caused by the extraordinary item or prior-period adjustment is shown "next to" the extraordinary item or prior-period adjustment. For example, assume that an extraordinary gain of $100,000 causes a company's income tax to increase by $25,000; thus, the net result is a gain of $75,000. The recommended reporting procedure is as follows:

> Extraordinary item:
> Gain on sale of investment in affiliated company $100,000
> Less applicable income tax.   25,000 $75,000

Such reporting procedure is known as the net-of-tax basis. The objective of the procedure is to disclose the net, or after-tax, results of extraordinary items or prior-period adjustments.

The following statements of Gay Corporation, which show an extraordinary item, a prior-period adjustment, and the net-of-tax procedure, conform to the position advocated by the Accounting Principles Board.

GAY CORPORATION
Income Statement
For the Year Ended December 31, 19+8

Net sales		$1,000,000
Cost of goods sold	$600,000	
Operating expenses	250,000	850,000
Net operating income		$ 150,000
Income tax		70,000
Income before extraordinary item		$ 80,000
Extraordinary item:		
Gain on sale of investment in affiliated company	$100,000	
Less applicable income tax	25,000	75,000
Net income		$ 155,000

GAY CORPORATION
Statement of Retained Earnings
For the Year Ended December 31, 19+8

Retained earnings, December 31, 19+7:		
As previously reported		$3,000,000
Adjustment for 19+8 payment of damages in connection with alleged patent infringement during 19+4	$200,000	
Less reduction in income tax	100,000	100,000
As restated		$2,900,000
Net income for the year		155,000
Total		$3,055,000
Dividends		85,000
Retained earnings, December 31, 19+8		$2,970,000

Because of the danger that some readers of accounting reports are likely to assume that the income statement tells all that is to be told about gains and losses and are not aware of the significance of matters disclosed in the statement of retained earnings, a combined statement of income and retained earnings is frequently advocated. Such a statement, prepared in accordance with the position taken by the Accounting Principles Board, is shown on the opposite page.

Efforts to improve financial statements. During recent decades the attention given to financial reporting has expanded steadily. Financial statements are now widely circulated and an ever-growing number of individuals examines them to form opinions about financial position and results of operations. (For an example of financial statements included in an annual report to stockholders, see Appendix 1.)

During recent decades financial statements have improved. Not only has the disclosure of pertinent financial information expanded greatly, but accounting principles and procedures show evidence of refinement and improvement. In fact the time and resources devoted to the improvement of accounting principles and procedures have reached unprecedented levels. All of the major professional accounting associations support worthwhile research and committee projects which generally produce contributions to the literature of the field and to the sum-total of the knowledge about accounting. Several hundred thousand dollars are disbursed annually

GLOOM COMPANY
Statement of Income and Retained Earnings
For the Year Ended December 31, 19+8

Net sales		$2,000,000
Cost of goods sold	$1,300,000	
Operating expenses	500,000	1,800,000
Net operating income		$ 200,000
Income tax		95,000
Income before extraordinary item		$ 105,000
Extraordinary item:		
Write-off of goodwill		100,000
Net income		$ 5,000
Retained earnings, December 31, 19+7:		
As previously reported		$ 300,000
Adjustment for payment of additional income taxes for 19+5		50,000
As restated		$ 250,000
Total		$ 255,000
Dividends		25,000
Retained earnings, December 31, 19+8		$ 230,000

on such efforts. But dollars spent is a poor indicator of the extent of the total effort because, as a general rule, the association members who devote time and energy to such projects receive no pay for their services and talents. In addition, many state and federal agencies have responsibilities in the area of setting and improving standards of financial reporting. And they work diligently for improvement.

In spite of the impressive quantity of resources and quality of manpower being invested in this effort, progress has been slow. The lack of speed can be attributed in part to the fact that there are several organizations working more or less independently to achieve the same goal with either unclear or no authority to enforce their recommendations. Situations of this kind are not unfamiliar to a democracy. While they may retard the rate of progress, because they bring diverse interests and talents to bear on accounting problems, the ultimate solutions may be better than might be attained if a single, authoritative body had the sole responsibility for efforts in this area.

Some accountants believe that progress is retarded for a more basic reason, namely, because there is lack of agreement concerning the *purpose* of financial statements. It is generally conceded that, in setting up any measurement system, it is imperative at the outset to specify the purpose for which the measurements are intended. Accounting, of course, is a measurement system. Such general assertions as "accounting should provide the user of financial statements with meaningful information," or that "financial statements should provide useful information," though often uttered, are so broad as to be of little or no help in deciding which principle or procedure from among the alternatives is best.

Contributing to the difficulty of securing agreement on the matter of *purpose* is the fact that financial statements are used for a variety of purposes, such as:

To measure management performance.

To gauge debt-paying ability.

To provide the stockholders with an accountability report about the resources placed at the disposal of management.

To assist investors in making predictions about future earnings.

To provide a measurement of social benefits produced by businesses.

It may prove unrealistic to hope that agreement will ever be reached about the best single or primary *purpose* to be served by financial statements. Lacking such consensus, financial statements will continue to be *general purpose* in character. It is important that a user of financial statements recognize this basic feature of the product of the accounting process. As a result of efforts to satisfy a variety of needs, many compromises have been made, so that we do not have as logical and as orderly a set of accounting principles and supporting procedures as we would have if accountants concentrated on the preparation of a single-purpose report as their objective. The general-purpose approach has contributed also to the existence of a number of alternative principles and procedures. Without agreement about purpose, progress toward a reduction in the number of alternatives and the resolution of controversies will be difficult.

Concluding note. If you perceive the meaning and implications of the following statements, and if called upon can provide some elaboration thereon, you have made an excellent start in understanding the accounting process.

- Accounting is essentially a cost-based system in contrast to a value-based system.
- One should not attribute great precision to the income-determination process. An income figure is an approximation.
- As a general rule, the worth or value of a business will not be revealed by its balance sheet.
- At the present time, financial statements can be characterized as general-purpose statements.
- Judgment is required in the application of accounting principles and procedures.
- When accounting principles and procedures are applied, some trade-off between objectivity, usefulness, and feasibility is inevitable.
- Consistency of application is a key element to which much of the value of financial statements can be attributed.
- Interpretation of financial statements requires judgment.

ASSIGNMENT
MATERIAL

QUESTIONS

1. If we designate those served by accounting as "insiders" and "outsiders," which group has the greatest need for accounting data based on accounting principles?

2. Does the emphasis the accountant places on consistency mean that accounting methods, once adopted, can never be changed?

3. How useful, or helpful, are broadly stated accounting principles?

4. Cite any one of the broad principles listed in the chapter and give an example of an accounting practice that would be incompatible with the principle cited.

5. Under what circumstances are departures from historical cost acceptable to the accountant?

6. Why is so little attention given to present (actual) values in the preparation of conventional financial statements?

7. Is appreciation of asset values *income* as accountants define the term?

8. A manufacturing company has expended a total of $3,000 worth of its material, labor, and expense in constructing a machine for its own use. The machine, if bought in the open market, would have cost $4,000. Is it sound accounting to capitalize this machine at the market price?

9. State the guidelines for recurring transactions.

10. Contrast the current operating concept and the all-inclusive concept.

11. Describe how an extraordinary loss would be shown in the financial statements on a net-of-tax basis.

12. List the uses made of financial statements according to the chapter.

SHORT EXERCISES

E15-1. Under each of the circumstances described below, determine the amount that should be shown in the financial statements.

(a) Merchandise inventory

Cost	$1,000
Replacement cost	1,025
Realizable value	1,100

(b) Equipment

Cost..	$5,000
Replacement cost—outside supplier....................	5,200
Replacement cost—built in own plant	4,400
Resale value	4,600

(c) Patent

Cost..	$10,000
Replacement cost....................................	15,000
Estimated market value..............................	-0-
Commercial value of product covered by patent	-0-

(d) Gross margin

Regular sales.......................................	$50,000
Installment sales....................................	10,000
Cost of goods sold—all customers	40,000
Collections from installment customers................	6,000

(e) Gross margin—Installment sales method

Installment sales during period	$10,000
Cost of goods sold on installment plan................	6,000
Collections from installment customers................	3,000

(f) Income from construction in progress—Long-term contract

Total contract price.................................	$100,000
Cost incurred during fiscal year just ended	40,000
Aggregate cost incurred to date......................	40,000
Estimated cost to complete contract..................	40,000
Per cent work completed	50%

E15-2. Determine the income from operations and the net income for each of the following cases. (Ignore the matter of income taxes.)

	(a)	(b)	(c)	(d)
Revenue from sales	$500,000	$500,000	$500,000	$500,000
Cost of goods sold	300,000	300,000	300,000	300,000
Operating expenses..........	100,000	100,000	100,000	100,000
Prior-period adjustment.......	40,000 (debit)		30,000 (credit)	
Write-off of goodwill.........	50,000			
Loss from devaluation of foreign currency		30,000		
Gain from sale of plant.......			15,000	
Loss from write-down of inventory				20,000
Unusual loss from uncollectible receivables		18,000		
Foreign exchange gain				5,000

E15-3. Make use of the data given for E15-2 (c). Assume that the statement of retained earnings for the preceding year (19+2) showed an ending balance of $100,000. Also assume that the dividends for the current year amount to $20,000. Prepare the statement of retained earnings for the current year, 19+3. (Use ABC Company in heading and ignore income taxes.)

E15-4. Make use of the data given for E15-2(b). Assume that the proper income tax rate is 50 per cent. Determine the income before extraordinary items and the net income, following the net-of-tax procedure.

PROBLEMS

Problem A15-1. From the data given below, prepare the statement of retained earnings for Frame Company for the year ended December 31, 19+5. The retained earnings as of December 31, 19+4, were reported in last year's financial statements as $44,400.

19+5 Data

Gross margin.	$200,000
Operating expenses.	125,000
Interest revenue.	2,000
Rent revenue.	18,000
Advances from customers—Year-end balance	3,000
Dividends.	8,000
Unrealized appreciation on long-lived assets	25,000
Payment of additional income taxes for 19+2.	20,000
Loss on sale of investment in affiliated company	50,000
Reduction in income tax resulting from sale of investment in affiliated company.	12,500
Special credit from savings resulting from manufacture of equipment for company's use	7,000
Liability for 19+5 income taxes	23,000

Problem A15-2. From the data given below, prepare a combined statement of income and retained earnings for Nonautomatic Corporation for the year ended December 31, 19+8. Consider the sale of investments to be an extraordinary item.

Sales	$ 50,200
Cost of goods sold	27,820
Operating expenses.	16,130
Interest revenue.	560
Dividends (paid)	5,000
Income tax liability at end of 19+8.	17,293
Income tax applicable to current operations, including interest	2,043
Increase in replacement cost of property, plant, and equipment	20,000
Gain on sale of investments (taxable at 25%)	16,000
Retained earnings, December 31, 19+7.	136,540
Assessment for additional income taxes for 19+4 and 19+5	11,250

Problem A15-3. The following statement of retained earnings was prepared with no consideration given to the position taken by the Accounting Principles Board in its Opinion No. 9. Furthermore, as indicated, the net-of-tax procedure was not adopted and certain generally accepted accounting principles have been disregarded.

OPTIMUM COMPANY
Statement of Retained Earnings
For the Year Ended December 31, 19+8

Retained earnings, December 31, 19+7 . . . . $180,000
Add:
  Net income for the year $27,000
  Unrealized appreciation in land 30,000
  Premium arising from issuance of additional share of
    capital stock 5,000
  Refund of portion of 19+4 income taxes 8,000   70,000
Total $250,000
Deduct:
  Dividends $10,000
  Loss on disposal of equipment of discontinued product
    line 20,000   30,000
Retained earnings, December 31, 19+8 . . . . $220,000

The income tax rate for 19+8 is 30 per cent. You may assume that the following computation of the income tax liability for 19+8 is correct.

Net operating income $30,000
Deduct loss on disposal of equipment of discontinued product line . 20,000
Taxable income $10,000

Estimated income tax liability. . . . . $ 3,000

Prepare the statement of retained earnings as you believe it should be prepared.

Problem A15-4. In the course of your examination of the records of Shadford Company for the years ended December 31, 19+6, 19+7, and 19+8, you discover the following errors:

(1) The merchandise inventory on December 31, 19+6, was understated in the amount of $1,600 as a result of errors in the extensions on inventory sheets.

(2) Unexpired insurance of $850, applicable to 19+8, was ignored on December 31, 19+7.

(3) Premium of $3,000 on the issuance of $200,000 face amount of ten-year bonds, dated July 1, 19+6, was treated as current revenue on that date.

(4) A customer's order for merchandise in the amount of $3,400 was treated as a credit sale when received on December 18, 19+8, although the related goods were not shipped until January, 19+9, and were included in the December 31, 19+8 inventory.

(5) On January 1, 19+7, an item of equipment costing $2,600, with accumulated depreciation thereon of $1,200, was sold for $1,600 cash. The amount received was recorded as Miscellaneous Income, and depreciation on the asset was taken for 19+7 and 19+8 at an annual rate of 10% of cost.

(6) Interest receivable, in the amount of $420, was not recorded on December 31, 19+7; it was collected in 19+8.

The amounts of net income for the years ended December 31, 19+6, 19+7, and 19+8, as determined by Shadford Company, were as follows:

19+6	$18,900
19+7	16,200
19+8	6,800

(a) Compute the correct net income for Shadford Company for the years ended December 31, 19+6, 19+7, and 19+8.

(b) Prepare the necessary correcting entry or entries as of December 31, 19+8, assuming that the books have not been closed for 19+8. As needed, use a special account titled "Correction of Prior Years' Net Income" for correction items assignable to years prior to 19+8.

Problem A15-5. Some novel procedures were used during the first year following the organization of Spoof Company, as indicated below.

$50,000 of par value stock was issued.
> The premium thereon was credited to Miscellaneous Income.

$200,000 of orders for merchandise were obtained by the company's salesmen.
> Unfilled Orders was debited for the amount of each order.
> Inventory was credited for the cost of goods ordered.
> Deferred Gross Margin was credited for the gross margin thereon.
>> (The gross margin was uniform on all transactions, being 40 per cent of selling price.)

$160,000 of the above orders were shipped to the customers.
> Cost of Goods Sold was debited for cost.
> Deferred Gross Margin was debited.
> Unfilled Orders was credited.

$150,000 was collected from customers for completed orders.
> Cash was debited.
> Sales was credited.

$170,000 of purchase orders were placed with suppliers.
> Goods on Order was debited.
> Accounts Payable was credited.

$150,000 of goods ordered were received from suppliers.
> Inventory was debited.
> Goods on Order was credited.

$145,000 was paid on account to suppliers for goods received.
> Accounts Payable was debited.
> Cash was credited.

Procedures for commissions to salesmen—rate, 20%:
> Sales Commissions debited when the purchase order was received from the customer.
> Accrued Commissions credited.

> Accrued Commissions debited.
> Cash credited when the amount owed by the customer was collected in full.

The trial balance as of the end of the first year is shown below.

SPOOF COMPANY
Trial Balance
December 31, 19+8

Cash	27,000	
Unfilled orders	40,000	
Deferred gross margin		16,000
Inventory	30,000	
Goods on order	20,000	
Accounts payable		25,000
Accrued commissions		10,000
Capital stock		50,000
Sales		150,000
Cost of goods sold	96,000	
Sales commissions	40,000	
Miscellaneous income		2,000
	253,000	253,000

Submit a corrected trial balance.

Problem B15-1. The income statement and statement of retained earnings of Sunday Corporation, set forth in preliminary form by a new employee, are shown below.

SUNDAY CORPORATION
Income Statement
For the Year Ended December 31, 19+8

Net sales		$600,000
Cost of goods sold	$360,000	
Operating expenses	215,000	
Income tax	3,000	578,000
Net income		$ 22,000

SUNDAY CORPORATION
Statement of Retained Earnings
For the Year Ended December 31, 19+8

Retained earnings, December 31, 19+7		$200,000
Net income—per above		22,000
Total		$222,000
Deduct:		
Uninsured fire loss	$15,000	
Dividends	10,000	25,000
Retained earnings, December 31, 19+8		$197,000

After reviewing the above draft, the management of Sunday Corporation decided to use the combined statement form for 19+8 and following years. Prepare such a statement for 19+8. The applicable income tax rate is 30 per cent, and you may assume that the corporation's income tax liability at the end of 19+8 is $3,000.

Problem B15-2. The following data are taken from the accounts of Space Company. They show the debits to all of the company's asset accounts during 19+8.

Cash

Proceeds from sale of treasury stock	$ 5,000
Collections on accounts receivable	180,000
Advances from customers (Note 1)	1,800
Bank loan	10,000
Cash sales	33,000
Proceeds from sale of long-term investment	18,000

Accounts receivable

Sales on account	$184,000

Inventory

Purchases, including cost of delivered special-order merchandise (see Note 1)	$112,000

Land

Write-up to appreciated value		$ 20,000
Beginning-of-year account balance	$60,000	
End-of-year account balance	80,000	

Equipment

Cost of equipment constructed by company	$ 50,000
Saving as a result of construction of equipment	10,000

Long-term investment

No debits during year.		
Beginning-of-year account balance	$36,000	
End-of-year account balance	24,000	

Note 1: When a customer wishes to buy merchandise which is not in stock, the company collects the full price from the customer, which is accounted for as an advance, and issues a special purchase order for the merchandise. The company directs the supplier to ship the merchandise direct to the customer. By the end of the year, shipments of special-order merchandise, which cost $600, covered one-half of the 19+8 advances.

Prepare a schedule showing the amount of revenue earned by the company in 19+8.

Problem B15-3. A new employee of Trackside Company has been in charge of recording transactions since July 1. An analysis of the sales, inventory, and cost of goods sold accounts covering the period since July 1 follows.

Sales

Credits:

Cash sales	$ 42,000
Cash collections from credit customers:	
For sales before July 1	28,000
For sales since July 1	72,000
Merchandise shipped on consignment	21,000
Order received from State of Kansas	12,000
Sale of stated value treasury stock	7,000
Collections from customers whose accounts had been written off as uncollectible	800
Appreciation of inventory	9,000

Debits:

Return of sales price to cash customers for merchandise returned	$ 240

Cost of goods sold

Debits:

Cost of goods sold (Selling prices set at 150% of cost). . . . . . . $ 94,000*
Cost of goods shipped on consignment.   14,000
Cost of treasury stock sold   4,000

Credits:

Returns from cash customers   240

* You may assume that this figure is correct.

Inventory

Debits:

Purchases $150,000
Returns from cash customers   240
Appreciation   9,000

Credits:

Cost of goods sold   94,000
Cost of goods shipped on consignment.   14,000

(Note: The merchant receiving the goods on consignment had not disposed of any of such merchandise as of the date the above analysis was prepared.)

Although some of the account balances would be incorrect, you may assume that if a trial balance were taken at this time it would balance. You may also assume that correct recording procedures were followed prior to July 1.

Prepare journal entries to correct the sales, inventory, and cost of goods sold accounts. Use August 1, 19+3, as the date for the correcting entries.

Problem B15-4. R. P. Brown, who operates a small retail store, has followed the practice of recording sales revenue when cash is collected from customers and merchandise purchases and expenses (other than depreciation) when cash is disbursed. He has prepared the following income statement for 19+8.

R. P. BROWN
Income Statement
For the Year Ended December 31, 19+8

Cash received from customers $92,200
Cost of goods sold:
  Merchandise inventory, December 31, 19+7 . . . . $ 9,600
  Cash paid for merchandise   63,600
  Total. $73,200
  Deduct merchandise inventory, December 31, 19+8   13,800   59,400
Gross margin. $32,800
Expenses paid $21,200
Depreciation expense   2,000   23,200
Net income . . . . $ 9,600

Using the following additional information, prepare a corrected income statement. Show computations of sales, cost of goods sold, and expenses.

(a) Accounts payable—Merchandise:

December 31, 19+7 .... $ 3,600
December 31, 19+8   4,100

(b) Liability for expenses:

December 31, 19+7 .... $ 1,600
December 31, 19+8   1,900

(c) Accounts receivable (all collectible):

December 31, 19+7 .... $10,400
December 31, 19+8   8,800

Problem B15-5. The following financial statements with five supporting footnotes have been submitted to you by the president of Off Base Company who wishes to sell to you the 6,000 shares of Off Base stock he owns, so that he can retire. You may assume that the facts set forth in the statements and footnotes are accurate.

(a) Reconstruct the comparative balance sheet to conform with generally accepted accounting principles.

(b) Estimate the 19+4 net income earned by the company.

OFF BASE COMPANY
Comparative Balance Sheet
December 31, 19+4 and 19+3

Assets

	19+4	19+3
Current assets:		
Cash	$ 20,000	$ 25,000
Short-term investments in marketable securities, at market values (cost, $8,000 as of 12/31/+4 and $14,000 as of 12/31/+3)	10,000	15,000
Accounts receivable—net of allowance for uncollectibles, $1,000 as of 12/31/+4 and $800 as of 12/31/+3	44,000	39,200
Inventory—at replacement cost—Note 1	66,000	52,500
Prepaid expenses	3,000	2,300
	$143,000	$134,000
Property, plant, and equipment:		
Land—at appraised value—Note 2	$ 25,000	$ 24,000
Plant—at appreciated values—Note 3	72,600	66,000
Equipment—at trade-in values—Note 4	14,000	19,000
	$111,600	$109,000
Intangibles:		
Estimated value of goodwill	$ 50,000	$ 40,000
	$304,600	$283,000

Equities

Current liabilities:

Accounts payable	$ 48,000	$ 45,000
Wages and salaries payable	9,080	12,100
	$ 57,080	$ 57,100

Other equities:

Accumulated depreciation—Plant	$ 14,520	$ 9,900

Stockholders' equity:

Capital stock—Note 5	$160,000	$150,000
Surplus	73,000	66,000
	$233,000	$216,000
	$304,600	$283,000

OFF BASE COMPANY
Surplus Statement
For the Year Ended December 31, 19+4

Balance, December 31, 19+3		$66,000
Add:		
Net income	$ 8,000	
Increase in goodwill	10,000	
Excess of issuance price over stated value	5,000	23,000
Total		$89,000
Deduct dividends		16,000
Balance, December 31, 19+4		$73,000

Note 1: Replacement costs were 10 per cent above cost as of 12/31/+4 and 5 per cent above cost as of 12/31/+3.

Note 2: The land was acquired through issuance of $20,000 of stated-value capital stock when the corporation was organized.

Note 3: The plant was constructed in 19+1 when the cost of living index was 100. The plant account balance has been revised each year to keep pace with the change in the cost of living index.

Cost of Living Index

19+1	100	19+3	110
19+2	105	19+4	121

The plant has an expected useful life of twenty years, with no resale or scrap value anticipated. It is the company's policy to take a full year's depreciation on assets put into service during the year.

Note 4: The record of equipment purchases follows:

	Cost
19+1	$20,000
19+2	10,000
Total	$30,000

The equipment has an expected useful life of ten years, with no scrap value or trade-in value at the end of its useful life. However, a well-established trade-in market exists for used equipment that has some remaining useful life.

Note 5: The $10 stated value capital stock was issued as follows:

At organization date: 13,000 shares for $130,000 cash; 2,000 shares for land.

During 19+4: 1,000 shares for $15,000 cash.

16

Sources and Uses of Working Capital

Changes in working capital and causes thereof. Suppose that you were given the following comparative balance sheet:

THE A COMPANY
Comparative Balance Sheet
December 31, 19+2 and 19+1

	December 31,	
	19+2	19+1
Assets		
Cash	$ 4,700	$ 3,000
Accounts receivable	11,500	12,000
Merchandise	9,000	8,000
Land	6,600	5,000
	$31,800	$28,000
Equities		
Accounts payable..........................	$ 4,500	$ 7,000
Capital stock	25,000	20,000
Retained earnings.........................	2,300	1,000
	$31,800	$28,000

If you were asked to prepare a statement detailing the changes in the elements of working capital, you would use the balances in the current asset and current liability accounts and would prepare the following schedule.

THE A COMPANY
Schedule of Working Capital
December 31, 19+2 and 19+1

	December 31, 19+2	December 31, 19+1	Changes in Working Capital Increase	Changes in Working Capital Decrease
Current assets:				
Cash............................	$ 4,700	$ 3,000	$1,700	
Accounts receivable............	11,500	12,000		$ 500
Merchandise..................	9,000	8,000	1,000	
Total current assets..........	$25,200	$23,000		
Current liabilities:				
Accounts payable	4,500	7,000	2,500	
Working capital	$20,700	$16,000		
Increase in working capital				4,700
			$5,200	$5,200

This chapter deals with a statement which shows the *causes* of the change in working capital; but, before the statement is illustrated, it will be helpful to look at the comparative balance sheet below, in which the changes in working capital accounts are shown in one pair of columns and the changes in other accounts are shown in another pair of columns. Observe that the net debits in the working capital accounts and the net credits in the other accounts are equal.

THE A COMPANY
Comparative Balance Sheet
With Classification of Changes in Account Balances
December 31, 19+2 and 19+1

	December 31, 19+2	December 31, 19+1	Changes in Account Balances In Working Capital Accounts Debit	Changes in Account Balances In Working Capital Accounts Credit	Changes in Account Balances In Other (Noncurrent) Accounts Debit	Changes in Account Balances In Other (Noncurrent) Accounts Credit
Assets						
Cash	$ 4,700	$ 3,000	$1,700			
Accounts receivable	11,500	12,000		$ 500		
Merchandise	9,000	8,000	1,000			
Land	6,600	5,000			$1,600	
	$31,800	$28,000				

Equities

Accounts payable	$ 4,500	$ 7,000	2,500	
Capital stock	25,000	20,000		$5,000
Retained earnings.	2,300	1,000		1,300
	$31,800	$28,000		
Net debits in working capital accounts			4,700	
Net credits in noncurrent accounts				4,700
	$5,200	$5,200	$6,300	$6,300

Because of the equality of the net debits and net credits in the two types of accounts, i.e., the working capital accounts and the noncurrent accounts, by referring to the noncurrent accounts in the ledger and determining what caused the changes in them, we shall at the same time ascertain the causes of the change in working capital. The causes of the changes in the noncurrent accounts and the related effects on working capital are shown below.

	Changes in Noncurrent Account Balances		Working Capital Result	
	Debit	Credit	Increase	Decrease
Land:				
Cause of change—Land purchased	$1,600			
Effect on working capital—Decrease				$1,600
Capital stock:				
Cause of change—Additional stock issued . .		$5,000		
Effect on working capital—Increase			$5,000	
Retained earnings:				
Cause of change—Net income for the year .		1,300		
Effect on working capital—Increase			1,300	
	$1,600	$6,300	$6,300	$1,600
Net credits to noncurrent accounts and increase in working capital	4,700			4,700
	$6,300	$6,300	$6,300	$6,300

The credits in the noncurrent accounts indicate the sources of working capital that came into the business during the year; the noncurrent account debit reflects the use of working capital; the excess of the credits over the debit is the amount of the increase in working capital for the year, $4,700. This amount agrees with the increase in working capital shown in the schedule of working capital on page 364.

The causes of the increase in working capital are shown below.

THE A COMPANY
Sources and Uses of Working Capital
For the Year Ended December 31, 19+2

Working capital sources:		
Operations	$1,300	
Issuance of capital stock	5,000	$6,300
Working capital uses:		
Purchase of land		1,600
Increase in working capital—per schedule (page 364)		$4,700

This statement is often referred to as a *funds statement,* and the title "Statement of Application of Funds" is well known to accountants and statement users. However, that title is subject to criticism because it does not clearly indicate the nature of the statement.

Purpose of the statement. The primary purpose of the statement of sources and uses of working capital is to show what caused the change in working capital during a period. It is of particular interest to bankers and other grantors of short-term credit. A schedule of working capital, such as the one on page 364, shows the change in working capital but it does not answer the question: What caused this change? The answer to this question may be very important.

Suppose that three prospective borrowers submitted reports to a banker showing working capital of $50,000 at the beginning of the year and $60,000 at the end of the year. One submitted a statement of sources and uses of working capital showing:

Working capital sources:	
Operations...	$15,000
Working capital uses:	
Payment of dividends...............................	5,000
Increase in working capital	$10,000

This statement would probably create a favorable impression.

The second applicant submitted the following statement:

Working capital sources:		
Operations..................................	$ 8,000	
Issuance of five-year notes	25,000	$33,000
Working capital uses:		
Purchase of land.............................	$18,000	
Payment of dividends..........................	5,000	23,000
Increase in working capital		$10,000

This statement would probably create a less favorable impression. The banker would observe the smaller amount of working capital provided by operations and the greater proportion thereof paid out in dividends. He might want to ask the management why they thought the expenditure for land advisable. And he probably would be particularly interested in an answer to the following question: Unless they can increase the inflow of working capital from operations or will reduce their dividends, how do they expect to pay off the $25,000 of notes in five years without impairing their working capital?

The third submitted a statement showing:

Working capital sources:		
Operations..................................	$ 2,000	
Issuance of five-year notes	20,000	$22,000
Working capital uses:		
Payment of dividends..........................		12,000
Increase in working capital		$10,000

This statement would create a very unfavorable impression. It does not seem to be good financial management to borrow money in order to pay dividends equal to six times the small amount of working capital provided by operations. And, with such results of operations and such a dividend policy, how does the management expect to pay the five-year notes, to say nothing of an additional bank loan?

Additional features illustrated. The following comparative balance sheet is the basis of this illustration.

THE B COMPANY
Comparative Balance Sheet
December 31, 19+2 and 19+1

	December 31, 19+2	December 31, 19+1	Increase— Decrease*
Assets			
Cash	$ 6,600	$ 3,500	$3,100
Accounts receivable	5,900	6,200	300*
Merchandise	19,000	16,500	2,500
Investment securities	7,000	9,000	2,000*
Goodwill	—	2,500	2,500*
	$38,500	$37,700	$ 800
Equities			
Accounts payable	$ 1,500	$ 1,900	$ 400*
Long-term notes payable	—	5,000	5,000*
Capital stock	34,500	30,000	4,500
Capital in excess of par value	450	—	450
Retained earnings	2,050	800	1,250
	$38,500	$37,700	$ 800

The first step is to prepare the schedule of working capital.

THE B COMPANY
Schedule of Working Capital
December 31, 19+2 and 19+1

	December 31, 19+2	December 31, 19+1	Changes in Working Capital Increase	Changes in Working Capital Decrease
Current assets:				
Cash	$ 6,600	$ 3,500	$3,100	
Accounts receivable	5,900	6,200		$ 300
Merchandise	19,000	16,500	2,500	
Total current assets	$31,500	$26,200		
Current liabilities:				
Accounts payable	1,500	1,900	400	
Working capital	$30,000	$24,300		
Increase in working capital				5,700
			$6,000	$6,000

To determine what caused the increase in working capital, we prepare the following analysis of the noncurrent accounts. The information required was obtained from the noncurrent accounts in the ledger. (It is necessary sometimes to examine explanations or documents that support the entries in the accounts. However, in many cases the causes of changes in the balances of noncurrent accounts are apparent, making it unnecessary to refer to the ledger accounts or other sources of accounting information.)

THE B COMPANY
Analysis of Changes in Noncurrent Accounts
For the Year Ended December 31, 19+2

	Debit—	Working Capital Result		
	Credit*	Increase	Decrease	No Effect
Investment securities:				
12/31/+1	9,000			
Sale of securities at cost	2,000*	2,000		
12/31/+2	7,000			
Goodwill:				
12/31/+1	2,500			
Write-off to Retained Earnings	2,500*			2,500*
12/31/+2	—			
Long-term notes payable:				
12/31/+1	5,000*			
Payment	5,000		5,000	
12/31/+2	—			
Capital stock:				
12/31/+1	30,000*			
Par of stock issued	4,500*	4,500a		
12/31/+2	34,500*			
Capital in excess of par value:				
12/31/+1	—			
Premium on stock issued	450*	450a		
12/31/+2	450*			
Retained earnings:				
12/31/+1	800*			
Net income	4,750*	4,750		
Dividends	1,000		1,000	
Goodwill write-off	2,500			2,500
12/31/+2	2,050*			
		11,700	6,000	—
Increase in working capital			5,700	
		11,700	11,700	

a—The par value of the stock issued and the premium thereon are marked "a" to indicate that they are to be shown together in the statement of sources and uses of working capital.

As shown in the preceding analysis of noncurrent accounts, some changes have no effect on the amount of working capital. Consider the case of the goodwill write-off. The only accounts affected are the goodwill and retained earnings accounts, neither being a working capital account. Such changes are extended to the No Effect column. The amounts entered in the No Effect column should add to zero.

The increase in working capital shown in the foregoing analysis agrees with the increase shown in the schedule of working capital, thus showing that the analysis of noncurrent accounts provides all of the information required for the preparation of the statement of sources and uses of working capital.

THE B COMPANY
Sources and Uses of Working Capital
For the Year Ended December 31, 19+2

Working capital sources:			
Operations			$4,750
Issuance of capital stock:			
Par		$4,500	
Premium		450	4,950
Sale of investment securities			2,000 $11,700
Working capital uses:			
Payment of long-term debt			$5,000
Payment of dividends			1,000 6,000
Increase in working capital			$ 5,700

Contents of the statement of sources and uses of working capital. The sources and uses statement is a summary, covering a period of time, of the transactions that resulted in a change in the *amount* of working capital. To understand this statement, it is important to realize that some transactions and entries have no effect on the amount of working capital.

Transactions that affect current asset and/or current liability accounts *only* do not change the amount of working capital. For example, a purchase of securities to be held as short-term investments causes an increase in one current asset account (Short-term Investments) and an equal decrease in another current asset (Cash). Because transactions of this nature have no effect on the *amount* of working capital, they are not reflected in the *statement* of sources and uses of working capital; they will, of course, affect the *schedule* of working capital.

Some transactions affect noncurrent accounts only. For instance, the issuance of $100,000 of common stock in retirement of an equal par value of preferred stock would have no effect on working capital. The resulting account changes would not appear in the statement of sources and uses of working capital.

Some changes in noncurrent accounts result from mere book entries debiting one noncurrent account and crediting another. The write-off of goodwill in the preceding illustration is an example. Working capital was not affected.

The entries that are relevant for sources-and-uses-statement purposes are those affecting one or more working capital accounts and one or more noncurrent accounts. Such entries reflect a change in the amount of working capital.

Working capital provided by operations may be greater than net income. Some charges to expense accounts reduce the net income without having any bearing on the working capital. For instance, depreciation of plant and equipment reduces the net income but has no effect on working capital.

> Although depreciation is an expense, the charge for depreciation does not involve any utilization of working capital. Therefore, to determine the amount of working capital provided by operations, it is necessary to add the net income for the period and the depreciation charges made during the period. However, such "adding back" of depreciation does not make it a source of working capital; it is an adjustment to net income to determine the amount of working capital provided by operations.

To illustrate, assume that a man began business on January 1, and that his financial condition at that date was as follows:

Assets:
Cash	$100
Machine	500
Owner's equity.	$600

He did a cash business; all sales were cash sales and cash was paid for all purchases of merchandise and miscellaneous expenses. At the end of the year he prepared the following summary of cash receipts and disbursements and an income statement. Note that all of the merchandise purchased was sold before year end.

Cash Summary

Beginning balance		$ 100
Cash receipts:		
Sales.		2,000
Total		$2,100
Cash disbursements:		
Purchase of merchandise.	$800	
Miscellaneous expenses	200	1,000
Ending balance		$1,100

Income Statement

Sales		$2,000
Deduct cost of goods sold		800
Gross margin.		$1,200
Deduct:		
Miscellaneous expenses	$200	
Depreciation.	50	250
Net income		$ 950

The data show that, although the net income was $950, the working capital of the business, which in this instance consisted of cash, was increased $1,000 by operations. Thus, to determine the increase in working capital resulting from operations, it is necessary to add the $950 net income and the $50 depreciation charge.

The above analysis relating to depreciation charges also applies to charges made for the amortization of intangible assets; such expense charges are added to net income to determine the working capital generated by operations.

The following comparative balance sheet is the basis of an illustration showing working capital provided by operations in excess of net income.

THE C COMPANY
Comparative Balance Sheet
December 31, 19+2 and 19+1

	December 31,		Increase—
Assets	19+2	19+1	Decrease*
Cash	$ 11,200	$ 8,500	$2,700
Accounts receivable	21,300	23,500	2,200*
Allowance for uncollectibles	(1,350)	(1,425)	75
Merchandise inventory	35,000	30,600	4,400
Long-term investments	16,000	12,000	4,000
Land	10,000	10,000	—
Building	60,000	60,000	—
Accumulated depreciation—Building	(12,000)	(9,000)	3,000*
Furniture and fixtures	8,000	7,000	1,000
Accumulated depreciation—Furniture and fixtures	(3,200)	(2,400)	800*
	$144,950	$138,775	$6,175
Equities			
Accounts payable	$ 15,000	$ 18,000	$3,000*
Notes payable	10,000	7,500	2,500
Real estate mortgage payable	40,000	40,000	—
Capital stock	50,000	45,000	5,000
Reserve for contingencies	15,000	12,000	3,000
Retained earnings	14,950	16,275	1,325*
	$144,950	$138,775	$6,175

( ) Deduction.

Again, the first step is to prepare the schedule of working capital.

THE C COMPANY
Schedule of Working Capital
December 31, 19+2 and 19+1

	December 31,		Changes in Working Capital	
	19+2	19+1	Increase	Decrease
Current assets:				
Cash	$11,200	$ 8,500	$ 2,700	
Accounts receivable	21,300	23,500		$ 2,200
Allowance for uncollectibles	(1,350)	(1,425)	75	
Merchandise inventory	35,000	30,600	4,400	
Total current assets	$66,150	$61,175		
Current liabilities:				
Accounts payable	$15,000	$18,000	3,000	
Notes payable	10,000	7,500		2,500
Total current liabilities	$25,000	$25,500		
Working capital	$41,150	$35,675		
Increase in working capital				5,475
			$10,175	$10,175

An analysis of the noncurrent accounts is shown below.

THE C COMPANY
Analysis of Changes in Noncurrent Accounts
For the Year Ended December 31, 19+2

	Debit—Credit*	Increase	Decrease	No Effect
		Working Capital Result		
Long-term investments:				
12/31/+1	12,000			
Additional investment	4,000	4,000		
12/31/+2	16,000			
Accumulated depreciation—Building:				
12/31/+1	9,000*			
Depreciation for the year	3,000*	3,000a		
12/31/+2	12,000*			
Furniture and fixtures:				
12/31/+1	7,000			
Purchase	1,000		1,000	
12/31/+2	8,000			
Accumulated depreciation—F. & F.:				
12/31/+1	2,400*			
Depreciation for the year	800*	800a		
12/31/+2	3,200*			
Capital stock:				
12/31/+1	45,000*			
Stock issued	5,000*	5,000		
12/31/+2	50,000*			
Reserve for contingencies:				
12/31/+1	12,000*			
Transfer from Retained Earnings	3,000*			3,000*
12/31/+2	15,000*			
Retained earnings:				
12/31/+1	16,275*			
Net income	6,675*	6,675a		
Dividend—In cash	5,000		5,000	
Transfer to Reserve for Contingencies	3,000			3,000
12/31/+2	14,950*			
		15,475	10,000	—
Increase in working capital			5,475	
		15,475	15,475	

Because the increase in working capital shown in the schedule of working capital agrees with the increase shown in the analysis of changes in noncurrent accounts, the following statement may be prepared.

THE C COMPANY
Sources and Uses of Working Capital
For the Year Ended December 31, 19+2

Working capital sources:
Operations:

Net income for the year	$6,675	
Add: Depreciation—Building	3,000	
Depreciation—Furniture and fixtures	800	$10,475
Issuance of capital stock		5,000 $15,475

Working capital uses:

Investment in long-term securities	$ 4,000	
Purchase of furniture and fixtures	1,000	
Payment of dividend	5,000	10,000
Increase in working capital		$ 5,475

Decrease in working capital. The following comparative balance sheet is the basis of an illustration showing a decrease in working capital.

THE D COMPANY
Comparative Balance Sheet
December 31, 19+2 and 19+1

	December 31,		Increase—
Assets	19+2	19+1	Decrease*
Cash	$ 3,000	$ 3,400	$ 400*
Accounts receivable	6,000	5,000	1,000
Inventory	18,000	20,000	2,000*
Prepayments	500	600	100*
Furniture	13,500	6,000	7,500
Accumulated depreciation—Furniture	(2,300)	(1,800)	500*
	$38,700	$33,200	$5,500
Equities			
Accounts payable	$ 2,100	$ 2,300	$ 200*
Capital stock	25,000	20,000	5,000
Retained earnings	11,600	10,900	700
	$38,700	$33,200	$5,500

( ) Deduction.

Following is the schedule of working capital. Note the inclusion of prepayments in the illustration.

THE D COMPANY
Schedule of Working Capital
December 31, 19+2 and 19+1

	December 31,		Changes in Working Capital	
	19+2	19+1	Increase	Decrease
Current assets:				
Cash	$ 3,000	$ 3,400		$ 400
Accounts receivable	6,000	5,000	$1,000	
Inventory	18,000	20,000		2,000
Prepayments	500	600		100
Total current assets	$27,500	$29,000		
Current liabilities:				
Accounts payable	2,100	2,300	200	
Working capital	$25,400	$26,700		
Decrease in working capital			1,300	
			$2,500	$2,500

The analysis of the noncurrent accounts follows.

THE D COMPANY
Analysis of Changes in Noncurrent Accounts
For the Year Ended December 31, 19+2

	Debit— Credit*	Working Capital Result		
		Increase	Decrease	No Effect
Furniture:				
12/31/+1	6,000			
Purchase	7,500		7,500	
12/31/+2	13,500			
Accumulated depreciation—Furniture:				
12/31/+1	1,800*			
Depreciation for the year	500*	500a		
12/31/+2	2,300*			
Capital stock:				
12/31/+1	20,000*			
Stock dividend	2,000*			2,000*
Issued for cash	3,000*	3,000		
12/31/+2	25,000*			
Retained earnings:				
12/31/+1	10,900*			
Net income	12,700*	12,700a		
Stock dividend	2,000			2,000
Cash dividend	10,000		10,000	
12/31/+2	11,600*			
		16,200	17,500	—
Decrease in working capital		1,300		
		17,500	17,500	

To show a decrease in working capital in the statement of sources and uses of working capital, it is best to reverse the sequence of the statement—that is, to show the uses section above the sources section.

THE D COMPANY
Sources and Uses of Working Capital
For the Year Ended December 31, 19+2

Working capital uses:			
Purchase of furniture		$ 7,500	
Payment of cash dividend		10,000	$17,500
Working capital sources:			
Issuance of capital stock		$ 3,000	
Operations:			
Net income for the year	$12,700		
Add operating charge not affecting working			
capital—Depreciation of furniture	500	13,200	16,200
Decrease in working capital			$ 1,300

Present status of statement. To an increasing degree, corporations are including a statement of sources and uses of working capital in their annual reports to stockholders. Many accountants favor the inclusion of such a statement with supporting interpretive comments by management. It is believed that information of this kind can be of great assistance to a statement reader in understanding the financial policies, plans, and operations of the company.

A statement that reports on the flow of working capital discloses significant aspects of the operations of a business. For this reason there is considerable support for the opinion that the statement of sources and uses of working capital should be ranked in importance along with the balance sheet and the income statement.

ASSIGNMENT
MATERIAL

QUESTIONS

1. What is the primary purpose of the statement of sources and uses of working capital?
2. If you were given comparative data regarding all ledger amounts except the current assets and current liabilities, would it be possible for you to prepare a statement of sources and uses of working capital?
3. Comment on the present status of the statement of sources and uses of working capital.
4. If, on October 15, a business borrows $5,000 from a bank by issuing a six-month interest-bearing note, will that transaction be shown as a source of working capital in the statement of sources and uses of working capital for the calendar year?
5. Would it be possible for a statement of sources and uses of working capital to show an increase in working capital if the business operated at a loss?
6. List three examples of transactions affecting noncurrent accounts that have no effect on working capital.
7. A company declares a cash dividend in $19+1$, payable in $19+2$. Will this action have any effect on the statement of sources and uses of working capital for $19+1$? For $19+2$?

SHORT EXERCISES

E16-1. The comparative balance sheet of Rover Corporation is presented below:

ROVER CORPORATION
Comparative Balance Sheet
December 31, $19+3$ and $19+2$

	December 31,	
	$19+3$	$19+2$
Assets		
Cash	$ 16,000	$ 12,000
Accounts receivable	18,100	19,000
Allowance for uncollectibles	430*	650*
Merchandise inventory	15,300	13,700
Land	35,000	25,000
Equipment	45,000	38,000
Accumulated depreciation—Equipment	8,400*	6,800*
	$120,570	$100,250

Equities

Accounts payable	$ 24,000	$ 18,000
Salaries payable	1,600	2,300
Mortgage payable	15,000	20,000
Common stock	60,000	50,000
Retained earnings	19,970	9,950
	$120,570	$100,250

*Deduction.

What were the net changes for 19+3 in (a) working capital accounts; and (b) noncurrent accounts?

E16-2. Rover Corporation (see E16-1) transferred $5,000 from Retained Earnings as the result of a stock dividend declared during the year ended December 31, 19+3. The company also paid a $2,000 cash dividend on December 31, 19+3. If depreciation for the year was $1,800, what was the effect of operations on working capital.

E16-3. An analysis of the noncurrent accounts of Childers, Inc., reveals the following changes during the year ended June 30, 19+8:

Long-term investments—Increased $5,000 as the result of an additional purchase.
Land—Decreased $10,000 as the result of a sale.
Equipment—Increased $15,000 as the result of a purchase. Cash of $5,000 was paid and a note due in 5 years given for the balance.
Accumulated depreciation—Equipment—Increased $2,500 by recording depreciation for the year.
Patents—Decreased $4,000 by amortization charged against income.
Notes payable—Increased $10,000 by purchase of equipment.
Common stock—Increased $5,000 by stock dividend.
Retained earnings—Decreased $12,000 as the result of operations and the stock dividend.

Compute the effect on working capital resulting from the changes in noncurrent accounts.

E16-4. For each of the transactions listed below, indicate whether it results in an increase or a decrease or has no effect on working capital:

(a) Declaration of a cash dividend.
(b) Issuance of common stock for cash.
(c) Payment of a cash dividend previously declared.
(d) Amortization of patents.
(e) Issuance of a stock dividend.
(f) Purchase of equipment, paying some cash and giving a long-term mortgage for the balance.
(g) Write-off of goodwill.
(h) Recording annual depreciation charges.
(i) Recording salaries payable.
(j) Recording estimated bad debt losses.

PROBLEMS

Problem A16-1. Following is the comparative balance sheet of North Curve Company.

NORTH CURVE COMPANY
Comparative Balance Sheet
December 31, 19+2 and 19+1

Assets	December 31, 19+2	December 31, 19+1
Cash	$ 5,000	$ 8,000
Accounts receivable	18,000	13,500
Land	6,200	5,000
Trademarks	900	800
	$30,100	$27,300

Equities		
Accounts payable	$ 7,600	$ 6,400
Common stock	19,000	18,000
Retained earnings	3,500	2,900
	$30,100	$27,300

Asset acquisitions during the year included land for $1,200 and trademarks for $100. Stock was issued at par for $1,000. Net income for the year was $600.

Required:

(a) A schedule of working capital.
(b) An analysis of changes in noncurrent accounts.
(c) A statement of sources and uses of working capital.

Problem A16-2. Following are comparative balance sheet data of July Corporation.

Debits	December 31, 19+2	December 31, 19+1
Cash	$ 3,900	$ 4,500
Accounts receivable	8,850	7,450
Merchandise inventory	21,350	24,600
Land	15,000	10,000
Goodwill	2,500	5,000
	$51,600	$51,550

Credits		
Accounts payable	$ 5,920	$ 5,180
Allowance for uncollectibles	400	350
Bonds payable	3,000	6,000
Capital stock	37,000	35,000
Retained earnings	5,280	5,020
	$51,600	$51,550

Some of the information regarding the noncurrent accounts is given below.

Net income for the year amounted to $4,510.
Dividends were paid totaling $1,750.
Goodwill was written off against retained earnings to the extent of $2,500.
Land was purchased for $5,000.
One-half of the bonds outstanding at the beginning of the year were retired.

Prepare:

(a) A schedule of working capital.
(b) An analysis of changes in noncurrent accounts.
(c) A statement of sources and uses of working capital.

Problem A16-3. Prepare a statement of sources and uses of working capital.

IOWA COMPANY
Comparative Balance Sheet
December 31, 19+2 and 19+1

| | December 31, | | Net Changes | |
Assets	19 + 2	19 + 1	Debit	Credit
Cash	$14,000	$16,800		$ 2,800
Accounts receivable	12,000	18,000		6,000
Prepaid expenses	6,000	4,000	$ 2,000	
Equipment	50,000	40,000	10,000	
Accumulated depreciation	24,000*	16,000*		8,000
	$58,000	$62,800		
Equities				
Expenses payable	$ 3,400	$ 4,200	800	
Long-term bank loan (due July 1, 19+2)		8,000	8,000	
Capital stock—5% dividend rate	40,000	40,000		
Retained earnings	14,600	10,600		4,000
	$58,000	$62,800	$20,800	$20,800

*Deduction.

IOWA COMPANY
Income Statement
For the Year Ended December 31, 19+2

Net sales		$80,000
Expenses:		
Depreciation expense	$ 8,000	
Other expenses	66,000	74,000
Net income		$ 6,000

Problem A16-4. From the following financial statements relating to Geometric Corporation prepare: (a) schedule of working capital; (b) analysis of changes in noncurrent accounts; and (c) statement of sources and uses of working capital. Where information on the causes of the changes in noncurrent accounts is lacking, use your best judgment regarding the probable causes.

GEOMETRIC CORPORATION
Comparative Balance Sheet
December 31, 19+2 and 19+1

	December 31,	
Assets	**19+2**	**19+1**
Cash	$13,770	$11,440
Accounts receivable	11,200	12,810
Merchandise inventory	34,930	30,650
Unexpired insurance	400	400
Long-term investments	18,000	21,000
Land	20,000	18,000
	$98,300	$94,300

Equities		
Accounts payable	$ 9,810	$ 9,740
Current installment due on bonds payable	2,000	2,000
Bonds payable	10,000	12,000
Capital stock	68,000	60,000
Retained earnings	8,490	10,560
	$98,300	$94,300

GEOMETRIC CORPORATION
Statement of Retained Earnings
For the Year Ended December 31, 19+2

Balance, December 31, 19+1		$10,560
Add:		
Net income	$5,430	
Gain on sale of long-term investments	600	6,030
Total		$16,590
Deduct:		
Stock dividend	$6,000	
Cash dividend	2,100	8,100
Balance, December 31, 19+2		$ 8,490

Problem A16-5. From the following data and the information provided by the statement on page 381 prepare a schedule of working capital and a statement of sources and uses of working capital.

Bonds of $100,000 face value were issued at 98 at the beginning of 19+2.
Depreciation and amortization were charged to operations during the year as follows:

By credit to accumulated depreciation accounts:

Buildings	$6,000
Equipment	6,500

By credit to the asset accounts:

Containers	$5,000
Patents	2,000

By credit to Discount on Bonds:

Discount on bonds . . . . $ 200

During the year, equipment which cost $10,000 was sold for its carrying value, $6,000. Land that cost $4,000 was sold for $4,300, and an additional parcel was purchased for $9,000.

BAY COMPANY
Comparative Balance Sheet
December 31, 19+2 and 19+1

	December 31,	
Assets	19+2	19+1
Cash . . . .$	7,150	$ 6,500
Accounts receivable	31,600	29,700
Allowance for uncollectibles	1,500*	1,200*
Inventory	38,020	38,300
Advances to salesmen	1,000	750
Unexpired insurance	250	300
Land	70,000	65,000
Buildings	155,000	110,000
Accumulated depreciation—Buildings.	16,000*	10,000*
Equipment	110,000	100,000
Accumulated depreciation—Equipment	13,500*	11,000*
Containers—less depreciation	22,000	25,000
Patents—less amortization	28,000	30,000
Long-term investments in stocks		25,000
Discount on bonds	1,800	
	$433,820	$408,350

Equities

Accounts payable . . . .$	14,000	$ 35,500
Notes payable	5,000	27,000
Bank loans		20,000
Bonds payable—19+8	300,000	200,000
Capital stock	100,000	100,000
Retained earnings	14,820	25,850
	$433,820	$408,350

*Deduction.

Analysis of Retained Earnings

Balance, December 31, 19+1		$25,850
Add:		
Net income—19+2		5,670
Gain on sale of land		300
Total		$31,820
Deduct:		
Dividends paid	$15,000	
Loss on sale of investments	2,000	17,000
Balance, December 31, 19+2		$14,820

Problem B16-1. From the following balance sheet accounts and supplementary data relating to Economy Company, prepare a schedule of working capital, an analysis of the changes in the noncurrent accounts, and a statement of sources and uses of working capital.

	December 31,	
Debits	19+2	19+1
Cash	$10,400	$ 8,600
Accounts receivable	12,560	16,400
Merchandise inventory	26,300	19,000
Long-term investments	10,000	12,000
	$59,260	$56,000

Credits		
Accounts payable	$ 3,300	$ 8,230
Allowance for uncollectibles	490	650
Common stock	46,000	40,000
Capital in excess of stated value—Common stock		
issuances	5,200	4,000
Retained earnings.............................	4,270	3,120
	$59,260	$56,000

Net income for the year amounted to $1,750. Investments, costing $2,000, were sold for $2,000. Six hundred shares of common stock, stated value $10, were issued at $12 per share. Dividends of $600 were paid during the year.

Problem B16-2. From the following balance sheet accounts and supplementary data relating to Standing Company, prepare an analysis of changes in noncurrent accounts and a statement of sources and uses of working capital.

	December 31,	
Debits	19+2	19+1
Cash	$ 22,640	$ 24,600
Accounts receivable	33,540	29,200
Inventory	37,000	40,800
Equipment	38,000	30,000
	$131,180	$124,600

Credits		
Accounts payable	$ 26,520	$ 35,880
Allowance for uncollectibles	1,860	1,720
Accumulated depreciation—Equipment	15,400	12,000
Long-term bank loan	10,000	
Capital stock	40,000	40,000
Reserve for contingencies.......................		5,000
Retained earnings.............................	37,400	30,000
	$131,180	$124,600

During the year the company obtained a long-term bank loan. A portion of the proceeds from the loan was invested in new equipment. The Reserve for Contingencies was closed and the balance returned to Retained Earnings. The net income for the year amounted to $12,400. Cash dividends paid during the year amounted to $10,000.

Problem B16-3.

ILLINOIS CORPORATION
Comparative Balance Sheet
June 30, 19+2 and 19+1

Assets	June 30, 19+2	June 30, 19+1
Cash	$ 25,140	$ 21,360
U.S. Securities—short-term	54,860	65,940
Accounts receivable	32,280	36,700
Inventories	57,200	54,800
Land	36,600	21,600
Goodwill	22,000	24,000
	$228,080	$224,400

Equities	19+2	19+1
Accounts payable	$ 17,380	$ 25,200
Wages payable	5,300	4,280
5% cumulative preferred stock—$100 par	36,000	30,000
Capital in excess of par value—Preferred stock issuances	3,600	3,300
Common stock—No par value	132,000	120,000
Reserve for contingencies	22,000	16,000
Retained earnings	11,800	25,620
	$228,080	$224,400

The company declared and paid the following dividends:

   $1,500 cash dividends on preferred stock.
   $8,700 cash dividends on common stock.

The corporation issued an additional 60 shares of preferred stock at $105 per share.

The goodwill is being amortized; annual charges therefor, in the amount of $2,000, are shown in the income statement.

All other changes in noncurrent accounts are the result of transactions typically recorded in such accounts.

Required:

   (a) Analysis of changes in noncurrent accounts.
   (b) Statement of sources and uses of working capital.

Problem B16-4. Data from the comparative balance sheet of Green Corporation are shown below.

	December 31,		
Debits	19+2	19+1	Difference
Cash	13,000	15,000	(2,000)
Accounts receivable	33,000	30,000	3,000
Allowance for uncollectibles	900*	800*	(100)
Service and repair parts	24,000	20,000	4,000
Long-term investments:			
Land	-0-	12,000	(12,000)
Serial bonds ($2,000 matures each July 1			
starting in 19+3)	10,000	10,000	—
Property, plant, and equipment	60,000	50,000	10,000
Accumulated depreciation	26,000*	22,000*	(4,000)
	113,100	114,200	

Credits			
Accounts payable for service and repair parts	10,100	8,200	(1,900)
Dividends payable	3,000	-0-	(3,000)
Advances from customers	1,000	1,000	—
Convertible bonds—due 19+25	15,000	25,000	10,000
Common stock	60,000	50,000	(10,000)
Retained earnings	24,000	30,000	6,000
	113,100	114,200	

*Deduction.

Supplementary Information

The company reported a net loss of $3,000 for 19+2, which included an extraordinary loss of $4,000 from the sale of land held as a long-term investment.

During 19+2, the company declared a $3,000 cash dividend payable January 15, 19+3.

The company overlooked the fact that during 19+2 it performed the services required to earn the $1,000 of advances received from customers. At the end of 19+2 the company should have recorded the following adjusting entry:

    Advances from customers 1,000
        Revenue from services........................   1,000

During 19+2 the company wrote off $500 of uncollectible accounts. The income statement for 19+2 shows the bad-debts expense as $600.

During 19+2 the company junked $1,000 of fully depreciated equipment and made the following entry:

    Accumulated depreciation 1,000
        Equipment   1,000

A $200 insurance premium for a two-year policy expiring July 1, 19+4, was recorded as a 19+2 expense.

All other changes in noncurrent accounts are the result of transactions typically recorded in such accounts.

Required:

(a) Schedule of working capital.

(b) Statement of sources and uses of working capital.

Problem B16-5. The following statement of sources and uses of working capital was prepared before the company's auditors completed their examination of the financial statements.

VIDEO RANGE COMPANY
Sources and Uses of Working Capital
For the Year Ended December 31, 19+2

Working capital uses:		
Purchase of office furniture	$ 1,000	
Investment in land	5,000	
Retirement of preferred stock	10,000	$16,000
Working capital sources:		
Operations:		
Net loss	$ 6,000	
Deduct charges not affecting working capital:		
Depreciation	8,000	2,000
Decrease in working capital		$14,000

During the course of the audit engagement, the auditors discovered the following:

(a) On July 1, 19+2, the company paid $800 rent in advance for the two-year period ending June 30, 19+4. The $800 was recorded as an expense of 19+2.

(b) The company forgot to record the annual charge for patent amortization in the amount of $800.

(c) No recognition was given in the accounts for merchandise in transit shipped f.o.b. shipping point. The amount of such merchandise was $1,100.

(d) No recognition was given in the accounts for wages payable as of December 31, 19+2. The amount payable was $1,500.

(e) When the tentative balance sheet was prepared by the company, all of the serial bonds payable were classified under the Long-term Liabilities caption in spite of the fact that $5,000 of such bonds mature in 19+3.

(f) No entry was made when the company scrapped $6,000 of fully depreciated equipment during 19+2.

(g) Uncollectible accounts in the amount of $700 had not been written off against the Allowance for Uncollectibles.

(h) The following entry should have been recorded and dated December 30, 19+2:

```
19+3
Jan. 2   Cash . . . . . . . . . . . . . . . . . . . . . . . . . . . .   15,000
              Bank loans . . . . . . . . . . . . . . . . . . . .             15,000
         Six months' bank loan.
```

Prepare a corrected statement of sources and uses of working capital.

Cash-flow Analysis

The income statement and cash flow. The income statement is a very significant report on the results of operations. It shows the resource inflow arising from revenues and the resource outflow necessitated by expenses. The resulting net income (or loss) is a measure of the success or progress of the business entity.

The flow of cash, the receipts and disbursements, is another "stream of business activity" that is very important. Inadequate attention and skill in the matter of cash utilization and planning can produce serious consequences. For example, the fact that a particular firm's net income indicates a profitable year does not necessarily mean that the company has cash available to pay dividends, to meet maturing long-term debt, or to make needed plant and equipment additions. The point to be made is that an income statement indicates the presence or lack of profitable operations, but it does not indicate where management has been receiving and spending its cash. There is a tendency, too often evident, to regard the income statement as an indicator of cash flow.

A cash-flow statement shows the individual sources and uses of cash and thus yields information that is not directly provided in the income statement. Thus the cash flow statement *supplements,* but does not replace, the traditional financial statements. The following income statement of First Service Company will illustrate this important matter.

FIRST SERVICE COMPANY
Income Statement
For the Year Ended December 31, 19+4

Net sales		$50,000
Expenses:		
Salaries	$35,000	
Rent	3,600	
Depreciation	4,000	
Other	4,400	47,000
Net income		$ 3,000

It is not possible to tell from an examination of the income statement whether, as a result of the operations for 19+4, the cash increased, decreased, or remained unchanged. With the use of additional data, however, the income statement can be converted to show the cash receipts and cash disbursements associated with the revenue and expense transactions.

Cash flow related to operations. Unless all sales are for cash, the cash receipts during any given period will be affected by the promptness with which the customers settle their accounts. If the accounts receivable balances are increasing, the cash receipts from customers will be less than the net sales for the period by the dollar amount of the increase in accounts receivable. That is, a company would be selling more than it would be collecting in cash from customers during the period. If the customers are reducing their indebtedness (accounts receivable decreasing), the cash receipts will be greater than the net sales by the dollar amount of the decrease in accounts receivable. Thus the cash receipts from customers may be computed as follows:

Net sales − Increase in accounts receivable = Cash receipts from customers.

or

Net sales + Decrease in accounts receivable = Cash receipts from customers.

First Service Company had the following accounts receivable:

	December 31,	
	19+4	19+3
Accounts receivable	$6,000	$4,500

The 19+4 cash receipts from customers can be computed as follows:

Net sales	$50,000
Deduct increase in accounts receivable	1,500
Cash receipts from customers	$48,500

Expenses other than depreciation, depletion, and similar noncash expenses can be converted to cash disbursements if consideration is given to all related accruals or prepayments. The only such item in the case of First Service Company was accrued salaries.

	December 31,	
	19+4	19+3
Salaries payable	$ 300	$1,000

The 19+4 cash disbursement for salaries can be computed as follows:

Salaries expense.	$35,000
Add decrease in accrual.	700
Cash disbursement for salaries	$35,700

The conversion computations for an expense can be stated as follows:

Expense − Increase in related liability = Cash disbursement for expense.

or

Expense + Decrease in related liability = Cash disbursement for expense.

If there is a prepayment relating to any particular expense, the conversion computation may be stated as follows:

Expense − Decrease in related prepayment = Cash disbursement for expense.

or

Expense + Increase in related prepayment = Cash disbursement for expense.

If there is *both* a liability and a prepayment relating to an expense, the conversion computation would be a combination of the above, which can be stated as follows:

Expense, minus increase or plus decrease in related liability, minus decrease or plus increase in related prepayment, equals cash disbursement for expense.

It should be remembered that some expenses, such as depreciation, do not require any cash outlay at the time of expense recognition.

Cash from operations. The conversion of the income statement of First Service Company to a cash basis is shown below. It is based on the computations presented in the preceding paragraphs.

FIRST SERVICE COMPANY
Conversion of Income Statement to Cash Basis
For the Year Ended December 31, 19+4

	Income Statement	Add Deduct*	Cash Basis
Net sales	$50,000		
Deduct increase in accounts receivable		$1,500*⎫	$48,500
Expenses:			
Salaries	$35,000		
Add decrease in accrual.		700 ⎫	$35,700
Rent	3,600		3,600
Depreciation.	4,000	Noncash	
Other	4,400		4,400
Total	$47,000		$43,700
Net income	$ 3,000		
Cash earnings			$ 4,800

Assuming that 1,000 shares of the company's stock are outstanding, the frequently computed (but often misleading) cash earnings per share amount to $4.80, whereas the earnings (net income) per share amount to $3.00.

Cash earnings. Many companies make some mention of cash earnings, or cash flow, in their annual reports. To compute such cash earnings or cash-flow data, very often the noncash expenses such as depreciation are merely added back to net income. For the First Service Company, for example, the cash earnings would be reported as $7,000; that is, the net income plus depreciation. Basically this procedure is faulty because it ignores adjustments for changes in receivables, liabilities, accruals, and prepayments related to operations. Moreover, so-called cash earnings do not include significant nonoperating receipts and expenditures.

When companies show cash earnings or cash flow in their annual reports, the data are reported in a variety of ways, including graphic presentations, tables, and per-share amounts. Two such graphic presentations taken from annual reports to stockholders are shown on the following page.

Weaknesses of cash earnings. The principal weakness of cash-earnings data is that they are only a part of the flow of cash receipts and disbursements. Cash earnings are computed by the conversion of revenues and expenses to a cash basis. But the cash account is affected by significant receipts and disbursements other than those associated with revenue and expense. Such receipts and disbursements include debt financing and repayment, purchase and sale of investments, additions to and disposals of plant and equipment, acquisition and disposal of treasury stock, and dividends to stockholders. With cash earnings telling only a part of the story about the flow of cash, it is dangerous to reach any conclusions about their availability for some particular purpose such as expansion, replacements, or dividends. A company with better-than-average cash earnings may be burdened with more-than-average debt. If annual payments on the principal are required, this could leave the company with no cash available for dividends or for the replacement of depreciable assets for some period of time.

Another weakness associated with the computation and disclosure of cash earnings is the apparent inclination of many to believe that cash earnings are better than net income as a measure of the company's real earning power. The author of a well-regarded accounting research study concludes as follows: *

"Many of the comments made in connection with cash-flow analysis leave the reader with the impression that somehow or other the 'cash earnings' are superior as an indication of the company's 'real earning power.' Calculations of the Price/Cash Earnings ratio are sometimes made and presented as a substitute for or supplement to the Price/Earnings ratio in evaluating a company's stock. It should be self-evident that a cash-flow earnings figure cannot be considered a substitute for or an improvement upon the net income, calculated with a proper and reasonable deduction for depreciation, depletion, amortization, and the like."

Finally, since the addition of depreciation expense to net income is quite often the only addition made to derive so-called cash earnings, one might conclude, incor-

---

*Perry Mason, *"Cash Flow" Analysis and The Funds Statement* (New York: American Institute of Certified Public Accountants, Accounting Research Study No. 2, 1961), pp. 38-39.

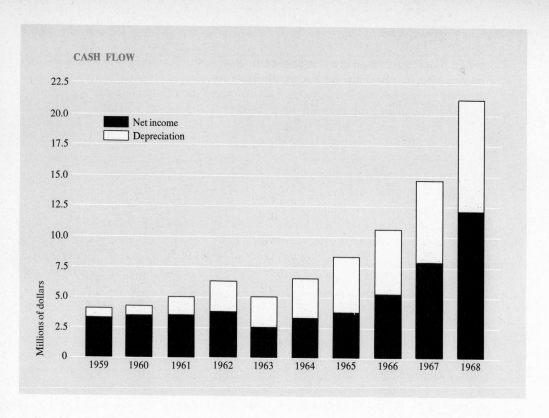

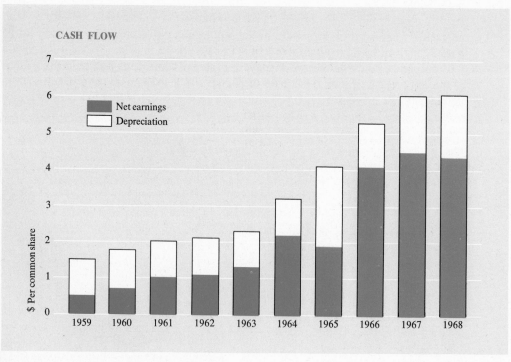

rectly, that depreciation is a source of cash. However, it is revenue that is the *ultimate* source of cash, not depreciation, as illustrated below.

Cash revenue		$100,000
Operating expenses:		
Cash expenses	$100,000	
Depreciation expense	10,000	110,000
Net loss		$ (10,000)

The illustration shows that the net cash inflow is zero despite $10,000 in depreciation. If depreciation were a source of cash, then the illustration would have to show a net cash inflow of $10,000, which it does not.

Complete cash-flow statement. In the First Service Company example, the cash earnings for 19+4 amounted to $4,800. However, this inflow of cash did not result in an increase in the cash balance or provide a source for dividends to stockholders, as is so often assumed to be the consequences of cash earnings. In this particular case, cash declined during the year as shown by the full report on the cash flow presented below.

FIRST SERVICE COMPANY
Cash-Flow Statement
For the Year Ended December 31, 19+4

Cash uses:		
Payment of loan	$6,000	
Purchase of land	1,000	$7,000
Cash sources:		
Cash earnings (See page 388)		4,800
Decrease in cash		$2,200

The relevant financial statements of First Service Company are presented below. The changes in the land and loan payable accounts, as shown by the comparative balance sheet, confirm the cash uses of $6,000 and $1,000 reported in the cash-flow statement.

FIRST SERVICE COMPANY
Comparative Balance Sheet
December 31, 19+4 and 19+3

	December 31,		Net Changes	
Assets	**19+4**	**19+3**	**Debit**	**Credit**
Cash	$ 2,000	$ 4,200		$2,200
Accounts receivable	6,000	4,500	$1,500	
Land	3,000	2,000	1,000	
Equipment	20,000	20,000		
Accumulated depreciation	12,000*	8,000*		4,000
	$19,000	$22,700		
Equities				
Salaries payable	$ 300	$ 1,000	700	
Loan payable (noninterest)		6,000	6,000	
Capital stock	10,000	10,000		
Retained earnings	8,700	5,700		3,000
	$19,000	$22,700	$9,200	$9,200

*Deduction.

FIRST SERVICE COMPANY
Income Statement
For the Year Ended December 31, 19+4

Sales		$50,000
Expenses:		
Salaries	$35,000	
Rent	3,600	
Depreciation.	4,000	
Other	4,400	47,000
Net income		$ 3,000

Working papers. In more complex situations, accountants generally use some form of special working papers to accumulate the information needed for the cash-flow statement. The example shown on page 393 is based on the financial statements of First Service Company. The data in the last two columns would be used to prepare the cash-flow statement. In this instance, the statement has been previously presented on page 391.

The operation of the Adjustments columns is indicated by the keyed supporting explanations in the working papers. The objective of the Adjustments columns is to convert the income statement amounts to a cash basis, following the computational rules noted and illustrated earlier in the chapter.

As shown, the net changes in the balance sheet accounts that are not related to revenue and expense transactions are extended to the Cash columns of the working papers.

Conversion of cost of sales to cash disbursements. In order to determine the cash disbursements for merchandise acquired, it is first necessary to determine the total purchases of merchandise for the period. To do this one must relate the change in inventory to the cost of goods sold. If the merchandise inventory is decreasing, the total purchases of merchandise inventory will be smaller than the cost of goods sold by the dollar amount of the decrease in inventory. That is, a company would be selling more inventory than it is purchasing during the period. If the merchandise inventory is increasing, a company would be buying more inventory than it is selling during the period. The computational procedure is:

Cost of goods sold − Decrease in inventory
$$= \text{Purchases of merchandise inventory.}$$

or

Cost of goods sold + Increases in inventory
$$= \text{Purchases of merchandise inventory.}$$

One can convert the cost of goods sold to cash disbursements for merchandise by relating the change in the beginning-of-year and end-of-year accounts payable for merchandise to the purchases of merchandise for the period. If the accounts payable for merchandise are increasing, the cash disbursements for merchandise are

FIRST SERVICE COMPANY
Cash-Flow Statement Working Papers
For the Year Ended December 31, 19+4

	Year's Changes—Net		Adjustments		Cash	
	Debit	Credit	Debit	Credit	Uses	Sources
Income statement accounts:						
Sales		50,000	A 1,500			48,500
Salaries	35,000		B 700		35,700	
Rent	3,600				3,600	
Depreciation	4,000			C 4,000		
Other expenses	4,400				4,400	
Net income	3,000			D 3,000		
	50,000	50,000			43,700	48,500
Cash earnings—forward					4,800	
					48,500	48,500
Cash earnings						4,800
Balance sheet accounts:						
Cash		2,200				2,200
Accounts receivable	1,500			A 1,500		
Land	1,000				1,000	
Equipment		4,000	C 4,000			
Accumulated depreciation						
Salaries payable	700			B 700		
Loan payable	6,000				6,000	
Capital stock						
Retained earnings		3,000	D 3,000			
	9,200	9,200	9,200	9,200	7,000	7,000

Adjustments

A—Deduct increase in accounts receivable.
B—Add decrease in accrued salaries.
C—Noncash expense.
D—Offset duplicate amounts.

smaller than the total merchandise purchased by the dollar amount of the increase in accounts payable. That is, a company would be buying more merchandise than it is paying for during the period. If the accounts payable for merchandise are decreasing, a company would be paying for more merchandise than it is buying during the period. The computational procedure is:

Merchandise purchases − Increase in accounts payable for merchandise
= Cash disbursements for merchandise.

or

Merchandise purchases + Decrease in accounts payable for merchandise
= Cash disbursements for merchandise.

The following example illustrates the computation.

		December 31,	
		19+5	19+4
(1)	Given data:		
	Merchandise inventory	$ 700	$ —
	Accounts payable for merchandise	500	—
	Cost of goods sold for year	10,000	

(2) Computation of purchases of merchandise:	
Cost of goods sold	$10,000
Add increase in inventory	700
Purchases of merchandise	$10,700

(3) Computation of cash payments for purchases:	
Purchases of merchandise	$10,700
Deduct increase in accounts payable for merchandise	500
Cash disbursements for merchandise	$10,200

Illustration continued. In order to expand the illustration, the financial statements of First Service Company for the next year, 19+5, will be used to determine the cash flow. Assume that the company expands its operations to include merchandising activities for the year 19+5.

FIRST SERVICE COMPANY
Comparative Balance Sheet
December 31, 19+5 and 19+4

	December 31,		Net Changes	
Assets	19+5	19+4	Debit	Credit
Cash	$ 8,800	$ 2,000	$ 6,800	
Accounts receivable	5,000	6,000		$ 1,000
Inventory	700		700	
Prepaid rent	300		300	
Land	3,000	3,000		
Equipment	24,000	20,000	4,000	
Accumulated depreciation	16,000*	12,000*		4,000
	$25,800	$19,000		

	December 31,		Net Changes	
Equities	19+5	19+4	Debit	Credit
Accounts payable—for merchandise..........	$ 500			500
Notes payable—for new equipment..........	1,200			1,200
Salaries payable........................	900	$ 300		600
Capital stock..........................	12,000	10,000		2,000
Retained earnings......................	11,200	8,700		2,500
	$25,800	$19,000	$11,800	$11,800

*Deduction.

FIRST SERVICE COMPANY
Income Statement
For the Year Ended December 31, 19+5

Sales (including merchandise sales)		$52,000
Expenses:		
Cost of goods sold.........................	$10,000	
Salaries	27,600	
Rent	3,600	
Depreciation..............................	4,000	
Other	4,300	49,500
Net income		$ 2,500

The working papers on page 396 show how the data for the 19+5 cash-flow statement are developed. The nature of the adjustments is indicated by the keyed description of them at the bottom of the working papers. It should be mentioned that the adjustments are not entered in the journals or ledger but only in the working papers. In practice the accountant would analyze the outstanding liability accounts in order to determine what other account or accounts to adjust for the change in liabilities. In this instance, the increase in the notes payable was attributable, as indicated, to the purchase of new equipment and the accounts payable relate entirely to merchandise purchases. Although the equipment account increased by $4,000, as disclosed by the comparative balance sheet, only $2,800 of cash was spent on equipment during 19+5, because $1,200 is still owed on the new equipment.

The working papers show the sources of cash inflow to be earnings ($7,600) and the issuance of additional shares of capital stock ($2,000). As noted above, cash in the amount of $2,800 was disbursed for new equipment and the cash account increased $6,800 during the year.

Cash-flow data and cash forecasting. Cash-flow data are useful in reporting what has happened in the management of a company's cash resources. The data are also helpful in developing a forecast of the cash flow, which is important for many reasons but especially because:

- It alerts management to the need to negotiate borrowing arrangements.
- It signals availability of excess funds and thus points up the desirability of investment planning.
- It indicates the timing feasibility of discretionary programs requiring significant cash outlays.
- It stimulates planning generally.

FIRST SERVICE COMPANY
Cash-Flow Statement Working Papers
For the Year Ended December 31, 19+5

	Year's Changes—Net		Adjustments		Cash	
	Debit	Credit	Debit	Credit	Uses	Sources
Income statement accounts:						
Sales		52,000		A 1,000		53,000
Cost of goods sold	10,000		B 700	C 500	10,200	
Salaries	27,600			D 600	27,000	
Rent	3,600		E 300	D 600	3,900	
Depreciation	4,000			F 4,000		
Other expenses	4,300				4,300	
Net income	2,500			G 2,500		
Cash earnings—forward	52,000	52,000			45,400	53,000
					7,600	
					53,000	53,000
Cash earnings						7,600
Balance sheet accounts:						
Cash	6,800				6,800	
Accounts receivable		1,000	A 1,000			
Inventory	700			B 700		
Prepaid rent	300			E 300		
Land						
Equipment	4,000			H 1,200	2,800	
Accumulated depreciation		4,000	F 4,000			
Accounts payable		500	C 500			
Notes payable—For new equipment		1,200	H 1,200			
Salaries payable		600	D 600			
Capital stock		2,000				2,000
Retained earnings		2,500	G 2,500			
	11,800	11,800	10,800	10,800	9,600	9,600

Adjustments

A—Add decrease in accounts receivable.
B—Add increase in inventory.
C—Deduct increase in accounts payable.
D—Deduct increase in accrued salaries.
E—Add increase in prepaid rent.
F—Noncash expense.
G—Offset duplicate amounts.
H—Deduct unpaid liability for new equipment.

Cash forecasts can be developed for any period of time—a month, a quarter, a year, or longer. Forecasts for shorter periods are likely to be more reliable. Reliability is also affected by the precision with which certain business policies and practices are set forth and enforced within the company. The following policies are among those that should facilitate the preparation of meaningful cash forecasts:

A strict policy of settling all bills within the discount period.

Careful coordination between the volume of sales and the release of purchase orders for replacement merchandise.

Established collection policies and credit-granting standards.

Agreement on maximum and minimum cash balances.

A system requiring management approval for any asset acquisition costing more than a specified amount.

In the process of developing cash forecasts, many companies, in addition to making some judgmental allowance for expected economic conditions, attempt to discover and make use of some economic indicators that have correlated in the past with the company's experience.

Forecasting techniques. It is important to understand that the heart of cash forecasting is planning, with adequate managerial control and follow-up to maximize the chances for prediction to approximate reality. The forms, schedules, or working papers used to accumulate the data bearing on the cash forecast are not a critical part of the forecasting process. Any device that the accountant finds workable has merit. For example, a form basically like the cash-flow working papers illustrated in this chapter can be used to build up a cash forecast. Similarly, the form used for the cash forecast statement may follow that shown for the cash-flow statement on page 391. When the same statement form is used for the forecast and the historical statement, the data can be presented in comparative form. Such a comparative presentation provides an indication of the excellence of the forecasting process.

Cash-forecast working papers. To illustrate the development of a cash forecast for one month, January of 19+4, certain data are assumed for Rapid Service Company. The completed cash-forecast working papers are presented on page 399. The following comments indicate the procedure followed in preparing the working papers.

HISTORICAL DATA

The data in the first four money columns are taken from the accounting records or financial statements, whichever is more convenient. Such historical information is placed in the working papers to assist in forecasting the January results.

FORECAST OF CHANGES

Sales   According to the company's past experience, January is the slowest month of the year. As a general rule, January sales of service amount to about 85 per cent of the preceding month, and this percentage is used for the forecast. In this case the forecast for January sales is 85 per cent of $4,800, or $4,080. This amount is entered in the January, 19+4, columns as a credit.

Salaries   Salaries have increased 10 per cent over last January. The salaries for January of 19+4 are expected to equal 110 per cent of $2,800, or $3,080. In December of 19+3, $200 of overtime was paid. No overtime is expected during January of 19+4. The estimate is entered in the working papers.

Rent   Effective January 1, 19+4, the monthly rental is $210. This amount is entered in the working papers.

Depreciation   No change. The monthly charge of $180 is entered in the working papers.

Other Expenses Other expenses have been averaging about 11 per cent of sales. This relationship is used for the January forecast, rounded to the nearest ten dollars, or 11% of $4,080 = $450.

Net Income   The estimated amounts indicate a net income for January of $160. (Since this is significantly below the net income earned last January, management should review the expenses for savings and possibly should consider changing its billing rates.)

*Accounts   Past experience indicates that January is a poor collection
Receivable*   month and that the receivables at the end of January will probably be $500 more than at the end of December. The $500 increase that is forecast is placed in the January, 19+4, columns as a debit.

Land   No change is anticipated. Hence no amount is entered in the forecast columns of the working papers.

Equipment   No change is anticipated.

*Accumulated   The change is the depreciation for the month, $180.
Depreciation*

*Accrued   Payday falls on January 28, 19+4, so there will be a smaller
Salaries*   accrual at the end of January. It will amount to $200. As a result, there will be a $300 change in the salaries payable. This reduction is entered as a debit in the January, 19+4, columns.

*Loan   The loan matures on January 15, 19+4. The loan will not
Payable*   be renewed. Its reduction is therefore noted with the other predicted changes.

Capital Stock   No change is anticipated.

*Retained   Increased by the estimated net income.
Earnings*

RAPID SERVICE COMPANY
Cash-Forecast Working Papers
For the Month of January 19+4

	Historical January, 19+3	Historical December, 19+3	Forecast for January, 19+4	Adjustments Debit	Adjustments Credit	Cash Forecast Uses	Cash Forecast Sources	January 31, 19+4 Forecasted Cash Balance
Income statement accounts:								
Sales	4,000	4,800	4,080	A 500			3,580	
Salaries	2,800	3,280	3,080	B 300		3,380		
Rent	200	200	210			210		
Depreciation	180	180	180		C 180			
Other expenses	420	490	450			450		
Net income	400	650	160		D 160			
	4,000 4,000	4,800 4,800	4,080 4,080			4,040	3,580	
Forecasted cash earnings—Deficit—forward							460	
						4,040	4,040	
Forecasted cash earnings—Deficit						460		
		December 31, 19+3						
Balance sheet accounts:								
Cash		3,000	1,460				1,460	1,540
Accounts receivable		7,500	500		A 500			
Land		4,000						
Equipment		20,000						
Accumulated depreciation		12,000	180	C 180				
Salaries payable		500	300		B 300			
Loan payable (noninterest)		1,000	1,000			1,000		
Capital stock		15,000						
Retained earnings		6,000	160	D 160				
		34,500 34,500	1,800 1,800	1,140	1,140	1,460	1,460	

Adjustments

A—Expected increase in receivables.
B—Expected decrease in accrued salaries.
C—Noncash expense.
D—Offset duplicate amounts.

Cash   The cash change can be computed after all other changes have been estimated. The amount of the change is the balancing amount for the January, 19+4, columns for the balance sheet accounts, or $1,460 credit.

The estimated cash balance as of January 31, 19+4, is $3,000 − $1,460, or $1,540.

Cash-forecast statement. A statement form suitable for the presentation of the cash forecast to management is submitted below. The data are taken from the working papers.

RAPID SERVICE COMPANY
Cash Forecast
For the Month of January, 19+4

Cash balance, December 31, 19+3 . . . . $3,000
Deduct:
    Forecasted cash earnings for January—Deficit . . . . $ 460
    Payment of loan 1,000 1,460
Estimated cash balance, January 31, 19+4 . . . . $1,540

If desired, the details supporting the cash earnings can be included in the statement.

It is generally agreed that if the benefits from cash forecasting are to be maximized, the underlying planning process must be undertaken seriously and continuously; effective forecasting is not something that can be done well if done casually and occasionally.

ASSIGNMENT
MATERIAL

QUESTIONS

1. Why is the income statement generally a poor indicator of cash flows in a firm?
2. What does a cash-flow statement report and what is the relationship between a cash-flow statement and the traditional financial statements?
3. How may the net sales reported by a firm selling on account be converted to a cash basis?
4. What is the major weakness of cash-earnings data?
5. Why are cash earnings not a better measure than net income of a company's real earning power?
6. What is the rule for converting reported expenses, other than noncash items, to a cash basis?
7. Discuss the computational procedures involved in determining the cash outflow for merchandise.
8. List four advantages of cash forecasting to a firm.
9. Name several policies which will help a firm to prepare meaningful cash forecasts.
10. What is the relationship between a cash-flow statement and a cash forecast?
11. What are the key elements in effective cash forecasting?
12. Why do both income statement and balance sheet accounts appear on the cash-flow statement working papers?

SHORT EXERCISES

E17-1. The records of Pavenel Corporation show the following for the last two fiscal periods:

	June 30,	
	19+4	19+3
Prepaid insurance	$640	$850
Interest payable	320	570

Compute the cash payments for insurance and interest for the year ended June 30, 19+4, if the income statement for the year shows insurance expense of $1,300 and interest expense of $500.

E17-2. The income statement of Rowland Company is presented below:

ROWLAND COMPANY
Income Statement
For the Year Ended December 31, 19+3

Net sales		$18,600
Expenses:		
Salaries	$7,000	
Rent	2,000	
Depreciation	2,500	
Other expenses	3,500	15,000
Net income		$ 3,600

Convert the income statement to a cash basis using the following data pertaining to changes in account balances during the year: (a) Accounts Receivable decreased $2,200; (b) Salaries Payable increased $500; and (c) Prepaid Rent increased $200.

E17-3. Data pertaining to Murphy Company are presented below:

	December 31,	
	19+8	19+7
Merchandise inventory	$10,000	$12,000
Accounts payable (all for merchandise)	6,300	7,500

If the cost of goods sold for the year ended December 31, 19+8, is $56,000, what were the cash disbursements for merchandise for the year?

E17-4. Selected account balances for Lindsey Corporation are presented below:

	April 30,	
	19+7	19+6
Equipment	$15,000	$11,000
Land	20,000	25,000
Notes payable	5,000	

The company paid a $5,000 dividend during the year ended April 30, 19+7. Prepare a cash-flow statement for the year, assuming cash earnings produced a deficit of $6,500.

E17-5. The general ledger of Cox Corporation contains the following balances as of March 31, 19+7: Cash, $43,000; Accounts Receivable, $38,000; and Accounts Payable, $33,000.

Forecast data for April and May are presented below:

	April	May
Sales (80% on account)	$51,000	$54,000
Purchases (90% on account)	36,000	29,000
Operating expenses (includes depreciation of $1,500 per month)	23,000	24,000

Compute the forecast cash balance at May 31, 19+7, assuming credit sales and purchases are paid in the month following the sale or purchase.

PROBLEMS

Problem A17-1. Selected account balances from the ledger of Armstrong Corporation are presented below:

Account	Balance, December 31, 19+7	Balance, December 31, 19+6
Accounts receivable	$37,500	$33,000
Merchandise inventory	27,000	29,000
Prepaid rent	300	400
Prepaid insurance	650	500
Accounts payable	14,200	12,000
Interest payable	350	800
Sales	97,000	
Cost of goods sold	74,000	
Rent expense	500	
Insurance expense	700	
Interest expense	980	

Required:

Computation of the following for the year ended December 31, 19+7.

(a) Cash collected from customers.
(b) Purchases of merchandise inventory.
(c) Cash payments for insurance premiums.
(d) Cash payments for rent.
(e) Cash payments for interest.

Problem A17-2. Financial statements of Olanta Corporation are presented below:

OLANTA CORPORATION
Income Statement
For the Year Ended March 31, 19+7

Net sales		$71,752
Cost of goods sold		47,500
Gross margin		$24,252
Expenses:		
Salaries	$6,015	
Rent	3,600	
Depreciation—Building	2,625	
Depreciation—Equipment	550	
Insurance	800	
Advertising	2,600	
Office expense	1,000	
Interest expense	750	17,940
Net income		$ 6,312

OLANTA CORPORATION
Comparative Balance Sheet
March 31, 19+7 and 19+6

	March 31,	
Assets	**19+7**	**19+6**
Cash	$ 8,800	$ 6,600
Accounts receivable	21,350	18,850
Merchandise inventory	22,300	21,200
Prepaid insurance	720	800
Land	10,000	9,000
Buildings	55,000	50,000
Accumulated depreciation—Buildings	15,125*	12,500*
Equipment	6,000	5,000
Accumulated depreciation—Equipment	3,050*	2,500*
	$105,995	$96,450

Equities		
Accounts payable	$ 21,700	$19,767
Notes payable		8,000
Interest payable	600	500
Bonds payable	20,000	15,000
Capital stock	46,200	42,000
Retained earnings	17,495	11,183
	$105,995	$96,450

*Deduction.

Convert the income statement to a cash basis.

Problem A17-3. On July 1, 19+5, Abbeville Company's records show the following balances: Cash, $28,000; Accounts Receivable, $55,000; and Accounts Payable, $43,000. The following data are forecast for the next three months:

	Sales	Merchandise Purchases	Operating Expenses
July	$90,000	$60,000	$20,000
August	80,000	45,000	22,000
September	95,000	66,000	25,000

All sales of the company are on account, with 25 per cent collected in the month of sale and the balance collected in the following month.

Merchandise purchases are on account. One-third of the purchases are paid for in the month of purchase; the balance is paid in the following month.

Operating expenses, which are paid in the month incurred, include depreciation of $2,000 per month.

Required:

A schedule showing the forecast cash balance at the end of each of the next three months.

Problem A17-4. The following information is taken from the general ledger of Eatonton, Inc.

	December 31,	
	19+8	19+7
Debits		
Cash	$ 6,300	$ 6,700
Marketable securities	10,500	8,000
Accounts receivable	26,600	22,100
Prepaid rent	1,000	
Machinery	35,000	35,000
Goodwill	9,000	10,000
	$88,400	$81,800
Credits		
Accumulated depreciation—Machinery	$18,700	$16,400
Salaries payable	1,400	1,150
Taxes payable	475	620
Common stock	50,000	40,000
Capital in excess of par	5,000	3,000
Retained earnings	12,825	20,630
	$88,400	$81,800

The company's income statement for the year ended December 31, 19+8, is presented below:

EATONTON, INC.
Income Statement
For the Year Ended December 31, 19+8

Sales		$67,396
Expenses:		
Depreciation	$ 2,300	
Rent	12,000	
Salaries	28,604	
Taxes	3,890	
Advertising	18,710	
Utilities	1,682	
Amortization of goodwill	1,000	
Office expense	7,015	75,201
Net loss		$ 7,805

Required:

Cash-flow statement working papers for the year ended December 31, 19+8.

Problem A17-5. Comparative balance sheets of Villa Rica Company are presented below:

VILLA RICA COMPANY
Comparative Balance Sheet
December 31, 19+6 and 19+5

Assets	19+6	19+5
Cash	$ 21,000	$ 17,500
Accounts receivable	13,000	18,500
Merchandise inventory	18,200	14,300
Investments	14,100	8,000
Land	15,000	20,000
Buildings	55,000	32,000
Accumulated depreciation—Buildings	24,600*	19,600*
Equipment	40,000	28,000
Accumulated depreciation—Equipment	19,000*	14,700*
	$132,700	$104,000

Equities		
Accounts payable	$ 25,290	$ 22,300
Mortgage payable	24,500	28,000
Common stock	50,000	30,000
Retained earnings	32,910	23,700
	$132,700	$104,000

*Deduction.

All accounts payable are for merchandise purchases.
The firm's income statement for the year ended December 31, 19+6, shows the following:

VILLA RICA COMPANY
Income Statement
For the Year Ended December 31, 19+6

Net sales		$115,750
Cost of goods sold		70,000
Gross margin		$ 45,750
Operating expenses:		
Salaries expense	$15,450	
Advertising expense	5,600	
Depreciation expense—Buildings	5,000	
Depreciation expense—Equipment	4,300	
Taxes expense	2,700	
Office expense	1,940	
Interest expense	1,550	36,540
Net income		$ 9,210

Required:

Cash-flow statement working papers for the year ended December 31, 19+6.

Problem A17-6. Monticello Corporation follows the practice of preparing quarterly cash forecasts. The following data pertain to the quarter ended March 31, 19+4.

	Quarter Ended March 31, 19+4	
Income statement accounts:		
Sales..		61,080
Salaries....................................	24,300	
Rent......................................	5,000	
Advertising	12,300	
Depreciation.............................	5,450	
Amortization of patent...................	500	
Insurance.................................	1,400	
Office expense	4,970	
Net income	7,160	
	61,080	61,080

	March 31, 19+4	
Balance sheet accounts:		
Cash......................................	5,200	
Accounts receivable.......................	6,400	
Prepaid advertising	1,050	
Equipment................................	60,000	
Accumulated depreciation—Equipment		30,500
Patent....................................	4,000	
Salaries payable		875
Common stock		25,000
Retained earnings		20,275
	76,650	76,650

The corporation's income statement for the second quarter of 19+3 is presented below:

MONTICELLO CORPORATION
Income Statement
For Quarter Ended June 30, 19+3

Sales		$43,700
Expenses:		
Salaries.................................	$18,200	
Rent....................................	3,000	
Advertising	8,600	
Depreciation............................	4,700	
Amortization of patent..................	500	
Insurance...............................	900	
Office expenses.........................	3,800	39,700
Net income		$ 4,000

Additional Data

1. Sales for the second quarter of 19+4 are forecast at 60 per cent above the same quarter in the previous year.
2. Salaries are expected to increase 10 per cent over the first-quarter level. There will be $400 salaries payable on June 30, 19+4.
3. Second-quarter advertising expense will be twice the amount for the same quarter last year. There will be no prepaid advertising at June 30, 19+4.

4. All other expenses will be the same as their first-quarter level.

5. June 30, 19+4 accounts receivable are expected to be 25 per cent greater than the balance at the beginning of the quarter.

6. New equipment to be delivered on June 30, 19+4, is to be purchased for $10,000 cash.

7. The balance in the patent account on June 30, 19+4, after amortization for the second quarter, is to be written off to Retained Earnings.

Required:

Cash-forecast working papers for the second quarter of 19+4.

Problem B17-1. The selected account balances below are taken from the records of Pinewood Company.

	December 31,	
	19+9	19+8
Accounts receivable	37,100	46,500
Merchandise inventory	29,600	26,900
Investments	6,000	9,000
Buildings	60,000	75,000
Accumulated depreciation—Buildings	23,600	22,100
Accounts payable	33,300	24,800
Sales	168,000	157,000
Cost of goods sold	126,000	118,000
Gain on sale of building	1,000	

All accounts payable are for merchandise purchases. During the year the firm sold a building that had cost $15,000. It had been depreciated for 5 years based on a 30-year life.

Required:

Computation of the following for the year ended December 31, 19+9:

(a) Cash collected from customers.
(b) Disbursements for merchandise inventory.
(c) Proceeds from sale of the building.

Problem B17-2. Ahoskie Corporation's income statement for the year ended June 30, 19+3, is presented below:

AHOSKIE CORPORATION
Income Statement
For the Year Ended June 30, 19+3

Net sales		$140,200
Cost of goods sold		100,700
Gross margin		$ 39,500
Expenses:		
Salaries	$20,100	
Rent	4,000	
Insurance	700	
Office expense	3,960	28,760
Net income		$ 10,740

Comparative balance sheet data for June 30, 19+2 and 19+3, are presented below:

	June 30,	
	19+3	19+2
Debits		
Cash	$ 20,680	$15,300
Accounts receivable	21,352	27,880
Merchandise inventory	44,710	28,602
Land	17,000	20,000
	$103,742	$91,782
Credits		
Accounts payable	$ 7,300	$16,460
Salaries payable	940	560
Common stock	60,000	50,000
Retained earnings	35,502	24,762
	$103,742	$91,782

All accounts payable are for merchandise purchases.

Convert the income statement to a cash basis.

Problem B17-3. The financial statements below pertain to Dillon Company.

DILLON COMPANY
Comparative Balance Sheet
June 30, 19+6 and 19+5

	June 30,	
Assets	19+6	19+5
Cash	$24,000	$19,000
Accounts receivable	18,000	27,000
Prepaid rent	800	400
Equipment	60,000	40,000
Accumulated depreciation	26,000*	17,000*
	$76,800	$69,400
Equities		
Salaries payable	$ 2,300	$ 1,800
Notes payable	10,000	5,000
Common stock	47,000	47,000
Retained earnings	17,500	15,600
	$76,800	$69,400

*Deduction.

DILLON COMPANY
Income Statement
For the Year Ended June 30, 19+6

Net sales		$79,400
Expenses:		
Depreciation expense	$ 9,000	
Other expenses	68,500	77,500
Net income		$ 1,900

Required:

A cash-flow statement for the year ended June 30, 19+6. Show supporting computations.

Problem B17-4. Gaffney Corporation's after-closing trial balances as of December 31, 19+1 and 19+2, are presented below:

GAFFNEY CORPORATION
After-Closing Trial Balances
December 31, 19+2 and 19+1

	December 31,			
	19+2		19+1	
	Debit	Credit	Debit	Credit
Cash	24,500		29,700	
Accounts receivable	33,100		32,280	
Merchandise inventory	49,800		39,600	
Investments.	20,000		18,000	
Land	25,000		15,000	
Buildings	134,000		120,000	
Accumulated depreciation—Buildings. . .		23,800		19,500
Equipment	28,000		25,000	
Accumulated depreciation—Equipment .		8,200		6,900
Accounts payable		19,000		22,120
Mortgage payable.		25,570		35,460
Common stock		200,000		170,000
Capital in excess of par		20,000		16,000
Retained earnings.		17,830		9,600
	314,400	314,400	279,580	279,580

All accounts payable are for merchandise purchases.

The corporation's income statement for the year ended December 31, 19+2, shows the following:

GAFFNEY CORPORATION
Income Statement
For the Year Ended December 31, 19+2

Sales		$419,430
Expenses:		
Cost of goods sold.	$340,000	
Depreciation expense—Buildings	4,300	
Depreciation expense—Equipment	1,300	
Selling expense	45,000	
General expense	19,000	
Interest expense	1,600	411,200
Net income		$ 8,230

Required:

(a) Cash-flow statement working papers for the year ended December 31, 19+2.
(b) A cash-flow statement for the year ended December 31, 19+2.

Problem B17-5. The general ledger of Wilmington Sales Company contains the following data as of December 31, 19+2.

Account	Debit	Credit
Cash	35,100	
Accounts receivable	54,900	
Notes receivable	5,000	
Merchandise inventory	25,500	
Prepaid expenses	1,000	
Equipment	83,000	
Accumulated depreciation—Equipment		26,000
Accounts payable		46,150
Notes payable		15,000
Interest payable		750
Common stock		80,000
Retained earnings		36,600
	204,500	204,500

Sales forecast for January and February, 19+3, are $83,000 and $90,000, respectively. Cost of goods sold is expected to average 65 per cent of sales. The inventory at the end of January should equal one-half of the following month's needs.

All sales are on account and are collected as follows:

In the month of sale 60%
In the first month following the month of sale 30%
In the second month following the month of sale 10%

Accounts receivable on January 1, 19+3, are composed of the following:

December, 19+2 sales $39,900
November, 19+2 sales 15,000
$54,900

All accounts payable on January 1, 19+3, are for merchandise purchases, all of which are on account. Fifty per cent of such purchases are paid in the month of purchase and the balance in the following month.

A $5,000 noninterest-bearing note receivable is due on January 30, 19+3. A note payable of $15,000, plus interest of $750, is due on January 1, 19+3. There will be no interest payable on January 31, 19+3.

New equipment costing $12,000 is to be delivered on January 31, 19+3. The entire price is to be paid upon delivery.

Operating expenses of $22,200 are forecast for January. This includes depreciation of $2,800. There will be prepaid expenses of $1,400 on January 31, 19+3.

Required:

Cash-forecast working papers for January, 19+3. Show supporting computations for changes in Accounts Receivable. Merchandise Inventory, and Accounts Payable.

Basic Concepts Associated
with Manufacturing Operations

Introduction. In preceding chapters we have dealt with accounting as applied to service organizations and merchandising enterprises. Manufacturing is another major area of business activity. This chapter will acquaint the student with some basic features of accounting for manufacturing operations.

In accounting for manufacturing operations, great reliance is placed on cost information. For example, if management does not know how much it costs to manufacture its goods, the cost of the manufactured goods sold and the cost of the inventory of manufactured products on hand could not be set forth in the financial statements. Similarly, if management is not aware of the costs of alternative production methods, possible cost savings may be lost.

Although cost is defined broadly as a sacrifice for benefits received or to be received, the noun *cost* is usually modified by an adjective: historical cost, production department cost, expired cost (expense), unexpired cost (asset), and replacement cost are examples. Which cost concept is relevant depends on the purpose to be served by the cost information. In accounting for a manufacturing firm, two fundamental purposes of cost information are:

(1) Product costing.

> The concern here is primarily with gathering and recording financial data for the purpose of preparing financial statements for those outside the firm. That is, product costing is used to determine cost of goods sold (via the cost of goods manufactured) for the income statement and to determine inventory costs for the balance sheet. Also, in product costing, historical costs normally are used and manufacturing costs are kept separate from costs incurred in connection with selling and administrative activity.

(2) Planning and control.

> The aim here is primarily to provide relevant information to management for decision-making purposes. For such purposes the distinction between relevant and irrelevant costs, as well as between variable and fixed costs, is especially useful. These and other cost classifications are discussed in this chapter.

Manufacturing costs. A merchandising concern buys its goods ready for resale. A manufacturing concern also buys goods, but the goods purchased are raw materials which are not ready for resale. To change the raw materials to finished goods ready for sale requires expenditures for labor and for a great variety of other manufacturing costs. Therefore, provision must be made for accounts in which to record such costs.

The accountant usually views manufacturing costs as consisting of three classes: direct materials (often called raw materials), direct labor, and manufacturing (factory) overhead.

Direct materials are all raw materials that are directly traceable to the finished goods. Those raw materials that enter into and become part of the finished product are obviously direct materials, for they are directly identifiable with the finished goods. Supplies used in the operation of the factory are not classified as direct materials because they do not become part of, nor are they traceable to, the finished product; factory supplies such as glue and screws are classified as indirect materials.

Direct labor is all factory labor that is directly identifiable with the finished product; normally it is that factory labor that converts the direct materials into finished goods. The nature of direct labor can best be understood by contrast with indirect labor. Employees who work on the product with tools, or who operate machines in the process of production, are direct laborers; but superintendents and foremen, who supervise the production process, and janitors and engineers, whose services are incidental to the process of production, are indirect laborers.

Manufacturing (factory) overhead is all factory costs that are not directly traceable to the finished product; hence it includes all manufacturing costs other than direct materials and direct labor. The term *factory overhead cost* is synonymous with indirect manufacturing costs. Examples of manufacturing overhead are indirect labor, indirect materials (e.g., factory supplies), depreciation of the factory buildings and equipment, the power used in production, taxes and expired insurance on the assets used in manufacture, and repairs and upkeep of the factory.

Selling and administrative expenses. A manufacturing business can incur selling and general and administrative expenses. Such operating expenses must not be commingled with the manufacturing costs. They are not part of the cost of manufacturing a product. As indicated by the illustration on page 415, they are shown in the income statement below gross margin as they are for a merchandising concern.

FINANCIAL STATEMENTS

STATEMENT OF COST OF GOODS MANUFACTURED: Whereas a merchandising firm acquires inventory for resale, a manufacturing firm transforms raw materials through the production process into finished goods ready for sale. The cost of the goods fully completed during the fiscal period is called the cost of goods manufactured.

If all units of product were both started and completed during the period, the cost of goods completed is simply the sum of the costs of direct materials, direct labor, and manufacturing (factory) overhead used to carry on the manufacturing process. Accountants refer to them as "utilized" costs. However, if some goods are only partially completed—called goods (work) in process—at the end of the period, their cost is deducted from the total production costs for the period to determine the cost of the units completed. Similarly, there may have been partially completed goods in process at the beginning of the current period. Any prior period's manufacturing costs applicable to such partially finished goods are added to the current period's production cost to determine the total cost of goods completed in the current period. Therefore, the cost of fully completed goods during a time period (the cost of goods manufactured) is calculated as follows:

$$
\begin{pmatrix} \text{Cost of} \\ \text{goods} \\ \text{manufactured} \end{pmatrix} = \underbrace{ \begin{pmatrix} \text{Direct} \\ \text{material} \\ \text{cost} \end{pmatrix} + \begin{pmatrix} \text{Direct} \\ \text{labor} \\ \text{cost} \end{pmatrix} + \begin{pmatrix} \text{Factory} \\ \text{overhead} \\ \text{cost} \end{pmatrix} }_{\substack{\text{Production costs utilized} \\ \text{during the current period}}} + \begin{pmatrix} \text{Cost of} \\ \text{beginning} \\ \text{goods in} \\ \text{process} \end{pmatrix} - \begin{pmatrix} \text{Cost of} \\ \text{ending} \\ \text{goods in} \\ \text{process} \end{pmatrix}
$$

The above equation is formalized by the statement of cost of goods manufactured, as shown below.

THE ABC COMPANY
Statement of Cost of Goods Manufactured
For the Year Ended December 31, 19+2

Direct material cost	$ 895,750
Direct labor cost	662,550
Factory overhead cost	441,700
Production cost utilized during period	$2,000,000
Add beginning goods in process, December 31, 19+1	215,250
Total production cost	$2,215,250
Deduct ending goods in process, December 31, 19+2	120,000
Cost of goods manufactured	$2,095,250

THE ABC COMPANY
Income Statement
For the Year Ended December 31, 19+2

Net sales		$2,955,000
Deduct cost of goods sold:		
Beginning finished goods inventory,		
December 31, 19+1	$ 200,000	
Cost of goods manufactured	2,095,250	
Goods available for sale....................	$2,295,250	
Deduct ending finished goods inventory,		
December 31, 19+2	170,000	2,125,250
Gross margin................................		$ 829,750
Operating expenses:		
Selling expense..........................	$ 390,100	
General and administrative expense	259,400	649,500
Net income		$ 180,250

INCOME STATEMENT: The income statements of manufacturing companies do not necessarily differ from those of merchandising companies except in one particular: in determining the cost of goods sold, manufacturing companies use the cost of goods manufactured while merchandising companies use the cost of goods purchased, as shown below:

Manufacturing Firm

$$\begin{pmatrix} \text{Cost of} \\ \text{goods} \\ \text{sold} \end{pmatrix} = \begin{pmatrix} \text{Cost of} \\ \text{beginning} \\ \text{finished goods} \\ \text{inventory} \end{pmatrix} + \begin{pmatrix} \text{Cost of} \\ \text{goods} \\ \text{manufactured} \end{pmatrix} - \begin{pmatrix} \text{Cost of} \\ \text{ending} \\ \text{finished goods} \\ \text{inventory} \end{pmatrix}$$

Merchandising Firm

$$\begin{pmatrix} \text{Cost of} \\ \text{goods} \\ \text{sold} \end{pmatrix} = \begin{pmatrix} \text{Cost of} \\ \text{beginning} \\ \text{merchandise} \\ \text{inventory} \end{pmatrix} + \begin{pmatrix} \text{Cost of} \\ \text{merchandise} \\ \text{purchased} \end{pmatrix} - \begin{pmatrix} \text{Cost of} \\ \text{ending} \\ \text{merchandise} \\ \text{inventory} \end{pmatrix}$$

The equation for the manufacturing firm is formalized in the income statement, as shown above.

BALANCE SHEET: The balance sheet of a merchandising firm shows only one merchandise inventory account, and it shows property, plant, and equipment associated with selling and administrative functions only. In contrast, the balance sheet of a manufacturing firm shows three inventory amounts (finished goods, goods in process, and raw materials) and property, plant, and equipment associated with both manufacturing and the selling and administrative functions. A balance sheet for a manufacturing firm follows.

THE ABC COMPANY
Balance Sheet
December 31, 19+2

Assets

Current assets:

Cash		$240,000	
Accounts receivable	$ 400,000		
Less allowance for uncollectibles	10,000	390,000	
Inventories:			
Finished goods	$ 170,000		
Goods in process	120,000		
Materials	90,000	380,000	
Prepaid insurance		3,000	$1,013,000

Property, plant, and equipment:

Land		$100,000	
Plant and equipment	$1,350,000		
Less accumulated depreciation	387,500	962,500	1,062,500
			$2,075,500

Equities

Current liabilities:

Accounts payable		$ 228,000	
Salaries and wages payable		67,750	$ 295,750

Stockholders' equity:

Capital stock		$1,000,000	
Retained earnings		779,750	1,779,750
			$2,075,500

Product cost. Note, in the preceding statement of cost of goods manufactured, that the direct materials, direct labor, and manufacturing overhead costs were not charged directly to expense. During the manufacturing process the services associated with direct labor and factory overhead are utilized in converting direct materials into finished goods. Such conversion increases future economic benefits, in that goods fully or partially completed are worth more than basic raw materials. The increase in future economic benefits justifies the accountant's treatment of direct material, direct labor, and factory overhead costs as assets, not expenses, when the associated services are utilized in production.

The costs of factors used (costs utilized) in manufacturing are called product costs. The costs shown in the cost of goods manufactured statement on page 414 are all product costs. Product costs are assets in the form of goods in process or finished goods inventories. When finished goods are sold, the related product costs are treated as expenses via cost of goods sold in order to match revenue and expense. The distinction between cost incurred and cost utilized is set forth in the illustration on the following page.

During an accounting period, factory costs incurred probably will not equal product costs because of the time lag between cost incurrence and cost utilization.

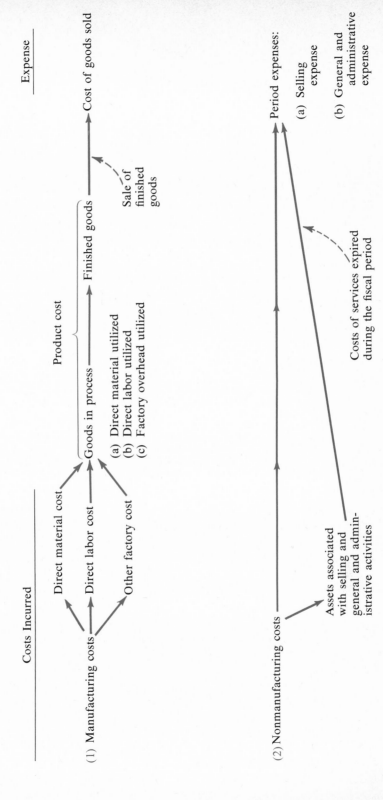

The cost of raw materials purchased is a factory cost incurred, but it is not a product cost until the raw materials are used in production. The purchase of factory equipment is a factory cost incurred, but not a product cost. When the services of the equipment are utilized in production, then the cost of these services (depreciation) is treated as a product cost via factory overhead cost. On the other hand, there is no time lag between incurrence and utilization in the case of direct labor; therefore, the accountant treats direct labor cost incurred as a product cost immediately.

The statement of cost of goods manufactured, shown on page 414, includes only those costs which are product costs. The income statement, shown on page 415, shows those product costs that have become expense via cost of goods sold.

To summarize the distinctions made in the preceding paragraphs:

The items shown in the statement of cost of goods manufactured (page 414) are product costs: the manufacturing costs utilized in production.

The product costs which have reached the status of expense are reported in the income statement (page 415) as cost of goods sold.

The total of the manufacturing costs incurred during a fiscal period is not shown in the traditional financial statements.

The data from the preceding statements plus the manufacturing costs incurred are tied together in the illustration on the next page.

The determination of product cost is generally easier for a merchandising concern than for a manufacturing concern. The accountant for a merchandising concern determines product cost by ascertaining costs of merchandise purchased ready for sale—usually a fairly simple matter. Conceptually, transportation, storage, handling, and like charges are product costs because they can be traced to or associated with the merchandise acquired for sale. If such incidental outlays are not included as part of inventory cost, it is because the amounts involved are insignificant and, therefore, are immediately assigned to expense, for practical reasons.

In contrast, to determine the product costs of a manufacturing company can be a most complex matter. First, it must be decided which of the many and varied costs incurred can be traced to or associated with the manufacturing activity. For example, is some part of the salary of the company's president a manufacturing cost and hence a product cost? Is some part of the cost of operating the personnel department a product cost? If so, how is the share determined? In short, to classify costs and expenses by such broad categories as manufacturing, selling, and general and administrative, though a necessary task since selling expenses and general and administrative expenses are not product costs, may not be an easy task. Many activities carried on by a business can be said to contribute in some measure to more than one of the three categories noted above. These costs must be distributed if the cost of goods manufactured is to be shown. Such cost distributions require judgment and practical considerations. As a result, the amounts reported in the financial statements for inventories and for cost of goods sold should be recognized as approximations.

Product Cost

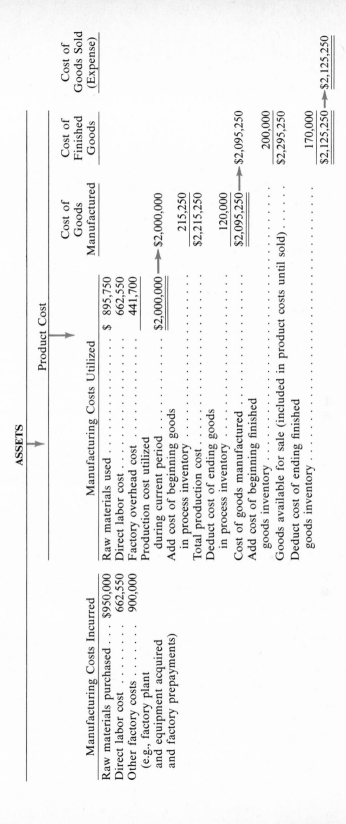

Manufacturing Costs Incurred	Manufacturing Costs Utilized	Cost of Goods Manufactured	Cost of Finished Goods	Cost of Goods Sold (Expense)
Raw materials purchased . . . $950,000	Raw materials used . . . . $ 895,750			
Direct labor cost 662,550	Direct labor cost 662,550			
Other factory costs 900,000	Factory overhead cost 441,700			
(e.g., factory plant and equipment acquired and factory prepayments)	Production cost utilized during current period $2,000,000	$2,000,000		
	Add cost of beginning goods in process inventory	215,250		
	Total production cost	$2,215,250		
	Deduct cost of ending goods in process inventory	120,000		
	Cost of goods manufactured	$2,095,250	$2,095,250	
	Add cost of beginning finished goods inventory		200,000	
	Goods available for sale (included in product costs until sold)		$2,295,250	
	Deduct cost of ending finished goods inventory		170,000	
			$2,125,250	$2,125,250

419

Production and service departments. Most manufacturing companies are divided into production departments and service departments. In a production department, work is done directly on the products manufactured. The segmentation of the factory into production departments usually is based on (1) types of products produced (Department 1 produces ball-point pens and Department 2 produces pencils); (2) kinds of manufacturing processes used (preparation department, assembly department, and finishing department); or (3) product components (one department produces the barrels and another department produces the caps for ball-point pens).

In contrast to production departments, service departments provide services that aid other departments of the firm. Although the service departments do not provide direct work on the products manufactured, they provide services necessary for the producing departments to function properly. Examples of service departments include the maintenance department, the personnel department, and the company cafeteria.

Each production and service department is a cost center—an area of operating activity for which responsibility can be assigned for the work performed and the costs incurred. The assignment of costs to departments may improve the operating performance of a business because it facilitates the fixing of responsibility for various functions. Thus to treat the department as a cost center is useful for both planning and control purposes, as discussed in Chapter 22 dealing with responsibility accounting.

Departments are also useful for purposes of income determination and product costing. As products pass through production departments, they must have departmental costs assigned to them to provide the data necessary for preparation of financial statements. Also, departmental costs may show whether a company's product pricing policy is in line with its costs.

Factory overhead allocation to departments. Generally it is not difficult to assign direct material and direct labor costs to departments and to products. Problems do arise when the indirect factory overhead costs are assigned to departments and thus to products. Because factory overhead costs are not readily identifiable with departments, they are allocated (prorated) to the departments by an averaging process:

$$\textit{Allocation rate} = \frac{\textbf{Total of one item of overhead cost to be allocated}}{\textbf{Allocation base}}$$

$$\begin{matrix}\textbf{Overhead cost allocated} \\ \textbf{to a department}\end{matrix} = \begin{matrix}\textbf{Allocation} \\ \textbf{rate}\end{matrix} \times \begin{matrix}\textbf{Amount of allocation base} \\ \textbf{in the department}\end{matrix}$$

The allocation plan should be based on a logical relationship between the cost to be allocated and some measure (base) that, hopefully, is indicative of benefits received or to be received by each production and service department. Possible allocation bases for certain items of manufacturing overhead are shown in the distribution schedule on page 421. For example, in the distribution schedule the

THE ABC COMPANY
Manufacturing Overhead Distribution Schedule
For the Year Ended December 31, 19+2

| Item | Total Amount | Distribution | | | | Basis of Distribution |
| | | Production Departments | | | Service Department—Maintenance | |
		Dept. A	Dept. B	Dept. C		
Primary allocation:						
Indirect labor	$153,250	$ 81,250	$ 36,000	$ 36,000	$ —	Payroll data
Heat, light, and power	30,000	11,000	7,000	8,000	4,000	Cubic space
Machinery repairs and maintenance	67,950	—	—	—	67,950	Direct
Depreciation:						
Building	32,000	12,000	8,000	10,000	2,000	Floor space used
Machinery and equipment	60,000	20,000	14,000	18,000	8,000	Time used
Insurance premiums expired	8,500	4,100	2,200	1,400	800	Insurable value of assets
Property taxes	12,000	6,000	3,000	2,000	1,000	Assessed valuation
Factory supplies used	42,000	14,000	14,000	14,000	—	Equally among production departments
Miscellaneous factory costs	36,000	9,000	9,000	9,000	9,000	Equally
Total manufacturing overhead	$441,700	$157,350	$ 93,200	$ 98,400	$92,750	
Secondary allocation:						
Distribution of service department cost to production departments	—	37,650	23,000	32,100	92,750*	Hours worked for production departments
Total distributed to production departments	$441,700	$195,000	$116,200	$130,500		

*Deduction.

factory depreciation on machinery and equipment is allocated (assuming that each department shares the same machinery and equipment) according to the time the machinery and equipment is used in each department, as shown below with regard to Department A.

$$\textit{Allocation rate} = \frac{\textbf{Total depreciation cost of machinery and equipment}}{\textbf{Total time machinery and equipment used}}$$

$$\textbf{\$3 per hour} = \frac{\textbf{\$60,000}}{\textbf{20,000 hours}}$$

$$\begin{array}{c}\textbf{Depreciation cost} \\ \textbf{allocated} \\ \textbf{to Department A}\end{array} = \begin{array}{c}\textbf{Allocation} \\ \textbf{rate}\end{array} \times \begin{array}{c}\textbf{Actual length of time the machinery and} \\ \textbf{equipment are used in Department A}\end{array}$$

$$\textbf{\$3} \times \textbf{6666 hours} = \textbf{\$20,000 (rounded)}$$

Once the factory overhead costs have been allocated to the production and service departments (primary allocation), the service department costs are allocated to the production departments (secondary allocation). This secondary allocation is necessary because no products are produced by service departments and, therefore, service department costs cannot be *directly* assigned to products. Because products are manufactured by the production departments, all manufacturing costs (both production and service department costs) are assigned to the production departments. In other words, service department costs are *indirect* costs of the product (factory overhead) and are allocated on the basis of benefits received by the production departments from the service departments. The total cost of each service department is related to a base, such as hours worked for the production departments, and the resulting rate is used to allocate the service department cost to the production departments (see illustration on the preceding page allocating the maintenance cost to the production departments).

Allocation of actual factory overhead to products. After the service department costs have been allocated to the production departments, the actual factory overhead costs are totaled for each production department. In the preceding illustration the departmental totals were:

Department	Actual Factory Overhead
A	$195,000
B	116,200
C	130,500

These costs must, in turn, be assigned to the products which pass through the departments.

Assume that 3,250 units of product were manufactured in Department A during 19+2. Returning to the illustration, the actual factory overhead cost per unit for that department is $60 ($195,000 ÷ 3,250 units).

Applying factory overhead cost to products. Because it takes time to accumulate and allocate factory overhead following the procedures just described, accurate data about departmental costs and product unit cost would not be available promptly. Such delay would, in turn, delay the preparation of financial statements, whether prepared monthly, quarterly, or annually, because product unit cost data are needed to determine the cost of goods sold and the goods in process and finished goods inventories. To overcome such delay, accountants may use an approximation method involving factory overhead rates based on planned (budgeted) factory overhead. The determination of such an overhead rate is illustrated below. It relates to Department A of The ABC Company.

$$Overhead\ rate = \frac{Budgeted\ factory\ overhead}{Budgeted\ direct\ labor\ hours}$$

$$\$4 = \frac{\$200,000}{50,000\ (hours)}$$

The denominator, or application base, used in the computation of the rate is some type of business activity that is logically related to factory overhead. The base used in the example, direct labor hours, is suitable if it is reasonable to believe, in the given circumstances, that a change in the number of direct labor hours used in the production process would be accompanied by a similar change in factory overhead.

The amounts used in the determination of the factory overhead rate are based on some concept of normal business activity. For the determination of such normal amounts, reliance on annual averages of expected business activity over several years would be acceptable.

To illustrate the use of overhead rates, assume that 49,000 direct labor hours were used in Department A during the year following the establishment of the $4 overhead rate. The overhead applied to products manufactured in the department would amount to $196,000 ($4 × 49,000 hours). If 3,250 units of product were produced in Department A, the applied factory overhead cost per unit would be $60.31 ($196,000 ÷ 3,250).

At the $4 application rate, $196,000 of factory overhead would be applied to the production of Department A and unit cost data would be available without delay. Should it develop that the *actual* factory overhead for the year differed from the amount applied, which would be the usual case, an adjustment for the difference would be required. Such disposition of the underapplied or overapplied factory overhead cost is discussed in Chapter 21.

To further illustrate applied factory overhead cost, assume that the following data pertain to two different products manufactured in Department A:

Product #1—25,000 actual direct labor hours used, 2,000 units produced
Product #2—24,000 actual direct labor hours used, 1,250 units produced

Assuming a $4 applied factory overhead rate per direct labor hour, the factory overhead cost *applied* to the products manufactured in Department A is as follows:

	Total Amount	Per Unit
Product #1:		
Total applied overhead ($4 × 25,000)	$100,000	
Applied overhead per unit ($100,000 ÷ 2,000)		$50.00
Product #2:		
Total applied overhead ($4 × 24,000)	96,000	
Applied overhead per unit ($96,000 ÷ 1,250)		76.80
Total applied overhead ($4 × 49,000) Department A	$196,000	

Referring to the preceding discussion, the $4 overhead rate is called an *applied* overhead rate and the $196,000 estimated factory overhead cost is called *applied* factory overhead cost. In accounting jargon, the term "applied factory overhead cost" generally refers to *estimated* factory overhead cost, *not* actual factory overhead cost, allocated to products.

Variable and fixed costs and expenses. *Variable cost* is that part of total cost that varies in direct proportion to changes in *production* volume, assuming a relevant production volume range. As production volume changes, total variable cost changes proportionately so that the variable cost per unit produced remains constant. Stated in other words, variable cost per unit does not change with changes in production volume. For example, suppose that production is at 10,000 units when total variable cost is $30,000. A 10 per cent increase in volume (10% of 10,000) to 11,000 units causes total variable cost to change proportionately (10% of $30,000) to $33,000; however, note that at both the 10,000 and 11,000 volume levels the variable cost per unit remains constant at $3 ($30,000 ÷ 10,000 units and $33,000 ÷ 11,000 units). Thus, total variable cost and variable cost per unit are graphed as follows:

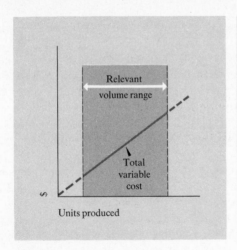 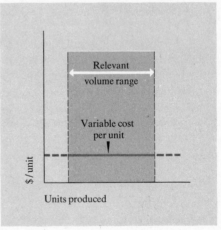

The proportionate change in total variable cost with changes in production volume is assumed only over a company's normal operating range of volume—the relevant range. At unusually high and low production volume levels, total variable costs may not change proportionately. For example, direct labor is normally a variable cost, but at an extremely high level of production volume the addition of more workmen may not increase production volume proportionately because of the crowded working conditions. Also, even over the relevant volume range the concept of proportionate changes in total variable cost is an approximation that holds only on the average.

Variable expense is that part of total expense that varies in direct proportion to changes in *sales* volume, assuming a relevant sales volume range. Whereas variable *cost* varies with changes in production volume, variable *expense* varies with changes in sales volume. Sales volume can be measured either in dollars or in quantities (units) sold.

Graphically, variable expense looks the same as variable cost (see above) except that the horizontal axis is stated in terms of sales volume (not units produced).

Fixed cost is that part of total cost that remains constant as *production* volume changes, assuming a relevant production volume range and a short-run time period. Fixed costs include such costs as the salaries of factory executives, straight-line depreciation on factory plant and equipment, and factory rent on a long-term lease.

Given a long enough time period, all costs are variable; hence fixed costs exist only in the short run. For example, factory rent cost is fixed only for the term of the lease. Straight-line depreciation is fixed only for the useful life of the factory equipment. The salary of a factory executive is fixed until his contract expires or possibly until top management takes an action changing it.

The short run is a period of time that is not long enough to permit a company to increase production volume by acquiring additional capacity. Capacity is the company's upper limit of output brought about by existing plant and equipment, management, and financing. Over the short run, a company operates with given capacity because capacity can be changed only over a long period of time; therefore, the costs related to capacity normally are fixed costs in the short run. Thus short-run increases in production volume result in increased variable costs with fixed costs remaining constant.

With a constant total fixed cost, the greater the production volume the smaller the fixed cost per unit of volume. The total fixed cost is spread over more units as production volume increases and fixed cost per unit decreases. If factory depreciation is $10,000 annually, then with production of 5,000 units the fixed cost per unit is $2 ($10,000 ÷ 5,000); with 8,000 units, fixed cost per unit is $1.25 ($10,000 ÷ 8,000); and with 10,000 units it is $1 per unit. Consequently, total fixed cost and fixed cost per unit are graphed as shown on page 426.

Besides assuming a short-run time period, the concept of fixed cost also assumes a normal operating range of volume (the relevant range). Over the relevant range, changes in production volume have no effect on fixed costs because capacity usually is not affected. However, at extreme production volume levels, total fixed cost may not remain constant. An extreme increase in output may necessitate changes in plant and equipment and cause changes in total fixed costs.

Fixed expense is that part of total expense that remains constant as *sales* volume changes, assuming a relevant sales volume range and a short-run time period. Fixed period expenses include the annual salaries of administrative and sales executives and the straight-line depreciation on the salesmen's cars and on office equip-

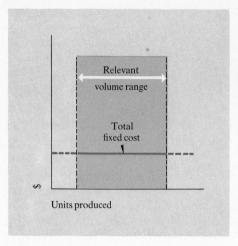

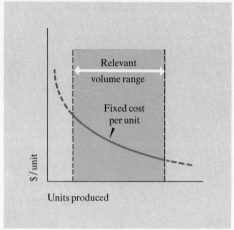

ment. Graphically, fixed expense looks the same as fixed cost (see above), except that the horizontal axis is stated in terms of units sold (not units produced).

Relevant costs and expenses. When costs and expenses are used for decision making, it is important to exclude those costs and expenses that are not relevant to the particular decision at hand. A cost or an expense is relevant if it is *different* under the given alternatives and if it is a *future* cost or expense. For example, if factory depreciation remains constant no matter whether a new product line is added or not, then depreciation is irrelevant to the decision to add the new product. Similarly, a cost that has already occurred cannot be revoked and has no effect on a particular decision today, except possibly for tax purposes. For example, the fact that a company paid $100,000 for factory equipment five years ago is irrelevant to the decision to buy new equipment today.

The concept of relevant costs and expenses is explained more fully in a later chapter.

Summary of cost and expense classifications. The cost and expense concepts previously discussed are summarized below.

    I. Function
        (1) Manufacturing costs
        (2) Selling expenses
        (3) General and administrative expenses
    II. Traceability
        (1) Direct costs
            (a) Direct materials
            (b) Direct labor
        (2) Indirect costs
            (a) Factory overhead cost

III. Recognition of expense
    (1) Product cost
    (2) Period expense
IV. Departmental costs
    (1) Production department costs
    (2) Service department costs
 V. Volume changes
    (1) Production volume
        (a) Variable cost
        (b) Fixed cost
    (2) Sales volume
        (a) Variable expense
        (b) Fixed expense
VI. Decision making
    (1) Relevant costs and expenses
    (2) Irrelevant costs and expenses

ASSIGNMENT

MATERIAL

QUESTIONS

1. What is wrong with a narrow definition of cost?
2. What is the difference between the balance sheet of a merchandising firm and the balance sheet of a manufacturing firm?
3. What is the difference between the income statement of a merchandising firm and the income statement of a manufacturing firm?
4. Why do accountants make the distinction between product costs and period expenses?
5. How can depreciation be an expense to a merchandising firm and a cost (asset) to a manufacturing firm?
6. Why is it necessary to allocate service department costs to production departments? Is such allocation useful for decision making?
7. Other than labor costs, why do manufacturing costs incurred tend to differ from manufacturing costs utilized? Why do labor costs incurred normally equal labor costs utilized?
8. How should the accountant select a base for allocating factory overhead cost to departments? to products?
9. What is the difference between variable cost and variable expense? between fixed cost and fixed expense? Why is the distinction between cost and expense important?
10. What is the concept of the short-run time period and why is it important?

SHORT EXERCISES

E18-1. Classify the following items as either (a) direct materials cost, (b) direct labor cost, (c) manufacturing overhead cost, or (d) selling and administrative expense, by writing the appropriate letter in the space provided.

    <u> c </u> 0. Factory foreman's salary
    <u>   </u> 1. Depreciation on office equipment
    <u>   </u> 2. Salary of janitor who cleans the factory building
    <u>   </u> 3. Metal used in production
    <u>   </u> 4. Salaries of factory machine operators
    <u>   </u> 5. Salesmen's commissions
    <u>   </u> 6. Glue, nails, screws, and bolts used in production

E18-2. What is wrong with the following statement of cost of goods manufactured?

DICKENSON COMPANY
Statement of Cost of Goods Manufactured
December 31, 19+6

Direct materials cost	$ 200,000
Direct labor cost	400,000
Manufacturing overhead cost	300,000
Production cost utilized during period	$ 900,000
Add beginning finished goods, December 31, 19+5	700,000
Total production cost	$1,600,000
Deduct ending finished goods, December 31, 19+6	600,000
Cost of goods manufactured	$1,000,000

E18-3. Application Company uses an applied factory overhead rate based on budgeted machine hours. It was estimated at the beginning of the year that total factory overhead cost and machine hours would be $500,000 and 100,000, respectively, for the current fiscal year. If 25,000, 20,000, 15,000, and 55,000 machine hours were used in the company's four production departments during the year, what was the applied factory overhead for each department? If 15,000 units of the 25,000 units of product produced in Department #1 were sold, what was the applied factory overhead cost allocated to ending inventory and to the units sold for Department #1?

E18-4. Variable Company produced 300,000 units and sold 200,000 units of a product during the current year (no beginning inventory). The total cost to produce the product was $2,550,000, which included total fixed costs of $1,500,000.

    (a) What was the variable cost per unit? Show all your work.
    (b) What was the total variable *expense* for the year?
    (c) What was the fixed cost per unit?
    (d) What was the total fixed *expense* for the year?
    (e) What was the difference between variable cost per unit and variable expense per unit? between fixed cost per unit and fixed expense per unit?

PROBLEMS

Problem A18-1. The data below pertain to W. S. Mitchell Company for the fiscal year ended December 31, 19XX. Note that the data are not in any particular sequence, but are all mixed up. You are asked to prepare a cost of goods manufactured statement and an income statement. In the preparation of the income statement, show the component parts of the cost of goods sold section.

Selling expenses	$100,000
Beginning goods in process inventory	200,000
Ending finished goods inventory	600,000
Direct material cost	150,000
General and administrative expenses	80,000
Ending goods in process inventory	250,000
Factory overhead cost	180,000
Beginning finished goods inventory	500,000
Direct labor cost	200,000
Net sales	600,000

Problem A18-2. You are given data for the year 19+1 for Pearlman Company.

	19+1
Total manufacturing costs	$300,000
Fixed manufacturing costs	100,000
Units produced (no goods in process inventories)	10,000
Units sold	9,000

Using the relationships from the above data, you are asked to predict costs and expense (cost of goods sold) for the next year (19+2) if production and sales are expected to be 15,000 and 16,000 units, respectively. Specifically, you are asked to determine for the year 19+2 the following (show your calculations):

        (a) Variable cost per unit.   (c) Total fixed cost.
        (b) Total variable cost.   (d) Cost of goods sold.

Problem A18-3. You are given below an abbreviated listing of expenditures made by Radosevich Company, followed by some possible ways each expenditure could be classified.

    (1) Payment for three-year rental of factory equipment
    (2) Direct materials and labor utilized
    (3) Salesmen's travel
    (4) Purchase of factory materials
    (5) General office salaries
    (6) Employer's payroll taxes for factory workers
    (7) Overtime paid to factory workers
    (8) Factory fire insurance for the fiscal year
    (9) Shipping supplies used
  (10) Rework of defective product by factory workers
  (11) President's salary
  (12) Total outlay for advertising allowed

Factory Cost Incurred	Factory Cost Utilized		Expense	
	Variable	Fixed	Variable	Fixed
A	B	C	D	E

List the expenditures by number, and after each number write a letter (A,B,C,D, or E) indicating the classification you think should be selected for that particular expenditure. Also explain *why* you selected the classification for each expenditure.

Problem A18-4. You are given cost data below that are used in calculating cost of goods manufactured. However, some cost data are missing, as indicated by the question marks. You are to solve for the missing data and in so doing to show all your calculations, not just the final answers. Note that the three sets of costs given below (see columns *a, b,* and *c*) are unrelated to one another. Ignore the dashes (—) in each column.

	(a)	(b)	(c)
Cost of goods manufactured . . . . $	?	$630,000	$?
Ending goods in process inventory	80,000	120,000	—
Factory overhead cost	60,000	150,000	?
Direct material cost	70,000	?	50,000
Production cost utilized during period	—	?	150,000
Beginning goods in process inventory	?	100,000	—
Direct labor cost	80,000	300,000	60,000
Total production cost	310,000	—	—
Increase in goods in process inventory	—	—	10,000

Problem A18-5. An incomplete manufacturing overhead distribution schedule for Proration Company is presented below.

	Total Cost	Service Departments		Producing Departments	
		Maintenance	Cafeteria	Dept. #1	Dept. #2
Indirect materials and labor	$1,300,000	$90,000	$60,000	$500,000	$650,000
Factory depreciation (based on square footage)	189,000				
Property taxes (based on book value)	100,000				
Insurance	22,950				
Power	2,080				
Sundry factory costs	8,000				
	$1,622,030				
Distribution of service departments to production departments:					
Maintenance	—				
Cafeteria	—				
	$1,622,030				

The above overhead costs can be allocated to the departments based on the data below:

Basis of Allocation	Maintenance	Cafeteria	#1	#2
Kilowatt hours used ($.08 per kw. hours used)	5,000	4,000	7,000	10,000
Maintenance hours worked in production departments			4,000	6,000
Book value (5% of book value)	$200,000	$400,000	$600,000	$ 800,000
Value of assets ($.90 per $100 value of assets)	$300,000	$450,000	$800,000	$1,000,000
Number of employees using cafeteria . . .			22	28
Square footage used	2,000	3,000	4,000	5,000
Sundry	$\frac{1}{8}$	$\frac{3}{8}$	$\frac{2}{8}$	$\frac{2}{8}$

Required:

(a) Complete the manufacturing overhead distribution schedule.
(b) If overhead is applied to the production in the two producing departments on the basis of $15 per direct labor hour used, what is the difference between actual (derived in part (a) of problem) and applied factory overhead for the two producing departments? Assume that 46,000 and 65,000 direct labor hours were used in Departments #1 and #2, respectively.
(c) Show how the rate of $.08 per kilowatt hour was derived.

Problem B18-1. For the year 19+1, Swinth Company manufactured 5,000 finished units of product. There were no goods in process inventories. During the year, $50,000 of raw materials were purchased and $30,000 worth were issued to production. Factory labor costs were $60,000. On January 1, 19+1, new equipment for the factory was acquired at a cost of $200,000. The useful life of the equipment was estimated to be 10 years, with no expected salvage value, and the equipment was to be depreciated on a straight-line basis. On July 1, 19+1, $20,000 was paid for two years' rental service of specialized factory equipment needed by the company. The fiscal period for the company ends December 31.

Required:

(a) What was the total factory cost incurred and the total factory cost utilized for the year 19+1?
(b) If 3,000 units were sold during 19+1 (assume no beginning finished goods inventory), what was the cost of goods sold and the cost of the ending finished goods inventory for the year 19+1?

Problem B18-2. Financial data for Maurer Company for the year 19+1 are presented below:

Ending materials inventory	$ 50,000
Equipment	1,000,000
General and administrative expenses	61,000
Income taxes payable	52,000
Ending goods in process inventory	100,000
Retained earnings	270,000
Net sales	700,000
Accounts receivable	300,000
Labor utilized	206,000
Common stock	800,000
Beginning goods in process inventory	49,000
Selling expenses	134,000
Ending finished goods inventory	60,000
Allowance for uncollectibles	55,000
Factory overhead utilized	150,000
Beginning finished goods inventory	40,000
Accumulated depreciation	400,000
Accounts payable	28,000
Materials utilized	35,000
Cash	95,000

Given the above data, you are asked to prepare (a) a statement of cost of goods manufactured, (b) an income statement, and (c) a balance sheet.

Problem B18-3. A fire destroyed most of the accounting records of Crumpler Company, but the following cost data were saved:

Ending finished goods inventory	$ 60,000
Labor utilized	300,000
Cost of goods sold	890,000
Materials utilized	250,000
Decrease in finished goods inventory	140,000
Ending materials inventory	50,000
Factory overhead utilized	280,000
Materials purchased	260,000
Ending goods in process inventory	180,000

Using the above incomplete data, (a) determine the beginning inventory costs for materials, goods in process, and finished goods, and (b) prepare a schedule of cost of goods sold. Show all of your calculations in arriving at your final figures. (Hint: Try working backwards from the given cost of goods sold figure.)

Problem B18-4. Brooks Manufacturing Company produces one product. The chief accountant for the firm is worried that the monthly financial statements are misleading because of seasonal variations in factory overhead costs and in production. He believes that the company should use an estimated annual factory overhead rate in applying overhead to production. His analysis shows that direct labor hours and factory overhead cost tend to move together; hence, he recommends using an annual overhead rate of $5 per direct labor hour.

In order to present his case to management, he asks you to (a) compute actual monthly overhead rates (actual factory overhead cost divided by direct labor hours); (b) compute the monthly and the total applied factory overhead cost ($5 rate times direct labor hours); (c) compare the monthly and total applied factory overhead to the monthly and total actual factory overhead; and (d) make recommendations, based on your analysis, as to whether the company should use the annual factory overhead rate.

The accountant provides you with the worksheet below to make your analysis.

Months	Direct Labor Hours	Actual Factory Overhead Cost	Monthly Overhead Rate	Applied Factory Overhead Cost	Difference Between Actual and Applied
January	9,000	$ 63,000			
February	11,000	71,500			
March	13,000	81,250			
April	15,000	90,000			
May	17,000	93,500			
June	21,000	105,000			
July	31,000	147,250			
August	41,000	153,750			
September	33,000	140,250			
October	19,000	85,500			
November	15,000	83,000			
December	11,000	66,000			
	236,000	$1,180,000		$	$

Problem B18-5. Clark Manufacturing Company has been using actual factory overhead cost in costing its two products. However, the chief accountant has pointed out that the monthly financial statements are misleading because of seasonal variations in actual factory overhead cost and in production. He recommends that the company use an estimated annual overhead rate for applying factory overhead cost to production. The chief accountant has gathered the following representative data to determine the applied overhead rate to use:

	Production Department #1	Production Department #2	Total
Factory overhead costs (includes service department costs) . . .	$500,000	$800,000	$1,300,000
Direct labor hours	20,000	200,000	220,000
Machine hours.	100,000	20,000	120,000

Required:

(a) Compute factory overhead rates based on direct labor hours and machine hours for each production department.

(b) Compute plant wide factory overhead rates (both departments combined) based on direct labor hours and machine hours.

(c) Present your arguments as to the factory overhead rate or rates that you think Clark Manufacturing Company should use.

19

Manufacturing Cost Systems–
Job Order Costing

The need for cost accounting systems. As a general rule, a manufacturing concern is engaged in the production and marketing of more than one kind of product. Also, as a general rule, several kinds of raw materials are used, and the manufacturing process comprises several distinct production steps. In short, the business activity associated with manufacturing operations often is neither simple nor of the size that would be described as a "small" business. If it were necessary to make a physical count of the inventories and to develop unit cost data each time financial statements were prepared, management would no doubt have some reservations about the adequacy of such an accounting system in any situation of even moderate size and complexity.

The discussion and illustrations in the preceding chapter referred to beginning and ending inventories of goods in process and finished goods. If these inventories are determined by physical count, the periodic inventory method is being used. If day-by-day inventory records are kept of the inventory inflows, outflows, and current balances, then a perpetual inventory method is being used. Under the periodic inventory method, until the ending inventories are determined by physical count, data needed for the preparation of financial statements are not available. Under the perpetual inventory method, inventory taking need not precede the preparation of financial statements because the required data are available in the accounts. However, physical inventory counts should be made from time to time, at least annually, as a check on the accuracy of the perpetual inventory records.

Because of its advantages, most large manufacturing firms use the perpetual inventory method. Here are some of its advantages:

(1) Perpetual inventory records provide timely cost data for managerial decision making. For example, management decisions with regard to the quantity of materials needed to be purchased, the cash needed for the purchase of materials, and the goods in process and finished goods inventory levels to be maintained are facilitated by up-to-date information about inventories on hand.

(2) The preparation of interim financial statements (statements prepared during the year, e.g. monthly) is facilitated because the inventory figures are readily available without investing the time and expense required for a physical count.

(3) The quantities of inventory that should be on hand are shown, thereby reducing the likelihood of unexplained disappearances in inventories.

(4) As shown later in the chapter, perpetual inventory records provide information about the costs required to make the general ledger transfers from materials inventory to Goods in Process, To Finished Goods, and to Cost of Goods Sold.

The fundamental procedures of cost accounting will become apparent from a description of job order cost accounting in this chapter and of process cost accounting in the next chapter.

Job order costing. Job order or specific order cost accounting is characterized by the accumulation of production costs by separate and distinct jobs. This system is particularly suitable for firms that manufacture according to specific customer orders or for stock (i.e., manufacturing for inventory purposes with sales made out of stock on hand). For example, a furniture manufacturer may receive an order for one custom-made chair, and the company would assign an order number to the job and accumulate costs under that number. Or, the furniture manufacturer may receive an order for fifty of the same custom chairs, and a job order number would be assigned to the entire lot. Note that each product or product lot is sufficiently different so that each job is identifiable.

Specific order cost accounting is used by manufacturing firms that engage in discontinuous production in which a variety of different jobs are going on at once, and in which each job requires different amounts of material, labor, and overhead. Industries using job order cost systems include machinery, furniture, lumber products, and construction.

Cost flows. Materials inventory and manufacturing (factory) overhead accounts are set up in the general ledger to accumulate the costs for materials (debit Materials Inventory and credit Accounts Payable) and manufacturing overhead (debit Manufacturing

Overhead and credit such accounts as Cash, Accounts Payable, Prepaid Insurance—Factory, and other unexpired factory assets). Because there is no time lag between labor cost incurrence and utilization, a labor cost account need not be used to accumulate labor cost incurred. Instead, a liability account, Factory Payroll Payable, is credited for the cost of labor utilized in production, and the corresponding debit is to Goods in Process. The actual payment of the labor cost is recorded by a debit to Factory Payroll Payable and a credit to Cash (for the present we shall ignore withholding taxes). At the end of the fiscal period, any credit balance in the factory payroll payable account represents the liability for wages earned but not paid. Such a liability arises when the pay date occurs after the end of the accounting fiscal period.

As the services related to direct material, direct labor, and factory overhead are utilized in production, the cost of the services is accounted for in the general ledger account Goods (Work) in Process. The production costs are transferred from the two basic cost accounts and the payroll account to the goods in process account (debit Goods in Process and credit the respective Materials Inventory, Factory Payroll Payable, and Manufacturing Overhead).

When the goods are completed, the applicable production costs are transferred from the goods in process account to the finished goods account (debit Finished Goods and credit Goods in Process). When the finished goods are sold, the production costs of the goods are transferred to the expense account Cost of Goods Sold (debit Cost of Goods Sold and credit Finished Goods).

The preceding cost entries are facilitated by the use of perpetual inventory records for raw materials (both direct and indirect materials), goods in process, and finished goods. Thus the cost flows can be shown, as on the next page, by arrows (the head of an arrow denotes a debit, the tail represents a credit).

Applied factory overhead cost. As discussed in the preceding chapter, actual factory overhead cost is not directly traceable to particular units of a product, and there is a time lag after utilization before actual factory overhead cost can be determined. Similarly, *actual* factory overhead cost is not directly traceable to particular jobs and it cannot be readily determined as jobs are completed; therefore, applied (estimated) factory overhead cost is used in job order costing. How applied factory overhead cost is determined and used in a job order system is summarized below.

(1) An activity base is selected that tends to vary with factory overhead cost. It is assumed that such a related base reflects the factors that cause changes in overhead costs. For example, if direct labor cost (or direct labor hours or machine hours) tends to vary with overhead cost, it can be used as the activity base needed to derive the applied factory overhead rate.

(2) The volume of activity for the base selected is estimated for the next fiscal year. Generally it is either the volume *expected* next year or the *normal* annual volume (an annual average volume estimated over several years). Thus the expected or normal labor cost for next year, say $8,000, would be a measure of the estimated activity volume.

CHART SHOWING FLOW OF COSTS

Goods in Process

Direct materials	Goods completed
Direct labor	
Applied overhead	

Finished Goods

	Completed goods sold

Cost of Goods Sold

Materials Inventory

Materials purchased	Materials utilized in production

Factory Payroll Payable

Labor payments	Labor utilized in production

Manufacturing Overhead

(Actual)	(Applied)
Indirect labor utilized	Estimated factory overhead utilized in production
Indirect materials utilized	
Other indirect costs utilized	

Accounts Payable

Cash

Prepaid Insurance—Factory

Accumulated Depreciation—Factory

Utility Cost—Factory

438

(3) Factory overhead costs are projected for next year at the estimated (expected or normal) activity volume. Assume that this estimate is $4,800.

(4) The estimated factory overhead cost is divided by the estimated activity level to derive an applied factory overhead rate. For example, the estimated factory overhead cost of $4,800 divided by the estimated direct labor cost of $8,000 indicates an applied overhead rate of .6.

(5) As each job is completed during the year, the *actual* direct labor cost for each job is multiplied by the applied factory overhead rate to determine the factory overhead cost to be applied to each job. For example, if job #80 had direct labor cost of $250, the applied factory overhead cost would be $150 ($250 × .6). Obviously, the cost of a job is the sum of its direct materials, direct labor, and applied factory overhead costs.

(6) For purposes of inventory costing, factory overhead is applied to any uncompleted jobs at the end of the fiscal period. For example, assume that job #82 utilized $200 of labor and it is not finished. The applied factory overhead would be $120 ($200 × .6).

Subsidiary cost records. General ledger accounts were used in the preceding section to show cost flows in a job order cost accounting system. The cost data needed to make the entries in the general ledger accounts are provided by subsidiary records. That is, general ledger accounts are summary (control) accounts in which entries are based on total dollar amounts aggregated, usually on a monthly basis, from detailed subsidiary cost records. Subsidiary records are kept (1) to avoid unwieldy amounts of data in the general ledger, (2) to provide a check on bookkeeping accuracy, and (3) to provide easier access to current data (i.e., if the control accounts are being used, the subsidiary records are available for use, and vice versa).

The *job cost sheet* is the basic subsidiary record underlying the goods in process account. For each job there is a job cost sheet, which shows the details of the costs for direct materials and direct labor utilized during production and the applied (estimated) factory overhead cost for a particular job. A job cost sheet is shown on page 440.

A file of all the job cost sheets provides a subsidiary ledger to the goods in process account. Consequently, at the end of the fiscal period, the cost of the ending goods in process inventory is merely the sum of the total costs from the cost sheets for all jobs that remain uncompleted. Similarly, the sum of the total costs for all jobs that are completed, as shown by the job cost sheets, provides the data for the entry debiting Finished Goods and crediting Goods in Process (usually done monthly).

In those cases where manufacturing is done by specific customer order, a file of the completed job cost sheets may serve as the subsidiary ledger to the finished goods account. Thus the ending inventory cost for finished goods is simply the sum of the costs from the job cost sheets for those finished goods still on hand at the end of the fiscal period. Instead of job cost sheets, inventory cards or a formal ledger are used as the subsidiary ledger to the finished goods account when goods are manufactured for stock.

Job Cost Sheet

Description: _____	Job Order No. _____
For stock _____	Due Date _____
Customer _____	Date completed _____
Date ordered _____	Quantity completed _____
Quantity ordered _____	

Direct Materials Cost			Applied Overhead Cost	
Date	Reference	Amount	Date	Amount

Direct Labor Cost			Cost Summary	
Date	Reference	Amount	Direct materials	$ _____
			Direct labor	_____
			Applied overhead	_____
			Total	$ _____
			Cost per unit	$ _____

Besides the job cost sheet, other supporting documents and records are the following:

(1) Sellers' invoices or company receiving reports (a report verifying the quantity and condition of purchased materials received), summarized monthly, provide the data necessary to make the general ledger entry debiting Materials Inventory and crediting Accounts Payable.

(2) Materials (stores) ledger cards (see next page), which show the detailed inflows, outflows, and ending balances pertaining to materials inventory, serve as the subsidiary records supporting the general ledger account Materials Inventory.

(3) Materials (stores) requisitions (see next page), which are used as the authority to issue materials to production, provide the material cost data that are recorded in the materials ledger cards and in the job cost sheets. The materials requisitions, or a summary sheet of the requisitions, also serve as a basis for the monthly general ledger entry debiting Goods in Process (direct materials) and Manufacturing Overhead (indirect materials) and crediting Materials Inventory.

(4) Work tickets (see next page) provide a record of each factory workman's time, pay rate, and total labor cost for each job. Thus the work tickets provide the direct labor cost data that are recorded on the job cost sheets. The work tickets, or a summary sheet of the work tickets, also provide the data needed to make the monthly general ledger entry debiting Goods in Process (direct labor) and Manufacturing Overhead (indirect labor) and crediting Factory Payroll Payable.

(5) Factory overhead analysis sheets (see next page), which provide the detailed data pertaining to *actual* factory overhead costs, serve as the subsidiary records supporting the general ledger account Manufacturing Overhead. The factory overhead costs recorded in the analysis sheets are obtained from materials requisitions (indirect materials), work tickets (indirect labor), and miscellaneous invoices. A monthly summary of the overhead analysis sheets provides the data needed for the general ledger entry debiting Manufacturing Overhead and crediting various accounts.

A manufacturing company may use a factory overhead cost sheet for each department. In this way departmental responsibility for overhead costs can be maintained. On the other hand, there may be no need to maintain specific departmental records for direct material and direct labor costs because such data can be obtained from the materials requisitions and work tickets.

Materials Ledger Card

Description_____   Part No._____

		Received			Issued			Balance		
Date	Reference	Quantity	Unit Cost	Amount	Quantity	Unit Cost	Amount	Quantity	Unit Cost	Amount

Materials Requisition

Job No._____   Requisition No._____

Department_____   Date_____

Authorized by_____

Description	Quantity	Unit Cost	Amount

Work Ticket

Employee No._____   Rate $_____   Date_____

Operation No._____   Amount $_____   Job No._____

Department No._____

Time	Pieces
Stop_____ Start_____ Total hours_____ Clock No._____	Accepted_____ Rejected_____ Total_____ Inspector_____

| **Factory Overhead Cost Sheet** Department_____ | | | | | | | | |
Date	Reference	Indirect materials	Indirect labor	Insurance	Depreciation	Taxes	Utilities	Other

The preceding financial documents serve (1) to control the use of manufacturing resources (e.g., perpetual materials inventory records provide control over the issuance of materials to production); (2) to provide the stimulus for action (e.g., materials requisitions initiate the action to issue materials to production); and (3) to provide the basis for useful information for decision-making purposes (e.g., the documentation of the cost flows provides the basis for the preparation of financial statements and for comparisons of actual cost data with expected cost data, both of which are useful in decision making).

The general ledger cost entries with the supporting financial documents and subsidiary ledgers are summarized below.

Summary Entry in General Ledger			Basic Document Underlying Entry	Subsidiary Records
(0) Materials inventory	x		Seller's invoice, receiving	Materials cards
Accounts payable		x	report, or purchase	or materials
			requisition	ledger
(1) Goods in process	x		Materials requisitions	Job cost sheet,
Manufacturing overhead	x		or summary of	factory overhead
Materials inventory		x	requisitions	cost sheets, and
				stores cards
(2) Goods in process	x		Work tickets or summary	Job cost sheet
Manufacturing overhead	x		of tickets	and factory
Factory payroll payable		x		overhead cost
				sheets
(3) Goods in process	x		Applied factory overhead	Job cost sheet
Manufacturing overhead		x	rate	
(4) Manufacturing overhead	x		Invoices and memos	Factory overhead
Accounts payable		x		cost sheets
Cash		x		
Prepayments—Factory		x		
Other accounts		x		

Summary Entry in General Ledger		Basic Document Underlying Entry	Subsidiary Records
(5) Finished goods	X	Completed jobs cost sheets	File of completed jobs cost sheets, finished goods ledger, or finished goods cards
Goods in process	X		
(6) Cost of goods sold	X	Sales invoices or shipping orders	File of job cost sheets associated with goods sold, finished goods inventory cards, or finished goods ledger
Finished goods	X		

An illustration of job costing. Assume that a furniture manufacturer worked on three jobs (Job #80, Job #81, and Job #82) during the month of August. Further assume that Job #80 and Job #81 were started in July and completed in August, and that the finished product that resulted from Job #80 was sold at the end of August. Finally, assume that factory overhead is applied to production at a rate of 60 per cent of direct labor cost. Because no entries were made for the manufacturing costs utilized during August, you are asked to record the necessary cost entries, given the data below, and prepare a statement of cost of goods manufactured for the month of August.

	Job #80	Job #81	Job #82	Total
		Job Cost Sheets		
Beginning goods in process	$ 500	$ 800	$—	$1,300
Costs utilized during August:				
Direct materials	200	100	220	520
Direct labor	250	160	200	610
Manufacturing overhead applied	150	96	120	366
Subtotal	$1,100	$1,156	$540	$2,796
Indirect materials (actual)				$ 135
Indirect labor (actual)				180
Various indirect factory costs (actual)				120

Solution:

(1) Goods in process (direct)	520	
Manufacturing overhead (indirect)	135	
Materials inventory		655
Issuance of direct and indirect materials to production.		
(2) Goods in process (direct)	610	
Manufacturing overhead (indirect)	180	
Factory payroll payable		790
Direct and indirect labor utilized in production.		
(3) Goods in process (60% of $610)	366	
Manufacturing overhead		366
Application of factory overhead at 60% of direct labor cost.		

(4) Manufacturing overhead   120
       Miscellaneous accounts (Accounts payable,
        Cash, Accumulated depreciation—
        Factory, etc.)   120
       To record actual factory overhead cost utilized.

(5) Finished goods 2,256
       Goods in process ($1,100 for Job #80
        plus $1,156 for Job #81) 2,256
       To record completion of jobs #80 and #81.

(6) Cost of goods sold (Job #80). 1,100
       Finished goods 1,100
       To record cost of goods sold.

FURNITURE COMPANY
Statement of Cost of Goods Manufactured
Month Ended August 31, 19xx

Direct material cost . . . . $ 520
Direct labor cost   610
Manufacturing overhead (applied).   366
Production cost utilized during August $1,496
Add beginning goods in process 1,300
Total production cost $2,796
Deduct ending goods in process (Job #82)   540
Cost of goods manufactured. $2,256

Although the foregoing illustration is simplified because of only three jobs, it does show how the job cost sheets provide the necessary data for recording transfers from Goods in Process to Finished Goods to Cost of Goods Sold. The same method of accounting would be used for a company with 1,000 jobs: sum up the job cost sheets for all jobs uncompleted (ending goods in process), for all jobs completed and still on hand (ending finished goods), and for all jobs of which the finished goods have been sold (cost of goods sold).

The illustration also assumed that each job was the result of a specific customer order, so that upon completion of a job all the units (or one unit) were sold to the specific customer. However, in manufacturing for stock, the units completed for a particular job may not all be sold during the same time period; hence to determine the cost of goods sold it is necessary to calculate an average cost per unit completed in each job. Thus, if job #190 had total manufacturing costs of $800, and if 20 units were completed, the cost per unit would be $40; if 5 of the units were sold, the cost of goods sold pertaining to job #190 would be $200 (5 × $40).

Underapplied and overapplied overhead. Note that in the preceding illustration there is a $69 difference between the actual factory overhead cost ($435) and the applied factory overhead cost ($366), as summarized below:

Manufacturing Overhead

(Actual)	(Applied)
135	366
180	
120	
435	

The difference is called the factory overhead variance, and in this instance it represents underapplied (underabsorbed) factory overhead: only $366 was applied to production, which was $69 under the actual factory overhead cost of $435. Similarly, if actual factory overhead cost is less than applied factory overhead cost, then the overhead variance represents overapplied (overabsorbed) overhead; in comparison to actual factory overhead cost, too much overhead was applied to production.

In the usual situation there will be month-to-month variation between actual and applied factory overhead cost. This variation should be expected because actual monthly factory overhead cost is affected by fluctuations in actual production volume and seasonal overhead costs. In contrast, applied factory overhead cost for any month (or any interim period) is really an *average* cost (i.e., the estimated average annual applied rate times the actual monthly activity level) that smooths out seasonal variations. On the other hand, by the end of the fiscal year the monthly differences between the applied and actual factory overhead costs should tend to offset one another so that any year-end factory overhead variance should be minor.

If monthly financial statements are prepared, any factory overhead variance should be shown in the balance sheet: underapplied factory overhead would be shown as the last item under current assets and overapplied factory overhead would be shown as the last item under current liabilities. Applied, not actual, factory overhead would be shown on the *monthly* statement of cost of goods manufactured, as shown on page 444, and, therefore, also shown on the *monthly* income statement as part of the cost of goods sold.

The reason for showing a monthly factory overhead variance in the current section of the balance sheet is that the monthly variances largely represent random departures from normal operating overhead costs that should tend to net out and result in a small or zero variance by year end. If monthly overhead variances were shown on the monthly income statements, monthly net income would vary with the random fluctuations in the overhead variance and possibly would mislead investors, creditors, and other readers of the income statement.

At the end of the fiscal year, any factory overhead variance usually is shown in the income statement rather than in the balance sheet. One treatment is to write off any year-end overhead variance to cost of goods sold: underapplied factory overhead is debited to Cost of Goods Sold and overapplied factory overhead is credited to Cost of Goods Sold, as shown below:

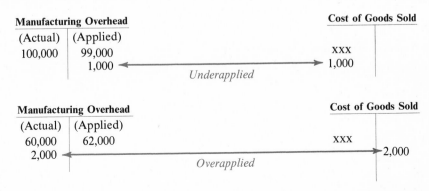

Theoretically, one can argue that any year-end factory overhead variance should be prorated to cost of goods sold, finished goods, and goods in process in proportion to the amount of applied factory overhead contained in the ending balance of each of these three accounts. The contention is that the balance sheet and income statement should reflect *actual* historical overhead cost, which is accomplished by prorating the factory overhead variance to the three accounts. However, in most cases the prorating is not done because the factory overhead variance generally is small at year end, so that the added accuracy in prorating is not significant.

ASSIGNMENT
MATERIAL

QUESTIONS

1. What is the function of the following cost accounting records?
   (a) Factory overhead analysis sheets
   (c) Job cost sheets
   (b) Materials requisitions
   (d) Materials ledger cards

2. Why is job order costing not used by firms engaged in mass production? Are there any situations where such firms may use job order costing?

3. In the cost flows of a job order system, why are part of the materials and labor costs first taken to Manufacturing Overhead instead of Goods in Process?

4. Why are both general ledger cost accounts and subsidiary cost records kept? For managerial decision-making purposes, which source (general ledger accounts or subsidiary records) of data would be the more useful?

5. Why do firms that manufacture for stock, instead of by specific customer order, not use a file of completed job cost sheets as the subsidiary ledger to the finished goods account?

6. A specific job-order number can refer to the cost of manufacturing one unit of a product or to the cost of manufacturing several units of the same product (a job lot). How does the cost accounting for a job lot differ from the cost accounting for one unit of product?

7. Would the following circumstances result in underapplied or overapplied factory overhead cost? Explain.
   (a) More factory overhead cost utilized than expected.
   (b) An applied overhead rate that is too high.
   (c) Production that is greater than expected.

8. What is the difference between the accounting treatment of factory overhead in monthly as opposed to year-end financial statements? Discuss.

9. Is there any difference between a theoretical approach as opposed to a practical approach in the treatment of the factory overhead variance at year end? Discuss.

10. Note that in the job-order cost flows there is a cost account set up for materials (Materials Inventory) and for factory overhead (Manufacturing Overhead). However, for labor there is a liability account (Factory Payroll Payable) instead of a cost account. Why is no cost account set up for labor? (Hint: Remember the distinction between costs incurred and utilized.)

SHORT EXERCISES

E19-1. For the month of February, the costs of Job #81 were as follows:

> Direct materials utilized: 10,000 pounds @ $.70 a pound
> Direct labor utilized: 3,000 hours @ $3.50 an hour
> Factory overhead applied: $5 per direct-labor hour
> Units completed: 5,000
> Units sold: 1,500

(a) What was the cost of goods manufactured with regard to Job #81?

(b) What was the cost of the ending inventory of finished goods with regard to Job #81?

(c) What was the cost of goods sold with regard to Job #81?

E19-2. You are given below the factory payroll payable account for Harmon Company for the month of February:

Factory Payroll Payable

19,000	Balance 3,000
	20,000

(a) In general journal form, make the entry for the labor payment.

(b) If direct labor cost utilized was $18,000 during February, make the general journal entry recording the total labor cost utilized.

(c) Why is there a difference between total debits and credits in the above account? Explain.

E19-3. For the month of January, you are given below the manufacturing overhead account for Wilt-the-Stilt Company:

Manufacturing Overhead Cost

4,800	5,000

(a) The actual factory overhead costs utilized during January consisted of $3,000 equipment depreciation, $500 indirect materials, $1,000 indirect labor, and $300 factory insurance. Make one compound general journal entry to record the actual overhead costs.

(b) In general journal form, record the applied factory overhead cost for the month of January.

(c) Why do the total debits not equal the total credits in the above account? Explain.

E19-4. During the fiscal period, the following charges were made to the goods in process account for Jo Jo Company:

Goods in Process

Balance.	—
Direct materials	200,000
Direct labor.	500,000
Factory overhead	300,000

The costs charged to the goods in process account consisted of the following three jobs:

	Units Completed	Direct Materials	Direct Labor
Job #10	10,000	$50,000	$110,000
Job #11	25,000	80,000	200,000
Job #12	20,000	70,000	190,000

(a) If factory overhead was applied to production based on direct labor cost, what was the factory overhead applied rate?

(b) If 4,000 and 8,000 units of Jobs #10 and #11, respectively, were sold during the year, what was the cost of goods sold for those two jobs?

PROBLEMS

Problem A19-1. Tuggle Manufacturing Company uses a job order cost system. You are required to do the following:

(a) Prepare entries in general journal form for the following transactions that relate to the month of April, assuming no beginning inventories:

1. Materials costing $50,000 were purchased on credit.
2. Materials issued to production were as follows:

Job #110	$3,000
Job #111	2,000
Job #112	5,000
Indirect materials	1,000

3. Labor utilized in production was as follows:

Job #110	$5,000
Job #111	8,000
Job #112	7,000
Indirect labor	4,000

4. Wages of $18,000 were paid to the factory workers.
5. Manufacturing overhead is applied to production on the basis of 80% of direct labor cost.
6. Actual miscellaneous factory overhead costs utilized during the month were $10,000.
7. Jobs #110 and #111 were completed during the month.
8. The product from Job #110 was shipped and invoiced at the end of the month at a profit of 20% of cost.

(b) What is the cost of the ending inventory of goods in process? Of finished goods?

(c) What is the overhead variance for the month?

Problem A19-2. The March 1, 19xx inventory balances for Pollay Manufacturing Company are given below:

Materials inventory.	$ 6,000
Goods in process	5,000
Finished goods	14,000

The cost transactions for the month of March were as follows:

1. Materials purchased for cash were $30,000.
2. Direct and indirect materials utilized were $18,000 and $2,000, respectively.
3. Direct and indirect labor utilized were $16,000 and $1,000, respectively.
4. Applied factory overhead cost was $12,800, and miscellaneous actual factory overhead cost was $9,000.
5. Factory wages paid at the end of the month were $15,000.
6. The total cost of jobs completed and transferred to finished goods was $30,000.
7. The cost of the goods sold for the month was $40,000.

Required:

(a) Set up T-accounts and post the beginning balances and the transactions for the month of March.

(b) What was the ending balance in the factory payroll account, what does it mean, and where is it shown in the financial statements?

(c) What was the ending balance in the manufacturing overhead account, what does it mean, and where is it shown in the financial statements?

Problem A19-3. The following data pertain to Saunders Manufacturing Company.

Cost of goods sold (includes applied overhead cost) . . . . $	90,000
Net sales	150,000
Stockholders' equity	1,020,000
Net long-lived assets	1,000,000
Selling and administrative expenses	45,000
Actual factory overhead cost.	40,000
Current liabilities	190,000
Current assets	200,000
Applied factory overhead cost.	30,000

Required:

(a) Prepare a balance sheet and an income statement, assuming that the income statement figures above pertain to the month of January and that the balance sheet figures are as of January 31, 19xx.

(b) Prepare an income statement, assuming that the above income statement figures pertain to the year ended December 31, 19xx.

(c) Explain the difference between the income statements in part (a) and part (b).

Problem A19-4. You are given below some incomplete cost data for Pinet Company as of January 31, 19xx:

Materials Inventory		Goods in Process	
Jan. 1 Bal. 20,000		Jan. 1 Bal. 10,000	
60,000		Dir. matl. 35,000	
		Dir. labor 46,000	

Factory Payroll Payable		Finished Goods	
	50,000	Jan. 1 Bal. 35,000	

Factory Overhead Cost		Cost of Goods Sold	
Ind. matl. 10,000		125,000	

In addition to the above data, you find out that the company applies factory overhead at the rate of 80% of direct labor cost, that miscellaneous actual factory overhead costs were $30,000, and that the January 31 ending balance of Goods in Process was $15,000.

Show all computations for:

1. The total cost of the materials issued to production.
2. The cost of the indirect labor utilized.
3. The cost of January 31, 19xx ending materials inventory balance.
4. The total cost of the goods in process transferred to finished good.
5. The cost of the January 31, 19xx ending finished goods inventory balance.
6. The amount by which factory overhead was overapplied or underapplied.

(Hint: Complete the postings of the T-accounts to solve for unknowns.)

Problem A19-5. Tidwell Manufacturing Company uses a job-order cost system. The applied factory overhead rate of 85% of direct labor cost is the same for each job. The incomplete cost data for two jobs are given below:

	Job #450	Job #451
Direct materials	$ 40,000	$?
Direct labor	?	?
Factory overhead applied	?	34,000
Total	$132,500	$90,000

Required:

1. What was the direct labor cost for Job #451?
2. What was the direct materials cost for Job #451?
3. What was the direct labor cost for Job #450?
4. What was the applied factory overhead cost for Job #450?

Problem B19-1. You are given below cost data pertaining to Churchill Manufacturing Company.

Goods in process:
Beginning inventory balance.	$20,000
Direct materials cost	15,000
Direct labor cost	18,000
Applied factory overhead.	16,200
Ending inventory balance	25,000
Indirect material cost	6,000
Indirect labor cost	8,000

Required:

1. Based on the above data, make the cost entries (general journal form) transferring the three cost elements to Goods in Process and from Goods in Process to Finished Goods.

2. Set up T-accounts and post the general journal entries to them. Number the entries in the T-accounts.
3. Assuming that it is based on direct labor cost, what is the applied factory overhead rate? Show your calculations.
4. Make the general journal entry transferring the underapplied or overapplied factory overhead to Cost of Goods Sold.

Problem B19-2. Pichler Company manufactures its products for stock rather than by specific customer orders. Job numbers are assigned to each job lot.

(a) Prepare entries in general journal form for the following transactions that relate to the month of January, assuming no beginning inventories:

1. Materials were purchased on account for $3,000.
2. Three jobs were placed into production:

> Job #609 for 10 units of Model W
> Job #610 for 5 units of Model X
> Job #611 for 20 units of Model Y

3. Materials issued to production were as follows:

Job #609	$400
Job #610	500
Job #611	300
Indirect materials	200

4. Labor utilized in production was as follows:

Job #609	$400
Job #610	750
Job #611	560
Indirect labor	300

5. Factory overhead was applied to production based on direct labor hours used. At the beginning of the year, it was estimated that factory overhead cost would be $500,000 and that direct labor hours would be 100,000. The direct labor hours for January were as follows:

Job #609	100
Job #610	150
Job #611	140

6. Actual miscellaneous factory overhead costs for the month were $800.
7. Jobs #609 and #611 were completed during the month.
8. At the end of the month, cash was paid for the materials purchased and for the labor utilized.
9. At the end of the month, 6 units of Job #609 and 4 units of Job #611 were sold at a 20% markup on cost.

(b) What was the cost of the ending inventory of goods in process as of January 31 (show calculations)?
(c) What was the cost of the ending inventory of finished goods as of January 31 (show calculations)?

Problem B19-3. The manager of Fitch Company presents you with the following inventory data for the year 19+8:

	1/1/+8	12/31/+8
Materials inventory......................	$ 50,000	$ 60,000
Goods in process inventory	100,000	80,000
Finished goods inventory..................	200,000	170,000

Additional cost data are as follows:

Direct labor hours utilized	30,000
Materials purchased	$25,000
Applied factory overhead rate per direct labor hour	2
Factory supplies used	1,000
Factory utility costs	4,000
Direct labor utilized	90,000
Factory depreciation	30,000
Factory insurance for the year	10,000
Indirect labor cost	12,000
Miscellaneous indirect costs	1,000

Required:

(a) Using the above data, you are asked to reconstruct the cost entries (in general journal form) for the year 19+8.

(b) What is the amount of the overhead variance at year end? (Show calculations) Explain what the variance means.

(c) Close the overhead variance to Cost of Goods Sold.

Problem B19-4. The job cost sheets of Weltmer, Inc., for the month of March were as follows:

	Job #960	Job #961	Job #962	Job #963	Job #964	Job #965
Goods in process, March 1, 19xx:						
Direct materials			$ 200	$ 125		
Direct labor			300	240		
Applied factory overhead			195	156		
Finished goods, March 1, 19xx:						
Direct materials	$1,500	$560				
Direct labor	2,000	700				
Applied factory overhead	1,300	455				
Costs utilized in March:						
Direct materials			910	1,100	$3,000	$400
Direct labor			1,200	1,400	3,500	600
Applied factory overhead			780	910	2,275	

Jobs #962, #963, and #964 were completed during March. Based on direct labor cost, applied factory overhead cost was added to the job cost sheets for those jobs completed during March. Actual factory overhead cost at the beginning of March was $3,000 and actual overhead for March was $1,500.

Required:

(a) Prepare a statement of cost of goods manufactured for the month ended March 31, 19xx.

(b) Check the cost-of-goods-manufactured figure by adding together the costs of the jobs completed during March. Show your calculations.

(c) Set up a T-account for manufacturing overhead and enter the actual and applied overhead costs as of March 31, 19xx.

Problem B19-5. You are given below some incomplete cost data for Sterling Corporation as of January 31, 19xx:

Materials Inventory		Goods in Process	
Jan. 1 Bal. 8,000	22,000	Jan. 1 Bal. 11,000	

Factory Payroll Payable		Finished Goods	
	45,000	Jan. 1 Bal. 40,000	
		75,000	

Factory Overhead Cost		Cost of Goods Sold	
Ind. matl. 8,000	25,000		
Ind. labor 12,000			
Misc. 4,000			

In addition, you are told that the January 31 ending balances were as follows: Materials Inventory $9,000, Factory Payroll Payable $15,000, and Finished Goods $32,000.

Show all computations for:

1. The cost of the materials purchased.
2. The cost of the direct materials utilized during January.
3. The amount of cash paid for factory wages.
4. The cost of the direct labor utilized during January.
5. The January 31 ending inventory of goods in process.
6. The cost of goods sold.
7. Factory wages owed at January 31, 19xx.

(Hint: Complete the postings of the T-accounts to solve for unknowns.)

20

Manufacturing Cost Systems–
Process Costing

Introduction. Process cost accounting is characterized by the accumulation of production costs by specific manufacturing operations, or steps, called processes. A manufacturing process generally is associated with a department where the product costs are uniformly applied to each unit of output worked on in that department. Thus process costing is used by firms that mass produce like products by passing each unit through a series of uniform manufacturing processes until it is completed in the last process. For example, a firm's product may be manufactured by passing sequentially through a preparation department (Process #1), then the assembly department (Process #2), and finally the finishing department (Process #3). Industries using process cost accounting systems include petroleum refining, chemicals, meat packing, ore refining, and canneries.

Since process costing is used for the continuous production of mass quantities of like units, where each unit of product receives the same treatment, broad averages are used to determine the unit costs needed for inventory-costing purposes. The direct material, direct labor, and factory overhead costs utilized in production over the fiscal period, divided by the appropriate physical units produced, provide the unit costs necessary to cost the ending goods in process and the goods completed in a particular process. In contrast, a job order system does not use broad averages because many jobs consist of only one or a few units of the same product, and each job uses varying amounts of material, labor, and factory overhead.

Cost flows. In process costing, a goods in process account is set up in the general ledger for each manufacturing process or department. Direct and indirect materials may be issued to all or only some of the processes (debit the appropriate goods in process accounts for those processes in which materials were used, debit Manufacturing Overhead for the indirect materials, and credit Materials Inventory), while the labor services usually are utilized in each of the manufacturing processes (debit each goods in process account, debit Manufacturing Overhead for the indirect labor, and credit Factory Payroll Payable). Factory overhead is applied to each process, based on either an overall or a departmental overhead rate (debit each goods-in-process account and credit Manufacturing Overhead).

The cost flows may be such that the product passes through each process in sequence: Process #1 to Process #2 to Process #3, and so on, until the cost of the finished goods is transferred from the last goods in process account to the finished goods account. Sequential process costing is used by manufacturing firms that produce a product or products that receive uniform processing: chemical products, refined ores, and the like. An illustration of sequential process costing is shown on the next page, assuming that direct materials are used in all three processes.

In other instances the cost flows may be such that two or more products pass sequentially through different groups of processes: product *A* passes through Processes #1 and #2 and product *B* passes through Processes #3 and #4. Or the products may pass through some processes and not through other processes: product *A* passes through Processes #1, #3, and #4 and product *B* passes through Processes #2 and #4.

Subsidiary cost records. Other than the job cost sheet, the basic cost documents used in job order costing are also used in process costing: sellers' invoices for materials purchased, materials ledger cards, materials requisitions, work tickets, factory overhead cost sheets, and sales invoices. In place of the job cost sheet, a production report is used in process costing to summarize the production costs and units of production in each process. A production report is shown on page 465; however, it contains data that have not yet been explained.

Process Cost Flows

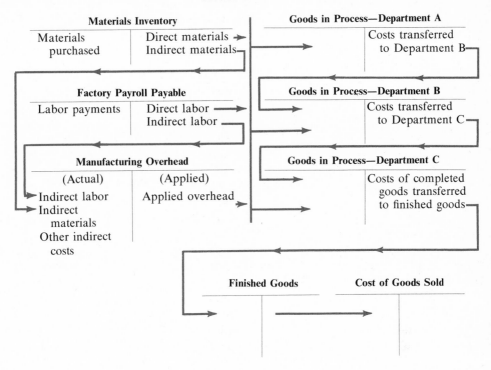

Process Cost Entries

(1) Goods in process—Department A x
    Goods in process—Department B x
    Goods in process—Department C x
    Manufacturing overhead x
        Materials inventory xx

(2) Goods in process—Department A x
    Goods in process—Department B x
    Goods in process—Department C x
    Manufacturing overhead x
        Factory payroll payable xx

(3) Goods in process—Department A x
    Goods in process—Department B x
    Goods in process—Department C x
        Manufacturing overhead xx

(4) Manufacturing overhead xx
        Various accounts xx

(5) Goods in process—Department B x
        Goods in process—Department A x

Process Cost Entries

(6)   Goods in process—Department C x
        Goods in process—Department B x

(7)   Finished goods x
        Goods in process—Department C x

(8)   Cost of goods sold xx
        Finished goods xx

Illustration—No goods in process at beginning or end of period. Assume that, during 19+1 (the first year of its operations), a company produced 8,000 units of commodity *X*, and that there were no goods in process at the beginning or at the end of the year. The unit cost of the product can be determined as follows:

Direct materials	$ 26,000
(This cost is the total of the materials requisitions.)	
Direct labor	34,000
(Since all direct labor costs in the factory were utilized in the manufacture of commodity *X*, the entire direct labor payroll for 19+1 may be regarded as a cost of commodity *X*.)	
Manufacturing overhead	40,800
(Based on an estimated factory overhead rate of 120% of direct labor cost: 120% of $34,000.)	
Total	$100,800

Unit Costs—19+1

Direct materials ($26,000 ÷ 8,000)	$ 3.25
Direct labor ($34,000 ÷ 8,000)	4.25
Manufacturing overhead ($40,800 ÷ 8,000)	5.10
Total cost per unit	$12.60

Assume that, of the 8,000 units of commodity *X* that were fully completed, 2,000 units were sold during the fiscal period. The above cost of $12.60 per unit is used to cost out the ending inventory of finished goods and the cost of goods sold:

Ending inventory of finished goods (6,000 × $12.60)	$ 75,600
Cost of goods sold (2,000 × $12.60)	25,200
Total	$100,800

Equivalent units (production). The preceding illustration was simplified by the exclusion of beginning and ending goods in process inventories. With no in-process inventories, the number of units completed was a correct measure of production work accomplished. Because each unit completed received the same manufacturing treatment, the total manufacturing costs utilized could be averaged over the total units completed. However, given the existence of goods in process inventories, the number of units completed may not be the correct measure of the production work accomplished during a stated period of time. In such a case, one cannot derive per-unit costs by dividing manufacturing costs utilized during the period by the number of units completed during the period.

To illustrate the effect of ending goods in process inventories on the computation of unit costs, assume that the actual cost to manufacture one unit started and fully completed during the fiscal period is $10. Further assume that at the end of the fiscal period there are units in process that are only 25 per cent complete in the manufacturing process. What is the cost per unit of the ending goods in process inventory? A solution would be to weight the cost of a partly completed unit in terms of the cost of a fully completed unit. Thus, if it costs $10 to manufacture a unit started and fully completed during the fiscal period, then logically a unit that is 25 per cent complete could be assigned a cost of $2.50 (25% of $10). This assumes, however, that the cost of a unit started and fully completed during the fiscal period has been previously determined.

In order to calculate the cost of a fully completed unit, manufacturing costs utilized over the fiscal period are divided, not by the number of units completed during the period, but by the number of equivalent units produced by the utilization of the manufacturing costs. Equivalent units are physical units weighted by the proportion of work done on them during the current period. Because units started and completed have 100 per cent of the work done on them during the fiscal period, they automatically are in terms of equivalent units. In contrast, goods in process inventories represent units on which less than 100 per cent of the work was performed during the current period. Hence the percentage of product completion during the current fiscal period is used to weight the units in goods in process inventories and thus convert them to equivalent finished units.

For example, if there are 1,000 units in beginning goods in process inventory that are 40 per cent complete, the equivalent units in the beginning inventory are 400 units (40% of 1,000); 1,000 units 40 per cent complete are equivalent to 400 fully completed units. If these 1,000 uncompleted units on hand at the beginning of the period are completed during the period, the equivalent production is 600 units (60% of 1,000); 40 per cent of the work was done last period and 60 per cent (100% − 40%) of the work was done in the current period. Similarly, if there are 2,000 units of uncompleted product in the ending goods in process inventory that are 20 per cent complete, the equivalent production is 400 units (20% of 2,000); 2,000 units 20 per cent complete are equivalent to 400 fully completed units. Finally, if there are 10,000 units started and fully completed during the current period, the equivalent production is 10,000 units (100% of 10,000). These results are summarized below:

	Physical Flow ×	Percentage of Completion— Current Period =	Equivalent Units
Beginning goods in process completed during period	1,000	60%	600
Units started and completed	10,000	100%	10,000
Ending goods in process inventory . .	2,000	20%	400
	13,000		11,000

Assume that the above equivalent units pertain to $220,000 manufacturing costs utilized over the fiscal period. The problem is to determine how much of the $220,000 is assigned to the ending goods in process and to the completed goods. In order to solve the problem, we calculate the cost of a fully completed unit by dividing the manufacturing costs utilized by the pertinent equivalent production:

$$\frac{\$220,000}{11,000} = \$20 \text{ cost per equivalent finished unit}$$

The cost of an equivalent finished unit is then weighted by the percentage of product completion to derive the unit cost applicable to goods in process inventories.

Using the above data, there were 2,000 units in ending goods in process that were 20 per cent complete. If it costs $20 to complete one unit during the fiscal period, then a unit that is 20 per cent complete should be assigned a cost of $4 (20% of $20), and the cost of the ending goods in process would be $8,000 ($4 × 2,000). Or, the 2,000 units in ending goods in process are equivalent to 400 complete units (20% of 2,000) at $20 each ($20 × 400 = $8,000):

Cost of ending goods in process:

$$\textbf{(20\% of \$20 = \$4)} \times \textbf{2,000}$$

or

$$\textbf{\$20} \times \textbf{400 units} \qquad = \textbf{\$8,000}$$

The same weighting treatment is used to cost the goods completed, assuming that the beginning goods in process will be the first units completed (*fifo*):

Completion costs of *current* period:

From beginning goods in process:

$$\textbf{(60\% of \$20 = \$12)} \times \textbf{1,000}$$

or

$$\textbf{\$20} \times \textbf{600 units} \qquad = \textbf{\$12,000}$$

Started and completed:

$$\textbf{(100\% of \$20 = \$20)} \times \textbf{10,000}$$

or

$$\textbf{\$20} \times \textbf{10,000 units} \qquad = \underline{\textbf{200,000}}$$

$$\underline{\underline{\textbf{\$212,000}}}$$

The sum of the cost of the ending goods in process inventory and the cost to complete the units finished during the period total $220,000:

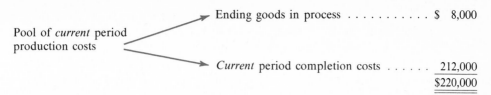

Pool of *current* period production costs	Ending goods in process . . . . $ 8,000
	Current period completion costs 212,000
	$220,000

Illustration—Materials and labor at different stages of completion. Assume that during 19+2 the company completed 9,000 units of commodity X, that there were no beginning goods in process, and that 400 units were in process at the end of the year. The ending goods in process were in the following stages of completion:

Direct materials 75%
Direct labor 50%

The company's costs for the year were:

Direct materials . . . . $ 28,830
Direct labor 37,720
Manufacturing overhead—120% of direct labor cost 45,264
Total $111,814

The costs shown above cannot be divided by 9,000 (the number of units completed) to determine the unit costs of completed goods because some of these costs were utilized in the production associated with ending goods in process. Equivalent-production data must be compiled following the procedure discussed in the preceding section. However, in this illustration involving process cost accounting, it is assumed that the stage of completion for the material content of the in-process inventory differs from the stage of completion for direct labor. For example, in the computation on the following page, 75 per cent of the material requirements have been supplied for the 400 units in the ending in-process inventory, leaving only 25 per cent to be supplied during the next period to complete the material requirements. For the labor element, half of the required work has been performed on the goods in process inventory.

The results of the 19+2 production activity are shown by the following T-accounts:

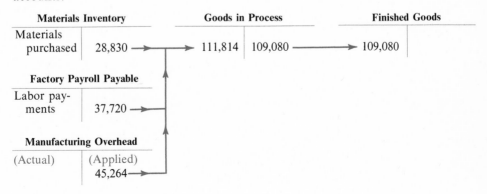

Equivalent Production—19+2

	Physical Flow	Equivalent Units	
		Direct Materials	Direct Labor
Units started and completed in 19+2............	9,000	9,000	9,000
Add goods in process at end of 19+2	400		
Direct material:			
75% of the material requirements have been placed in production, which is equivalent to the material requirements for 75% of 400 finished units, or		300	
Direct labor:			
50% of the total labor costs have been utilized which is equivalent to the labor costs for 50% of 400 units, or			200
Total	9,400	9,300	9,200

Unit Costs—19+2

Direct materials ($28,830 ÷ 9,300) .... $ 3.10
Direct labor ($37,720 ÷ 9,200) 4.10
Manufacturing overhead (120% of $4.10) 4.92

Total cost per unit.................................... $12.12

Distribution of Total Costs—19+2

Finished goods (9,000 × $12.12) $109,080
Ending goods in process, December 31, 19+2:
Direct materials:
(75% of $3.10 = $2.325) × 400 or simply
equivalent units of 300 × $3.10...................... $930

Direct labor:
(50% of $4.10 = $2.05) × 400 or simply
equivalent units of 200 × $4.10...................... 820

Manufacturing overhead:
(120% of $2.05 = $2.46) × 400 or equivalent
units of 200 × $4.92 or simply 120% of $820 984   2,734

Total $111,814

Illustration—Goods in process at beginning and end of period. Continuing with the previous illustration, assume that the costs for 19+3 were as follows:

Direct materials	$ 30,600
Direct labor	40,400
Manufacturing overhead—120% of direct labor cost	48,480
Total	$119,480

The company completed 10,000 units in 19+3. There were 400 units in beginning goods in process for 19+3, which were the ending goods in process for the previous period (19+2). There were 500 units in process at the end of the year, in the following stages of completion:

Direct materials	100%
Direct labor	60%

The computation of the equivalent production for 19+3 is shown below:

		Equivalent Units	
	Physical Flow	Direct Materials	Direct Labor
Units completed during 19+3:			
From beginning goods in process	400		
Direct materials:			
75% of the material requirements were placed in production last period; therefore, 25% placed in production this period to complete the units, which is equivalent to the material requirements for 25% of 400 finished units, or		100	
Direct labor (50% of 400)			200
Started and completed in 19+3	9,600	9,600	9,600
Ending goods in process	500		
Direct materials (100% of 500)		500	
Direct labor (60% of 500)			300
Total	10,500	10,200	10,100

To calculate the unit costs for 19+3, divide the production costs by the appropriate equivalent units:

	Unit cost
Direct materials ($30,600 ÷ 10,200)	$ 3.00
Direct labor ($40,400 ÷ 10,100)	4.00
Manufacturing overhead (120% of $4.00)	4.80
Total cost per unit	$11.80

Given the above unit costs and the equivalent production for beginning and ending goods in process inventories, the production costs for 19+3 are distributed as follows:

```
Completed goods:
  To complete beginning goods in process:
    Direct materials:
      (25% of $3.00 = $.75) × 400 or simply equivalent units
      of 100 × $3.00 . . . . . . . . . . . . . . . . . . . . . . . .    $   300
    Direct labor:
      (50% of $4.00 = $2.00) × 400 or simply equivalent units
      of 200 × $4.00 . . . . . . . . . . . . . . . . . . . . . . .        800
    Manufacturing overhead (120% of $800) . . . . . . . . . .           960   $  2,060
  Goods started and completed in 19+3 (9,600 × $11.80) . . . . . .              113,280
  Ending goods in process, December 31, 19+3:
    Direct materials:
      (100% of $3.00 = $3.00) × 500 or simply equivalent
      units of 500 × $3.00 . . . . . . . . . . . . . . . . . . . . .    $1,500
    Direct labor:
      (60% of $4.00 = $2.40) × 500 or simply equivalent units
      of 300 × $4.00 . . . . . . . . . . . . . . . . . . . . . . .       1,200
    Manufacturing overhead (120% of $1,200) . . . . . . . . . .         1,440    4,140
    Production costs utilized during period . . . . . . . . . . . . . . .      $119,480
```

The above calculations show the total manufacturing costs for 19+3, but they do not show the total cost of the completed goods. The cost of the beginning goods in process for 19+3, $2,734, which is the same as the ending goods in process for 19+2, must be included.

Total Cost of Completed Goods

Beginning goods in process balance	$ 2,734
To complete beginning goods in process	2,060
Goods started and completed in 19+3	113,280
Cost of goods manufactured	$118,074

Using the statement form from Chapter 18 (see page 414), the cost of goods manufactured can be presented as follows:

Direct material cost	$ 30,600
Direct labor cost	40,400
Factory overhead cost	48,480
Production cost utilized during period	$119,480
Add beginning goods in process, December 31, 19+2	2,734
Total production cost	$122,214
Deduct ending goods in process, December 31, 19+3	4,140
Cost of goods manufactured	$118,074

Assuming that the above costs pertain to Department A of a particular company, a production report is shown on the next page summarizing the production costs.

DEPARTMENT A
Production Report
For the Year Ending December 31, 19+3

	Physical Flow	Equivalent Units Direct Materials	Equivalent Units Direct Labor
Units:			
Beginning goods in process	400		
Units started or transferred in	10,100		
Units to be accounted	10,500		
Units completed:			
From beginning goods in process	400	100	200
Started and completed	9,600	9,600	9,600
Total completed	10,000		
Ending goods in process	500	500	300
Units accounted	10,500	10,200	10,100

	Total	Direct Materials	Direct Labor	Applied Overhead	Total Cost per Unit
Costs:					
Beginning goods in process	$ 2,734				
Current period's costs	119,480	$30,600	$40,400	$48,400	
Costs to be accounted	$122,214				
Cost per equivalent unit		$3	$4	$4.80	$11.80
		$\left(\frac{\$30,600}{10,200}\right)$	$\left(\frac{\$40,400}{10,100}\right)$	(120% of $4)	
Ending goods in process	$ 4,140	$1,500	$1,200	$1,440	
		(500 × $3)	(300 × $4)	$\left(\begin{array}{l}120\% \text{ of} \\ \$1,200\end{array}\right)$	
Completed goods:					
Started and completed	$113,280				(9,600 × $11.80)
Beginning goods in process					
balance	2,734				
Complete beginning goods in					
process	2,060	$300	$800	$960	
		(100 × $3)	(200 × $4)	$\left(\begin{array}{l}120\% \text{ of} \\ \$800\end{array}\right)$	
Cost of goods manufactured	$118,074				
Costs accounted	$122,214				

Actual factory overhead. In the preceding illustration an applied factory overhead rate was used because it was assumed that there were seasonal fluctuations in production and in overhead costs. On the other hand, if production is generally uniform and there are only minor seasonal variations in overhead costs, then actual factory overhead can be used in place of applied factory overhead.

Percentage of completion. In order to calculate equivalent units, it is necessary to know the extent of completion of the goods in process. An estimate of the degree of completion can be made by having inspectors, such as production engineers, analyze the manufacturing operations to determine how much work needs to be done to complete the goods in process. However, in some industries where production is uniform, it is assumed that there are no significant goods in process inventories and all production costs are assigned to completed goods. Also, if estimates of the degree of completion are very difficult or very costly to make, the percentage of completion may be based on reasonable assumptions.

Assumptions. The discussion in this chapter about the accounting for a process cost system was based on the following assumptions:

(1) The percentage of completion for any goods in process inventory is assumed to be either determinable or based on reasonable estimates.

(2) Manufacturing costs are assumed to be uniformly utilized throughout production (with the exception of materials in some cases), which means that the percentage of product completion can be used to assign cost to a unit partially completed during the current time period. That is, if the cost of a unit fully completed during the period is $3, and if ending goods in process inventory is one-third complete, then it is assumed that the cost per unit of ending goods in process inventory is $1 ($\frac{1}{3}$ of $3). Based on this assumption, equivalent finished units can be used to derive unit costs necessary for product costing and income determination.

(3) Any beginning goods in process inventory on hand is assumed to be fully completed during the current period of production, i.e., *fifo* (first-in, first-out) inventory costing is assumed.

(4) Applied factory overhead is used in place of actual factory overhead cost, because it is assumed that seasonal fluctuations in production and in overhead costs exist.

(5) The costs associated with spoilage, scrap, addition or loss of unit weight, joint production, and other complicated cost accounting problems are assumed not to exist. Such problems are discussed in cost accounting courses.

ASSIGNMENT
MATERIAL

QUESTIONS

1. The selection of a job order or a process cost system for a particular manufacturing firm depends on its manufacturing technology. What does this statement mean? Explain.

2. What are the differences between the cost flows of a job order system and of a process cost system? Explain.

3. Manufacturing costs that are direct costs under a process cost system may be indirect costs under a job order system, and vice versa. What does this statement mean? Explain.

4. Job order cost systems emphasize total cost, while process cost systems emphasize average cost. What does this statement mean? Explain.

5. What is equivalent production?

6. Why are separate unit costs calculated for materials and labor?

7. In a process cost system, how would service department costs be handled?

8. In a process cost system, there is no need to use applied factory overhead rates. Do you agree with this statement? Explain.

9. The basic report of a job order system is the job cost sheet. What is the basic report of a process cost system and why is it important?

10. In a process cost system, the percentage of completion is used to assign cost to a unit partially completed during the fiscal period. Why is this an assumption? Explain.

SHORT EXERCISES

E20-1. What is wrong with the calculation below? Explain.

Units of beginning goods in process.	5,000
Units started in production	45,000
Total units of production	50,000
Units of ending goods in process.	10,000
Units completed.	40,000
Beginning goods in process cost	$ 40,000
Production cost utilized during period	460,000
Total production cost	$500,000 ÷ 40,000 = $12.50
Ending goods in process cost ($12.50 × 10,000) .	125,000
Cost of goods manufactured.	$375,000

E20-2. Fill in the blanks below:

(a) If 200,000 units were started and completed during the period, they would be equivalent to _____ finished units.

(b) Ending inventory of 4,000 units that is 20 per cent complete during the period is equivalent to _____ finished units.

(c) Beginning inventory of 10,000 units that were 40 per cent complete at the beginning of the period would be equivalent to _____ finished units last period and _____ finished units this period (assuming *fifo*).

(d) If materials are added to production at the end of the production process, then ending goods in process of 10,000 units that are 75 per cent complete as to labor and overhead would be equivalent to _____ finished units with regard to materials and _____ finished units with regard to labor and overhead.

E20-3. You are given the following process cost data:

	Physical Flow	Equivalent Units Materials	Equivalent Units Labor & Overhead
Completed:			
Beginning goods in process	80,000	—	32,000
Started and completed	300,000	300,000	300,000
Ending goods in process	40,000	40,000	24,000
	420,000	340,000	356,000

(a) Were materials added to production at the beginning of the production process, continuously, or at the end of the production process? Explain.

(b) What is the percentage of completion for labor and overhead with regard to beginning goods in process? started and completed? ending goods in process? Make sure you show how the percentages were derived.

(c) How many units were started in production during the period?

E20-4. You are given below the process flows for Sequential Company:

Materials Inventory		
xxx	20,000	

Goods in Process—#1	
8,000	25,000
15,000	
12,000	

Finished Goods	
50,000	40,000

Factory Payroll Payable	
xxx	50,000

Goods in Process—#2	
25,000	60,000
5,000	
25,000	
20,000	

Cost of Goods Sold	
40,000	

Manufacturing Overhead	
xxx	40,000

Goods in Process—#3	
60,000	50,000
7,000	
10,000	
8,000	

(a) In general journal form, make entries to record the above cost flows.

(b) What is the ending inventory for each of the goods in process accounts and for finished goods?

PROBLEMS

Problem A 20-1. Knapper, Inc., manufactures a product in two production processes. The following transactions took place during January, 19+4.

(1) Purchased material on credit for $50,000.

(2) Materials issued to production were as follows: Process #1, $10,000; Process #2, $15,000; factory supplies, $5,000.

(3) Labor utilized was as follows: Process #1, $20,000; Process #2, $18,000; indirect labor, $8,000.

(4) Applied factory overhead for the month was based on 80 per cent of direct labor cost.

(5) Actual factory overhead for the month was as follows: factory depreciation, $4,000; factory insurance, $2,000; factory machinery repairs, $8,000 (paid to a maintenance firm).

(6) Product costing $30,000 was completed in Process #1 and transferred to Process #2.

(7) Product costing $70,000 was completed in Process #2 and transferred to finished goods.

(8) Product costing $65,000 was sold during the month.

Required:

(a) In general journal form, make entries for the January transactions of Knapper, Inc.

(b) Compute the ending inventory for the following accounts (show your work): Goods in Process—#1, Goods in Process—#2, and Finished Goods.

Problem A 20-2. Assume that Buckholz Corporation started (i.e., put into production) 50,000 units of product during the fiscal period. For each of the cases below, calculate the equivalent production for Buckholz Corporation (show your calculations).

1. The number of units fully completed during the period was 50,000; there were no beginning goods in process.

2. Ending goods in process consisted of 10,000 units 25 per cent complete at the end of the period; there were no beginning goods in process.

3. Beginning goods in process consisted of 4,000 units 25 per cent complete at the beginning of the period. Ending goods in process consisted of 8,000 units 75 per cent complete at the end of the period.

4. Beginning goods in process consisted of 2,000 units 40 per cent complete as to labor and overhead and 80 per cent complete as to materials at the beginning of the period. Ending goods in process consisted of 4,000 units 20 per cent complete as to labor and overhead and 60 per cent complete as to materials at the end of the period.

Problem A 20-3. Quirk Manufacturing Company has two manufacturing processes. In Process #1 all of the materials were added at the beginning of the process, while in Process #2 all of the materials were added at the end of the process. The percentage of completion with regard to labor and overhead was as follows:

	Process #1	Process #2
Beginning goods in process	60% complete at beginning of period	30% of work done in the current period to complete
Ending goods in process	45% complete at end of period	50% complete at end of period

Given the physical flows below, calculate the equivalent production for the two processes (show your calculations):

	Process #1	Process #2
Beginning goods in process	100,000	60,000
Started or transferred in	800,000	700,000
Units to be accounted	900,000	760,000
Ending goods in process	200,000	140,000
Completed or transferred out	700,000	620,000
Units accounted	900,000	760,000

(Hint: In calculating the equivalent production for materials, make sure you take into account the time period when the materials were or will be added to production. For example, if all materials were added last period, they would be weighted zero this period.)

Problem A20-4. Heller Manufacturing Company uses a process cost system. The company manufactures one product in one process. The cost data for the year 19+2 are given below:

Goods in process:
Beginning units . . . .   —
Units started   20,000
Ending units (100% complete as to materials and 80% complete as
  to labor and overhead).   8,000
Materials cost $217,000
Labor cost $450,064
Manufacturing overhead cost $225,032

Required:

Prepare a production report for Heller Manufacturing Company as of December 31, 19+2.

Problem A20-5. Farmland Mixers, Inc., opened a new feed plant on March 1. Mixing operations consist of two processes with the following mixing ratios:

Process 1:	Wheat	10 bushels
	Milo	10 "
		20 bushels
Process 2:	Secret mix	5 "
	Feed	25 bushels

There were no beginning inventories of wheat, milo, secret mix, or feed. The two processes had no beginning or ending inventories for the month of March. The month's records indicate the following:

Wheat purchased—100,000 bushels @ $1.20
Milo purchased—100,000 bushels @ $1.60
Secret mix purchased—60,000 bushels @ $2.10
Process #1 direct labor . . . . $ 800
Process #2 direct labor   4,000
Factory overhead (250% of direct labor cost)   12,000
Feed produced—200,000 bushels
Feed sold—175,000 bushels

Required:

(a) Set up T-accounts for the three ingredients, for the two processes, and for the feed inventory, and record the cost flows.

(b) Make up a schedule of all the ending inventories.

(Hint: Use the mixing ratios to determine the inputs.)

Problem B20-1. Knudson Company has a process cost system in which production begins in the preparation process, then moves to the finishing process, and then to finished goods. At the beginning of the year Knudson Company had the following beginning inventory balances: materials, $200,000; preparation process, $21,000; finishing process, $35,000; finished goods, $35,000. The following transactions took place during the year 19+5:

1. Materials issued to production were as follows: preparation process, $80,000; finishing process, $50,000; indirect materials, $20,000.

2. Factory labor utilized was as follows: preparation process, $100,000; finishing process, $150,000; indirect labor, $50,000.

3. Actual factory overhead costs utilized over the year were: factory utilities, $3,000; factory depreciation, $20,000; factory insurance, $10,000; miscellaneous factory costs, $6,000.

4. Because factory overhead costs and production are fairly uniform, the firm does not use applied factory overhead. Thus, actual factory overhead cost was distributed to the processes as follows: preparation process, $60,000; finishing process, $49,000.

5. At year end, there were ending goods in process of $75,000 in the preparation process. The other units were transferred to the finishing process.

6. At year end, there were ending goods in process of $190,000 in the finishing process. The other units were transferred to finished goods.

7. The ending inventory of finished goods was $65,000.

Required:

Set up T-accounts. Post the beginning balances and the above transactions.

Problem B20-2. For each of the cases below, calculate the equivalent production for Harshaw Corporation.

1. The number of units started was 100,000; ending goods in process consisted of 40,000 units that were ⅗ complete; no beginning goods in process.

2. Beginning goods in process consisted of 30,000 units ⅖ complete at the beginning of the period; ending goods in process consisted of 40,000 units ⅕ complete; 80,000 units were completed.

(Continued)

3. Beginning goods in process consisted of 75,000 units in which 80 per cent of the work was done in the current period to complete them; 90,000 units were started; ending goods in process consisted of 25,000 units that were 25 per cent complete.
4. There were 200,000 units started; beginning goods in process consisted of 20,000 units $\frac{4}{5}$ complete as to materials and $\frac{1}{5}$ complete as to labor and overhead at the beginning of the period; ending goods in process consisted of 125,000 units $\frac{3}{5}$ complete as to materials and $\frac{2}{5}$ complete as to labor and overhead.

Problem B20-3. Stettler Company uses a sequential process cost system in which costs flow from Process 1 to Process 2 to Process 3. The following data are provided: Materials *A* and *B* were added in Process 1, material *C* was added in Process 2, and material *D* was added in Process 3. Assume that costs were added continuously, that there were no in-process inventories, and that actual factory overhead cost was 120 per cent of direct labor cost.

Data for August:

Materials used:		Labor utilized:	
A	$2,800	Process 1	$16,000
B	4,400	Process 2	12,000
C	3,600	Process 3	24,000
D	3,200		

Required:

(a) Set up T-accounts for each process and show the cost flows.
(b) Assuming 10,000 units of finished product were produced, what is the unit cost of the product after it leaves each process?
(c) Prepare a production report indicating, for each process, the total and unit costs.

Problem B20-4. You are given below the cost and the quantity data for Lewis Manufacturing Company. Material is added at the beginning of the process, the *fifo* method is used, and completed goods are transferred to finished goods.

Beginning goods in process inventory, April 1, 19xx:
  2,000 units, 50% completed:
    Materials . . . . $ 4,000
    Labor and factory overhead 6,000
  Costs during April:
    Materials, 9,000 units 18,000
    Labor and factory overhead 61,880
  Ending goods in process inventory, April 30, 19xx—800 units, 40% completed.

Required:

(a) How many units were completed? Show all calculations.
(b) What was the total cost of the goods completed? Show all calculations.
(c) What was the cost of the ending goods in process inventory? Show all calculations.
(d) What was the *average* cost per finished unit? (Hint: Don't forget to include the $10,000 from beginning goods in process.)

Problem B20-5. The equivalent production and the manufacturing costs for Kirschman Company for the year ended December 31, 19+1, are presented below:

	Physical Flow	Equivalent Units Materials	Equivalent Units Labor
Ending goods in process	50,000	40,000	30,000
Completed goods:			
Beginning goods in process	10,000	2,000	4,000
Started and completed	70,000	70,000	70,000
	130,000	112,000	104,000

Beginning goods in process cost . . . . $ 80,000
Materials cost 688,000
Labor cost 686,400
Factory overhead cost—80% of direct labor cost.

Required (show all calculations):

(a) The unit costs of manufacturing for 19+1.
(b) The cost of the ending goods in process and the completion costs for 19+1.
(c) The total cost of the completed goods.

21

Target Costs

Historical costs. It is important to remember that the cost data accumulated and presented by the accounting methods described in the preceding chapters are historical; that is, the cost data are based on past transactions. Carefully compiled and promptly available historical cost data are needed and useful, but there are limitations to the usefulness of historical information, particularly from the point of view of management. Some of the limitations inherent in historical cost information are noted in the following observations:

> Historical information provides an inadequate basis for the measurement of efficiency. It is true that some impressions about efficiency can be obtained through historical comparisons; for example, unit costs for the month just ended can be compared with unit costs data for the same month last year. But how is it determined whether operations of the same month last year— the basis used for comparison—were efficient? If there have been changes in wage rates, material prices, or the volume of production—to mention just a few of the things that can change—the difference in unit costs is not a reliable indication even for deciding whether recent operations have been more or less efficient. In short, what conclusions about efficiency can be reached from the fact that the unit cost of a given product or operations is $2 above last year?

In some industries, prices must be announced for the finished product before production is started. This is typical for businesses making annual model changes. If there is some relationship between costs and selling prices, the costs that are most relevant are not historical costs.

Standard costs. A system whereby predetermined costs are developed and used as a basis for comparison with actual costs is believed to overcome some of the limitations of historical costs. Predetermined costs, usually referred to as standard costs, are computed before production occurs but only after necessary study and analysis have provided the accountant with the basis for a conclusion about what the costs should be.

The degree of difficulty in compiling standard costs is influenced by many factors, such as the size of the business, the complexity of the manufacturing process, and the stability of business conditions. The build-up of predetermined unit costs involves a detailed analysis of the material specifications. Information about the kinds, grades, quantities, and expected prices of the materials is developed. Each step in the manufacturing process is studied to determine the class and amount of direct labor required. Wage rates are then considered. The final cost segment to be estimated is manufacturing overhead. Here the accountant often faces a great challenge to his ingenuity. It is possible, however, with study and experience, to arrive at predetermined costs for factory overhead that have considerable validity.

The predetermined costs thus developed are short-run cost targets. They are the "should be" costs that represent short-run goals, thus providing an excellent basis for efficiency measurements.

Even though great care is used in computing predetermined costs, it is likely that the actual costs will deviate from the standard. Such deviations, or differences, are referred to as *variances*. When actual costs exceed standard costs, the variance is unfavorable. A favorable variance arises when the actual costs are below standard costs. Variances are signals, alerting management to seek out the reasons for the variances and, when necessary, to initiate remedial action. In this way management can improve its decision making by learning how successful its past decisions have been. Moreover, the feedback of actual financial data for comparison with standards aids management in determining whether the firm is meeting top management's objectives.

Although variances are signals for management action, the *consistent absence* of variances may also be a signal to management. For example, zero variances may be the result of cost manipulation.

Finally, it must be stressed that unless standards are continually revised they will be no more effective than a mere comparison of this year's historical costs with past years' historical costs. In other words, the use of a standard cost system assumes up-to-date standards.

Basic features of a standard cost system. There are two basic features of a standard cost system:

(1) The inventory account balances in the materials inventory, goods in

process, and finished goods accounts are normally stated at standard (predetermined) prices.

(2) The cost transfers from the finished goods account to the cost of goods sold account are stated at standard cost.

The following example will indicate the nature of variances and the distinctive features of the recording procedure when cost standards have been established. Data:

Standard price per unit of acquired materials	$	1
Actual cost of acquired materials—400 units @ $.98		392

Accounting entry:

Materials inventory (400 × $1)	400	
Materials price variance		8
Accounts payable		392

The example shows that purchases are charged to the materials inventory account at standard price. Any price variation is isolated in a variance account when the purchase is recorded. By recording the material price variance at the time of purchase, control is facilitated because any corrective action can be taken immediately. This also leads to bookkeeping economy, since the inventory clerk needs only to keep track of quantities of materials. He need not keep track of actual material prices, for the price variances are isolated in the materials price variance accounts and he knows the standard prices used to cost out the materials.

A quantity variance may exist if the quantity of materials used in the production of finished goods differs from the predetermined standard quantity.

The several variances that may arise and the factors that determine the dollar amount of each variance are noted below.

Direct materials:

Price variance = **Difference between the actual material price paid and the standard material price per unit multiplied by the actual quantity of materials *purchased*.**

Quantity variance = **Difference between the actual material quantity *used* (not purchased) in production and the standard material quantity multiplied by the standard material price per unit.**

Direct labor:

Rate variance = **Difference between the actual labor rate paid and the standard labor rate per hour multiplied by the *actual* labor hours used in production.**

Efficiency (time) variance = **Difference between the actual labor hours used in production and the standard labor hours multiplied by the *standard* wage rate per hour.**

Manufacturing overhead:
  Total factory overhead
      variance   = **Difference between the actual factory overhead and the stand-
                    ard factory overhead.**

In the recording of variances, debit variances are unfavorable and credit vari-
ances are favorable.

Illustration. Following is a simple illustration of the operation of a standard cost system.
State Company manufactures one product. The following standard unit costs have
been established:

Standard Cost Card

Direct materials—2 units at $1 . . . . $ 2
Direct labor—1 hour at $3   3
Manufacturing overhead—applied per direct labor hour or 1 hour at $5.   5
  Standard cost per finished unit. $10

Data for the period

Goods in process—no beginning or ending inventories . . . . .   -0-
Units manufactured   190
Units sold   185
Direct materials:
  Actual purchase price per unit—$.98.
  Actual quantity purchased   400
  Actual quantity used in production   390
  Standard quantity for 190 units manufactured   380
    (Standard cost card shows that it should take 2 units of
    material to produce 1 unit of finished product; therefore,
    the standard quantity is 190 × 2.)

Direct labor:
  Actual hourly labor rate paid—$3.05.
  Actual labor hours worked   180
  Standard labor hours for 190 units manufactured   190
    (Standard cost card shows that it should take 1 hour of
    labor to produce 1 unit of product; therefore, standard
    labor hours are 190 × 1.)

Manufacturing overhead:
  Actual factory overhead cost. $1,000
  Applied overhead (at standard) for 190 units manufactured
    ($5 per hour × 190 standard hours)   950

Cost entries:

(1) Materials inventory ($1 × 400)   400
       Materials price variance [($.98 − $1) × 400]   8
       Accounts payable ($.98 × 400)   392

(2) Goods in process   390
       Materials inventory ($1 × 390)   390

(3) Goods in process ($3 × 180)   540
         Labor rate variance [($3.05 − 3.00) × 180] . . . .
         Factory payroll payable ($3.05 × 180)   549

(4) Manufacturing overhead (Actual costs)   1,000
         Various accounts   1,000

(5) Goods in process   950
         Manufacturing overhead ($5 × 190 hours)   950

(6) Finished goods ($10 × 190)   1,900
         Materials quantity variance [$1 × (390 − 380)]   10
         Labor efficiency variance [$3 × (180 − 190)]   30
         Goods in process ($390 + $540 + $950)   1,880

(7) Manufacturing overhead variance ($1,000 − $950)   50
         Manufacturing overhead   50

(8) Cost of goods sold   1,850
         Finished goods ($10 × 185)   1,850

The cost flows are summarized in the illustration on the next page.

Comments about illustration. To compute standard quantities, actual equivalent production is multiplied by the standard (predetermined) inputs per unit of finished output. The standard cost card indicates the inputs of material and labor that *should* be used to produce one unit of finished product; hence, to compute standard quantities, actual output is converted into the inputs that should have been utilized to produce that actual output. These standard quantities can be directly compared with the quantities of actual input to derive quantity variances. For example, the standard cost card in the illustration indicates that it should take two units of material and one hour of labor per unit of finished output. With actual output of 190 units, the standard quantity of materials is 380 units (2 × 190) and the standard labor hours are 190 (1 × 190).

The illustration also points out that the materials quantity variance and the labor efficiency variance are isolated when the product is transferred from goods in process to finished goods. This approach assumes that these two variances cannot be reasonably determined until the goods are completed or that management prefers to have them isolated at that time.

For purposes of managerial control, it is desirable to isolate the two variances as soon as possible. Thus, where it is possible, management should have the materials quantity variance and labor efficiency variance isolated at the time any excess material and labor are added to goods in process (or at least isolated before the production is completed). For example, the inventory clerk may issue materials based on standard requirements for a job, and any additional materials will be issued only if the production foreman signs excess materials requisitions, which pinpoint the quantity variances. Such excess quantities of materials are charged at standard prices to the materials quantity variance account. An illustration of a standard cost system in which the materials quantity variance and the labor efficiency variance are isolated when the costs are transferred to goods in process is presented on page 480. Following this plan, goods in process costs are based on both standard prices and quantities of materials, and on both standard rates and hours for labor.

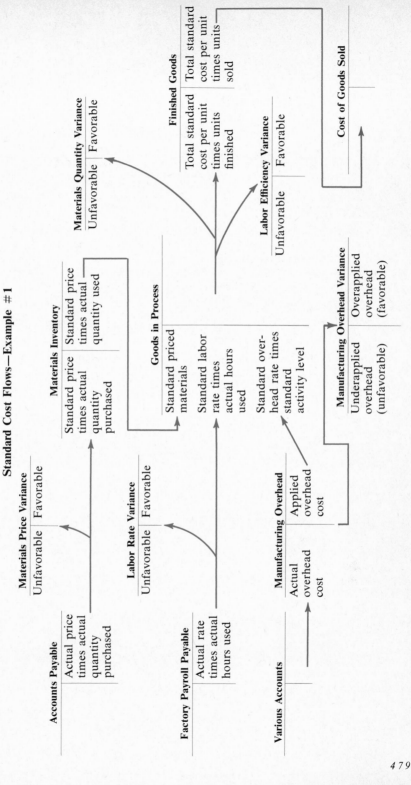

Standard Cost Flows—Example #1

Accounts Payable

Actual price times actual quantity purchased

Materials Price Variance

Unfavorable	Favorable

Materials Inventory

Standard price times actual quantity purchased	Standard price times actual quantity used

Materials Quantity Variance

Unfavorable	Favorable

Factory Payroll Payable

Actual rate times actual hours used

Labor Rate Variance

Unfavorable	Favorable

Goods in Process

Standard priced materials

Standard labor rate times actual hours used

Standard overhead rate times standard activity level

Finished Goods

Total standard cost per unit times units finished	Total standard cost per unit times units sold

Labor Efficiency Variance

Unfavorable	Favorable

Various Accounts

Manufacturing Overhead

Actual overhead cost	Applied overhead cost

Manufacturing Overhead Variance

Underapplied overhead (unfavorable)	Overapplied overhead (favorable)

Cost of Goods Sold

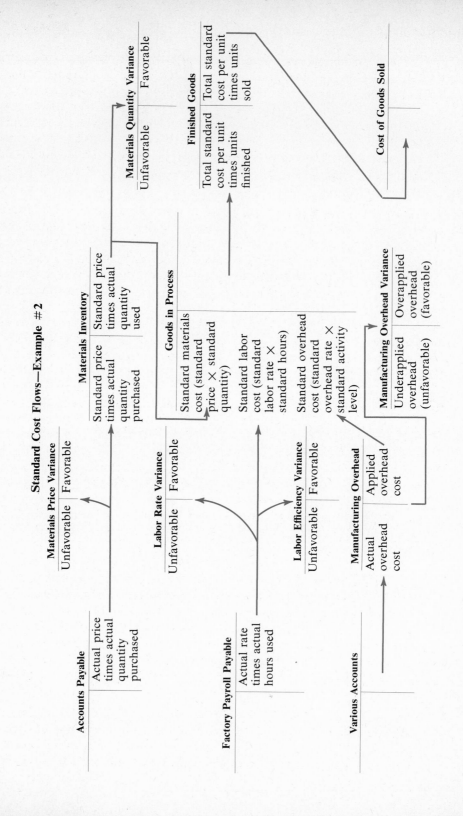

Standard Cost Flows—Example #2

Finally, the preceding illustration (Example #2) also points out that to calculate applied factory overhead under standard costing, the *standard* activity level (e.g., standard direct labor hours or cost) is multiplied by the standard factory overhead rate. In previous chapters, the applied factory overhead was the *actual* activity level (e.g., actual direct labor hours or cost) times the standard factory overhead rate. However, the actual activity level may reflect inefficiencies that should not be included in applied factory overhead because, at year end, applied overhead serves as the yardstick for determining, and subsequently analyzing, the total factory overhead variance.

Variance analysis. With the standard cost system isolating the discrepancies between planned and actual costs, management has an excellent opportunity through the use of variance data to seek out the causes for differences between expectation and achievement. However, interpreting variances is not a simple matter. If variances are misinterpreted by management and improper actions are taken, then the standard cost system, a potentially effective managerial device, can in fact prove to be a harmful tool.

There are certain kinds of background information about any standard cost system that, if known, will improve the chances for a correct interpretation of variances. For instance, a causal relationship exists between variances and the level at which standards are set. Standards may be set at "ideal" levels, the attainment of which cannot be expected. Or, standards may be set at levels thought to be attainable. There is no rule or requirement that forces management to establish standards at any particular level. Practices in this regard vary among companies. The point is, variances from ideal standards carry different implications from those carried by variances from attainable standards.

It should also be recognized that some variances may be an indication merely that external conditions have changed since the standards were adopted. For instance, suppliers may have announced new price schedules, or property tax rates may have changed. Under such circumstances it would be desirable to revise the standards to avoid the showing of variances resulting from conditions beyond the control of management or employees.

The standard-setting procedure followed by a company may also be pertinent. If the employees who are in a position to incur costs are excluded from the standard-setting process, they may be inclined to work against the system. On the other hand, if they have participated in the setting of standards and believe that the goals are attainable, the opportunity for management to use variance data as a measurement of performance and to stimulate efficiency may be greatly improved.

The analysis of specific variances should be undertaken for the purpose of locating the reasons for the off-standard results. The reasons set forth in the following paragraphs are illustrative.

MATERIAL VARIANCES: Material price variances may be the fault of the purchasing department. Price variances may be attributable to the ordering of uneconomical quantities of material or the ordering of the wrong quality of material. Improper attention to the location of the supplier may have resulted in above-standard transportation charges. But it is unwise to assume that price variances are always attributable to the actions of the purchasing department. Poor scheduling by the production department may have put such pressure on the purchasing department that it was forced to release purchase orders on unfavorable terms in order to avoid any delay of the manufacturing activities. It is also unwise to assume that a favorable price variance is to the credit of some employee or department. It may merely indicate that market prices have declined.

Material quantity variances may be traceable to the level of efficiency and skill of the working force, to spoilage from improper handling and storage, or to defective materials. Although quantity variances generally are more controllable than price variances, quantity variances may be difficult to analyze if there are several contributing causes. It may be noted at this point that offsetting variances, some favorable and some unfavorable, may cause the net variance to be insignificant and thus possibly lead management to the improper conclusion that no substandard performance exists.

LABOR VARIANCES: Labor variances may be attributable to changes in wage rates, to the wrong category of workers assigned to a task, to improper hiring practices, and to inadequate training programs. An especially difficult analytical problem may arise as a result of the factory working under overtime conditions. The effectiveness of personnel policies can also have a considerable effect on labor variances.

FACTORY OVERHEAD VARIANCES: In the previous chapter it was pointed out that, during the fiscal period, factory overhead variances may occur because of seasonal fluctuations in production and individual factory overhead costs. However, by the end of the fiscal period, the seasonal variations should tend to average out so that the total factory overhead variance is small or zero, i.e., applied and actual factory overhead should approximate one another. Thus any interim-period factory overhead variance is shown on the balance sheet and any year end factory overhead variance generally is written off, for convenience, to Cost of Goods Sold.

On the other hand, factory overhead variances can arise from other than seasonal factors. For example, actual and standard applied factory overhead costs may differ because of unexpected price changes in individual overhead items, poor cost estimates of individual overhead items, differences between the actual and standard activity level used in applying factory overhead cost to goods in process, and differences between planned and actual production levels.

For purposes of analysis, the total factory overhead variance can be broken down into component parts. Such procedures are discussed in cost accounting courses.

Management by exception. It should be apparent from the above paragraphs that not all variances are signals for action. To treat all so-called unfavorable variances as sufficient reason for some penalty action would, in many cases, be quite shortsighted on the part of management. Thus management is concerned about the unusual and important financial variations from the expected; management is concerned about such exceptions because its time is limited and valuable and should not be spent analyzing all variances. Consequently, management attempts to analyze exceptional variations in order to identify the causes and make remedial decisions affecting the future.

Management by exception necessitates the establishment of criteria to determine whether variances are exceptional enough to warrant analysis by management. For example, the proportion of the dollar amount of a variance to the total standard cost may be used as a criterion. That is, based on past and expected operations, management may ignore all variances of less than 10 per cent as immaterial and random; variances of 10 per cent or more would be exceptions requiring management analysis.

In general, management is more concerned about efficiency variances (material quantity and labor efficiency variances) than about price variances, because the former are more controllable by management. For instance, unusual material price increases generally are not within the control of the purchasing agent.

Management should be concerned not only about exceptional unfavorable variances but also about unusual favorable variances. Analysis may indicate that standards are out of date or that certain types of management policies that led to the favorable variances should be continued in the future.

Disposition of variances. When a standard cost system is in use and variances exist, the inventory account balances at the end of an accounting period will not be stated at actual costs. Thus, in theory, the variances should be prorated to the inventory cost accounts and to Cost of Goods Sold in order to reflect actual costs. However, the usual practice is to write off the variances at the end of the fiscal period to expense, e.g., Cost of Goods Sold. The practice of writing off variances, for convenience, to Cost of Goods Sold is acceptable so long as the standards are up to date and are not based on unattainable (ideal) performance.

Using the State Company data from the previous illustration, the variances are closed to Cost of Goods Sold as follows:

Cost of goods sold	31	
Labor efficiency variance	30	
Materials price variance	8	
Labor rate variance		9
Materials quantity variance		10
Manufacturing overhead variance		50

The labor efficiency and materials price variances are favorable; to close them, therefore, the two variance accounts are debited as shown. Because labor rate and materials quantity variances are unfavorable, they are closed by credits. The manufacturing overhead variance represents underapplied factory overhead cost of $50 ($1,000 actual minus $950 applied), which is an unfavorable debit variance. The $50 variance is closed by a debit to Cost of Goods Sold and a credit to Manufacturing Overhead Variance. The standard cost of goods sold of $1,850 plus the $31 net adjustment for the closing of all the variances results in a $1,881 ending balance for Cost of Goods Sold.

ASSIGNMENT

MATERIAL

QUESTIONS

1. What are the arguments in favor of using standard costs over historical costs? Discuss.

2. Do you think standard costs should be set at *ideal* levels of attainment? Discuss.

3. Why is the difference between actual and standard materials (or labor) costs segmented into *two* variances? Discuss.

4. Some accountants record the materials price at time of purchase, while other accountants record the variance when materials are issued to production. What are the advantages and disadvantages of these two different approaches to the recording of the materials price variance? Discuss.

5. Some accountants record the materials quantity and the labor efficiency variances when the goods are completed, while other accountants record the two variances when materials and labor are put into production. What are the advantages and disadvantages of the two different approaches? Discuss.

6. How is the concept of management by exception related to a standard cost system? Discuss.

7. A materials price variance may be the responsibility of the sales manager or the production manager instead of the purchasing manager. What does this statement mean? Discuss.

8. What is done with the cost variances at the end of the fiscal period? Discuss.

9. The standard quantity of materials (or standard labor hours) is based on equivalent production. What does this statement mean? Discuss.

10. The materials price variance and the labor rate variance formulas are not mathematically sound. In contrast, the formulas for the materials quantity variance and the labor efficiency variance are mathematically sound. What do these statements mean? Discuss. (Hint: In the variance formulas, mathematically only the variable under analysis should vary and the other variable should be held constant.)

SHORT EXERCISES

E21-1. What is wrong with the variance analysis of materials shown below?

Actual cost of materials ($4 actual price × 1,000 lbs. of materials issued to production) $4,000

Standard cost of materials ($3 standard price × 1,100 standard lbs. of materials issued to production).   3,300

Unfavorable materials variance . . . . $ 700

E21-2. The standard cost card for Target Company is presented below:

Standard Cost Card

Direct materials—4 lbs. @ $3 . . . . $12

Direct labor—2 hours @ $5   10

Factory overhead—$4 per direct labor hour   8

Standard cost per finished unit. $30

During the fiscal period, 10,000 units of product were manufactured in which 42,000 actual pounds of materials and 19,000 actual direct labor hours were used.

(a) How was the $8 standard factory overhead cost per unit calculated? Show all of your work.

(b) What was the standard quantity of materials used in production?

(c) What was the standard cost of materials used in production?

(d) What were the standard labor hours used in production?

(e) What was the standard cost of labor used in production?

(f) What was the materials quantity variance? Was it favorable or unfavorable?

(g) What was the labor efficiency variance? Was it favorable or unfavorable?

E21-3. Standard Company uses a standard cost system in accounting for its manufacturing operations. Given the company's cost flows for the fiscal period, as shown below, make general journal entries recording the manufacturing costs.

Accounts Payable		Materials Price Variance		Materials Inventory	
xxx	20,000	500		19,500	12,000

Materials Quantity Variance		Factory Payroll Payable		Labor Rate Variance	
	400	xxx	30,000		1,000

Goods in Process		Labor Efficiency Variance		Various Accounts	
12,000	48,400	200		xxx	21,000
31,000					
20,200					

Factory Overhead		Factory Overhead Variance		Finished Goods	
21,000	20,200	800		48,600	25,000
	800				

Cost of Goods Sold	
25,000	

E21-4. Using the cost flow data of Standard Company (see E21-3 above), make one compound general journal entry closing out the variance accounts to Cost of Goods Sold. What is the cost of goods sold figure after the closing of the variance accounts?

PROBLEMS

Problem A 21-1. Bentz Company uses a standard cost system. The company's cost data for the month of July were as follows:

Pounds of steel purchased	18,000
Pounds of steel used in production	15,500
Standard pounds required for production	16,000
Purchase price per pound of steel—$2.05	
Standard price per pound of steel—$2.00	

Required:

(a) Assuming that Bentz Company separates the materials price variance at time of purchase and separates the materials quantity variance by taking it out of Goods in Process, make general journal entries to record the purchase of the materials, the issuance of materials to production, and the separation of the materials quantity variance.

(b) Assuming that Bentz Company maintains its goods in process account at standard cost (standard price × standard quantity), make general journal entries to record the purchase of materials and the issuance of materials to production.

(c) Discuss the differences between the two standard cost systems used in (a) and in (b).

Problem A 21-2. The management of Dakin Corporation, a manufacturing concern, has requested an explanation of the manufacturing variances that occurred during the month of April. The following data are supplied:

Actual manufacturing overhead—$1,100
Standard direct labor rate per hour—$3.15
Actual material quantity purchased and used—600
Standard applied overhead rate per standard direct hour—$5
Standard direct labor hours used in production—200
Actual material purchase price—$2.50
Actual direct labor hours used in production—210
Standard materials price—$2.25
Actual direct labor rate per hour—$3
Standard quantity of material used in production—580

Required:

(a) Prepare a schedule of the factory variances using the format given below.

Variance Description	Calculations	Variance Amount	
		Unfavorable	Favorable

(b) Discuss two possible causes for *each* favorable or unfavorable variance.

Problem A 21-3. Blocker, Inc., uses a standard cost system. The company's cost data for the month of May were as follows:

```
Actual direct labor hours used  . . . . . . . . . . . . . . . . . . . . . . . . . .  2,705
Standard direct labor hours used . . . . . . . . . . . . . . . . . . . . . . .  2,715
Actual direct labor cost—$8,520.75
Actual factory overhead cost—$15,900
Standard direct labor hour rate—$3
Factory overhead rate per standard direct labor hour—$6
```

Required:

(a) Assuming that Blocker, Inc., does *not* maintain its Goods in Process at standard cost (standard rate × standard hours), make general journal entries to record the labor cost utilized in production, the labor efficiency variance, and the manufacturing overhead variance.

(b) Assuming that Blocker, Inc., *does* maintain its Goods in Process at standard cost (standard rate × standard hours), make general journal entries to record the labor cost utilized in production and the manufacturing overhead variances.

(c) Using only the given data, explain why each of the three variances is favorable or unfavorable.

Problem A21-4. Newton Manufacturing Company has a standard cost system. The management asks you to provide a schedule showing the variance computations, given the data below.

```
Actual factory overhead cost . . . . . . . . . . . . . . . . . .  $1,100.00
Actual quantity of material issued to production—200
Standard direct labor hours used in production—100
Materials price variance . . . . . . . . . . . . . . . . . . . . . . . . .  24.00 favorable
Labor efficiency variance . . . . . . . . . . . . . . . . . . . . . . . .  45.00 unfavorable
Actual quantity of materials purchased—400
Factory overhead variance . . . . . . . . . . . . . . . . . . . . . . .  50.00 favorable
Actual labor hours used in production—115
Materials quantity variance  . . . . . . . . . . . . . . . . . . . . . .  30.00 unfavorable
Labor rate variance  . . . . . . . . . . . . . . . . . . . . . . . . . . . . .  23.00 unfavorable
Standard price of materials  . . . . . . . . . . . . . . . . . . . . . .  1.50
```

You soon discover that you are missing some data; hence, before you can make up the variance schedule, you have to solve for the missing data.

Required:

(a) From the above data only, find the average actual price paid for materials. Show all calculations.

(b) What was the standard quantity of materials issued to production?

(c) What was the standard labor rate per direct labor hour?

(d) What was the actual labor rate per direct labor hour?

(e) What was the standard factory overhead rate?

(Hint: Use the variance formulas and solve for unknowns.)

Problem A21-5. Trillich, Inc., manufactures a product with the brand name of "Trills." The company uses a standard-cost system.

Standard Cost per Unit of Trills

```
Materials:   A—2 pounds @ $2 . . . . . . . . . . . . . . . . . . . . . . . . . . .  $ 4
             B—3 units @ $4  . . . . . . . . . . . . . . . . . . . . . . . . . . .    12
Labor . . . . . .  2 hours @ $5 . . . . . . . . . . . . . . . . . . . . . . . . .    10
Manufacturing overhead . . . . . . . . . . . . . . . . . . . . . . . . . . . . .     6
                                                                                   ———
                                                                                   $32
```

Material *A* was added at the beginning and material *B* was added at the end of the manufacturing process. The beginning goods in process consisted of 800 units that were 50 per cent complete as to labor and factory overhead. The ending goods in process of 400 units were 25 per cent complete as to labor and overhead. There were 18,000 units of Trills started and completed during the fiscal period.

Twenty tons of material *A* were purchased at a cost of $92,000, and 37,000 pounds were used in production. Material *B* was purchased for $237,000, or $3.95 per unit, and 56,000 units were used in production. Actual labor and factory overhead costs were $180,320 and $112,300, respectively. Actual labor hours used in production were 36,800.

Required:

(a) Compute materials variances, labor variances, and the total factory overhead variance. (Hint: Use equivalent units to calculate standard quantities and hours.)
(b) Assuming that the materials quantity variance and the labor efficiency variance are not recorded until finished goods are recorded, set up T-accounts and trace the cost flows.

Problem B21-1. Krogh, Inc., provides you with financial data on three types of materials it used in production during March.

Material E:
 Purchase price per gallon—32.9¢
 Standard price per gallon—33.5¢
 Gallons purchased and used—2,200
 Standard gallons used in production—2,000

Material F:
 Pounds purchased at $1.30—7,500
 Standard pounds used in production—7,400
 Actual pounds used in production—7,000
 Standard price per pound—$1.26

Material G:
 Amount paid for 20 tons—$750
 Standard price per ton—$40
 Actual tons used at standard price—$600
 Standard pounds used in production—28,000

Required:

(a) Calculate the materials price and quantity variances for each of the three types of materials. Show all calculations.
(b) Using only the given data, discuss why the variances were favorable or unfavorable for material E.
(c) Make the general journal entries recording the purchase of materials and the separation of the materials quantity variance from goods in process for material G.

Problem B21-2. The management of L'Ecuyer Manufacturing Company has requested an explanation of the manufacturing variances that occurred during the month of February. The following data are supplied:

Standard labor hours used in production—305
Standard factory overhead rate per standard labor hour—$8.20
Standard quantity of material used in production—2,215
Actual manufacturing overhead cost—$2,550
Actual labor hours used in production—312
Standard materials price—$12.40
Standard labor rate per hour—$3.10
Actual materials price—$12.50
Actual labor rate per hour—$3.05
Actual quantity of materials purchased and used—2,200

Required:

(a) Prepare a schedule of the factory variances using the format given below.

Variance Description	Calculations	Variance Amount	
		Unfavorable	Favorable

(b) Discuss two possible causes for *each* favorable or unfavorable variance.

Problem B21-3. Dennis Corporation uses a standard cost system. Manufacturing overhead is applied to production based on standard direct labor hours. You are given the following data:

Actual direct labor cost for 8,550 hours	$20,349.00
Actual factory overhead cost.	7,468.00
Standard direct labor rate per hour	2.40
Standard direct labor hours used—8,600	
Standard factory overhead rate	.85

Required:

(a) Assuming that Dennis Corporation separates the labor rate variance when recording labor cost in Goods in Process and separates the labor efficiency variance by taking it out of Goods in Process, make general journal entries to record the labor cost utilized in production, the labor efficiency variance, and the manufacturing overhead variance.

(b) Assuming that Dennis Corporation maintains its goods in process account at standard cost (standard rate × standard hours), make general journal entries to record the labor cost utilized in production and the manufacturing overhead variance.

(c) Discuss the differences between the two standard cost systems used in (a) and (b).

Problem B21-4. The data below pertain to the Reilly Company for the year 19xx. The company uses a standard-cost system in its production of one product.

Standard Cost Card

Materials: *A*—2 pounds @ $3		$ 6.00
B—1 unit @ $2		2.00
Labor. . . . . . . .1 hour @ $3.50		3.50
Manufacturing overhead		1.50
		$13.00

19xx data:

> Goods in process—no beginning or ending inventories
> Units manufactured—75,000
> Units sold @ $20—72,500
> Pounds of material *A* purchased @ $3.02—160,000
> Units of material *B* purchased @ $1.99—78,000
> Actual pounds of material *A* used in production—152,000
> Actual units of material *B* used in production—76,000
> Actual direct labor costs of production—$260,000
> Actual direct labor hours used in production—80,000
> Manufacturing overhead cost—$118,000
> All variances closed to Cost of Goods Sold at year end

Required:

> (a) General journal entries for the year 19xx. Assume that the company does *not* maintain its goods in process account at standard cost (standard price × standard quantity).
>
> (b) Year-end general journal entries to dispose of all variances.

Problem B21-5. The Handigadget Manufacturing Company produces Handigadgets. The standards for 100 units of product are as follows:

<u>Standard Cost per 100 Handigadgets</u>

Materials . . . . 5 lbs. sheet aluminum @ $2.80	$14.00
Labor. . . . . 2 hours of direct labor @ $3	6.00
Factory overhead . . . . . . 150% of standard direct labor cost	9.00
Total.	$29.00

Material is added at the beginning of the manufacturing process. During May, 4,500 pounds of sheet aluminum were purchased at a cost of $12,510 and 4,000 pounds were issued to production. During the month, 1,620 direct labor hours were worked at an average wage of $3.02 per hour. Actual manufacturing overhead for May was $7,131.

The $193.50 beginning goods in process (May 1) consisted of 900 Handigadgets, 50 per cent complete with regard to labor and factory overhead. During May, 80,000 Handigadgets were completed. As of May 31, ending goods in process consisted of 700 Handigadgets that were 50 per cent complete as to labor and factory overhead.

Required:

> (a) Compute materials variances, labor variances, and the total factory overhead variance. (Hint: Use equivalent units to calculate standard pounds and hours.)
>
> (b) Assuming that the materials quantity variance and the labor efficiency variance are not recorded until finished goods are recorded, set up T-accounts and trace the cost flows.

22

Responsibility Accounting

Introduction. Except in the chapter on standard costs, we have been concerned up to this point with the accumulation of costs for purposes of costing products and determining net income for the preparation of financial statements for investors, creditors, and others outside the firm. However, another important part of accounting is the control of internal operations. Control is defined as the determination of whether business operations are being carried out according to management plans. For example, the comparison of actual and standard costs is a control device.

An important aspect of controlling business operations is the assignment of responsibility to individuals. The responsibility for material price variances rests with the purchasing agent. The responsibility for material quantity variances is assigned to the production manager. Each one of these individuals has the obligation, and is answerable to higher management, to hold costs at or below a specified level. Thus, to have particular persons responsible for certain costs makes the control of those costs easier.

Responsibility accounting is the segmentation of the business firm into supervisory areas (responsibility centers) in which only those costs, expenses, or revenues and expenses that are under the control of a supervisor are assigned to that supervisor; they become his responsibility. An important point is that those costs or expenses not under the control of a particular supervisor should not be assigned to him as his responsibility.

Under responsibility accounting, expenditures are accumulated by cost and expense centers, which are segments of the firm for which management desires cost and expense data. Typical cost centers of a firm include factory service and production departments; typical expense centers are the general office and delivery departments. In addition, there are segments of the firm called profit centers for which *both* revenues and expenses are isolated. A profit center is an independent business segment of the firm, and is usually called a "division." A firm, for example, might have two divisions: an electrical appliance manufacturing division and a computer manufacturing division, each having a division manager who is held responsible for revenues, expenses, and assets used in the operation of his division.

Ideally, responsibility accounting motivates a manager to control costs, for he knows that the costs he incurs will be traced to him and that he will not be charged for those costs not under his control. In general, the manager will feel that he is being treated fairly if his performance is evaluated in terms of those factors over which he has control.

Traditional reporting. As pointed out in Chapter 18, direct costs are assigned to production and service departments; indirect costs are allocated to the production and service departments; service department costs are allocated to the production departments; and each production department cost is assigned to the finished product. Thus, to calculate the cost of goods sold (expense) for each product line, the production cost per unit is multiplied by the number of units sold; and, if selling and administrative expenses are allocated to the product lines, the result is an income statement segmented by product lines. The main purpose, generally, is to provide data for financial statements. A traditional report is shown below.

	Total	Product #1	Product #2	Product #3
Net sales	$355,000	$200,000	$30,000	$125,000
Deduct cost of goods sold	200,000	110,000	18,000	72,000
Gross margin.	$155,000	$ 90,000	$12,000	$ 53,000
Deduct selling and administrative expenses	98,000	40,000	20,000	38,000
Net income (loss)	$ 57,000	$ 50,000	$ (8,000)	$ 15,000

For purposes of control, the traditional reports are inadequate for two reasons. First is the arbitrary allocations of indirect costs. To achieve cost allocation, indirect costs are prorated to cost centers by means of some rational method of identification. The problem, however, is that there are several rational ways to allocate an indirect cost and that the selection of one allocation method is really an arbitrary choice. For example, note the several possible allocation bases for each indirect cost listed below.

Indirect Cost to Be Distributed	Bases for Distribution
Depreciation of equipment	Floor space; value of equipment; direct charge to department using equipment
Machine maintenance	Cost of machines; direct charges to departments where maintenance work is done
Taxes and insurance on building	Value of assets; square feet occupied
Power and light	Kilowatts per meter; capacity of equipment
Personnel department	Number of employees; time spent working on department problems; number of employees hired
Cafeteria	Total number of employees in department; number of employees in department using cafeteria

Secondly, the traditional report emphasizes the net income from each product after allowing for all expenses associated with the product. When such a report is used to judge performance, product managers normally would be evaluated on the basis of the total product net income, the percentage of product net income to sales, or some other similar measure. However, the emphasis on product net income overlooks the possibility that such reports are based on the allocation to the product lines of indirect expenses that are not under the control of the product manager. For instance, the net loss for Product #2 in the example might be the result of allocations of indirect expenses over which the product manager has no control. The product manager probably has no control over such indirect expenses as top executive salaries, outlays for basic research and development, and the expenses of operating the personnel department that are allocated to his product. Such traditional reports are not compatible with responsibility accounting.

Controllable costs and expenses. Controllable costs and expenses are those subject to regulation by a manager because of his direct influence over the incurrence of such costs and expenses, assuming a given time period and a given responsibility center. The latter two assumptions are necessary because controllable costs are affected by (1) the particular responsibility center and (2) the particular time period.

A cost or expense that is uncontrollable with regard to one responsibility center may be controllable at another responsibility center. Thus outlays associated with product research may or may not be controllable by the division manager. Similarly, a cost that is controllable over a long period of time may not be controllable over a short period of time. A division manager may not be able to control the current charge for depreciation of factory equipment, but at the end of, say, five years when he buys new equipment, his decision will influence subsequent depreciation charges. Given a long enough time period, all costs are at least partially controllable.

As a first approximation, fixed costs are often assumed to be uncontrollable and variable costs controllable; however, the degree of controllability really depends on the particular responsibility center and the particular time period involved. The cost of renting production equipment is an uncontrollable annual fixed cost to the product manager, but it is controllable by the division manager if he has the authority to buy new equipment to replace the rental equipment. For this cost the responsibility of the division manager outranks that of the product manager. The cost is uncontrollable at one responsibility center and controllable at a higher responsibility center. Similarly, the product manager may have no control over the annual budget for advertising his product, but he may have some control in that he can decide on the kind of advertising and the spending rate for advertising up to the total amount he is allowed. At some higher management level the decision is made to limit outlays for advertising to some fixed amount; advertising expense is controllable at this management level. Thus some costs and expenses are fixed at the discretion of management and are therefore controllable (at least partially) by management: budgeted outlays for advertising and research are examples.

Contribution margin. Contribution margin is defined as the dollar amount that remains when variable expenses are subtracted from net sales, and is available to meet fixed expenses, any remainder being net income. Contribution margin is expressed either as a total dollar amount, as an amount per unit of product sold, or as a percentage of sales:

	Total Amount	Percentage	Per Unit (7,000 units)
Sales	$140,000	100%	$20.00
Variable expenses	98,000	− 70	14.00
Contribution margin	$ 42,000	30%	$ 6.00
Fixed expenses	30,000		
Net income	$ 12,000		

Note that, if fixed expenses are truly fixed, net income varies with the amount of contribution margin (assuming that sales and variable expenses per unit are constant). For example, if the sales price per unit is increased $2, contribution margin and profit are increased $2 per unit, or $14,000 ($2 × 7,000). Similarly, if 2,000 more units of product are sold, contribution margin and profit increase $12,000 ($6 contribution margin per unit times 2,000 units). The point is that, with known fixed expenses, known sales price per unit, and known variable expense per unit, management can analyze the changes in contribution margin to determine the effects on profits of alternative short-run decisions.

Contribution-margin analysis is also useful in determining which products, sales territories, and the like should be emphasized or dropped by management. In the short run with given fixed expenses, if a product or sales territory has sales revenue greater than variable expenses (a positive contribution margin), the product is contributing towards the overall profitability of the firm. Even if there is a net loss (fixed expenses exceed contribution margin), so long as the contribution margin is positive, the product should be retained in the short run. Fixed expenses that are truly fixed are irrelevant because they cannot be changed in the short run and are not germane to the decision of emphasizing or de-emphasizing products, sales territories, and the like.

Assume that a company sells the following three products and that we are using contribution-margin analysis to determine the profitability of the products.

	Total	Product #1	%	Product #2	%	Product #3	%
Sales	$350,000	$80,000	100%	$70,000	100%	$200,000	100%
Variable expenses .	262,000	60,000	75	42,000	60	160,000	80
Contribution margin . .	$ 88,000	$20,000	25%	$28,000	40%	$ 40,000	20%
Fixed expenses .	71,000	12,000		29,000		30,000	
Net income (loss). . . .	$ 17,000	$ 8,000		$(1,000)		$ 10,000	

With given fixed expenses and plant facilities, contribution-margin analysis shows that Product #2 is contributing $28,000 to overall profits even though there is an apparent net loss of $1,000. If Product #2 were dropped, the $29,000 fixed expense would have to be covered by the other products and there would be a drop in overall profit of $28,000.

	Keep Product #2	Drop Product #2	Advantage in Keeping Product #2
Contribution margin	$28.000	$ —	$28,000
Less fixed expense	(29,000)	(29,000)	—
Difference.	$(1,000)	$(29,000)	$28,000

Contribution-margin analysis also shows that Product #2 may have the greatest potential for increasing profits because of its 40 per cent contribution-margin ratio. For every dollar of sales, Product #2 contributes $.40, Product #1 contributes $.25, and Product #3 contributes $.20 to profit. Because it has the highest contribution-margin ratio, management should analyze the market for Product #2 to determine if sales volume can be increased through advertising and other sales promotion techniques. Management should also analyze the possibilities of increasing the contribution margin of Products #1 and #3 by reducing variable expenses per unit or by increasing sales prices. On the other hand, this is not to say that management should always push the product with the highest contribution-margin ratio, because there are other factors that must be considered. Some pertinent considerations might be the total units of each product that can be sold, the production time necessary for producing each product, the capacity of the existing plant to produce the different products, and the social responsibilities of the firm (for example, a drug concern manufacturing vaccines should not base its decisions solely on profits).

Contribution margin and responsibility accounting. Traditional internal accounting reports prepared for management about segments of the firm tend to follow the functional lines of external accounting statements: sales minus cost of goods sold minus operating expenses equal net income. Such reports as shown on page 492 do not reflect responsibility accounting, nor do they take into account the behavior of expenses via contribution-margin analysis. Thus more useful information can be provided to management if internal reports on segments of the firm are based on responsibility accounting and are designed to set forth the contribution margin. Such a report is presented below, for which data from the traditional internal report on page 492 are classified as controllable and noncontrollable variable and fixed expenses.

| | Firm Totals | Non-controllable Expenses | Sales and Controllable Expenses | | | | | |
| | | | Product #1 | | Product #2 | | Product #3 | |
			Amount	%	Amount	%	Amount	%
Net sales	$355,000		$200,000	100%	$30,000	100%	$125,000	100%
Variable expenses . .	210,000	$10,000	140,000	70	10,000	33	50,000	40
Contribution margin	$145,000	$(10,000)*	$ 60,000	30%	$20,000	67%	$ 75,000	60%
Fixed expenses	88,000	50,000	12,000		11,000		15,000	
Net income	$ 57,000	$(60,000)	$ 48,000		$ 9,000		$ 60,000	

*( ) denotes negative amount.

Note that the traditional report shows a net loss of $8,000 for Product #2, while the proposed report shows net income of $9,000 and a contribution margin of $20,000 for Product #2. The difference is due to the removal of noncontrollable expenses from the product columns (see the separate column for noncontrollable expenses).

There are some fixed expenses that are fixed by management decision. Such expenses remain constant as sales volume changes because top management plans to spend a certain fixed amount for the current year. However, in some cases the product managers have some control over these so-called "discretionary" fixed expenses, and they, therefore, can be assigned to the product lines (see the $12,000, $11,000, and $15,000 fixed expenses assigned to product lines above). For example, if the product manager can influence spending up to a certain budgeted amount for product advertising and research, the expense would be assigned to his product line. On the other hand, those fixed expenses that are not assigned to the product segments are the result of joint costs that benefit overall operations: top executive salaries, basic research and development expenses, and administrative expenses associated with the central office are examples. These are not identifiable with any segment except under arbitrary allocation methods.

Finally, the proposed report highlights the contribution margin of each product. Product #2 should not be dropped in the short run, for its contribution margin is positive. Also, the total and percentage contribution margins provide a starting point for further management analysis to determine how to increase the firm's overall profitability. For example, note that Product #2, the least profitable product under the traditional report, has the highest contribution-margin ratio.

Variable (direct) costing. Conventional cost accounting, as explained in Chapters 18 through 21, is primarily concerned with the preparation of financial statements for investors, creditors, and others outside the business firm. Conventional cost accounting for external reporting includes in product cost all those manufacturing costs associated with the production of finished goods: direct material, direct labor, and factory overhead. Also, because factory overhead cost usually is applied to production by the use of an absorption (applied or estimated) overhead rate, conventional cost accounting is sometimes called absorption costing.

Whereas conventional cost accounting generally stresses external reporting, variable costing emphasizes internal reporting to management. Variable costing, when combined with responsibility accounting, facilitates the preparation of internal reports, such as the report proposed on page 496.

Variable costing is a cost accounting procedure whereby production costs are separated into variable and fixed components and only the variable production costs (direct materials, direct labor, and variable factory overhead costs utilized in production) are treated as product costs. Under variable costing, fixed factory overhead cost is immediately expensed (treated as a period expense); therefore, fixed factory overhead cost does not pass through the asset accounts associated with goods in process and finished goods inventories (product costs) as it does under conventional costing. The difference between conventional and variable costing is illustrated below.

	Conventional Costing Amount	Conventional Costing Per Unit	Variable Costing Amount	Variable Costing Per Unit	Difference Amount	Difference Per Unit
Direct material cost	$20,000	$20	$20,000	$20	$ —	$—
Direct labor cost	30,000	30	30,000	30	—	—
Variable factory overhead cost	25,000	25	25,000	25	—	—
Fixed factory overhead cost	15,000	15	—	—	15,000	15
Total manufacturing cost	$90,000	$90	$75,000	$75	$15,000	$ 15
Ending inventory for balance sheet (200 units):						
200 × $90	$18,000					
200 × $75			$15,000		$ 3,000	
Expense:						
Cost of goods sold (800 units):						
800 × $90	72,000					
800 × $75			60,000		(3,000)	
Fixed factory overhead as a period expense	—		15,000			
	$90,000		$90,000			
Income statement effect—Net income	$3,000 higher		$3,000 lower			
Balance sheet effect—Assets and retained earnings	$3,000 higher		$3,000 lower			

The case for variable costing for internal reporting. The basic argument for variable costing is that it provides more useful information for short-run decision making than does conventional costing. In the first place, variable production costs are closely identified with specific units of production: if production increases (or decreases), variable costs tend to increase (or decrease). Thus variable costs indicate the extent to which factory plant and equipment (physical capacity) are being utilized. In contrast, fixed factory overhead cost is not readily identified with units of production, but it is related to the capacity to produce over a given time period. That is, variable factory costs are utilized because production occurs, while fixed factory overhead cost is utilized over the fiscal period whether production occurs or not. Because fixed factory overhead costs are not closely identified with units of production, the allocation of fixed overhead to production under conventional costing can distort net income and hinder decision making (this is illustrated in the next section). On the other hand, variable costing does not have this problem, because fixed factory overhead cost is treated as a period expense and is not allocated to production.

In the second place, under variable costing a firm's costs and expenses are classified into variable and fixed components; this classification is carried over to the income statement and thereby highlights contribution margin. Under variable costing, cost-and-expense data are recorded and reported in a form that facilitates the use of responsibility accounting and the analysis of cost-volume-profit relationships, which are discussed in Chapter 23. On the other hand, conventional (absorption) costing does not distinguish between variable and fixed costs and expenses and does not emphasize contribution margin. Thus it is contended that variable costing provides more useful information for decision making than does conventional costing.

The case against variable costing for internal reports. Those accountants who are against the use of variable costing for internal reporting contend that, if fixed factory overhead costs are necessary for production, then they should be included in product cost. In other words, because variable costing excludes fixed factory overhead cost from product cost, goods in process and finished goods inventories are understated in terms of historical cost.

A second argument against variable costing is that it provides information to management that may be misleading in product-pricing decisions. The contention is that management should set prices so as to cover all costs, including fixed factory overhead costs, and not just the variable costs.

Finally, there is the contention that the separation of costs and expenses into variable and fixed components is not an easy task and that much of the separation ends up being arbitrary. Moreover, even if costs and expenses can be meaningfully separated into variable and fixed components, conventional accounting reports for management can be modified to show variable expenses, fixed expenses, and contribution margin in the same manner as variable costing reports.

The net income effect in internal reports. Conventional cost accounting applies fixed factory overhead cost to ending inventory on hand and to cost of goods sold, while variable costing charges all of fixed factory overhead cost to expense during the current time period, regardless of the quantity of inventory on hand. Thus if, during the current period, production exceeds sales, resulting in an increase in inventory, the profit under conventional costing normally will be higher than under variable costing. The reason is that conventional costing charges part of fixed factory overhead to the increased ending inventory (an asset), which obviously is not expensed (net income higher) during the current period.

For example, in the illustration on page 497, production (1,000 units) exceeded sales (800 units) and the ending inventory (200 units) was charged with fixed factory overhead cost of $3,000 (200 × $15) under conventional costing, which did not reach the income statement. Under variable costing, all of the fixed factory overhead cost was charged not to ending inventory but to expense. Consequently, both ending inventory and net income were $3,000 lower under variable costing than under conventional costing.

The reverse is true if sales exceed production, resulting in a decrease in inventory. Fixed factory overhead cost contained in beginning inventory cost is released as expense (cost of goods sold) under conventional costing, so that net income normally is lower than it would be under variable costing.

AN ILLUSTRATION: In order to see, for internal reporting purposes, the difference between conventional and variable costing when units produced differ from units sold, assume the following data:

Units of Product

	Year 1	Year 2
Beginning inventory of finished goods	—	3,000
Finished goods produced	7,000	4,000
Goods available for sale	7,000	7,000
Ending inventory of finished goods	3,000	1,000
Finished goods sold	4,000	6,000

Standard Unit Costs

Variable costs of manufacturing (direct material, direct labor, and variable factory overhead)	$20
Applied fixed factory overhead	30
Conventional cost per unit	$50

Other Data

Sales price per unit	$80
Actual fixed factory overhead per year	$210,000
Selling and administrative expense per year (assumed to be fixed)	$ 20,000

The above data are used to calculate conventional and variable cost income statements for the two years, as shown on page 500.

During the first year, production (7,000 units) exceeded sales (4,000 units) and resulted in the conventional income statement showing net income $90,000 higher than the variable costing income statement. The difference is explained by the increase in inventory (from 0 to 3,000 units) and the allocation of fixed factory overhead ($30 × 3,000 = $90,000) to the ending inventory under conventional costing.

Conventional Costing

Year 1

Sales (4,000 × $80)		$320,000
Cost of goods sold:		
Beginning finished goods	$ —	
Cost of goods manufactured (7,000 × $50)	350,000	
Goods available for sale	$350,000	
Ending finished goods (3,000 × $50)	150,000	200,000
Gross margin		$120,000
Operating expenses:		
Selling and administrative expenses		20,000
Net income		$100,000

Year 2

Sales (6,000 × $80)		$480,000
Cost of goods sold:		
Beginning finished goods (3,000 × $50)	$150,000	
Cost of goods manufactured (4,000 × $50)	200,000	
Goods available for sale	$350,000	
Ending finished goods	50,000	
Difference	$300,000	
Underapplied factory overhead ($210,000 − $120,000)	90,000	390,000
Gross margin		$ 90,000
Operating expenses:		
Selling and administrative expenses		20,000
Net income		$ 70,000

Variable Costing

Year 1

Sales (4,000 × $80)		$320,000
Variable cost of goods sold:		
Beginning finished goods	$ —	
Cost of goods manufactured (7,000 × $20)	140,000	
Goods available for sale	$140,000	
Ending finished goods (3,000 × $20)	60,000	80,000
Manufacturing contribution margin		$240,000
Fixed factory overhead	$210,000	
Operating expenses:		
Selling and administrative expenses	20,000	230,000
Net income		$ 10,000

Year 2

Sales (6,000 × $80)		$480,000
Cost of goods sold:		
Beginning finished goods (3,000 × $20)	$ 60,000	
Cost of goods manufactured (4,000 × $20)	80,000	
Goods available for sale	$140,000	
Ending finished goods (1,000 × $20)	20,000	120,000
Manufacturing contribution margin		$360,000
Fixed factory overhead	$210,000	
Operating expenses:		
Selling and administrative expenses	20,000	230,000
Net income		$130,000

In contrast, variable costing assigned all of the fixed factory overhead to expense, which caused the net income figure to be lower:

$$\begin{matrix}\textbf{Difference in profit}\\ \textbf{between conventional}\\ \textbf{and variable costing}\end{matrix} = \left(\begin{matrix}\textbf{units}\\ \textbf{produced}\end{matrix} - \begin{matrix}\textbf{units}\\ \textbf{sold}\end{matrix}\right) \times \left(\begin{matrix}\textbf{fixed factory overhead}\\ \textbf{applied per unit}\end{matrix}\right)$$

$$= \left(\textbf{change in inventory}\right) \times \left(\begin{matrix}\textbf{fixed factory}\\ \textbf{overhead applied}\\ \textbf{per unit}\end{matrix}\right)$$

$$\textbf{\$90,000} = \textbf{(7,000 - 4,000)} \times \textbf{\$30}$$

$$= \textbf{3,000} \times \textbf{\$30}$$

During the second year, sales (6,000 units) exceeded production (4,000 units), so that part of the goods sold were from beginning inventory (2,000 units) and caused the net income under conventional costing to be $60,000 lower than under variable costing. That is, under conventional costing for Year 2, fixed factory overhead cost in beginning inventory (3,000 × $30 = $90,000) was expensed as part of cost of goods sold, which reduced net income, and part of fixed factory overhead was charged to ending inventory (1,000 × $30 = $30,000), which increased net income; the result was a net reduction of $60,000 in net income.

In contrast, under variable costing for Year 2, beginning and ending inventory included no fixed factory overhead cost because it was charged to expense, instead of ending inventory, in both years:

$$\begin{matrix}\textbf{Difference in profit}\\ \textbf{between conventional}\\ \textbf{and variable costing}\end{matrix} = \left(\begin{matrix}\textbf{units}\\ \textbf{produced}\end{matrix} - \begin{matrix}\textbf{units}\\ \textbf{sold}\end{matrix}\right) \times \left(\begin{matrix}\textbf{fixed factory overhead}\\ \textbf{applied per unit}\end{matrix}\right)$$

$$\textbf{\$60,000} = \textbf{(4,000 - 6,000)} \times \textbf{\$30}$$

NET INCOME DISTORTION: Although the foregoing illustration is exaggerated in order to contrast conventional and variable costing, it does point out the difficulty in analyzing net income under conventional cost accounting. Sales increased from $320,000 in Year 1 to $480,000 in Year 2 (a 34 per cent increase), yet the conventional income statement showed a decline in net income from $100,000 to $70,000 (a 30 per cent decrease) despite constant total fixed expense and a constant variable expense per unit. Under such circumstances, it is difficult for management to understand and the accountant to explain what caused the decline in net income. How do you explain to management that net income decreased as the result of the conventional cost accounting allocation of fixed factory overhead cost to finished goods inventory?

In contrast, the net income figure under variable costing is easier to analyze because it tends to change with and in the same direction as changes in volume. In the preceding illustration, the 34 per cent increase in sales from Year 1 to Year

2 was accompanied by a 1,200 per cent increase in net income ($10,000 to $130,000) under variable costing. The large percentage increase in net income is explained by the large contribution-margin ratio (75%), so that, once fixed expenses were covered by sales, every additional sales dollar provided $.75 toward profits. Thus the variable cost statements not only are easier to analyze than conventional statements, they also provide additional information that is useful for managerial decision making.

On the other hand, those accountants who favor conventional costing would contend that the preceding illustration indicates the preferability of conventional costing over variable costing. Those advocating conventional costing would argue that the underapplied fixed factory overhead cost of $90,000 for the second year informs management about the cost of excess capacity (idle plant), which variable costing does not do.

Variable costing and external reporting. If variable costing provides useful information to management, it would seem that it should also provide useful information to investors, creditors, and others outside the business entity. However, traditionally, accountants have not been willing to use variable costing in the preparation of external financial statements. The basic argument is that fixed factory overhead cost is a necessary cost to produce finished goods and, therefore, it should be included in product cost. If fixed factory overhead cost is excluded from product cost, as in variable costing, then the goods in process and finished goods inventories on the balance sheet are understated and the historical cost assumption is violated. Also, over long periods of time, production and sales volume approximate one another so that net income under variable costing and conventional costing are approximately the same.

ASSIGNMENT

MATERIALS

QUESTIONS

1. Under responsibility accounting, why is the firm segmented into responsibility centers? Discuss.

2. Is the allocation of indirect expenses to product lines useful for managerial decision-making purposes? Discuss.

3. Whether a cost or expense is controllable by a manager depends on the particular responsibility center and the particular time period. What does this statement mean? Discuss.

4. What is meant by a discretionary cost or expense? Discuss.

5. A fixed expense or cost is controllable and a variable expense or cost is uncontrollable. Do you agree with this statement? Discuss.

6. Assuming a short-run time period, what is the decision rule for deciding whether a product line should be dropped or retained? Discuss.

7. The product line with the greatest contribution-margin ratio is the product line that management should emphasize. Do you agree with this statement? Discuss.

8. For purposes of internal reporting to management, why do some accountants prefer variable costing to conventional costing? Discuss.

9. What is meant by the statement that the net income figure reported to management under conventional costing is unduly influenced by production? Discuss.

10. If variable costing is useful in providing relevant financial data for managerial decision making, would it also be useful in providing relevant financial data for investors, creditors, and others outside the business firm? Discuss.

SHORT EXERCISES

E22-1. Given the cost data on page 504, evaluate the performance of the manager in charge of Production Department #4.

	Production Department #4		
	Actual Costs	Budgeted Costs	Difference
Direct materials	$ 50,000	$ 51,000	$ (1,000)
Direct labor	100,000	103,000	(3,000)
Factory overhead:			
Variable factory overhead . .	32,000	30,000	2,000
Depreciation of factory building	5,000	5,000	—
Share of service department costs	40,000	20,000	20,000
	$227,000	$209,000	$18,000 unfavorable

E22-2. The management of Discontinue Company wants to drop product lines #4 and #6. Although the company's overall net income for the fiscal year was $300,000, product lines #4 and #6 incurred net losses of $10,000 and $20,000, respectively, as shown below. The variable expenses for product lines #4 and #6 were $151,000 and $170,000, respectively. Should these two product lines be dropped? Explain, and show your calculations.

	Product #4	Product #6
Sales	$150,000	$230,000
Deduct cost of goods sold	100,000	170,000
Gross margin.	$ 50,000	$ 60,000
Deduct selling and administrative expenses	60,000	80,000
Net loss	$(10,000)	$(20,000)

E22-3. The internal income statement for Conventional Company for the year ended December 31, 19+3, is presented below:

	Total	Product #1	Product #2
Sales	$300,000	$100,000	$200,000
Cost of goods sold	170,000	60,000	110,000
Gross margin.	$130,000	$ 40,000	$ 90,000
Operating expenses.	80,000	20,000	60,000
Net income	$ 50,000	$ 20,000	$ 30,000

Variable expenses are 60 and 65 per cent of sales from Products #1 and #2, respectively, and $20,000 of the total variable expenses are noncontrollable. Products #1 and #2 have controllable fixed expenses of $4,000 and $6,000, respectively. Given these data and the format below, convert the conventional internal income statement to one based on responsibility accounting.

	Totals	Non-controllable Expenses	Product #1 Amount	%	Product #2 Amount	%
			Sales and Controllable Expense			
Sales						
Variable expenses.						
Contribution margin						
Fixed expenses						
Net income.						

E22-4. The management of Confused, Inc., cannot understand why the internal income statement for the year shows net income of $30,000 when only 10,000 units of product were sold out of the 20,000 units produced (no beginning inventory). Management also points out that fixed factory overhead costs were not even covered. In order to explain the situation, the controller of the company prepared a variable cost income statement that could be compared with the conventional income statement, as shown below:

	Conventional Costing	Variable Costing
Sales ($30 × 10,000)	$300,000	$300,000
Variable expenses.	210,000	210,000
Contribution margin	$ 90,000	$ 90,000
Deduct:		
Fixed factory overhead.	$ 50,000	$100,000
Fixed operating expense	10,000	10,000
Total fixed	$ 60,000	$110,000
Net income (loss)	$ 30,000	$ (20,000)

(a) Explain what caused the difference between the net income under conventional costing and the net income under variable costing. Show your calculations.
(b) Which statement do you believe provides the more useful information to management? Discuss.

PROBLEMS

Problem A22-1. Wescoe Chair Manufacturing, Inc., produces several lines of chairs in which wood is the basic raw material. The company is segmented into cost and expense centers with a manager in charge of each center.

The manager in charge of production is unhappy because of the manner in which his performance is evaluated. His performance for last year was rated unsatisfactory; however, he contends that this is the result of being held responsible for costs over which he has no control.

You are asked to evaluate his contention, given the following data:

(1) The purchase price of wood increased last year.
(2) A new labor contract had been signed by the personnel department last year in which labor costs went up $.25 per direct labor hour.
(3) The sales prices of the chairs remained the same.
(4) The material quantity variance and the labor efficiency variance last year were below previous years' variances.
(5) The quantity of chairs produced had increased, but there was no significant change in sales.
(6) Variable and fixed factory overhead rates were unchanged.

Required:

(a) Discuss in general the production manager's complaint.
(b) How would *each* of the six factors above affect the evaluation of his performance? Discuss.

Problem A22-2. Laurence Manufacturing Company produces several products including a plastic jayhawk. Each jayhawk is sold to retail stores for $.80. The company's cost of manufacturing one unit is $.775, as shown below:

	Per Finished Unit
Direct materials	$.150
Direct labor	.250
Factory overhead (150% of direct labor cost)	.375
Total	$.775

Both the sales manager and the production manager are unhappy with this product because they both receive bonuses based on net income. With selling expense of $.10 a unit, each plastic jayhawk incurs a $.075 loss.

The sales manager contends that the product should be dropped. He states that the price cannot be increased because of strong competition.

The production manager contends that factory overhead cost will remain the same if the product is dropped. Thus the factory overhead rate would have to be increased over the remaining products should the plastic jayhawk be dropped. He suggests allocating factory overhead over a direct materials base because this would reduce the unit cost of the jayhawks and would result in a profit per unit.

Required:

(a) Discuss the sales manager's contention that the plastic jayhawk product should be dropped. Use figures to support your discussion.

(b) Discuss the production manager's contention that the overhead allocation base should be changed.

(c) What do you think of paying bonuses to the sales and production managers based on net income? Discuss.

Problem A22-3. Sherr Manufacturing Company produces a number of different products that are classified according to product lines. Each product line is under the responsibility of a manager. At the end of each year, profitability statements are prepared for each product line. Each product-line manager receives a bonus based on the improvement in the product line's return on sales (net income ÷ sales) from the previous year.

The manager of one of the product lines is unhappy because he will not receive a bonus this year, because the product line's rate of return on sales dropped from 7.42 per cent last year to 6.43 per cent this year, as shown below:

	Year 2	Year 1
Net sales	$700,000	$600,000
Deduct cost of goods sold	425,000	375,500
Gross margin	$275,000	$224,500
Deduct selling and administrative expenses	230,000	180,000
Net income	$ 45,000	$ 44,500
Rate of return on sales	6.43%	7.42%

The product-line manager contends that the above statements are misleading. He argues that he has no control over the fixed factory overhead contained in cost of goods sold ($153,000 and $175,000 for Years 1 and 2, respectively) and the fixed selling and administrative expenses ($120,000 and $160,000 for Years 1 and 2, respectively). Thus, he feels the rate of return should be based on sales minus controllable expenses divided by sales.

Required:

(a) Assuming that the variable expenses are controllable by the product-line manager, prepare income statements and rates of return on sales based on responsibility accounting.

(b) Present arguments for or against the product-line manager receiving a bonus for Year 2.

(c) What do you think of the bonus method used by the company? Discuss.

Problem A22-4. The income statements for the last two years for R. M. Olsen Company are shown below:

	19+9	19+8
Net sales	$450,000	$300,000
Deduct cost of goods sold	330,000	220,000
Gross margin	$120,000	$ 80,000
Deduct operating expenses:		
Selling and administrative expenses	$ 27,000	$ 25,000
Underapplied factory overhead	36,000	—
Total	$ 63,000	$ 25,000
Net income	$ 57,000	$ 55,000

Management cannot understand why a 50 per cent increase in sales increased net income by only 4 per cent. You are asked to advise management as to what happened to cause the small increase in net income, given the following additional data:

Units sold	30,000	20,000
Units produced	24,000	30,000
Sales price per unit	$ 15	$ 15
Standard variable expense per unit	5	5
Actual fixed factory overhead	180,000	180,000
Standard fixed factory overhead per unit	6	6
Overhead variances are closed to Cost of Goods Sold.		

Required:

(a) Prepare income statements using variable (direct) costing for the two years.

(b) By comparing net income under conventional (absorption) and variable (direct) costing, explain the small increase in net income shown by the conventional income statements.

Problem A22-5. The president of a small company, Carey, Inc., received a letter from a prominent stockholder asking him how reported net income could decline $2,000 when reported sales increased from $30,000 last year to $45,000 this year. The president of the company looked at the income statements for the last two years and could not explain what happened.

The president of the company has asked you to prepare an explanation of why reported net income showed a decline from last year. Because he does not want you to be influenced by the published income statements for the last two years, he asks you to prepare conventional income statements in order to verify the figures on the published statements. You are given the following data:

	19+2	19+1
Units sold @ $15 per unit	3,000	2,000
Units produced	2,000	3,000
Standard variable production cost per unit	$ 5	$ 5
Actual fixed factory overhead	18,000	18,000
Selling and administrative expenses (assumed to be fixed) .	2,500	2,500
Standard fixed factory overhead per unit	6	6
Overhead variances are written off to Cost of Goods Sold.		

Required:

(1) Prepare comparative income statements for the last two years using conventional (absorption) costing. The statements should agree with the published income statements.

(2) Prepare an analysis explaining how net income could decline $2,000 when sales increased $15,000. In your analysis, explain why the $2,000 decline in net income is misleading.

Problem B22-1. Porter, Inc., manufactures several different product lines. Each product line is under the responsibility of a manager. The product-line managers are paid bonuses based on the net income of their product lines.

One of the product-line managers is complaining because his bonus will be smaller than last year as a result of a decline in the net income of his product line. He contends that he is not being evaluated fairly because allocations of fixed expenses distort the net income of his product line. He argues that the method of allocating fixed expenses should be changed so that his product line will not be charged with an excessive amount of allocated fixed expense. That is, he feels that the other product lines are not carrying a fair share of the allocated fixed expense.

Required:

(a) Is this allocation of fixed expenses to the product lines consistent with responsibility accounting? Discuss.

(b) Do you agree with the product-line manager's contention that his share of allocated fixed expenses should be reduced in order to provide a more equitable allocation? Discuss.

(c) What is your recommendation as to how each manager's performance should be evaluated? Discuss.

Problem B22-2. L. M. Jones Company produces two different product lines. The company has a manager in charge of each product line. The manager of product line #2 is complaining about the accounting system. He feels that his product line has had a better year than last year, but the income statement for his product line shows a $15,000 net loss for the current year.

	Total	Product Line #1	Product Line #2
Sales	$1,700,000	$900,000	$800,000
Deduct manufacturing cost of sales . .	1,530,000	790,000	740,000
Gross margin	$ 170,000	$110,000	$ 60,000
Operating expenses	137,000	62,000	75,000
Net income (loss)	$ 33,000	$ 48,000	$ (15,000)

You have been asked to analyze the income statements of the two product lines and determine whether the complaint by the product-line manager is justified. In your analysis you find that the overall contribution margins for product lines #1 and #2 are 30 per cent and 40 per cent, respectively. You also discover that variable expenses generally tend to be controllable by the managers, and that noncontrollable fixed expenses for product lines #1 and #2 are $200,000 and $190,000, respectively.

Required:

(a) Income statements for the two product lines based on responsibility accounting.
(b) A written explanation supporting or refuting the product-line manager's complaint.

Problem B22-3. You are given the following financial data for Thaete Manufacturing for the last three years.

	Year 1	Year 2	Year 3
Units of beginning finished goods	—	10,000	—
Units produced	80,000	60,000	40,000
Units sold	70,000	70,000	40,000
Units of ending finished goods	10,000	—	—
Net income under variable costing	$1,700,000	$1,700,000	$500,000

Standard Cost Card

Direct materials	$ 8
Direct labor	5
Variable factory overhead	7
Fixed factory overhead	10
Standard cost per finished unit	$30

The company uses variable (direct) costing for internal reporting to management and conventional (absorption) costing for external reporting. Thus, at year end, it is necessary to convert the cost data from the variable cost system to a conventional cost basis for external reporting.

Required:

(a) Using the above data, convert the net income figures under variable costing to net income figures under absorption costing. Show all calculations for all three years.
(b) For each year, write an explanation as to why net income differed or was the same under the two costing methods.
(c) Would net income in Year 3 be the same under both conventional and variable costing if there were 10,000 units of finished goods on hand at the beginning of the period? Discuss.

Problem B22-4. Samuel Hobbs Liquors, Inc., produces a blended whiskey called Sam Hobbs. The company uses *fifo* for costing its inventory and writes off factory overhead variance to Cost of Goods Sold at year end. Operating statistics for 19+8 were as follows:

Cases produced—30,000
Cases of inventory, January 1, 19+8—1,000
Cases of inventory, December 31, 19+8—6,000
Cases sold—25,000
Selling price per case . . . . $ 30
Actual material cost per case   7

Actual labor cost per case . . . . $ 6
Actual variable factory overhead per case   4
Applied fixed factory overhead per case   6
Actual fixed overhead costs 162,000
Actual fixed selling and administrative expenses   60,000
Actual variable selling and administrative expenses—10 per cent of
   sales

While costs were the same in 19+8 as in 19+7, materials cost during 19+9 rose 10 per
cent and labor cost rose 5 per cent. All other costs remained unchanged. Despite an increase
in the selling price of 6 per cent in 19+9, 6,000 more cases were sold than in 19+8. However,
production was cut back in 19+9 by 4,000 cases.

Required:

(a) Comparative income statements for 19+8 and 19+9, using conventional (absorp-
     tion) costing.
(b) Comparative income statements for 19+8 and 19+9 using variable (direct) costing.
(c) For each year, an explanation of the differences in net income under the two
     methods.

Problem B22-5. Flaherty Manufacturing Company has several product lines with a manager in charge
of each line. Each product-line manager is paid a bonus based on the net income generated
by his product line.

In analyzing one product line, the president of the company noted that sales declined
from $800,000 last year to $600,000 for the current year. However, the product-line manager
received a larger bonus than last year because net income increased from $90,000 last year
to $120,000 for the current year.

Based on the decline in sales, the president wonders whether the product-line manager
should have received a larger bonus this year. Also, the president of the company wants
to know why net income increased when sales declined. He asks you to analyze the situation
and to prepare a written report explaining how net income increased when sales declined.
You are given the following data:

	Year 2	Year 1
Units sold @ $20	30,000	40,000
Units produced	50,000	30,000
Units of beginning finished goods inventory	—	10,000
Standard variable production cost per unit	$ 8	$ 8
Standard fixed factory overhead per unit	5	5
Actual fixed factory overhead cost	200,000	200,000
Selling and administrative expenses (assumed to be fixed)	140,000	140,000
All factory overhead variances are written off to Cost of		
Goods Sold.		

Required:

(a) Prepare income statements for the two years using conventional (absorption) cost-
     ing.
(b) Prepare income statements for the two years using variable (direct) costing.
(c) Prepare a written report, supported by figures, explaining why net income increased
     when sales declined.
(d) What do you think about the bonus method? Discuss.

Cost-Volume-Profit Analysis

Introduction. The management of a business firm is continually faced with such short-run questions as: What are the total sales needed to earn x dollars of profit? Should an attempt be made to increase profits through sales promotion or changing product prices? What are the total sales needed to cover total expenses? Is it profitable to enter a foreign market? Should an existing product line be dropped? Is sales territory #4 really contributing toward overall company profits?

To answer such questions the management must know how net income is affected by particular cost and revenue decisions. Management needs to know about the behavior and interrelationships among cost, volume, and profit over the short-run time period. In essence, this means knowledge about contribution margin.

Before discussing cost-volume-profit analysis, let us first review the necessary terminology:

(1) *Variable expense* is that total expense that varies in direct proportion to changes in sales volume, assuming a relevant sales volume range.
(2) *Fixed expense* is that total expense that remains constant as sales volume changes, assuming a relevant sales volume range and a short-run time period.

(3) *Volume* is some type of business activity per period of time, and usually refers to the dollar amount or the quantity sold or produced over a time period.

(4) *Relevant volume* is the normal operating range of volume for a business firm, which excludes extremely high and low levels of volume.

(5) The *short run* is that period of time over which it is assumed that increases in volume are brought about by increases in variable costs and expenses, because the time period is not long enough to permit increases in capacity (fixed costs and expenses exist only during the short run).

(6) *Contribution margin* is the dollar amount that is obtained when variable expenses are subtracted from net sales, and is available to meet fixed expenses, any remainder being equal to net income. Contribution margin is stated as an absolute amount, as a percentage of sales (contribution-margin ratio), or as an amount per unit of sales volume (contribution margin per unit).

The break-even point. SINGLE-PRODUCT ANALYSIS: The break-even point is where total revenue equals total expense and net income is zero. The break-even point is helpful in management planning for new products, new markets, and the like, for it informs management about the minimum sales necessary for these new operations merely to meet expenses. Break-even analysis also provides useful information to management about how well actual volume compares with actual or planned break-even volume.

For a one-product firm or for one product of a multi-product firm, the break-even point can be computed in terms of units of product. In the following illustration it takes sales of 10,000 units of product to break even:

	Amount	Per Unit (10,000 units)
Break-even sales	$100,000	$10
Variable expense	60,000	6
Contribution margin	$ 40,000	$ 4
Fixed expense	40,000	
Net income	$ —	

Note that, at the break-even point, total contribution margin ($40,000) equals total fixed expense ($40,000). With a constant sales price ($10) and variable expense per unit ($6), contribution margin per unit is also constant ($4) and total contribution margin at the break-even point equals contribution margin per unit times the number of units to break even ($4 × 10,000). Therefore, the formula for calculating the break-even point in units of product is total fixed expense divided by the contribution margin per unit:

Total contribution margin = Total fixed expense
$40,000 = $40,000

Contribution margin per unit	×	**Units of product to break even**	=	**Total fixed expense**
$4	×	10,000	=	$40,000

$$\textit{Units of product to break even} = \frac{\textbf{Total fixed expense}}{\textbf{Contribution margin per unit}}$$

$$10,000 = \frac{\$40,000}{\$4}$$

The break-even point in units multiplied by the sales price equals the break-even point in terms of dollars of sales:

$$\textit{Break-even sales} = \frac{\textbf{Break-even}}{\textbf{units}} \times \frac{\textbf{Sales price}}{\textbf{per unit}}$$

Graphically, the break-even point can be shown in two ways, as illustrated below:

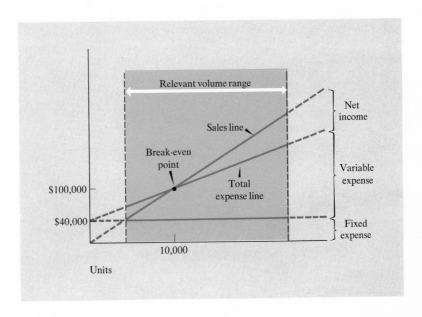

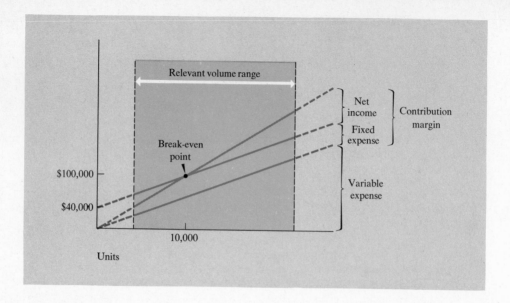

The second graph is preferred because it shows the contribution margin. The first graph is the traditional one.

MULTI-PRODUCT ANALYSIS: For a firm that sells more than one product, the overall break-even point is calculated in terms of dollars of sales instead of units of product. The reason is that units of product are not a common base for calculating the break-even point for a multi-product firm. The break-even point in units of product is usually different for each product because the products are dissimilar, with different sales prices and expenses per unit. The sales dollar, however, is a common denominator for the calculation of an overall break-even point for a multi-product firm.

Assume that the following data are the totals for a multi-product firm:

	Amount	Percentage
Sales (break-even)	$500,000	100%
Variable expense	350,000	70
Contribution margin	$150,000	30%
Fixed expense	150,000	
Net income	$ —	

As with the one-product firm, total contribution margin at the break-even point equals total fixed expense. However, since units of product are not a common base, total contribution margin is the contribution-margin ratio multiplied by the break-even sales. The contribution-margin ratio is the total contribution margin divided by the total sales ($150,000/$500,000 = 30%), or 1 minus the variable-expense ratio:

$$\left(1 - \frac{\$350,000}{\$500,000} = 30\%\right).$$

Consequently, the break-even formula for the multi-product firm is total fixed expense divided by the contribution-margin ratio.

Total contribution margin = Total fixed expense

$150,000 = $150,000

| **Total break-even** $\times$ **sales** | **Contribution- margin ratio** | = **Total fixed expense** |

$500,000 $\times$ 30% = $150,000

$$\text{Total break-even sales} = \frac{\text{Total fixed expense}}{\text{Contribution-margin ratio}}$$

$500,000 = $150,000 ÷ 30%

Graphically, the break-even point is shown by a sales line drawn at a 45-degree angle and expenses drawn as before. The sales line does not change, for it is a common denominator base that measures dollars of sales regardless of different prices. The vertical axis measures sales and expenses while the horizontal axis measures sales. The horizontal axis is scaled so that it includes the normal operating range (relevant sales range), as shown below:

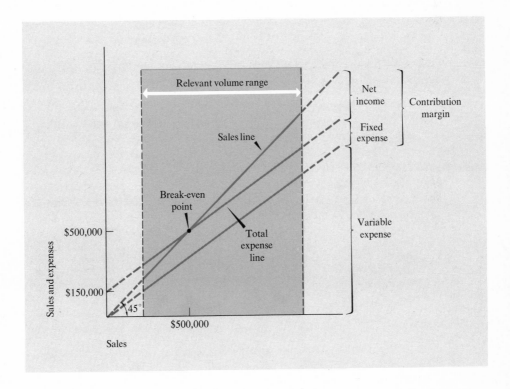

The margin of safety. When evaluating, for example, the revenue potential of an existing or new product, or a new sales territory, or a different marketing strategy, management is concerned about how much the actual or planned sales can decline before losses occur. Since losses occur when sales drop below the break-even point, the margin of safety is defined as the excess of actual or planned sales over actual or planned break-even sales.

In the example below, actual sales can decline $50,000 (the margin of safety) before losses occur:

	Actual Volume		Break-even Volume	
	Amount	Percentage	Amount	Percentage
Sales	$250,000	100%	$200,000	100%
Variable expenses	150,000	60	120,000	60
Contribution margin	$100,000	40%	$ 80,000	40%
Fixed expenses	80,000		80,000	
Net income	$ 20,000	8%	$ —	

Or, in percentage terms, actual sales can decline 20 per cent before losses occur. Thus the margin of safety stated as a percentage is equal to 1 minus the ratio of break-even sales to actual sales:

$$\text{\textit{Margin-of-safety percentage}} = 1 - \frac{\textbf{Break-even sales}}{\textbf{Actual sales}}$$

$$20\% = 1 - \frac{\$200,000}{\$250,000}$$

One can find the margin-of-safety percentage also by dividing the percentage of net income to sales by the contribution-margin ratio:

$$\text{\textit{Margin-of-safety percentage}} = \frac{\textbf{Percentage of net income to sales}}{\textbf{Contribution-margin ratio}}$$

$$20\% = 8\% \div 40\%$$

Target profit. There is more to cost-volume-profit analysis than just break-even analysis. For example, management may want to know the overall sales necessary to generate net income of $20,000. In the illustration below, it takes sales volume of $150,000 to earn the $20,000 target profit:

	Amount	Percentage
Sales	$150,000	100%
Variable expense	90,000	60
Contribution margin	$ 60,000	40%
Fixed expense	40,000	
Net income	$ 20,000	

Note that total contribution margin ($60,000) equals fixed expense ($40,000) plus the target profit ($20,000). Thus the formula for calculating the sales volume necessary to achieve the target profit for a multi-product firm is the sum of fixed expense plus target profit divided by the contribution-margin ratio, as shown below (divided by contribution margin per unit for single-product analysis):

$$\text{Sales needed for target profit} \times \text{Contribution-margin ratio} = \text{Total fixed expense} + \text{Target profit}$$

$$\$150,000 \times 40\% = \$40,000 + \$20,000$$

$$\textit{Sales needed for target profit} = \frac{\text{Total fixed expense} + \text{Target profit}}{\text{Contribution-margin ratio}}$$

$$\$150,000 = \frac{\$40,000 + \$20,000}{40\%}$$

The target profit is shown graphically below:

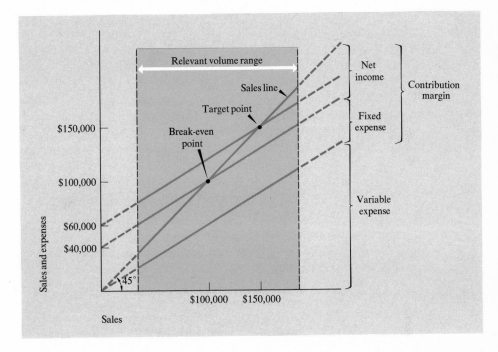

Note that it would be improper to conclude from the graph that an unlimited increase in sales volume will lead to unlimited profits. Conventional cost-volume-profit analysis is applicable only within the relevant volume range. Beyond the relevant range, economic theory indicates that straight-line assumptions are not valid, because of the likelihood of increasing expenses and declining sales.

Short-cut analysis. SINGLE-PRODUCT ANALYSIS. Contribution-margin analysis allows the accountant to answer quickly the management's questions as to how net income will be affected by changes in selling prices, expenses per unit, or sales volume. The use of contribution-margin analysis means that the accountant does not have to prepare a new income statement each time management asks a question about cost-volume-profit changes. With given fixed expenses, net income tends to vary with changes in contribution margin, and the latter can be analyzed to determine the effects of changes in cost-volume-profit relationships.

Assume that the data below pertain to product *X* and management wishes to know how profits would be affected by certain proposed changes.

	Actual	
	Amount	Per unit (10,000 units)
Sales	$50,000	$5
Variable expense	40,000	4
Contribution margin	$10,000	$1
Fixed expense	4,000	
Net income	$ 6,000	

Suppose management asks you what the effect on profits would be if the price per unit were increased $1 and volume remained at 10,000 units. You could immediately state that net income would increase $10,000 because total contribution margin would increase from $10,000 to $20,000 ($2 new contribution margin per unit times 10,000 units). Now suppose that management asks the same question, except that volume would decline 4,000 units. In this instance you could quickly state that net income would increase $2,000 because total contribution margin would increase from $10,000 to $12,000 ($2 new contribution margin per unit times 6,000 units). Similarly, if management asks what the effect on profits would be if there were an increase in variable expense of $.50 a unit, you could point out that at 10,000 units profit would decrease $5,000. That is, contribution margin would decline from $10,000 to $5,000 ($.50 new contribution margin per unit times 10,000 units).

MULTI-PRODUCT ANALYSIS: Whereas the short-cut analysis of the single-product case focuses on the change in the contribution margin per unit, the same type of analysis is used in the multi-product case, except that attention is directed toward the change in the contribution-margin ratio. In order to illustrate short-cut analysis in the multi-product case, assume the following data.

	Actual Volume		Break-even Volume	
	Amount	Percentage	Amount	Percentage
Sales	$600,000	100%	$250,000	100%
Variable expense	480,000	80	200,000	80
Contribution margin	$120,000	20%	$ 50,000	20%
Fixed expense	50,000		50,000	
Net income	$ 70,000		$ —	

At an overall sales volume of $600,000, suppose management wishes to know what the effect on profits would be if the variable-expense ratio were reduced 1 per cent by an increase in fixed expense of $2,000. Your instant answer is that net income would increase $4,000 because the increase in contribution margin from $120,000 to $126,000 (.21 new contribution-margin ratio times $600,000 in sales) would more than offset the $2,000 increase in fixed expense.

Assume that management wishes to know how a 20 per cent increase in fixed expense would affect the $250,000 break-even point. You can immediately state that the break-even sales would also have to increase 20 per cent ($250,000 × 1.20 = $300,000) in order to cover the higher fixed expense. That is, total contribution margin equals total fixed expense at the break-even point, and, if fixed expense increases 20 per cent, then contribution margin must increase 20 per cent (from $50,000 to $60,000) to maintain the equality. Since contribution margin varies with sales, a 20 per cent increase in contribution margin necessitates a 20 per cent increase in sales to break even. Thus, in both the single-product and the multi-product case, an x per cent increase in fixed expenses necessitates an x per cent increase in break-even sales. The 20 per cent increase in fixed expense and break-even sales is shown below:

	New Break-even
Sales ($250,000 × 1.20)	$300,000
Variable expense ($200,000 × 1.20)	240,000
Contribution margin ($50,000 × 1.20)	$ 60,000
Fixed expense ($50,000 × 1.20)	60,000
Net income	$ —

Generalizations on cost-volume-profit analysis. After analyzing the cost-volume-profit relationships of a firm, the accountant can make recommendations to management about possible ways to increase profitability. For example, suppose a firm is highly mechanized so that fixed expenses are a large proportion of total expenses, the variable-expense ratio is relatively low, and the contribution-margin ratio is relatively high, as shown below.

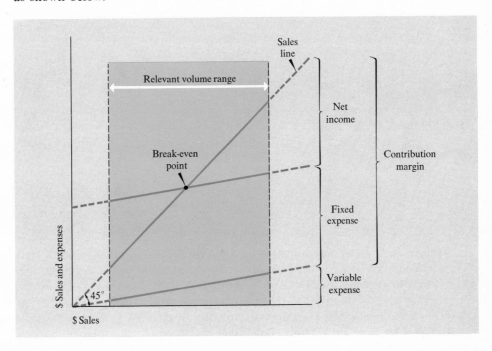

In such a situation the accountant can recommend that management attempt to increase profits by increasing sales volume or by reducing fixed expense. When sales volume exceeds the break-even point, such a firm is highly profitable because of the high contribution margin. Note the large gap between sales and total expense beyond the break-even point. Consequently, management should investigate the possibilities of increasing sales volume through advertising and other sales-promotion techniques. Also, management might be able to bring about an increase in profits by a reduction in fixed expense or by a trade-off of fixed expense for variable expense (i.e., reduce fixed expense more than the increase in variable expense). Although there are several possibilities, the accountant is saying: "Here are two recommendations that appear to be good starting points in attempting to increase company profits."

Now suppose the accountant is analyzing a firm that has a high proportion of variable expense to total expense, a low proportion of fixed expense to total expense, and a low contribution-margin ratio, as shown below:

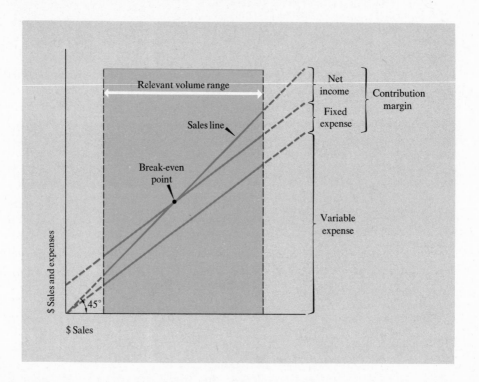

In this case the accountant can recommend to management that two good strategies in attempting to increase profits would be to increase sales price or to reduce variable expense. Note the small gap between sales and total expense beyond the break-even point. That is, the contribution-margin ratio is so low that an increase in sales volume does not increase profits very much; hence, as a starting point, management should attempt to increase the contribution-margin ratio. For example, it may be possible to reduce variable expense by replacing expensive labor with machinery. Or the firm's markets might be such that an increase in sales prices would not lower sales volume and would thus increase profits.

Finally, suppose management is faced with a problem in that one of its products is not even covering its variable expense, as illustrated.

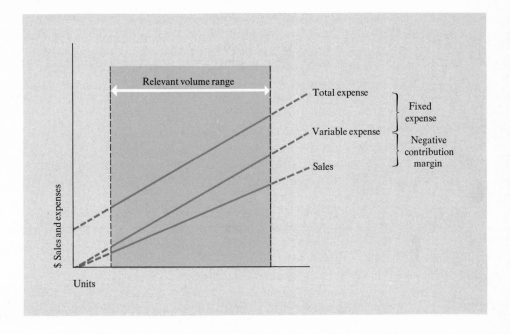

Given the above situation, the firm should drop the product, because it is not providing any positive contribution margin. Losses are minimized at zero volume as shown by the increasing losses as volume increases. On the other hand, if it is possible to bring about changes in the short run that result in a positive contribution margin, then the product could be retained. For example, the sales price might be increased without reduction of volume, or total expenses might be reduced. Also, the recommendation to drop the product is based on the assumption that variable expenses are relevant and fixed expenses irrelevant to the decision; however, the accountant should make sure that this assumption is not distorting the analysis.

Once the accountant has analyzed the cost-volume-profit structure of a firm, he can make recommendations to management which he feels are the most likely to increase company profits. However, this does not mean that the recommendations necessarily will turn out to be the best strategies management can employ. For example, the firm with a high contribution-margin ratio may not be able to increase sales volume in the short run because of a lack of plant capacity. Thus cost-volume-profit analysis is a good starting point, but further analysis, especially of qualitative factors, must be carried on in each situation.

Assumptions. Short-run analysis of a firm's cost-volume-profit relationships does not provide exact answers to management's financial problems. It provides approximate answers, given the underlying assumptions, and the assumptions have to be kept in mind at all times. Nevertheless, the technique is useful as a starting point in evaluating performance and in planning for the future.

The assumptions underlying cost-volume-profit analysis are summarized below:

(1) Revenue and expense are assumed to be linear functions (straight lines) of volume over the relevant range, so that sales prices, variable-expense ratios, and total fixed expenses are constant as volume changes. Cost-volume-profit analysis can be used in a nonlinear case, but then traditional contribution-margin analysis has to be modified.

(2) Variable and fixed expenses can be meaningfully separated. In actuality the separation is a difficult problem. Various approaches to the separation of variable and fixed expenses include judgmental separation based on analysis of the accounting records, the use of scatter graphs, an analysis of the change in total expense over representative high-low volume levels, and the use of such statistical techniques as least squares and multiple regression.

(3) Technological changes and efficiency are assumed to be constant. However, through a series of analyses under different efficiency conditions, the effect of changes in efficiency on net income can be approximated.

(4) Volume is assumed to be the common and relevant base for comparing sales and expenses. Obviously this is a simplification because external factors (wars, business conditions, and strikes) and qualitative factors (trade-union effects or the necessity of maintaining a wide product line to satisfy customers) also influence net income. Thus cost-volume-profit analysis is only a starting point for further analysis.

(5) Variable (direct) costing, not absorption costing, is assumed to be the proper approach for cost-volume-profit analysis. That is, *actual* fixed factory overhead cost, which is treated as a period expense, is used in cost-volume-profit analysis instead of *applied* fixed factory overhead cost.

(6) For a multi-product firm, the proportion of each product's sales to total company sales is assumed to be constant (i.e., the sales mix is constant). That is, for a particular situation, cost-volume-profit analysis depends on the fixed relationship of high and low sales-mix products. However, the effect of different product sales mixes can be studied by a series of analyses under varying sales-mix conditions.

ASSIGNMENT

MATERIAL

QUESTIONS

1. What does cost-volume-profit analysis attempt to do? Discuss.
2. Why is cost-volume-profit analysis referred to as short-run analysis? Discuss.
3. Is break-even analysis synonymous with cost-volume-profit analysis? Discuss.
4. In cost-volume-profit analysis, the *conventional* model used by the accountant is not applicable to volume levels outside of the relevant operating range. What does this statement mean? Discuss.
5. Assuming a short-run time period, why does total net income fluctuate with total contribution margin? Explain and illustrate.
6. Assuming a short-run time period, why does a y per cent increase in fixed expenses result in a y per cent increase in break-even sales? Discuss.
7. In cost-volume-profit analysis, why does single-product analysis differ from multi-product analysis? Discuss.
8. Graphically, the accountant's model of the firm seems to imply unlimited profits. What does this statement mean? Do you agree with the statement? Discuss.
9. Cost-volume-profit analysis for the multi-product firm implies a constant sales mix. What does this statement mean? Discuss.
10. Does the break-even point indicate the lower limit below which a product line, sales territory, or the like, should be dropped? Discuss.

SHORT EXERCISES

E23-1. You are given a cost-volume-profit graph of a firm.

(a) Identify each number in the graph.
(b) How does the graph differ from the traditional cost-volume-profit graph?

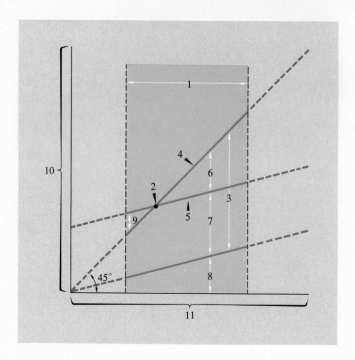

E23-2. Determine the amounts needed to complete the blanks.

(a) Single-product firms:

	Sales	Variable Expense	Fixed Expense	Net Income	Units Sold	Contribution per Unit
1.	$_____	$_____	$_____	$140,000	15,000	$50 − $30 = $20
2.	600,000	450,000	_____	70,000	10,000	_____
3.	900,000	_____	_____	100,000	30,000	10.00
4.	_____	250,000	100,000	_____	20,000	7.50

(b) Multi-product firms:

	Sales	Variable Expense	Fixed Expense	Net Income	Contribution Margin %
1.	$600,000	$540,000	$_____	$25,000	_____%
2.	100,000	_____	_____	10,000	40
3.	_____	280,000	100,000	_____	30
4.	_____	_____	50,000	10,000	20

E23-3. Make-or-Buy Company produces and sells several products. One of its products, called Leno, is produced at the following per-unit costs: $2 direct materials, $12 direct labor, $8 variable factory overhead, and $4 fixed factory overhead. An offer was recently received from another company to manufacture Leno for Make-or-Buy Company at a cost of $24. Management has decided to accept this offer since the $24 purchase price is less than the $26 total cost per unit to produce the product. Evaluate the decision.

E23-4. Assume that One Product Company manufactures a product at a variable cost of $30 per unit. Annual fixed costs are $104,000. The company has an operating capacity of 15,000 units, but annual production and sales have been about 10,000 units. The product is sold for $50 a unit. The company recently received an offer of $35 a unit from a foreign distributor to market 3,000 units of the product. Management rejected the offer because the $38 [($104,000 ÷ 13,000) + $30] average production cost per unit was higher than the $35 price the foreign distributor was willing to pay. Evaluate the decision.

PROBLEMS

Problem A23-1. Answer the following short questions and show all your calculations.

(1) If total fixed expense is $205,000 and contribution margin is $5 per unit, how many units of product must be sold to break even?

(2) If a multi-product firm has total fixed expenses of $240,640, and the overall contribution-margin ratio is 32 per cent, what total sales are necessary to break even?

(3) If total fixed expense is $567,000, target profit is $80,000, and the overall contribution-margin ratio is 40 per cent, what are the actual sales needed to attain the target profit?

(4) If break-even sales are $554,760, and if actual sales are 40,200 units at $15 per unit, what is the total dollar amount of the margin of safety? What is the margin-of-safety percentage?

(5) If net income is 8 per cent of sales, the contribution margin is 40 per cent, and break-even sales are $352,000, what are the actual sales?

Problem A23-2. Crownover Company manufactures and sells one product. The product is sold at $16 per unit. Normal production and sales volume are 120,000 units of product. The expenses associated with one unit of product are as follows:

Cost of goods sold:	
Direct materials	$ 3.20
Direct labor	4.35
Variable factory overhead	3.10
Fixed factory overhead ($282,000 ÷ 120,000 units)	2.35
Selling and administrative expenses:	
Variable	1.35
Fixed	.65
	$15.00

Management wants to try to increase profits by increasing sales volume. The market-research staff believes sales volume can be increased under four different plans:

(1) To increase annual advertising $40,000 would, it is estimated, increase sales volume 10 per cent. The sales price would remain the same at $16 per unit.

(2) To reduce the selling price by 25¢ a unit and increase annual advertising $6,000, it is estimated, would increase sales volume 10 per cent.

(3) To reduce the selling price 50¢ per unit should increase sales volume 15 per cent.

(4) To reduce the selling price by 75¢ per unit should increase sales volume 20 per cent.

Prepare an analysis of each of the four plans and show which is the most favorable.

Problem A23-3. Gustafson Company sells pencils to stationery stores on the east coast for $2.50 per box of 200. Last year the company had sales of $500,000, fixed expenses of $200,000, and variable expenses of $175,000 (on a per-box basis).

Management wishes to expand its market to the midwest. Since the company has excess capacity, the only additional expenses would be the new salesmen needed for the new market. The estimated expense of the additional salesmen, who would be paid a fixed salary, is $60,000.

(1) If last year's performance in the eastern market is expected to be the same for the current year, how many additional boxes of pencils must be sold in the midwestern market to provide $37,500 in additional profits over last year? Show all computations.

(2) If the price per box were lowered to $2 for both markets, how many boxes would have to be sold to provide $37,500 in additional profits over last year?

(3) Management estimates that if the price per box is reduced from $2.50 to $2 in the eastern market, 290,000 boxes can be sold in that market. Given this strategy for the eastern market, how many boxes must be sold at $2.50 each in the midwestern market to provide $160,500 in total company profits?

Problem A23-4. Masterson Manufacturing produces and sells three products. The operating results for the year are as follows:

	Product #1	Product #2	Product #3	Total
Sales	$50,000	$100,000	$10,000	$160,000
Variable expenses	35,000	80,000	5,000	120,000
Contribution margin	$15,000	$ 20,000	$ 5,000	$ 40,000
Fixed expenses				15,500
Net income				$ 24,500

(1) What is the overall break-even sales figure?

(2) Using the above data, what is the proportion of *each* product's sales to total sales (sales mix)?

(3) Based on total sales of $160,000, assume that the sales mix changes to the following: Product #1, 35 per cent; Product #2, 40 per cent; Product #3, 25 per cent. What is the new overall break-even sales figure?

(4) Explain *why* the break-even sales in part (3) either increased or decreased.

Problem A23-5. G. Sorter Company manufactures a single product. The company's annual normal production is 500,000 units of output, or, in terms of standard input, 100,000 direct labor hours. The normal plant capacity of 100,000 direct labor hours is based on a single eight-hour-a-day work shift.

Last year's internal income statement for the company is presented on page 527.

G. SORTER COMPANY
Income Statement
For the Year Ended December 31, 19+1

Sales (700,000 units @ $2.50)		$1,750,000
Variable expenses:		
Direct materials	$280,000	
Direct labor (140,000 hours @ $3.50)	490,000	
Factory overhead:		
Overtime premiums (40,000 hours @ $1.75)	70,000	
Miscellaneous	210,000	1,050,000
Contribution margin		$ 700,000
Fixed expenses		550,000
Net income		$ 150,000

Management is concerned about the overtime premiums (one-half of the normal labor rate) paid last year, and asks the chief accountant to prepare an analysis of the effect on profits on a second work shift. The accountant estimates that the second shift would increase costs as follows: an additional factory supervisor at $15,000 per year, a night-shift bonus of $.30 per direct labor hour, and an increase in fixed expenses (mostly selling and administrative expenses) of $19,800.

(1) Instead of paying overtime premiums last year, would profits have been greater if a second work shift had been used for the 40,000 above-normal direct labor hours?

(2) In comparison to last year, the forecast for this year includes the following: a 20 per cent increase in units sold, a 5 per cent increase in direct materials cost per unit, and a direct labor rate increase of $.16 per hour. Assuming that this forecast is correct, how much can be saved by use of a second work shift?

(3) Assuming that the day shift can best handle the normal capacity of 100,000 direct labor hours, and assuming that the overtime premium is $1.75, at what capacity level above 100,000 hours should the company switch to the second shift? (Hint: Find the number of direct labor hours that equate the cost of overtime to the cost of the second shift.)

Problem B23-1. Answer the following short questions and show all your calculations.

(1) If total fixed expense is $558,625, sales price per unit is $21.50, and variable expense per unit is $11.25, how many units of product must be sold to break even? What is the dollar amount of break-even sales?

(2) Fixed expenses are expected to be $120,000 and variable expenses are expected to be 40 per cent of sales. Sales at 100 per cent capacity are estimated to be $600,000. How would you construct a graph to show break-even sales and target sales if target profit is $75,000?

(3) A company's total fixed expense for the current year is $50,000. Next year the fixed expenses are expected to increase to $52,500. In percentage terms, how will the increase in fixed expenses affect break-even sales? Discuss.

(4) For the current year a company has sales of $800,000, net income of $70,000, and a contribution-margin ratio of 40 per cent. What is the total fixed expense of the company? What is the margin-of-safety percentage?

Problem B23-2. The management of Helgeson, Inc., has hired you as a management consultant. You are asked to analyze the company's cost-volume-profit relationships in order that management can analyze different strategies in an attempt to increase profits.

You point out to management that, before different strategies can be analyzed, financial data are needed to determine the company's basic cost-volume-profit structure. Thus you ask for a breakdown of expenses into variable and fixed components. Instead you are given the following data for two representative years:

	19+2	19+1
Sales	$800,000	$750,000
Total expenses	720,000	680,000
Net income	$ 80,000	$ 70,000

Given only the above data, answer the following questions (show all calculations):

(1) What is the contribution-margin ratio? (Hint: Analyze the changes between the two years.)
(2) What is the variable-expense ratio?
(3) What are the total variable expenses for 19+2 and 19+1?
(4) What are the total fixed expenses?
(5) What are the break-even sales?

Problem B23-3. Schweppe Manufacturing produces and sells four products. The operating results for the year are as follows:

	Product #1	Product #2	Product #3	Product #4
Sales	$600,000	$150,000	$200,000	$50,000
Variable expenses	360,000	120,000	100,000	45,000
Contribution margin	$240,000	$ 30,000	$100,000	$ 5,000
Fixed expenses	140,000	27,000	43,000	3,000
Net income	$100,000	$ 3,000	$ 57,000	$ 2,000

(1) What is the overall break-even sales?
(2) Using the above data, what is the proportion of *each* product's sales to total sales (sales mix)?
(3) Assume that the sales mix changes to the following: Product #1, 45 per cent; Product #2, 20 per cent; Product #3, 25 per cent; Product #4, 10 per cent. What is the new overall break-even sales?
(4) Explain *why* the break-even sales in part (3) either increased or decreased.

Problem B23-4. Skinner, Inc., produces and sells three products. The operating results for the year just ended are as follows:

	Product #1	Product #2	Product #3
Sales	$500,000	$100,000	$300,000
Variable expenses	400,000	60,000	210,000
Contribution margin	$100,000	$ 40,000	$ 90,000
Fixed expenses	60,000	50,000	55,000
Net income	$ 40,000	$ (10,000)	$ 35,000

Sales consisted of 20,000, 5,000, and 10,000 units, respectively, for Products #1, #2, and #3.

Mr. Skinner, the president of the company, wants to drop Product #2 and undertake a large advertising campaign to push the sales of Product #1. His reasoning is that Product #2 is unprofitable and that Product #1 generates the most profit.

The treasurer of the company contends that Product #2 should be pushed, not dropped, since it has the highest contribution-margin ratio.

The assistant to the president argues that the company should push Product #3, since it has the highest contribution margin per unit.

(1) Evaluate all three positions and state which one you think is the best. Include financial data in your analysis.
(2) What other factors should be considered? Discuss.

Problem B23-5. Turner Company produces and sells one product in the midwestern and eastern markets. The company normally sells 300,000 units of product per year at the following expenses per unit:

Cost of goods sold:
Direct materials . . . . $ 3.20
Direct labor 4.35
Variable factory overhead 3.10
Fixed factory overhead ($705,000 ÷ 300,000) 2.35
Operating expenses:
Variable selling 1.35
Fixed administration ($195,000 ÷ 300,000) 65
$15.00

(1) Turner Company receives an offer from Blades Company to produce the product for Turner Company's customers in the eastern market. Blades Company is willing to produce and ship the product for $14.50 per unit. In such a case Turner Company would merely forward its eastern sales orders to Blades Company. Turner Company would still bill the eastern customers at the regular price and collect all receivables. The annual normal sales to the eastern market are 100,000 units of product. If Turner Company were to accept this offer, total fixed factory overhead would be reduced 30 per cent in the production of the 200,000 units and variable selling expense would be cut 40 per cent on the sale of the 100,000 units. Should Turner Company accept or reject the offer? (Hint: Try calculating the costs avoided.)
(2) Would your answer to part (1) change if the company were able to rent its idle plant facilities at $400,000 per year, if total fixed factory overhead cost remained the same, and if variable selling expense per unit were cut 40 per cent?

24

Price-level Changes
and Supplementary Statements

The unstable dollar. In a period of inflation there is an increase in the price level. Goods and services cost more; conversely, dollars are worth less because they have less purchasing power. In a period of deflation, there is a decrease in the price level; dollars are worth more because they have more purchasing power.

To illustrate a period of inflation, assume that commodities A, B, and C and services S and T provide us with a suitable statistical sample of the goods and services produced and sold in our economy. The following tabulation shows that a 60 per cent increase in the price level has occurred during the period of years between 19— and 19+5.

				Prices		
Item	19—	19+1	19+2	19+3	19+4	19+5
A	$ 10	$ 11	$ 11	$ 13	$ 15	$ 16
B	25	27	29	32	37	40
C	16	19	21	23	24	26
S	34	36	40	45	48	54
T	15	17	20	20	22	24
	$100	$110	$121	$133	$146	$160

In 19+5, $160 would be needed to purchase the same "package" of commodities and services that could have been purchased with $100 in 19—. During this hypothetical inflationary period, the purchasing power of the dollar declined.

It is a well-known fact that changes do occur in the level of prices. This condition is demonstrated by the following chart. If we use the word "size" to denote purchasing power, the size of the dollar changes; the dollar is unstable.

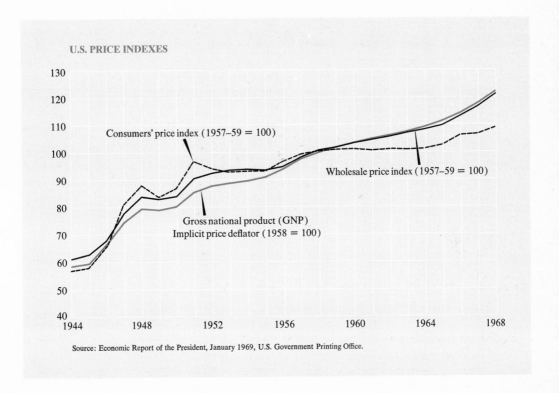

U.S. PRICE INDEXES

Consumers' price index (1957–59 = 100)

Wholesale price index (1957–59 = 100)

Gross national product (GNP)
Implicit price deflator (1958 = 100)

Source: Economic Report of the President, January 1969, U.S. Government Printing Office.

The stable-dollar assumption. As noted in Chapter 2, accounting is based on an assumption that changes in the purchasing power of the dollar will be insignificant and hence may properly be ignored. As a consequence, accounting regards all dollars as identical, whether the account balances are stated in 1945 dollars, 1955 dollars, today's dollars, or a mixture of dollars. But 1945 dollars are not the same as 1955 dollars or today's dollars. 1945 dollars were worth more—that is, they had greater general purchasing power—than 1955 dollars or today's dollars. One hundred dollars in 1945 purchased more goods and services than $100 will purchase today.

Dollars can be thought of as units of measurement; assets, liabilities, revenues, and expenses are stated in terms of dollars. Inches and pounds are also units of measurement. Units of measurement are useful in stating quantities. Amounts stated in a stable unit of measurement may be added, subtracted, or compared. For instance, the production of a factory may be stated in pounds. If this year's average daily production amounted to 200 pounds and the average daily production of some earlier year amounted to 100 pounds, the comparison tells us that production has doubled. We have confidence in such a comparison because a pound this year weighs as much as a pound of an earlier year. The size of a pound doesn't change with the passage of time. The same cannot be said of a dollar.

If a unit of measurement is to serve its function properly, it should be stable. It would be confusing to have pounds consist of 21 ounces in some years, 17 ounces in other years, and 14 ounces in the current year. If the weight of a pound varied from year to year, it would be questionable whether historical data stated in pounds should be added, subtracted, or compared with current data. If the pound were subject to such variation, it would be necessary to know the dimensions or the sizes of the pounds before meaningful comparisons could be made. In order to assure comparability, it would be necessary to adjust or convert data stated in pounds of different sizes to pounds of the same size. Without such conversion it would not be possible to conclude with any certainty, for example, that 200 present-day pounds represented twice as much as 100 pounds of some earlier period.

Inflation and comparison problems. Because the size of the dollar may change with the passage of time, comparisons of dollar amounts, without any adjustment to improve comparability, may be misleading. For example, the following comparison, covering the 25-year period shown in the chart on page 531, suggests that there has been no change in the inventory.

	December 31,	
	1943	1968
Inventory	$100,000	$100,000

Such a conclusion is probably wrong.

To continue, the following comparison taken from the balance sheets of a business might be construed to mean that the business had as much purchasing power in its cash balance in 1968 as it had 25 years earlier.

	1943 Balance Sheet	1968 Balance Sheet
Cash	$100,000	$100,000

If the purchasing power of the dollar has changed during the 25-year period, and it has, then we are comparing amounts stated in unequal units of measurement. As indicated by the chart on page 531, a 1968 dollar had about one-half as much purchasing power as did a dollar in 1943 (1943 price index divided by the 1968 price index). In other words, one 1943 dollar is equivalent to approximately two 1968 dollars (1968 price index divided by the 1943 price index). In the above comparison of cash balances, this fact is not revealed. The following comparison, in which the 100,000 1943 dollars have been converted to 1968 dollars to improve comparability, should be more meaningful, because it can be interpreted to mean that the company is holding about one-half as much purchasing power in its cash balance in 1968 as it did in 1943.

	1943 Balance Sheet Data			1968
	Unadjusted	Conversion Ratio	Stated in 1968 Dollars	1968 Balance Sheet
Cash	$100,000	2	$200,000	$100,000

Comparative statements. Many of the dollar amounts shown in comparative financial statements are "old" dollars. Therefore, comparative statements are likely to be misunderstood because of variations in the purchasing power of the dollar.

An increasing number of businesses regularly present partial or complete comparative financial statements covering a considerable number of years. Comparative financial statements for a 10-year period are fairly common. Some companies regularly report selected accounting data for a period exceeding 25 years. There are instances where selected yearly data, such as sales, are shown in each annual report since the date of organization of the corporation.

But when there have been significant movements in the general price level, the annual data covering a period of several years are not as comparable as they appear to be. Actually, they often are subject to serious misinterpretation because of the significant variations in the size of the dollar.

The following suggestion, which has received considerable support, has been advanced as a means of making comparative data more meaningful.

> Prepare statements in the customary manner, with no consideration of changes in the price level.
>
> In addition, prepare supplementary statements in which historical dollars have been converted to the size of today's dollars by the use of index numbers.

A hypothetical index of the general price level covering the years 19— through 19+5 is shown below; 19— is the base year, and the numbers indicate the price level of each year in relation to the base year. The index was developed from the data on prices tabulated on page 530. It was assumed there that commodities A, B, and C and services S and T provided us with a suitable sample of the goods and services produced and sold in our economy.

Year	Price Index
19—	100
19+1	110
19+2	121
19+3	133
19+4	146
19+5	160

A general price index does not purport to measure the price changes that occur in any single business. But even so, comparative statements prepared by the use of index numbers developed to indicate changes in the general price level provide information that should be a useful supplement to conventional statements. By the use of index numbers, dollar amounts of past years can be converted into today's dollars. When converted, the old dollar amounts are comparable with today's dollars in terms of general purchasing power. To illustrate, annual sales data for the years 19— through 19+5 are converted into 19+5 dollars by the use of the price index numbers on page 533.

| | | | | Sales | | |
Year	Price Index	Conversion Ratio		Per Books		In 19+5 Dollars (Rounded)
19—	100	160/100	×	$125,000	=	$200,000
19+1	110	160/110	×	137,000	=	200,000
19+2	121	160/121	×	150,400	=	200,000
19+3	133	160/133	×	165,300	=	200,000
19+4	146	160/146	×	181,800	=	200,000
19+5	160	160/160	×	200,000	=	200,000

The last column shows the sales in terms of 19+5 dollars. The converted amounts make its plain that the sales performance under review was probably not one of growth or expansion, as might have been the conclusion if the analysis had been confined to the unadjusted data.

It is probably apparent that the conversion ratios are developed from the price index numbers. In converting an "old" dollar amount into an equivalent number of current-year dollars, the index number applicable to the current year is used as the numerator and the index number applicable to the "old" year is used as the denominator.

$$\text{Conversion ratio} = \frac{\text{Price index of current year}}{\text{Price index for year when amount was originally recorded}}$$

Liabilities and inflation. Although the dollar amount for a given liability is fixed, it does not follow that a comparison such as that presented below is the most meaningful comparison that can be made.

	19—	19+5
Long-term loan	$50,000	$50,000

The comparison implies that nothing affecting the loan has happened between 19— and 19+5 (19+5 being the current year). But, if the general price level has increased during this period (causing the purchasing power of the dollar to decrease), something has happened; the purchasing power of the dollars borrowed was greater than the purchasing power of the dollars that will repay the loan. Normally the borrower spends the money borrowed and hence uses the amount of purchasing power provided by the loan. When the loan matures, the borrower is committed to repay the same number of dollars borrowed, not the same amount of purchasing power. Thus, during a period of rising prices it generally works out that creditors will have lost purchasing power and debtors will have gained purchasing power. Inflation tends to be less harmful financially to those in debt because they can pay back the money borrowed with "cheaper" dollars, that is, with dollars of smaller size in terms of purchasing power. It can be said that an increase in the price level reduces outstanding liabilities, not in terms of dollars, but in terms of purchasing power.

Consider the above long-term loan under the assumption that the price level had increased 60 per cent between 19— and 19+5. Although $50,000 was borrowed and must be repaid, the effective reduction in the liability that has occurred is not disclosed by a comparison using unadjusted data. If the amounts shown for the long-term liability in the 19— and 19+5 columns are stated in dollars depicting equivalent purchasing power, the comparison is made more meaningful. Because the amount in the 19— column is the one that is out of date, it should be converted to equivalent 19+5 dollars to improve comparability.

	19—	19+5	Per Cent Decrease*
Unadjusted data:			
Long-term loan....................	$50,000	$50,000	-0-%
Adjusted data:			
Long-term loan stated in 19+5 dollars# ...	$80,000	$50,000	37½%*

$$\#\,50{,}000 \ 19\text{— dollars} \times \frac{160}{100} = 80{,}000 \ 19{+}5 \text{ dollars.}$$

Using the adjusted data, the comparison indicates that in 19— the size of the loan was equivalent to 80,000 19+5 dollars. Actually the burden associated with the above long-term debt has declined by about 37½% between 19— and 19+5. This reduction is revealed by the comparison using the adjusted data.

Converting the financial statements of the current year. The point has been made in the preceding paragraphs that the usefulness of comparative statements may be impaired by changes in the purchasing power of the dollar. The same point can be raised about the financial statements of the current year. They report all dollars as though they were identical. Usually, however, some of the account balances in any given set of financial statements are the result of transactions of prior years. The property, plant, and equipment account balances can be cited as examples. Thus when, during the preparation of financial statements, account balances originating in the current year and stated in current dollars are added to or subtracted from account balances originating in prior years, a commingling of different size dollars is the result. Consider the following account balances shown in a conventional balance sheet:

Accounts receivable	$550,000
Land	550,000

If the land was acquired several years ago, it is probable that the " accounts receivable dollars" and the "land dollars" are dissimilar. Assume that the land was acquired in 19+1, when the general price index was 110, and that the index number for the current year (19+5) is 160. The account balances can be stated in equivalent purchasing-power dollars for 19+5 as follows:

Accounts receivable	$550,000
Land [$550,000 × (160/110)]	800,000

Notice the different impression of relative size when both account balances are stated in 19+5 dollars.

Similar comments may be made regarding the amounts reported in income statements. In the following simplified income statement for a service enterprise, the depreciation expense is listed along with the other amounts as though all of the dollars shown in the statement represented the same purchasing power. If the equipment being depreciated was acquired several years ago, it is likely that the "depreciation dollars" and the other dollars shown in the income statement are dissimilar and not comparable.

Conventional Income Statement
For the Year Ended December 31, 19+5

Revenue from services		$480,000
Expenses:		
Wages and salaries	$272,000	
Supplies purchased and used during the year	80,000	
Depreciation of equipment	80,000	432,000
Net income		$ 48,000

If it is assumed that the equipment being depreciated was acquired five years ago at a cost of $800,000, when the general price index was 100, the following conversions will state the equipment and depreciation amounts in 19+5 dollars. The index number for the current year is assumed to be 160.

		19+5 Dollars
Equipment	$800,000 × 160/100 =	$1,280,000
Accumulated depreciation	400,000 × 160/100 =	640,000
Depreciation charge for the current year	80,000 × 160/100 =	128,000

Since the other amounts shown in the illustrative income statement are expressed in 19+5 dollars, a supplementary income statement, with all dollars of equivalent size, would appear as follows:

Supplementary Income Statement
Adjusted for General Price-Level Changes
For the Year Ended December 31, 19+5

Revenue from services		$480,000
Expenses:		
Wages and salaries	$272,000	
Supplies purchased and used during the year	80,000	
Depreciation of equipment	128,000	480,000
Net income		$ -0-

Additional supplementary statements are shown on the following pages. The object of such supplementary statements, to repeat, is to show all amounts in dollars of uniform size. All old dollars are converted to current-year dollars.

Supplementary balance sheet. Autopark Company was organized during 19—, when the prevailing price level was indicated by an index number of 100. The company issued capital stock for $25,000.

Autopark Company commenced business operations by parking cars on rented property. In 19+4 (four years after the company was organized) a parking lot was purchased for $11,000. During 19+6 a parking structure was built, financed in part by a long-term mortgage loan. The structure was not ready for use until the first week of 19+7.

The conventional balance sheet for December 31, 19+10, is shown below. The income statement for 19+10 is omitted for the time being in order to simplify the illustration.

AUTOPARK COMPANY
Balance Sheet
December 31, 19+10

Assets		Equities		
Cash	$ 9,400	Liabilities:		
Parking lot	11,000	Mortgage payable		$ 8,000
Parking structure	36,000	Stockholders' equity:		
Accumulated depreciation	14,400*	Capital stock	$25,000	
		Retained earnings	9,000	34,000
	$42,000			$42,000

*Deduction.

Data for Supplementary Balance Sheet
19+10 Dollars

Year		Price Index
19—	Autopark Company organized	100
19+4	Parking lot purchased for cash	110
19+6	Parking structure built; financed in part with a mortgage loan (structure first used in January, 19+7)	120
19+9	Last year	140
19+10	Current year	147

		Conversion Ratio	19+10 Dollars
Account balances stated in 19— dollars:			
Capital stock	$25,000	147/100	$36,750
Account balances stated in 19+4 dollars:			
Parking lot	11,000	147/110	14,700
Account balances stated in 19+6 dollars:			
Parking structure	36,000	147/120	44,100
Accumulated depreciation	14,400	147/120	17,640
Account balances stated in 19+10 dollars:			
Cash			9,400
Mortgage payable			8,000

A supplementary balance sheet, with all amounts stated in 19+10 dollars, is presented on the next page.

AUTOPARK COMPANY
Supplementary Balance Sheet
Adjusted for General Price-Level Changes
December 31, 19+10

Assets

Cash	$ 9,400
Parking lot	14,700
Parking structure	44,100
Accumulated depreciation	17,640*
	$50,560

Equities

Liabilities:

Mortgage payable	$ 8,000

Stockholders' equity:

Capital invested by stockholders	$36,750	
Balance of stockholders' equity	5,810	42,560
		$50,560

*Deduction.

The presentation of the Stockholders' Equity section in the supplementary balance sheet differs from that in the conventional balance sheet. In a conventional balance sheet, the capital stock account shows the par or stated value of the shares issued or, in the case of no-par stock without a stated value, the amount received for the shares issued. In the supplementary statement, the account description is changed to Capital Invested by Stockholders and the historical amount is restated to show 19+10 dollars. The Balance of Stockholders' Equity is a balancing amount which should not be described as retained earnings or realized surplus.

The amounts in the above supplementary statement are stated in 19+10 dollars. Thus all of the dollars are comparable, since they are of equivalent size. The extent to which a supplementary statement may alter one's impression of the relative sizes of the various amounts is shown by the following comparative percentage analysis of the conventional and supplementary balance sheets.

December 31, 19+10 Balance Sheet Data

	Conventional		Supplementary	
	Amount	Per Cent of Total	Amount	Per Cent of Total
Cash	$ 9,400	22.4%	$ 9,400	18.6%
Parking lot	11,000	26.2	14,700	29.1
Parking structure	36,000	85.7	44,100	87.2
Accumulated depreciation	14,400*	34.3*	17,640*	34.9*
	$42,000	100.0%	$50,560	100.0%
Mortgage payable..........	$ 8,000	19.0%	$ 8,000	15.8%
Capital invested by stockholders .	25,000	59.5	36,750	72.7
Balance of stockholders' equity ..	9,000	21.5	5,810	11.5
	$42,000	100.0%	$50,560	100.0%

*Deduction.

In the conventional balance sheet, the parking lot is shown at $11,000. The supplementary balance sheet shows this asset as $14,700. Both amounts are expressions of cost; one amount is stated in 19+4 dollars ($11,000) and the other in 19+10 dollars ($14,700). It seems appropriate at this point to mention that, just as the 11,000 historical dollars may not be an indication of current value, neither may the adjusted amount of 14,700 dollars indicate current value. Both amounts are expressions of historical cost, with the cost stated in dollars of different purchasing power.

Supplementary income statement. The conventional income statement for Autopark Company for 19+10 is presented below.

AUTOPARK COMPANY
Income Statement
For the Year Ended December 31, 19+10

Parking revenue—all cash		$40,000
Expenses:		
Depreciation	$ 3,600	
Other (including interest)—all cash	34,400	38,000
Net income (income taxes are ignored)		$ 2,000

As discussed previously, the conventional measurement of net income may be misleading because some of the amounts shown in the income statement are not stated in today's dollars. In the above income statement, the depreciation expense illustrates this point. The annual charge for depreciation is 10 per cent of the cost of the parking structure, which was built with 19+6 dollars. Because the price level in 19+10 is 22½ per cent above the 19+6 level, we can state the depreciation expense in 19+10 dollars by adding 22½ per cent to the $3,600 amount (or by using the 147/120 conversion ratio). As adjusted, the depreciation expense is $4,410. We can achieve the same result by taking 10 per cent of the converted amount for the parking structure (10 per cent of $44,100).

Data for Supplementary Income Statement
In 19+10 Dollars

	19+6 Dollars	Conversion Ratio	19+10 Dollars
Account balances stated in 19+6 dollars:			
Depreciation expense	$3,600	147/120	$ 4,410
Account balances stated in 19+10 dollars:			
Parking revenue			40,000
Expenses—Other			34,400

The supplementary income statement follows.

AUTOPARK COMPANY
Supplementary Income Statement
Adjusted for General Price-Level Changes
For the Year Ended December 31, 19+10

Parking revenue		$40,000
Expenses:		
Depreciation	$ 4,410	
Other (including interest)	34,400	38,810
Net income (income taxes are ignored)		$ 1,190

The net income reported by the supplementary statement is about 40 per cent less than that reported by the conventional statement.

Supplementary comparative balance sheet. The procedure demonstrated in the preparation of a supplementary balance sheet may be used to set forth supplementary comparative balance sheet data in dollars that are uniform in terms of general purchasing power. The following comparative statement of Autopark Company is based on the same assumed facts as presented earlier in the chapter.

AUTOPARK COMPANY
Comparative Balance Sheet
December 31, 19+10 and 19+9

Assets

	19+10	19+9
Cash	$ 9,400	$ 3,800
Parking lot	11,000	11,000
Parking structure	36,000	36,000
Accumulated depreciation	14,400*	10,800*
	$42,000	$40,000

Equities

	19+10	19+9
Liabilities:		
Mortgage payable	$ 8,000	$ 8,000
Stockholders' equity:		
Capital stock	25,000	25,000
Retained earnings	9,000	7,000
	$42,000	$40,000

*Deduction.

The amounts used in the December 31, 19+10 supplementary balance sheet on page 538 are appropriate for the 19+10 column of the supplementary comparative balance sheet and need not be recomputed for this illustration. The amounts shown in the 19+9 column need to be stated in 19+10 dollars. Such conversions are noted below.

Price Index and Historical Data—Same as on Page 537

Year		Price Index
19—	Autopark Company organized	100
19+4	Parking lot purchased for cash	110
19+6	Parking structure built; financed in part with a mortgage loan (structure first used in January, 19+7)	120
19+9	Last year	140
19+10	Current year	147

19+9 Data for Supplementary Comparative Balance Sheet

	19+9 Conventional Statement	Conversion Ratio	19+10 Dollars
Account balances stated in 19— dollars:			
Capital stock	$25,000	147/100	$36,750
Account balances stated in 19+4 dollars:			
Parking lot	$11,000	147/110	$14,700
Account balances stated in 19+6 dollars:			
Parking structure	$36,000	147/120	$44,100
Accumulated depreciation	10,800	147/120	13,230
Account balances stated in 19+9 dollars:			
Cash	$ 3,800	147/140	$ 3,990
Mortgage payable	8,000	147/140	8,400
Balance of stockholders' equity—the balancing amount			$ 4,410

AUTOPARK COMPANY

Supplementary Comparative Balance Sheet
19+10 Dollars
December 31, 19+10 and 19+9

Assets

	19+10	19+9
Cash	$ 9,400	$ 3,990
Parking lot	14,700	14,700
Parking structure	44,100	44,100
Accumulated depreciation	17,640*	13,230*
	$50,560	$49,560

Equities

	19+10	19+9
Liabilities:		
Mortgage payable	$ 8,000	$ 8,400
Stockholders' equity:		
Capital invested by stockholders	36,750	36,750
Balance of stockholders' equity	5,810	4,410
	$50,560	$49,560

*Deduction.

Price-level adjustment of monetary items. When supplementary comparative balance sheets are prepared, the beginning and ending balances of the portion of the stockholders' equity described as Balance of Stockholders' Equity may be reconciled as follows:

AUTOPARK COMPANY
Statement of Changes in Balance of Stockholders' Equity
For the Year Ended December 31, 19+10

Balance of stockholders' equity, December 31, 19+9, per above	$4,410
Add:	
Net income—per supplementary statement on page 539	1,190
Price-level adjustment of monetary items	210
Balance of stockholders' equity, December 31, 19+10, per above	$5,810

This statement is like the statement of retained earnings, which shows last year's balance, the changes during the year, and the ending balance. Notice the item described as "Price-level adjustment of monetary items." Monetary items consist of cash, receivables, and liabilities. The $210 amount shown in the above statement is the difference between the prior-year book balances of the monetary items and their converted balances, as shown below.

| | 19+9 Book Balances | | Conversion Ratio | 19+10 Dollars | Differences |
	Debit	Credit			
Monetary items:					
Cash.	$3,800		147/140	$3,990	$190 debit
Mortgage payable		$8,000	147/140	8,400	400 credit
Price-level adjustment of monetary items					$210 credit

The nature of the price-level adjustment of monetary items can be explained as follows. Last year Autopark Company had a bank balance of $3,800 when the general price index was 140. During the next year (19+10), the price level increased 5 per cent, which carried the price index to 147. When cash is held during a period of rising prices, a loss in purchasing power occurs. A cash balance of $3,800 × 1.05, or $3,990, is required in 19+10 to equal the purchasing power of last year's cash balance of $3,800. Holding cash of $3,800 has caused a purchasing power loss of $190.

Purchasing power gains and losses can also arise from liabilities. In the Autopark Company example, less purchasing power is required in 19+10 to settle the mortgage liability than was required in 19+9. In effect, the burden of the liability has lessened as a result of the change in the price level. In the illustration, this "gain" in purchasing power amounted to $400.

The price-level adjustment of monetary items is the difference between the $400 gain in purchasing power from the liability and the $190 loss of purchasing power in the cash balance. Such gains and losses in purchasing power are not included in conventional income statements. For that reason they are included in the statement of changes illustrated above and are not shown in the supplementary income statement on page 539.

It should be noted that, if the price level declines, opposite results occur. Thus a declining price level would produce a gain in purchasing power in the cash balance (the same would be true for receivables) and a loss in purchasing power in connection with liabilities.

Account balances in mixed dollars. In the Autopark Company illustration, each account balance was traceable to a single year. For example, the parking lot was purchased in 19+4 and the parking structure was built in 19+6. It is not uncommon, however, for an account balance to be the result of entries made during several years. Consider the case of a company which has purchased five parcels of land during a 10-year period, each parcel costing $100,000. The following details are taken from the company's accounting records.

Land

Year of Purchase	Cost
19—	$100,000
19+4	100,000
19+6	100,000
19+9	100,000
19+10	100,000
Account balance	$500,000

Assume that the same price-index data used in the preceding examples are applicable in this case.

Year	Price Index
19—	100
19+4	110
19+6	120
19+9	140
19+10	147

The land account can be stated in 19+10 dollars by making the following conversions:

Year of Origin	Recorded Dollars	Conversion Ratios	19+10 Dollars
19—	$100,000	147/100	$147,000
19+4	100,000	147/110	133,636
19+6	100,000	147/120	122,500
19+9	100,000	147/140	105,000
19+10	100,000	147/147	100,000
Balance	$500,000		$608,136

Inventories and cost of goods sold. Autopark Company is a service enterprise, and hence there have been no inventories of merchandise and no cost of goods sold. If supplementary statements are prepared for a merchandising concern, the procedure is the same. Each account balance is analyzed in order to identify the amounts by year of origin. Any old amounts are converted to current year's general purchasing power, so that all dollars shown in the supplementary statements will be of the same size.

Balance Sheet Data
(Conventional Accounting)

	December 31,	
	19+10	19+9
Current assets:		
Merchandise inventory	$ 12,000	$ 10,000

19+10 Income Statement Data
(Conventional Accounting)

Sales			$118,000
Cost of goods sold:			
Beginning inventory.	$ 10,000		
Purchases.	90,000		
Total goods available	$100,000		
Deduct ending inventory	12,000	88,000	
Gross margin.			$ 30,000

Price Level Index

10+9 140
19+10 147

The above dollar amounts are stated in 19+10 dollars, with the exception of the December 31, 19+9 inventory of $10,000. This dollar balance can be converted to 19+10 dollars as follows:

19+9 Dollars	Conversion Ratio	19+10 Dollars
$10,000	147/140	$10,500

A supplementary income statement would show the beginning inventory at $10,500, with the result that the gross margin would be reported as $29,500. In a supplementary comparative balance sheet for December 31, 19+9 and 19+10, last year's inventory would be stated at $10,500.

Materiality. Small amounts were used in the illustrations in this chapter to help keep the data simple. A recent annual report to stockholders provides a better indication of the potential materiality of the effect of price-level changes. The Indiana Telephone Corporation reports its telephone plant and related depreciation expense in both historical dollars and today's dollars. The amounts in its 1968 report were as follows:

	Conventional Accounting	Adjusted for General Price-Level Changes
Telephone plant	$26,342,475	$31,144,241
Depreciation expense	1,319,194	1,546,636

Concluding comments about supplementary statements. Although financial statements show dollars of "mixed or varying dimensions," it is doubtful whether statement users so interpret the dollars. It is natural to regard all dollars as reflecting the current year's general purchasing power. Thus the $500,000 balance in the land account presented on page 543 would probably be thought of in terms of general purchasing power associated with present-day dollars. The same interpretation would probably apply to the property, plant, and equipment category generally. Similarly, dollar amounts shown in income statements probably are interpreted by statement users as dollars of uniform size, although the depreciation expense, as a general rule, is based on dollars expended in earlier years—often under a price structure not typical of the present period.

Thus there is an inherent weakness in the accounting process and in the resulting conventional financial statements. The weakness is the treatment of all dollars in the accounts as identical dollars. The consequences of changes in the price level are not disclosed in financial statements, a condition which no doubt contributes to the apparent widespread unawareness of the significance of an unstable dollar. Supplementary companion statements in which the dollars are stated in terms of their current general purchasing power might help to cure this situation. With companion supplementary statements, the conventional statements are less vulnerable to criticism and are thus strengthened. Of course, the value of supplementary statements depends on the rate and extent of change in the "size" of the dollar. During periods of relative stability, there would be few, if any, benefits from supplementary statements. On the other hand, during a period of inflation or deflation, when interpretation of financial statements is more difficult, supplementary statements could make a significant contribution toward improving the general level of understanding of the results of operations and the financial position of business entities.

In 1951 a committee of the American Accounting Association studied the matter of price-level changes and financial statements. It concluded that the primary financial statements should, at the present stage of accounting development, continue to reflect historical dollar costs. However, the committee expressed an opinion that "management may properly include in periodic reports to stockholders comprehensive supplementary statements which present the effects of the fluctuation in the value of the dollar upon net income and upon financial position."

The Accounting Principles Board of the American Institute of Certified Public Accountants, at its April 28, 1961 meeting, agreed that the assumption by accountants that fluctuations in the general purchasing power of the dollar may be ignored is unrealistic, and that, therefore, the Director of Accounting Research should be instructed to set up a research project to study the problem and to prepare a report containing recommendations for the disclosure of the effect of price-level changes upon the financial statements. The opinions of the research staff as set forth in the completed research study include the following: (1) It is feasible to give recognition to the effects of price-level changes on financial statements; (2) disclosure of such effects would not be misleading or dangerous to investors; and (3) the forms of disclosure favored were supplementary statements, parallel columns, or detailed supporting schedules (including charts and graphs). Subsequently, in June of 1969, the Accounting Principles Board issued a statement in which the Board (1) acknowledged the usefulness of price-level-adjusted financial statements, (2) gave its approval to supplementary price-level-adjusted financial statements, and (3) expressed its belief that use of general price-level information is not required at this time to achieve a fair presentation of financial position and results of operations.

The advisability of publishing supplementary price-level-adjusted statements has been questioned in some quarters on the ground that they would be of little usefulness because the public is generally unaware of the fact that financial statements based on the stable-dollar assumption may be misleading. It also is contended that the concurrent publication of conventional and supplementary statements showing differing results of operations and differing financial position might result in more confusion than enlightenment, and might undermine the public confidence in certi-fied statements prepared in accordance with generally accepted accounting principles. Possibly, as a starter, the disclosure of price-level-adjusted information should be limited to selected data, such as sales, net income, and earnings per share. This approach should minimize the chance for confusion which might arise initially from the presentation of two complete sets of statements.

It seems to the authors that the matter of supplementary financial statements is deserving of the increasing attention and encouragement which it is receiving. Although only a few companies now include supplementary price-level-adjusted data in their annual reports, it is expected that the practice will become more widely adopted, particularly as the purpose and nature of supplementary statements become more generally understood by the public. It is emphasized, however, that the authors are not advocating that conventional financial statements be changed or eliminated. It is merely suggested that under certain conditions additional, or companion, state-ments could provide useful supplementary information.

ASSIGNMENT
MATERIAL

QUESTIONS

1. State the stable-dollar assumption which is associated with the accounting process.

2. Discuss the relationship between stability and comparability with regard to units of measurement.

3. Why is it that comparisons of dollar amounts in financial statements may be misleading?

4. Does the following comparison, based on amounts taken from the balance sheets of a business, mean that the business had as much purchasing power in its cash balance in 1960 as in 1940?

	1940 Balance Sheet	1960 Balance Sheet
Cash	$100,000	$100,000

5. What is the purpose of supplementary statements of the type illustrated in this chapter?

6. Is it necessary to change accounting principles and the conventional financial statements in order to minimize chances for confusion and misunderstanding because the dollar is an unstable unit of measurement?

7. Why is it that inflation tends to be less harmful financially to those in debt?

8. If a supplementary balance sheet were prepared by the use of an index which indicates changes in the purchasing power of the dollar, would the balances shown therein for the assets be indicative of current values?

9. Data for the current year and the two preceding years are given below.

	Sales	General Price Index
Two years ago	$240,000	150
Last year	300,000	200
Current year	325,000	225

(a) For comparative purposes, you are to state the sales in terms of current-year dollars.

(b) What is revealed by a comparison of the restated amounts?

SHORT EXERCISES

E24-1. In the following table the cash balance of Zolo Corporation for prior years is being converted to 19+8 dollars. Supply the missing figures.

		Conversion		Cash		In 19+8
Year	Index	Ratio		Per Books		Dollars
19+5	(a)	140/100	×	$12,000	=	$ (b)
19+6	110	(c)	×	11,000	=	(d)
19+7	(e)	140/135	×	(f)	=	14,000
19+8	(g)	(h)	×	(i)	=	18,000

E24-2. In 19+7, the general price-level index was 170. The income statement of Player Company for the year shows a net income of $14,000 after adjustment for price-level changes. The adjusted statement shows a depreciation deduction of $10,200. Depreciation, the only noncash expense, was $6,600 on the unadjusted income statement and represented depreciation on assets acquired in the first year of operation. Determine (a) the price level for the year the depreciable assets were acquired; and (b) the income for 19+7 before price-level adjustments.

E24-3. A partial income statement of Converse Company for 19+6 is presented below:

CONVERSE COMPANY
Partial Income Statement
For the Year Ended December 31, 19+6

Sales		$40,000
Cost of goods sold:		
Beginning inventory.	$14,000	
Purchases.	30,000	
Total	$44,000	
Deduct ending inventory	11,000	33,000
Gross margin.		$ 7,000

All sales were for cash. Compute the gross margin after adjustment for an increase in the price level from 150 to 160 during the year. Round all amounts to the nearest dollar.

E24-4. The stockholders' equity of Supreme Corporation increased $3,300 during 19+4 as the result of price-level adjustments of monetary items, consisting of Cash, Marketable Securities, and Mortgage Payable. There was a total loss of $6,000 in the purchasing power of the cash and marketable securities. What is the balance owed on the mortgage on December 31, 19+4, if the adjusted amount of the liability as stated in the supplementary comparative balance sheet is $43,200?

PROBLEMS

Problem A24-1. Convert the following historical account balances to 19+5 dollars.

Year	Sales	Dividends	Price Index
19—	$188,000	$30,000	100
19+1	205,000	30,000	110
19+2	225,600	30,000	121
19+3	239,400	33,000	133
19+4	245,230	33,000	146
19+5	255,000	36,000	160

Carry computations to the nearest dollar.

Problem A24-2. The conventional balance sheet of Campus Apartment Company for December 31, 19+5, is presented below. The company was organized during 19—, when the prevailing price level was indicated by an index number of 100.

CAMPUS APARTMENT COMPANY
Balance Sheet
December 31, 19+5

Assets

Cash		$ 24,000
Land		84,000
Apartment building	$504,000	
Accumulated depreciation	100,800	403,200
		$511,200

Equities

Current liabilities:		
Accounts payable		$ 9,000
Long-term liabilities:		
Mortgage payable		320,000
Stockholders' equity:		
Capital stock	$150,000	
Retained earnings	32,200	182,200
		$511,200

Additional Data

Year		Price Index
19—	Campus Apartment Company organized and stock issued	100
19+1	Land purchased for cash	105
19+2	Building constructed and occupied; financed in part with a mortgage	120
19+5	Current year	147

Prepare a supplementary balance sheet as of December 31, 19+5, with all amounts stated in 19+5 dollars. Carry computations to the nearest dollar.

Problem A24-3. The conventional balance sheet of Campus Apartment Company is given on page 550. The date is December 31, 19+6, which is one year beyond the date of the balance sheet of Campus Apartment Company shown in Problem A24-2.

CAMPUS APARTMENT COMPANY
Balance Sheet
December 31, 19+6

Assets

Cash		$ 90,000
Land		84,000
Apartment building	$504,000	
Accumulated depreciation	126,000	378,000
		$552,000

Equities

Current liabilities:		
Accounts payable		$ 18,000
Long-term liabilities:		
Mortgage payable		320,000
Stockholders' equity:		
Capital stock	$150,000	
Retained earnings	64,000	214,000
		$552,000

Prepare a supplementary comparative balance sheet, with all amounts stated in 19+6 dollars. You will need to give consideration to the data set forth in Problem A24-2. The price index for 19+6 is 155. Carry computations to the nearest dollar.

Problem A24-4. Prepare a supplementary comparative income statement for Vending Corporation in 19+6 (current) dollars.

VENDING CORPORATION
Comparative Income Statement
For 19+6 and 19+5

	19+6	19+5
Revenue from coin machines	$456,000	$432,000
Expenses:		
Depreciation—Building	$ 28,800	$ 28,800
Depreciation—Machines.......................	14,400	14,400
All other	396,000	376,800
Total expenses	$439,200	$420,000
Net income	$ 16,800	$ 12,000

The building was acquired in 19+4. The machines are being depreciated at a rate of 10 per cent per year; $72,000 was invested in machines in 19+4 and another $72,000 was invested in 19+5.

Year	Price Index
19—	100
19+4...	120
19+5...	125
19+6...	130

Problem A24-5. Conventional financial statements of ZYX Company are presented below.

ZYX COMPANY
Comparative Balance Sheet
December 31, 19+10 and 19+9

Assets

	19+10	19+9
Current assets:		
Cash	$ 48,000	$ 41,800
Long-lived assets:		
Land.	22,440	22,440
Building	105,000	105,000
Accumulated depreciation	29,400*	25,200*
	$146,040	$144,040

Equities

	19+10	19+9
Long-term liabilities:		
Mortgage payable	$ 80,000	$ 80,000
Stockholders' equity:		
Capital stock	50,000	50,000
Retained earnings	16,040	14,040
	$146,040	$144,040

*Deduction.

ZYX COMPANY
Income Statement
For the Year Ended December 31, 19+10

Revenue		$80,000
Expenses:		
Depreciation.	$ 4,200	
All other	73,800	78,000
Net income		$ 2,000

Price Index and Historical Data

Year		Price Index
19—	Company organized	100
19+1	Land acquired.	102
19+3	Building constructed	105
19+4	Mortgage obtained	106
19+9	Last year	125
19+10	Current year	120

Required:

Supplementary comparative balance sheet adjusted for changes in the general price level.

Supplementary income statement.

Statement of changes in "balance of stockholders' equity."

Problem B24-1. The conventional income statement of Avenue Apartment Company is presented below. Prepare a supplementary income statement in current dollars.

AVENUE APARTMENT COMPANY
Income Statement
For the Year Ended December 31, 19+4

Rent		$300,000
Expenses:		
Depreciation—Building	$ 96,000	
Depreciation—Equipment	63,000	
All other	123,000	282,000
Net income		$ 18,000

Data from the company's ledger are set forth below.

Building		Equipment	
19+1 2,400,000		19+1 240,000	
		19+3 75,000	

The price index covering a recent period of years follows:

Year	Price Index
19—	115
19+1	120
19+2	122
19+3	125
19+4	132

Problem B24-2. The balance sheet of Substandard Building Corporation is presented below.

SUBSTANDARD BUILDING CORPORATION
Balance Sheet
December 31, 19+5
Assets

Current assets:			
Cash		$ 9,000	
Rent receivable		2,400	$ 11,400
Long-lived assets:			
Land		$ 22,880	
Building	$275,000		
Accumulated depreciation	33,000	242,000	264,880
			$276,280

Equities

Current liabilities:			
Taxes payable			$ 8,000
Long-term liabilities:			
Mortgage payable			150,000
Stockholders' equity:			
Capital stock	$100,000		
Retained earnings	18,280	118,280	
			$276,280

The corporation was organized and the capital stock issued when the price level was indicated by an index number of 100. The land was acquired for cash when the price index was 104. The building was completed and occupied when the price index was 110. The mortgage financing was secured when the index was at 108. The index is at 120 in 19+5.

Prepare a supplementary balance sheet as of December 31, 19+5, with all amounts adjusted for general price-level changes. Carry computations to the nearest dollar.

Problem B24-3. This problem is a continuation of Problem B24-2. Prepare a supplementary comparative balance sheet as of December 31, 19+6 and 19+5. The price index applicable to 19+6 is 126. During 19+6, Substandard Building Corporation purchased some additional land and issued additional stock.

SUBSTANDARD BUILDING CORPORATION
Balance Sheet
December 31, 19+6
Assets

Current assets:

Cash	$ 29,000	
Rent receivable	3,000	$ 32,000

Long-lived assets:

Land		$ 29,750	
Building	$275,000		
Accumulated depreciation	44,000	231,000	260,750
			$292,750

Equities

Current liabilities:

Taxes payable	$ 8,400

Long-term liabilities:

Mortgage payable	150,000

Stockholders' equity:

Capital stock	$112,500	
Retained earnings	21,850	134,350
		$292,750

Problem B24-4. The conventional income statement of Higman Company is presented below. Prepare a supplementary income statement adjusted for general price-level changes.

HIGMAN COMPANY
Income Statement
For the Year Ended December 31, 19+4

Sales		$300,000
Cost of goods sold:		
Beginning inventory	$ 26,250	
Purchases	210,000	
Total	$236,250	
Deduct ending inventory	44,250	192,000
Gross margin		$108,000
Expenses:		
Depreciation—Building	$ 32,000	
Depreciation—Equipment	21,000	
All other expenses	39,000	92,000
Net income		$ 16,000

The company's building was acquired in 19+1 at a cost of $800,000. The equipment was purchased as follows: $60,000 in 19+1 and $45,000 in 19+3.

A general price index covering a recent period of years is set forth below.

19+1.................	120	19+3.................	125
19+2.................	122	19+4.................	132

Problem B24-5. Comparative trial balances are set forth below. State the account balances in 19+10 dollars. Also prepare a statement of changes in "balance of stockholders' equity" for the year ended December 31, 19+10.

RST COMPANY
Trial Balances
December 31, 19+10 and 19+9

	December 31,			
	19+10		19+9	
Cash	48,000		41,800	
Land	22,440		22,440	
Building	105,000		105,000	
Accumulated depreciation		29,400		25,200
Bonds payable...............		80,000		80,000
Capital stock		50,000		50,000
Retained earnings..............		14,040		7,615
Revenue		80,000		87,500
Depreciation expense	4,200		4,200	
Other expense	73,800		76,875	
	253,440	253,440	250,315	250,315

Other Data

Year		Price Index
19—	Company organized and stock issued	100
19+1	Land acquired	102
19+3	Building constructed	105
19+4	Bonds issued	106
19+9	Last year	125
19+10	Current year	120

Income Tax Considerations

The usefulness of income tax knowledge. Obviously, knowledge of income taxes is a must for the tax specialist—attorney or accountant. But anyone faced with the necessity of making business decisions needs more than accounting data and the ability to evaluate such data; he also needs an awareness of the tax consequences of his decisions. The decision-maker can, and in some complex cases should, rely on the tax specialist for an appraisal of tax consequences. But the better the tax background of managers of business, the greater is their ability to understand and profit from the advice and counsel of the tax specialist.

Those interested in financial statements will find their comprehension level improved by an appreciation of the impact of income taxes on business. Stockholders and investors become more knowledgeable in the pursuit of their interests when they have developed a sensitivity to income taxes. The majority of adults, without regard to occupation or source of income, are involved with income taxes as taxpayers. Furthermore, income tax rules and regulations are such that informed taxpayers often can, through various proper and timely actions, affect the amount of their tax liability.

The magnitude of the income tax collections makes it desirable for the thoughtful citizen to have some familiarity with the subject. There are broad and vital considerations that should concern everyone. For instance, what is the impact of high income tax rates on individual initiative? How does the income tax relate to the size of the federal government and its role in the economic affairs of the nation in such areas as employment levels and price stability? Indeed, the question may well be put, who would not benefit from some exposure to the topic of income taxes?

With such considerations in mind, the remainder of the chapter will be devoted to a short history of the federal income tax and its purposes, a brief discussion of how tax rules are applied, and a more lengthy discussion of some areas that are of particular concern to both the accountant and the business manager.

The history of the federal income tax. Although a federal income tax was proposed as early as 1815 and such a tax was actually collected during the War Between the States, the history of the present law properly begins with the Revenue Act of 1894. In the historic case of *Pollack v. The Farmer's Loan and Trust Company,* the Supreme Court held that the tax under this law was unconstitutional. The Constitution provides that "no capitation or other direct tax shall be laid, unless in proportion to the census or enumeration hereinbefore directed to be taken." Obviously, an income tax cannot be apportioned as required by this provision. For example, no one can say that the amount of tax collected in one state whose population entitles it to 30 representatives will be three times as great as the amount of tax collected in another whose population entitles it to 10 representatives.

The Court found that the income tax at issue was a direct tax in the constitutional sense and hence invalid. Thus it was established that a federal income tax could come into being only through an amendment to the Constitution. The necessary amendment, the Sixteenth, was passed by Congress in 1909 and was ratified by the required number of State legislatures early in 1913. The Sixteenth Amendment gave Congress the "power to lay and collect taxes on incomes, from whatever source derived without apportionment . . . and without regard to any census or enumeration." The government lost little time in tapping this source with the Revenue Act of 1913. Since that time, over forty revenue acts and other laws containing tax provisions have been enacted. The most recent of these acts at the time of this printing is the Tax Reform Act of 1969.

The original purpose of the income tax was simply to raise revenue. But over the course of 55 years and forty revenue acts, the goals of the income tax laws have been broadened to include nonrevenue objectives such as the following:

(1) Redistribution of national income
(2) Control of inflation or deflation
(3) Attainment of full employment
(4) Encouragement of foreign trade
(5) Economic stimuli to certain industries
(6) Granting of subsidies for noneconomic purposes
(7) Growth of small businesses

Just as the objectives of the income tax have kept expanding, so, too, the rate of taxation has been increasing. Back in 1913, the normal rate for individuals was

1 per cent; the *minimum* is now 14 per cent. The combined normal and surtax in 1913 was only 7 per cent on incomes over $1,000,000; today the rate for an individual is 70 per cent on taxable income in excess of $100,000. The current rate of 22 per cent on the first $25,000 of net corporate income and 48 per cent on net income exceeding that amount dwarfs the 1913 rate of 1 per cent. (The current rates above do not give consideration to the additional 10 per cent surcharge enacted in 1968.) Although there have been many refinements of the tax law through the years, this marked increase in tax rates has been the most significant development.

Almost as significant as the increase in rates has been the broadening of the tax base so that more and more income has been taxed. Broadening the tax base is viewed by many as the most effective means of obtaining greater amounts of tax revenue.

As a consequence of the increase in rates and the broadening of the base, there has been a sharp rise in the number of returns filed and the amount of revenue collected. The growth of the income tax revenue is particularly striking; in the period from 1940 to 1960 alone, the government's income tax revenues rose from $2,082,000,000 to $62,209,000,000. After 1932 the total number of tax returns filed annually for individuals and fiduciaries grew from less than 4,000,000 to over 74,000,000 in 1968. With the government's increased reliance on the income tax as the prime source of revenue, the federal income tax gives every sign of being with us for many years to come.

A PROFILE VIEW OF FEDERAL INCOME TAXES

Before the accountant or businessman can appreciate the impact of federal income taxes, he must acquire some general knowledge of basic income-tax concepts. To provide this background, some of the income tax fundamentals—the classes of taxpayers, tax rates, gross income, deductions, taxable income, and other concepts—are briefly presented.

Classes of taxpayers. There are four major classes of taxable entities, or kinds of taxpayers: individuals, corporations, estates, and trusts. Each of these must file a return and pay a tax on its taxable income.

Partnerships and sole proprietorships are not taxable entities, even though they are separate business entities for accounting purposes. Their income is taxed to the individual owners involved. A partnership has to file a return, but it is for information only, showing how the partners shared the income.

Corporations, on the other hand, are taxed separately. Individual stockholders who receive after-tax profits from the corporation in the form of dividends must report those dividends in their own individual returns. As a consequence, many stockholders claim that corporate profits are subject to double taxation.

Corporations that meet certain qualifications can avoid the separate corporate tax by electing to be treated as a partnership for tax purposes. Such partnership-type corporations are commonly referred to as *Subchapter S Corporations,* from the portion of the Internal Revenue Code that affords them the election.

Income tax rates. Although there are four kinds of taxable entities, there are only two rate structures, the individual and the corporate. Estates, trusts, and individuals use the individual rate structure.

The federal individual income tax is a progressive tax. This means that those with the lowest taxable income are subject to the lowest rates, while those with higher taxable incomes are subjected to progressively higher tax rates. There is general agreement that the United States income tax rate structure is steeply progressive. Rates go from 14 per cent all the way to 70 per cent, and that maximum applies to all taxable income over $100,000. A glance at a schedule of tax rates will show how this works.

TAX RATE SCHEDULE
(In force at time of this printing but without giving consideration to 10 per cent surcharge enacted in 1968)
(Married person filing joint return)

Taxable Income	Tax (Before Credits)
$ 0 to $ 1,000	14%
1,000 to 2,000	$ 140 plus 15% on amount over $ 1,000
2,000 to 3,000	290 plus 16% on amount over 2,000
3,000 to 4,000	450 plus 17% on amount over 3,000
4,000 to 8,000	620 plus 19% on amount over 4,000
8,000 to 12,000	1,380 plus 22% on amount over 8,000
12,000 to 16,000	2,260 plus 25% on amount over 12,000
16,000 to 20,000	3,260 plus 28% on amount over 16,000
20,000 to 24,000	4,380 plus 32% on amount over 20,000
24,000 to 28,000	5,660 plus 36% on amount over 24,000
28,000 to 32,000	7,100 plus 39% on amount over 28,000
32,000 to 36,000	8,660 plus 42% on amount over 32,000
36,000 to 40,000	10,340 plus 45% on amount over 36,000
40,000 to 44,000	12,140 plus 48% on amount over 40,000
44,000 to 52,000	14,060 plus 50% on amount over 44,000
52,000 to 64,000	18,060 plus 53% on amount over 52,000
64,000 to 76,000	24,420 plus 55% on amount over 64,000
76,000 to 88,000	31,020 plus 58% on amount over 76,000
88,000 to 100,000	37,980 plus 60% on amount over 88,000
100,000 to 120,000	45,180 plus 62% on amount over 100,000
120,000 to 140,000	57,580 plus 64% on amount over 120,000
140,000 to 160,000	70,380 plus 66% on amount over 140,000
160,000 to 180,000	83,580 plus 68% on amount over 160,000
180,000 to 200,000	97,180 plus 69% on amount over 180,000
200,000 and over	110,980 plus 70% on amount over 200,000

The progressive tax is designed to accomplish an equitable distribution of the burden of taxation by distributing the tax load according to the ability to pay. The progressive income tax also helps create economic stability. Inflationary and deflationary trends are minimized; an inflationary expansion of income is dampened by an automatic increase in taxes and a decrease in personal income is softened by an automatic reduction in taxes which results in a smaller decline in disposable income. These are the advantages pointed out by supporters of the progressive tax rates.

The progressive income tax also has many critics. They charge that the progressive tax discourages personal initiative by minimizing incentives. For example, suppose a married executive is making $24,000 in taxable income and paying $5,660 a year in taxes, or an average tax of 23.5 per cent (see schedule). Also suppose that he is offered a more responsible position with an annual taxable income of $28,000 a year. If he takes the new position, his new tax bill will be $7,100, or an average tax of 25.4 per cent. With this small increase in average tax rates, the executive might feel that the salary increase is worth the added work and responsibility. But he might feel differently if he judges his salary increase in terms of marginal tax rates; every dollar of taxable income that he makes over $24,000 will be taxed at a 36 per cent rate. Since he could keep only 64 per cent of his raise, he might not feel that the new position is worth it. The higher up the income ladder one goes, the more one encounters this situation. Whether the progressive tax discourages initiative to the degree some claim it does is open to debate, but there is no doubt that it promotes the search for tax-exempt and tax-favored income.

The schedule on page 558 is not the only tax schedule. This schedule reflects the split-income privilege accorded married taxpayers. Married persons filing separately use a different schedule wherein the dollar amount of the brackets are exactly half the bracket amounts in the joint schedule.

Further, schedules are provided for (1) single persons and (2) so-called heads-of-household. The schedule for single persons is designed so that they will not pay a tax more than 20% greater than a married couple with the same income filing jointly. Some additional relief is granted heads-of-household.

Compared to the individual rate tables, corporate taxation is quite simple. There is a normal tax of 22 per cent on taxable income up to and including $25,000 and an additional 26 per cent surtax on all taxable income over $25,000. In the same way that the marginal tax has an impact on individual decisions, the combined normal and surtax rate of 48 per cent affects corporate decisions. For example, a $26,000 corporate taxable income is taxed at an average rate of 23 per cent, but the last $1,000 earned is taxed at the marginal rate of 48 per cent. If the corporation can defer the last $1,000 until a later year, possibly it can keep $780 of the $1,000 instead of $520. (Again, no consideration has been given to the 10 per cent surcharge enacted in 1968 because it may prove to be temporary.)

Individual gross income. As defined in the Internal Revenue Code, gross income includes "all income from whatever source derived." This general definition is somewhat misleading; there are many items that do not constitute income for tax purposes. Among them are gifts, bequests, social security benefits, certain money damages, and other items. Of course, most of the money an individual receives is included. Wages, dividends, business income, rents, bonuses, and tips are all subject to the income tax.

Deductions. Certain expenses can be subtracted from the taxpayer's gross income in computing his net taxable income; these are called *income tax deductions.* These deductions are of two types: (1) deductions from gross income to arrive at adjusted gross income and (2) deductions from adjusted gross income to arrive at net taxable income.

The deductions from gross income are generally of a business nature. They include expenses for salaries and wages paid, advertising, depreciation, expenses attributable to earning rents, losses from the sale of property, and certain other expenses. By subtracting these deductions from gross income, the taxpayer determines his adjusted gross income.

The next step is to compute taxable net income by subtracting deductions from adjusted gross income. Here the taxpayer has a choice: He can subtract either his itemized deductions (local and state taxes, charitable contributions, medical expenses, interest payments, and certain other expenses) *or* a standard deduction.

The standard deduction is a percent of adjusted gross income with a maximum as follows: 10% and $1,000 until 1971; 13% and $1,500 in 1971; 14% and $2,000 in 1972; and 15% and $2,000 thereafter. (There is also a low-income allowance which as the name implies, is only effective at minimum income levels.) The majority of high-income taxpayers consider itemizing their deductions, because of the limits on the standard deduction. On the other hand, most lower-income taxpayers claim the standard deduction.

Each individual taxpayer is allowed a separate deduction for personal exemptions, in addition to either the standard deduction or itemized deductions just mentioned. A taxpayer is entitled to an exemption for himself and one for each of his dependents (his wife and minor children are typical dependents), with additional exemptions for old age (over 65) and blindness. The deduction is $625 for 1970; $650 for 1971; $700 for 1972; and $750 for later years.

What is left after all deductions from adjusted gross income is taxable income, against which the appropriate tax rate is applied. (If a surcharge is in effect, there is additional "tax on the tax.") The result is the tax that must be paid, unless the taxpayer is eligible for certain credits he can subtract from this figure. Examples include a credit allowed elderly taxpayers equal to a stated per cent of certain classes of "retirement" income and a credit for foreign taxes.

Capital gains and losses. One of the most interesting and important aspects of our tax system is the special tax treatment of gains and losses from the sale of capital assets. This special treatment results in a tax that is sometimes one-half (and often less than half) of what the tax would be on a like amount of ordinary income. Because of this special treatment, most taxpayers and their advisers make an effort to get capital gains income instead of ordinary income. Although the ways of doing this are varied and complex, here is a thumbnail sketch of the capital-gains-and-losses situation.

The tax statute defines capital assets. The definition does not correspond very closely with business, economic, or accounting terminology. The capital assets most commonly held by taxpayers include shares of stock, bonds, a personal residence, and land. Business inventories are not capital assets.

The next question is how to measure capital gain and loss. Gain (or loss) is measured by the difference between the selling price and the capital asset's "basis."

Basis rules are quite complicated. For our purposes, we shall use the most common standard of basis: the cost of purchased property.

Another requirement for special tax treatment is that the capital gains must be long-term gains; in tax terms, this means that the assets must have been held for more than six months prior to sale.

Only *net* long-term capital gains are given special treatment. Very specific rules are followed to arrive at net capital gain and loss figures. These so-called "offsetting" rules are necessarily subjects for a tax manual. For our purposes, keep in mind that, in general, long-term gains are offset by long-term losses and short-term gains by short-term losses.

Here is an example of a capital gains situation: The taxpayer buys a share of Big Steel (a capital asset) at $40 (his basis). He also buys a share of Telephone at $60 (his basis). Seven months later he sells Big Steel for $70 and Telephone for $50. Result: Taxpayer has a long-term capital gain of $30 on Big Steel ($70 minus $40) and a long-term capital loss of $10 on Telephone ($60 minus $50). After offsetting these two figures, he has a net long-term capital gain of $20.

If capital losses exceed capital gains, so that there is a net capital loss, the loss can be used to offset up to $1,000 of taxpayer's other taxable income each year. But only 50 cents of each $1.00 of long-term loss may be so offset. Any net capital losses (subject to the same limitation) that are not used fully can be carried forward and used in succeeding years.

The tax law for capital gains is tailored to meet a certain purpose. With a maximum tax rate on capital gains of 29.5 per cent for 1970, 32.5 per cent for 1971 and 35 per cent thereafter, those with "risk capital" are encouraged to make capital investments. They might not do so if their gains were taxed at the high ordinary income rates. By holding down the tax on capital gains, capital investment is encouraged and the whole economy benefits.

Corporate taxation. The corporation is taxed generally in the same way as an individual: Gross income less allowable deductions equals net taxable income. Aside from the deductions which are obviously not applicable to corporations (personal exemptions and the standard deduction), there are other important differences:

(1) The capital gain subject to tax is computed differently, but the tax is limited to 30 per cent of the gain.

(2) There is a more stringent limit on corporate deductions for charitable contributions.

(3) Dividends received are treated much more liberally in corporate tax returns than for individuals.

(4) There are also other special deductions that corporations are allowed to take: organizational expenses; a percentage of dividends received from certain foreign corporations; and others.

Aside from these basic differences, corporate taxable income equals gross income minus the usual deductions.

Corporations engaged in a trade or business are permitted to carry back losses or carry them forward. For example, should a company suffer a net loss of $50,000 in 19+8, the loss can be carried back to 19+5 and deducted from the earnings of that year. The 19+5 income tax is refigured and the difference between the tax paid and the revised tax for 19+5 is refunded.

Losses may be carried back and deducted from the earnings of the three preceding years. But suppose that the 19+8 loss is greater than the earnings of the three preceding years? Any unused loss may then be carried forward and deducted from earnings of the next five years. If a company's losses exceed the earnings of the three preceding years, with the result that the company has a loss carryforward, future earnings equal to the loss carryforward are tax-free. This tax status can be a matter of considerable importance when future earnings prospects of a currently unprofitable company are evaluated.

The operation of the carryback-carryforward provisions is illustrated in the following table, in which a company that was profitable during the years 19+5 through 19+7 turns unprofitable for 19+8 and 19+9.

	19+5	19+6	19+7	19+8	19+9
Taxable income (loss*)	$10,000	$15,000	$5,000	$50,000*	$25,000*
Loss carryback	10,000*	15,000*	5,000*	30,000	
Loss carryforward.				$20,000*	$45,000*

If the company should earn $45,000 during the next two years, there would be no income tax on the earnings because of the carryforward privilege.

BUSINESS INCOME VERSUS TAXABLE INCOME

Taxable income is a statutory concept that is governed by considerations of public policy; business income follows the generally accepted principles of accounting. Taxable income is computed for one purpose, the payment of taxes; business income is designed to measure the results of operations. Even though both are termed "income," the dissimilar objectives of the two income concepts cause real differences. Many think that there should be greater conformity. For example, a committee of the American Accounting Association stated that "the interest of government, business and the public would best be served if the definition of business income subject to tax were made as nearly as possible coincidental with net income under generally accepted accounting principles." It will be quite some time before these differences are reconciled, if ever.

Tax returns can depart from income statements in two principal ways: (1) some items of revenue and expense that are properly included in the computation of business income are excluded from the computation of taxable income; and (2) a taxpayer can elect to report certain items of revenue or expense in his tax return differently from the way he reports them in his income statement.

The following examples deal more specifically with some of the differences between taxable income and that shown in the books and financial statements.

Differences in concepts. As stated above, the computation of taxable income excludes certain items of business income and expense. These exclusions are dictated by considerations having little relevance to accounting principles. Here is a list of the main exclusions:

(1) Although it is actually business income, interest received on state or municipal bonds is not taxed by the federal government for constitutional reasons.

(2) Only "ordinary and necessary" business expenses are tax deductible. What the Internal Revenue Service means by "ordinary and necessary" does not always coincide with the businessman's interpretation. Result: Some business expenses cannot be deducted for tax purposes.

(3) Only reasonable amounts can be deducted for salaries and other compensation. But for accounting purposes, salaries and wages are considered a business expense no matter how large and unreasonable they are by Internal Revenue Service standards.

(4) Life insurance proceeds are not included in taxable income. On the other hand, deductions for insurance premiums are not allowed.

The government's effort to stimulate investments through tax deductions also contributes to the differences between accounting and taxable income. An example is the percentage depletion allowance. By allowing certain taxpayers a special depletion deduction computed as a percentage of their annual gross income from the exploitation of wasting assets, the government permits these taxpayers to recover more than the original cost of their income-producing property in some cases. This type of depletion has no counterpart in the accounting field.

The taxpayer's method of accounting. To appreciate how the use of different methods for tax and accounting purposes causes income measurement and reporting problems, we must look into the general rules governing the taxpayer's accounting procedures.

Section 446 of the Code provides that "taxable income shall be computed under the method of accounting on the basis of which the taxpayer regularly computes his income in keeping his books." Generally, the taxpayer uses either the cash method or the accrual method (see page 27). Whichever one the taxpayer uses, it must "clearly reflect income" or the government will prescribe a method that does. Most businesses use the accrual method.

If Section 446 were the only Code provision dealing with methods of accounting, there would be little problem. The taxpayer's business and taxable income would be kept on the same basis and differences between the two incomes would be confined to the expense and income differences mentioned earlier. But this is not the case.

Different methods for books and taxes. The taxpayer often may, and sometimes must, use an accounting method for tax purposes other than his regular method. In such situations he will use two methods for the same item of income or expense—one method for his books and financial statements and another to determine his taxable income. This practice obviously widens the gap between the two incomes.

Here are two situations in which the taxpayer may be forced to use a different method for tax-computation purposes:

(1) Generally, prepaid income is taxable in the year received; it makes no difference that the taxpayer may be on the accrual basis. For example, advance payments of rent are taxed when received, even though accrual-basis taxpayers do not include them as income in financial statements until the year they are earned.

(2) Accountants estimate future costs related to current revenue and regard them as current expenses. An example is the cost of performance under warranty and service contracts. In figuring taxable income, whether he is on a cash basis or an accrual basis, the taxpayer is usually not allowed to deduct the future costs until they have become fixed and determinable.

Elective methods. The Code also permits the taxpayer to adopt for income tax purposes, with respect to certain specific items, accounting methods that are different from those used in his books and financial statements. These elective methods include the installment sales method, accelerated depreciation, the deferred-payment sales method, various development expenses, and other items.

The *lifo* inventory method can also be elected for tax purposes, but if it is, it must also be used for accounting purposes.

The installment sales method and accelerated depreciation are two outstanding examples of elective methods.

(1) The installment sales method of reporting income allows taxpayers who receive income from installment sales, and who are using the accrual method in the books and financial statements, to report as income for tax purposes amounts based on collections. This permits an accrual-basis taxpayer, who would otherwise be taxed in the year of sale, to postpone the payment of taxes.

(2) The Code allows a deduction for depreciation in computing taxable income. Two methods of computing depreciation—the straight-line method and the sum of years' digits method—are discussed on pages 231–232. Other accelerated depreciation methods besides the sum of years' digits method are also available. Even though he uses one of the accelerated methods for tax purposes, the taxpayer can continue using the straight-line method in his books. If this is done, there is a difference between taxable and book income.

When one of the elective methods is used, the taxpayer must maintain such records as are necessary to support his determination of taxable income.

Financial reporting problems created by tax elections. Whenever a method is elected for tax purposes that is different from that used for accounting purposes, a problem arises in connection with the reporting of net income in the taxpayer's income statement. In particular, the question concerns the proper amount to show for income tax expense. The nature of the problem can be seen if the income of a corporation is computed under two different conditions:

Case A—The company adopts straight-line depreciation for its books and its tax return.

Case B—The company adopts straight-line depreciation for its books and sum of years' digits depreciation for its tax return.

Data for illustration:

Cost of equipment $150,000
Useful life . . . . 5 years
Salvage value . . . . None
Income tax rate 50%

Case A: **Same depreciation methods.**

			Year			Total for
	1	2	3	4	5	5 Years
Net income before depreciation and income tax	$200,000	$200,000	$200,000	$200,000	$200,000	$1,000,000
Depreciation expense—Straight-line	30,000	30,000	30,000	30,000	30,000	150,000
Net income before income tax	$170,000	$170,000	$170,000	$170,000	$170,000	$ 850,000
Income tax expense	85,000	85,000	85,000	85,000	85,000	425,000
Net income	$ 85,000	$ 85,000	$ 85,000	$ 85,000	$ 85,000	$ 425,000

Case B: **Different depreciation methods.**

			Year			Total for
	1	2	3	4	5	5 Years
Taxable income before depreciation	$200,000	$200,000	$200,000	$200,000	$200,000	$1,000,000
Depreciation—Sum of years' digits	50,000	40,000	30,000	20,000	10,000	150,000
Taxable income	$150,000	$160,000	$170,000	$180,000	$190,000	$ 850,000
Income tax—50%	$ 75,000	$ 80,000	$ 85,000	$ 90,000	$ 95,000	$ 425,000

Income Statement Data

(Assuming for the moment that the proper measure of income tax expense is the tax shown in the tax return)

			Year			Total for
	1	2	3	4	5	5 Years
Net income before depreciation and income tax	$200,000	$200,000	$200,000	$200,000	$200,000	$1,000,000
Depreciation expense—Straight-line	30,000	30,000	30,000	30,000	30,000	150,000
Net income before income tax	$170,000	$170,000	$170,000	$170,000	$170,000	$ 850,000
Income tax expense—per schedule above	75,000	80,000	85,000	90,000	95,000	425,000
Net income	$ 95,000	$ 90,000	$ 85,000	$ 80,000	$ 75,000	$ 425,000

A comparison of the net income amounts in Cases A and B shows that the five-year total is the same, but that the annual amounts have a different pattern. In the Case B situation, investors and creditors would probably be puzzled by the increasing income tax charges and the declining net income, since the income statements would show that the company's business was steady.

The question confronting the accountant is this: Should the adoption of different methods for book and tax purposes affect the net income shown in the financial statements? As indicated by the illustration, the aggregate depreciation taken over the life of the asset is the same under both methods; so is the income tax for the five-year period. (The aggregate income tax would be different if there were changes in tax rates during the five-year period.) The question is whether something should be done to remove the influence of a tax election from the income statement.

This kind of distortion can be removed from the income statement when the following policy is adopted:

> Whenever a different method is elected for tax purposes only, show as income tax expense, not the amount of tax actually payable, but the amount that would be payable if the accounting method used in the books had been used also for tax purposes.

Accountants refer to this policy as *income tax allocation*. It is widely practiced. If we apply income tax-allocation procedures to Case B, the earnings distortion will be removed and the net income reported in the income statement will agree with that reported in Case A. The accounting for income taxes in Case B, following tax-allocation procedures, is shown by the following entries. Note that in each year the amount credited to the income tax payable account equals the actual tax liability.

Year 1 tax expense:

Income tax expense	85,000	
Income tax payable		75,000
Deferred income tax		10,000

Tax for year 1 paid:

Income tax payable	75,000	
Cash		75,000

Year 2 tax expense:

Income tax expense	85,000	
Income tax payable		80,000
Deferred income tax		5,000

Tax for year 2 paid:

Income tax payable	80,000	
Cash		80,000

Year 3 tax expense:

Income tax expense	85,000	
Income tax payable		85,000

Tax for year 3 paid:

Income tax payable	85,000	
Cash		85,000

Year 4 tax expense:

Income tax expense	85,000	
Deferred income tax	5,000	
Income tax payable		90,000

Tax for year 4 paid:

Income tax payable	90,000	
Cash		90,000

Year 5 tax expense:

Income tax expense	85,000	
Deferred income tax	10,000	
Income tax payable		95,000

Tax for year 5 paid:

Income tax payable	95,000	
Cash		95,000

The five-year history of the deferred income tax account, which is shown among the liabilities in the balance sheet, is presented below.

DEFERRED INCOME TAX

Year		Year	
4	5,000	1	10,000
5	10,000	2	5,000

The following question may now be raised: Why would a company want to elect a different method just for income tax purposes if, because of the accountant's use of tax-allocation procedures, the election had no effect on net income? The attraction lies with the difference in timing of cash disbursements for income taxes. The tax payments under Cases A and B are set forth below.

	Cash Payments for Income Taxes	
Year	Case A	Case B
1	$ 85,000	$ 75,000
2	85,000	80,000
3	85,000	85,000
4	85,000	90,000
5	85,000	95,000
	$425,000	$425,000

Given a choice, most businessmen will select the Case B schedule of payments because it gives them longer use of some of the funds ultimately payable to the government for taxes. Whenever a payment can be postponed without penalty or cost, that alternative will generally appeal to the businessman.

THE IMPACT OF INCOME TAXES ON BUSINESS DECISIONS

When corporate and individual tax rates were insignificant, businessmen could afford to make decisions without regard to income taxes. However, for today's businessman, net income *after* taxes is the primary measure of his business success. Therefore, tax economy and planning have become business functions as necessary as marketing, advertising, or sales.

One key fact helps explain why this is so: a tax dollar saved is even more profitable than an extra dollar earned. An extra dollar of income before taxes has to be shared with the tax collector. If, for example, a taxpayer is in the 50 per cent bracket (that is, he must earn a $2 profit to retain $1), a tax saving of $1 is worth as much as a $2 increase in net operating income. To put it another way, to obtain the same net income effect as that produced by a few hundred or thousand dollars in tax savings, very substantial increases in sales might be required. Assume a tax saving of $10,000. The required increases in sales, assuming various rates of net income, are shown below.

If the company's per cent of net income to sales is	To increase the net income as much as it would be increased by the assumed tax savings, or	The required increase in sales would be
20%	$10,000	$ 50,000
15%	10,000	66,667
10%	10,000	100,000
5%	10,000	200,000
2%	10,000	500,000

With tax dollars at stake in practically every type of business decision, many businessmen seek guidance from tax specialists. These specialists are usually from the accounting or legal professions. Aside from their importance in terms of dollar savings, tax specialists are often helpful for other reasons.

One reason is that income taxes are sometimes too complicated for the average businessman. Often it takes a man with time and special training just to fill out the tax return and compute the tax for even a small business.

Another reason is that tax-saving opportunities usually must be recognized when they arise, or they are lost. Again the average businessman lacks the necessary time and training. If he engages a tax specialist, the specialist can plan tax strategies and make sure that no tax-saving opportunities are missed. The businessman can then implement his adviser's suggestions by making decisions at the right time and in the right way.

Evasion and avoidance. Before we go into specific examples of the impact of taxes on business, an explanation of the difference between tax avoidance and tax evasion is in order. Tax evasion is illegal, but tax avoidance is allowed. The whole purpose of tax avoidance is to prevent a needless tax liability coming into existence. Whatever means is used to accomplish this end is unimportant, assuming that it is legal apart from tax considerations. The significant point is that no tax liability is incurred. The tax evader, on the other hand, denies or fails to report a tax liability that is already in existence. Because it is sometimes difficult to know if a tax liability has been incurred, the distinction between tax evasion and tax avoidance is not always easy to make. None of the tax matters covered in this section is based on either a tax-evading "scheme" or a strained interpretation of the tax laws. Tax avoidance, as dealt with here, is both a proper and a profitable activity.

Effect of taxes on business organization. One of the businessman's first decisions—what legal form his business will have—has income tax overtones. He knows the three basic business forms: the sole proprietorship, the partnership, and the corporation. The businessman also knows that he cannot restrict himself to legal considerations but must study the tax consequences of his final choice. Here are some of the points he should consider.

As noted earlier, the sole proprietor must pay a tax on the entire taxable income of his business. The partner must also pay his proportionate share on the taxable income of the partnership. If the businessman decides to incorporate his business, a new taxpayer comes into existence. The corporation (unless it elects *Subchapter S* treatment) must report and pay a tax on its income, and the stockholders must also include their dividend income in their individual returns. In other words, distributed corporate earnings are taxed twice.

Before he decides on the form of his business, the businessman and his tax assistant should estimate how he would fare from a tax standpoint under the alternative business forms. For example, suppose that he is trying to decide whether to organize his business as a corporation or as a sole proprietorship. He plans on receiving $10,000 a year as compensation for his services if he operates as a corporation. He expects that the revenue of the business will be $100,000 a year and that operating expenses other than his salary will be $60,000. Although most businesses retain some of their earnings for expansion, in this case the plan is to distribute all of its net income. Here is a comparison of the income tax status of the two forms of organization being considered (the 1968 enacted surcharge is ignored):

Operating Results

	Corporation		Sole Proprietorship	
Sales		$100,000		$100,000
Deduct expenses:				
Owner's salary	$10,000		$ 0	
Other expenses	60,000	70,000	60,000	60,000
Net income before corporate income tax		$ 30,000		
Deduct corporate income tax		7,900		
Net income distributed to owner		$ 22,100		$ 40,000

Owner's Income and Tax Payments

	Corporation	Sole Proprietorship
Salary	$10,000	
Dividends	22,100	
Total income	$ 32,100	$ 40,000
Income tax ($5,000 deductions and exemptions and joint return used) . .		9,920
Income tax ($5,000 deductions and exemptions: $200 dividend exclusion; and joint return used)	6,704	
Disposable income	$ 25,396	$ 30,080

This example does not prove that the sole proprietorship always has an income tax advantage over the corporation. It merely shows how the comparison between the forms should be made. In the final analysis, many other tax features should be weighed. Following are a few of these features.

In our example, we assumed that the corporation distributed all of its earnings; this is not the usual case. Corporations may retain part of their earnings. Even though there are limits, it still means that a corporation can hold on to some of its earnings and avoid distributing taxable dividends. Unlike a partnership or sole proprietorship, where *all* business income is reported by the owners, the corporation can control the flow of income to its stockholders by retaining earnings.

Other corporate tax features are the various tax-favored pension, profit-sharing, and insurance plans that are designed for use in corporations. Although sole proprietors and partners can set up similar plans, theirs are much more restricted than the plans that can be established by corporations.

Whatever business form is finally chosen, it is certain that income taxes should play a significant role in the decision.

The timing of income and expenses for tax purposes. One of the ways income taxes can be controlled is through prudent spending and selling policies. The proper timing of receipts and expenditures is one of the simplest and most effective ways of controlling taxable income. The guidelines for the businessman are:

(1) Avoid bunching income in one year and expenses in another.
(2) If a big-income year is anticipated, hold off discretionary expenses so that they can be deducted in the high-income year.
(3) If there is to be an increase or decrease in tax rates, accelerate or defer income and expenses accordingly.
(4) Avoid having long-term capital gains and long-term capital losses in the same year. Long-term capital gains are desirable; offsetting losses water them down.

These simple guidelines are among the most effective of all tax-saving devices. They further illustrate the influence of income taxes on basic business decisions.

Effect of taxes on financing arrangements. If an enterprise is incorporated, the way it is financed can have an effect on its net income and its income tax expense in subsequent years. The reason is that interest on bonds and other forms of indebtedness is deductible while dividends on stock are not. Thus, when a corporation needs funds, it will often find borrowing more advantageous than issuing stock.

A simple example will illustrate this point. Suppose that a company in the 48 per cent tax bracket is considering the following alternatives for obtaining $200,000 on which it expects to earn 10 per cent: (1) issuance of 6 per cent preferred stock, or (2) borrowing at the rate of 5 per cent.* The after-tax results of the two alternatives are shown below.

	Issue Stock	Borrow
Earnings ($200,000 × 10%)	$20,000	$20,000
Deduct interest ($200,000 × 5%)	-0-	10,000
Taxable income	$20,000	$10,000
Deduct corporate income tax:		
($20,000 × 48%)	9,600	
($10,000 × 48%)		4,800
Earnings after taxes	$10,400	$ 5,200
Deduct preferred dividends ($200,000 × 6%)	12,000	-0-
Earnings available to reinvest or distribute to the common stockholders	$ (1,200)	$ 5,200

Taxes have a major bearing on many other financial-planning decisions. For instance, the decision whether to buy or lease is also affected by taxes. Leasing arrangements may allow rental deductions in excess of the depreciation deductions that would be available to the company if it were to buy property.

Taxes and inventories. Taxes also influence the choice of method of inventory valuation. Inventory valuation is a major factor in the determination of taxable income. You will recall that the book value of goods in inventory at the end of the year affects the company's cost of goods sold. This, in turn, has an effect on the net income figures. To put it another way, the lower the valuation placed on the ending inventory, the lower the taxable income. Thus different methods of inventory valuation can cause substantial differences in taxable income. The last-in, first-out (*lifo*) method of valuation has received much attention in recent years and has been adopted by many taxpayers because of its tax advantages.

The effect of taxes on the form of business transactions. Many business transactions are purposely framed in a way that will qualify them for tax-favored treatment. For example, when a taxpayer sells his business, he will usually try to allocate a large part of his selling price to goodwill. This is done because goodwill is taxed at the lower

---

*Interest rates are generally lower than dividend rates on preferred stock.

capital gains rate. On the other hand, a buyer of a business wants a major part of the purchase price allocated to the depreciable assets; his total depreciation deductions depend on what he pays for them. Another instance in which terms and conditions are influenced by taxes is the sale of land under an installment contract. If more than 30 per cent of the purchase price is received in the first year, the gain from the sale cannot be prorated over the period during which the installment payments are received. The installment seller must see that the combined down payment and installment collections during the first year do not exceed 30 per cent of the sale price if he wants tax-favored treatment.

Income taxes and hold-or-sell decisions. In reaching a decision about holding or selling income-producing assets, the owner usually should give consideration to income tax consequences. In doing so, he would, as a general rule, regard the income from the asset as incremental (or marginal) income. That is, the income would be regarded as taxable at the highest rate paid by the owner. To illustrate, assume that an individual in the 60 per cent tax bracket has owned an apartment building for 15 years. Data relating to the building are given below:

Cost.	$120,000
Useful life when new	20 years
Present remaining useful life	5 years
Undepreciated cost (tax basis)	$30,000
Salvage value	None
Annual rental income after all expenses except depreciation	$20,000
Depreciation expense	6,000
Income before tax	$14,000
Income tax—60%	8,400
After-tax income from building	$ 5,600
Remaining life of building in years	5
Total prospective after-tax income from building	$28,000

Assume further that the asset qualifies for treatment as a capital asset and that the owner receives an offer of $80,000 for the property. His after-tax gain would be computed as follows:

Sale price	$80,000
Basis	30,000
Capital gain	$50,000
Tax—25% (assumed rate)	12,500
After-tax gain	$37,500

The sale alternative is attractive on two counts:

It offers the larger after-tax income.

The larger after-tax income is available now; if the building is held, the owner must wait up to five years for some of the income.

What are the after-tax earnings prospects of the purchaser if he is in the 40 per cent tax bracket?

Annual rental income after all expenses except depreciation......	$20,000
Depreciation expense ($80,000 ÷ 5).....................	16,000
Income before tax	$ 4,000
Income tax—40%.................................	1,600
After-tax income from building........................	$ 2,400
Average investment in building—$80,000 initially and $0 when asset is fully depreciated gives a simple average of..............	$40,000
After-tax return on investment	6%

Concluding note. This introduction to income taxes will have been worthwhile if opinions such as the following are the result:

Income taxes cannot wisely be ignored in business affairs.

Income taxes are so complicated that one should never conclude quickly and with supreme confidence that he knows and has considered all of the tax consequences of a given course of action.

It is a sign of wisdom in many cases to seek tax advice from those with training and experience in the subject.

ASSIGNMENT
MATERIAL

QUESTIONS

1. Mention some of the goals of income tax laws.
2. Name the four major classes of taxable entities.
3. How is the income of a partnership taxed under the federal income tax law?
4. Discuss some theoretical advantages of a progressive income tax.
5. Describe in general terms the operation of the loss carryback-carryforward privilege.
6. Name the two principal ways in which tax return income can differ from the net income before income tax shown in the income statement.
7. May a corporation adopt a different method of depreciation for its books and financial statements from that adopted for income tax purposes?
8. What is the objective of income tax-allocation procedures?
9. Distinguish between tax evasion and tax avoidance.
10. Explain why income taxes may affect the type of business organization used by a businessman.
11. Explain why income taxes may affect the financing arrangements adopted by a business.
12. Mention some of the ways by which a businessman, by the timing of receipts and expenditures, may affect his taxable income.

SHORT EXERCISES

E25-1. Goren Company reports taxable income as follows for the first seven years of operation:

19+2	$ 3,000 profit
19+3	6,000 profit
19+4	5,000 loss
19+5	8,000 loss
19+6	4,000 profit
19+7	11,000 profit
19+8	6,000 loss

What is the taxable income for each year after application of the loss carryback-carryforward provisions?

E25-2. Griffin Corporation purchased for $10,000 an asset having a useful life of 10 years on January 1, 19+3. What is the first-year tax advantage (computed to the nearest dollar) of the sum of years' digits method over the straight-line method, assuming a constant tax rate of 50 per cent? What is the tax advantage of the method over the ten-year period?

E25-3. Minnesota Corporation, which does not use income tax-allocation procedures, uses the straight-line method to depreciate certain assets for income-statement purposes. The use of a different method for tax depreciation resulted in the following differences between the net income reported in the income statement and net income reported in the tax return:

	Net Income	
	Income Statement	Tax Return
19+3...........................	$ 6,000	$ 4,000
19+4...........................	8,000	7,000
19+5...........................	12,000	9,000
19+6...........................	13,000	14,000
19+7...........................	15,000	18,000

By what amounts would the December 31, 19+7 balance sheet differ if the company had used tax-allocation procedures beginning January 1, 19+3? The corporation's tax rate is 50 per cent.

E25-4. Ken Knight sold for $35,000 a capital asset that cost $40,000 and had accumulated depreciation of $15,000. Assuming that he is in the 70 per cent tax bracket, compute his tax savings as a result of the capital gains provisions of the tax law, assuming that his capital gain rate is 25%.

PROBLEMS

Problem A 25-1. Early in 19+1, Dart Company purchased specialized production facilities for $800,000. It was anticipated at the time of purchase that the product manufactured by the specialized facilities would be in demand for only four years and that the facilities would have no scrap value thereafter.

During each of the four years (19+1 through 19+4) the company earned $600,000 before depreciation and income tax. The company used the sum of the years' digits method of depreciation for income tax purposes and the straight-line method for its books, and followed income tax-allocation procedures.

(a) Compute the net income for the years 19+1, 19+2, 19+3, and 19+4, following income tax-allocation procedures. You may assume a 50 per cent income tax rate.

(b) Set up a T-account for Deferred Income Tax and show the entries that appeared therein following income tax-allocation procedures.

Problem A 25-2. The owner of a marina has been advised by the controlling governmental agency that his operating license, which expires in 4 years, will not be renewed. He has received a cash offer of $156,000 for the property and asks you to prepare a suitable analysis to assist him in deciding whether to sell or hold the asset.

The marina has a tax basis of $60,000. His income from owning the marina, which has been averaging $45,000 a year, is taxed in the 60 per cent bracket. However, any gain from its sale will be taxed at 25 per cent. It seems unlikely that any salvage value will be realized from the property.

After giving consideration to the analysis mentioned above, state one consideration that could influence the decision.

Problem A 25-3. Fancy Company has just been organized. Its depreciable asset, which cost $180,000, has an estimated useful life of 3 years. The management is considering the following alternatives:

(1) Adopt the sum of the years' digits method of depreciation for both book and income-tax purposes.
(2) Adopt the sum of the years' digits method of depreciation for income tax purposes and the straight-line method for the books.

Assume the following:

	Year		
	1	2	3
Revenues—cash	$200,000	$220,000	$240,000
Cash expenses	110,000	115,000	120,000
Income tax rate	50%	50%	50%

Management asks you to prepare estimates of the following:

(a) Net income for Years 1, 2, and 3 under each alternative, and assuming that income tax-allocation procedures are not adopted.
(b) Net cash inflow from operations for Years 1, 2, and 3 under each alternative, and assuming that the income tax is paid at each year-end.
(c) Net income for Years 1, 2, and 3 under alternative 2, assuming that income tax-allocation procedures are adopted.

Problem A 25-4. (a) For each of the following forms of business organization, estimate the amount of gross income that A will have to report on his individual tax return. The corporate income tax rate is 50 per cent.

	Corporation	Partnership
Sales		$500,000	$500,000
Expenses:		
Salary to A	$ 15,000	
Other	435,000	450,000	435,000
Net operating income		$ 50,000	$ 65,000
Income tax expense		25,000	
Net income		$ 25,000	
Dividends		$ 20,000	
Drawings by A			$ 15,000

Under the corporate form of organization, A will own 50 per cent of the outstanding stock. Under the partnership form of organization, A will have a 50 per cent interest in the partnership.

(b) Assume the facts set forth in (a) and that the business is organized as a corporation. Assume further that the corporation can earn 12 per cent before corporate income tax on an additional investment of $100,000.

A is willing to make an additional investment of $100,000 in the business and is considering the following alternative arrangements:

(1) A long-term loan of $100,000 at 6 per cent interest.
(2) An investment of $100,000 for an additional 1,000 shares of stock. After issuance of the additional 1,000 shares, 5,000 shares will be outstanding.

Assuming that the corporation will distribute as additional dividends all incremental after-tax income from its use of the $100,000, estimate the increase in A's taxable income under each alternative.

Problem B25-1. B is trying to decide whether to operate his business as an individual proprietorship or as a corporation. Compute the total income tax that will be assessed on the business income earned under both forms of business organization. You may assume that business income is the same as taxable income.

Assume the following income tax rates.

	Taxable Income	Tax Rates
Corporate	$ 0—$25,000	22%
	25,001 and above	48
Individual	$ 0—$ 2,000	—
	2,001— 5,000	25%
	5,001— 7,500	30
	7,501— 10,000	35
	10,001— 15,000	40
	15,001— 25,000	50
	25,001— 50,000	60

	Corporation	Individual Proprietor
Sales	$200,000	$200,000
Expenses:		
Salary to owner . . . . $ 12,000		
Other 175,000	187,000	175,000
Net operating income	$ 13,000	$ 25,000
Dividends	$ 8,000	
Drawings		$ 15,000

Problem B25-2. Assume that the income tax rate is 50 per cent. Apply the carryback-carryforward provisions to the taxable income data set forth below and estimate the liability for income tax for 19+6 and 19+7.

Year	Taxable income (Loss*)
19+1	$10,000
19+2	20,000
19+3	5,000
19+4	40,000*
19+5	25,000*
19+6	15,000
19+7	40,000

Problem B25-3. Rookie Company follows income tax-allocation procedures. Data from the company's accounts are shown below.

	Net Income	Liability for Income Taxes
19+1	$200,000	$176,000
19+2	180,000	172,000
19+3	210,000	218,000
19+4	220,000	244,000

Deferred Income Tax

19+3	8,000	19+1	24,000
19+4	24,000	19+2	8,000

Compute the following: (a) The income tax expense shown in the company's income statements for 19+1, 19+2, 19+3, and 19+4; and (b) the net income that would have been reported if the company had not followed income tax-allocation procedures.

Problem B25-4. The only income-producing asset of XYZ Company is its patent. The patent has a remaining legal and commercial life of five years. Under existing legal agreements, the patent will earn a royalty income of $10,000 per annum for the next five years.

XYZ COMPANY
Balance Sheet
December 31, 19+4

Assets			Equities	
Cash and royalties			Capital stock	$15,000
receivable		$10,000	Retained earnings............	15,000
Patent—at cost........	$68,000			
Less accumulated				
amortization	48,000	20,000		
		$30,000		$30,000

A has an opportunity to acquire control of the patent (1) by purchasing it from the corporation for $30,000, or (2) by purchasing all of the outstanding capital stock from the stockholders for $40,000 (the receivables are collectible).

If A elects to acquire the outstanding capital stock, he will permit the company to continue its ownership of the patent for the remaining life of the patent. At the end of the five-year period, the corporation would be liquidated.

If A acquires the outstanding capital stock, as owner of all of the capital stock he would have the following alternatives:

(a) Have the corporation declare annual dividends equal to its net income for each year.
(b) Have the corporation adopt a no-dividends policy.

Compute total payments for income taxes traceable to A's control of the patent under each of the three alternative plans described above. Use the following flat income tax rates:

Corporation 25%
Individual:
    Ordinary income 40%
    Capital gains 20%
        (Assume that capital losses in excess of capital gains are deductible from
        ordinary income.)

Problem B25-5. Refer to Problem B25-4 and compute the aggregate disposable income to the original
stockholders of XYZ Company under each of the alternatives set forth therein.
    You may assume the following:

(a) The patent is a capital asset of the corporation. Any gain on its sale will be taxed
    at the capital gain rate of 25 per cent. The tax basis of the patent is the same
    as its book value, $20,000.
(b) The shares of stock held by the taxpayers have a basis of $15,000. Any excess above
    the basis received from the disposal of the shares will be taxed as a capital
    gain, at one-half the rate applicable to ordinary income, but not above 25 per
    cent.

You may assume further that, if alternative (1) is selected, the stockholders will imme-
diately liquidate the company.

Consolidated Statements

Parent-subsidiary relationship. A parent-subsidiary relationship exists when one firm, known as the parent, acquires a majority of the voting stock of another company, known as the subsidiary. Such an arrangement may be attractive for many reasons. For instance, the use of subsidiaries to conduct particular segments of a business may result in lower income taxes than if the operations were combined and carried on by a single corporation. Or, the use of subsidiaries may improve management effectiveness if the operations of a business are widely diversified; for example, a grocery chain may operate a bakery and one or more canning plants, or a fruit company may own banana plantations and ocean-going freight ships; under such circumstances, a separate corporation for each kind of business activity can have directors and officers having specialized knowledge of the particular operations. Or, it may be prudent to limit the risks of a hazardous venture by making its liabilities a claim against only the assets of a single company instead of those of the entire organization. Or, part of the operations may be subject to governmental regulations; for instance, an automobile finance company may organize a subsidiary to insure the cars that are security for its receivables.

A parent company may acquire the stock of a subsidiary in the following ways:

(1) By organizing a new corporation; the parent thus supplies the initial capital and in return receives newly issued shares of the subsidiary's capital stock.

(2) By purchasing the capital stock of a going business from its stockholders.

(3) By issuing additional shares of its stock in exchange for the outstanding capital stock of another corporation. Thus the stockholders of the company which becomes a subsidiary become stockholders of the parent company.

When a parent-and-subsidiary relationship exists, it may be desirable to prepare consolidated financial statements for the group of companies as a whole.

CONSOLIDATED BALANCE SHEET

Assume that Company P organizes a subsidiary, Company S, and invests $50,000 in the capital stock of the subsidiary. The balance sheet of the parent company just after the investment is shown below.

COMPANY P
Balance Sheet
December 31, 19—

Assets		Equities		
Cash	$ 30,000	Accounts payable		$ 27,000
Accounts receivable	25,000			
Inventory	65,000	Stockholders' equity:		
Investment in stock of		Capital stock	$100,000	
Company S	50,000	Retained earnings . . .	43,000	143,000
	$170,000			$170,000

Assume further that the subsidiary completes the following transactions on the date it is organized.

Capital stock is issued to the parent company:

Cash	50,000	
Capital stock		50,000

Inventory is purchased, partly on account:

Inventory	30,000	
Cash		22,000
Accounts payable		8,000

Land is purchased for cash:

Land	15,000	
Cash		15,000

The balance sheet of the subsidiary, after those transactions, is shown below:

COMPANY S
Balance Sheet
December 31, 19—

Assets		Equities	
Cash	$13,000	Accounts payable	$ 8,000
Accounts receivable	15,000		
Merchandise inventory	30,000	Stockholders' equity:	
		Capital stock	50,000
	$58,000		$58,000

Whenever a company owns the majority of the voting stock of another company, it is in a position to control the business activities of the subsidiary company. In essence, parent and subsidiary companies operate as a single business unit. Because they so operate, it is generally considered more meaningful if their financial statements are consolidated so as to depict the unity of operation and control.

When a consolidated balance sheet is prepared, the amounts set forth in the balance sheets of the parent and subsidiary companies are combined after those offsetting account balances that are traceable to intercompany investment and intercompany debt have been eliminated. Thus a consolidated balance sheet includes the assets controlled by the parent through its ownership of the subsidiary's capital stock, and the subsidiary's debts to creditors other than the parent company.

The following working papers show the consolidation of the balance sheets of Company P and its subsidiary just after the subsidiary company was organized.

COMPANY P AND SUBSIDIARY
Consolidated Balance Sheet Working Papers
December 31, 19—

	Balance Sheets		Intercompany Eliminations		Consolidated Balance Sheet
	Company P	Company S			
Assets					
Cash	30,000	13,000			43,000
Accounts receivable	25,000	15,000			40,000
Merchandise inventory . .	65,000	30,000			95,000
Investment in Company S	50,000		A 50,000		
	170,000	58,000			178,000
Equities					
Accounts payable	27,000	8,000			35,000
Common stock:					
Company P	100,000				100,000
Company S		50,000	A 50,000		
Retained earnings.	43,000				43,000
	170,000	58,000	50,000	50,000	178,000

Intercompany Eliminations

A—Parent's Investment in Company S and the subsidiary's Capital Stock.

Without the $50,000 elimination in the working papers, the consolidated assets would be overstated. The investment in the subsidiary's capital stock gives the parent indirect ownership of the subsidiary's assets. To include both the assets of the subsidiary and the parent's investment in the capital stock of the subsidiary in the consolidated balance sheet would result in a duplication. If the investment is eliminated, the related capital stock account in the subsidiary's balance sheet must be eliminated also to preserve the debit-credit equality. A consolidated balance sheet is a statement showing the financial position of a group of affiliated companies, with all accounts reflecting intercompany relationships eliminated.

The consolidated balance sheet follows.

COMPANY P AND SUBSIDIARY

Consolidated **Balance Sheet**
December 31, 19—

Assets		Equities		
Cash	$ 43,000	Accounts payable		$ 35,000
Accounts receivable	40,000			
Merchandise inventory	95,000	Stockholders' equity:		
		Common stock	$100,000	
		Retained earnings	43,000	143,000
	$178,000			$178,000

A parent's unconsolidated balance sheet and a consolidated balance sheet serve different purposes. An unconsolidated balance sheet should be used when it is desired to show the financial position of the parent company from a legal standpoint as a separate corporate entity. A consolidated balance sheet may be used when the legal reality of separate corporate entities can safely be ignored and it is desired to show, in a single statement, the financial position of a group of affiliated companies as a business unit.

Balance sheet subsequent to organization of subsidiary. At the date of organization, the subsidiary had no retained earnings; therefore, the retained earnings shown in the consolidated balance sheet in the foregoing illustration were those of the parent only. We shall now illustrate the treatment of subsidiary retained earnings accumulated since organization, bearing in mind that they are part of the retained earnings of the group of affiliated companies as a whole.

Intercompany relationships other than the subsidiary stock ownership, such as intercompany votes, may exist; they should be eliminated in the preparation of consolidated balance sheets.

COMPANY P AND SUBSIDIARY
Consolidated Balance Sheet Working Papers
December 31, 19+1

	Balance Sheets		Intercompany	Consolidated Balance
	Company P	Company S	Eliminations	Sheet
Assets				
Cash	25,000	18,000		43,000
Accounts receivable	28,000	17,000		45,000
Notes receivable (from Company S)	5,000		A 5,000	
Merchandise inventory	69,000	36,000		105,000
Investment in Company S	50,000		B 50,000	
	177,000	71,000		193,000

	Balance Sheets		Intercompany Eliminations		Consolidated Balance Sheet
	Company P	Company S			
Equities					
Accounts payable	26,000	9,000			35,000
Notes payable					
(to Company P)		5,000	A 5,000		
Stockholders' equity:					
Capital stock:					
Company P	100,000				100,000
Company S		50,000	B 50,000		
Retained earnings	51,000	7,000			58,000
	177,000	71,000	55,000	55,000	193,000

Intercompany Eliminations

A—Intercompany notes.
B—Parent's Investment in Company S and the subsidiary's Capital Stock.

Following is the consolidated balance sheet:

COMPANY P AND SUBSIDIARY
Consolidated **Balance Sheet**
December 31, 19 + 1

Assets		**Equities**		
Cash	$ 43,000	Liabilities:		
Accounts receivable	45,000	Accounts payable		$ 35,000
Merchandise inventory	105,000			
		Stockholder's equity:		
		Capital stock	$100,000	
		Retained earnings . . .	58,000	158,000
	$193,000			$193,000

CONSOLIDATED INCOME STATEMENT, STATEMENT OF RETAINED EARNINGS, AND BALANCE SHEET

Preparation of the statements. When the consolidated income statement is prepared, the balances of the revenue and expense accounts of the parent and subsidiary are combined after revenue and expense account balances, or any portions thereof, resulting from intercompany transactions, have been eliminated. In the following illustration, two kinds of intercompany transactions affecting the income statement are shown:

    (A) Intercompany sales.

                During 19 + 1 the parent company made $20,000 of sales to its subsidiary. The merchandise sold cost the parent $15,000. Before year end, the subsidiary sold the goods to its customers for $25,000. The sales would result in the following account balances:

	In the Books of	
	Company P	Company S
Sales	$20,000	$25,000
Cost of goods sold	15,000	20,000

From the standpoint of the combined entity, such intercompany sales are merely transfers of inventory between the related companies, and their effect should be eliminated when consolidated statements are prepared. The sales shown in a consolidated income statement should be only those made to nonaffiliated customers, in other words, to "outsiders." Thus, only $25,000 of the sales would be included in the income statement. The related cost of goods sold would be $15,000, the cost to the affiliated group. In order to obtain this result, an elimination is made by a working paper debit to Sales and a credit to Cost of Goods Sold for $20,000.

(B) Intercompany dividends.

During 19+1 Company S paid a $1,000 dividend, which was received by Company P, the only stockholder of Company S, and credited to Dividend from Company S. Dividends received by the parent from the subsidiary are income to the parent, but they are eliminated in the computation of consolidated net income. From the standpoint of the combined entity, such dividends are merely a transfer of assets from one company to the other.

Illustration. Working papers for the preparation of consolidated statements (income, retained earnings, and balance sheet) for 19+1, the year following the organization of Company S as a subsidiary, are shown on page 586.

Following are the consolidated statements of income and retained earnings. The consolidated balance sheet would be the same as that on page 584.

COMPANY P AND SUBSIDIARY
Consolidated **Income Statement**
For the Year Ended December 31, 19+1

Sales	$286,000
Cost of goods sold	215,000
Gross margin.	$ 71,000
Expenses	50,000
Net income	$ 21,000

The consolidated statement of retained earnings shows the consolidated retained earnings at the beginning of the period, the consolidated net income for the period, any dividends declared by the parent company during the period, and the consolidated retained earnings at the end of the period.

COMPANY P AND SUBSIDIARY
Consolidated Working Papers
For the Year Ended December 31, 19+1

	Company P	Company S	Intercompany Eliminations	Consolidated
INCOME STATEMENT:				
Sales	189,000	117,000	A 20,000	286,000
Cost of goods sold	146,000	89,000	A 20,000	215,000
Gross margin	43,000	28,000		71,000
Expenses	30,000	20,000		50,000
Net income from operations	13,000	8,000		21,000
Dividend from Company S	1,000		B 1,000	
Net income	14,000	8,000		21,000
STATEMENT OF RETAINED EARNINGS:				
Retained earnings—beginning of year	43,000			43,000
Net income—per above	14,000	8,000		21,000
Total	57,000	8,000		64,000
Dividends:				
Company P	6,000			6,000
Company S		1,000	B 1,000	
Retained earnings—end of year	51,000	7,000		58,000
BALANCE SHEET:				
Assets				
Cash	25,000	18,000		43,000
Accounts receivable:				
Trade	28,000	17,000		45,000
From Company S	5,000		C 5,000	
Inventory	69,000	36,000		105,000
Investment in Company S	50,000		D 50,000	
	177,000	71,000		193,000
Equities				
Accounts payable:				
Trade	26,000	9,000		35,000
To Company P		5,000	C 5,000	
Capital stock:				
Company P	100,000			100,000
Company S		50,000	D 50,000	
Retained earnings—per above	51,000	7,000		58,000
	177,000	71,000	76,000	193,000
			76,000	

Intercompany Eliminations

A—Intercompany sales. B—Intercompany dividends. C—Intercompany receivable and payable. D—Intercompany stockholding.

COMPANY P AND SUBSIDIARY
Consolidated Statement of Retained Earnings
For the Year Ended December 31, 19+1

Retained earnings, December, 31, 19—	$ 43,000
Net income	21,000
Total	$ 64,000
Deduct dividends	6,000
Retained earnings, December 31, 19+1	$ 58,000

Intercompany profit in ending inventory. Assume that one of the affiliated companies makes sales to the other company at a profit. From the selling company's standpoint, the profit is made at the time of sale; but from the consolidated standpoint, profits are made only by sales to outsiders. Therefore, if, at the end of the period, any inter-company-sold goods remain in the purchasing company's inventory, any intercompany profit thereon must be eliminated in the preparation of consolidated statements. The elimination affects the balance sheet valuation of the inventory and the sales and cost of goods sold shown in the income statement. To illustrate, assume that we are preparing consolidated statements of Company A and its subsidiary Company B for the year 19+5; the parent company made sales of $18,000 to the subsidiary during the year, the merchandise sold cost the parent $14,000, and the merchandise remained in the year-end inventory of the subsidiary. Thus the year-end inventory of Company B contained intercompany profit of $4,000 which, from a consolidated point of view, was unrealized profit and which, therefore, should be eliminated from the consolidated financial statements.

The above sales would result in the following account balances:

	In the Financial Statements of	
	Parent	Subsidiary
Sales	$18,000	
Cost of goods sold	14,000	
Inventory		$18,000

The required elimination is indicated below.

	In the Financial Statements of			
	Parent	Subsidiary	Elimination	Consolidated
Sales	18,000		18,000	
Cost of goods sold	14,000			14,000
Inventory		18,000	4,000	14,000

Observe that, as a consequence of the above elimination, the intercompany sales and related cost of goods sold are excluded from the consolidated income statement and that the inventory acquired by an intercompany transaction is reduced to what it cost the company making the intercompany sale, or $14,000.

In the example, the intercompany sale was made by the parent. The need to eliminate intercompany sales and any unrealized profits therefrom also exists when a subsidiary has made sales to its parent or to another subsidiary of the parent.

Subsequent realization of intercompany profit. To show the subsequent realization of inter-
company profit, we shall continue the foregoing illustration through 19+6. During
19+6 the merchandise acquired from the parent in 19+5 was sold to outsiders for
$20,000, which was $2,000 above the cost to the subsidiary but $6,000 above the
cost to the parent. The consolidated income statement for 19+6 should include the
following:

Sales	$20,000
Cost of goods sold	14,000
Gross margin.	$ 6,000

The cost of goods sold was determined as follows:

Cost paid by subsidiary when it purchased the goods from its parent	$18,000
Less intercompany profit element therein	4,000
Cost to parent	$14,000

Thus, the profit taken in 19+6 would include the $4,000 of profit associated with
last year's intercompany sales, which was not included in last year's consolidated
income statement because the merchandise had not been sold to outsiders.

Minority interest. Assume that when Company P organized Company S, as described on
page 581, it had taken only 90 per cent of the stock issued by the subsidiary, paying
$45,000 therefor, and that the remaining 10 per cent had been issued to stockholders
outside the affiliated companies. The holders of that 10 per cent are called *minority
stockholders,* and their interest in the subsidiary is called the *minority interest.*

The preparation of consolidated financial statements would still be justified be-
cause the parent company, as owner of 90 per cent of the voting stock, would be
able to control the operations of the subsidiary. However, in such a case there would
be a minority interest to account for in the consolidated statements. The assumed
data for the previous illustrations are used again, but modified to show the effect
of a 10 per cent minority interest. Only working papers are shown. The first illustra-
tive working papers relate to the date when the subsidiary was organized. The second
illustrative working papers cover the first year. In a consolidated balance sheet the
minority interest is shown as a separate category just above the Stockholders' Equity
section. As indicated in the working papers on page 590, the consolidated net income
for 19+1 is $20,200 (observe the $800 deduction for the minority interest) and the
minority interest as of December 31, 19+1, amounts to $5,700.

OTHER ACQUISITION METHODS

In the material developed thus far concerning consolidated statements, the sub-
sidiary was acquired as a result of the parent company organizing a new corporation.
As noted on page 580, there are two additional ways a parent company may acquire
the stock of a subsidiary:

By purchasing, usually for cash, the capital stock of a going business from its
stockholders. The stockholders of the acquired company are then no longer
stockholders of either the parent or the subsidiary company.

COMPANY P AND SUBSIDIARY
Consolidated Balance Sheet Working Papers
December 31, 19—

	Balance Sheets		Intercompany Eliminations	Minority Interest	Consolidated Balance Sheet
Assets	Company P	Company S			
Cash	35,000	13,000			48,000
Accounts receivable	25,000				25,000
Inventory	65,000	30,000			95,000
Investment in Company S	45,000		A 45,000		
Land		15,000			15,000
	170,000	58,000			183,000
Equities					
Accounts payable	27,000	8,000			35,000
Capital stock:					
Company P	100,000				100,000
Company S		50,000	A 45,000	5,000	
Retained earnings	43,000				43,000
Minority interest				5,000	5,000
	170,000	58,000	45,000	5,000	183,000
			45,000		

Intercompany Eliminations

A—Parent's Investment in Company S and the subsidiary's Capital Stock.

COMPANY P AND SUBSIDIARY
Consolidated Working Papers
For the Year Ended December 31, 19+1

	Company P	Company S	Intercompany Eliminations	Minority Interest	Consolidated
INCOME STATEMENT:					
Sales	189,000	117,000	A 20,000		286,000
Cost of goods sold	146,000	89,000	A 20,000		215,000
Gross margin	43,000	28,000			71,000
Expenses	30,000	20,000			50,000
Net income from operations	13,000	8,000			21,000
Dividend from Company S	900		B 900		
Minority interest—10% of $8,000				800	800
Net income	13,900	8,000		800	20,200
STATEMENT OF RETAINED EARNINGS:					
Retained earnings—beginning of year	43,000				43,000
Net income—per above	13,900	8,000	B 900	800	20,200
Total	56,900	8,000			63,200
Dividends:					
Company P	6,000				6,000
Company S		1,000	B 900	100	
Retained earnings—end of year	50,900	7,000		700	57,200
BALANCE SHEET:					
Assets					
Cash	30,000	18,000			48,000
Accounts receivable:					
Trade	28,000	2,000			30,000
From Company S	5,000		C 5,000		
Inventory	69,000	36,000			105,000
Investment in Company S	45,000		D 45,000		
Land		15,000			15,000
	177,000	71,000			198,000
Equities					
Accounts payable:					
Trade	26,100	9,000			35,100
To Company P		5,000	C 5,000		
Capital stock:					
Company P	100,000				100,000
Company S		50,000	D 45,000	5,000	
Retained earnings—per above	50,900	7,000		700	57,200
Minority interest				5,700	5,700
	177,000	71,000	70,900	5,700	198,000
			70,900		

Intercompany Eliminations

A—Intercompany sales. B—Intercompany dividends. C—Intercompany receivable and payable. D—Intercompany stockholding.

By issuing additional shares of parent company stock in exchange for the outstanding capital stock of the "to-be" subsidiary company. The stockholders of the acquired company then become stockholders of the parent company.

Some of the consolidation rules that are peculiar to these additional acquisition methods are noted below.

Subsidiary acquired by purchase of stock of a going business. When the parent organizes a subsidiary, the subsidiary, being a new corporation, has no retained earnings at the date the parent-subsidiary relationship is established. But when the acquired company is a going business, the subsidiary will usually have some retained earnings at the time the parent-subsidiary relationship is established. An important question is: What disposition is made of the subsidiary's retained earnings as of the date of acquisition when consolidated statements are prepared? The answer is: Such retained earnings are eliminated. If the subsidiary was acquired by the purchase of stock, then the retained earnings of the subsidiary as of the date of acquisition are not included in consolidated retained earnings; only the retained earnings earned after the company became a subsidiary are included in consolidated retained earnings.

COST OF INVESTMENT EQUALS BOOK VALUE: As an example, assume that Company P paid $100,000 for all of the outstanding capital stock of Company S at a time when the stockholders' equity of Company S consisted of the following:

Capital stock	$ 75,000
Retained earnings.	25,000
Total stockholders' equity	$100,000

As indicated in the consolidated working papers on page 592, if a consolidated balance sheet were prepared at acquisition date, the investment account on the parent's books, which has a balance of $100,000, and the capital stock and retained earnings accounts on the subsidiary's books, which equal $100,000, are eliminated.

Now assume a time interval during which the parent's and subsidiary's retained earnings increased to $70,000 and $35,000, respectively. As indicated by the consolidated working papers on page 593, the retained earnings which the subsidiary earned since becoming a subsidiary, $10,000 in this instance, are included in consolidated retained earnings. Thus the consolidated retained earnings amount to $80,000 (the $70,000 retained earnings of the parent and the $10,000 increment to the subsidiary's retained earnings since acquisition).

COST OF INVESTMENT DIFFERENT FROM BOOK VALUE: In the preceding illustration, the parent company paid book value for the subsidiary's capital stock, that is, $100,000. Now suppose that the parent paid more than book value for the subsidiary's capital stock. What is done with the excess when consolidated statements are prepared?

COMPANY P AND SUBSIDIARY
Consolidated Balance Sheet Working Papers
At Acquisition

	Balance Sheets		Intercompany Eliminations	Consolidated Balance Sheet
	Company P	Company S		
Assets				
Assets other than investment in subsidiary	250,000	150,000		400,000
Investment in Company S	100,000		A 100,000	
	350,000	150,000		400,000
Equities				
Liabilities	100,000	50,000		150,000
Capital stock:				
Company P	200,000			200,000
Company S		75,000	A 75,000	
Retained earnings:				
Company P	50,000			50,000
Company S		25,000	A 25,000	
	350,000	150,000	100,000	400,000

Intercompany Eliminations

A—Parent's Investment in Company S and the subsidiary's Capital Stock and Retained Earnings as of the date of acquisition.

COMPANY P AND SUBSIDIARY
Consolidated Balance Sheet Working Papers
Subsequent to Acquisition

	Balance Sheets		Intercompany Eliminations	Consolidated Balance Sheet
	Company P	Company S		
Assets				
Assets other than investment in subsidiary	270,000	160,000		430,000
Investment in Company S	100,000		A 100,000	
	370,000	160,000		430,000
Equities				
Liabilities	100,000	50,000		150,000
Capital stock:				
Company P	200,000			200,000
Company S		75,000	A 75,000	
Retained earnings:				
Company P	70,000			70,000
Company S:				
At acquisition		25,000	A 25,000	
Increase since		10,000		10,000
	370,000	160,000	100,000 100,000	430,000

Intercompany Eliminations

A—Parent's Investment in Company S and the subsidiary's Capital Stock and Retained Earnings as of the date of acquisition.

Presumably the assets of the subsidiary are worth more than their book value—at least the parent company thought so, or it would not have paid more than book value for the subsidiary's capital stock. Accordingly, the excess of cost over book value is assigned to one or more of the assets of the subsidiary to show what the parent company paid for the subsidiary's assets when it acquired ownership; such assignment is done in the consolidated working papers as shown on page 595. In effect the assets of the subsidiary are adjusted for consolidated statement purposes to reflect the cost paid by the parent. In the illustration, the parent paid $115,000 for all of the outstanding stock of the subsidiary, which was $15,000 above book value. Observe how the excess of cost over book value is set forth in the working papers. It was assumed that such excess was due to the fact that the land was currently worth $50,000; hence the excess was properly assignable to the land owned by the subsidiary.

Subsidiary acquired by exchange of shares. In most instances in which the parent-subsidiary relationship is established by an exchange of shares, the accountant follows what is known as a "pooling of interests" approach when he prepares consolidated statements. When the exchange-of-shares method is used, the stockholders of the acquired company become stockholders of the parent company. Thus, in effect, the stockholders of two companies join together and become stockholders of the parent company.

When the stockholder interests are thus "pooled" or combined, the parent company records its investment in the subsidiary at the aggregate par or stated value of the shares it issues, without regard to the value of such shares. To illustrate, let us return to the example on page 592 and assume that Company P, instead of paying $100,000 for its investment in the subsidiary, issued 7,500 shares of its $10 par value stock in exchange for all of the outstanding stock of Company S. The entry for such exchange transaction is:

Investment in Company S	75,000	
Capital stock		75,000
Issuance of 7,500 shares of $10 par value stock in exchange		
for the stock of Company S.		

The consolidated working papers on page 596 indicate the required intercompany elimination. Note that, under the conditions set forth, namely, the pooling of interest case, subsidiary retained earnings at acquisition can be included in consolidated retained earnings. The inclusion of the subsidiary's retained earnings is based on the contention that the exchange of shares that results in a pooling of interests is more a matter of form than substance, because usually the combined businesses will carry on the same kind of business activities with the same assets, employees, and stockholders as before the combination. As indicated earlier, such inclusion would not be acceptable if the shares of the subsidiary had been acquired by purchase rather than by an exchange of shares.

COMPANY P AND SUBSIDIARY
Consolidated Balance Sheet Working Papers
At Acquisition

	Balance Sheets		Adjustments and Eliminations		Consolidated Balance Sheet
Assets	Company P	Company S			
Cash	65,000	15,000			80,000
Accounts receivable	70,000	40,000			110,000
Inventory	100,000	60,000			160,000
Investment in Company S:					
Book value at acquisition	100,000			A 100,000	
Excess of cost over book value	15,000			B 15,000	
Land		35,000	B 15,000		50,000
	350,000	150,000			400,000
Equities					
Accounts payable	100,000	50,000			150,000
Capital stock:					
Company P	200,000				200,000
Company S		75,000	A 75,000		
Retained earnings:					
Company P	50,000				50,000
Company S		25,000	A 25,000		
	350,000	150,000	115,000	115,000	400,000

Adjustments and Eliminations

A—Parent's Investment in Company S and the subsidiary's Capital Stock and Retained Earnings.
B—Assignment of excess of cost over book value to the land account.

595

COMPANY P AND SUBSIDIARY
Consolidated Balance Sheet Working Papers
At Acquisition

Assets	Balance Sheets Company P	Balance Sheets Company S	Intercompany Eliminations	Consolidated Balance Sheet
Assets other than investment in subsidiary...	275,000	150,000		425,000
Investment in Company S	75,000		A 75,000	
	350,000	150,000		425,000
Equities				
Liabilities	100,000	50,000		150,000
Capital stock:				
Company P	200,000			200,000
Company S		75,000	A 75,000	
Retained earnings	50,000	25,000		75,000
	350,000	150,000	75,000	75,000	425,000

Intercompany Eliminations

A—Parent's Investment in Company S and the subsidiary's Capital Stock.

Suppose that the aggregate par or stated value of the shares issued is different from the aggregate par or stated value of the shares received in exchange. How is such difference handled in the preparation of consolidated financial statements?

If the aggregate par or stated value of the shares issued is less than the aggregate par or stated value of the shares received in exchange, the difference is shown as additional paid-in capital.

To illustrate, return to the preceding example and assume that 6,000 shares of $10 par value stock are issued in exchange for all of the outstanding stock of Company S.

> *Entry for investment on books of Company P:*
> Investment in Company S 60,000
>   Capital stock   60,000

> *Working paper intercompany elimination:*
> Capital stock—Company S 75,000
>   Investment in Company S   60,000
>   Additional paid-in capital   15,000

If the aggregate par or stated value of the shares issued is greater than the aggregate par or stated value of the shares received in exchange, the difference is charged to additional paid-in capital; if none exists, or if it is insufficient, then retained earnings are charged.

To illustrate, assume that 9,000 shares of $10 par value stock are issued in exchange for all of the outstanding shares of Company S.

> *Entry for investment on books of Company P:*
> Investment in Company S 90,000
>   Capital stock   90,000

Working paper intercompany elimination:

Capital stock—Company S	75,000	
Retained earnings	15,000	
Investment in Company S		90,000

Limitations of usefulness of consolidated statements. Consolidated statements were devised for the purpose of giving interested parties an overall view of the financial position and operating results of a group of affiliated companies without requiring them to examine the statements of all of the related companies and to attempt to piece them together into a composite picture. For this purpose, consolidated statements have a real usefulness; but they do not serve all of the purposes for which individual company statements may be used or required. Creditors of the parent and subsidiary companies can obtain little information of value to them because consolidated statements do not detail the assets, liabilities, revenues, and expenses of the several companies.

There are also limitations to the usefulness of consolidated statements as a source of information to the parent company's stockholders. Because the balance sheet does not show the financial position of the parent as a separate legal entity, it does not disclose such facts as the ratio of subsidiary stock investments to total assets or stockholders' equity and the parent's working capital. The consolidated retained earnings statement does not show the retained earnings of the parent, which is generally the legal limit for dividends. The consolidated net income presumably includes an undisclosed amount of subsidiary earnings, which are not available for parent company dividends until transferred to the parent by subsidiary dividends.

It is customary to show as finished goods inventory in the consolidated balance sheet the total finished goods inventories of all companies and to combine the other inventories in a similar manner. However, if intercompany sales are made and finished goods of one company become raw materials of another company, such an inventory classification may be misleading and give a false impression of the liquidity of the inventories.

Ratio analyses based on consolidated data may result in misleading impressions. Such ratios are composites; the good and bad features of individual companies are not disclosed by them. For instance, assume the following facts about working capital.

	Current Assets	Current Liabilities	Working Capital Ratio
Company P	$60,000	$20,000	3.0
Company S	30,000	25,000	1.2
Consolidated	$90,000	$45,000	2.0

The precarious working capital position of the subsidiary is not disclosed; and, if the consolidated working capital were assumed to be that of the parent, the assumption is unwarranted.

For these and other reasons, a parent company may publish its own statements as well as consolidated statements. The trend, however, seems to be toward consolidated statements only.

ASSIGNMENT
MATERIAL

QUESTIONS

1. What is a consolidated balance sheet?
2. What is a subsidiary company?
3. When preparing a balance sheet for a parent company, under what circumstances should the accountant use the unconsolidated form and when may he use the consolidated form?
4. Is the capital stock of a fully owned subsidiary shown in the consolidated balance sheet? Explain your answer.
5. Mention some reasons why subsidiaries may be created.
6. Why are the inventories of affiliated companies reduced in consolidated statements by the amount of any intercompany profit therein?
7. When a parent company acquires a subsidiary by purchasing outstanding shares from stockholders, what disposition is made of the subsidiary's retained earnings as of the date of acquisition when consolidated statements are prepared?
8. Describe the different ways by which a parent company may acquire the stock of a subsidiary.
9. What is a minority interest?
10. Discuss the limitations of consolidated statements.

SHORT EXERCISES

E26-1. The December 31, 19+2 balance sheets of Parent Company and Subsidiary Company show the following assets:

	Parent Company	Subsidiary Company
Assets		
Current assets:		
Cash..................................	$ 40,000	$ 30,000
Accounts receivable—Customers	90,000	60,000
Allowance for uncollectibles	(1,800)	(1,000)
Advances to Subsidiary Company.............	8,000	—
Inventory..............................	150,000	100,000
Prepaid expenses........................	1,800	1,000
	$288,000	$190,000
Long-term investments:		
Investment in Subsidiary Company...........	$300,000	
Property, plant, and equipment:		
Land..................................	$100,000	$ 50,000
Buildings	300,000	200,000
Accumulated depreciation.................	(140,000)	(60,000)
Equipment.............................	150,000	120,000
Accumulated depreciation.................	(68,000)	(40,000)
	$342,000	$270,000
	$930,000	$460,000

Parent Company owns 80 per cent of the common stock of Subsidiary Company.

All of the inventory of Subsidiary Company was purchased from Parent Company. The inventory cost Parent Company $85,000.

The chief accountant of Parent Company must prepare a consolidated balance sheet. Determine the total that will be shown for the asset side of the consolidated balance sheet.

E26-2. The Stockholders' Equity sections of the December 31, 19+4 balance sheets of South Company and its wholly owned subsidiary, East Company, are presented below.

	South Company	East Company
Stockholders' equity:		
Capital stock	$400,000	$200,000
Retained earnings	120,000	50,000

As of December 31, 19+4, East Company was indebted to South Company for $15,000. Show the Stockholders' Equity section of the December 31, 19+4 consolidated balance sheet under each of the following conditions:

(a) East Company was organized by South Company.

(b) South Company purchased its interest in East Company several years after East Company was organized and when East Company's retained earnings amounted to $20,000.

(c) South Company acquired its interest in East Company by a pooling-of-interests transaction and when East Company's retained earnings amounted to $10,000.

E26-3. From the following selected data, prepare a consolidated income statement for the year ended December 31, 19+4.

	Prime Company	Sub Company
Sales, including $15,000 of sales by Prime Company to its wholly owned subsidiary, Sub Company	$480,000	$235,000
Cost of goods sold	280,000	145,000
Operating expenses.	170,000	70,000
Dividends declared.	10,000	5,000
Dividend income—From Sub Company	5,000	
Intercompany profit in ending inventory.		-0-

E26-4. Below are data from the unconsolidated statements of retained earnings of Company P and of its subsidiary, which is 90 per cent owned. The subsidiary was organized by Company P, which has held its 90 per cent interest since the date of organization. There is no unrealized intercompany profit at either December 31, 19+5, or December 31, 19+6.

	Company	
	P	S
Retained earnings, December 31, 19+5	$300,000	$100,000
Net income, including dividend income	14,500	8,000
Total	$314,500	$108,000
Dividends.	7,500	5,000
Retained earnings, December 31, 19+6	$307,000	$103,000

(a) Compute the consolidated retained earnings as of December 31, 19+5, and December 31, 19+6.

(b) Prepare the consolidated statement of retained earnings for the year ended December 31, 19+6.

PROBLEMS

Problem A 26-1. The condensed balance sheets of Saginaw Corporation and Valley Company appeared as follows on December 31, 19+2.

Assets	Saginaw Corporation	Valley Company
Current assets	$100,000	$ 50,000
Investment in Valley Company	100,000	
Property, plant, and equipment—net of accumulated depreciation	200,000	110,000
	$400,000	$160,000

Equities		
Current liabilities.	$ 60,000	$ 30,000
Long-term liabilities	40,000	20,000
Stockholders' equity:		
Capital stock	200,000	100,000
Retained earnings	100,000	10,000
	$400,000	$160,000

Saginaw Corporation organized Valley Company one year ago and holds all of the outstanding capital stock of the subsidiary.

(a) Prepare the December 31, 19+2 consolidated balance sheet.

(b) Assume that the following data relate to the next year, which ends December 31, 19+3.

	Saginaw Corporation	Valley Company
Net income	$25,000	$10,000
Dividends paid	10,000	5,000

Compute the consolidated retained earnings as of December 31, 19+3.

(c) As an alternative to (b), assume that Saginaw Corporation made intercompany sales to Valley Company of $5,000, on which there was $500 of intercompany profit, and that the goods are included in the December 31, 19+3 inventory of Valley Company. Compute the consolidated retained earnings as of December 31, 19+3.

Problem A 26-2. The condensed balance sheets of Alpha Corporation and Gamma Company on December 31, 19+8, are presented below.

	Alpha Corporation	Gamma Company
Assets		
Current assets	$ 20,600	$ 10,100
Investment in Gamma Company	117,000	
Property, plant, and equipment—net	134,500	122,400
	$272,100	$132,500
Equities		
Current liabilities	$ 46,800	$ 18,200
Capital stock	150,000	100,000
Retained earnings	75,300	14,300
	$272,100	$132,500

On December 31, 19+3, Alpha Corporation acquired 90 per cent of the capital stock of Gamma Company at a cost of $112,000. On this date the balances of the retained earnings accounts of the two companies were:

Alpha Corporation $48,900
Gamma Company $30,000

Required:

(1) The amount of minority interest which would be included in the December 31, 19+8 consolidated balance sheet.

(2) The Stockholders' Equity section of the December 31, 19+8 consolidated balance sheet.

Problem A 26-3. The trial balances presented below were taken from the records of Bryce Company and its subsidiary, Zion Company, as of the end of their fiscal years.

BRYCE COMPANY and ZION COMPANY
Trial Balances
April 30, 19+8

	Bryce Company	Zion Company
Debits		
Cash	96,800	18,600
Accounts receivable—net	99,700	22,200
Inventory, April 30, 19+8	116,400	10,800
Investment in Zion Company	40,000	
Equipment	172,100	58,700
Cost of goods sold	294,500	67,600
Operating expenses	90,600	26,600
Dividends	20,000	10,000
	930,100	214,500
Credits		
Accounts payable	87,700	18,200
Accumulated depreciation—Equipment	131,600	5,600
Capital stock	300,000	50,000
Retained earnings, April 30, 19+7	26,300	
Sales	376,500	140,700
Dividends from subsidiary	8,000	
	930,100	214,500

Bryce Company acquired 80 per cent of the capital stock of Zion Company on May 1, 19+7, the date of organization of the latter company.

During the year ended April 30, 19+8, Zion Company purchased merchandise from Bryce Company at a billed price of $85,000, which was the cost of this merchandise to the seller. On April 30, 19+8, Zion Company had not paid for $8,200 of the billed price of this merchandise.

Prepare consolidated working papers for Bryce Company and Zion Company for the year ended April 30, 19+8.

Problem A 26-4. The June 30, 19+8 balance sheets of Vapor Company and Trail Corporation are presented below.

VAPOR COMPANY and TRAIL CORPORATION
Balance Sheets
June 30, 19+8

	Vapor Company	Trail Corporation
Assets		
Cash	$ 28,400	$ 6,800
Accounts receivable, net of allowance for uncollectibles	46,100	10,200
Advance to Trail Corporation	25,000	
Inventory	83,500	18,500
Prepaid expenses	6,400	2,600
Investment in Trail Corporation	30,000	
Land	15,000	6,400
Buildings, net of accumulated depreciation	108,600	20,100
Furniture and equipment, net of accumulated depreciation	138,900	12,300
	$481,900	$76,900

Equities

Accounts payable	$ 18,900	$14,200
Income tax payable	62,400	4,300
Advance from Vapor Company		25,000
Capital stock	300,000	25,000
Retained earnings	100,600	8,400
	$481,900	$76,900

Vapor Company acquired its 90 per cent interest in Trail Corporation on July 1, 19+4, on which date the balance of retained earnings of Trail Corporation was $1,400. On this date there was evidence that the land owned by Trail Corporation was worth more than its book value.

On June 30, 19+8, the inventory of Trail Corporation included merchandise purchased from Vapor Company for $6,400, which was $1,800 above cost to Vapor Company.

Required:

(A) Consolidated balance sheet working papers as of June 30, 19+8.
(B) The Equities portion of the consolidated balance sheet as of June 30, 19+8.

Problem A26-5. The trial balances presented below were taken from the books of Booth Company and its subsidiary, Harly Corporation, on December 31, 19+7. Booth Company acquired 90 per cent of the capital stock of Harly Corporation on December 31, 19+6, on which date Harly Corporation's retained earnings account showed a credit balance of $26,400. On this date there was evidence that the land owned by Harly Corporation was overvalued.

BOOTH COMPANY and HARLY CORPORATION
Trial Balances
December 31, 19+7

	Booth Company	Harly Corporation
Debits		
Cash	32,400	14,500
Accounts receivable—net	51,600	33,100
Inventories, December 31, 19+7	72,500	37,400
Prepaid expenses	3,800	1,800
Investment in Harly Corporation	75,000	
Land	22,400	25,400
Buildings	103,600	39,100
Equipment	180,700	61,400
Cost of goods sold	416,200	218,300
Expenses	219,700	97,900
Dividends paid	35,000	10,000
	1,212,900	538,900
Credits		
Accumulated depreciation—Buildings	17,900	10,600
Accumulated depreciation—Equipment	72,900	24,200
Accounts payable	138,000	57,700
Capital stock	200,000	60,000
Retained earnings, December 31, 19+6	64,800	26,400
Sales	710,300	360,000
Dividend from subsidiary	9,000	
	1,212,900	538,900

During the year ended December 31, 19+7, Harly Corporation purchased merchandise from Booth Company for $152,000. This merchandise had cost Booth Company $128,000. The December 31, 19+7 inventory of the subsidiary included one-fourth of the merchandise purchased from the parent during the year.

(a) Prepare consolidated working papers for the year ended December 31, 19+7.

(b) Prepare a consolidated income statement and a consolidated statement of retained earnings for the year ended December 31, 19+7, and a consolidated balance sheet as of December 31, 19+7.

Problem B26-1. The adjusted trial balances of a parent and its 100 per cent owned subsidiary are presented below. The investment was acquired when the subsidiary was organized.

Adjusted Trial Balances
June 30, 19+4

	Propjet Company		Subsonic Company	
Cash	31,000		22,750	
Accounts receivable	24,000		32,400	
Advances to subsidiary	10,000			
Inventory	26,000		33,300	
Investment in Subsonic Company . . .	75,000			
Property, plant, and equipment—net of accumulated depreciation of $60,000 (combined)	80,840		50,000	
Accounts payable		27,460		8,250
Advances from parent				10,000
Capital stock		200,000		75,000
Retained earnings, June 30, 19+3 . . .		4,940		45,000
Dividends	14,000		4,500	
Sales		350,000		232,000
Cost of goods sold	220,000		137,500	
Expenses	106,060		89,800	
Dividends from subsidiary		4,500		
	586,900	586,900	370,250	370,250

The advances are noninterest-bearing. Intercompany sales were $35,000. However, there was no intercompany profit in the inventories.

Prepare consolidated financial statements.

Problem B26-2. The Stockholders' Equity sections of the December 31, 19+7 balance sheets of Ann Company and its subsidiary, Arbor Corporation, are presented below.

	Ann Company	Arbor Corporation
Stockholders' equity:		
Capital stock	$300,000	$100,000
Retained earnings	78,000	24,300

Ann Company acquired 95 per cent of the capital stock of Arbor Corporation on December 31, 19+4, for $104,985, when the total stockholders' equity of Arbor Corporation was $106,300.

Determine the amounts at which the following items would be shown in the December 31, 19+7 consolidated balance sheet. Show all pertinent computations.
(1) Difference between the cost of the subsidiary stock and the book value thereof.
(2) Minority interest.
(3) Consolidated retained earnings.

Problem B26-3. The condensed balance sheets of June Corporation and May Company appeared as follows on June 30, 19+8:

	June Corporation	May Company
Assets		
Cash	$ 37,000	$ 8,400
Accounts receivable—net	72,600	10,600
Inventory	101,000	16,200
Property, plant, and equipment—net of accumulated depreciation	121,400	28,900
Investment in May Company	49,500	
	$381,500	$64,100
Equities		
Accounts payable	$ 26,300	$ 9,100
Bonds payable—19+20	100,000	
Capital stock	200,000	50,000
Retained earnings	55,200	5,000
	$381,500	$64,100

The investment in May Company represents the cost of 90 per cent of the capital stock of May Company acquired by June Corporation on June 30, 19+8.
Included in the accounts payable of June Corporation is $1,200 due to May Company.

(a) Prepare the June 30, 19+8 consolidated balance sheet.
(b) Assume that the following data relate to the year ended June 30, 19+9:

	June Corporation	May Company
Net income	$20,000	$10,000
Dividends paid	5,000	-0-

Compute the consolidated retained earnings as of June 30, 19+9.

(c) As an alternative, assume that May Company also paid a dividend, as indicated by the following revised data which relate to the year ended June 30, 19+9:

	June Corporation	May Company
Net income	$21,800	$10,000
Dividends paid	5,000	2,000

Compute the consolidated retained earnings as of June 30, 19+9.

Problem B26-4. Condensed balance sheets are presented below.

December 31, 19+8

Assets	Main Company	Sub Company
Current assets	$ 90,000	$ 60,000
Investment in Sub Company	240,000	
Property, plant, and equipment	470,000	240,000
	$800,000	$300,000

Equities		
Current liabilities	$ 60,000	$ 30,000
Capital stock	500,000	200,000
Retained earnings	240,000	70,000
	$800,000	$300,000

Prepare a condensed consolidated balance sheet for each of the following separate cases.

Case I.   The parent purchased all of the stock of its subsidiary for $240,000 when the retained earnings of Sub Company amounted to $20,000. There was evidence which indicated that the plant assets of Sub Company were worth more than their book value.

Case II.   The parent purchased 80 per cent of the subsidiary's stock for $240,000 when the retained earnings of Sub Company amounted to $100,000.

Case III.   Several years ago the parent purchased 100 per cent of the subsidiary's stock for $240,000 when the retained earnings of Sub Company amounted to $40,000. Intercompany profit in the inventory of Sub Company was as follows:

December 31, 19+7 .... $4,000
December 31, 19+8 .... $3,000

Problem B26-5. Lindsay Company organized Howe Company as of July 1, 19+3, and acquired 90 per cent of the subsidiary's capital stock for $90,000.

The following trial balance data were taken from the records of the affilitated companies on June 30, 19+8.

Debits	Lindsay Company	Howe Company
Cash	47,640	19,810
Accounts receivable	62,500	35,160
Allowance for uncollectibles	1,800*	1,000*
Inventories, June 30, 19+8	62,800	41,640
Investment in Howe Company	90,000	
Land	50,000	15,640
Buildings	68,450	39,250
Accumulated depreciation—Buildings	21,600*	14,160*
Fixtures and equipment	74,500	32,640
Accumulated depreciation—Fixtures and equipment	31,200*	18,500*
Cost of goods sold	478,800	220,560
Selling expenses	72,460	31,300
Administrative expenses	81,420	42,800
Dividends	30,000	10,000
	1,063,970	455,140

Credits

Accounts payable	83,760	17,340
Wages payable	4,200	
Capital stock	250,000	100,000
Retained earnings, June 30, 19+7	32,660	22,400
Sales	684,350	315,400
Dividends received	9,000	
	1,063,970	455,140

*Deduction.

During the year ended June 30, 19+8, Lindsay Company sold Howe Company merchandise for $182,500. The inventories of Howe Company included intercompany profit in the following amounts:

June 30, 19+7	$4,100
June 30, 19+8	$2,200

Use what you need of the data presented to (a) determine the consolidated retained earnings as of June 30, 19+7, that is, at the beginning of the current fiscal year; and (b) prepare the consolidated income statement for 19+8.

27

Introduction to Capital Budgeting

Introduction. Short-run analysis is characterized by financial decision making under conditions of given fixed costs, as previously discussed with regard to cost-volume-profit analysis and responsibility accounting. The short run is that time period which is not long enough to permit acquisition of new capacity, such as plant and equipment. It follows that the long-run time period is that period over which capacity conditions can change. During the long run a company can acquire new plant and equipment, new financing, and new management; hence costs associated with capacity are not constant (fixed) during the long run.

A company's long-run investments in land, plant and equipment, research programs, and the like are extremely important for three basic reasons: (1) long-run investments associated with capacity usually entail large dollar amounts; (2) the decision to acquire plant and equipment commits a company to that decision for several years, with a loss of flexibility (a company cannot afford to buy new plant and equipment every month or year); and (3) the commitment of funds to acquire land or equipment causes those funds to be unavailable for other investment opportunities. Other alternatives are foregone because of the acceptance of particular long-run investments.

Capital budgeting techniques provide a scientific and systematic approach to important long-run investment decisions. The term *capital budgeting* refers to the fact that investment money (capital) is scarce and must be budgeted among competing investment alternatives. The management of a business does not have unlimited investment money available to take advantage of all investment opportunities. Instead, management strives to allocate limited investment capital to those investments that promise the greatest future benefits to the company.

Capital budgeting techniques aid in answering questions such as the following: Should management keep or replace existing equipment? Given limited investment money and *x*-number of feasible investment projects, which should management select? Should management invest in a long-run research and development program?

Cash flows. Capital budgeting decisions are long-run decisions and, as such, they should be evaluated in terms of their effect on the firm's *future long-run profitability*. One can determine how a particular capital-budgeting decision will affect future long-run profitability by making an analysis of the *amount* and the *timing* of the *future net cash inflows* that result from making the investment.

The *timing* of the expected cash inflows from an investment proposal is important because such inflows can be invested and can earn interest over the expected life of the investment. Thus, as will be explained more fully later, long-run decisions must take into account the effect of interest. The importance of the timing of net cash inflows from proposed long-term investments means that annual net income should not be used to evaluate such investments. Net income is a short-run measure of profitability that is based on matching revenues and expenses over the fiscal year regardless of cash flows (accrual accounting). Thus net income does not reflect the long-run profitability of capital-budgeting decisions.

Under accrual accounting, the amount of revenue applicable to a given period of time generally differs from the cash receipts generated by the revenue-producing transactions. This condition is attributable to the time lag between the date of sale and the date of collection when sales are made on account. Similarly, the amount of expense applicable to a given period of time generally differs from the related cash disbursements made during the same time period. Depreciation provides the most obvious example of the difference in timing between a cash outlay and the related charges for expense. Usually the cash outlay for a depreciable asset occurs at or near the time the asset is acquired, while the depreciation charges are spread over the useful life of the asset. The aggregate depreciation charges tend to equal the capitalized cash outlays for depreciable assets, but the timing of the two amounts will differ significantly. To repeat, it is the prospective cash flows attributable to an investment, not the resulting revenues and expenses, that deserve attention when investment proposals are being evaluated.

To isolate the prospective relevant cash flows requires considerable analytical skill. The objective is to determine the *change* in cash flows that can reasonably be expected to result from the proposed investment and to assign the change to future time periods. If a company can expect to receive $10,000 a year for the next ten years whether or not a proposed investment is made, that cash flow is irrelevant to the investment decision. Likewise, if a company is committed to spend $5,000 a year for the next ten years whether or not a proposed investment is made, such cash outflow is irrelevant. But if, as a result of a proposed investment, the cash inflow or outflow will change, then the cash flow becomes relevant and the amount of the change should be isolated for analysis.

Suppose the accountant is attempting to determine whether the company should replace an existing machine with a new one. The relevant cash flows identified with the old machine are the cash inflows expected from the sale of the goods produced by the machine (plus any other expected cash flows associated with the old machine) minus the expected cash operating outlays (and any other related cash expenditures) associated with the old machine. Similarly, the relevant cash flows identified with the new machine are the expected cash inflows generated by the machine minus the cash outlays to acquire the new asset and to operate it. The net cash flows of the old machine and the new are then compared to determine which alternative is preferable from a quantitative viewpoint.

In the following example there is an expected net cash inflow from replacing an old machine with a new one.

| | Relevant Cash Flow Identified With | | |
	New Machine	Old Machine	Difference
Aggregate cash inflow	$75,000	$50,000	$25,000
Aggregate cash outflow	50,000	35,000	15,000
Net cash flow	$25,000	$15,000	
Net cash difference from machine replacement			$10,000

Although the example demonstrates the use of relevant cash flows, investment decisions should *not* be based on *aggregate* cash flows because then the time value of money is ignored.

The time value of money. The preceding illustration gave no consideration to the timing of the cash flows. It treated all dollars as equivalent without regard as to when they were to be spent or received. However, a dollar expected in the future is not equivalent to a dollar receivable today because of the time value of money.

A rational person prefers a dollar today to a dollar receivable in the future. A dollar in hand can be invested immediately to earn interest, and to grow to more than one dollar in the future. If a 6 per cent return is available, having $5,000 today would be preferable to receiving $5,000 one year from now. The $5,000 could be invested immediately, would earn $300 interest ($5,000 × .06 × 1), and would amount to $5,300 at the end of one year. With a 6 per cent interest rate, $5,000 today would be preferable to any amount less than $5,300 receivable at the end of one year, ignoring income tax considerations.

Note how the interest calculation in the preceding example converted present-day dollars ($5,000) into equivalent future dollars ($5,300 one year hence). With 6 per cent interest available, the alternative of receiving $5,000 today is equivalent to receiving $5,300 at the end of one year.

Given the fact that money has time value, when deciding which of two amounts is preferable, and the amounts are receivable (or payable) at different dates, it is necessary to make allowance for the time difference. One can accomplish this by comparing the amounts *at the same point in time,* as is shown by the following examples.

Which is the most attractive alternative, assuming that money can earn 6 per cent per annum?

(A) $5,000 today or $5,200 one year hence.

To make the comparison, state both amounts at their value one year hence:

	Now	One Year Hence
(a)	**$5,000 × 1.06 =**	**$5,300**
(b)		**$5,200**

Answer: Accept $5,000 now because it will amount to more than $5,200 one year hence.

(B) $5,000 today or $5,400 one year hence.

	Now	One Year Hence
(a)	**$5,000 × 1.06 =**	**$5,300**
(b)		**$5,400**

Answer: Accept $5,400 one year hence because it is more than $5,000 will amount to when invested at 6% for one year.

(C) $5,000 today or $5,300 one year hence.

Answer: They are equivalent, assuming, of course, no risk of loss either through investment or while waiting.

The time value of money acknowledges the fact that money has a cost, called interest, just as does land (rent), labor (wages), and owners' risk (profit). Money is an economic good because it is scarce and useful; therefore, money is in demand and commands a price in the form of interest. If $1,000 is kept in a safety deposit box for one year, the opportunity of investing the money at, say, 6 per cent and earning interest has been foregone. It has cost $60 ($1,000 × .06 × 1) to keep the money idle.

Compound interest. Simple interest is the interest earned on the *original* amount invested (principal); hence the principal and the interest payments remain the same for each interest period. For example, an investment of $2,000 at 6 per cent *simple* interest for two years would earn total interest of $240, as shown below.

	Principal	×	Interest Rate	×	Time	=	Simple Interest
End of Year 1	$2,000	×	.06	×	1	=	$120
End of Year 2	$2,000	×	.06	×	1	=	120
							$240

Because only the principal earns interest, a rational person would withdraw any simple interest earned and invest it elsewhere so that the invested interest would earn future interest. Otherwise the simple interest previously earned lies idle and does not earn anything in subsequent years. In the example above suppose that the $120 interest earned by the end of year 1 is withdrawn and invested at 6 per cent, which would produce $7.20 more interest, or a total of $247.20 over the two years:

	Simple Interest Earned On Original Principal	Simple Interest Earned On Investment Of Previously Earned Interest	Total Interest Earned
End of Year 1	$2,000 × .06 × 1 = $120	—	$120.00
End of Year 2	$2,000 × .06 × 1 = $120	$120 × .06 × 1 = $7.20	127.20
			$247.20

Obviously, financial institutions do not want investors to withdraw interest earned on savings, since earned interest left in savings accounts provides the financial institution with a larger pool of capital that can be used for loans and investments. Consequently, most financial institutions pay compound interest to induce savers to leave earned interest in savings accounts. Compound interest is interest earned on any previously earned interest plus the original principal. Periodically as interest becomes due (either annually, semiannually, quarterly, monthly, or daily), it is added (compounded or converted) to the principal and the larger accumulated amount (called the compound amount, compound sum, or future value) earns interest. In the previous example, the saver would not have to withdraw his $120 interest earned at the end of the first year if the financial institution paid interest at 6 per cent compounded annually.

	Interest Per Year	Compound Interest	Compound Amount
End of Year 1 .... $2,000 × .06 × 1 =	$120.00	$120.00	$2,120.00
End of Year 2 .... $2,120 × .06 × 1 =	127.20	247.20	2,247.20

Where:

Compound Amount at End of Period	=	Compound Amount at Beginning of Period	×	1 + Interest Rate
$2,120.00	=	$2,000.00	×	1.06
2,247.20	=	2,120.00	×	1.06

Compound Interest	=	Compound Amount at End of Period	−	Original Principal
$120.00	=	$2,120.00	−	$2,000.00
247.20	=	2,247.20	−	2,000.00

The determination of the compound amount supplies the answer to the following question: If a certain amount of money is invested today at a given rate of interest, how much will be accumulated at the end of a given number of years? Or, given the dollar amount of the investment today, the interest rate, and the time period, what is the future value (compound amount) of the investment?

Interest tables are available which show the compound amount or future value of $1 at various rates and time periods. An abbreviated table will be found below. To calculate the compound amount of an investment made today, multiply the sum invested by the compound amount of $1 at the given interest rate and time period obtained from compound tables, or

Compound future amount of an investment today = Principal × **Compound amount of $1 at given interest rate and time period (available from compound tables)**

For example, to calculate the compound amount of $50,000 at 6 per cent interest for five years, multiply $50,000 by 1.3382, which is the compound amount of $1 at 6 per cent for five years according to the table. The compound amount is $66,910.

Compound Amount (Future Value) of $1
Interest Rates

Periods	1%	2%	3%	4%	5%	6%	7%	8%	9%	10%
1	1.0100	1.0200	1.0300	1.0400	1.0500	1.0600	1.0700	1.0800	1.0900	1.1000
2	1.0201	1.0404	1.0609	1.0816	1.1025	1.1236	1.1449	1.1664	1.1881	1.2100
3	1.0303	1.0612	1.0927	1.1249	1.1576	1.1910	1.2250	1.2597	1.2950	1.3310
4	1.0406	1.0824	1.1255	1.1699	1.2155	1.2625	1.3108	1.3605	1.4116	1.4641
5	1.0510	1.1041	1.1593	1.2167	1.2763	1.3382	1.4026	1.4693	1.5386	1.6105
6	1.0615	1.1262	1.1941	1.2653	1.3401	1.4185	1.5007	1.5869	1.6771	1.7716
7	1.0721	1.1487	1.2299	1.3159	1.4071	1.5036	1.6058	1.7138	1.8280	1.9487
8	1.0829	1.1717	1.2668	1.3686	1.4775	1.5938	1.7182	1.8509	1.9926	2.1436
9	1.0937	1.1951	1.3048	1.4233	1.5513	1.6895	1.8385	1.9990	2.1719	2.3579
10	1.1046	1.2190	1.3439	1.4802	1.6289	1.7908	1.9672	2.1589	2.3674	2.5937
11	1.1157	1.2434	1.3842	1.5395	1.7103	1.8983	2.1049	2.3316	2.5804	2.8531
12	1.1268	1.2682	1.4258	1.6010	1.7959	2.0122	2.2522	2.5182	2.8127	3.1384
13	1.1381	1.2936	1.4685	1.6651	1.8856	2.1329	2.4098	2.7196	3.0658	3.4523
14	1.1495	1.3195	1.5126	1.7317	1.9799	2.2609	2.5785	2.9372	3.3417	3.7975
15	1.1610	1.3459	1.5580	1.8009	2.0789	2.3966	2.7590	3.1722	3.6425	4.1772
16	1.1726	1.3728	1.6047	1.8730	2.1829	2.5404	2.9522	3.4259	3.9703	4.5950
17	1.1843	1.4002	1.6528	1.9479	2.2920	2.6928	3.1588	3.7000	4.3276	5.0545
18	1.1961	1.4282	1.7024	2.0258	2.4066	2.8543	3.3799	3.9960	4.7171	5.5599
19	1.2081	1.4568	1.7535	2.1068	2.5270	3.0256	3.6165	4.3157	5.1417	6.1159
20	1.2202	1.4859	1.8061	2.1911	2.6533	3.2071	3.8697	4.6610	5.6044	6.7275
25	1.2824	1.6406	2.0938	2.6658	3.3864	4.2919	5.4274	6.8485	8.6231	10.8347
30	1.3478	1.8114	2.4273	3.2434	4.3219	5.7435	7.6123	10.0627	13.2677	17.4494
35	1.4166	1.9999	2.8139	3.9461	5.5160	7.6861	10.6766	14.7853	20.4140	28.1024
40	1.4889	2.2080	3.2620	4.8010	7.0400	10.2857	14.9745	21.7245	31.4094	45.2593
45	1.5648	2.4379	3.7816	5.8412	8.9850	13.7646	21.0025	31.9204	48.3273	72.8905
50	1.6446	2.6916	4.3839	7.1067	11.4674	18.4202	29.4570	46.9016	74.3575	117.3909

Present value. An understanding of compound interest leads to an understanding of present value, because present value is merely the opposite of compounding. With a known future amount, the present value is the dollar amount that would have to be invested today to accumulate the future amount. The unknown to be calculated in compounding is the future amount, while the unknown in present value calculations is the amount of the present investment. Thus, at this point, present value is defined as the equivalent dollar value today of a known future amount, assuming a given interest rate and time period.

An investment of $1,000 at 6 per cent interest for two years grows to a compound amount of $1,123.60 ($1,000 × 1.1236). However, this may be turned around and stated in terms of present value: What is the present value of $1,123.60 due two years hence, if the interest rate is 6 per cent compounded annually? The present value is $1,000, for it would take an investment of $1,000 today to have $1,123.60 at the end of two years at 6 per cent interest compounded annually. Thus a known investment of $1,000 today is equivalent to a future value of $1,123.60; a known future amount of $1,123.60 is equivalent to a present value of $1,000, assuming a 6 per cent interest rate compounded annually for two years.

Assuming a 6 per cent interest rate compounded annually, the illustration below may provide an insight to the present value concept by showing how present value is the opposite of compounding. Compounding is an accumulation of compound amounts (future values) as time moves forward. Given a future amount, present value is the movement back in time to derive the smaller equivalent dollar amount today of that future amount. In terms of the illustration on page 615, compounding is moving up the hill as time progresses, and present value is moving down the hill as time retrogresses.

The formula for compounding provides the formula for present value, which is used to derive tables showing the present value of $1 at various rates of interest and time periods. An abbreviated present value table of $1 is shown on page 616. Thus, to find the present value of a known future amount, multiply the future amount by the present value of $1 for the appropriate time period and interest rate, or

$$\textit{Present value} \;=\; \begin{array}{c}\textbf{Future value}\\ \textbf{or compound amount}\end{array} \;\times\; \begin{array}{l}\textbf{Present value of \$1 at a}\\ \textbf{given interest rate and}\\ \textbf{time period (obtained from}\\ \textbf{present value tables)}\end{array}$$

For example, the present value of $3,207.10 at 6 per cent interest compounded annually for 20 years is $1,000.

$$\$1,000 = \$3,207.10 \times .3118$$

Present value of an annuity. The previous discussion of compounding and present value has dealt with a single lump-sum cash flow. We have discussed the compound or future amount of a known lump-sum investment today and the present value of a known

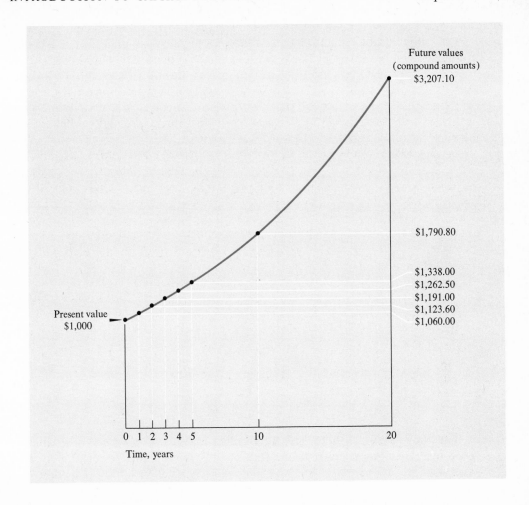

Future values
(compound amounts)
$3,207.10

$1,790.80

$1,338.00
$1,262.50
$1,191.00
$1,123.60
$1,060.00

Present value
$1,000

0 1 2 3 4 5   10   20

Time, years

lump-sum future amount. However, usually there are several cash flows, not one, occurring over the life of a long-term investment or loan.

The compound and present value tables previously illustrated can be used to calculate the future value and present value of a series of cash flows. For example, to find the present value of equal cash flows of $1,000 to be received at the end of each year for three years, with interest at 6 per cent compounded annually, add the present value of a lump sum of $1,000 at the end of each year for three years:

	Cash Flow	Present Value of $1 at 6% Interest	Present Value
Year 1 . . . . =	$1,000 ×	.9434	= $ 943.40
Year 2 . . . . =	$1,000 ×	.8900	= 890.00
Year 3 . . . . =	$1,000 ×	.8396	= 839.60
		2.6730	$2,673.00

Present Value of $1
Interest Rates

Periods	1%	2%	3%	4%	5%	6%	7%	8%	9%	10%
1	.9901	.9804	.9709	.9615	.9524	.9434	.9346	.9259	.9174	.9091
2	.9803	.9612	.9426	.9246	.9070	.8900	.8734	.8573	.8417	.8264
3	.9706	.9423	.9151	.8890	.8638	.8396	.8163	.7938	.7722	.7513
4	.9610	.9238	.8885	.8548	.8227	.7921	.7629	.7350	.7084	.6830
5	.9515	.9057	.8626	.8219	.7835	.7473	.7130	.6806	.6499	.6209
6	.9420	.8880	.8375	.7903	.7462	.7050	.6663	.6302	.5963	.5645
7	.9327	.8706	.8131	.7599	.7107	.6651	.6227	.5835	.5470	.5132
8	.9235	.8535	.7894	.7307	.6768	.6274	.5820	.5403	.5019	.4665
9	.9143	.8368	.7664	.7026	.6446	.5919	.5439	.5002	.4604	.4241
10	.9053	.8203	.7441	.6756	.6139	.5584	.5083	.4632	.4224	.3855
11	.8963	.8043	.7224	.6496	.5847	.5268	.4751	.4289	.3875	.3505
12	.8874	.7885	.7014	.6246	.5568	.4970	.4440	.3971	.3555	.3186
13	.8787	.7730	.6810	.6006	.5303	.4688	.4150	.3677	.3262	.2897
14	.8700	.7579	.6611	.5775	.5051	.4423	.3878	.3405	.2992	.2633
15	.8613	.7430	.6419	.5553	.4810	.4173	.3624	.3152	.2745	.2394
16	.8528	.7284	.6232	.5339	.4581	.3936	.3387	.2919	.2519	.2176
17	.8444	.7142	.6050	.5134	.4363	.3714	.3166	.2703	.2311	.1978
18	.8360	.7002	.5874	.4936	.4155	.3503	.2959	.2502	.2120	.1799
19	.8277	.6864	.5703	.4746	.3957	.3305	.2765	.2317	.1945	.1635
20	.8195	.6730	.5537	.4564	.3769	.3118	.2584	.2145	.1784	.1486
25	.7798	.6095	.4776	.3751	.2953	.2330	.1842	.1460	.1160	.0923
30	.7419	.5521	.4120	.3083	.2314	.1741	.1314	.0994	.0754	.0573
35	.7059	.5000	.3554	.2534	.1813	.1301	.0937	.0676	.0490	.0356
40	.6717	.4529	.3066	.2083	.1420	.0972	.0668	.0460	.0318	.0221
45	.6391	.4102	.2644	.1712	.1113	.0727	.0476	.0313	.0207	.0137
50	.6080	.3715	.2281	.1407	.0872	.0543	.0339	.0213	.0134	.0085

The above example shows that the formula for the present value of a series of expected cash flows is equal to the sum of the present values of each individual cash flow:

$$
\begin{aligned}
\left.\begin{array}{c} \textbf{\textit{Present value}} \\ \textbf{\textit{of a series of}} \\ \textbf{\textit{cash flows}} \end{array}\right\} &= \left(\begin{array}{ccc} \textbf{Cash flow} & & \textbf{Present value of \$1} \\ \textbf{end of first} & \times & \textbf{at given interest} \\ \textbf{period} & & \textbf{rate for 1 period} \end{array}\right) \\[2mm]
&+ \left(\begin{array}{ccc} \textbf{Cash flow} & & \textbf{Present value of \$1} \\ \textbf{end of second} & \times & \textbf{at given interest} \\ \textbf{period} & & \textbf{rate for 2 periods} \end{array}\right) \\[2mm]
&+ \left(\begin{array}{ccc} \textbf{Cash flow} & & \textbf{Present value of \$1} \\ \textbf{end of third} & \times & \textbf{at given interest} \\ \textbf{period} & & \textbf{rate for 3 periods} \end{array}\right) \\[2mm]
&+ \\
&\quad\cdot \\
&\quad\cdot \\
&\quad\cdot
\end{aligned}
$$

The computation of the present value of a series of cash flows is simplified if an annuity exists. An annuity is a series of *equal* cash receipts or payments made at *uniform* intervals of time at a *constant* interest rate. For simplicity, the assumption is made that the cash flows of an annuity occur at the *end* of each payment (or receipt) period and that each payment (receipt) period is equal to the compound interest period.

In the previous example, the $1,000 cash inflow is a constant amount that occurs at equal intervals of one year for three years, with interest compounded annually. Hence, an annuity exists. Note that in the example the present value of $1 at the end of each year for three years totals 2.673 (.9434 + .8900 + .8396), and that $1,000 multiplied by 2.673 equals the present value of a series of equal cash flows at equal intervals of time. Thus the present value of an annuity is equal to the constant cash flow each period multiplied by the sum of the present values of $1 for each period. However, the latter summation is available from present value of annuity tables; an abbreviated form appears on page 618.

$$\begin{matrix} \textit{Present value of} \\ \textit{an annuity} \end{matrix} = \begin{matrix} \textbf{Constant cash flow} \\ \textbf{each period} \end{matrix} \times \begin{matrix} \textbf{Present value of an annuity} \\ \textbf{of \$1 at a given interest} \\ \textbf{rate and number of periods} \\ \textbf{(obtained from present value} \\ \textbf{of annuity tables)} \end{matrix}$$

$$\textbf{\$2,673} \quad = \quad \textbf{\$1,000} \quad \times \quad \textbf{2.673}$$

The net present value method. The acceptance or rejection of a particular investment is decided by comparison of the present value of the expected net cash inflows to be generated by the investment with the present cash cost of making the investment. If net present value is defined as the difference between the present value of the expected net cash inflows and the cost to acquire the investment, then the investment will be accepted quantitatively if it has a positive net present value, rejected if it has a negative net present value, and either accepted or rejected if it has a zero net present value.

A positive net present value means that the present value of the expected net cash inflows exceeds the cost today to acquire the investment and that the firm's financial position and earnings should be improved if the investment is made. For example, suppose that the management of a firm has some idle cash which it would like to invest in land for speculative purposes. The land costs $10,000 today; management forecasts that the land could be sold for $20,000 in 10 years, and estimates that the cost of money is 10 per cent. Upon consulting the present value tables it would appear that the investment should not be made: the net present value is a negative $2,290, as shown below.

$$\begin{matrix} \textit{Present value} \\ \textit{of investment} \end{matrix} = \begin{matrix} \textbf{Expected} \\ \textbf{cash inflow} \end{matrix} \times \begin{matrix} \textbf{Present value of \$1 at 10\%} \\ \textbf{for 10 years (obtained from} \\ \textbf{present value tables)} \end{matrix}$$

$$\textbf{\$7,710} \quad = \quad \textbf{\$20,000} \quad \times \quad \textbf{.3855}$$

$$\begin{matrix} \textit{Net present value} \\ \textit{of investment} \end{matrix} = \begin{matrix} \textbf{Present value of} \\ \textbf{expected cash inflow} \end{matrix} - \begin{matrix} \textbf{Cost to acquire} \\ \textbf{investment today} \end{matrix}$$

$$\textbf{-\$2,290} \quad = \quad \textbf{\$7,710} \quad - \quad \textbf{\$10,000}$$

Present Value of An Annuity of $1
Interest Rates

Periods	1%	2%	3%	4%	5%	6%	7%	8%	9%	10%
1	0.9901	0.9804	0.9709	0.9615	0.9524	0.9434	0.9346	0.9259	0.9174	0.9091
2	1.9704	1.9416	1.9135	1.8861	1.8594	1.8334	1.8080	1.7833	1.7591	1.7355
3	2.9410	2.8839	2.8286	2.7751	2.7232	2.6730	2.6243	2.5771	2.5313	2.4869
4	3.9020	3.8077	3.7171	3.6299	3.5460	3.4651	3.3872	3.3121	3.2397	3.1699
5	4.8534	4.7135	4.5797	4.4518	4.3295	4.2124	4.1002	3.9927	3.8897	3.7908
6	5.7955	5.6014	5.4172	5.2421	5.0757	4.9173	4.7665	4.6229	4.4859	4.3553
7	6.7282	6.4720	6.2303	6.0021	5.7864	5.5824	5.3893	5.2064	5.0330	4.8684
8	7.6517	7.3255	7.0197	6.7327	6.4632	6.2098	5.9713	5.7466	5.5348	5.3349
9	8.5660	8.1622	7.7861	7.4353	7.1078	6.8017	6.5152	6.2469	5.9952	5.7590
10	9.4713	8.9826	8.5302	8.1109	7.7217	7.3601	7.0236	6.7101	6.4177	6.1446
11	10.3676	9.7868	9.2526	8.7605	8.3064	7.8867	7.4987	7.1390	6.8052	6.4951
12	11.2551	10.5753	9.9540	9.3851	8.8633	8.3838	7.9427	7.5361	7.1607	6.8137
13	12.1337	11.3484	10.6350	9.9856	9.3936	8.8527	8.3577	7.9038	7.4869	7.1034
14	13.0037	12.1062	11.2961	10.5631	9.8986	9.2950	8.7455	8.2442	7.7862	7.3667
15	13.8651	12.8493	11.9379	11.1184	10.3797	9.7122	9.1079	8.5595	8.0607	7.6061
16	14.7179	13.5777	12.5611	11.6523	10.8378	10.1059	9.4466	8.8514	8.3126	7.8237
17	15.5623	14.2919	13.1661	12.1657	11.2741	10.4773	9.7632	9.1216	8.5436	8.0216
18	16.3983	14.9920	13.7535	12.6593	11.6896	10.8276	10.0591	9.3719	8.7556	8.2014
19	17.2260	15.6785	14.3238	13.1339	12.0853	11.1581	10.3356	9.6036	8.9501	8.3649
20	18.0456	16.3514	14.8775	13.5903	12.4622	11.4699	10.5940	9.8181	9.1285	8.5136
25	22.0232	19.5235	17.4131	15.6221	14.0939	12.7834	11.6536	10.6748	9.8226	9.0770
30	25.8077	22.3965	19.6004	17.2920	15.3725	13.7648	12.4090	11.2578	10.2737	9.4269
35	29.4086	24.9986	21.4872	18.6646	16.3742	14.4982	12.9477	11.6546	10.5668	9.6442
40	32.8347	27.3555	23.1148	19.7928	17.1591	15.0463	13.3317	11.9246	10.7574	9.7791
45	36.0945	29.4902	24.5187	20.7200	17.7741	15.4558	13.6055	12.1084	10.8812	9.8628
50	39.1961	31.4236	25.7298	21.4822	18.2559	15.7619	13.8007	12.2335	10.9617	9.9148

The problem can also be stated in terms of future amounts. If management can earn 10 per cent on its invested money, the firm would be better off financially if it invested the money at 10 per cent for 10 years, which would result in a cash inflow of $25,938, rather than investing in the land, which would bring in cash of $20,000 ten years hence:

$$
\begin{matrix}
\textit{Future value} \\
\textit{(Compound amount)} \\
\textit{of investment}
\end{matrix}
=
\begin{matrix}
\textbf{Investment} \\
\textbf{cost today}
\end{matrix}
\times
\begin{matrix}
\textbf{Compound amount of \$1 at 10} \\
\textbf{per cent for 10 years (obtained} \\
\textbf{from compound tables)}
\end{matrix}
$$

$$ \$25,938 \quad = \quad \$10,000 \quad \times \quad 2.5938 $$

In addition to assisting management in deciding whether to accept or reject investment opportunities, the net present value method can be used to choose the best investment alternative or alternatives from among several. Suppose that management wished to select the one best investment from among the following four alternatives:

	Investment	Expected Net Cash Inflow at End of Each Year for 10 Years
Investment #1	$ 40,000	$10,000
Investment #2	100,000	15,000
Investment #3	70,000	11,000
Investment #4	63,000	14,000

The solution is to calculate the present value of the expected cash inflow from each investment and compare it to the amount invested. In general, the investment alternative with the greatest net present value is the one that is preferred from a quantitative viewpoint.

Note that the expected cash inflows from each investment are constant each year. Hence we can use the present value of annuity tables. Assuming a 10 per cent cost of money, investments #2 and #3 are eliminated because of negative net present values, and investment #4 is preferred over investment #1 because of its greater net present value.

	Present Value of Investment	=	Annual Cash Inflow	×	Present Value of an Annuity of $1 at 10% for 10 Years (Obtained from Present Value of Annuity Tables)
Investment #1 ..	$61,446	=	$10,000	×	6.1446
Investment #2 ..	92,169	=	15,000	×	6.1446
Investment #3 ..	67,591	=	11,000	×	6.1446
Investment #4 ..	86,024	=	14,000	×	6.1446

	Net Present Value	=	Present Value of Investment	−	Investment
Investment #1	+$21,446	=	$61,446	−	$ 40,000
Investment #2	− 7,831	=	92,169	−	100,000
Investment #3	− 2,409	=	67,591	−	70,000
Investment #4	+ 23,024	=	86,024	−	63,000

In contrast to the net present value method, the payback-period method (original cost of investment divided by the constant annual net cash flow generated by the investment) would rank investment #1 ($40,000 ÷ $10,000 = 4 years) over investment #4 ($63,000 ÷ $14,000 = 4.5 years). The payback period is based on the rationale that the shorter the time period in which the original investment cost is recovered, the better the investment. Because it is simple to understand and easy to calculate, the payback period is probably the most widely used capital-budgeting method in industry. However, as the illustration indicates, the payback period can lead to incorrect investment decisions because it fails to take into account the time value of money and it completely neglects the net cash inflows generated after the payback period.

The cost of capital. The calculation of the net present value of an investment assumes a given rate of interest, called the cost of capital. The cost of capital is defined as the *minimum* desired rate of return on investment proposals. If the cost of capital is 10 per cent, a firm must earn at least 10 per cent on its investment projects in order to maintain its present financial position. Consequently, for any given long-term investment alternative:

A *positive* net present value indicates that the alternative is quantitatively *acceptable.* The investment is attractive because it is expected to earn a rate of return that is above the cost of capital.

A *negative* net present value indicates that the alternative is quantitatively *unacceptable.* The investment is rejected because it is expected to earn a rate of return that is less than the cost of capital.

Qualitative factors. Long-run investment decisions are based not only on quantitative factors, but also on qualitative factors. Qualitative factors are those which cannot be measured in terms of dollars and cents with an acceptable degree of precision.

To reach a quantitative decision, the net present value of prospective long-run investments is calculated. The quantitative decision is either supplemented or offset by the analysis of qualitative factors that influence the investment proposals. Thus, the final investment decision is based on both quantitative and qualitative considerations. Some of the more important qualitative factors to consider are the following:

A company may accept an investment proposal with a slight negative net present value in order to keep its labor force busy and avoid the risks associated with laying off workers and attempting to rehire them later, which might cause labor problems.

A company may accept an investment project that is quantitatively unacceptable because it broadens the company's product line and thus provides better customer service, which may increase over all company sales.

An equipment replacement illustration. Assume that management wishes to determine whether or not an old piece of equipment should be replaced. The company accountants assemble the following data to be analyzed:

	Old Asset	New Asset
Expected cash inflow per year	$40,000	$40,000
Expected cash outflows per year:		
Direct material cost	10,000	9,000
Direct labor cost	20,000	15,000
Variable factory overhead cost	8,000	6,000
Fixed factory overhead cost	9,000	9,000
Cost to acquire new equipment today	—	70,000
Salvage value of old equipment today	15,000	—
Salvage value end of 10 years	5,000	10,000
Estimated useful life	10 years	10 years
Cost of capital	10%	10%

Which cash flows are relevant to the replacement decision? The expected cash revenue of $40,000 and the fixed factory overhead cost of $9,000 are irrelevant because they are the same for both alternatives and do not affect the decision. The new machine results in a cost saving per year of $1,000 ($10,000 − $9,000) for direct material, $5,000 ($20,000 − $15,000) for direct labor, and $2,000 ($8,000 − $6,000) for variable factory overhead. The total of $8,000 in cost savings per year for 10 years is equivalent to an annual cash inflow of $8,000 for the new equipment. Also, the $70,000 cost to acquire the new equipment is relevant, for it is not the same under both alternatives (the $70,000 cost is not incurred if the old equipment is retained in service).

The $15,000 salvage value (estimated amount to be recovered from disposal of the old asset) today is relevant, for it is realized only if the new equipment is purchased; therefore, the cash inflow from the salvage, in effect, reduces the cost today of acquiring the new equipment. The $10,000 salvage value of the new equipment at the end of 10 years is a relevant cash inflow in favor of the new equipment. Finally, the $5,000 salvage value of the old equipment at the end of 10 years is relevant for it is foregone if the new equipment is purchased; hence, it is treated as a cash outflow (a cost) of the new equipment. The cash flows are summarized graphically below.

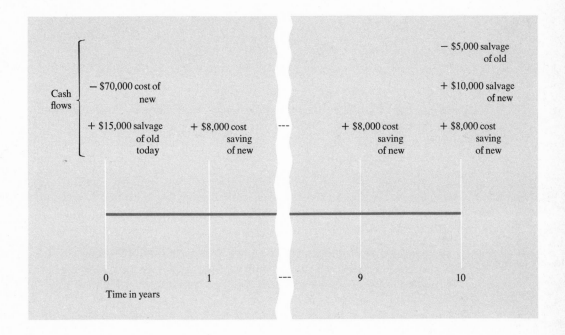

The cost of acquiring the new equipment and the salvage value of the old equipment today are both in terms of present-day dollars; no present value computations are necessary. The cost savings of $8,000 are constant each year and, therefore, can be converted to present value dollars by the use of present value of annuity tables. The $10,000 salvage of the new equipment and the $5,000 salvage of the old equipment occur in year 10. Therefore, tables for present value of $1 can be used to convert the salvage values into equivalent dollars today. The present value calculations are summarized on page 622.

		Present value of an	Present value of	
Annual cash	×	annuity of $1 at 10%	= annual cost	
cost savings		for 10 years	savings of new	Summary
$ 8,000	×	6.1446	= $49,156.80	+ $49,156.80

		Present value of $1		
Cash inflow from	×	at 10% at end of	= Present value of	
salvage of new		10 years	salvage of new	
$10,000	×	.3855	= $ 3,855.00	+ 3,855.00

			Present value of	
		Present value of $1	salvage of old	
Cash inflow from	×	at 10% at end of	= foregone if new	
salvage of old		10 years	purchased	
$ 5,000	×	.3855	= $ 1,927.50	− 1,927.50

Cost today to				
acquire new	−	Salvage value of	= Net cost of	
equipment		old equipment today	new equipment	
$70,000	−	$15,000	= $55,000.00	− 55,000.00
				− $ 3,915.70

The calculations show that the purchase of the new equipment is rejected quantitatively, for the present value of the expected cash inflows is less than the net cost of acquiring the new equipment. That is, there is a negative net present value of $3,915.70. On the other hand, qualitative considerations must be taken into account before a final decision is reached.

Assumptions underlying net present value. The quantitative analysis associated with capital budgeting, as discussed earlier in this chapter, rested on certain assumptions, the most important of which are presented below.

(1) The expected cash inflows and outflows were assumed to be known with certainty. In reality it is difficult to forecast future cash flows, and undoubtedly a range of expected cash flows would be used in the analysis.

(2) The cost of capital was assumed to be given. Actually the calculation of the cost of capital is very difficult. It requires a weighted average to be taken of the cost of financing from common stock, preferred stock, retained earnings, and debt.

(3) The cash flows discussed in this chapter were assumed to be on an after-tax basis. Capital budgeting techniques must take into account the effect of income taxes on cash receipts, cash disbursements, depreciation expense, salvage values, book gains and losses on old equipment, and so forth. That is, tax payments are cash payments which are relevant cash flows.

(4) Cash flows were assumed to occur at the end of each time period, and

each time period was assumed to correspond to the compound interest period.

(5) Out of several competing investment proposals, the preferred investment was assumed to be the one with the greatest net present value. In more advanced courses, it is pointed out that there are unusual circumstances where this may not be true (e.g., capital rationing and substantial cost differentials).

ASSIGNMENT

MATERIAL

QUESTIONS

1. Why does a rational person prefer to receive a dollar today rather than a dollar in the future?
2. What is capital budgeting?
3. If accrual accounting is used by accountants in the preparation of financial statements, why not then use accrual accounting data to solve capital budgeting problems?
4. What is the difference between simple and compound interest?
5. If the paying of compound interest costs more than the paying of simple interest, why do savings institutions pay compound interest?
6. In your own words discuss what *present value* means and why it is a useful concept.
7. Make up an example to show that present value is merely the opposite of compounding.
8. What are annuity tables? When and why are they used?
9. Suppose that you have a table showing the present value of $1, but that you do not have a table showing the present value of an annuity. How can you convert the lump-sum present value factors given in your table into present value factors of an annuity?
10. If the time value of money is such an important concept, why is it not used in cost-volume-profit analysis?

SHORT EXERCISES

E27-1. Assume that you can invest money at 7 per cent compounded annually. Further assume that you have four different investment opportunities, listed below, all of which have the same initial cost. Which one of the four investment alternatives do you prefer? (Show all computations.)

    (a) The receipt of $12,000 five years from now.
    (b) The receipt of $2,000 at the end of each year for the next five years.
    (c) The receipt of $8,700 today.
    (d) The receipt of the following net cash inflows at the end of each successive year
        as follows: $1,000; $2,000; $5,000; $2,000; and $1,000.

E27-2. The management of Acquisition Company has decided to acquire a new piece of equipment. The cost of the equipment is $100,000, and it is expected to generate annual net cash inflows of $20,000 for seven years. The decision to buy the equipment was based on the equipment's net future cash inflows of $140,000 ($20,000 × 7 years) being greater than its $100,000 cost today. Assuming that the cost of capital is 10 per cent, evaluate management's decision to acquire the equipment.

E27-3. The management of Procurement Company uses the payback period (original cost divided by annual net cash inflow) to determine whether capital expenditures should be made. A payback period of eight years or less is considered acceptable. Using this criterion, management decided to acquire a new piece of equipment that cost $80,000 and was expected to generate annual net cash inflows of $10,000 over its expected thirteen-year life. In other words, the payback period was acceptable ($80,000 ÷ 10,000 = 8 years). If the cost of capital is 8 per cent, evaluate the decision to acquire the new equipment.

E27-4. The management of Alternative Company uses an average rate of return on cost (annual net cash inflow ÷ original cost) in choosing between different investment alternatives. Management used this method to choose Investment B over Investment A, as shown below. Assuming a cost of capital of 9 per cent, evaluate the decision.

	Investment A	Investment B
Expected annual net cash inflow from investment		
(11 year life) . . . . (a)	$ 20,000	$16,800
Cost. . . . . (b)	100,000	80,000
Average rate of return . . . . (a ÷ b)	20%	21%

PROBLEMS

Problem A27-1. Solve the following short problems.

   (a) If the interest rate is 3 per cent compounded annually, $10,000 invested today would accumulate to how much in 7 years? What is your answer if the interest rate is 8 per cent compounded annually?

   (b) Solve problem (a) if the interest rate is 3 per cent simple annual interest and the annual interest is not withdrawn.

   (c) If the interest rate is 6 per cent compounded annually, how much money must be invested today to accumulate to $12,000 in 10 years? What is your answer if the interest rate is 10 per cent compounded annually?

   (d) If the interest rate is 5 per cent compounded annually, how much do you need to invest today to insure that your mother can withdraw $6,000 at the end of each year for the next 10 years?

   (e) If the interest rate is 4 per cent compounded annually, a $5,000 deposit at the beginning of each year for the next 5 years will accumulate to how much money? (Hint: You can sum up the compound factors for $1 to derive a compound annuity factor.)

   (f) If $1 today is worth $25 in year *n*, $1 to be received in year *n* is worth how much today? (Hint: Present value is the opposite of compounding, so try 1 over the compound factor.)

Problem A 27-2. Solve the following two short problems.

(a) You have the opportunity to invest $7,000 today that will return cash of $1,000 after the first year, $1,200 after the second year, $1,500 after the third year, $2,000 after the fourth year, and $2,200 after the fifth year. If you want to earn at least 6 per cent on your invested money, should you make this proposed investment?

(b) You wish to decide between an investment of $65,000 in one of two alternatives. The first alternative results in cash receipts of $10,000 at the end of each year for 10 years. The second alternative results in the receipt of $200,000 at the end of 15 years. If you wish to earn at least 8 per cent on your investment, which alternative should you choose?

Problem A 27-3. Quandry Corporation must earn 7 per cent on its money in order to maintain its present position. Its management is contemplating a $400,000 investment in new equipment. Management estimates that the new equipment will be used for 7 years, at the end of which the estimated salvage value should be $50,000. Estimated yearly cash revenues and expenses are presented below. Should the investment be accepted?

Year	Cash Revenue	Cash Expense	Maintenance (cash outlays)	Overhauls (cash outlays)
1	$170,000	$100,000	$ 1,000	$ —
2	180,000	120,000	4,000	—
3	200,000	130,000	10,000	—
4	275,000	185,000	2,000	25,000
5	290,000	200,000	5,000	—
6	300,000	200,000	11,000	—
7	250,000	190,000	2,000	25,000

Problem A 27-4. Alexander Corporation is considering the replacement of some of its major equipment. Although management has made its choice as to which equipment to purchase, it has not decided whether the replacement is financially sound. Given the data below, advise Alexander Corporation on whether the replacement should be made.

	Present Equipment	New Equipment
Undepreciated cost	$2,000,000	—
Acquisition cost	—	$10,000,000
Useful life	10 years remaining	10 years
Salvage value now	$3,000,000	—
Salvage 10 years hence	—	$2,500,000
Expected annual cash revenues	$2,000,000	$2,750,000
Expected annual cash costs:		
Direct materials	$400,000	$400,000
Direct labor	300,000	100,000
Variable factory overhead	200,000	300,000
Fixed factory overhead	250,000	250,000
Expected annual cash maintenance	$500,000	$100,000
Cost of capital	10%	10%

Problem A 27-5. The management of A. J. Baxter Company has decided that computer operations are becoming necessary. Management can purchase or rent either Computer A or Computer B; hence there are four alternatives. Given the data on the next page, show which alternative is the most advantageous and rank all four alternatives.

	Computer A		Computer B	
	Purchase	Rent	Purchase	Rent
Acquisition cost	$5,000,000	—	$7,000,000	—
Rental cost		$1,000/hour used		$1,200/hour used
Estimated useful life . . .	5 years	—	5 years	—
Estimated salvage value				
5 years hence	$500,000	—	$1,000,000	—
Estimated cash main-				
tenance per year	$225,000	—	$100,000	—
Estimated cash savings				
per year	$4,000,000	$4,000,000	$4,750,000	$4,750,000
Cost of capital	5%	5%	5%	5%
Estimated hours of use:				
Year 1		1,000		800
2		1,200		1,000
3		1,400		1,300
4		1,600		1,400
5		1,800		1,600

Problem B27-1. Solve the following short problems.

(a) A father is attempting to determine how much money he can accumulate for his son's future college education. If he has $6,000 to invest today at 5 per cent compounded annually, and if his son will need the money 8 years from now, how much will he be able to accumulate?

(b) If a $10,000 loan has to be paid 5 years from now, how much must be invested today at 4 per cent interest compounded annually to insure the payment of the loan?

(c) How much will the father in problem (a) accumulate if he invests $6,000 at the beginning of each year for 8 years? (Hint: You can sum up the compound factors for $1 to derive a compound annuity factor.)

(d) The management of a company wishes to reduce outstanding debt by paying $9,000 at the end of each year for 5 years. If management can invest money at 6 per cent interest compounded annually, how much would have to be invested today to insure the annual debt payments?

(e) Suppose that you owe $3,000 plus 4 per cent interest compounded annually to be paid 4 years from now. If the creditor can invest money at 7 per cent interest compounded annually, how much should he be willing to accept today to cancel the debt?

(f) If you have $8,424.80 to invest today at 6 per cent interest compounded annually, how much could you withdraw at the end of each year for 5 years in order to exhaust your investment fully? (Hint: Substitute the given data in the present value of an annuity formula given in the chapter and solve for the annual payment.)

Problem B27-2. You are given below data pertaining to three investment alternatives. If the cost of capital is 6 per cent, which investments are quantitatively acceptable? In comparison to each alternative, what is the basic cause for the differences in acceptability?

Investment	Cost Today	Future Cash Flows			
		Year 1	Year 2	Year 3	Year 4
#1	$14,000	$4,000	$4,000	$4,000	$4,000
#2	14,000	6,000	5,000	4,000	3,000
#3	14,000	2,000	3,000	4,000	5,000

Problem B27-3. The management of Tolefson Company has decided to add a new production line, and the choice is narrowed to either production line A or production line B. Given the data below, which production-line alternative is quantitatively better? Is the better alternative quantitatively acceptable?

	Alternative A	Alternative B
Acquisition cost	$500,000	$600,000
Estimated useful life	8 years	8 years
Salvage value 8 years hence	$ 50,000	$200,000
Estimated annual cash revenues	$250,000	$300,000
Estimated annual cash costs:		
Direct materials	$ 50,000	$ 60,000
Direct labor	70,000	40,000
Variable factory overhead	30,000	50,000
Maintenance	10,000	60,000
Cost of capital	10%	10%

Problem B27-4. The management of D. J. K. Corporation has decided to acquire a new truck, which can be either purchased or leased. Given the data below and that the cost of capital is 7 per cent, should management purchase or lease the truck? Would your answer be different if the rental charge was $1,000 per year plus $.10 per mile?

Purchase:

Acquisition cost	$27,000
Estimated life	5 years
Salvage 5 years hence	$5,000

	Year 1	Year 2	Year 3	Year 4	Year 5
Estimated cash cost savings	$40,000	$50,000	$60,000	$40,000	$30,000
Estimated cash maintenance	1,000	2,000	2,000	4,000	5,000

Lease:

Rental expense	$.10 per mile
Maintenance expense	paid by owner

	Year 1	Year 2	Year 3	Year 4	Year 5
Estimated cash cost savings	$40,000	$50,000	$ 60,000	$40,000	$30,000
Estimated mileage	60,000	90,000	100,000	70,000	40,000

Problem B27-5. The owners of Ralph Smith Company are considering the expansion of their facilities. The proposed facilities are estimated to have a useful life of 50 years, after which time the salvage value is estimated to be zero. Given the data below, should the expansion be undertaken?

	Present Facilities	Present and Expanded Facilities
Initial cost	$900,000	$1,400,000
Estimated annual cash revenues	200,000	300,000
Estimated annual cash expenses	100,000	150,000
Remodeling costs—Year 10	75,000	100,000
Remodeling costs—Year 20	100,000	125,000
Remodeling costs—Year 30	150,000	200,000
Remodeling costs—Year 40	175,000	200,000
Cost of capital	8%	8%

28

Analysis of Financial Statements

Introduction. A recurring theme throughout this book has been that the field of accounting exists to provide useful financial data for decision-making purposes. The use of financial data for managerial decision making has been previously discussed, especially with regard to target costs, responsibility accounting, cost-volume-profit analysis, and capital budgeting. The discussion now turns to how accounting data in the form of financial statements can provide useful information for persons outside the business firm who do not have access to internal accounting records. It should be obvious, however, that the information contained in financial statements is also useful to management, especially when used with pertinent internal accounting data.

Why are financial statements analyzed? Management and such outsiders as investors, creditors, labor unions, and government agencies analyze financial statements not only to determine the overall financial status of a company but also to determine relationships that indicate financial strengths and weaknesses that are pertinent to their particular interests. Thus, financial statements are analyzed in an effort to find answers to a variety of practical and important questions, such as the following: What are the earnings record and prospects? What is the short-term debt-paying ability of the business? Is there any danger of default on the long-term liabilities? Is the amount of debt large in comparison to owners' equity? In general, is management doing a good job of running the business?

Sources of financial data. Financial statements and other financial data can be found in annual* and quarterly reports prepared and published by business firms. The Securities and Exchange Commission requires certain companies to file detailed annual reports (SEC Form 10-K), which can be obtained for purposes of analysis. Investment advisory services, such as Moody's Investors Service, Inc., Standard and Poor's Corporation, and The Value Line Investment Survey, publish financial statements and analyses of companies. Finally, various financial analyses are published by Dun and Bradstreet, Robert Morris Associates, stock brokerage houses, credit agencies, trade agencies, financial newspapers, and financial periodicals.

Comparative statements. In order to determine financial trends, balance sheets and income statements for a company should be compared over the last five to ten years. In their annual reports, many companies now show balance sheet and income statement data for several years side by side to facilitate trend analysis. If such comparative statements are not available in an annual report, the data can be obtained from several annual reports and listed side by side on a spread sheet.

From the comparative financial statements, dollar and percentage changes can be calculated for key financial figures to determine: (1) the primary elements that caused the change; (2) whether the trend of the change is favorable or unfavorable; and (3) whether, based on expected business conditions, the trend is likely to continue in the near future.

To illustrate comparative analysis, suppose that your analysis of a particular company shows that net income has been increasing about 4 per cent per year for the last five years. Some conclusions resulting from your analysis of the income data might be:

(1) Much of the recent increase in net income is the result of nonoperating gains which are unlikely to recur in the near future.
(2) The trend is upward, but in comparison to similar companies the rate of increase is below average.
(3) In view of an expected business recession next year, the below-average historical growth in earnings, and no expectation of nonoperating gains, net income next year is unlikely to show any increase.

As an example, some comparative financial statements for "Vivian & Sons, Inc.," are presented on pages 632 and 633. Like most published financial statements, they do not show breakdowns of cost of goods sold, of operating expenses, or of the variable and fixed components of expenses. Generally the lack of detail is rationalized by the desire to avoid bulky financial statements, to avoid giving too much data to competitors, and to avoid confusing the readers of the statements with too much detail. However, for the purpose of financial-statement analysis, it would be especially helpful if expenses were broken down between fixed and variable components so that cost-volume-profit analysis could be used by outsiders.

Ratio analysis. Financial statements contain a maze of dollar amounts that are difficult to interpret when viewed as a whole or individually. Relevant financial relationships

---

*See Appendix 1 for an example of an annual report.

may be overlooked in an overall examination because of the complexity of such a large mass of financial data. Similarly, an analysis of each dollar amount by itself overlooks key relationships because meaningful comparisons are not made. Also, individual dollar amounts by themselves often are relatively insignificant.

So that readers will not be "blinded" by the mass of figures contained in financial statements, financial-statement analysis should entail the use of ratio analysis. A financial ratio is a comparison of two related pieces of financial data of a firm, the ratio being derived from the common fraction of the two in percentage form. An example would be the current ratio of Vivian & Sons, Inc., as of December 31, 19+6.

$$\textit{Current ratio} = \textbf{Current Assets} \div \textbf{Current Liabilities}$$
$$\textbf{1.79} = \textbf{\$905,000} \div \textbf{\$504,950}$$

Through the use of ratios, one can focus attention on financial inter-relationships:

(1) By relating sections of a financial statement to other sections of the same statement.

Example: Current assets are compared with current liabilities (current ratio) as an indicator of a firm's ability to meet short-term debts.

(2) By relating financial data in one statement to data in another statement.

Example: Net income from the income statement is compared with common stockholders' equity from the balance sheet to determine a rate of return on owners' equity.

(3) By relating an evaluation of a particular section of a statement to an overall evaluation of the firm to determine if the latter confirms the former.

Example: A company may have only a "fair" current ratio, but the overall profitability and financial position may be good enough to offset the current ratio and may lead to the conclusion that the company can meet its short-term debts satisfactorily.

On the other hand, the analyst must be careful to avoid conclusions based on ratio analysis *alone*. Because ratio analysis has certain weaknesses (discussed on pages 645–646), conclusions based on ratio analysis should be verified by funds-flow analysis, comparative-statement analysis (to determine trends), and the like.

Financial analysis for investors in common stocks. Varying degrees of risk are associated with investments in common stock. Having determined the risk class of common stock in which he is willing to invest his money, the investor is primarily interested in stock-price appreciation and dividend payments. Because both of these factors are influenced by net income, much of the analysis undertaken to determine the attractiveness of an investment in common stock focuses attention on the earnings record of the company under consideration. That is, net income is a measure of operating efficiency and thus provides some indication as to whether a particular common stock is a good investment.

VIVIAN & SONS, INC.
Comparative Balance Sheets
December 31, 19+1—19+6

Assets

	19+1	19+2	19+3	19+4	19+5	19+6
Current assets:						
Cash	$ 70,000	$ 45,000	$ 37,400	$ 54,600	$ 20,000	$ 5,000
Net accounts receivable	100,000	150,000	170,000	200,000	275,000	400,000
Inventory	80,000	200,000	210,000	250,000	300,000	500,000
Total current assets	$250,000	$395,000	$ 417,400	$ 504,600	$ 595,000	$ 905,000
Long-lived assets:						
Land	$ 80,000	$ 80,000	$ 170,000	$ 170,000	$ —	$ —
Plant and equipment	$400,000	$500,000	$ 602,000	$ 802,000	$1,002,000	$1,102,000
Accumulated depreciation	100,000	125,000	155,100	195,200	245,300	300,400
Net	$300,000	$375,000	$ 446,900	$ 606,800	$ 756,700	$ 801,600
Total long-lived assets	$380,000	$455,000	$ 616,900	$ 776,800	$ 756,700	$ 801,600
	$630,000	$850,000	$1,034,300	$1,281,400	$1,351,700	$1,706,600

Equities

	19+1	19+2	19+3	19+4	19+5	19+6
Current liabilities:						
Accounts payable	$ 10,000	$ 35,000	$ 40,000	$ 45,000	$ 54,800	$ 125,350
Short-term loans	—	15,000	20,000	35,000	60,000	300,000
Taxes payable	20,000	40,000	46,400	54,000	65,200	79,600
Total current liabilities	$ 30,000	$ 90,000	$ 106,400	$ 134,000	$ 180,000	$ 504,950
Long-term liabilities						
Bonds payable—6%	$ —	$100,000	$ 250,000	$ 450,000	$ 450,000	$ 450,000
Stockholders' equity:						
Common stock—20,000 shares	$400,000	$400,000	$ 400,000	$ 400,000	$ 400,000	$ 400,000
Retained earnings	200,000	260,000	277,900	297,400	321,700	351,650
Total stockholders' equity	$600,000	$660,000	$ 677,900	$ 697,400	$ 721,700	$ 751,650
	$630,000	$850,000	$1,034,300	$1,281,400	$1,351,700	$1,706,600
Market price per share of common stock, December 31	$ 5	$ 12	$ 19	$ 27	$ 49	$ 80
Annual dividends	—	—	51,700	61,500	73,500	89,450

VIVIAN & SONS, INC.
Comparative Income Statements
For the Years Ended December 31, 19+1—19+6

	19+1	19+2	19+3	19+4	19+5	19+6
Net sales	$600,000	$900,000	$950,000	$1,000,000	$1,100,000	$1,210,000
Cost of goods sold	400,000	630,000	646,000	670,000	737,000	806,000
Gross margin	$200,000	$270,000	$304,000	$ 330,000	$ 363,000	$ 404,000
Operating expenses:						
Selling expense	$ 90,000	$100,000	$108,000	$ 110,000	$ 112,000	$ 115,000
General and administrative expenses	60,000	64,000	65,000	58,000	61,000	63,000
Total	$150,000	$164,000	$173,000	$ 168,000	$ 173,000	$ 178,000
Net operating income	$ 50,000	$106,000	$131,000	$ 162,000	$ 190,000	$ 226,000
Other expense:						
Interest expense	—	6,000	15,000	27,000	27,000	27,000
Net income before taxes	$ 50,000	$100,000	$116,000	$ 135,000	$ 163,000	$ 199,000
Income tax	20,000	40,000	46,400	54,000	65,200	79,600
Net income	$ 30,000	$ 60,000	$ 69,600	$ 81,000	$ 97,800	$ 119,400

EARNINGS PER SHARE AND IMPORTANT RELATIONSHIPS: The net income of a company minus any dividends on preferred stock equals the amount of income applicable to common stockholders. This divided by the average number of common stock shares outstanding equals the earnings per share of common stockholders.

$$\textit{Earnings per share} = \frac{\textbf{Net income minus preferred dividends}}{\textbf{Average number of common shares outstanding}}$$

Although earnings-per-share figures are probably the most widely published and used financial figures, their value is overrated. In the first place, the financial operations of a business cannot really be condensed into one figure called earnings per share. Secondly, comparisons of the earnings per share of different companies can be distorted by the effects of different accounting procedures with regard to inventory, depreciation, capitalization vs. expensing of outlays, and the like. The point is, the financial data from which the earnings per share is derived must be analyzed.

Financial analysts compare earnings per share and the related dividends per share to other financial data in the hope of determining key relationships that may indicate the investment merits of a company's common stock. Three such widely used relationships are the price-earnings ratio, the payout ratio, and the dividend yield.

$$\textit{Price-earnings ratio} = \frac{\textbf{Market price per share of common stock}}{\textbf{Earnings per share}}$$

$$\textit{Payout ratio} = \frac{\textbf{Dividends per share}}{\textbf{Earnings per share}}$$

$$\textit{Dividend yield} = \frac{\textbf{Dividends per share}}{\textbf{Market price per share of common stock}}$$

From the price-earnings ratio a multiplier is derived that shows the evaluation that investors place on the company's earnings. For example, a common stock with a market price of $100 and earnings per share of $5 has a price-earnings ratio of 20; the stock market values every dollar of earnings twenty times. As an indicator of whether a company's common stock is underpriced or overpriced, its price-earnings ratio can be compared with the price-earnings ratios of similar companies, of the industry, and the popular stock averages (indexes). Also, a comparison of the price-earnings ratios of a company for several years can be used in trend analysis for predicting future price-earnings ratios and therefore future stock prices.

A company's payout ratio reflects its management's policy as to whether dividends should be a large or a small percentage of net income. A company that is experiencing substantial growth in earnings (net income) may have a small payout ratio because the management is reinvesting funds in the business. The reinvestment of funds should increase future net income and should be reflected in higher stock prices in the future. An investor interested in stock-price appreciation may well invest in such a company even though the payout ratio is low. In contrast, an investor who is interested primarily in dividends should invest in the common stock of a company with a high payout ratio.

An investor who is interested primarily in dividend income can compute dividend yields on proposed investment alternatives in common stock to aid him in deciding which is the best. He probably would be interested in those common stocks that have a high dividend yield and a high payout ratio. However, the dividend yield is not the entire yield, for its does not take into account stock-price appreciation.

From the financial data on pages 632–633, the three ratios discussed above are calculated as follows:

		19+6	19+5	19+4	19+3	19+2	19+1
Market price per share, December 31. . . .	(a). . .	$80.00	$49.00	$27.00	$19.00	$12.00	$5.00
Earnings per share (annual net income ÷ 20,000 shares).	(b). . .	$ 5.97	$ 4.89	$ 4.05	$ 3.48	$ 3.00	$1.50
Dividends per share (annual dividends ÷ 20,000 shares outstanding)	(c). . .	$ 4.47	$ 3.68	$ 3.08	$ 2.59	—	—
Price-earnings ratio (multiplier)	(a ÷ b) .	13	10	7	5	4	3
Dividend yield (per cent).	(c ÷ a) .	6%	8%	11%	14%	—	—
Payout ratio (per cent)	(c ÷ b) .	75%	75%	76%	74%	—	—

This analysis shows that the company has experienced excellent growth, as earnings per share almost quadrupled from 19+1 to 19+6. The stock market has reacted favorably to the increase in earnings, as shown by the increase in the price-earnings ratio from 3 in 19+1 to 13 in 19+6. Although the dividend yield has been declining, both the yield and payout ratio seem high for a company growing this fast.

If the investor expects earnings to grow at about 20 per cent per year, the estimated earnings per share would be $7.16 ($5.97 × 1.2) for 19+7. If the estimate in growth is correct, the expected growth in earnings should be reflected in an increase in the market price of the stock for 19+7. Suppose that the investor expects the price-earnings ratio to increase to 20 for 19+7, but, to be on the safe side, he decides to use the 19+6 price-earnings ratio of 13. Based on his expectations, he would value the 19+7 stock price at about $93 ($7.16 × 13). If his estimates were correct, he could buy the stock today at about $80 and sell it next year at $93; a $13 price increase per share.

PROFITABILITY RATIOS: In addition to the calculations pertaining to percentage increases in net income (comparative analysis) and the earnings-per-share figures, the investor should analyze a firm's profitability further by making a comparison of net income to such related financial bases as stockholders' equity and total assets. Even though earnings per share and the percentage increase in net income may both be great, a firm may be unattractive from the investor's viewpoint because its net income is such a small percentage of stockholders' equity. Thus the investor should also analyze net income in terms of the following profitability ratios:

$$\text{Rate of return on common stock equity} = \frac{\text{Net income (after taxes) minus preferred dividends}}{\text{Common stockholders' equity}}$$

$$\text{Rate of return on total assets} = \frac{\text{Net income (after taxes) + interest expense}}{\text{Total assets}}$$

The rate of return on common stock equity (Common stock + Capital in excess of par or stated value + Retained earnings) measures the profitability of the capital committed to the business by the common stockholders. Since capital is invested and business is conducted with the object of earning income, the return on equity is a basic measure of business success and managerial efficiency.

The rate of return on total assets measures the relationship between the after-tax income applicable to *all* those who have supplied funds to a firm and the invested funds themselves as reflected in total assets. This measure is indicative of management's ability to earn a satisfactory return on all funds committed to the business. Because creditors provide funds to the firm, consistency requires that the numerator in this calculation be net income (after taxes) plus interest expense.

The investor in common stock should be aware of the fact that the rate of return on total assets affects the rate of return on common stockholders' equity. If a company borrows money and pays a rate of interest that is less than the return on total assets, then the return on common stockholders' equity will be increased and it will be higher than the return on total assets. Thus a company may have a relatively low return on total assets but, through low-cost debt financing, may have a relatively high return on stockholders' equity. This is simply to say that the return on common stockholders' equity depends upon the return on total assets together with the proportion of total capital supplied by debt and preferred stock (see page 285 where leverage is discussed).

Finally, the investor should understand that both of the above rates of return are affected by the "old" dollar book values of the depreciable assets (historical cost minus accumulated depreciation). As a result, some analysts also calculate a rate of return on sales (net income ÷ sales) under the assumption that sales are more reflective of present-day dollars. However, the return on sales neglects the fact that some firms have a large sales volume and a low markup while other firms have a low sales volume and a high markup.

From the data for Vivian & Sons, Inc., the two ratios discussed above can be calculated as follows:

	19+6	19+5	19+4	19+3	19+2	19+1
Net income . . . . . (a) . . .	$ 119,400	$ 97,800	$ 81,000	$ 69,600	$ 60,000	$ 30,000
Common stockholders' equity . . . . (b) . . .	$ 751,650	$ 721,700	$ 697,400	$ 677,900	$660,000	$600,000
Rate of return on common stockholders' equity . . . (a ÷ b) . .	15.9%	13.6%	11.6%	10.3%	9.1%	5.0%
Net income + interest . . . (a) . . .	$ 146,400	$ 124,800	$ 108,000	$ 84,600	$ 66,000	$ 30,000
Total assets . . . . (b) . . .	$1,706,600	$1,351,700	$1,281,400	$1,034,300	$850,000	$630,000
Rate of return on total assets . . . (a ÷ b) . .	8.6%	9.2%	8.4%	8.2%	7.8%	4.8%

These calculations confirm the substantial increase in earnings per share that were calculated previously. Not only are earnings per share increasing at a fast rate, they are also a favorable percentage in relation to the stockholders' equity base. Although the return on total assets is lower than the return on common stockholders' equity, so long as the return on the total assets remains above the interest expense (6 per cent), the return on common stockholders' equity will be benefited (by the leverage factor).

DEBT-TO-EQUITY RATIO: One measure of the common stockholders' risk in a firm is the relation between the funds supplied by creditors to the funds supplied by owners, as shown below:

$$Debt\text{-}to\text{-}equity \ ratio = \frac{\textbf{Total debt}}{\textbf{Stockholders' equity}}$$

Because debt consists of fixed obligations that must be met by the firm in order to avoid insolvency, the higher the debt-to-equity ratio the greater the financial risk that the firm cannot pay its debts. Because of the greater risk, a high debt-to-equity ratio may also preclude a company from obtaining additional debt financing, which results in the loss of financing flexibility.

Although a high debt-to-equity ratio increases financial risk, it can be attractive to stockholders for the following reasons:

(1) It can increase the rate of return on stockholders' equity via leverage.
(2) The voting control of the common stockholders may be maintained by avoidance of new stock flotations.
(3) Because the proportion of stockholders' investment to total financing is small, the creditors are bearing most of the financial risk.

Thus each investor has to weigh the merits of a high debt-to-equity firm by balancing the potential advantages of leverage against the added risk.

The debt-to-equity ratios for Vivian & Sons, Inc., are calculated as follows:

		19+6	19+5	19+4	19+3	19+2	19+1
Total debt	(a) . .	$954,950	$630,000	$584,000	$356,400	$190,000	$ 30,000
Stockholders' equity .	(b) . .	$751,650	$721,700	$697,400	$677,900	$660,000	$600,000
Debt-to-equity ratio .(a ÷ b) .		127%	87%	84%	53%	29%	5%

What the above ratios indicate is that, in order to finance its expanding operations, the debt position of the company was over-extended. Debt financing was increased so fast that by 19+4 the possibility of obtaining additional long-term loans was not feasible. Consequently, management increased the firm's short-term debt financing in 19+5 and especially in 19+6 to help finance the company's expansion.

The large proportion of long-term debt and the increased use of short-term debt increase the possibility that the company may not have the funds to meet interest payments and the retirement of the debt. Short-term debt may be more risky than long-term debt because of the frequent need to replace or renew the financing. An important question is whether the company will be able to continue its profitable operations with the heavy burden of debt. To help answer this question, funds-flow analysis is discussed in the next section.

FUNDS-FLOW ANALYSIS: Clues to the general financial approach used by management in providing financing for a firm can be obtained through analysis of where management is obtaining and using its funds (working capital). In other words, analysis of working-capital flows is useful in evaluating managerial efficiency because profitability and financial position are affected by how management obtains financing and by the types of assets acquired by management. Thus funds-flow analysis is useful not only to common stockholders, but to all those persons who are interested in financial statement analysis.

Since the investor in common stock is concerned primarily with profitability, his analysis of working capital via funds flow, via liquidity ratios (discussed on pages 641–642), and via current asset turnovers (discussed on pages 643–644) should attempt to provide answers to the following types of questions: Is the company hurting its future profitability—

(1) By keeping too much cash on hand, some of which could be reinvested at a favorable rate of return?
(2) By not using debt and/or preferred stock to increase the rate of return on stockholders' equity via leverage?
(3) By paying dividends when such cash should have been reinvested in the business?
(4) By neglecting to replace old plant and equipment?
(5) By expanding operations too fast?
(6) By increasing long-term debt too fast?
(7) By overlooking short-term financing opportunities?
(8) By failing to consider the issuance of additional shares of common stock as a means of additional financing?
(9) By tying up cash in excess inventory?
(10) By tying up cash in accounts receivable that should have been collected?

Many companies do not include funds-flow statements in their annual reports, and if they do, it is unlikely that they will be comparative funds-flow statements covering several years. Thus the investor in common stock should use a spread sheet and either list the data from the annual funds-flow statements for five to ten years or construct his own funds-flow statements from the comparative financial statements. For example, from the comparative financial statements on pages 632–633, comparative fund-flow statements may be prepared, using the techniques discussed in Chapter 16.

VIVIAN & SONS, INC.
Comparative Sources and Uses of Working Capital
For the Years Ended December 31, 19+2—19+6

	19+6	19+5	19+4	19+3	19+2
Working capital sources:					
Funds from operations*	$174,500	$147,900	$121,100	$ 99,700	$ 85,000
Issuance of bonds	—	—	200,000	150,000	100,000
Sale of land	—	170,000	—	—	—
Total sources	$174,500	$317,900	$321,100	$249,700	$185,000

	19+6	19+5	19+4	19+3	19+2
Working capital uses:					
Acquisition of plant and equipment.......	$100,000	$200,000	$200,000	$102,000	$100,000
Acquisition of land	—	—	—	90,000	—
Payment of dividends	89,450	73,500	61,500	51,700	—
Total uses	$189,450	$273,500	$261,500	$243,700	$100,000
Increase (decrease) in working capital	($ 14,950)	$ 44,400	$ 59,600	$ 6,000	$ 85,000

*Depreciation is assumed to be the only nonfund expense. Hence, to compute funds from operations, depreciation expense is added to net income. For instance, funds from operations for 19+6 equal $119,400 + $55,100.

The funds-flow analysis confirms the previous analysis of the debt-to-equity ratios. The company's expansion was financed primarily by the issuance of long-term debt through 19+4, by the sale of land in 19+5, and by internal financing obtained from profitable operations (funds from operations) in 19+6. Also, the balance sheets show a great increase in short-term debt the last two years. Considering the size of the long-term debt and the extent of the recent increase in short-term debt, the risk of insolvency has increased.

Up to this point the contention has been that the company has overextended its debt position. However, it was previously pointed out (page 636) that each investor has to weigh the advantages of leverage against the added risk. Thus the analyst may reach the opposite conclusion, that the growth in net income for Vivian & Sons, Inc., indicates management's ability to take advantage of the expansion, and that the company is not really overextended in terms of debt. In other words, two analysts can reach different conclusions based on the same financial data, because some subjectivity cannot be avoided in financial statement analysis.

As the sources of working capital are analyzed, the question arises why management did not issue additional common stock. This strategy would have taken advantage of a rising price for the company's common stock to bring in additional cash. It would have reduced the high debt-to-equity ratio and given management some flexibility in obtaining future financing.

The use of working capital was primarily for new plant and equipment and the payment of dividends. Although the expansion in plant and equipment probably was too fast, management was attempting to expand its facilities in order to take advantage of its growth potential. However, management should refrain from any further extensive plant and equipment expansion until the debt-to-equity imbalance is corrected.

The payment of large dividends was not sound strategy. Because the company was experiencing substantial and profitable growth, the funds paid out in dividends would have been better used if they had been reinvested in the business. The reinvested funds would have earned a good rate of return on equity and would have reduced the need for such an extensive increase in debt. Similarly, management's maintenance of a 75 per cent payout ratio is much too high for a growth company such as this. In fact, 75 per cent is a high payout for a nongrowth company.

The failure to issue additional common stock, the payment of exorbitant dividends, and the small number of common shares outstanding, seem to indicate that the company may be controlled by a small group of stockholders. That is, additional common stock may not have been issued because the small group of controlling shareholders did not want to share voting control with new stockholders. Similarly, the large dividends may have been at the insistence of the small group of controlling shareholders.

The possibility of issuing additional common stock and the expectation of the continuance of funds inflows from operations indicate that sound management of the firm could result in an improvement in the present precarious debt position. The big question, however, is whether the present management is capable of making the necessary decisions to avoid insolvency.

Finally, the funds-flow analysis should be supplemented by an analysis of the composition and movement of the current assets. This subject is discussed in the section dealing with short-term creditor analysis.

THE THEORETICAL VALUE OF COMMON STOCK: In theory one can estimate the value of a share of common stock by using the approach to capital budgeting decisions described in Chapter 27. The present-value concept must be used because there are time lags between the acquisition of a common stock today and the expected cash inflows to be generated from the investment in the future. Thus the theoretical value of a common stock today is equal to the present value of all its expected dividends over the investment period, plus the present value of the expected cash from the sale of the stock at the end of the investment period.

$$\begin{array}{l}\textit{Theoretical value}\\ \textit{of common stock}\end{array} = \begin{array}{c}\textbf{Present value of the}\\ \textbf{expected dividends over}\\ \textbf{the holding period}\end{array} + \begin{array}{c}\textbf{Present value of the expected}\\ \textbf{cash from the sale of}\\ \textbf{the stock at the end of}\\ \textbf{the holding period}\end{array}$$

If the cost today is greater than the theoretical value, then quantitatively the stock investment should be rejected because it has a negative net present value. A positive net present value would indicate that, quantitatively, the stock investment is acceptable.

$$\begin{array}{c}\textbf{Net present value}\\ \textbf{of common stock}\end{array} = \begin{array}{c}\textbf{Theoretical value}\\ \textbf{of common stock}\end{array} - \begin{array}{c}\textbf{Price of common}\\ \textbf{stock today}\end{array}$$

Using the data for Vivian & Sons, Inc., assume that an investor wishes to determine whether it is profitable for him to buy some of the company's common stock today, hold it for one year (19+7), and then sell it. The first step is to estimate the value of the common stock one year hence.

Over the last two years, the company's earnings and dividends have been growing at a simple annual rate of about 20 per cent. If this rate continues, the earnings and dividends per share should equal $7.16 and $5.36, respectively, at the end of 19+7.

Estimated earnings per share: $5.97 × 1.2 = $7.16
Estimated dividends per share: $4.47 × 1.2 = $5.36

Assume that the investor estimates that the 19+7 price-earnings ratio will be 13. The expected market value of the stock, then, at the end of 19+7 should be $93.

Estimated market price = Estimated earnings per share × Estimated price-earnings ratio
$$\$93 = \$7.16 \times 13$$

Assuming a desired minimum rate of return of 10 per cent, the present value of $1 at the end of one year is .9091 (see page 616), and the theoretical value of the common stock is equal to $90.

Theoretical value of common stock if held for one year = $\begin{bmatrix}\text{Estimated dividends for one year}\end{bmatrix} \times \begin{bmatrix}\text{Present value of \$1 for one year at 10 per cent}\end{bmatrix} + \begin{bmatrix}\text{Expected market price at end of one year}\end{bmatrix} \times \begin{bmatrix}\text{Present value of \$1 for one year at 10 per cent}\end{bmatrix}$

$$\$90 = (\$5.36 \times .9091) + (\$93 \times .9091)$$

If the stock is selling for $80 today, the theoretical value of $90 is greater than cost and the investment is quantitatively acceptable.

Financial analysis for short-term creditors. Short-term creditors are concerned primarily with the ability of the firm to generate sufficient cash to pay current liabilities and to have enough cash left over to meet current operating needs. Consequently, short-term creditors focus attention on a company's cash position and its near-cash resources, that is, the current assets, and their relation to short-term liabilities. Working capital is an indication of the ability of a business to pay its current liabilities as they mature. It is sometimes called a measure of short-term solvency. However, short-term creditors are also interested in the flow of working capital from operations. If the in-flow exceeds the out-flow, there is less concern about a company's ability to meet current liabilities. In the final analysis, whether a company can meet its short-term debts depends largely on whether operating receipts exceed operating outlays as indicated by working capital from operations.

LIQUIDITY RATIOS: Creditors want a firm's working capital to be sufficient to meet current needs. But the amount of working capital is not an adequate measure of sufficiency. Any test of the adequacy of working capital must take into consideration the possibility of shrinkages in the realizable values of the current assets; in the event of forced liquidation, the inventory may have to be disposed of at a loss; and, in the event of a general business recession, it may be difficult to dispose of the inventory and to collect the receivables. Consequently, short-term creditors normally calculate the following two liquidity ratios:

$$\textit{Current ratio} = \frac{\textbf{Current assets}}{\textbf{Current liabilities}}$$

$$\textit{Acid-test or quick ratio} = \frac{\textbf{Cash + Marketable securities + Accounts receivable}}{\textbf{Current liabilities}}$$

During a business recession, a firm may suffer operating losses (or reduced profitability) and may have difficulty obtaining short-term credit; hence, to meet its operating needs, current assets may be depleted. The current ratio indicates how much current assets can be reduced and still meet the firm's current liabilities. For example, a current ratio of 4 to 1 means that the current assets could be reduced three-fourths and still have sufficient current assets to cover current liabilities. Consequently, a low current ratio, such as 1 to 1 or below, indicates that a firm would have difficulty obtaining cash through a reduction of inventory and accounts receivable and still have cash available to meet normal operating needs. Obviously, a high current ratio is favored by short-term creditors, but from a managerial viewpoint it may indicate excessive cash tied up in current assets that could profitably be used elsewhere in the firm.

In analyzing the current ratio, the short-term creditor should be aware of the practice of many firms to improve their current ratio immediately preceding the end of the fiscal period—so-called window dressing. For example, the firm may postpone purchases of materials until the beginning of next year, or pay off loans at the end of the year with the idea of borrowing again at the beginning of next year. Also, the creditor should be aware of the effect on the current ratio of seasonal fluctuations and general business conditions. For example, many firms end their fiscal period during the slack season when cash and receivables are high and inventory low, which improves their liquidity position.

One of the main shortcomings of the current ratio is that it does not reveal the *distribution* (or composition) of current assets. Normally it takes more time to convert inventory into cash than to convert marketable securities or accounts receivable. Similarly, prepayments are current assets that usually cannot be converted readily, if at all, into cash. In contrast, such current assets as cash, marketable securities, and accounts receivable are called quick assets because they normally can be easily and quickly converted into cash; they are highly liquid. A comparison of the most liquid current assets with the current liabilities is provided by the acid-test or quick ratio.

Using Vivian & Sons, Inc., data, the current ratios and the acid-test ratios are shown as follows:

	19+6	19+5	19+4	19+3	19+2	19+1
Current assets . . . . . . (a)	$905,000	$595,000	$504,600	$417,400	$395,000	$250,000
Quick assets . . . . (b)	$405,000	$295,000	$254,600	$207,400	$195,000	$170,000
Current liabilities . . . . (c)	$504,950	$180,000	$134,000	$106,400	$ 90,000	$ 30,000
Current ratio . . . . .(a ÷ c)	1.8	3.3	3.8	3.9	4.4	8.3
Acid-test ratio . . . . .(b ÷ c)	.8	1.6	1.9	1.9	2.2	5.7

The unfavorable trend of both the current ratio and the acid-test ratio confirms the working-capital problem indicated by the funds-flow analysis. With a current ratio of 1.8 in 19+6, the company's current assets could shrink 44 per cent $(1 - \frac{1}{1.8})$ and still have current assets available to meet current liabilities. However, the .8 acid-test ratio for 19+6 shows that there are not sufficient quick assets to meet current liabilities.

THE MOVEMENT OF CURRENT ASSETS: Both the current ratio and the acid-test ratio will be misleading if accounts receivable are too high because of slow credit collections. Similarly, the current ratio will be misleading if a firm's inventory is too high because it is not being turned over (sold) as fast as it should be. Because the liquidity ratios overlook the movement of current assets, short-term creditors should also analyze the receivables turnover and the inventory turnover.

$$\textit{Receivables turnover} = \frac{\text{Net sales}}{\frac{1}{2} \times \left(\begin{array}{c}\text{Beginning accounts} \\ \text{receivable}\end{array} + \begin{array}{c}\text{Ending accounts} \\ \text{receivable}\end{array}\right)} = \frac{\text{Net sales}}{\text{Average receivables}}$$

$$\begin{array}{c}\textit{Average number of} \\ \textit{days to collect} \\ \textit{receivables}\end{array} = \frac{\text{365 days in a year}}{\text{Receivables turnover}}$$

$$\textit{Inventory turnover} = \frac{\text{Cost of goods sold}}{\frac{1}{2} \times \left(\begin{array}{c}\text{Beginning} \\ \text{inventory}\end{array} + \begin{array}{c}\text{Ending} \\ \text{inventory}\end{array}\right)} = \frac{\text{Cost of goods sold}}{\text{Average inventory}}$$

The accounts receivable turnover approximates the average number of times accounts receivable were converted into cash during the fiscal period; therefore, it provides evidence as to the quality of a firm's receivables in terms of liquidity. A declining turnover may mean that the dollar amount of accounts receivable shown on the balance sheet includes "old" receivables that may be difficult to collect. The receivables are not so current (liquid) as they appear to be on the balance sheet.

Dividing 365 days by the receivables turnover will show the average collection period, which can then be compared with the firm's credit terms. For example, if it takes 80 days to collect receivables, and if credit terms are 30 days, this would indicate that the credit department is lax in its collections.

Because cost of goods sold represents the goods transferred out of inventory, cost of goods sold divided by the average inventory on hand during the fiscal period approximates the average number of times the inventory was replaced. Consequently, a declining inventory turnover may mean that:

(1) There is "old" inventory on hand that may not be readily salable.
(2) The firm has too much cash tied up in inventory that could be profitably used elsewhere, which results in a high inventory carrying cost.
(3) The risk of obsolete inventory has increased.

A high turnover of inventory indicates liquidity of inventory. Given a certain percentage of gross margin, the gross margin earned during a year increases as the turnovers increase. However, increasing the turnover by reducing the inventory may ultimately have the disastrous effect of alienating customers who become dissatisfied with the assortment.

The short-term creditor should be aware that both turnovers are only rough indicators of the movement of current assets. Seasonal fluctuations in accounts receivable and inventory may mean that the average figures used in the turnover calculations are not representative data. There is also the problem that some of the turnover data may not be available from the published financial statements. For example, the income statement may not show cost of goods sold, and the analyst would have to estimate inventory turnover by dividing net sales by inventory. Also, the accounts receivable turnover should be based on credit sales, but the financial statements show only total net sales. Finally, the ideal way to determine the movement of accounts receivable into cash is by the preparation of an aging schedule, but an outsider does not have the necessary data to do this.

Using Vivian & Sons, Inc., data, the turnovers are calculated as follows:

		19+6	19+5	19+4	19+3	19+2	19+1
Net sales	(a)	$1,210,000	$1,100,000	$1,000,000	$950,000	$900,000	$600,000
Average accounts receivable	(b)	$ 337,500	$ 237,500	$ 185,000	$160,000	$125,000	$100,000
Receivables turn-over	(a ÷ b) . . .	3.6	4.6	5.4	5.9	7.2	6.0
Number of days uncollectible [365 ÷ (a ÷ b)] . .		101	79	68	62	51	61
Cost of goods sold . . .	(a)	$ 806,000	$ 737,000	$ 670,000	$646,000	$630,000	$400,000
Average inventory . . .	(b)	$ 400,000	$ 275,000	$ 230,000	$205,000	$140,000	$ 80,000
Inventory turnover . .	(a ÷ b) . . .	2.0	2.7	2.9	3.2	4.5	5.0

The downward trend of both turnovers provides evidence that the liquidity ratios probably are misleading and are even less favorable than previously indicated. The results tend to confirm the previous funds-flow analysis.

Assuming 30-day credit terms, the 101-day average collection period for 19+6 is unfavorable. With the desperate need for working capital, there is urgent need for a revamping of the collection policies of the firm. Also, there is the possibility that the firm may be granting too much credit to customers with low credit standing.

Normally a low inventory turnover and a decreasing trend in the turnover indicates a decrease in the liquidity of the inventory. However, in the case of Vivian & Sons, Inc., sales have been increasing rapidly, and, with a gross margin of about 33 per cent of sales, the net income trend has been favorable. Thus the low inventory turnover must be the result of too rapid inventory accumulation in relation to expanding sales. More than enough inventory is on hand and there should be no substantial increase in the near future; too much cash has been tied up in inventory through failure properly to control inventory levels. Again, this is an indication of inefficiency in the management of the firm.

Long-term creditors. Long-term creditors are primarily interested in whether a company has the ability to meet interest payments over the life of a loan and to repay the loan at maturity. Consequently, the debt-to-equity ratio (previously discussed) is important to long-term creditors because it indicates the margin of safety provided by common stockholder financing. In the event of liquidation, creditors have legal claims to the assets before the common stockholders; hence, the lower the debt-to-equity ratio, the greater the proportion of stockholder financing and the greater the equity buffer protecting the long-term creditors.

Long-term creditors also calculate the number of times interest has been earned as an indicator of the ability of a company to meet its interest payments.

$$\frac{\textbf{Number of times}}{\textbf{interest earned}} = \frac{\textbf{Net income + Income taxes + Interest expense}}{\textbf{Interest expense}}$$

This ratio measures how much net income before interest and income tax could decline and still provide coverage of the total interest expense. Normally, the greater the ratio the less the risk that the company will not be able to meet its interest payments. Note that the ratio is calculated before income taxes because interest is deductible for income tax purposes; therefore, income taxes do not affect the ability to pay interest.

Using Vivian & Sons, Inc., data, the number of times interest earned is calculated as follows:

	19+6	19+5	19+4	19+3	19+2
Net income	$119,400	$ 97,800	$ 81,000	$ 69,600	$ 60,000
Interest expense . . . . (*a*)	27,000	27,000	27,000	15,000	6,000
Income taxes	79,600	65,200	54,000	46,400	40,000
Total . . . . (*b*)	$226,000	$190,000	$162,000	$131,000	$106,000
Times interest earned . . (*b* ÷ *a*)	8.4	7.0	6.0	8.7	17.7

The times-interest-earned ratios show a favorable trend upward during the last three years and are relatively high. For example, the 19+6 earnings before interest and income taxes could decline 88 per cent $(1 - \frac{1}{8.4})$ and the earnings would still cover total interest expense.

The firm's profitable operations make the times-interest-earned ratios look very favorable. However, it is cash, not net income, that is used to pay interest charges. Whether a firm has the cash to pay interest is better determined by funds-flow analysis. As previously discussed, the firm has a favorable generation of working capital from operations, which should be sufficient to meet the interest payments, provided that management refrains from further current expansion of plant and equipment, from paying large dividends, and from carrying excessive inventories and accounts receivable.

Weaknesses of ratio analysis. The use of ratio analysis is not as popular today as it once was. This decline probably is the result of an expanding awareness of the weaknesses of ratio analysis, some of which are listed below:

(1) By the time the outsider has obtained financial statements, the data are out of date.

(2) Ratio analysis uses historical data, and there is some question whether historical data can provide a relevant basis for making predictions.

(3) Diverse accounting treatments of inventory, depreciation, capitalization vs. expensing of outlays, and the like, make meaningful comparisons of companies via ratio analysis questionable.

(4) Ratio analysis by itself overlooks the dynamic aspects of the flow of funds through a firm, which is so helpful in evaluating management efficiency.

(5) Ratio analysis normally uses financial data that are not adjusted for changes in the level of general prices, which can distort the analysis.

(6) There has been a tendency to develop a multiplicity of ratios, some of which have little or no significance. If two dollar amounts have little or no significance in relation to each other, a ratio expression of their relation is no more significant. For instance, it is claimed by some that the ratio of current assets to long-term debt is meaningful, but it is difficult to see why.

(7) There are ratios in use that can give misleading results. For example, the turnover of working capital is often regarded as a very significant ratio (net sales divided by the working capital). An increase in the ratio is usually interpreted as desirable. But an increase in turnover may be caused by either an increase in sales or a *decrease* in the working capital. An increase in working-capital turnover caused by a decrease in working capital may be an undesirable trend.

On the other hand, when properly used, ratio analysis can be very helpful in evaluating a company's financial operations. The idea, however, is not to look at each ratio by itself, but to integrate ratio analysis with comparative analysis and funds-flow analysis. Comparative analysis and funds-flow analysis can indicate favorable or unfavorable trends, but they need to be supplemented by ratio analysis to confirm and determine the reasons for such trends.

ASSIGNMENT

MATERIAL

QUESTIONS

1. Why should one take time to calculate and analyze financial ratios when all of the financial data needed can be simply read from the financial statements? Discuss.

2. Is it possible that a high inventory turnover may be unfavorable? Discuss.

3. In calculating the rate of return on total assets, why is interest added to net income and why are preferred dividends ignored in the numerator of this ratio? Discuss.

4. How does the funds statement aid the financial analyst?

5. In analyzing the ratio of total debt to common stockholders' equity for a particular company, why will a common stock investor probably have a view different from a creditor's view of this ratio? Discuss.

6. Suppose that you were analyzing a particular company and found that the profitability trends and ratios were excellent, yet the company badly needed working capital. How could such a situation occur? Discuss.

7. Why might a company want to show short-term investments in government securities as a subtraction from taxes payable on the balance sheet, instead of showing them under current assets? Discuss.

8. The fact that the number of days to collect accounts receivable has been increasing does not necessarily mean that the credit manager is at fault. The fault could lie with the sales manager. What is meant by the foregoing statements? Discuss.

9. Suppose that, even though business in general has been in recession for the last two years, you still want to invest some money in common stocks, and you have narrowed your investment alternatives to two companies. In analyzing the two companies, their profitability, liquidity, and risk seem to be about equal. On the other hand, you notice that one company uses *lifo* and accelerated depreciation, and that all research and development costs are charged to expense. The other company uses *fifo* and straight-line depreciation, and its research and development costs are capitalized. Based only on this information, which company may be the better investment? Discuss.

10. Management is bargaining with a labor union over whether there should be a substantial increase in wages. The labor union negotiator contends that the company can afford to pay a large increase in wages because the return on common stockholders' equity has been increasing and is now about 20 per cent. Management argues that the company is not really that profitable, because the return on sales (net income after taxes ÷ sales) has remained constant at 14 per cent. What probably caused the differences between the two rates of return? Discuss.

SHORT EXERCISES

E28-1. You are given below some financial data for Ratio Company:

Total assets	$1,000,000
Income taxes	40,000
Sales	1,200,000
Interest expense	10,000
Common stockholders' equity	400,000
Preferred dividends	20,000
Net income before income taxes	100,000

(a) Calculate the rate of return on common stockholders' equity. (Show all of your calculations.)
(b) Calculate the rate of return on total assets.
(c) Calculate the rate of return on sales.
(d) Can you make any generalizations about the results of your rate-of-return calculations?

E28-2. A cash dividend was declared during December, 19+1. If the cash dividend was paid during January, 19+2, how would the dividend payment affect the current ratio? That is, would it increase, decrease, or not affect it, under the circumstances given below? Explain.

(a) The current ratio was 3:1 prior to the dividend payment.
(b) The current ratio was 1:3 prior to the dividend payment.
(c) The current ratio was 1:1 prior to the dividend payment.
(d) What conclusions can you reach from the effects on the current ratio?

E28-3. Assume that a friend of yours wants to invest in the common stock of a company because of the increasing trend of its net income, as shown below. However, he is puzzled as to why the earnings per share and the market price of the common stock declined in 19+5 in spite of an increase in net income. Write a brief report to your friend explaining what happened.

	19+5	19+4	19+3	19+2	19+1
Common shares outstanding	300,000	100,000	100,000	100,000	100,000
Net income	$450,000	$375,000	$300,000	$261,000	$210,000
Earnings per share	1.50	3.75	3.00	2.61	2.10
Market price per share	31.00	75.00	45.00	33.00	24.00

E28-4. Assume that you are analyzing a company to determine whether you should make a short-term loan. Further assume that you have calculated some ratios, given below, to help you determine whether the loan should be granted. Considering only the ratios given, would you lend the company money? Discuss.

	19+6	19+5	19+4	19+3
Current ratio	3 to 1	2.5 to 1	2.2 to 1	2 to 1
Acid test	.7 to 1	.85 to 1	.9 to 1	1 to 1
Inventory turnover	5	6	7	8
Accounts receivable turnover	4	5	6	7

PROBLEMS

Problem A 28-1. The following are the financial statements of Schugart Company:

SCHUGART COMPANY
Comparative Balance Sheets
December 31, 19+5 and 19+4

	19+5	19+4
Assets		
Current assets:		
Cash	$ 20,000	$ 30,000
Marketable securities	24,000	20,000
Accounts receivable	60,000	40,000
Inventory	100,000	80,000
Total current assets	$204,000	$170,000
Long-lived assets:		
Plant and equipment	$200,000	$200,000
Accumulated depreciation	160,000	150,000
Net	$ 40,000	$ 50,000
Total long-lived assets	$ 40,000	$ 50,000
	$244,000	$220,000
Equities		
Current liabilities:		
Accounts payable	$ 30,000	$ 20,000
Taxes payable	20,000	40,000
Total current liabilities	$ 50,000	$ 60,000
Long-term liabilities:		
Mortgage bonds—5¼%	$ 80,000	$ 80,000
Stockholders' equity:		
Preferred stock—6%	$ 20,000	$ 20,000
Common stock*	50,000	50,000
Retained earnings	44,000	10,000
Total stockholders' equity	$114,000	$ 80,000
	$244,000	$220,000

*Common shares outstanding were 500 for the years 19+5 and 19+4.

SCHUGART COMPANY
Income Statement
For the Year Ended December 31, 19+5

Net sales		$240,000
Cost of goods sold:		
Beginning inventory	$ 80,000	
Purchases	120,000	
Goods available for sale	$200,000	
Ending inventory	100,000	100,000
Gross margin		$140,000
Operating expenses:		
Selling expense	$ 30,000	
General and administrative expense	40,000	70,000
Net operating income		$ 70,000
Other expense:		
Interest expense		4,200
Net income before taxes		$ 65,800
Income taxes		29,800
Net income		$ 36,000

Required:

Calculate for the year 19+5 the following ratios:

(1) Current ratio.
(2) Acid-test ratio.
(3) Accounts receivable turnover.
(4) Number of days uncollectibles (assume a 360-day year).
(5) Inventory turnover.
(6) Number of times interest earned.
(7) Earnings per share (common stock).
(8) Rate of return on common stockholders' equity.
(9) Rate of return on total assets.
(10) Total debt to stockholders' equity.

Problem A 28-2. State whether *each* of the transactions below the three given ratios increases, decreases, or has no effect on the ratio, and then in four or five sentences explain *why*.

(1) Current ratio:
  (a) Inventory was purchased on account.
  (b) A cash dividend on common stock was declared.
  (c) An account payable was paid.
  (d) A building was sold at a loss.
(2) Earnings per share on common stock:
  (a) The common stock was split 2-for-1.
  (b) A 10 per cent stock (not cash) dividend was issued.
  (c) A cash dividend on preferred stock was declared.
  (d) A reserve for a pending law suit was appropriated from retained earnings.
(3) Number of days uncollectible.
  (a) An uncollectible account receivable was written off against the allowance account.
  (b) The accounts receivable turnover is increasing.

(c) An account receivable was collected.

(d) The entry for estimated bad debts was made at year end.

Problem A 28-3. For the years 19+3, 19+4, and 19+5, Bardwell, Inc., experienced a declining inventory turnover, so that management had been contemplating a reduction of its inventory purchases. However, during 19+6, management increased selling prices and the inventory turnover increased over that of 19+5. Management now believes that the increase in the inventory turnover for 19+6 indicates that there is no need to reduce inventory purchases and that the existing inventory position should be maintained.

Given the data below, evaluate management's policy with regard to maintaining the existing inventory position.

	19+6	19+5	19+4	19+3
Sales	$190,000	$160,000	$180,000	$200,000
Cost of goods sold	114,000	128,000	144,000	160,000
Gross margin	$ 76,000	$ 32,000	$ 36,000	$ 40,000
Inventory	$ 20,000	$ 20,000	$ 20,000	$ 20,000

Problem A 28-4. Mr. F. K. Easter has narrowed down his investment decision to buying the common stock of either Company K or Company U. His stockbroker has provided him with the following financial data about the two companies:

	19+6	19+5	19+4	19+3
Company K:				
Net income after taxes	$ 425,000	$ 370,000	$ 330,000	$ 300,000
Dividends on common stock	255,000	222,000	198,000	180,000
Market price per common share				
(50,000 shares outstanding)	85	59	46	36
Total stockholders' equity	2,125,200	2,053,333	2,062,500	2,000,000
Company U:				
Net income after taxes	$ 179,400	$ 138,000	$ 115,000	$ 100,000
Dividends on common stock	35,880	27,600	23,000	20,000
Market price per common share				
(20,000 shares outstanding)	179	104	58	25
Total stockholders' equity	1,196,000	862,500	638,888	500,000

The stockbroker recommends that Mr. Easter buy the common stock of Company U because of its growth potential. He points out that the net income of Company U has increased 30, 20 and 15 per cent, respectively, over the last three years. In contrast, the net income of Company K has increased 15, 12, and 10 per cent, respectively, over the last three years.

Required:

(1) Prepare an analysis of each company and discuss your findings in relation to the stockbroker's recommendation.

(2) Assume that, next year, net income is expected to increase 15 and 30 per cent, respectively, for Company K and Company U, and that the two companies are expected to maintain their present dividend policies. Furthermore, assume that the expected price-earnings ratios for next year are 15 and 25, respectively, for Company K and Company U. Finally, assume that Mr. Easter's minimum desired rate of return is 10 per cent. Based on these additional data, which common stock would you recommend that Mr. Easter buy? (Show all of your work.)

Problem A 28-5. Goss Corporation had a fire during January, 19+4, that destroyed most of its accounting records. Management asks you to try to prepare a balance sheet and an income statement for the year ended December 31, 19+3. You have been able to uncover the following accounting data:

GOSS CORPORATION
Balance Sheet
December 31, 19+3

Assets		Equities	
Current assets:		Current liabilities:	
Cash	$?	Accounts payable	$?
Accounts receivable	?	Long-term liabilities:	
Inventory	?	Notes payable-5%	$?
Total current assets	$?	Stockholders' equity:	
		Common stock	$200,000
Long-lived assets:		Retained earnings	300,000
Net plant and equipment	$?	Total	$500,000
Total assets	$?	Total equities	$?

GOSS CORPORATION
Income Statement
For the Year Ended December 31, 19+3

Net sales		$1,125,000
Cost of goods sold		?
Gross margin	$	?
Operating expenses		?
Net operating income	$	?
Other expense:		
Interest expense		?
Net income before taxes	$	?
Income tax (50% rate)		?
Net income	$	?

Other financial data:

(1) Accounts receivable at the beginning of 19+3 were $125,000 and, based on a 360-day year, it took 40 days to collect accounts receivable during 19+3.
(2) Gross margin was 30 per cent of sales for 19+3.
(3) Inventory at the beginning of 19+3 was $237,500, and the inventory turnover for 19+3 was 3.15.
(4) Total debt to equity for 19+3 was 50 per cent.
(5) For 19+3, operating expenses were 6 per cent of sales.
(6) Interest was earned 27 times during 19+3.
(7) The acid-test ratio for 19+3 was 3.75.

Required:

Reconstruct the December 31, 19+3 balance sheet and the income statement for the year 19+3 using the above financial data only. (Hint: Use the financial ratio formulas to solve for unknowns.)

Problem B28-1. Following are the financial statements of B. Bruns Company:

B. BRUNS COMPANY
Comparative Balance Sheets
December 31, 19+4 and 19+3

	19+4	19+3
Assets		
Current assets:		
Cash	$ 10,000	$ 14,900
Marketable securities	150,000	70,000
Accounts receivable	100,000	80,000
Inventory	200,000	150,000
Total current assets	$460,000	$314,900
Long-lived assets:		
Plant and equipment	$400,000	$400,000
Accumulated depreciation	300,000	280,000
Net	$100,000	$120,000
Total long-lived assets	$100,000	$120,000
	$560,000	$434,900
Equities		
Current liabilities:		
Accounts payable	$150,000	$ 80,000
Taxes payable	50,000	30,000
Total current liabilities	$200,000	$110,000
Long-term liabilities:		
Bonds payable—6%	$100,000	$100,000
Stockholders' equity:		
Preferred stock—5%	$ 50,000	$ 50,000
Common stock—10,000 shares	100,000	100,000
Capital in excess of par	20,000	20,000
Retained earnings	90,000	54,900
Total stockholders' equity	$260,000	$224,900
	$560,000	$434,900

B. BRUNS COMPANY
Income Statement
For the Year Ended December 31, 19+4

Sales	$810,000
Cost of goods sold	525,000
Gross margin	$285,000
Operating expenses	183,000
Net operating income	$102,000
Other expense:	
Interest expense	6,000
Net income before income taxes	$ 96,000
Income taxes	38,400
Net income	$ 57,600

Required:

(A) Calculate the following ratios for the year 19+4:
 (1) Current ratio.
 (2) Acid-test ratio.
 (3) Accounts receivable turnover.
 (4) Number of days uncollectible (assume a 360-day year).
 (5) Inventory turnover.
 (6) Number of times interest earned.
 (7) Earnings per share (common stock).
 (8) Rate of return on common stockholders' equity.
 (9) Rate of return on total assets.
 (10) Total debt to stockholders' equity.
(B) Prepare a funds (working capital) flow statement for the year ended December 31, 19+4.

Problem B28-2. You are given below an abbreviated balance sheet of W. Boutell Company:

W. BOUTELL COMPANY
Balance Sheet
December 31, 19+1

Assets		Equities	
Total assets	$1,000,000	Current liabilities	$ 50,000
		Long-term liabilities:	
		Bonds payable—8%	$ 350,000
		Stockholders' equity:	
		Preferred stock—7%	$ 200,000
		Common stock	300,000
		Retained earnings	100,000
			$ 600,000
	$1,000,000		$1,000,000

Required:

(1) Assume that W. Boutell Company had a 6 per cent rate of return on total assets for the year ended December 31, 19+1, and that the 7 per cent preferred dividend was paid. What was the rate of return on common stockholders' equity?

(2) Explain what caused the difference between the 6 per cent rate of return on total assets and the rate of return on common stockholders' equity calculated in part (1).

(3) Assume that W. Boutell Company had a 9 per cent rate of return on total assets for the year ended December 31, 19+1, and that the 7 per cent preferred dividend was paid. What was the rate of return on common stockholders' equity?

(4) Explain what caused the difference between the 9 per cent rate of return on total assets and the rate of return on common stockholders' equity calculated in part (3).

Problem B28-3. Following are condensed balance sheets for Mertz Company for the years 19+2 and 19+1:

MERTZ COMPANY
Comparative Balance Sheets
December 31, 19+2 and 19+1

	19+2	19+1
Assets		
Current assets	$ 985,000	$ 550,000
Long-lived assets	4,795,000	5,185,000
	$5,780,000	$5,735,000
Equities		
Current liabilities	$ 480,000	$ 240,000
Long-term liabilities:		
Notes payable—5%	$1,220,000	$1,660,000
Stockholders' equity:		
Common stock—100,000 shares	$1,500,000	$1,500,000
Additional paid-in capital	1,800,000	1,800,000
Retained earnings	780,000	535,000
Total stockholders' equity	$4,080,000	$3,835,000
	$5,780,000	$5,735,000
Common stock dividends per share	$ 1.80	$ 1.62

For the year 19+1, net income after taxes was $380,000. The common stock was selling for $46.50 and $53.80, respectively, for the years 19+1 and 19+2.

Required:

(1) Calculate earnings per share for both years.
(2) Calculate the price-earnings ratio for both years.
(3) Calculate the pay-out ratio for both years.
(4) Calculate the dividend yield on common stock for both years.
(5) Assume that the common stock of Mertz Company can be purchased today for $60 a share. Net income and dividends are expected to increase 10 per cent next year. The price-earnings ratio is expected to be 14 next year. Assuming that those estimates are correct, if your minimum desired rate of return is 10 per cent, could you profit by buying the stock today and selling it at the end of next year?

Problem B28-4. The comparative income statements for H. Anton, Inc., are presented below:

H. ANTON, INC.
Comparative Income Statements
For the Years Ended December 31, 19+1—19+3

	19+3		19+2		19+1	
Sales		$6,000,000		$4,502,000		$3,150,000
Cost of goods sold:						
Beginning inventory	$ 700,000		$ 800,000		$ 600,000	
Purchases	5,000,000		3,295,000		$2,300,000	
Goods available for sale..	$5,700,000		$4,095,000		$2,900,000	
Ending inventory.......	900,000	4,800,000	700,000	3,395,000	800,000	2,100,000
Gross margin		$1,200,000		$1,107,000		$1,050,000
Operating expenses		590,000		540,000		504,000
Net income		$ 610,000		$ 567,000		$ 546,000

A stockbroker friend of yours cannot understand how the sales of H. Anton, Inc., increased 47.5 per cent from 19+1 to 19+3, while net income increased only 9.9 per cent. The stockbroker hires you to analyze the above income statements and to tell him some possible reasons why net income did not increase more than it did.

Using the above financial data only, prepare a written report for the stockbroker explaining why the great increase in sales did not result in a great increase in net income.

Problem B28-5. Given the financial data below, reconstruct the balance sheet and the income statement for G. Staubus Company.

G. STAUBUS COMPANY
Balance Sheet
December 31, 19+9

Assets			Equities		
Current assets:			Current liabilities	$	?
Cash	$	?			
Net accounts receivable.		?	Long-term liabilities:		
Marketable securities		25,000	Bonds payable—6%	$	
Inventories		?			
Total current assets	$	?	Stockholders' equity:		
			Common stock		$200,000
Long-lived assets:			Retained earnings		$400,000
Net plant and equipment	$	?	Total stockholders' equity. . .		$600,000
Total assets	$	?	Total equities	$	?

G. STAUBUS COMPANY
Income Statement
For the Year Ended December 31, 19+9

Net sales	$	?
Cost of goods sold		?
Gross margin	$432,000	
Operating expenses		?
Operating income	$	?
Other expense:		
Interest expense		?
Net income before taxes	$	?
Income taxes (50% rate)		?
Net income	$	?

Other financial data for the year 19+9 include the following:

(1) The total debt to common stockholders' equity was 50 per cent.
(2) The average number of days to collect the accounts receivable was 40 (based on a 360-day year). The beginning accounts receivable balance was $150,000.
(3) The inventory turnover was 3 times. The beginning inventory balance was $335,000.
(4) Gross margin was 30 per cent of net sales.
(5) Interest was earned 12 times.
(6) The acid-test ratio was 2.24.
(7) Operating expenses were 20 per cent of sales.
(Hint: Use the ratio formulas to solve for unknowns.)

Appendix One

Sample Financial Statements

from Annual Reports

Several references were made in the text to the fact that corporations include a set of financial statements in their regular reports to stockholders. Two examples of such reporting are presented in this appendix. They were taken from the 1968 annual reports of Hoskins Manufacturing Company and The Trane Company.

In addition to financial statements and the footnotes thereto, annual reports include such important material as a message from the company's president, the opinion of the certified public accountant, informative disclosures about such matters as the company's products, research, new facilities, and future plans, and selected historical financial data.

The Financial Review presented on pages 660–661 is from the 1968 annual report of The Trane Company. This fine example shows the kinds of historical financial data that are now quite commonly included in annual reports to stockholders. Included in the Financial Review on page 660 is the "Statement of Source and Application of Funds." (The alternative title "Sources and uses of working capital" was used in this textbook when the statement was introduced in Chapter 16). It has become almost standard practice to include such a statement in annual reports to stockholders.

ASSETS	1968	1967
Current Assets:		
Cash	$ 482,461	$ 411,007
Certificates of deposit	493,230	292,570
U. S. Government, tax-exempt, and other securities, at cost (which approximates market) plus accrued interest	4,650,530	4,947,335
Accounts and notes receivable, less estimated doubtful accounts of $77,000 in 1968 and $60,000 in 1967	937,641	850,668
Inventories, at cost (first-in, first-out basis, except for raw metals and alloys aggregating $1,032,725 in 1968 and $978,286 in 1967 which are on a last-in, first-out basis) not in excess of market	2,256,267	2,177,733
Prepaid expenses	178,784	149,260
Total Current Assets	8,998,913	8,828,573
Land, Buildings and Equipment, at cost:		
Land	320,386	316,487
Buildings	1,435,047	1,395,639
Machinery and equipment	3,362,134	3,100,673
	5,117,567	4,812,799
Accumulated depreciation	2,648,027	2,436,886
	2,469,540	2,375,913
	$11,468,453	$11,204,486

CONSOLIDATED STATEMENT OF INCOME AND EARNINGS RETAINED FOR USE IN THE BUSINESS

for the years ended December 31, 1968 and 1967

INCOME	1968	1967
Sales, less returns and allowances	$13,367,437	$12,321,472
Interest and other income	231,216	213,538
	13,598,653	12,535,010
Cost of goods sold	9,039,369	8,071,551
Selling, general and administrative expenses	964,428	918,704
Depreciation (computed principally on accelerated methods)	353,151	307,775
	10,356,948	9,298,030
Income before income taxes	3,241,705	3,236,980
Estimated federal, state and Canadian income taxes	1,706,000	1,483,000
Net income—$1.08 a share in 1968 and $1.23 a share in 1967	1,535,705	1,753,980

EARNINGS RETAINED FOR USE IN THE BUSINESS

	1968	1967
At beginning of year	5,994,188	5,662,208
Dividends paid—$.90 a share in 1968 and $1.00 a share in 1967	(1,279,800)	(1,422,000)
At end of year	$ 6,250,093	$ 5,994,188

LIABILITIES	1968	1967
Current Liabilities:		
Accounts payable.	$ 318,590	$ 345,602
Accrued payroll, extra compensation, taxes, and other expenses.	1,303,518	1,283,643
Estimated liability for federal, state and Canadian income taxes, less U. S. Treasury tax notes at cost of $295,800 in 1968 and $395,504 in 1967.	217,965	202,766
Total Current Liabilities	1,840,073	1,832,011
Stockholders' Equity:		
Common stock, $2.50 par value—authorized 2,000,000 shares, issued 1,440,000 shares.	3,600,000	3,600,000
Earnings retained for use in the business.	6,250,093	5,994,188
	9,850,093	9,594,188
Less—18,000 shares of common stock in treasury, at cost.	221,713	221,713
	9,628,380	9,372,475
	$11,468,453	$11,204,486

NOTES TO FINANCIAL STATEMENTS — December 31, 1968

NOTE 1: The consolidated financial statements include the accounts of The Hoskins Manufacturing Company and its Canadian subsidiary. The assets, liabilities and net income of the subsidiary have been converted into U.S. dollars at appropriate rates of exchange.

NOTE 2: The Company has a pension plan covering substantially all of its employees. The total pension expense of $187,000 in 1968 and $206,200 in 1967 includes amortization of prior service costs over a period of approximately twenty years. The Company's policy is to fund pension costs accrued. The pension fund assets exceeded the actuarially computed value of vested benefits at December 31, 1968.

OPINION OF INDEPENDENT ACCOUNTANTS

To the Board of Directors, Stockholders and Employees of The Hoskins Manufacturing Company

In our opinion, the accompanying consolidated balance sheet and the related statement of consolidated income and earnings retained for use in the business present fairly the financial position of The Hoskins Manufacturing Company and its Canadian subsidiary company at December 31, 1968 and the results of their operations for the year, in conformity with generally accepted accounting principles applied on a basis consistent with that of the preceding year. Our examination of these statements was made in accordance with generally accepted auditing standards and accordingly included such tests of the accounting records and such other auditing procedures as we considered necessary in the circumstances.

Price Waterhouse & Co.

Detroit, Michigan
February 4, 1969

Consolidated Financial Summary 1959-1968

	1968	1967	1966	1965	1964
Net Sales	$197,498,000	$200,823,000	$187,779,000	$162,330,000	$136,937,0(
Net Earnings Before Taxes on Income	21,040,000	22,976,000	25,830,000	23,814,000	20,662,0(
Percent of Net Sales	10.7	11.4	13.8	14.7	15
Taxes on Income	11,305,000	11,601,000	12,550,000	11,734,000	10,422,0(
Net Earnings After Taxes	9,735,000	11,375,000	13,280,000	12,080,000	10,240,0(
Percent of Net Sales	4.9	5.7	7.1	7.4	7
Total Current Assets	102,043,000	108,463,000	99,462,000	80,779,000	69,904,0(
Total Current Liabilities	22,149,000	23,340,000	24,383,000	19,834,000	18,371,0(
Ratio of Current Assets to Current Liabilities	4.61	4.65	4.08	4.07	3.8
Working Capital	79,894,000	85,123,000	75,079,000	60,945,000	51,533,0(
Stockholders' Equity	106,112,000	100,040,000	92,265,000	83,004,000	74,370,0(
Long-Term Debt	30,675,000	40,571,000	26,965,000	11,430,000	6,918,0(
Percent of Capital Investment	22.4	28.9	22.6	12.1	8
Number of Stockholders	4,660	4,959	5,280	5,134	4,8
Common Shares Outstanding (At end of year and restated for stock distributions)	5,431,307	5,410,514	5,388,004	5,377,008	5,364,11

Per Common Share Outstanding
(Based on average shares outstanding)

	1968	1967	1966	1965	1964
Net Earnings	$1.80	$2.11	$2.47	$2.25	$1.9
Taxes on Income	2.09	2.15	2.34	2.18	1.9
Cash Dividends Paid	.80	.80	.80	.65	.5:
Stockholders' Equity	19.57	18.54	17.15	15.46	13.8
Stock Distribution	—	—	—	—	1 for

Consolidated Statement of Source and Application of Funds

FUNDS PROVIDED	1968	1967	1966	1965	1964
Net Earnings for the Year	$ 9,735,000	$ 11,375,000	$ 13,280,000	$ 12,080,000	$ 10,240,0(
Depreciation and Amortization	7,664,000	6,893,000	5,608,000	4,650,000	4,390,0(
Sale of Common Stock	828,000	816,000	289,000	315,000	271,0(
Long-Term Borrowing	807,000	21,519,000	16,200,000	5,110,000	291,0(
Total Funds Provided	19,034,000	40,603,000	35,377,000	22,155,000	15,192,0(
FUNDS APPLIED					
Expenditures for Property, Plant and Equipment, Net	8,850,000	17,452,000	16,269,000	8,385,000	4,850,0(
Retire Long-Term Debt	10,703,000	8,231,000	665,000	598,000	611,0(
Cash Dividends Declared	4,342,000	4,320,000	4,308,000	3,761,000	2,948,0(
Other	368,000	556,000	—	—	—
Total Funds Applied	24,263,000	30,559,000	21,242,000	12,744,000	8,409,0(
Increase or (decrease) in Working Capital	$ (5,229,000)	$ 10,044,000	$ 14,135,000	$ 9,411,000	$ 6,783,0(

1963	1962	1961	1960	1959
20,370,000	$117,535,000	$ 96,317,000	$102,461,000	$ 84,113,000
16,452,000	17,908,000	11,209,000	14,959,000	10,926,000
13.7	15.2	11.6	14.6	13.0
8,143,000	9,570,000	6,092,000	8,247,000	5,900,000
8,309,000	8,338,000	5,117,000	6,712,000	5,026,000
6.9	7.1	5.3	6.6	6.0
58,053,000	57,593,000	46,481,000	46,332,000	40,834,000
13,303,000	14,500,000	11,022,000	11,677,000	8,847,000
4.36	3.97	4.22	3.97	4.62
44,750,000	43,093,000	35,459,000	34,655,000	31,987,000
66,807,000	61,149,000	55,419,000	52,314,000	47,677,000
7,238,000	5,939,000	2,500,000	2,850,000	3,200,000
9.8	8.9	4.3	5.2	6.3
4,373	4,479	4,423	4,147	4,165
5,350,584	5,349,406	5,349,406	5,328,944	5,326,270
$1.55	$1.56	$ .96	$1.26	$ .94
1.52	1.79	1.14	1.55	1.11
.50	.475	.45	.36	.36
12.49	11.43	10.38	9.82	8.95
—	—	—	1 for 4	—

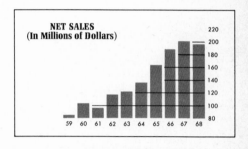

NET SALES
(In Millions of Dollars)

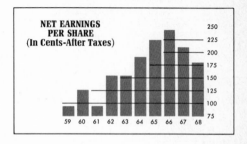

NET EARNINGS
PER SHARE
(In Cents-After Taxes)

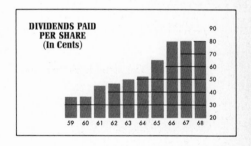

DIVIDENDS PAID
PER SHARE
(In Cents)

1963	1962	1961	1960	1959
8,309,000	$ 8,338,000	$ 5,117,000	$ 6,712,000	$ 5,026,000
4,374,000	4,008,000	3,737,000	3,424,000	2,979,000
25,000	—	388,000	46,000	42,000
1,988,000	4,000,000	—	—	—
14,696,000	16,346,000	9,242,000	10,182,000	8,047,000
9,675,000	5,543,000	5,687,000	5,044,000	3,689,000
689,000	561,000	350,000	350,000	350,000
2,675,000	2,608,000	2,401,000	2,120,000	1,918,000
—	—	—	—	—
13,039,000	8,712,000	8,438,000	7,514,000	5,957,000
1,657,000	$ 7,634,000	$ 804,000	$ 2,668,000	$ 2,090,000

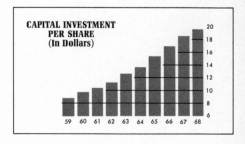

CAPITAL INVESTMENT
PER SHARE
(In Dollars)

661

Consolidated Balance Sheet
December 31, 1968 and 1967

	1968	1967
CURRENT ASSETS		
Cash.	$ 9,224,000	$ 15,452,000
Accounts receivable—less allowance for doubtful receivables of $1,091,000 and $878,000.	49,133,000	47,860,000
Inventories—at lower of cost (principally last-in, first-out) or market.	40,723,000	42,347,000
Prepaid expenses (see notes)	2,963,000	2,804,000
Total current assets.	102,043,000	108,463,000
PROPERTY, PLANT AND EQUIPMENT, at cost:		
Land.	1,575,000	1,518,000
Buildings.	45,026,000	41,453,000
Machinery and equipment.	45,106,000	43,145,000
	91,707,000	86,116,000
Less accumulated depreciation and amortization . . .	35,794,000	31,406,000
	55,913,000	54,710,000
OTHER ASSETS.	980,000	778,000
	$158,936,000	$163,951,000
CURRENT LIABILITIES	**1968**	**1967**
Accounts payable and accrued expenses.	$ 16,027,000	$ 17,362,000
Federal, state and foreign income taxes.	3,582,000	4,329,000
Dividend payable.	1,086,000	1,082,000
Current maturities of long-term debt and notes payable.	1,454,000	567,000
Total current liabilities (see notes).	22,149,000	23,340,000
LONG-TERM DEBT (see notes).	30,675,000	40,571,000
STOCKHOLDERS' EQUITY (see notes)		
Common stock, par value $2 per share Authorized, 7,500,000 shares Issued: 1968, 5,435,607 shares 1967, 5,412,214 shares.	10,871,000	10,824,000
Capital in excess of par value.	15,768,000	14,987,000
Retained earnings.	79,718,000	74,325,000
	106,357,000	100,136,000
Less treasury stock, at cost— 4,300 shares and 1,700 shares.	245,000	96,000
	106,112,000	100,040,000
	$158,936,000	$163,951,000

(See accompanying notes to financial statements)

Consolidated Statement of Earnings

Year Ended December 31, 1968 and 1967

	1968	1967
Net Sales	$197,498,000	$200,823,000
Costs and expenses (including depreciation of $7,647,000 and $6,893,000 computed by accelerated methods)		
Cost of goods sold	124,030,000	125,629,000
Selling, administrative and engineering expenses	50,323,000	50,221,000
Interest expense	2,105,000	1,997,000
Federal, state and foreign taxes on income (see notes) (including surtax of $900,000 in 1968)	11,305,000	11,601,000
	187,763,000	189,448,000
Net earnings for the year	$ 9,735,000	$ 11,375,000
Earnings per share of common stock:		
Based on average shares outstanding during the year	$1.80	$2.11
Based on assumption of conversion of outstanding convertible debentures and exercise of outstanding stock options	$1.77	$2.08

Consolidated Statement of Retained Earnings

Year Ended December 31, 1968 and 1967

	1968	1967
Balance at beginning of year	$ 74,325,000	$ 67,270,000
Net earnings for the year	9,735,000	11,375,000
	84,060,000	78,645,000
Cash dividends declared ($.80 per share)	4,342,000	4,320,000
Balance at end of year	$ 79,718,000	$ 74,325,000

(See accompanying notes to financial statements)

Notes to Financial Statements

SUBSIDIARY COMPANIES: The consolidated financial statements include the accounts of the Company and all wholly-owned subsidiaries. These subsidiaries, which are principally foreign companies, had net assets of $15,500,000 at December 31, 1968, including $8,500,000 in Canada and the balance largely in the United Kingdom and Western Europe. Sales and net earnings of these subsidiaries were $31,952,000 and $1,220,000 in 1968 and $29,301,000 and $4,000 in 1967, respectively.

STOCK OPTIONS: Under the 1956 and 1966 stock option plans, options have been granted to officers and key employees to purchase shares of common stock at prices not less than 95% of fair market value on the date of grant for options granted prior to 1964 and 100% of fair market value thereafter. Options generally become exercisable either one or five years after the date of grant, and terminate five or ten years thereafter. A summary of the 1956 and 1966 stock option plans is as follows:

	Number of Shares Under Option		Average Price Per Share	
	1956 Plan	1966 Plan	1956 Plan	1966 Plan
Outstanding at beginning of year	47,566	27,600		
Changes during the year:				
Granted	—	3,000	$ —	$57.38
Exercised	(20,770)	(2,000)	34.23	44.00
Terminated	(600)	(400)		
Outstanding at end of year	26,196	28,200	38.60	53.14
Exercisable at end of year	26,196	25,200		
Available for grant at end of year	—	26,800		

LONG-TERM DEBT: Amounts due consisted of the following (less current maturities of $1,454,000 and $474,000, respectively):

	December 31,	
	1968	1967
3¾% unsecured note, payable in annual installments of $250,000 to 1971	$ 500,000	$ 750,000
4⅝% unsecured notes, payable in annual installments of $200,000 to 1982	2,600,000	2,800,000
Mortgage notes payable in monthly installments to 1978 with interest rates of 2% to 6%	1,591,000	1,363,000
4% convertible subordinated debentures due in 1992	20,000,000	20,000,000
Notes payable—banks	4,000,000	13,000,000
Notes payable by foreign subsidiaries	1,984,000	2,658,000
	$30,675,000	$40,571,000

The subordinated debentures are convertible into common stock of the Company (unless previously redeemed) at $72.00 per share to September

15, 1992. The Company has reserved 277,778 shares of its authorized but unissued common stock for the possible future converison of these debentures. The Company is required to make annual sinking fund payments commencing in 1977 equal to 5% of the principal amount of debentures outstanding at September 15, 1976.

Notes payable—banks represent borrowings made under a $25,000,000 revolving credit agreement with interest payable at prime commercial rates. The notes may be renewed every 90 days to December 31, 1969. At any time up to that date, the Company may convert any portion of the revolving credit to term notes which will then bear interest at ¼ of 1% over prime commercial rates. The term notes will be payable in ten equal semiannual installments commencing June 30, 1970.

The notes payable by foreign subsidiaries bear interest at 5½% to 6½% and mature in varying annual amounts through 1978.

The Company may borrow up to $7,000,000 under 4-year revolving Euro-dollar loan agreements extending to 1972. Interest rates will be at prime rates in effect in the particular countries at the time such borrowings are made.

PENSIONS: The Company and its Canadian subsidiary maintain trusteed pension plans covering salaried and certain hourly-paid employees. These plans are noncontributory, except for two plans of the Canadian subsidiary.

The Company's policy is to fund accrued pension cost. The total pension expense for the year was $1,055,000. The amounts funded substantially exceed the actuarially computed value of estimated benefits vested under the plans at that date; accordingly, changes were made in actuarial assumptions which had the effect of increasing 1968 net income by approximately $140,000.

CHANGES IN CAPITAL:

	Common Stock	Capital in Excess of Par Value	Treasury Stock
Balances at beginning of year	$10,824,000	$14,987,000	$ 96,000
Issuance of 22,770 shares upon exercise of stock options	46,000	754,000	
Issuance of 623 shares in connection with the Trane Bonus Plan	1,000	27,000	
Purchases of 2,600 shares at cost			149,000
Balances at end of year	$10,871,000	$15,768,000	$245,000

RETAINED EARNINGS: Under the most restrictive provision of the Company's several borrowing agreements, approximately $28,674,000 of retained earnings is available at December 31, 1968 for cash dividends on, and purchases of the Company's common stock.

DEFERRED INCOME TAXES: To comply with the financial reporting requirements of the American Institute of Certified Public Accountants, the financial statements for the prior year have been restated to retroactively reflect a change in classification of deferred income taxes related to various transactions which had previously been recorded net of federal income tax reductions. This change had no effect on previously reported net earnings. Deferred tax provisions credited to net income were $355,000 in 1968 and $254,000 in 1967.

Opinion of Independent Accountants

PRICE WATERHOUSE & CO.

PRUDENTIAL PLAZA
CHICAGO 60601
January 20, 1969

To the Stockholders and Board of Directors
The Trane Company

In our opinion, the accompanying balance sheet and the related statements of earnings, retained earnings and source and application of funds present fairly the financial position of The Trane Company and subsidiaries consolidated at December 31, 1968 and 1967 and the results of their operations and the supplementary information on funds for those years, in conformity with generally accepted accounting principles consistently applied. Our examinations of these statements were made in accordance with generally accepted auditing standards and accordingly included such tests of the accounting records and such other auditing procedures as we considered necessary in the circumstances.

Price Waterhouse & Co.

STOCK TRANSFER AGENTS
Morgan Guaranty Trust Company
of New York
Harris Trust & Savings Bank,
Chicago, Illinois

REGISTRARS OF STOCK
Manufacturers Hanover Trust
Company, New York
The First National Bank of Chicago,
Chicago, Illinois

This Annual Report of The Trane Company has been prepared for and distributed to the stockholders solely for information. It must not be construed as an offer to buy or sell, or as solicitation of an offer to buy or sell, the securities of the Company.

Appendix Two

Chart of Accounts

Chart of accounts. As a general rule, the first accounting work performed for any business involves the development of an accounting system. The accountant studies the nature of the business, determines the types of transactions that probably will occur, and plans or selects the necessary forms and records in which the transactions of the business may be recorded.

One of the first steps in the development of an accounting system is the preparation of a chart of accounts. Such a chart lists the assets, liabilities, elements of the owners' equity, revenues, and expenses for which a separate record will be maintained.

It is advisable to number the accounts in a systematic manner so that the account numbers indicate classifications and relationships. Numbering systems differ, but the chart of accounts beginning on page 666 illustrates the general principle.

Observe that each account number contains four digits, and that the first digit at the left indicates a main classification, as shown below.

1--- Assets and related contra accounts.
2--- Liabilities.
3--- Stockholders' equity.
4--- Sales and related accounts.
5--- Purchases and related accounts (for a periodic inventory system).
6--- Operating expenses.
7--- Other revenue and expense.
8--- Income tax.

The second digit indicates a main subclassification, thus:

11-- Current assets and related contra accounts.
12-- Long-term investments.
13-- Property, plant, and equipment and related contra accounts.
14-- Intangible assets.
21-- Current liabilities.
24-- Long-term liabilities.

The third and fourth digits indicate further subclassifications and relationships, thus:

2180 Withholding and F.I.C.A. Tax Payable.
2181 Federal Unemployment Tax Payable.
2182 State Unemployment Tax Payable.

The third digit, 8, is common to a group of liability accounts for withholding and payroll taxes. The various taxes are differentiated by the fourth digit.

The third and fourth digits in many instances are selected for reasons of consistency, or to show relationships.

As examples of numbers chosen for the sake of consistency, observe the account numbers listed below. The first digit indicates whether the account represents an asset or a liability;

the fact that the item is current is indicated by the second digit; the final "30" indicates an account receivable or payable; the final "40" indicates a note receivable or payable.

1130   Accounts Receivable.
2130   Accounts Payable.

1140   Notes Receivable.
2140   Notes Payable.

Also observe that contra accounts, representing deductions from related accounts, are numbered with a final "8" or "9":

1130   Accounts Receivable.
1139   Allowance for Uncollectibles.

1350   Delivery Equipment.
1359   Accumulated Depreciation—Delivery Equipment.

4000   Sales.
4008   Sales Returns and Allowances.
4009   Sales Discounts.

As examples of account numbers assigned to show relationships, observe the following:

1191   Prepaid Insurance.
6591   Insurance Expense.

2155   Salaries Payable.
6555   Office Salaries.

Illustrative Chart of Accounts

CURRENT ASSETS:

1110   Cash.
1120   Temporary Investments.
1130   Accounts Receivable.
1139   Allowance for Uncollectibles.
1140   Notes Receivable.
1154   Interest Receivable.
1170   Inventory.
1190   Prepaid Rent.
1191   Prepaid Insurance.

LONG-TERM INVESTMENTS:

1210   Land.
1220   Investments in Bonds.

PROPERTY, PLANT, and EQUIPMENT:

1310   Parking Lot.
1320   Store Fixtures.
1329   Accumulated Depreciation—Store Fixtures.
1350   Delivery Equipment.
1359   Accumulated Depreciation—Delivery Equipment.

INTANGIBLE ASSETS:

1410   Patents.
1420   Goodwill.

CURRENT LIABILITIES:

2130   Accounts Payable.
2140   Notes Payable.

2154 Interest Payable.
2155 Salaries Payable.
2160 Estimated Income Tax Payable.
2170 Liability for Sales Taxes.
2180 Withholding and F.I.C.A. Tax Payable.
2181 Federal Unemployment Tax Payable.
2182 State Unemployment Tax Payable.
2195 Advances from Customers.
2196 Rent Received in Advance.

LONG-TERM LIABILITIES:

2410 Mortgage Payable.

STOCKHOLDERS' EQUITY:

3510 Capital Stock.
3511 Capital in Excess of Par Value.
3610 Retained Earnings.
3910 Dividends.

SALES AND RELATED ACCOUNTS:

4000 Sales.
4008 Sales Returns and Allowances.
4009 Sales Discounts.

PURCHASES AND RELATED ACCOUNTS:

5170 Purchases.
5178 Purchase Returns and Allowances.
5179 Purchase Discounts.
5200 Transportation In.
5500 Cost of Goods Sold.

OPERATING EXPENSES:

6001 Store Rent.
6002 Advertising.
6029 Depreciation Expense—Store Fixtures.
6059 Depreciation Expense—Delivery Equipment.
6070 Other Delivery Expense.
6071 Transportation Out.
6080 Salesmen's Commissions.
6090 Miscellaneous Selling Expenses.
6501 Office Expenses.
6511 Taxes, Other Than Income and Payroll.
6549 Bad Debts Expense.
6555 Office Salaries.
6585 Payroll Taxes Expense.
6591 Insurance Expense.

OTHER REVENUE:

7010 Rent of Land.
7054 Interest Revenue.

OTHER EXPENSE:

7154 Interest Expense.

INCOME TAX:

8160 Income Tax.

Appendix Three

Payroll Accounting

Federal old-age benefits taxes. The Social Security Act of 1935, as amended, provides for federal government disbursements called variously "old-age benefits," "old-age and survivors' benefits," "old-age insurance," and "old-age annuities." The payments include monthly benefits to retired workers, supplementary benefits to their wives, husbands, and dependent children, benefits for survivors of deceased wage earners, "disability benefits," hospital insurance benefits, and lump-sum payments in some cases.

The funds required for these disbursements are obtained from taxes levied under the Federal Insurance Contributions Act on employers and employees, in amounts based on wage payments for services performed in the United States, the Virgin Islands, Puerto Rico, Guam, and American Samoa, and on American vessels and aircraft. The tax also applies to U.S. citizens working outside the United States for American employers. Certain services are excepted. Payments made to an independent contractor for services are not wages.

The taxes levied on employees are withheld by the employers from wage payments; these tax withholdings, as well as the taxes levied on the employers, are remitted by the employers to the Internal Revenue Service. At the time of this writing, the rate is 4.8 per cent on employees and a matching 4.8 per cent on employers, for a total of 9.6 per cent. Because of possible revisions in the law, you should ascertain the rate currently in effect.

The tax is not levied on wages in excess of $7,800 paid to a worker by one employer during a calendar year. However, if an individual works for two or more employers during a calendar year, each employer is required to pay the tax on his wage payments to the employee up to $7,800 and to make similar deductions from the employee's wages. The employee can obtain a refund from the government for deducted taxes on his aggregate wages for the year in excess of $7,800; the employers cannot obtain a refund.

Every employer must apply to the Internal Revenue Service or the Social Security Administration for an "identification number" to be shown on his tax return. Each worker must apply to the Administration for an "account number," which is his social security number; the employer must be informed of the account number of each of his employees for use in his records and reports.

The law specifies that every employer withholding taxes must provide the employee with an annual statement on or before January 31 of the succeeding year which shows the total social security tax withheld.

If employment is terminated, the employer must give a final statement to the employee not later than 30 days after the final wage payment. Many employers find it convenient to report the tax deduction at the time of making each wage payment; methods of making such reports to employees are illustrated on pages 675 and 677.

The employer is required to maintain records that show the name, address, occupation, and social security number of every employee; also the total compensation due him at each pay date, any portion thereof subject to tax, the period covered by the payment, tips reported subject to tax, and the amount of the employee's pay deducted as tax. The employer must also keep copies of all returns and reports filed by him with government authorities.

Self-employed persons. Self-employed persons are covered by the old-age and survivors' insurance program. The tax on self-employment income is handled in all particulars as an integral part of the federal income tax. At the time of this writing, the F.I.C.A. rate for self-employed persons is 6.9 per cent, to be increased gradually to 7.9 per cent by 1987. It is applied to the first $7,800 of net earnings.

Federal unemployment insurance taxes. Taxes are levied against employers (but not against employees) under the Federal Unemployment Tax Act. Unemployment compensation payments are not made by the federal government directly to unemployed persons; the funds obtained by the collection of federal unemployment insurance taxes are used to make grants to the various states to assist them in carrying out their own unemployment compensation programs. Laws providing for unemployment compensation payments have been enacted by all the states, the District of Columbia, and Puerto Rico.

Unlike the federal old-age benefits tax, which is assessed against an employer with one or more employees in covered employment, the federal unemployment insurance taxes are assessed against only those employers who have four or more employees on at least one day of each of twenty calendar weeks in the calendar year. An employer who is subject to the tax is assessed on the basis of wages paid to those employees only who are engaged in the performance of nonexempt services.

The federal unemployment insurance tax rate is 3.1 per cent; wages in excess of $3,000 paid to any individual during the taxable year are not subject to the tax. Although the tax rate is 3.1 per cent, the employer is entitled to a credit for taxes paid to the states, the District of Columbia, and Puerto Rico under their unemployment compensation laws. This credit cannot be more than 90 per cent of the tax assessed by the federal government at a 3 per cent rate. Because of this provision in the federal law, the states have generally established a 2.7 per cent unemployment compensation tax rate. Since taxable wages are generally (though subject to some minor exceptions) computed in the same manner for both federal and state taxes, the tax rates are usually considered to be as follows:

Federal tax	.4%
State tax	2.7
Total	3.1%

Although the basic rate for most state taxes is 2.7 per cent, the tax actually payable to a state may be computed at a lower—and, in some cases, a higher—rate. Since one of the purposes of state unemployment legislation is to stabilize employment, the state laws contain provisions for merit-rating plans; under these provisions, an employer who establishes a good record for stable employment (thus reducing the claims upon state funds for unemployment compensation) may obtain the benefit of a state tax rate much lower than 2.7 per cent. In order to assure the employer of the enjoyment of the tax saving resulting from the reduced state rate, the federal law provides that an employer paying a state tax at a rate less than 2.7 per cent, as a result of the state's merit-rating plan, may deduct as a credit an amount computed at the 2.7 per cent rate or at the highest rate applicable to any taxpayer in the state, whichever is lower.

The employer must file his federal unemployment-tax return with the Internal Revenue Service on or before January 31 following the taxable calendar year. To assure himself of obtaining the full credit for state taxes, he should pay those taxes not later than January 31.

The present law calls for quarterly (instead of yearly) collections of federal unemployment taxes. The years 1970–1971 are a phasing-in period during which the first three quarterly payments are less than the amount of taxes actually due for the quarter. The remainder of taxes due for the entire year must be paid with the fourth quarter return. After 1971 the full quarterly tax must be paid for each quarter.

The employer's records should contain all information required to support his tax return.

State unemployment compensation taxes. Stimulated by the enactment of federal unemployment insurance legislation, all the states, the District of Columbia, and Puerto Rico have passed laws which have, in general, the following principal objectives:

(1) The payment of compensation, of limited amounts and for limited periods, to unemployed workers.
(2) The operation of facilities to assist employers in obtaining employees and to help workers obtain employment.
(3) The encouragement of employers to stabilize employment; the inducement offered is a reduction in the tax rate, through the operation of merit-rating systems.

Since the laws of the several states differ in many particulars, it is possible here to give only a general description. All the states levy a tax on employers; a very few also levy a tax on employees (in most cases, for payment of benefits in nonoccupational disability cases). The list of exempt services in the federal law is rather closely followed in most of the state laws. Whereas the federal unemployment insurance tax is assessed against only those employers who have four or more employees, many of the states assess taxes on employers of a smaller number of individuals—even as few as one. In most states the tax is not assessed on salaries in excess of $3,000. In general, the state tax rate is basically 2.7 per cent, but provision is made in some of the laws for increased rates. All state laws include merit-rating plans intended to effect lower taxes, by a reduction of the tax rate or by a credit against taxes, for employers who have established (during an experience period, usually of three years) a favorable record of stable employment. The *reserve ratio* plan is typical; in principle it operates as follows:

Assume that an employer's average annual payroll for three years has been $100,000. Assume, also, that the balance in the state's reserve account with this employer is $5,000; that is the excess of the taxes paid by this employer over the amounts of benefits paid by the state to his former employees.
The reserve ratio ($5,000 ÷ $100,000) is 5%.
The higher the reserve ratio, the lower the tax rate.

Most states require employers to file returns quarterly and to pay the tax by the end of the month following the close of the quarter. Because the amount of taxable wages paid to an individual is usually one of the factors determining the amounts of benefits payable to him when he is unemployed, employers may be required to file information returns showing the amount of compensation paid to each employee during the period.

Some states require employers to maintain a compensation record for each employee, showing, among other things, the period of employment, the reason for termination of employment, the cause of lost time, and the amounts of periodical payments of compensation to him during the period of employment. The specific requirements of each state are shown in its published regulations.

Federal income tax withholding. Employers of one or more employees are required to withhold federal income taxes from the wages of employees, except certain exempt wage payments.

The amount withheld from an employee's wages is affected by his income and by the number of exemptions ($600 each).
An individual is entitled to;

(1) An exemption for himself.
(2) An additional exemption if he is over 65 or will become 65 on or before January 1 of the following year.
(3) An additional exemption if he is blind.

If the employee is married, he can claim any of the above exemptions which his spouse could claim if she were employed—unless, of course, she is employed and claims them herself.

(4) An exemption for each dependent. No *additional* exemptions are allowed for aged or blind *dependents.*

(5) Employees with large itemized deductions may claim additional withholding exemptions called "withholding allowances."

A dependent is a person who is closely related to the taxpayer, has a gross income of less than $600 for the year, and received more than half of his support for the year from the taxpayer.

To determine the amount of tax to be withheld from an employee's compensation, the employer must know the number of exemptions claimed by the employee. Therefore, the employee is required to provide an Employee's Withholding Exemption Certificate to his employer.

If the employee's status as to exemptions changes during the year, he should give his employer an amended certificate; he is required to do so if the number of exemptions decreases, and he is permitted to do so if the number of exemptions increases.

The employer's report and payment procedures are summarized as follows:

Every employer must file a quarterly combined return for F.I.C.A. taxes and withheld income taxes. Except as noted in the following paragraph, the return and taxes are due and payable on or before the last day of the month following the calendar quarter covered by the return. Employers who had more than $2,500 in taxes for any month of a calendar quarter must make semimonthly deposits of the taxes during the next quarter. If the employer is not required to make semimonthly deposits but is liable for more than $100 in taxes in any month other than the last month of a calendar quarter, taxes must be deposited by the 15th of the following month. If an employer's tax liability for a quarter (reduced by any deposits for the quarter) is more than $100, he must deposit the unpaid balance by the last day of the month following the close of the calendar quarter; if the amount due is $100 or less, it may be deposited or paid with the quarterly return. Taxes may be deposited in any commercial bank qualified as a federal depositary or in a federal reserve bank. If all deposits have been made on time, the due date for the quarterly return is extended to the 10th day of the second month following the calendar quarter covered.

On or before January 31, the employer must give each of his employees a withholding statement showing the employee's total wages for the preceding year and the amount of income tax and social security tax withheld therefrom. If employment is terminated, the employer should give the employee, not later than 30 days after the last wage payment, a withholding statement covering the portion of the year during which he was employed.

With the return for the last calendar quarter, every employer must file a reconciliation of *income tax* withheld, to which copies of all withholding statements given to employees must be attached. The reconciliation form must be accompanied by a listing of the amounts of withheld income taxes as shown by the copies of the withholding statements.

Other payroll deductions. Employers may make other deductions from payrolls for such items as premiums for group hospital insurance, the purchase of government bonds for the employees, and payment of union dues.

Requirements of Federal Fair Labor Standards Act. This act establishes a minimum hourly wage rate and maximum hours of work per week for certain classes of employees engaged in interstate commerce or employed in certain enterprises engaged in interstate commerce. It provides that payment for overtime in excess of 40 hours during any work week shall be at the rate of one and one-half times the regular hourly wage.

The act also requires that employers subject to it shall maintain a record for each subject employee showing his name, address, date of birth (if under 19), sex, occupation, work week, regular rate of pay per hour, basis of wage payment (hour, week, month, piecework, and so on), hours worked per day and per work week, daily or weekly wages at his regular rate, weekly excess compensation for overtime worked, miscellaneous additions to or deductions from wages, total periodical wage payments, and date of payment.

Following are some examples showing application of the requirement for the payment of wages at one and one-half times the regular hourly rate for hours of work in excess of 40 hours during any work week.

(1) *A*'s regular hourly rate is $2.00. He works 45 hours during one week. His wages are computed as follows:

45 hours at $2.00	**$90.00**
5 hours at 1.00	5.00
Total	**$95.00**

(2) *B*'s wages are $117.00 a week for a regular work week of 39 hours (7 hours a day for 5 days, and 4 hours on Saturday). He works 45 hours during one week.

$117.00 ÷ 39 = $3.00 regular hourly rate.
45 hours at $3.00 = $135.00
5 hours at 1.50 = 7.50 (Excess payment for hours over 40)
Total $142.50

(3) *C* accepts a position with the understanding that he is to work 7 hours per day during each of the 6 days of his work week, and is to receive a weekly wage of $86; that the weekly wage includes overtime at time and one-half for the 2 hours over 40; and that if he works less than 42 hours, a corresponding deduction will be made. He works 50 hours during one week. To determine his regular hourly rate, we must remember that his regular work week consists of 42 hours, and that for 2 of these hours he is being paid one and one-half times the regular hourly rate; in other words, for the 2 hours regularly worked in addition to 40 hours, he is given the equivalent of 3 hours' pay. Therefore,

$86.00 ÷ 43 = $2.00, the regular hourly rate.

If he works the regular 42 hours, his wage is (theoretically) computed as follows:

42 hours at $2.00 = $84.00
2 hours at 1.00 = 2.00 (Excess for hours over 40)
Total $86.00

For the week that he works 50 hours, his wage is:

50 hours at $2.00 = $100.00
10 hours at 1.00 = 10.00 (Excess for hours over 40)
Total $110.00

If wages are paid monthly or semimonthly, recognition must be given to the fact that the time-and-one-half requirement applies to each work week separately. To illustrate, assume that an employee whose regular hourly rate is $2.00 was paid for the half-month ended Wednesday, July 15, and that he was entitled to no overtime payment for that period. We are now to compute his wage payment for the last half of July; we require the following information as to hours worked.

During prior payroll period:

Monday, July 13	 8
Tuesday, " 14	 8
Wednesday, " 15	 8

During current payroll period:

Thursday, July 16	 8
Friday, " 17	 7
Saturday, " 18	 5
Monday, " 20	 6
Tuesday, " 21	 7
Wednesday, " 22	 7
Thursday, " 23	 8
Friday, " 24	 6
Saturday, " 25	 7
Monday, " 27	 8
Tuesday, " 28	 8
Wednesday, " 29	 8
Thursday, " 30	 8
Friday, " 31	 8

His total wage payment for the semimonthly period is computed as follows:

(a) For the portion of the work week ended July 18:

Considering that work week as a whole, he worked 44 hours. Since, at the time of making the payment for the period ended July 15, it was not known whether he would work over 40 hours during the entire week, he was paid for the first 3 days at the regular rate. We now find that he worked 44 hours during that week, 20 of them during the current payroll period. Therefore, the payment to him now should be:

$$20 \text{ hours at } \$2.00 = \$40.00$$
$$4 \text{ hours at } \ \ 1.00 = \underline{\ \ \ 4.00}$$
$$\text{Total} \qquad \underline{\underline{\$44.00}}$$

(b) For the work week ended July 25:

During this week he worked 41 hours. For it he should be paid:

$$41 \text{ hours at } \$2.00 = \$82.00$$
$$1 \text{ hour at } \ \ 1.00 = \underline{\ \ \ 1.00}$$
$$\text{Total} \qquad \underline{\underline{\$83.00}}$$

(c) For the portion of the work week ended July 31:

Although he had already worked 40 hours during the week, there was no certainty on Friday night that he would work on Saturday. Therefore, he should be paid an amount computed as follows:

$$40 \text{ hours at } \$2.00 = \$80.00$$

His total wage payment for the semimonthly period is the total of the items shown below:

For partial work week ended July 18	$ 44.00
For work week ended July 25	83.00
For partial work week ended July 31	80.00
Total	$207.00

PAYROLL SUMMARY

For the Week Ended __August 7, 19—__   Date of Payment __August 9, 19—__

Employee No.	Income Tax Exemptions	Name	Day of Month 1 2 3 4 5 6 7 — Hours Worked	Total Hours	Hours Over 40	Hourly Wage Rates Regular	Hourly Wage Rates Excess	Wages Regular	Wages Excess	Wages Total	Deductions F.I.C.A.	Deductions Income Tax	Deductions Hospital Insurance	Net	Check No.
35	1	John Jones	7 8 6 8 7 7	43	3	4 00	2 00	172 00	6 00	178 00	8 54	22 50		146 96	5216
36	3	Frank Brown	7 7 7 7 7 7	42	2	3 30	1 65	138 60	3 30	141 90	6 81	16 30		118 79	5217
								6,128 40	336 80	6,465 20	300 34	807 86		5,357 00	

INDIVIDUAL EMPLOYMENT AND COMPENSATION RECORD

Name __John Jones__   Employee No. __35__

Address __2913 So. Burns Ave.,__   Social Security Acct. No. __325-10-0876__

__Chicago, 60611__   Date of Birth __8-17-38__

Phone __229-4631__   Occupation __Machinist__

Date Employed __8-1-__

Date of Severance _____

Cause _____

For Week In 19— Ended	Income Tax Exemptions	Lost Time Hours	Lost Time Cause	Hours Worked Total	Hours Worked Over-time	Regular Hourly Rate	Total Wages	Deductions F.I.C.A.	Deductions Income Tax	Deductions Hospital Insurance	Net	Check No.
Aug. 7	1	1	V	43	3	4 00	178 00	8 54	22 50		146 96	5216
14				42	2		172 00	8 26	22 50		141 24	5273

V—Voluntary time off.

674

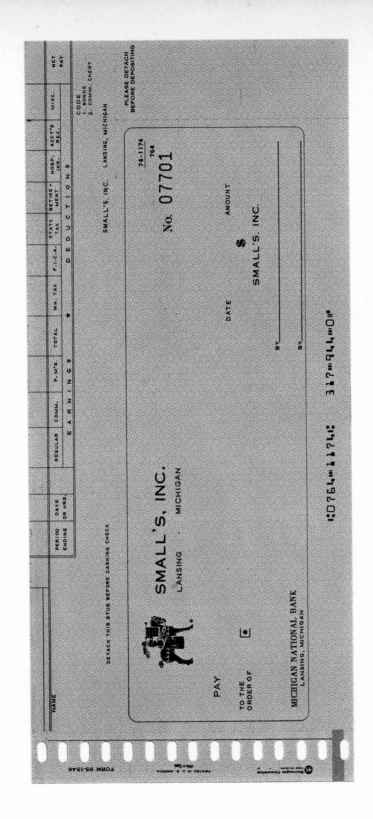

SMALL'S, INC.   LANSING, MICHIGAN

DETACH THIS STUB BEFORE CASHING CHECK

NAME													
PERIOD ENDING	DAYS OR HRS.	REGULAR	COMM.	P.M'S	TOTAL	WH. TAX	F.I.C.A.	STATE TAX	RETIRE-MENT	HOSP. INS.	ACCT'S REC.	MISC.	NET PAY
		E A R N I N G S			*	**D E D U C T I O N S**							

CODE
1. BONDS
2. COMM. CHEST

PLEASE DETACH
BEFORE DEPOSITING

74-1174
764

No. 07701

DATE _____

AMOUNT

$ _____

SMALL'S, INC.

BY _____

BY _____

SMALL'S, INC.
LANSING · MICHIGAN

PAY

TO THE
ORDER OF |*|

MICHIGAN NATIONAL BANK
LANSING, MICHIGAN

⑈07641174⑈ 317094400⑈

FORM 95-1346

PRINTED IN U. S. AMERICA

Payroll procedures. The payroll summary on page 674 provides information required for the entries in the ledger accounts applicable to wages and payroll deductions. The posting of column totals may be done directly from the payroll summary to the ledger; the debits and credits are shown below.

Wages (If it is desired to debit various accounts for amounts of
wages payable for different services, an analysis must be
made to obtain the information for this purpose) 6,465.20
F.I.C.A. tax payable 300.34
Income tax withholding payable 807.86
Payroll payable 5,357.00

One account, "Withholding and F.I.C.A. Tax Liabilities," may be used for both the social security and the income tax withholdings, since such withheld amounts are combined and reported, with the employer's share of the F.I.C.A. tax, on the same form to the same agency of the federal government.

The amount shown in the payroll summary of F.I.C.A. withholdings is not exactly 4.8 per cent of the payroll; that is presumably because some of the wage payments represented excesses over the $7,800 and are not subject to social security taxes.

The employer should compute his own liability for social security taxes in the manner shown below.

Total wages $6,465.20 $6,465.20
Wages (in excess of $7,800) not subject to F.I.C.A. taxes .
Wages (in excess of $3,000) not subject to unemploy-   208.10
ment taxes 3,808.10
Wages subject to taxes $6,257.10 $2,657.10

Taxes:
F.I.C.A.—4.8% of $6,257.10 . . . . $ 300.34
Federal unemployment—0.4% of $2,657.10 . . . .   10.63
State unemployment—2.7% of $2,657.10 . . . .   71.74
                                                                      $ 382.71

The entry to record the expense and the liabilities for these taxes may be as follows:

Payroll taxes expense (separate expense accounts may be used
if desired 382.71
F.I.C.A. tax payable 300.34
Federal unemployment tax payable 10.63
State unemployment tax payable 71.74

To meet the requirements of the law, it is also desirable to keep, for each employee, an individual employment and compensation record like the one shown on page 674.

To comply with legal requirements, payroll records with supporting data should be retained for four years.

Wage-payment reports to employees. As previously stated, many employers make reports to employees of payroll deductions at the time of each wage payment. In fact, a number of states require employers to give employees written statements of deductions with each payment.

If wages are paid by check, a stub may be attached to the check and the data may be shown on the stub, as shown on page 675.

If wages are paid in cash, the pay envelope may be printed as illustrated below:

THE BROWN COMPANY		
Employee's name _____		
Employee's number _____		
Date paid _____ 19 ___		
	Hours	Wages
Regular	_____	_____
Overtime	_____	_____
Total	_____	_____
Deductions:		
F.I.C.A. tax	_____	
Fed. Inc. tax	_____	
Savings bonds	_____	
Insurance	_____	
_____	_____	
_____	_____	
Total deductions	_____	
Cash enclosed	_____	

Index